A POPULAR HISTORY OF THE UNITED STATES OF AMERICA

FROM THE ABORIGINAL TIMES
TO THE PRESENT DAY

Embracing an Account of the Aborigines; the Norsemen in the New World; the Discoveries by the Spaniards, English, and French; the Planting of Settlements; the Growth of the Colonies; the Struggle for Liberty in the Revolution; the Development of the Nation; the Civil War; the Centennial of Independence; and the Recent Annals of the Republic.

THE WHOLE BROUGHT DOWN TO THE YEAR 1889.

BY
JOHN CLARK RIDPATH

Published by Left of Brain Books

Copyright © 2021 Left of Brain Books

ISBN 978-1-396-31802-3

First Edition

All rights reserved. No part of this publication may be reproduced, distributed, or transmitted in any form or by any means, including photocopying, recording, or other electronic or mechanical methods, without the prior written permission of the publisher, except in the case of brief quotations embodied in critical reviews and certain other noncommercial uses permitted by copyright law. Left of Brain Books is a division of Left of Brain Onboarding Pty Ltd.

Table of Contents

PREFACE.	1
INTRODUCTION	3
PART I. ABORIGINAL AMERICA.	5
CHAPTER I. The Red Men—Origin, Distribution, Character.	5
PART II. VOYAGE AND DISCOVERY. A. D. 986-1607.	19
CHAPTER II. The Icelanders and Norwegians in America.	19
CHAPTER III. Spanish Discoveries in America.	24
CHAPTER IV. Spanish Discoveries in America.—Continued.	32
CHAPTER V. The French in America.	47
CHAPTER VI. English Discoveries and Settlements.	56
CHAPTER VII. English Discoveries and Settlements.–Continued.	69
CHAPTER VIII. Voyages and Settlements of the Dutch.	79
PART III. COLONIAL HISTORY. A. D. 1607-1775.	83
PARENT COLONIES.	83
CHAPTER IX. Virginia.—The First Charter.	83
CHAPTER X. Virginia.-The Second Charter.	95
CHAPTER XI. Virginia.-The Third Charter.	99
CHAPTER XII. Virginia.—The Royal Government.	107
CHAPTER XIII. Massachusetts.—Settlement.	121
CHAPTER XIV. Massachusetts.—The Union.	133
CHAPTER XV. Massachusetts—King Philip's War.	141
CHAPTER XVI. Massachusetts.-War and Witchraft.	153
CHAPTER XVII. Massachusetts.—Wars of Anne and George.	160
CHAPTER XVIII. New York.—Settlement.	169
CHAPTER XIX. New York.—Administration of Stuyvesant.	178
CHAPTER XX. New York Under the English.	185
COLONIAL HISTORY.—CONTINUED.	199
MINOR EASTERN COLONIES.	199
CHAPTER XXI. Connecticut.	199
CHAPTER XXII. Rhode Island.	211

CHAPTER XXIII. New Hampshire.	218
COLONIAL HISTORY.—CONTINUED.	223
MINOR MIDDLE COLONIES.	223
CHAPTER XXIV. New Jersey.	223
Chapter XXV. Pennsylvania.	231
COLONIAL HISTORY.—CONTINUED.	239
MINOR SOUTHERN COLONIES.	239
CHAPTER XXVI. Maryland.	239
CHAPTER XXVII. North Carolina.	249
CHAPTER XXVIII. South Carolina.	256
CHAPTER XXIX. Georgia.	266
COLONIAL HISTORY.—CONTINUED.	278
FRENCH AND INDIAN WAR.	278
CHAPTER XXX. Causes.	278
CHAPTER XXXI. Campaigns of Washington and Braddock.	288
CHAPTER XXXII. Ruin of Acadia.	297
CHAPTER XXXIII. Expeditions of Shirley and Johnson.	300
CHAPTER XXXIV. Two Years of Disaster.	304
CHAPTER XXXV. Two Years of Successes.	308
CHAPTER XXXVI. Condition of the Colonies.	319
PART IV. REVOLUTION AND CONFEDERATION. A. D. 1775-1789.	325
CHAPTER XXXVII. Causes.	325
CHAPTER XXXVIII. The Beginning.	339
CHAPTER XXXIX. The Work of '76.	350
CHAPTER XL. Operations of '77.	368
CHAPTER XLI. France to the Rescue.	382
CHAPTER XLII. Movements of '79.	389
CHAPTER XLIII. Reverses and Treason.	395
CHAPTER XLIV. The End.	404
CHAPTER XLV. Confederation and Union.	418
PART V. NATIONAL PERIOD. A. D. 1789-1882.	426

CHAPTER XLVI. Washington's Administration, 1789-1797.	426
CHAPTER XLVII. Adams's Administration, 1797-1801.	438
CHAPTER XLVIII. Jefferson's Administration, 1801-1809.	443
CHAPTER XLIX. Madison's Administration, and War of 1812.	457
CHAPTER L. War of 1812.—Continued.	472
CHAPTER LI. The Campaigns of '14.	481
CHAPTER LII. Monroe's Administration.	492
CHAPTER LIII. Adams's Administration, 1825-1829.	500
CHAPTER LIV. Jackson's Administration, 1829-1837.	506
CHAPTER LV. Van Buren's Administration, 1837-1841.	516
CHAPTER LVI. Administrations of Harrison and Tyler, 1841-1845.	521
CHAPTER LVII. Polk's Administration, and the Mexican War, 1845-1849.	529
CHAPTER LVIII. Administrations of Taylor and Fillmore, 1849-1853.	550
CHAPTER LIX. Pierce's Administration, 1853-1857.	557
CHAPTER LX. Buchanan's Administration, 1857-1861.	563
CHAPTER LXI. Lincoln's Administration, and the Civil War, 1861-1865.	572
CHAPTER LXII. Causes.	577
CHAPTER LXIII. First Year of the War.	584
CHAPTER LXIV. Campaigns of '62.	592
CHAPTER LXV. The Work of '63.	611
CHAPTER LXVI. The Closing Conflicts.	628
CHAPTER LXVII. Johnson's Administration, 1865-1869.	653
CHAPTER LXVIII. Grant's Administration, 1869-1877.	665
CHAPTER LXIX. Hayes's Administration, 1877-1881.	754
CHAPTER LXX. Administrations of Garfield and Arthur.	770
CHAPTER LXXI. Cleveland's Administration, 1885–	798
CHAPTER LXXII. Harrison's Administration, 1889—	825
CHAPTER LXXIII. Conclusion.	859
APPENDIX A.	864

SIR JOHN MANDEVILLE'S ARGUMENT ON THE FIGURE OF THE EARTH.	864
APPENDIX B.	873
A PLAN OF PERPETUAL UNION, FOR HIS MAJESTY'S COLONIES IN NORTH AMERICA; PROPOSED BY BENJ. FRANKLIN, AND ADOPTED BY THE COLONIAL CONVENTION AT ALBANY, JULY 10TH, 1754.	873
APPENDIX C.	877
THE DECLARATION OF INDEPENDENCE, ADOPTED BY CONGRESS, JULY 4, 1776.	877
A Declaration by the Representatives of the United States of America, in Congress Assembled.	877
APPENDIX D.	882
ARTICLES OF CONFEDERATION.	882
Articles of Confederation and Perpetual Union	882
APPENDIX E.	893
CONSTITUTION OF THE UNITED STATES.	893
Amendments to the Constitution.	906
APPENDIX F.	912
WASHINGTON'S FAREWELL ADDRESS.	912
APPENDIX G.	928
THE EMANCIPATION PROCLAMATION. BY THE PRESIDENT OF THE UNITED STATES OF AMERICA.	928
PRONUNCIATION OF PROPER NAMES.	931

Preface.

Dear People of the United States:—

By this, my Preface, I offer to you a New History of your country—and mine. The work is presented in the form of an abridged narrative. My reasons for such a venture are brief, but, I trust, satisfactory:

First, to every American citizen some knowledge of the history of his country is indispensable. The attainment of that knowledge ought to be made easy and delightful.

Second, the Centennial of the Republic furnishes an auspicious occasion for the study of those great events which compose the warp and woof of the new civilization in the West.

This book is intended for the average American; for the man of business who has neither time nor disposition to plod through ten or twenty volumes of elaborate historical dissertation; for the practical man of the shop, the counter, and the plow. The work is dedicated to the household and the library of the working man. It is in scribed to the father, the mother, the son, and the daughter of the American family. If father, mother, son, and daughter shall love their country better—if they shall understand more clearly and appreciate more fully the founding, progress, and growth of liberty in the New World—the author will be abundantly repaid.

In the preparation of the work the following objects have been kept in view:

I. To give an accurate and spirited Narrative of the principal events in our National history from the aboriginal times to the present day.

II. To discuss the Philosophy of that history as fully as possible within the narrow limits of the work.

III. To avoid all Partiality, Partisanship, and Prejudice, as things dangerous, baneful, and wicked.

IV. To preserve a clear and systematic Arrangement of the several subjects, giving to every fact, whether of peace or war, its true place and importance in the narrative.

V. To give an Objective Representation by means of charts, maps, drawings, and diagrams, of all the more important matters in the history of the nation.

VI. To secure a Style and Method in the book itself which shall be in keeping with the spirit and refinement of the times.

Whether these important ends have been attained, dear People, it is not my province but yours to decide. I have labored earnestly to reach the ideal of such a work, and if success has not rewarded the effort, the failure has been in the execution rather than in the plan and purpose.

I surrender the book, thus undertaken and completed, to You—for whom it was intended. With diffidence I ask a considerate judgment and just recognition of whatever worth the work may be found to possess.

J. C. R.

INDIANA ASBURY UNIVERSITY,
January 1, 1883.

Introduction

1. THE history of every nation is divided into periods. For a while the genius of a people will be turned to some particular pursuit. Men will devote themselves to certain things and labor to accomplish certain results. Then the spirit of the age will change, and historical facts will assume a different character. Thus arises what is called A PERIOD IN HISTORY. In studying the history of the United States it is of the first importance to understand the periods into which it is divided.

2. First of all, there was a time when the New World was under the dominion of the aborigines. From ocean to ocean the copper-colored children of the woods ruled with undisputed sway. By bow and arrow, by flint and hatchet, the Red man supported his rude civilization and waited for the coming of the pale-faced races.

3. After the discovery of America, the people of Europe were hundreds of years in making themselves acquainted with the shape and character of the New World. During that time explorers and adventurers went everywhere and settled nowhere. To make new discoveries was the universal passion; but nobody cared to plant a colony. As long as this spirit prevailed, historical events bore a common character, being produced by common causes. Hence arose the second period in our history—the Period of Voyage and Discovery.

4. As soon as the adventurers had satisfied themselves with tracing sea-coasts, ascending rivers and scaling mountains, they began to form permanent settlements. And each settlement was a new State in the wilderness. Every voyager now became ambitions to plant a colony. Kings and queens grew anxious to confer their names on the towns and commonwealths of the New World. Thus arose a third period—the Period of Colonial History.

5. Then the colonies grew strong and multiplied. There were thirteen little sea-shore republics. The people began to consult about their privileges and to talk of the rights of freemen. Oppression on the part of

the mother-country was met with resistance, and tyranny with defiance. There was a revolt against the king; and the patriots of the different colonies fought side by side, and won their freedom. Then they built them a Union, strong and great. This is the Period of Revolution and Confederation.

6. Then the United States of America entered upon their career as a nation. Three times tried by war and many times vexed with civil dissensions, the Union of our fathers still remains for us and for posterity. Such is the Period of Nationality.

7. Collecting these results, we find five distinctly marked periods in the history of our country:

First. THE ABORIGINAL PERIOD; from remote antiquity to the coming of the White men.

Second. THE PERIOD OF VOYAGE AND DISCOVERY; A. D. 986-1607.

Third. THE COLONIAL PERIOD; A. D. 1607-1775.

Fourth. THE PERIOD OF REVOLUTION AND CONFEDERATION; A. D. 1775-1789.

Fifth. THE NATIONAL PERIOD; A. D. 1789-1888.

In this order the History of the United States will be presented in the following pages.

PART I.
Aboriginal America.

CHAPTER I.

The Red Men—Origin, Distribution, Character.

The primitive inhabitants of the New World were the Red men called INDIANS. The name *Indian* was conferred upon them from their real or fancied resemblance to the people of India. But without any such similarity the name would have been the same; for Columbus and his followers, believing that they had only rediscovered the Indies, would of course call the inhabitants Indians. The supposed similarity between the two races, if limited to mere personal appearance, had some foundation in fact; but in manners, customs, institutions, and character, no two peoples could be more dissimilar than the American aborigines and the sleepy inhabitants of China and Japan.

The origin of the North American Indians is involved in complete obscurity. That they are one of the older races of mankind can not be doubted. But at what date or by what route they came to the Western continent is an unsolved problem. Many theories have been proposed to account for the Red man's presence in the New World, but most of them have been vague and unsatisfactory. The notion that the Indians are the descendants of the Israelites is absurd. That half civilized tribes, wandering from beyond the Euphrates, should reach North America, surpasses human credulity. That Europeans or Africans, at some remote period, crossed the Atlantic by voyaging from island to island, seems altogether improbable. That the Kamtchatkans, coming by way of Behring's Strait, reached the frozen North-west and became the progenitors of the Red men, has no evidence other than conjecture to support it. Until further research shall throw additional light on the history and migrations of the primitive races of mankind, the origin of the Indians will remain shrouded in mystery. It is not unlikely that a more thorough knowledge of the North American languages may furnish a clue to the early history of the tribes that spoke them.

The Indians belong to the *Ganowanian*, or Bow-and-Arrow family of men. Some races cultivate the soil; others have herds and flocks others build cities and ships. To the Red man of the Western continent the chase was every thing. Without the chase he pined and languished and died. To smite with swift arrow the deer and the bear was the chief delight and profit of the primitive Americans. Such a race could live only in a country of woods and wild animals. The illimitable hunting-grounds—forest, and hill, and river—were the Indian's earthly paradise, and the type of his home hereafter.

The American aborigines belonged to several distinct families or nations. Above the sixtieth parallel of latitude the whole continent from Labrador to Alaska was inhabited by THE ESQUIMAUX. The name means *the eaters of raw meat.* They lived in snow huts, or in hovels, partly or wholly underground. Sometimes their houses were more artistically constructed out of the bones of whales and walruses. Their manner of life was that of fishermen and hunters. They clad themselves in winter with the skins of seals, and in summer with those of reindeers. Inured to cold and exposure, they made long journeys in sledges drawn by dogs, or risked their lives in open boats fighting with whales and polar bears among the terrors of the icebergs. By eating abundantly of oils and fat meats they kept the fires of life a-burning, even amid the rigors and desolations of the Arctic winter.

Lying south of the Esquimaux, embracing the greater part of Canada and nearly all that portion of the United States east of the Mississippi and north of the thirty-seventh parallel of latitude, spread the great family of THE ALGONQUINS. It appears that their original seat was on the Ottawa River. At the beginning of the seventeenth century the Algonquins numbered fully a quarter of a million. The tribes of this great family were nomadic in their habits, roaming from one hunting-ground and river to another, according to the exigencies of fishing and the chase. Agriculture was but little esteemed. They were divided into many subordinate tribes, each having its local name, dialect, and traditions. When the first European settlements were planted the Algonquin race was already declining in numbers and influence. Wasting diseases destroyed whole tribes. Of all the Indian nations the Algonquins suffered most from contact with the White man. Before his aggressive spirit, his fiery rum, and his destructive weapons, the warriors were unable to stand. The race has withered to a shadow; only a few thousands remain to rehearse the story of their ancestors.

Within the wide territory occupied by the Algonquins lived the powerful nation of THE HURON-IROQUOIS. Their domain extended over the country reaching from Georgian Bay and Lake Huron to Lakes Erie and Ontario, south of those lakes to the valley of the Upper Ohio, and eastward to the River Sorel. Within this extensive district was a confederacy of vigorous tribes, having a common ancestry, and generally—though not always—acting together in war. At the time of their greatest power and influence the Huron-Iroquois embraced no less than nine allied nations. These were the Hurons proper, living north of Lake Erie; the Eries and Andastes, south of the same water; the Tuscaroras, of Carolina, who ultimately joined their kinsmen in the North; the Senecas, Cayugas, Onondagas, Oneidas, and Mohawks, constituting the famous Five Nations of New York. The warriors of this great confederation presented the Indian character in its most favorable aspect. They were brave, patriotic, and eloquent; not wholly averse to useful industry; living in respectable villages; tilling the soil with considerable success; faithful as friends but terrible as enemies.

South of the country of the Algonquins were THE CHEROKEES and THE MOBILIAN NATIONS; the former occupying Tennessee, and the latter covering the domain between the Lower Mississippi and the Atlantic. The Cherokees were highly civilized for a primitive people, and contact with the whites seemed to improve rather than degrade them. The principal tribes of the Mobilians were the Yamassees and Creeks of Georgia, the Seminoles of Florida, and the Choctaws and Chickasaws of Mississippi. These displayed the usual characteristics of the Red men, with this additional circumstance, that below the thirty-second parallel of latitude evidences of temple-building, not practiced among the Northern tribes, began to appear.

Map I.
Aboriginal America.

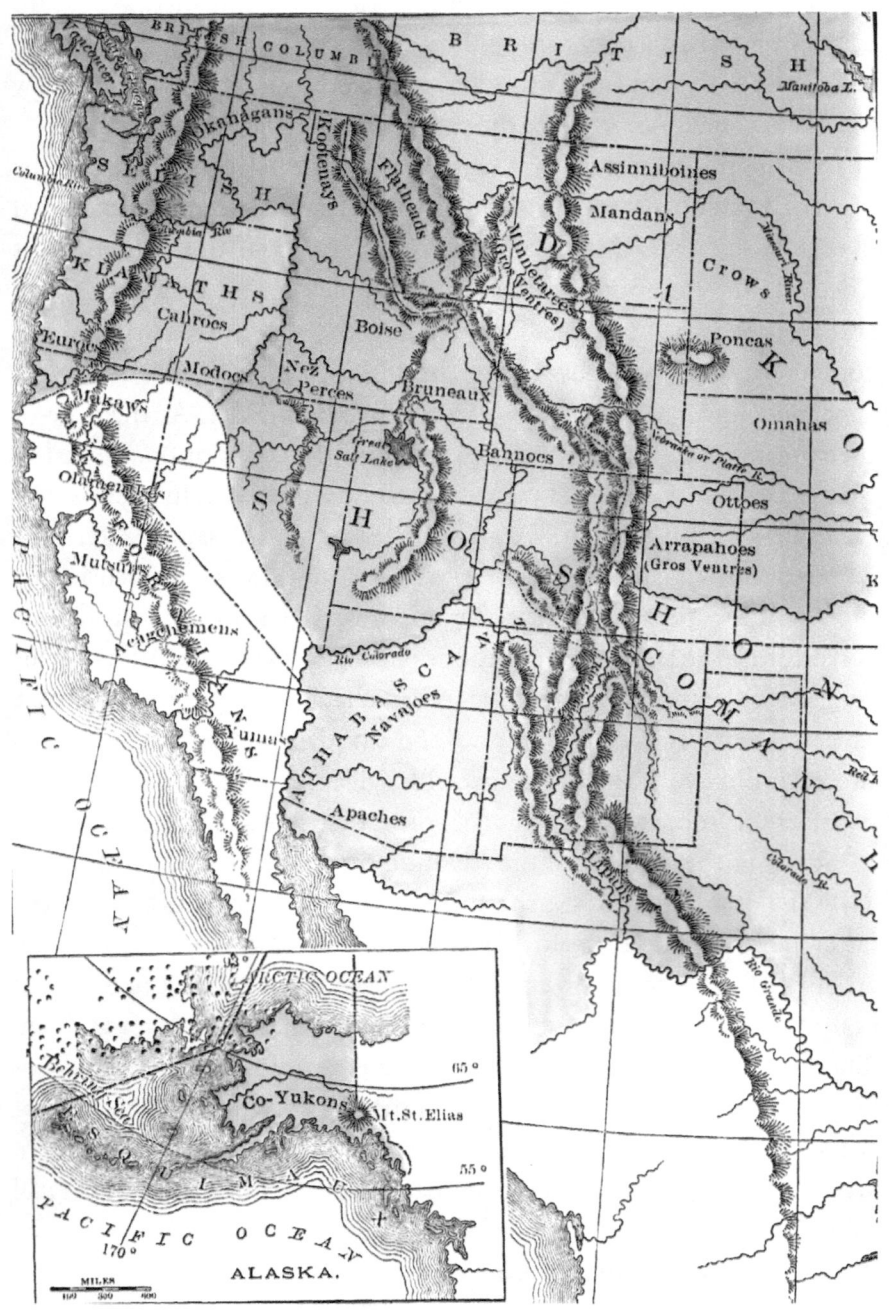

Showing the Distribution and Territorial Limits of the Indian Nations, in the New World.

West of the Father of Waters was the great and widely-spread race of THE DAKOTAS, whose territory extended from the Arkansas River to the country of the Esquimaux and westward to the Rocky Mountains. Their languages and institutions, differing much among the various tribes, are not so well understood as those of some other nations. South of the land of the Dakotas, in a district nearly corresponding with the present State of Texas, lived the wild COMANCHES, whose very name is a synonym for savage ferocity. Beyond the Rocky Mountains were the Indian nations of the Plains; the great family of THE SHOSHONEES, THE SELISH, THE KLAMATHS, and THE CALIFORNIANS. On the Pacific slope farther southward dwelt in former times the famous races of AZTECS and TOLTECS. These were the most civilized of the primitive Indian nations, but at the same time among the most feeble; the best builders in wood and stone, but the least warlike of any of the aborigines. Such is a brief sketch of the distribution of the copper-colored race in the New World. The territorial position of the various nations and tribes will be easily understood from an examination of the accompanying map.

The Indians were strongly marked with national peculiarities. The most striking characteristic of the race was *a certain sense of personal independence—willfulness of action—freedom from restraint.* To the Red man's imagination the idea of a civil authority which should subordinate his passions, curb his will, and thwart his purposes, was intolerable. Among this people no common enterprise was possible unless made so by the concurrence of free wills. If the chieftain entered the war-path, his kinsmen and the braves of other tribes followed him only because they chose his leadership. His authority and right of command extended no further than to be foremost in danger, most cunning in savage strategy, bravest in battle. So of all the relations of Indian life. The Medicine Man was a self-constituted physician and prophet. No man gave him his authority; no man took it away. His right was his own; and his influence depended upon himself and the voluntary respect of the nation. In the solemn debates of the Council House, where the red orators pronounced their wild harangues to groups of motionless listeners, only questions of expediency were decided. The painted sachems never thought of imposing on the unwilling minority the decision which had been reached in council.

Next among the propensities of the Red men was *the passion for war*. Their wars, however, were always undertaken for the redress of grievances, real or imaginary, and not for conquest. But with the Indian, a redress of grievances meant a personal vindictive, and bloody vengeance on the offender. The Indian's principles of war were easily understood, but irreconcilable with justice and humanity. The forgiveness of an injury was reckoned a weakness and a shame. Revenge was considered among the nobler virtues. The open, honorable battle of the field was an event unknown in Indian warfare. Fighting was limited to the surprise, the ambuscade, the massacre; and military strategy consisted of cunning and treachery. Quarter was rarely asked, and never granted; those who were spared from the fight were only reserved for a barbarous captivity, ransom, or the stake. In the torture of his victims all the diabolical ferocity of the savage warrior's nature burst forth without restraint.

In times of peace the Indian character shone to a better advantage. But the Red man was, at his best estate, an unsocial, solitary, and gloomy spirit. He was a man of the woods. He communed only with himself and the genius of solitude. He sat apart. The forest was better than his wigwam, and his wigwam better than the village. The Indian woman was a degraded creature, a drudge, a beast of burden; and the social principle was correspondingly low. The organization of the Indian family was so peculiar as to require a special consideration. Among civilized nations the family is so constructed that the lines of kinship diverge constantly from the line of descent, so that collateral kinsmen with each generation stand at a still greater remove from each other. The above diagram will serve to show how in a European family the lines of consanguinity diverge until the kinship becomes so feeble as to be no longer recognized. It will be observed that this fact of constant divergence is traceable to the establishment of *a male line of descent*.

In the Indian family all this is reversed. The descent is established *in the female line*; and as a consequence the ties of kinship converge upon each other until they all meet in the granddaughter. That is, in the aboriginal nations of North America, every grandson and granddaughter was the grandson and granddaughter of the whole tribe. This arose from the fact that all the uncles of a given person were reckoned as his fathers also; all the mother's sisters were mothers; all the cousins were sisters and brothers; all the nieces were daughters; all the nephews, sons, etc. This peculiarity of the Indian family organization is illustrated in the annexed diagram.

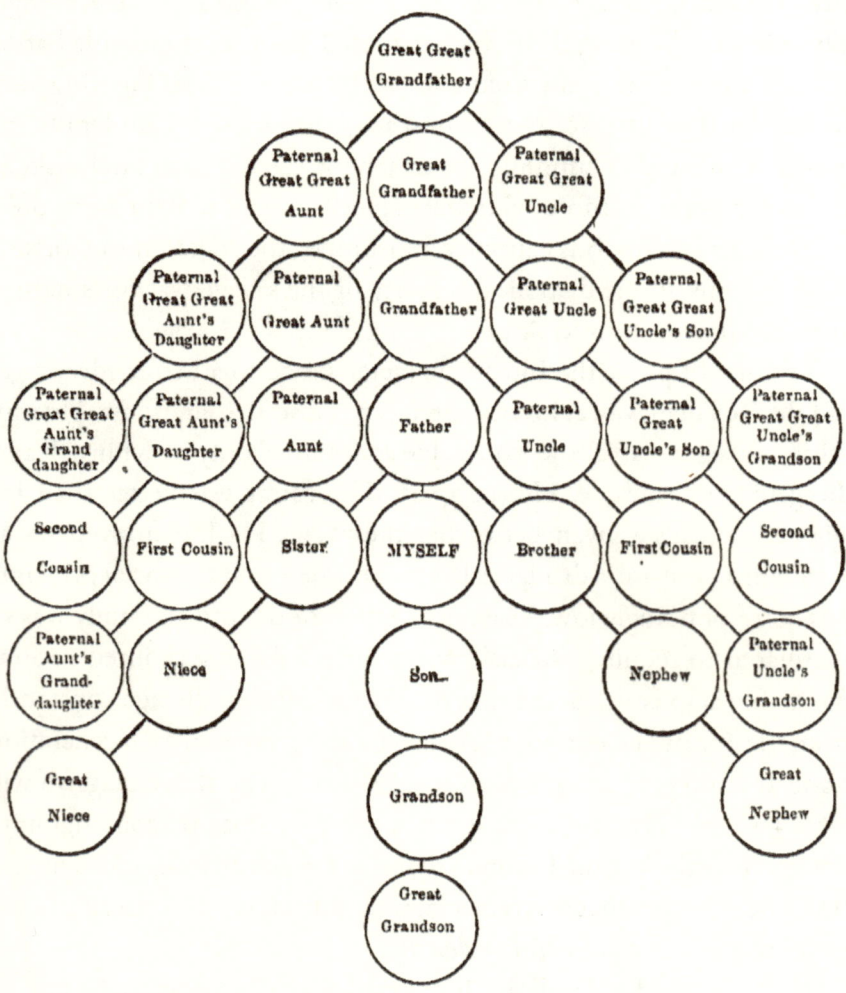

Diagram of European Kinship.

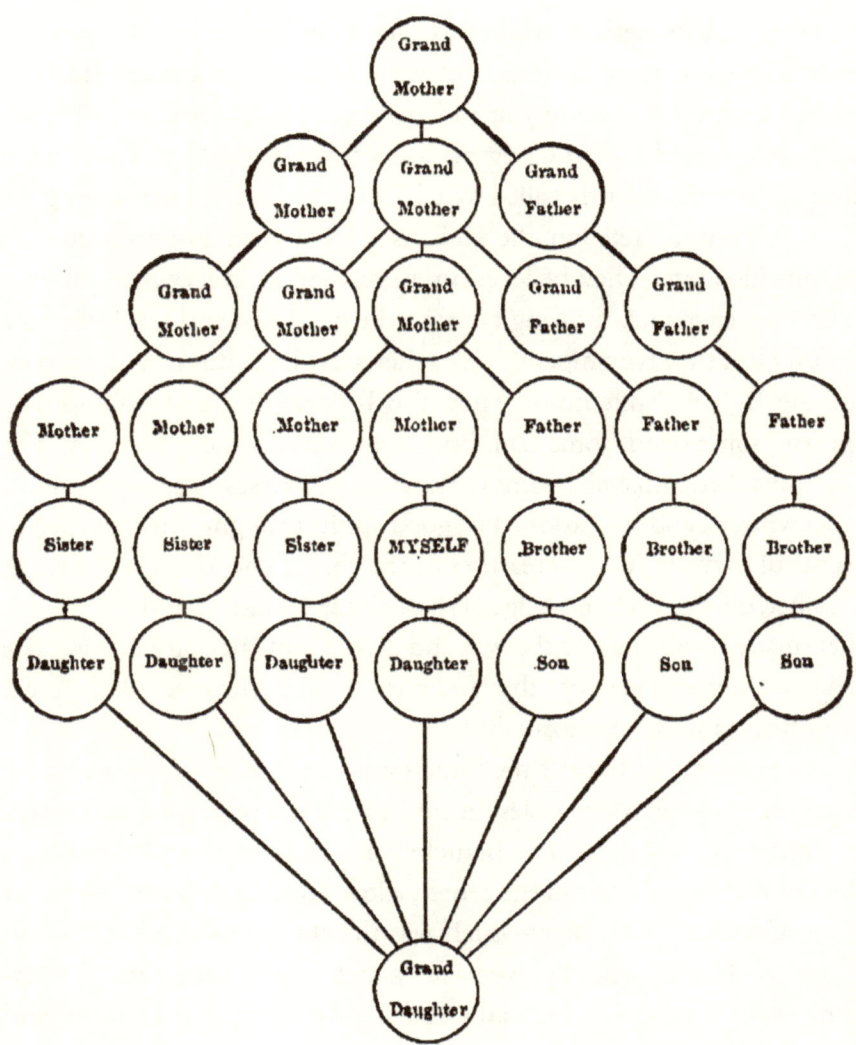

Diagram of Indian Kinship.

Civil government among the Indian nations was in its primitive stages of development. Each tribe had its own sachem, or chieftain, to whom in matters of peace and war a tolerable degree of obedience was rendered. At times confederations were formed, based either on ties of kinship or the exigencies of war. But these confederations were seldom enduring, and were likely at any time to be broken up by the barbarous passion and insubordination of the tribes who composed them. Sometimes a sachem would arise with such marked abilities, warlike prowess, and strength of will, as to gain an influence, if not a positive leadership over many nations. But with the death of the chieftain, or sooner, each tribe, resuming its independence, would return to its own ways. No general Indian Congress was known; but national and tribal councils were frequently called to debate questions of policy and right.

In matters of religion the Indians were a superstitious race, but seldom idolaters. They believed in a great spirit, everywhere present, ruling the elements, showing favor to the obedient, and punishing the sinful. Him they worshiped; to him they sacrificed. But not in temples, for the Indians built none. They also believed in many subordinate spirits—some good, some bad. Both classes frequented the earth. The bad spirits brought evil dreams to the Indian; diseases also, bad passions, cruel winters, and starvation. The good spirits brought sunshine, peace, plentiful harvests, all the creatures of the chase. The Medicine Man, or Prophet, obtained a knowledge of these things by fasting and prayer, and then made revelations of the will and purpose of the spirit world. The religious ceremonies of the Indians were performed with great earnestness and solemn formality.

In the matter of the arts the Indian was a barbarian. His house was a wigwam or hovel. Some poles set up in a circle, converging at the top, covered with skins and the branches of trees, lined and sometimes floored with mats, a fire in the center, a low opening opposite the point from which the wind blew—such was the aboriginal abode of North America. Indian utensils were few, rude, and primitive. Poorly-fashioned earthen pots, bags and pouches for carrying provisions, and stone hammers for pounding parched corn, were the stock and store. A copper kettle was a priceless treasure. The warrior's chief implement was his hatchet of stone or copper. This he always carried with him, and it was rarely free from the stain of blood. His weapon of offence and defence was the bow and arrow, by no means an insignificant or feeble instrument. The arrow pointed with stone or iron was frequently driven *entirely through* the ponderous buffalo. The range of the winged missile was two hundred yards or more, and the aim was one of fatal accuracy when the White man was the target. The Indian's clothing was a blanket, thrown over his shoulders, bound around him perhaps with a thong of leather. The material for his moccasins[1] and leggins was stripped from the red buck, elk, or buffalo. He was fond of hanging about his person an infinity of non-sensical trappings; fangs of rattlesnakes, claws of hawks, feathers of eagles, bones of animals, scalps of enemies. He painted his face and body, specially when the passion of war was on him, with all manner of glaring and fantastic colors. So the Prophet of his nation taught him; so he would be terrible to his enemies; so he would exemplify the peculiarities of his nation and be unlike the Pale face. All the higher arts were wanting. Indian writing consisted only of quaint and half-intelligible hieroglyphics rudely scratched on the face of rocks or cut in the bark of trees. The artistic sense of the savage could rise no higher than a coarse necessity compelled the flight.

Specimen of Indian Writing.

Translation: Eight soldiers (9), with muskets (10), commanded by a captain (1), and accompanied by a secretary (2), a geologist (3), three attendants (4, 5, 6), and two Indian guides, encamped here. They had three camp fires (13, 14, 15), and ate a turtle and a prairie hen (11, 12), for supper.

---

[1] The Algonquin word is *makisin*.

The language spoken by a people is always a matter of special interest and importance. The dialects of the North American races bear many and evident marks of resemblance *among themselves*; but little or no analogy to the languages of *other nations*. If there is any similarity at all, it is found between the Indian tongues and those spoken by the nomadic races of Asia. The vocabulary of the Red men was a very limited one. The principal objects of nature had special names, and actions were likewise specifically expressed. Abstract ideas but rarely found expression in any of the Indian languages; such ideas could only be expressed by a long and labored circumlocution. Words had a narrow but very intense meaning. There was, for instance, no general word signifying *to hunt* or *to fish*; but one word signified "to-kill-a-deer-with-an-arrow;" another, "to-take-fish-by-striking-the-ice." In most of the dialects there was no word for *brother*; but "elder-brother" and "younger-brother" could be expressed. Among many of the tribes the meanings of words and phrases were so restricted that the warrior would use one set of terms and the squaw another to express the same ideas. The languages were monosyllabic; but many of the monosyllables might be combined to form compounds resembling the polysyllables of European tongues. These compounds, expressing abstract and difficult ideas, were sometimes inordinately long,[2] the whole forming an *explanation* or *description* of the thing rather than a single word. Scholars have applied the term *agglutinative* to those languages in which such labored and tedious forms of expression occur. Of this sort are the tongues spoken by the nomadic races of Asia.

In personal appearance the Indians were strongly marked. In stature they were nearly all below the average of Europeans. The Esquimaux are rarely five feet high, but are generally thick-set and heavy. The Algonquins are taller and lighter in build; a straight and agile race, lean and swift of foot. Eyes jet-black and sunken; hair black and straight; beard black and scant; skin copper-colored, a reddish-black, cinnamon-hued, brown; high cheek bones; forehead and skull variable in shape and

---

[2] For instance, in the Massachusetts dialect, the form of speech meaning "our question" was this: Kum-mog-ko-don-at-toot-tum-moo-et-it-e-a-ong-an-nun-non-ash.

proportion; hands and feet small; body lithe but not strong; expression sinister, or rarely dignified and noble:—these are the well-known features and person of the Indian.

A North American Indian.³

Though generally sedate in manners and serious in behavior, the Red men at times gave themselves up to merry-making and hilarity. The dance was universal—not the social dance of civilized nations, but the dance of ceremony, of religion, and of war. Sometimes the warriors danced alone, but frequently the women joined in the wild exercise, circling around and around, chanting the weird, monotonous songs of the tribes. Many other amusements were common, such as running, leaping, wrestling, shooting at a mark, racing in canoes along swift rivers or placid lakes, playing at ball,

---

³ An authentic portrait of the celebrated Black Hawk, chief of the Sacs and Foxes.

or engaging in intricate and exciting games, performed with small stones resembling checkers or dice. To this latter sport was not unfrequently added the intoxication of gambling, in which the warriors, under the influence of their fierce passion, would often hazard and lose their entire possessions. In soberer moments, the Red men, never inclined to conversation, would sit in silence, communing each with his own thoughts or lost in a dream under the fascination of his pipe. The use of tobacco was universal and excessive; and after the introduction of intoxicating liquors by the Europeans the Indians fell into terrible drunkenness, only limited in its extent by the amount of spirits which they could procure. It is doubtful whether any other race has been so awfully degraded by drink.

Such is a brief sketch of the Red man—who *was* rather than *is*. The only hope of the perpetuity of his race seems now to center in the Choctaws, Cherokees, Creeks and Chickasaws of the Indian Territory. These nations, numbering in the aggregate about forty-eight thousand souls, have attained a considerable degree of civilization; and with just and liberal dealing on the part of the Government the outlook for the future is not discouraging. Most of the other Indian tribes seem to be rapidly approaching extinction. Right or wrong, such is the logic of events. Whether the Red man has been justly deprived of the ownership of the New World will remain a subject of debate; that he *has* been deprived, can be none. The Saxon has come. His conquering foot has trodden the vast domain from shore to shore. The weaker race has withered from his presence and sword. By the majestic rivers and in the depths of the solitary woods the feeble sons of the Bow and Arrow will be seen no more. Only their names remain on hill and stream and mountain. The Red man sinks and fails. His eyes are to the West. To the prairies and forests, the hunting-grounds of his ancestors, he says farewell. He is gone! The cypress and the hemlock sing his requiem.

PART II.
VOYAGE AND DISCOVERY.
A. D. 986-1607.

CHAPTER II.

THE ICELANDERS AND NORWEGIANS IN AMERICA.

THE western continent was first seen by white men in A. D. 986. A Norse navigator by the name of HERJULFSON, sailing from Iceland to Greenland, was caught in a storm and driven westward to Newfoundland or Labrador. Two or three times the shores were seen, but no landing was made or attempted. The coast was low, abounding in forests, and so different from the well-known cliffs of Greenland as to make it certain that another shore hitherto unknown was in sight. On reaching Greenland, Herjulfson and his companions told wonderful stories of the new lands seen in the west.

Fourteen years later, the actual discovery of America was made by LIEF ERICKSON. This noted Icelandic captain, resolving to know the truth about the country which Herjulfson had seen, sailed west ward from Greenland, and in the spring of the year 1001 reached Labrador. Impelled by a spirit of adventure, he landed with his companions, and made explorations for a considerable distance along the coast. The country was milder and more attractive than his own, and he was in no haste to return. Southward he went as far as Massachusetts, where the daring company of Norsemen remained for more than a year. Rhode Island was also visited; and it is alleged that the hardy adventurers found their way into New York harbor.

What has once been done, whether by accident or design, may easily be done again. In the years that followed Lief Erickson's discovery, other companies of Norsemen came to the shores of America. THORWALD,

Lief's brother, made a voyage to Maine and Massachusetts in 1002, and is said to have died at Fall River in the latter state.

Norse Explorations.

Then another brother, THORSTEIN by name, arrived with a band of followers in 1005; and in the year 1007, THORFINN KARLSEFNE, the most distinguished mariner of his day, came with a crew of a hundred and fifty men, and made explorations along the coast of Massachusetts,

Rhode Island, and perhaps as far south as the capes of Virginia. Other companies of Icelanders and Norwegians visited the countries farther north, and planted colonies in Newfoundland and Nova Scotia. Little however, was known or imagined by these rude sailors of the extent of the country which they had discovered. They supposed that it was only a portion of Western Greenland, which, bending to the north around an arm of the ocean, had reappeared in the west. The settlements which were made, were feeble and soon broken up. Commerce was an impossibility in a country where there were only a few wretched savages with no disposition to buy and nothing at all to sell. The spirit of adventure was soon appeased, and the restless Northmen returned to their own country. To this undefined line of coast, now vaguely known to them, the Norse sailors gave the name of VINLAND; and the old Icelandic chroniclers insist that it was a pleasant and beautiful country. As compared with their own mountainous and frozen island of the North, the coasts of New England may well have seemed delightful.

The men who thus first visited the shores of the New World were a race of hardy adventurers, as lawless and restless as any that ever sailed the deep. Their mariners and soldiers penetrated every clime. The better parts of France and England fell under their dominion. All the monarchs of the latter country after William the Conqueror—himself the grandson of a sea-king—are descendants of the Norsemen. They were rovers of the sea; freebooters and pirates; warriors audacious and headstrong, wearing hoods surmounted with eagles' wings and walruses' tusks, mailed armor, and for robes the skins of polar bears. Woe to the people on whose defenceless coasts the sea-kings landed with sword and torch! Their wayward life and ferocious disposition are well portrayed in one of their own old ballads:

> He scorns to rest 'neath the smoky rafter,
>   He plows with his boat the roaring deep;
> The billows boil and the storm howls after—
> But the tempest is only a thing of laughter,—
>   The sea-king loves it better than sleep!

A Norse Sea-King of the Eleventh Century.

During the twelfth, thirteenth, and fourteenth centuries occasional voyages continued to be made; and it is said that as late as A. D. 1347 a Norwegian ship visited Labrador and the north-eastern parts of the United States. The Norse remains which have been found at Newport, at Garnet Point, and several other places seem to point clearly to some such events as are here described; and the Icelandic historians give a uniform and tolerably consistent account of these early exploits of their countrymen. When the word America is mentioned in the hearing of the Icelandic schoolboys, they will at once answer, with enthusiasm, "Oh, yes; Lief Erickson discovered that country in the year 1001."

An event is to be weighed by its consequences. From the discovery of America by the Norsemen, nothing whatever resulted. The world was neither wiser nor better. Among the Icelanders themselves the place and the very name of Vinland were forgotten. Europe never heard of such a country or such a discovery. Historians have until late years been incredulous on the subject, and the fact is as though it had never been. The curtain which had been lifted for a moment was stretched again from sky to sea, and the New World still lay hidden in the shadows.[4]

---

[4] As to the reality of the Norse discoveries in America, the following from Humboldt's Cosmos, Vol. II., pp. 269-272, may be cited as conclusive: "We are here on historical ground. By the critical and highly praiseworthy efforts of Professor Rafn and the Royal Society of Antiquaries in Copenhagen, the Sagas and documents in regard to the expeditions of the Norsemen to Newfoundland, Nova Scotia, and Vinland have been published and satisfactorily commented upon. **** The discovery of the northern part of America by the Norsemen can not be disputed. The length of the voyage, the direction in which they sailed, the time of the sun's rising and setting, are accurately given. While the Caliphate of Bagdad was still flourishing, **** America was discovered about the year A. D. 1000, by Lief, the son of Eric the Red, at the latitude of forty-one and a-half degrees north."

CHAPTER III.

SPANISH DISCOVERIES IN AMERICA.

IT was reserved for the people of a sunnier clime than Iceland first to make known to the European nations the existence of a Western continent. Spain was the happy country under whose auspicious patronage a new world was to be added to the old; but the man who was destined to make the revelation was not himself a Spaniard: he was to come from genial Italy, the land of olden valor and the home of so much greatness. CHRISTOPHER COLUMBUS was the name of that man whom after ages have justly rewarded with imperishable fame.

The idea that the world is round was not original with Columbus. Others before him had held a similar belief; but the opinion had been so feebly and uncertainly entertained as to lead to no practical results. Copernicus, the Prussian astronomer, had not yet taught, nor had Galileo, the great Italian, yet demonstrated, the true system of the universe. The English traveler, Sir John Mandeville, had declared in the very first English book that ever was written (A. D. 1356) that the world is a sphere; that he himself, when traveling northward, had seen the polar star approach the zenith, and that on going southward the antarctic constellations had risen overhead; and that it was both possible and practicable for a man to sail around the world and return to the place of starting but neither Sir John himself nor any other seaman of his times was bold enough to undertake so hazardous an enterprise.[5] Columbus was, no doubt, the first *practical* believer in the theory of circumnavigation; and although he never sailed around the world himself, he demonstrated the possibility of doing so.

The great mistake with Columbus and others who shared his opinions was not concerning the figure of the earth, but in regard to its size. He believed the world to be no more than ten thousand or twelve thousand miles in circumference. He therefore confidently expected that after

---

[5] See Appendix A.

sailing about three thousand miles to the westward he should arrive at the East Indies; and to do that was the one great purpose of his life.

Christopher Columbus.

Christopher Columbus was born at Genoa, a seacoast town of North-western Italy, in A. D. 1435. He was carefully educated, and then devoted himself to the sea. His ancestors had been seamen before him. His own inclination as well as his early training made him a sailor. For twenty years he traversed the Mediterranean and the parts of the Atlantic adjacent to Europe; he visited Iceland; then went to Portugal, and finally to Spain. The idea of reaching the Indies by crossing the Atlantic had already possessed him. For more than ten years the poor enthusiast was a beggar, going from court to court, explaining to dull monarchs and bigoted monks the figure of the earth and the ease with which the rich islands of the East might be reached by sailing westward. He found one appreciative listener, afterward his constant and faithful friend—the noble and sympathetic Isabella, queen of Castile. Be it never forgotten that to the faith, and insight, and decision of a woman the final success of Columbus must be attributed.

CHART I.

1000   **1100**   **1200**   **1300**

Central Period of the Middle Ages.
                                    80. **The King**
24. **Conrad II.**   52. **Frederick Barbarossa.**
             The CRUSADES.
                99. **The Kingdom of Jerusalem established.**
       35. **Union of Castile and Leon.**   26. **Louis IX.**
                                        85. **Philip IV.**
     39. **Henry the Black.**   8. **Louis VI.**
                                            16. **Phi**
     56. **Henry IV.**
HOUSE OF CAPET IN FRANCE.   **The different Orders of Knighthood establisl**
                   37. **Louis VII.**   28.
   17 **Canute.**   71. **Conquest of Ireland.**
                     89. **Philip II.**
      40. **Hardicanute.**
        42. **Edward the Confessor.**
             66. **Harold.**   38. **Struggle of the Guelphs and Ghibellines.**
             66. **William I.**   **Wars of the Barons.**
                  35. **Stephen.**   15. **Magna Charta granted**
             87. **William Rufus.**
DANISH KINGS IN ENGLAND.   **Henry I.**
                  54. **Henry II.**   72. **Edward I.**
                     89. **Richard I.**   7. **Edwar**
                     99. **John.**   W
     The NORMANS. The PLANTAGENETS. **Heroic Age.**   27.

1. **LEIF ERICKSON**, an Icelandic navigator, sailing westward from Greenland, discovers the coast of Labrador, and makes explorations as far south as Rhode Island.

Bjarne Herjulfson driven by a storm within sight of the American coast A. D. 986.

2. **Thorwald Erickson** returns to America and remains three years.

5. **Thorstein Erickson** comes to America.

7. **Thorfinn Karlsefne** explores the coast of Massachusetts.

11. Expedition of **Freydis** to Vinland.

THE WESTERN CONTINENT UNKNOWN TO THE

21. **Erik Upsi** sent as bishop to Vinland.

DOUBTFUL ICELANDIC AND NORWEGIAN VOYAGES

70. Alleged discovery of America by **Madoc** the We

AMERICA UNDER THE ABORIGI

CHART I.

PERIOD OF VOYAGE AND DISCOVERY,
A. D. 986—1607.

ICELANDIC discoveries in *green*
SPANISH   "   " *yello*
ENGLISH   "   " *red.*
FRENCH   "   " *blue.*
DUTCH   "   " *brow*
PORTUGUESE   "   " *purp*

PERIOD OF VOYAGE AND DISCOVERY. A. D. 986-1607.

1400 **1500** **1600**

of Jerusalem overthrown.
35. **Columbus** born.
15. **John Huss.**
First book written in English, in which the author, Sir John Mandeville, declares the spherical figure of the earth and the practicability of circumnavigation.
98. **De Gama** doubles the Cape of Good Hope and reaches the East Indies.
48. **Treaty of Westphalia.**
80. Charles VI.
Printing Invented.
11-31. **Joan of Arc.**
Luther.
22. Charles VII.
The Reformation.
61. Louis XI.
E OF
9. **John Calvin.**
OIS.
72. St. Bartholomew.
77. Richard II.
15. **Francis I.**
Wars of the Roses.
80. Henry IV.
The LANCASTERS.
19. **Charles V.**
74. Ferdinand and Isabella.
10. Louis XIII.
The TUDORS.
The PURITANS.
43. **Louis XIV**
85. Henry VII.
The YORKS.
3. **James I.**
99. Henry IV.
9. **Henry VIII.**
13. Henry V.
47. Edward VI.
25. **Charles I.**
22. Henry VI.
53. Mary.
The STUARTS.
61. Edward IV.
83. Edward V.
58. **Elizabeth.**
ard III.
83. Richard III.

---

92. **Columbus** discovers the West Indies.
   Second voyage.
OPEAN NATIONS.
98. Third voyage.
93. **Discovers America.**
99. **Amerigo Vespucci** makes a voyage to South America.
he great plague depopulates Iceland, Greenland, and Vinland; communication with the New World is cut off.
12. **De Leon** explores Florida.
20. **Cortez** conquers Mexico.
25. **De Ayllon** in Carolina.
28. **De Narvaez** makes explorations in Florida.
39. **De Soto** in America.
65. **Melendez** founds St. Augustine.

97. **John Cabot** discovers North America.
98. **Sebastian Cabot** explores the American coast.
78. **Martin Frobisher's** voyages.
79. **Drake** on the Pacific coast.
83. **Gilbert's** voyage.
Raleigh's attempts at colonization.
company of Norsemen in America.
2. **Gosnold's** direct voyage.
3. **Pring's** voyage.
7. Settlement at **Jamestown**
77. **Columbus** visits Iceland and learns of the New World.
8. **Waymouth** in Maine.
20. The **Puritans** at **Plymouth.**

AL TRIBES.
24. **Verrazzani** explores the American coast.
34. **Cartier's** expedition.
42. **Roberval** in Canada.
62. **Ribault** with the Huguenots.
64. **Laudonniere's** enterprise.
98. **La Roche** in Nova Scotia.
4. **De Monts** and Champlain.
5. **Port Royal** founded.
8. Founding of **Quebec.**

9. **Hudson** in America.
14. Explorations of **Block** and **May.**
14. Founding of **New Amsterdam.**

1. Voyages of the **Cortereals.**
19. **Magellan** circumnavigates the globe.

The Night of October 11, 1492.

On the morning of the 3d day of August, 1492, Columbus, with his three ships, left the harbor of Palos. After seventy-one days of sailing, in the early dawn of October 12, Rodrigo Triana, who chanced to be on the lookout from the Pinta, set up a shout of "*Land!*" A gun was fired as the signal. The ships lay to. There was music and jubilee; and just at sunrise Columbus himself first stepped ashore, shook out the royal banner of Castile in the presence of the wondering natives, and named the island San Salvador. During the three remaining months of this first voyage the islands of Concepcion, Cuba and Hayti were added to the list of discoveries; and on the bay of Caracola, in the last named island, was erected out of the timbers of the Santa Maria a fort the first structure built by Europeans in the New World. In the early part of January, 1493, Columbus sailed for Spain, where he arrived in March, and was everywhere greeted with rejoicings and applause.

In September of the following autumn Columbus sailed on his second voyage. He still believed that by this route westward he should reach, if indeed he had not already reached, the Indies. The result of the second voyage was the discovery of the Windward group and the islands of Jamaica and Porto Rico. It was at this time that the first colony was established in Hayti and Columbus's brother appointed governor. After an absence of nearly three years, Columbus returned to Spain in the summer of 1496—returned to find himself the victim of a thousand bitter jealousies and suspicions. All the rest of his life was clouded with persecutions and misfortunes. He made a third voyage, discovered the island of Trinidad and the mainland of South America, near the mouth of the Orinoco. Thence he sailed back to Hayti, where he found his colony disorganized; and here, while attempting to restore order, he was seized by Bobadilla, an agent of the Spanish government, put in chains and carried to Spain. After a disgraceful imprisonment, he was liberated and sent on a fourth and last voyage in search of the Indies; but besides making some explorations along the south side of the Gulf of Mexico, the expedition accomplished nothing, and Columbus, overwhelmed with discouragements, returned once more to his ungrateful country. The good Isabella was dead, and the great discoverer found himself at last a friendless and despised old man tottering into the grave. Death came, and fame afterward.

Of all the wrongs done to the memory of Columbus, perhaps the greatest was that which robbed him of the name of the new continent. This was bestowed upon one of the least worthy of the many adventurers whom the genius and success of Columbus had drawn to the West. In the year 1499, AMERIGO VESPUCCI, a Florentine navigator of some daring but no great celebrity, reached the eastern coast of South America. It does not appear that his explorations there were of any great importance. Two years later he made a second voyage, and then hastened home to give to Europe the first published account of the Western World. Vespucci's only merit consisted in his recognition of the fact that the recent discoveries were not a portion of that India already known, but were in reality another continent. In his published narrative all reference to Columbus was carefully omitted; and thus through his own craft, assisted by the unappreciative dullness of the times, the name of this Vespucci rather than that of the true discoverer was given to the New World.

The discovery of America produced great excitement throughout the states of Western Europe. In Spain especially there was wonderful zeal and enthusiasm. Within ten years after the death of Columbus, the principal islands of the West Indies were explored and colonized. In the year 1510 the Spaniards planted on the Isthmus of Darien their first continental colony. Three years later, VASCO NUNEZ DE BALBOA, the governor of the colony, learning from the natives that another ocean lay only a short distance to the westward, crossed the isthmus and from an eminence looked down upon the Pacific. Not satisfied with merely seeing the great water, he waded in a short distance, and drawing his sword after the pompous Spanish fashion, took possession of the ocean in the name of the king of Spain.

Meanwhile, JUAN PONCE DE LEON, who had been a companion of Columbus on his second voyage, fitted out a private expedition of discovery and adventure. De Leon had grown rich as governor of Porto Rico, and while growing rich had also grown old. But there was a fountain of perpetual youth somewhere in the Bahamas—so said all the learning and intelligence of Spain—and in that fountain the wrinkled old cavalier would bathe and be young again. So in the year 1512 he set sail from Porto Rico; and stopping first at San Salvador and the neighboring islands, he came, on Easter Sunday, the 27th of March, in sight of an unknown shore. He supposed that another island more beautiful than the rest was discovered. There were waving forests, green leaves, birds of song and the fragrance of blossoms. Partly in honor of the day, called in the ritual of the Church Pascua Florida, and partly to describe the delightful landscape that opened on his sight, he named the new shore Florida—the Land of Flowers.

After a few days a landing was effected a short distance north of where, a half century later, were laid the foundations of St. Augustine. The country was claimed for the king of Spain, and the search for the youth-restoring fountain was eagerly prosecuted. The romantic adventurer turned southward, explored the coast for many leagues, discovered and named the Tortugas, doubled Cape Florida, and then sailed back to Porto Rico, not perceptibly younger than when he started.

The king of Spain rewarded Ponce with the governorship of his Land of Flowers, and sent him thither again to establish a colony. The aged veteran did not, however, reach his province until the year 1521, and then it was only to find the Indians in a state of bitter hostility. Scarcely had he landed when they fell upon him in a furious battle; many of the Spaniards were killed outright, and the rest had to betake themselves to the ships for safety. Ponce de Leon himself received a mortal wound from an arrow, and was carried back to Cuba to die.

CHAPTER IV.

SPANISH DISCOVERIES IN AMERICA.—CONTINUED.

THE year 1517 was marked by the discovery of Yucatan and the Bay of Campeachy by FERNANDEZ DE CORDOVA. While exploring the northern coast of the country, his company was attacked by the natives, and he himself mortally wounded. During the next year the coast of Mexico was explored for a great distance by GRIJALVA, assisted by Cordova's pilot; and in the year 1519, FERNANDO CORTEZ landed with his fleet at Tabasco and began his famous conquest of Mexico.

As soon as the news of the invasion spread abroad, the subjects of the Mexican empire were thrown into consternation. Armies of native warriors gathered to resist the progress of the Spaniards, but were dispersed by the invaders. After freeing the coast of his opponents, Cortez proceeded westward to Vera Cruz, a seaport one hundred and eighty miles south-east of the Mexican capital. Here he was met by ambassadors from the celebrated Montezuma, emperor of the country. From him they delivered messages and exhibited great anxiety lest Cortez should march into the interior. He assured them that such was indeed his purpose; that his business in the country was urgent; and that he must confer with Montezuma in person.

The ambassadors tried in vain to dissuade the terrible Spaniard. They made him costly presents, and then hastened back to their alarmed sovereign. Montezuma immediately despatched them a second time with presents still more valuable, and with urgent appeals to Cortez to proceed no farther. But the cupidity of the Spaniards was now inflamed to the highest pitch, and burning their ships behind them, they began their march towards the capital. The Mexican emperor by his messengers forbade their approach to his city. Still they pressed on. The nations tributary to Montezuma threw off their allegiance, made peace with the conqueror, and even joined his standard. The irresolute and vacillating Indian monarch knew not what to do. The Spaniards came in sight of the city—a glittering and splendid vision of spires and temples; and the poor Montezuma came forth to receive his remorseless enemies. On the morning of the 8th of November, 1519, the Spanish army marched over the causeway leading into the Mexican capital and was quartered in the great central square near the temple of the Aztec god of war.

Fernando Cortez.

It was now winter time. For a month Cortez remained quietly in the city. He was permitted to go about freely with his soldiers, and was even allowed to examine the sacred altars and shrines where human sacrifices were daily offered up to the deities of Mexico. He made himself familiar with the defences of the capital and the Mexican mode of warfare. On every side he found inexhaustible stores of provisions, treasures of gold and silver, and what greatly excited his solicitude, arsenals filled with bows and javelins. But although surrounded with splendor and abundance, his own situation became extremely critical. The millions of natives who swarmed around him were becoming familiar with his troops and no longer believed them immortal. There were mutterings of an outbreak which threatened to overwhelm him in an hour. In this emergency the Spanish general adopted the bold and unscrupulous expedient of seizing Montezuma and holding him as a hostage. A plausible pretext for this outrage was found in the fact that the Mexican governor of the province adjacent to Vera Cruz had attacked the Spanish garrison at that place, and that Montezuma himself had acted with hostility and treachery towards the Spaniards while they were marching on the city. As soon as the emperor was in his power, Cortez compelled him to acknowledge himself a vassal of the king of Spain and to agree to the payment of a sum amounting to six million three hundred thousand dollars, with an annual tribute afterwards.

In the mean time, Velasquez, the Spanish governor of Cuba, jealous of the fame of Cortez, had despatched a force to Mexico to arrest his progress and to supersede him in the command. The expedition was led by PAMPHILO DE NARVAEZ, the same who was afterwards governor of Florida. His forces consisted of more than twelve hundred well armed and well disciplined soldiers, besides a thousand Indian servants and guides. But the vigilant Cortez had meanwhile been informed by messengers from Vera Cruz of the movement which his enemies at home had set on foot against him, and he determined to sell his command only at the price of his own life and the lives of all his followers. He therefore instructed Alvarado, one of his subordinate officers, to remain in the capital with a small force of a hundred and forty men; and with the remainder, numbering less than two hundred, he himself hastily withdrew from the city and proceeded by a forced march to encounter De Narvaez on the sea-coast. On the night of the 26th of May, 1520, while the soldiers of the latter were quietly asleep in their camp near Vera Cruz, Cortez burst upon them with the fury of despair, and before they could rally or well understand the terrible onset, compelled the whole force to surrender. Then, adding the general's skill to the warrior's prowess, he succeeded in inducing the conquered army to join his own standard; and with his forces thus augmented to six times their original numbers he began a second time his march towards the capital.

While Cortez was absent on this expedition, the Mexicans of the capital rose in arms, and the possession of the country was staked on the issue of war. Alvarado, either fearing a revolt or from a spirit of atrocious cruelty, had attacked the Mexicans while they were celebrating one of their festivals, and slain five hundred of the leaders and priests. The people in a frenzy of astonishment and rage flew to their arms and laid siege to the palace where Alvarado and his men were fortified. The Spaniards were already hard pressed when Cortez at the head of his new army reached the city. He entered without opposition and joined Alvarado's command; but the passions of the Mexicans were now thoroughly aroused, and not all the diplomacy of the Spanish general could again bring them into subjection. In a few days the conflict began in earnest. The streets were deluged with the blood of tens of thousands; and not a few of the Spaniards fell before the vengeance of the native warriors. For months there was almost incessant fighting in and around the city and it became evident that the Spaniards must ultimately be overwhelmed and destroyed.

To save himself from his peril, Cortez adopted a second shameless expedient, more wicked than the first. Montezuma was compelled to go upon the top of the palace in front of the great square where the besiegers were gathered and to counsel them to make peace with the Spaniards. For a moment there was universal silence, then a murmur of vexation and rage, and then Montezuma was struck down by the javelins of his own subjects. In a few days he died of wretchedness and despair, and for a while the warriors, overwhelmed with remorse, abandoned the conflict. But with the renewal of the strife Cortez was obliged to leave the city. Finally a great battle was fought, and the Spanish arms and valor triumphed. In the crisis of the struggle the sacred Mexican banner was struck down and captured. Dismay seized the hosts of puny warriors, and they fled in all directions. In December of 1520, Cortez again marched on the capital. A siege, lasting until August of the following year, ensued; and then the famous city yielded. The empire of the Montezumas was overthrown, and Mexico became a Spanish province.

Among the many daring enterprises which marked the beginning of the sixteenth century, that of FERDINAND MAGELLAN is worthy of Special mention. A Portuguese by birth, a navigator by profession, this man, so noted for extraordinary boldness and ability, determined to discover a south-west rather than a north-west passage to Asia. With this object in view, he appealed to the king of Portugal for ships and men. The monarch listened coldly, and did nothing to give encouragement. Incensed at this treatment, Magellan threw off his allegiance, went to Spain—the usual resort of disappointed seamen—and laid his plans before Charles V. The emperor caught eagerly at the opportunity, and ordered a fleet of five ships to be immediately fitted at the public expense and properly manned with crews.

The voyage was begun from Seville in August of 1519. Sailing southward across the equinoctial line, Magellan soon reached the coast of South America, and spent the autumn in explorations, hoping to find some strait that should lead him westward into that ocean which Balboa had discovered six years previously. Not at first successful in this effort, he passed the winter—which was summer on that side of the equator—somewhere on the coast of Brazil. Renewing his voyage southward, he came at last to the eastern mouth of that strait which still bears the name of its discoverer, and passing through it found himself in the open and boundless ocean. The weather was beautiful, and the peaceful deep was called the Pacific.

Setting his prows to the north of west, Magellan now held steadily on his course for nearly four months, suffering much meanwhile from want of water and scarcity of provisions. In March of 1520 he came to the group of islands called the Ladrones, situated about midway between Australia and Japan. Sailing still westward, he reached the Philippine group, where he was killed in a battle with the natives. But the fleet was now less than four hundred miles from China, and the rest of the route was easy. A new captain was chosen, and the voyage continued by way of the Moluccas, where a cargo of spices was taken on board for the market of Western Europe. Only a single ship was deemed in a fit condition to venture on the homeward voyage; but in this vessel the crews embarked, and returning by way of the Cape of Good Hope arrived in Spain on the 17th day of September, 1522. The circumnavigation of the globe, long believed in as a possibility, had now become a thing of reality. The theory of the old astronomers, of Mandeville and of Columbus had been proved by actual demonstration.

The next important voyage undertaken to the shores of America was in the year 1520. LUCAS VASQUEZ DE AYLLON, who had been a judge in St. Domingo and had acquired great riches, conducted the expedition. He and six other wealthy men, eager to stock their plantations with slaves, determined to do so by kidnapping natives from the neighboring Bahamas. Two vessels were fitted out for the purpose, and De Ayllon commanded in person. When the vessels were nearing their destination, they encountered a storm which drove them northward about a hundred and fifty leagues, and brought them against the coast of South Carolina. The ships entered St. Helena Sound and anchored in the mouth of the Cambahee River. The name of Chicora was given to the country, and the river was called the Jordan. The timid but friendly natives, as soon as their fans had subsided, began to make presents to the strangers and to treat them with great cordiality. They flocked on board the ships and when the decks were crowded, De Ayllon, watching his opportunity, weighed anchor and sailed away. A few days afterward an avenging storm sent one of the ships to the bottom of the sea, and death came mercifully to most of the poor wretches who were huddled under the hatches of the other.

Going at once to Spain, De Ayllon repeated the story of his exploit to Charles V., who rewarded him with the governorship of Chicora and the privilege of conquest. Returning to his province in 1525, he found the natives intensely hostile. His best ship ran aground in the mouth of the Jordan, and the outraged Indians fell upon him with fury, killing many of the treacherous crew, and making the rest glad enough to get away with their lives. De Ayllon himself returned to St. Domingo humiliated and ruined. Thus ended the first disgraceful effort to enslave the Indians.

In the year 1526, Charles V. appointed the unprincipled PAMPHILO DE NARVAEZ governor of Florida, and to the appointment was added the usual privilege of conquest. The territory thus placed at his disposal extended from Cape Sable fully three-fifths of the way around the Gulf of Mexico, and was limited on the south-west by the mouth of the River of Palms. With this extensive commission De Narvaez arrived at Tampa Bay in the month of April, 1528. His force consisted of two hundred and sixty soldiers and forty horsemen. The natives treated them with suspicion, and, anxious to be rid of the intruders, began to hold up their gold trinkets and to point to the north. The hint was eagerly caught at by the avaricious Spaniards, whose imaginations were set on fire with the sight of the precious metal. They struck boldly into the forests, expecting to find cities and empires, and found instead swamps and savages. They reached the Withlacoochie and crossed it by swimming, they passed over the Suwanee in a canoe which they made for the occasion, and finally came to Apalachee, a squalid village of forty cabins. This, then, was the mighty city to which their guides had directed them.

Oppressed with fatigue and goaded by hunger, they plunged again into the woods, wading through lagoons and assailed by lurking savages, until at last they reached the sea at the harbor of St. Mark's. Here they expected to find their ships, but not a ship was there, or had been. With great labor they constructed some brigantines, and put to sea in the vain hope of reaching the Spanish settlements in Mexico. They were tossed by storms, driven out of sight of land and then thrown upon the shore again, drowned, slain by the savages, left in the solitary woods dead of starvation and despair, until finally four miserable men of all the adventurons company, under the leadership of the heroic De Vaca, first lieutenant of the expedition, were rescued at the village of San Miguel, on the Pacific coast, and conducted to the city of Mexico. The story can hardly be paralleled in the annals of suffering and peril.

But the Spaniards were not yet satisfied. In the year 1537 a new expedition was planned which surpassed all the others in the brilliancy of its beginning and the disasters of its end. The most cavalier of the cavaliers was FERDINAND DE SOTO, of Xeres. Besides the distinction of a noble birth, he had been the lieutenant and bosom friend of Pizarro, and had now returned from Peru loaded with wealth. So great was his popularity in Spain that he had only to demand what he would have of the emperor that his request might be granted. At his own dictation he was accordingly appointed governor of Cuba and Florida, with the privilege of exploring and conquering the latter country at his pleasure. A great company of young Spaniards, nearly all of them wealthy and high-born, flocked to his standard. Of these he selected six hundred of the most gallant and daring. They were clad in costly suits of armor of the knightly pattern, with airy scarfs and silken embroidery and all the trappings of chivalry. Elaborate preparations were made for the grand conquest; arms and stores were provided; shackles were wrought for the slaves; tools for the forge and workshop were abundantly supplied; bloodhounds were bought and trained for the work of hunting fugitives; cards to keep the young knights excited with gaming; twelve priests to conduct religious ceremonies; and, last of all, a drove of swine to fatten on the maize and mast of the country.

When, after a year of impatience and delay, everything was at last in readiness, the gay Castilian squadron, ten vessels in all, left the harbor of San Lucar to conquer imaginary empires in the New World. The fleet touched at Havana, and the enthusiasm was kindled even to a higher pitch than it had reached in Spain. De Soto left his wife to govern Cuba during his absence; and after a prosperous and exulting voyage of two weeks, the ships cast anchor in Tampa Bay. This was in the early part of June, 1539. When some of the Cubans who had joined the expedition first saw the silent forests and gloomy morasses that stretched before them, they were terrified at the prospect, and sailed back to the security of home; but De Soto and his cavaliers despised such cowardice, and began their march into the interior. During the months of July, August and September they marched to the northward, wading through swamps, swimming rivers and fighting the Indians. In October they arrived at the country of the Apalachians, on the left bank of Flint River, where they determined to spend the winter. For four months they remained in this locality, sending out exploring parties in various directions. One of these companies reached the gulf at Pensacola, and made arrangements that supplies should be sent out from Cuba to that place during the following summer.

In the early spring the Spaniards left their winter quarters and continued their march to the north and east. An Indian guide told them of a powerful and populous empire in that direction; a woman was empress, and the land was full of gold. A Spanish soldier, one of the men of Narvaez, who had been kept a captive among the Indians, denied the truth of the extravagant story; but De Soto only said that he would find gold or see poverty with his own eyes, and the freebooters pressed on through the swamps and woods. It was April, 1540, when they came upon the Ogechee River. Here they were delayed. The Indian guide went mad; and when the priests had conjured the evil spirit out of him, he repaid their benevolence by losing the whole company in the forest. By the 1st of May they had reached South Carolina, and were within a two days' march of where De Ayllon had lost his ships and men at the mouth of the Jordan. Thence the wanderers turned westward; but that De Soto and his men crossed the mountains into North Carolina and Tennessee is hardly to be believed. They seem rather to have passed across Northern Georgia from the Chattahouche to the upper tributaries of the Coosa, and thence down that river to the valleys of Lower Alabama. Here, just above the confluence of the Alabama and the Tombecbee, they came upon the fortified Indian town called Mauville, or Mobile, where a terrible battle was fought with the natives. The town was set on fire, and two thousand five hundred of the Indians were killed or burned to death. Eighteen of De Soto's men were killed, and a hundred and fifty wounded. The Spaniards also lost about eighty horses and all of their baggage.

The ships of supply had meanwhile arrived at Pensacola, but De Soto and his men, although in desperate circumstances, were too stubborn and proud to avail themselves of help or even to send news of their whereabouts. They turned resolutely to the north; but the country was poor, and their condition grew constantly worse and worse. By the middle of December they had reached the country of the Chickasas, in Northern Mississippi. They crossed the Yazoo; the weather was severe; snow fell and the Spaniards were on the point of starvation. They succeeded, however, in finding some fields of ungathered maize, and then came upon a deserted Indian village which promised them shelter for the winter. After remaining here till February, 1541, they were suddenly attacked in the dead of night by the Indians, who, at a preconcerted signal, set the town on fire, determined then and there to make an end of the desolating foreigners; but the Spanish weapons and discipline again saved De Soto and his men from destruction.

After gathering provisions and reclothing themselves as well as possible, the Spaniards set out again in early spring to journey still farther westward. The guides now brought them to the Mississippi. The point where the majestic Father of Waters was first seen by white men was at the lower Chickasaw Bluff, a little north of the thirty-fourth parallel of latitude; the day of the discovery cannot certainly be known. The Indians came down the river in a fleet of canoes, and offered to carry the Spaniards over; but the horses could not be transported until barges were built for that purpose. The crossing was not effected until the latter part of May.

De Soto's men now found themselves in the land of the Dakotas. Journeying to the north-west, they passed through a country where wild fruits were plentiful and subsistence easy. The natives were inoffensive and superstitious. At one place they were going to worship the woebegone cavaliers as the children of the gods, but De Soto was too good a Catholic to permit such idolatry. The Spaniards continued their march until they reached the St. Francis River, which they crossed, and gained the southern limits of Missouri, in the vicinity of New Madrid. Thence westward the march was renewed for about two hundred miles; thence southward to the Hot Springs and the tributaries of the Washita River. On the banks of this river, at the town of Atiamque, they passed the winter of 1541-42. The Indians were found to be much more civilized than those east of the Mississippi; but their civilization did not protect them in the least from the horrid cruelties which the Spaniards practiced. No consideration of justice, humanity or mercy moved the stony hearts of these polite and Christian warriors. Indian towns were set on fire for sport; Indian hands were chopped off for a whim; and Indian captives burned alive because, under fear of death, they had told a falsehood.

But De Soto's men were themselves growing desperate in their misfortunes. They turned again toward the sea, and passing down the tributaries of the Washita to the junction of that stream with the Red River, came upon the Mississippi in the neighborhood of Natchez. The spirit of De Soto was at last completely broken. The haughty cavalier bowed his head and became a prey to melancholy. No more dazzling visions of Peru and Mexico flitted before his imagination. A malignant fever seized upon his emaciated frame, and then death. The priests chanted a requiem, and in the middle of the solemn night his sorrowful companions put the dead hero's body into a rustic coffin, and rowing out a distance from shore sunk it in the Mississippi. Ferdinand de Soto had found a grave under the rolling waters of the great river with which his name will be associated for ever.

Before his death, De Soto had named Moscoso as his successor; and now, under the leadership of the new governor, the ragged, half-starved adventurers, in the vain hope of reaching Mexico, turned once more to the west. They crossed the country to the upper waters of the Red River, on the confines of Texas. Thence they turned northward into the territory of the Pawnees and the Comanches, ranging the hunting-grounds of those fierce savages until stopped by the mountains. In December of 1542, after almost endless wanderings and hardships, they came again to the Mississippi, reaching the now familiar stream a short distance above the mouth of Red River. They now formed the desperate resolution of building boats, and thus descending the river to the gulf. They erected a forge, broke off the fetters of the captives in order to procure iron, sawed timber in the forest, and at last completed seven brigantines and launched them. The time thus occupied extended from January to July of 1543. The Indians of the neighborhood were now for the last time plundered in order to furnish supplies for the voyage; and on the 2d day of July the Spaniards went on board their boats and started for the sea. The distance was almost five hundred miles, and seventeen days were required to make the descent. On reaching the Gulf of Mexico, they steered to the south-west; and keeping as close to the shore as possible, after fifty-five days of buffetings and perils along the dangerous coast, they came—three hundred and eleven famished and heart-broken fugitives—to the settlement at the mouth of the River of Palms; and thus ended the most marvelous expedition in the early history of our country.

Burial of de Soto.

The next attempt by the Spaniards to colonize Florida was in the year 1565. The enterprise was entrusted to PEDRO MELENDEZ, a Spanish soldier of ferocious disposition and criminal practices. He was under sentence to pay a heavy fine at the very time when he received his commission from the bigoted Philip II. The contract between that monarch and Melendez was to the effect that the latter should within three years explore the coast of Florida, conquer the country, and plant in some favorable district a colony of not less than five hundred persons, of whom one hundred should be married men. Melendez was to receive two hundred and twenty-five square miles of land adjacent to the settlement, and an annual salary of two thousand dollars. Twenty-five hundred persons collected around Melendez to join in the expedition. The fleet left Spain in July, reached Porto Rico early in August, and on the 28th of the same month came in sight of Florida.

It must now be understood that the real object had in view by Melendez was to attack and destroy a colony of French Protestants called Huguenots, who, in the previous year, had made a settlement about thirty-five miles above the mouth of the St. John's River. This was, of course, within the limits of the territory claimed by Spain and Melendez at once perceived that to extirpate these French heretics in the name of patriotism and religion would be likely to restore his shattered character and bring him into favor again. His former crimes were to be washed out in the blood of the innocents. Moreover, the Catholic party at the French court had communicated with the Spanish court as to the whereabouts and intentions of the Huguenots, so that Melendez knew precisely where to find them and how to compass their destruction.

It was St. Augustine's day when the dastardly Spaniard came in sight of the shore, but the landing was not effected until the 2d of September. The spacious harbor and the small river which enters it from the south were named in honor of the saint. On the 8th day of the same month, Philip II. was proclaimed monarch of all North America; a solemn mass was said by the priests; and there, in the sight of forest, and sky, and sea, the foundation-stones of the oldest town in the United States were put into their place. This was seventeen years before the founding of Santa

Fé by Antonio de Espego, and forty-two years before the settlement at Jamestown.

As soon as the new town was sufficiently advanced to be secure against accident, Melendez turned his attention to the Huguenots. The latter were expecting to be attacked, but had supposed that the Spanish fleet would sail up the St. John's, and make the onset from that direction. Accordingly, knowing that they must fight or die, all the French vessels except two left their covert in the river and put to sea, intending to anticipate the movements of the Spaniards; but a furious storm arose and dashed to pieces every ship in the fleet. Most of the crews, however, reached the shore just above the mouth of the river. Melendez now collected his forces at St. Augustine, stole through the woods and swamps, and falling unexpectedly on the defenceless colony, utterly destroyed it. Men, women and children were alike given up to butchery. Two hundred were killed outright. A few escaped into the forest, Laudonniere, the Huguenot leader, among the number, and making their way to the coast, were picked up by the two French ships which had been saved from the storm.

The crews of the wrecked vessels were the next object of Spanish vengeance. Melendez discovered their whereabouts, and deceiving them with treacherous promises of clemency, induced them to surrender. They were ferried across the river in boats; but no sooner were they completely in the power of their enemy than their hands were bound behind them, and they were driven off, tied two and two, toward St. Augustine. As they approached the Spanish fort the signal was given by sounding a trumpet, and the work of slaughter began anew. Seven hundred defenceless victims were added to the previous atrocious massacre. Only a few mechanics and Catholic servants were left alive. Under these bloody auspices the first permanent European colony was planted in our country. In what way the Huguenots were revenged upon their enemies will be told in another place.

The Spaniards had now explored the entire coast from the Isthmus of Darien to Port Royal in South Carolina. They were acquainted with the country west of the Mississippi as far north as New Mexico and Missouri, and east of that river they had traversed the Gulf States as far as the mountain ranges of Tennessee and North Carolina. With the establishment of their first permanent colony on the coast of Florida the period of Spanish voyage and discovery may be said to end.

Before closing this chapter, a brief account of the only important voyage made by the Portuguese to America will be given: At the time of the first discovery by Columbus, the unambitious John II. was king of Portugal. He paid but little attention to the New World, preferring the security and dullness of his own capital to the splendid allurements of the Atlantic. In 1495 he was succeeded on the throne by his cousin Manuel, a man of very different character. This monarch could hardly forgive his predecessor for having allowed Spain to snatch from the flag of Portugal the glory of Columbus's achievements. In order to secure some of the benefits which yet remained, King Manuel fitted out two vessels, and in the summer of 1501 commissioned GASPAR CORTEREAL to sail on a voyage of discovery. The Portuguese vessels reached America in the month of July, and beginning at some point on the shores of Maine, sailed northward, exploring the coast for nearly seven hundred miles. Just below the fiftieth parallel of latitude Cortereal met the icebergs, and could go no farther. Little attention was paid by him to the great forests of pine and hemlock which stood tall and silent along the shore, promising ship-yards and cities in after times. He satisfied his rapacity by kidnapping fifty Indians, whom, on his return to Portugal, he sold as slaves. A new voyage was then undertaken, with the avowed purpose of capturing another cargo of natives for the slave-mart of Europe; but when a year went by, and no tidings arrived from the fleet, the brother of the Portuguese captain sailed in hope of finding the missing vessels. He also was lost, but in what manner has never been ascertained. The fate of the Corte reals and their slave-ships has remained one of the unsolved mysteries of the sea.

CHAPTER V.

THE FRENCH IN AMERICA.

FRANCE was not slow to profit by the discoveries of Columbus. As early as 1504 the fishermen of Normandy and Brittany began to ply their vocation on the banks of Newfoundland. A map of the Gulf of St. Lawrence was drawn by a Frenchman in the year 1506. Two years later some Indians were taken to France; and in 1518 the attention of Francis I. was turned to the colonization of the New World. Five years afterward a voyage of discovery and exploration was planned, and JOHN VERRAZZANI, a native of Florence, was commissioned to conduct the expedition. The special object had in view was to discover a north-west passage to Asia.

In the month of January, 1524, Verrazzani left the shores of Europe. His fleet consisted at first of four vessels but three of them were damaged in a storm, and the voyage was undertaken with a single ship, called the Dolphin. For fifty days, through the buffetings of tempestuous weather, the courageous mariner held on his course, and on the 7th day of March discovered the main land in the latitude of Wilmington. He first sailed southward a hundred and fifty miles in the hope of finding a harbor, but found none. Returning northward, he finally anchored somewhere along the low sandy beach which stretches between the mouth of Cape Fear River and Pamlico Sound. Here he began a traffic with the natives. The Indians of this neighborhood were found to be a gentle and timid sort of creatures, unsuspicious and confiding. A half-drowned sailor who was washed ashore by the surf was treated with great kindness, and as soon as opportunity offered, permitted to return to the ship.

After a few days the voyage was continued toward the north. The whole coast of New Jersey was explored, and the hills marked as containing minerals. The harbor of New York was entered, and its safe and spacious waters were noted with admiration. At Newport, Rhode Island, Verrazzani anchored for fifteen days, and a trade was again opened with the Indians. Before leaving the place the French sailors repaid the confidence of the natives by kidnapping a child and attempting to steal a defenceless Indian girl.

Sailing from Newport, Verrazzani continued his explorations northward. The long and broken line of the New England coast was traced with considerable care. The Indians of the north were wary and suspicious. They would buy neither ornaments nor toys, but were eager to purchase knives and weapons of iron. Passing to the east of Nova Scotia, the bold navigator reached Newfoundland in the latter part of May. In July he returned to France and published an account, still extant, of his great discoveries. The name of New France was now given to the whole country whose sea-coast had been traced by the adventurous crew of the Dolphin.

Such was the distracted condition of France at this time, that another expedition was not planned for a period of ten years. In 1534, however, Chabot, admiral of the kingdom, selected JAMES CARTIER, a seaman of St. Malo, in Brittany, to make a new voyage to America. Two ships were fitted out for the enterprise, and after no more than twenty days of sailing under cloudless skies anchored on the 10th day of May off the coast of Newfoundland. Before the middle of July, Cartier had circumnavigated the island to the northward, crossed the Gulf of St. Lawrence to the south of Anticosti, and entered the Bay of Chaleurs. Not finding, as he had hoped, a passage out of this bay westward, he changed his course to the north again, and ascended the coast as far as Gaspé Bay. Here, upon a point of land, he set up a cross bearing a shield with the lily of France, and proclaimed the French king monarch of the country. Pressing his way still farther northward, and then westward, he entered the St. Lawrence, and ascended the broad estuary until the narrowing banks made him aware that he was in the mouth of a river. Cartier, thinking it impracticable to pass the winter in the New World, now turned his prows toward France, and in thirty days anchored his ships in the harbor of St. Malo.

So great was the fame of Cartier's first voyage that another was planned immediately. Three good ships were provided, and quite a number of young noblemen joined the expedition. Colonization rather than discovery was now the inspiring motive. The sails were set by zealous and excited crews, and on the 19th of May the new voyage was begun. This time there was stormy weather, yet the passage to Newfoundland was made by the 10th of August. It was the day of St. Lawrence, and the name of that martyr was accordingly given to the gulf, and afterward to the noble stream which enters it from the west. Sailing northward around Anticosti, the expedition proceeded up the river to the island of Orleans, where the ships were moored in a place of safety. Two Indians whom Cartier had taken with him to France in the previous year now gave information that higher up the river there was an important town on the island of Hochelaga. Proceeding thither in his boats, the French captain found it as the Indians had said. A beautiful village lay there at the foot of a high hill in the middle of the island. Climbing to the top of the hill, Cartier, as suggested by the scene around him, named the island and town Mont-Real. The country was declared to belong by right of discovery to the king of France; and then the boats dropped down the river to the ships. During this winter twenty-five of Cartier's men were swept off by the scurvy, a malady hitherto unknown in Europe.

With the opening of spring, preparations were made to return to France. The terrible winter had proved too much for French enthusiasm. The emblem of Catholicism, bearing the arms of France, was again planted in the soil of the New World, and the homeward voyage began; but before the ships had left their anchorage, the kindly king of the Hurons, who had treated Cartier with so much generosity, was decoyed on board and carried off to die. On the 6th day of July the fleet reached St. Malo in safety; but by the accounts which Cartier published on his return the French were greatly discouraged. Neither silver nor gold had been found on the banks of the St. Lawrence; and what was a new world good for that had not silver and gold?

Francis of La Roque, lord of ROBERVAL, in Picardy, was the next to undertake the colonization of the countries discovered by the French. This nobleman, four years after Cartier's return from his second voyage, was commissioned by the court of France to plant a colony on the St. Lawrence. The titles of viceroy and lieutenant-general of New France were conferred upon him, and much other vainglorious ceremony attended his preparations for departure. The man, however, who was chiefly relied on to give character and direction to the proposed colony was no other than James Cartier. He only seemed competent to conduct the enterprise with any promise of success. His name was accordingly added to the list, and he was honored with the office of chief pilot and captain general of the expedition.

The next thing to be done was to find material for the colony. This was a difficult task. The French peasants and mechanics were not eager to embark for a country which promised nothing better than savages and snow. Cartier's honest narrative about the resources of New France had left no room for further dreaming. So the work of enlisting volunteers went on slowly, until the government adopted the plan of opening the prisons of the kingdom and giving freedom to whoever would join the expedition. There was a rush of robbers, swindlers and murderers, and the lists were immediately filled. Only counterfeiters and traitors were denied the privilege of gaining their liberty in the New World.

In the latter part of May, 1541, five ships, under the immediate command of Cartier, left France, and soon reached the St. Lawrence. The expedition proceeded up the river to the present site of Quebec, where a fort was erected and named Charlesbourg. Here the colonists passed the winter. Cartier, offended because of the subordinate position which he held, was sullen and gloomy, and made no effort to prosecute discoveries which could benefit no one but the ambitious Roberval. The two leaders never acted in concert; and when La Roque, in June of the following year, arrived with immigrants and supplies, Cartier secretly sailed away with his part of the squadron, and returned to Europe. Roberval was left in New France with three shiploads of criminals who could only be restrained by whipping and hanging. During the autumn some feeble efforts were made to discover a northern passage; the winter was long and severe, and spring was welcomed by the colonists chiefly for the opportunity which it gave them of returning to France. The enterprise undertaken with so much pomp had resulted in nothing. In the year 1549 Roberval, with a large company of emigrants, sailed on a second voyage, but the fleet was never heard of afterward.

Dining-Hall of the French Colonists at Port Royal.

A period of fifty years now elapsed before the French authorities again attempted to colonize America. Meanwhile, private enterprise and religious persecution had co-operated in an effort to accomplish in Florida and Carolina what the government had failed to accomplish on the St. Lawrence. About the middle of the sixteenth century Coligni, the Protestant admiral of France, formed the design of establishing in America a refuge for the persecuted Huguenots of his own country. In 1562 this liberal and influential minister obtained from the sovereign, Charles IX., the coveted privilege of planting a colony of Protestants in the New World. JOHN RIBAULT of Dieppe, a brave and experienced sailor, was selected to lead the Huguenots to the land of promise. Sailing in February, the company reached the coast of Florida at a point where three years later St. Augustine was founded. The River St. John's, called by the Spaniards the St. Matthew, was entered by the French and named the River of May. The vessels then continued northward along the coast until they came to the entrance of Port Royal; here it was determined to make the settlement. The colonists were landed on an island, and a stone engraved with the arms of their native land was set up to mark the place. A fort was erected, and in honor of Charles IX. named Carolina—a name which a century afterward was retained by the English and applied to the whole country from the Savannah River to the southern boundary of Virginia. In this fort Ribault left twenty-six men to keep possession, and then sailed back to France for additional emigrants and stores. But civil war was now raging in the kingdom, and it was quite impossible to procure either supplies or colonists. No reinforcements were sent to Carolina, and in the following spring the men in the fort, discouraged with long waiting, grew mutinous, and killed their leader for attempting to control them. Then they constructed a rude brig and put to sea. After they had been driven about by the winds for a long time, they were picked up half starved by an English ship and carried to the coast of France.

Coligni did not yet despair of success in what he had undertaken. Two years after the first attempt another colony was planned, and LAUDONNIERE chosen leader. The character, however, of this second Protestant company was very bad. Many of them were abandoned men, of little industry and no prudence. The harbor of Port Royal was now shunned by the Huguenots, and a point on the River St. John's about fifteen miles west of where St. Augustine now stands was selected for the settlement. A fort was built here, and things were going well until a part of the colonists, under the pretext of escaping from famine, contrived to get away with two of the ships. Instead of returning to France, as they had promised, they began to practice piracy in the adjacent seas, until they were caught, brought back and justly hanged. The rest of the settlers, improvident and dissatisfied, were on the eve of breaking up the colony, when Ribault arrived with supplies of every sort, and restored order and content. It was at this time that the Spaniard Melendez, as already narrated, discovered the whereabouts of the Huguenots, and murdered the entire company.

It remained for DOMINIC DE GOURGES, a soldier of Gascony, to visit the Spaniards of St. Augustine with signal vengeance. This man fitted out three ships, mostly with his own means, and with only fifty daring seamen on board arrived in mid-winter on the coast of Florida. With this handful of soldiers he surprised successively three Spanish forts on the St. John's, and made prisoners of the inmates. Then, when he was unable to hold his position any longer, he hanged his leading captives to the branches of the trees, and put up this inscription to explain what he had done: "Not Spaniards, but murderers."

In the year 1598 the attention of the government of France was once more directed to the claims which French discovery had established in America. The MARQUIS OF LA ROCHE, a nobleman of influence and distinction, now obtained a commission authorizing him to found an empire in the New World. The prisons of France were again opened to furnish the emigrants, and the colony was soon made up. Crossing the Atlantic by the usual route, the vessels reached the coast of Nova Scotia, and anchored at Sable Island. A more dismal place could not have been found between Labrador and Mexico; yet here, on this desolate island, La Roche left forty men to form a settlement, while he himself, under the pre text of procuring more men and supplies, returned to France. Shortly after his arrival in that country he died; and for seven dreary years the new French empire, composed of forty criminals, languished on

Sable Island. Then they were mercifully picked up by some passing ships and carried back to France. Their punishment had been enough, and they were never remanded to prison.

But the time had now come when a colony of Frenchmen should actually be established in America. In the year 1603 the sovereignty of the country from the latitude of Philadelphia to one degree north of Montreal was granted to DE MONTS. The items of chief importance in the patent which he received from the king were a monopoly of the fur trade of the new country and religious freedom for Huguenot immigrants. De Monts, with two shiploads of colonists, left France early in March of 1604, and after a pleasant voyage reached the Bay of Fundy. The summer was spent in making explorations and in trafficking with the natives. De Monts seems to have been uncertain as to where he should plant his colony; but while in this frame of mind, Poutrincourt, the captain of one of the ships, being greatly pleased with a harbor which he had discovered on the north-west coast of Nova Scotia, asked and obtained a grant of the same, together with some beautiful lands adjacent, and he and a part of the crew went on shore. De Monts, with the rest of the colony, crossed to the west side of the bay, and began to build a fort on an island at the mouth of the St. Croix River. But in the following spring they abandoned this place, and returned to the harbor which had been granted to Poutrincourt. Here, on the 14th day of November, 1605, the foundations of the first permanent French settlement in America were laid. The name of Port Royal was given to the harbor and the fort, and the whole country, including Nova Scotia, the surrounding islands and the main land as far south as the St. Croix River, was called ACADIA.

Two years before the settlement was made at Port Royal, SAMUEL CHAMPLAIN, one of the most eminent and soldierly men of his times, was commissioned by a company of Rouen merchants to explore the country of the St. Lawrence and establish a trading-post. The traders saw that a traffic in the furs which those regions so abundantly supplied was a surer road to riches than rambling about in search of gold and diamonds. Under this commission, Champlain crossed the ocean, entered the gulf, sailed up the river, and with remarkable prudence and good judgment selected the spot on which Quebec now stands as the site for a fort. In the autumn of 1603, he returned to France, and published an interesting and faithful account of his expedition.

In the year 1608, Champlain again visited America, and on the 3d of July in that year the foundations of Quebec were laid. In the following year he and two other Frenchmen joined a company of Huron and Algonquin Indians who were at war with the Iroquois of New York. While marching with this party of warriors, he ascended the Sorel River until he came to the long, narrow lake which he was the first white man to look upon, and which has ever since borne the name of its discoverer.

Champlain was a religious enthusiast, and on that account the development of his colony was for some time hindered. In 1612 the Protestant party came into power in France, and the great Condé, the protector of the Protestants, became viceroy of the French empire in America. Now, for the third time, Champlain came to New France, and the success of the colony at Quebec was fully assured. Franciscan monks came over and began to preach among the Indians. These friars and the Protestants quarreled a good deal, and the settlement was much disturbed. A second time Champlain went with a war party against the Iroquois. His company was defeated, he himself wounded and obliged to remain all winter among the Hurons; but in the summer of 1617 he returned to the colony, in 1620 began to build, and four years afterward completed, the strong fortress of St. Louis. When the heavy bastions of this castle appeared on the high cliff above the town and river, the permanence of the French settlements in the valley of the St. Lawrence was no longer doubtful. To Samuel Champlain, more than to any other man—more than to the French government itself—the success of the North American colonies of France must be attributed.

CHAPTER VI.

ENGLISH DISCOVERIES AND SETTLEMENTS.

No day in the early history of the New World was more important than the 5th of May, 1496. On that day Henry VII., king of England, signed the commission of JOHN CABOT of Venice to make discoveries and explorations in the Atlantic and Indian Oceans, to carry the English flag, and to take possession of all islands and continents which he might discover. Cabot was a brave, adventurous man who had been a sailor from his boyhood, and was now a wealthy merchant of Bristol. The autumn and winter were spent in preparations for the voyage; five substantial ships were fitted, crews were enlisted, and everything made ready for the opening of the spring. In April the fleet left Bristol; and on the morning of the 24th of June, at a point about the middle of the eastern coast of Labrador, the gloomy shore was seen. This was the real discovery of the American continent. Fourteen months elapsed before Columbus reached the coast of Guiana, and more than two years before Ojeda and Vespucci came in sight of the main land of South America.

Cabot explored the shore-line of the country which he had discovered for several hundred miles. He supposed that the land was a part of the dominions of the Cham of Tartary; but finding no inhabitants, he went on shore, according to the terms of his commission, planted the flag of England, and took possession in the name of the English king. No man forgets his native land; by the side of the flag of his adopted country Cabot set up the banner of the *republic* of Venice— auspicious emblem of another flag which should one day float from sea to sea.

As soon as he had satisfied himself of the extent and character of the country which he had discovered, Cabot sailed for England. On the homeward voyage he twice saw on the right hand the coast of Newfoundland, but did not stop for further discovery. After an absence of but little more than three months, he reached Bristol, and was greeted with great enthusiasm. The town had holiday, the people were wild about the discoveries of their favorite admiral, and the whole kingdom took up the note of rejoicing.

The Crown gave him money and encouragement, new crews were enlisted, new ships fitted out, and a new commission more liberal in its provisions than the first was signed in February of 1498. Strange as it may seem, after the date of this second patent the very name of John Cabot disappears from the annals of the times. Where the remainder of his life was passed and the circumstances of his death are involved in complete mystery.

But Sebastian, second son of John Cabot, inherited his father's plans and reputation, and to his father's genius added a greater genius of his own. He had already been to the New World on that first famous voyage, and now, when the opportunity offered to conduct a voyage of his own, he threw himself into the enterprise with all the fervor of youth. It is probable that the very fleet which had been equipped for his father was entrusted to Sebastian. At any rate, the latter found himself, in the spring of 1498, in command of a squadron of well-manned vessels and on his way to the new continent. The particular object had in view was that common folly of the times, the discovery of a north-west passage to the Indies.

The voyage continued prosperously until, in the ocean west of Greenland, the icebergs compelled Sebastian to change his course. It was July, and the sun scarcely set at midnight. Seals were seen and the ships ploughed through such shoals of codfish as had never before been heard of. The shore was reached not far from the scene of the elder Cabot's discoveries, and then the fleet turned southward, but whether across the Gulf of St. Lawrence or to the east of Newfoundland is uncertain. New Brunswick, Nova Scotia and Maine were next explored. The whole coast-line of New England and of the Middle States was now for the first time since the days of the Norsemen traced by Europeans. Nor did Cabot desist from this work, which was bestowing the title of discovery on the crown of England, until he had passed beyond the Chesapeake. After all the disputes about the matter, it is most probable that Cape Hatteras is the point from which Sebastian began his homeward voyage.

MAP II

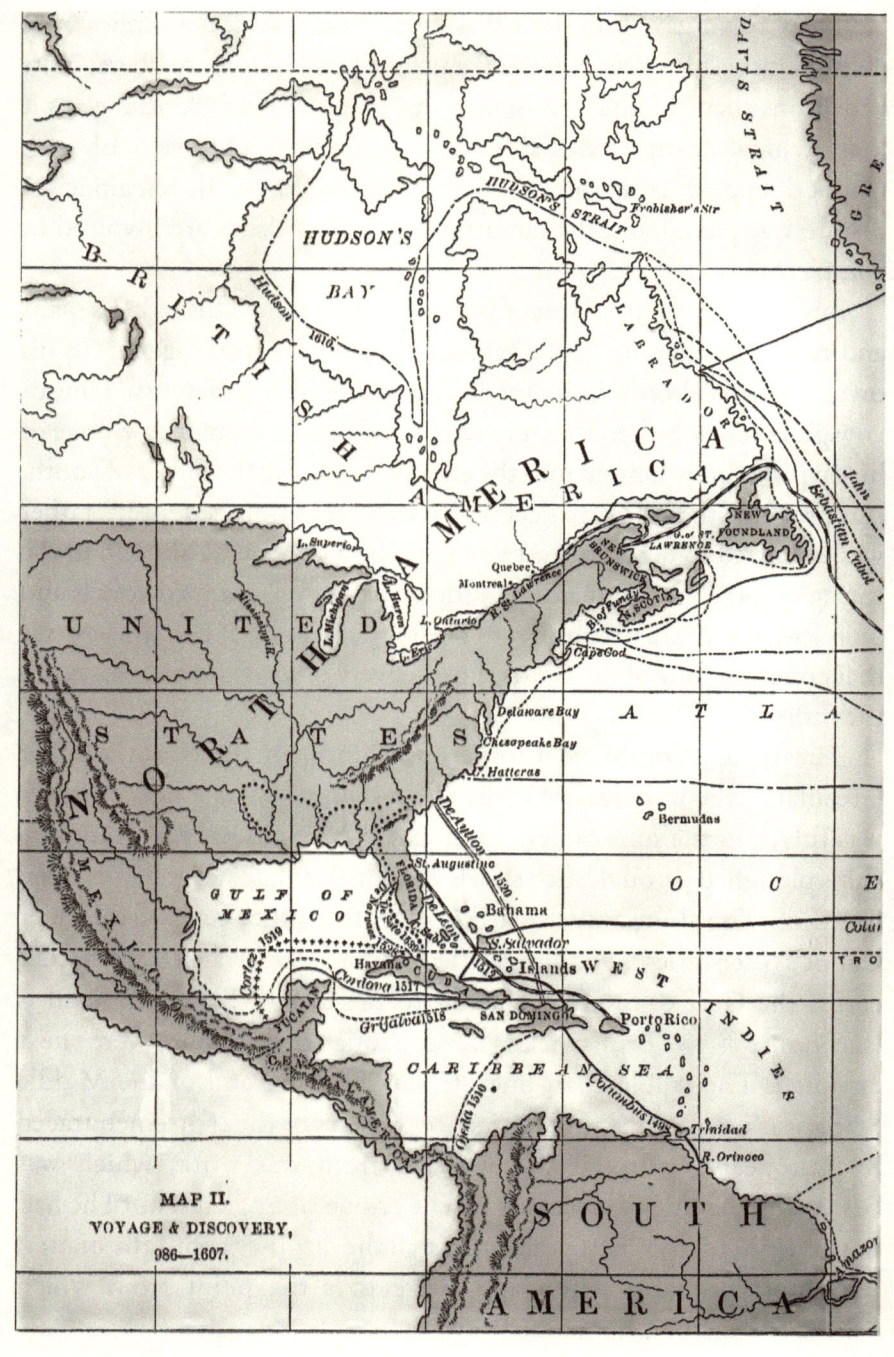

Voyage & Discovery, 986-1607.

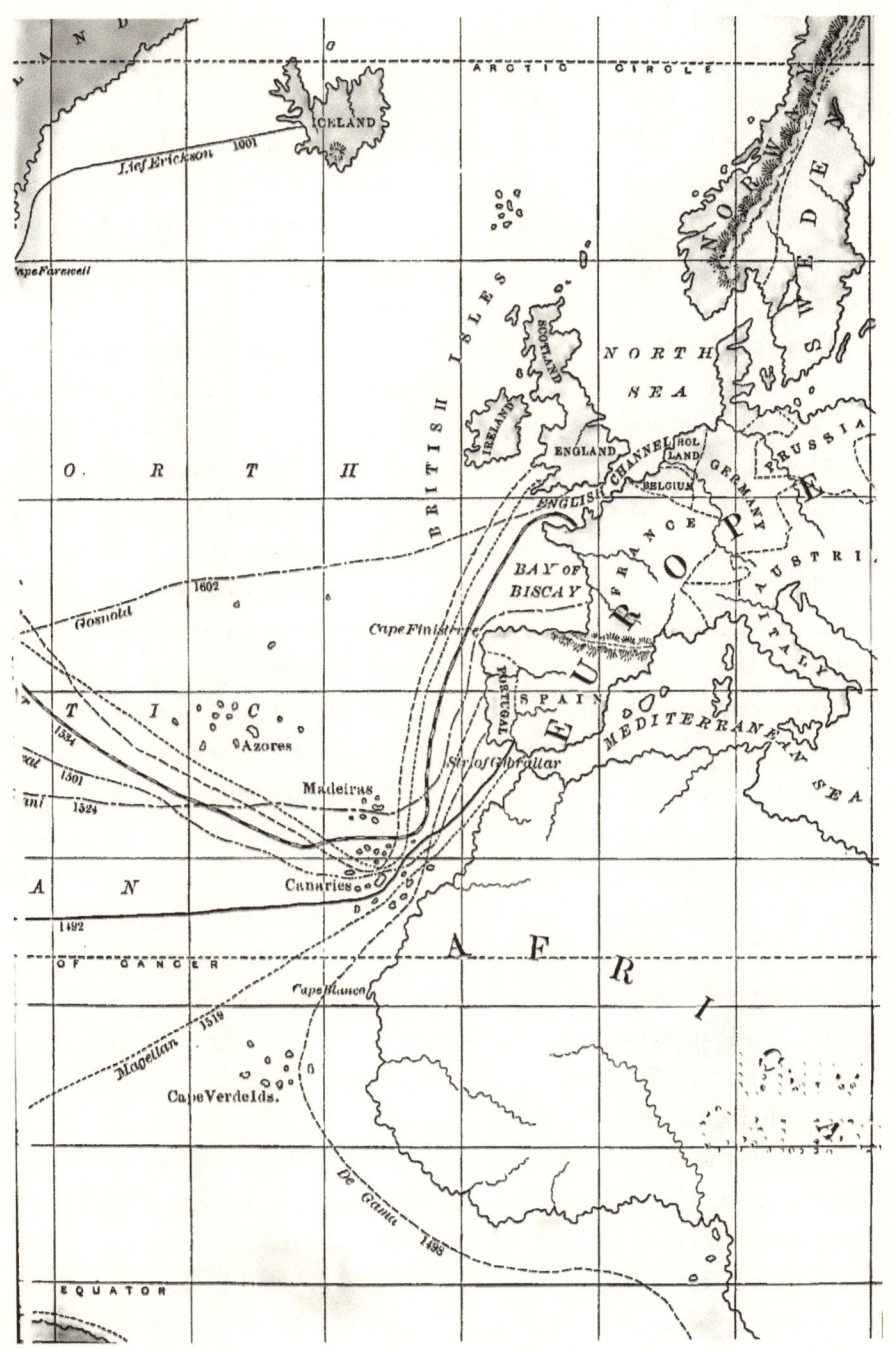

The future career of Cabot was as strange as the voyages of his boyhood had been wonderful. The scheming, illiberal Henry VII., although quick to appreciate the value of Sebastian's discoveries, was slow to reward the discoverer. The Tudors were all dark-minded and selfish princes. When King Henry died, Ferdinand the Catholic enticed Cabot away from England and made him pilot-major of Spain. While holding this high office he had almost entire control of the maritime affairs of the kingdom, and sent out many successful voyages. He lived to be very old, but the circumstances of his death have not been ascertained, and his place of burial is unknown.

The year 1498 is the most marked in the whole history of discovery. In the month of May, VASCO DE GAMA of Portugal doubled the Cape of Good Hope and succeeded in reaching Hindostan. During the summer the younger Cabot traced the eastern coast of North America through more than twenty degrees of latitude, thus establishing for ever the claim of England to the most valuable portion of the New World. In August, Columbus himself, now sailing on his third voyage, reached the mouth of the Orinoco. Of the three great discoveries, that of Cabot has proved to be by far the most important.

But several causes impeded the career of English discovery during the greater part of the sixteenth century. The next year after the New World was found, the pope, Alexander the Sixth, drew an imaginary line north and south three hundred miles west of the Azores, and issued a papal bull giving all islands and countries west of that line to Spain. Henry VII. of England was himself a Catholic, and he did not care to begin a conflict with his Church by pressing his own claims to the newly-found regions of the west. His son and successor, Henry VIII., at first adopted the same policy, and it was not until after the Reformation had been accomplished in England that the decision of the pope came to be disregarded, and finally despised and laughed at.

During the short reign of Edward VI. the spirit of maritime adventure was again aroused. In 1548 the king's council voted a hundred pounds sterling to induce the now aged Sebastian Cabot to return from Spain and become grand-pilot of England. The old admiral quitted Seville and once more sailed under the English flag. In the reign of Queen

Mary the power of England on the sea was not materially extended, but with the accession of Elizabeth a wonderful impulse was given to all enterprises which promised the aggrandizement of her kingdom.

The spirit of discovery now reappeared in that bold and skillful sailor, MARTIN FROBISHER. Himself poor, Dudley, earl of Warwick, came to his aid, and fitted out three small vessels to sail in search of a north-west passage to Asia. Three-quarters of a century had not sufficed to destroy the fanatical notion of reaching the Indies by sailing around America to the north. One of Frobisher's ships was lost on the voyage, another, terrified at the prospect, returned to England, but in the third the dauntless captain proceeded to the north and west until he attained a higher latitude than had ever before been reached on the American coast. Above the sixtieth parallel he discovered the group of islands which lies in the mouth of Hudson's Strait. Still farther to the north he came upon a large island which he supposed to be the mainland of Asia; to this he gave the name of Meta Incognita. North of this island, in latitude sixty-three degrees and eight minutes, he entered the strait which has ever since borne the name of its discoverer, then sailed for England, carrying home with him one of the Esquimaux and a stone which was declared by the English refiners to contain gold.

London was greatly excited. Queen Elizabeth herself added a vessel to the new fleet which in the month of May, 1577, departed for Meta Incognita to gather the precious metal by the shipload. Coming among the icebergs, the ships were for weeks together in constant danger of being crushed to atoms between the floating mountains. The summer was unfavorable. No ships reached as high a point as Frobisher had attained by himself on the previous voyage. The mariners were in consternation at the gloomy perils around them, and availed themselves of the first opportunity to get out of these dangerous seas and return to England.

Were the English gold-hunters satisfied? Not at all. Fifteen new vessels were immediately fitted out, the queen again bearing part of the expense, and as soon as the spring of 1578 opened the third voyage was begun. This time a colony was to be planted in the gold-regions of the north. Three of the ships, loaded with emigrants, were to remain in the promised land. The other twelve were to be freighted with gold-ore and return to London. When they reached the entrance to Hudson's Strait, they encountered icebergs more terrible than ever. Through a thousand perils the vessels finally reached Meta Incognita and took on cargoes of dirt. The provision-ship now slipped away from the fleet and returned to England. Affairs grew desperate. The north-west passage was forgotten. The colony which was to be planted was no longer thought of. Faith in the shining earth which they had stored in the holds gave way, and so, with disappointed crews on board and several tons of the spurious ore under the batches, the ships set sail for home. The El Dorado of the Esquimaux had proved an utter failure.

The English admiral, SIR FRANCIS DRAKE, sought fortune in a different manner. Without much regard for the law of nations, he began, in the year 1572, to prey upon the merchant-ships of Spain, and gained thereby enormous wealth. Five years later he sailed around to the Pacific coast by the route which Magellan had discovered, and became a terror to the Spanish vessels in those waters. When he had thus sufficiently enriched himself by a process not very different from piracy, he formed the daring project of tracing up the western coast of North America until he should enter the north-west passage from the Pacific, and thence sail east ward around the continent. With this object in view, he sailed northward along the coast as far as Oregon, when his sailors, who had been for several years within the tropics, began to shiver with the cold, and the enterprise, which could have resulted in nothing but disaster, was given up. Returning to the south, Drake passed the winter of 1579-80 in a harbor on the coast of Mexico. To all that portion of the western shores of America which he had thus explored he gave the name of New Albion; but the earlier discovery of the same coast by the Spaniards rendered the English claim of but little value. No colony of Englishmen had yet been established in the New World.

SIR HUMPHREY GILBERT was perhaps the first to conceive a rational plan of colonization in America. His idea was to form somewhere on the shores of the New Continent an agricultural and commercial state. With this purpose he sought aid from the queen, and received a liberal patent authorizing him to take possession of any six hundred square miles of unoccupied territory in America, and to plant thereon a colony of which he himself should be proprietor and governor. With this commission, Gilbert, assisted by his illustrious step-brother, WALTER RALEIGH, prepared a fleet of five vessels, and in June of 1583 sailed for the west. Only two days after their departure the best vessel in the fleet treacherously abandoned the rest and returned to Plymouth. Early in August, Gilbert reached Newfoundland, and going ashore, took formal possession of the country in the name of his queen. Unfortunately, some of the sailors discovered in the side of a hill scales of mica, and a judge of metals, whom Gilbert had been foolish enough to bring with him, declared that the glittering mineral was silver ore. The crews became insubordinate. Some went to digging the supposed silver and carrying it on board the vessels, while others gratified their piratical propensities by attacking the Spanish and Portuguese ships that were fishing in the neighboring harbors.

Meanwhile, one of Gilbert's vessels became worthless, and had to be abandoned. With the other three he left Newfoundland, and steered toward the south. When off the coast of Massachusetts, the largest of the remaining ships was wrecked, and a hundred men, with all the spurious silver ore, went to the bottom. The disaster was so great that Gilbert determined to return at once to England. The weather was stormy, and the two ships that were now left were utterly unfit for the sea; but the voyage was begun in hope. The brave captain remained in the weaker vessel, a little frigate called the Squirrel, already shattered and ready to sink. At midnight, as the ships, within hailing distance of each other, were struggling through a raging sea, the Squirrel was suddenly engulfed; not a man of the courageous crew was saved. The other ship finally reached Falmouth in safety.

But the project of colonization was immediately renewed by Raleigh. In the following spring that remarkable man obtained from the queen a new patent fully as liberal as the one granted to Gilbert. Raleigh was to become lord-proprietor of an extensive tract of country in America extending from the thirty-third to the fortieth parallel of north latitude. This territory was to be peopled and organized into a state. The frozen regions of the north were now to be avoided, and the sunny country of the Huguenots was to be chosen as the seat of the rising empire. Two ships were fitted out, and the command given to Philip Amidas and Arthur Barlow.

In the month of July the vessels reached the coast of Carolina. The sea that laved the long, low beach was smooth and glassy. The woods were full of beauty and song. The natives were generous and hospitable. Explorations were made along the shores of Albemarle and Pamlico Sounds, and a landing finally effected on Roanoke Island, where the English were entertained by the Indian queen. But neither Amidas nor Barlow had the courage or genius necessary to such an enterprise. After a stay of less than two months they returned to England to exhaust the rhetoric of description in praising the beauties of the new land. In allusion to her own life and reign, Elizabeth gave to her delightful country in the New World the name of VIRGINIA.

In December of 1584, Sir Walter brought forward a bill in Parliament by which his previous patent was confirmed and enlarged. The mind of the whole nation was inflamed at the prospects which Raleigh's province now offered to emigrants and adventurers. The plan of colonization, so far from being abandoned, was undertaken with renewed zeal and earnestness. The proprietor fitted out a second expedition, and appointed the soldierly Ralph Lane governor of the colony. Sir Richard Grenville commanded the fleet, and a company, not unmixed with the gallant young nobility of the kingdom, made up the crew. Sailing from Plymouth, the fleet of seven vessels reached the American coast on the 20th of June. At Cape Fear they were in imminent danger of being wrecked; but having escaped the peril, they six days afterward reached Roanoke in safety. Here Lane was left with a hundred and ten of the emigrants to form a settlement. Grenville, after making a few unsatisfactory explorations, returned to England, taking with him a Spanish treasure-ship which he had captured. Privateering and colonization went hand in hand.

Meanwhile, some Indians of a village adjacent to Roanoke had committed a petty theft, and the English wantonly burned the whole town as a measure of revenge. Jealousy and suspicion took the place of former friendships. Lane and some of his companions were enticed with false stories to go on a gold-hunting expedition into the interior; their destruction was planned, and only avoided by a hasty retreat to Roanoke. Wingina, the Indian king, and several of his chiefs were now in turn allured into the power of the English and inhumanly murdered. Hatred and gloom followed this atrocity, then despondency and a sense of danger, until the discouragement became so great that when Sir Francis Drake, returning with a fleet from his exploits on the Pacific coast, came in sight, the colonists prevailed on him to carry them back to England.

It was a needless and hasty abandonment, for within a few days a shipload of stores arrived from the prudent Raleigh; but finding no colony, the vessel could do nothing but return. Two weeks later Sir Richard Grenville himself came back to Roanoke with three well-laden ships, and made a fruitless search for the colonists. Not to lose possession of the country altogether, he left fifteen men upon the island, and set sail for home.

Baptism of Virginia Dare.

The ardor of the English people was now somewhat cooled. Yet they had before them truthful descriptions of the beauty and magnificence of the new country, and another colony, consisting largely of families, was easily made up. A charter of municipal government was granted by the proprietor, John White was chosen governor, and every precaution taken to secure the permanent success of the City of Raleigh, soon to be founded in the west. In July the emigrants arrived in Carolina. Avoiding the dangerous capes of Hatteras and Fear, they came safely to Roanoke; but a search for the fifteen men who had been left there a year before only revealed the fact that the natives, now grown savage, had murdered them. Nevertheless, the northern extremity of the ill-omened island was chosen as the site for the city, and on the 23d of the month the foundations were laid.

But disaster attended the enterprise. Jealousy between the settlers and the Indians grew into hostility, and hostility into war. Then a peace was concluded, and Sir Walter gave countenance to an absurd performance by which Manteo, one of the Indian chiefs, was made a peer of England, with the title of Lord of Roanoke. It was a silly and stupid piece of business. Notwithstanding the presence of this copper-colored nobleman, the colonists were apprehensive and gloomy. They pretended to fear starvation, and in the latter part of August almost compelled Governor White to return to England for an additional cargo of supplies. It was a great mistake. If White had remained, and the settlers had given themselves to tilling the soil and building houses, no further help would have been needed. The 18th of August was marked as the birthday of Virginia Dare, the first-born of English children in the New World. When White set sail for England, he left behind him a colony of a hundred and eight persons. What their fate was has never been ascertained. The story of their going ashore and joining the Indians is unlikely in itself, and has no historical evidence to support it.

The Invincible Armada was now bearing down upon the coasts of England. All the resources and energies of the kingdom were demanded for defence; and although Raleigh managed to send out two supply ships to succor his starving colony, his efforts to reach them were unavailing. The vessels which he sent with stores went cruising after Spanish merchantmen, and were themselves run down and captured by a man-of-war. Not until the spring of 1590 did the governor finally return to search for the unfortunate colonists. The island was a desert, tenantless and silent. No soul remained to tell the story of the lost.

In the mean time, Sir Walter, after spending two hundred thousand dollars of his own means in the attempt to found and foster a colony, had given up the enterprise. He assigned his exclusive proprietary rights to an association of London merchants, and it was under their auspices that White had made the final search for the settlers of Roanoke. From the date of this event very little in the way of voyage and discovery was accomplished by the English until the year 1602, when maritime enterprise again brought the flag of England to the shores of America. BARTHOLOMEW GOSNOLD was the man to whom belongs the honor of making the next explorations of our coast.

The old route from the shores of Europe to America was very circuitous. Ships from the ports of England, France and Spain sailed first southward to the Canary Islands, thence to the West Indies, and thence northward to the coast-line of the continent. Abandoning this path as unnecessarily long and out of the way, Gosnold, in a single small vessel called the Concord, sailed directly across the Atlantic, and in seven weeks reached the coast of Maine. The distance thus gained was fully two thousand miles. It was Gosnold's object to found a colony, and for that purpose a company of emigrants came with him. Beginning at Cape Elizabeth, explorations were made to the southward; Cape Cod was reached, and here the captain, with four of his men, went on shore. It was the first landing of Englishmen within the limits of New England. Cape Malabar was doubled, and then the vessel, leaving Nantucket on the right, turned into Buzzard's Bay. Selecting the most westerly island of the Elizabeth group, the colonists went on shore, and there began the first New England settlement.

It was a short-lived enterprise. A traffic was opened with the natives which resulted in loading the Concord with sassafras root, so much esteemed for its fragrance and healing virtues. Everything went well for a season but when the ship was about to depart for England, the settlers became alarmed at the prospect before them, and pleaded for permission to return with their friends. Gosnold acceded to their demands, and the island was abandoned. After a pleasant voyage of five weeks, and in less than four months from the time of starting, the Concord reached home in safety.

Gosnold and his companions gave glowing accounts of the country which they had visited, and it was not long until another English expedition to America was planned. Two vessels, the Speedwell and the Discoverer, composed the fleet, with MARTIN PRING for commander. A cargo of merchandise suited to the tastes of the Indians was put into the holds; and in April of 1603, a few days after the death of Queen Elizabeth, the vessels sailed for America. They came safely to Penobscot Bay, and afterward spent some time in exploring the harbors and shores of Maine. Then, turning to the south and coasting Massachusetts, Pring reached the sassafras region, and loaded his vessels at Martha's Vineyard. Thence he returned to England, reaching Bristol in October, after an absence of six months.

Two years later, GEORGE WAYMOUTH, under the patronage of the earl of Southampton, made a voyage to America, and passing Cape Cod on the left, came to anchorage among the islands of St. George, on the coast of Maine. He explored the harbor, and sailed up the river for a considerable distance, taking note of the fine forests of fir and of the beautiful scenery along the banks. A profitable trade was opened with the Indians, some of whom learned to speak English and returned with Waymouth to England. The voyage homeward was safely made, the vessels reaching Plymouth about the middle of June. This was the last of the voyages made by the English preparatory to the actual establishment of a colony in America. The time had at last arrived when, in the beautiful country of the Chesapeake, a permanent settlement should be effected.

CHAPTER VII.

ENGLISH DISCOVERIES AND SETTLEMENTS.—CONTINUED.

THE 10th of April, 1606, was full of fate in the destinies of the western continent. On that day King James I. issued two great patents directed to men of his kingdom, authorizing them to possess and colonize all that portion of North America lying between the thirty-fourth and forty-fifth parallels of latitude. The immense tract thus embraced extended from the mouth of Cape Fear River to Passamaquoddy Bay, and westward to the Pacific Ocean. The first patent was granted to an association of nobles, gentlemen and merchants residing at London, and called the LONDON COMPANY, while the second instrument was issued to a similar body which had been organized at Plymouth, in South-western England, and which bore the name of the PLYMOUTH COMPANY. To the former corporation was assigned all the region between the thirty-fourth and the thirty-eighth degrees of latitude, and to the latter the tract extending from the forty-first to the forty-fifth degree. The narrow belt of three degrees lying between the thirty-eighth and forty-first parallels was to be equally open to the colonies of either company, but no settlement of one party was to be made within less than one hundred miles of the nearest settlement of the other. The nature and extent of these grants will be fully understood from an examination of the accompanying map. Only the London Company was successful under its charter in planting an American colony.

The man who was chiefly instrumental in organizing the London Company was Bartholomew Gosnold. His leading associates were Edward Wingfield, a rich merchant, Robert Hunt, a clergyman, and John Smith, a man of genius. Others who aided the enterprise were Sir John Popham, chief-justice of England, Richard Hakluyt, a historian, and Sir Ferdinand Gorges, a distinguished nobleman. By the terms of the charter, the affairs of the company were to be administered by a Superior Council, residing in England, and an Inferior Council, residing in the colony. The members of the former body were to be chosen by the king, and to hold office at his pleasure; the members of the lower council were also selected by the royal direction, and were subject to removal by the same power. All legislative authority was likewise vested in the monarch. In the first organization of the companies not a single principle of self-government was admitted. The most foolish clause in the patent was that which required the proposed colony or colonies to hold all property in common for a period of five years. The wisest provision in the instrument was that which allowed the emigrants to retain in the New World all the rights and privileges of Englishmen.

In the month of August, 1606, the Plymouth Company sent their first ship to America. The voyage, which was one of exploration, was but half completed, when the company's vessel was captured by a Spanish man-of-war. In the autumn another ship was sent out, which remained on the American coast until the following spring, and then returned with glowing accounts of the country. Encouraged by these reports, the company, in the summer of 1607, despatched a colony of a hundred persons. Arriving at the mouth of the River Kennebec, the colonists began a settlement under favorable circumstances. Some fortifications were thrown up, a storehouse and several cabins built, and the place named St. George. Then the ships returned to England, leaving a promising colony of forty-five members; but the winter of 1607-8 was very severe; some of the settlers were starved and some frozen, the storehouse burned, and when summer came the remnant escaped to England.

The London Company had better fortune. A fleet of three vessels was fitted out, and the command given to Christopher Newport. On the 9th of December the ships, having on board a hundred and five colonists, among whom were Wingfield and Smith, left England. Newport, to begin with, committed the astonishing folly of taking the old route by way of the Canaries and the West Indies, and did not reach the American coast until the month of April. It was the design that a landing should be made in the neighborhood of Roanoke Island, but a storm prevailed and carried the ships northward into the Chesapeake. Entering the magnificent bay and coasting along the southern shore, the vessels came to the mouth of a broad and beautiful river, which was named in honor of King James. Proceeding up this stream about fifty miles, Newport noticed on the northern bank a peninsula more attractive than the rest for its verdure and beauty; the ships were moored, and the emigrants went on shore. Here, on the 13th day of May (Old Style), in the year 1607, were laid the foundations of Jamestown, the oldest English settlement in America. It was within a month of a hundred and ten years after the discovery of the continent by the elder Cabot, and nearly forty-two years after the founding of St. Augustine. So long a time had been required to plant the first feeble germ of English civilization in the New World.

After the unsuccessful attempt to form a settlement at the mouth of the Kennebec, very little was done by the Plymouth Company for several years; yet the purpose of planting colonies was not relinquished. Meanwhile, a new impetus was given to the affairs of North Virginia by the ceaseless activity and exhaustless energies of John Smith. Wounded by an accident, and discouraged, as far as it was possible for such a man to be discouraged, by the distractions and turbulence of the Jamestown colony, Smith left that settlement in 1609, and returned to England. On recovering his health he formed a partnership with four wealthy merchants of London, with a view to the fur-trade and probable establishment of colonies within the limits of the Plymouth grant. Two ships were accordingly freighted with goods and put under Smith's command. The summer of 1614 was spent on the coast of lower Maine, where a profitable traffic was carried on with the Indians. The crews of the vessels were well satisfied through the long days of July with the pleasures and profits of the teeming fisheries, but Smith himself found nobler work. Beginning as far north as practicable, he patiently explored the country, and drew a map of the whole coast-line from the Penobscot River to Cape Cod. In this map, which is still extant, and a marvel of accuracy considering the circumstances under which it was made, the country was called NEW ENGLAND—a name which Prince Charles confirmed, and which has ever since remained as the designation of the North eastern States of the republic. In the month of November the ships returned to Plymouth, taking with them many substantial proofs of a successful voyage.

Map III. English Grants. 1606-1732.

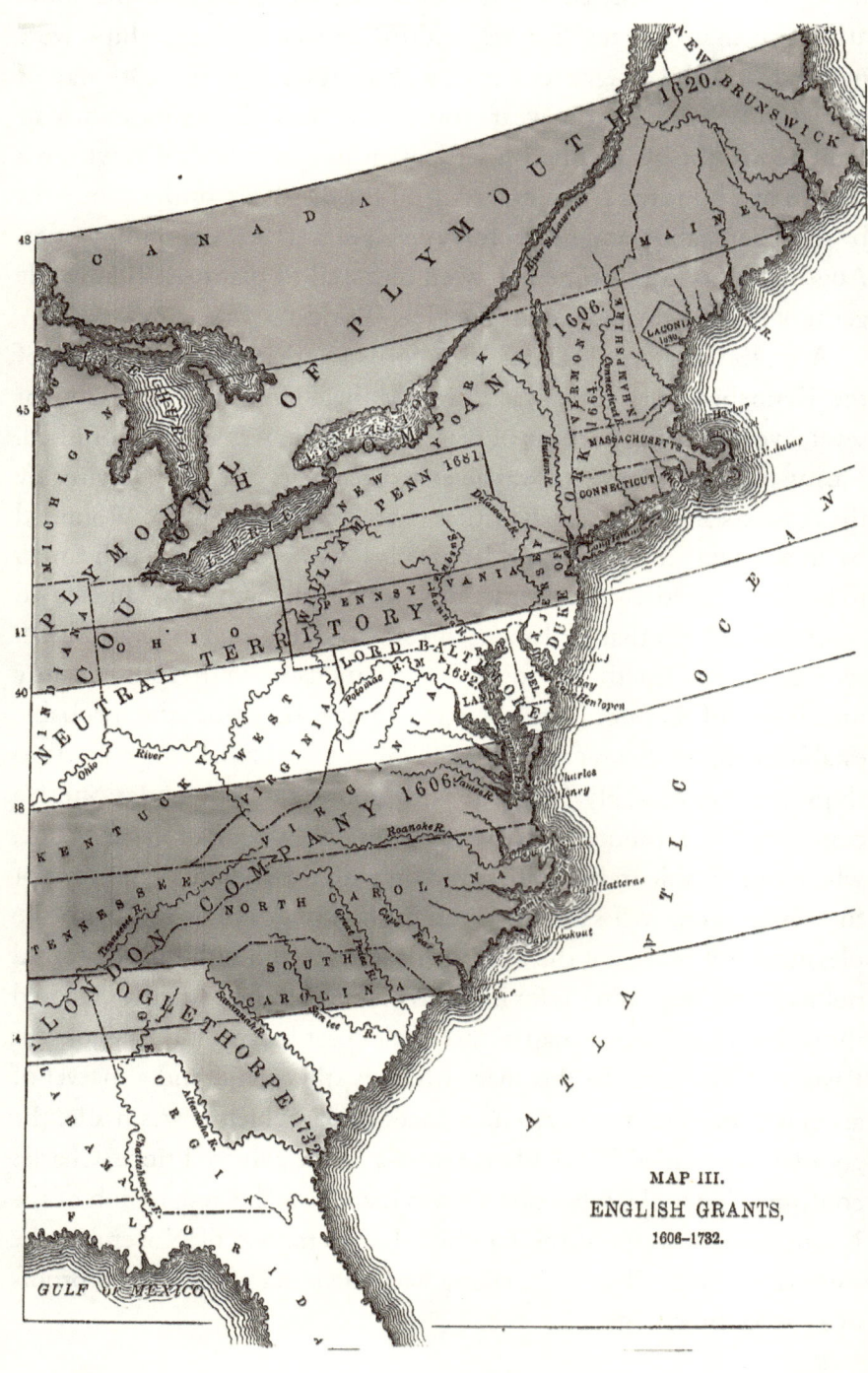

Smith now pleaded more strongly than ever in behalf of colonization. Some of his friends in the Plymouth Company gave him aid, and in 1615 a small colony of sixteen persons was sent out in a single ship. When nearing the American coast, they encountered a terrible storm, and after being driven about for two or three weeks were obliged to return to England. In spite of these reverses, the undaunted leader renewed the enterprise, and again raised a company of emigrants. Part of his crew became mutinous, betrayed him, and left him in mid-ocean. His own ship was run down and captured by a band of French pirates, and himself imprisoned in the harbor of Rochelle. Later in the same year he escaped in an open boat and made his way back to London. With astonishing industry, he now published a description of New England, and was more zealous than ever in inciting the company of Plymouth to energetic action. In these efforts he was much impeded. The London Company was jealous of its rival, and put obstacles in the way of every enterprise. The whole of the years 1617-18 was spent in making and unmaking plans of colonization, until finally, on the petition of some of its own leading members, the Plymouth Company was formally superseded by a new corporation called the COUNCIL OF PLYMOUTH, consisting of forty of the most wealthy and influential men of the kingdom. On this body were conferred, by the terms of the new charter, almost unlimited powers and privileges. All that part of America lying between the fortieth and the forty-eighth parallels of north latitude, and extending from ocean to ocean, was given to the council in fee simple. More than a million of square miles were embraced in the grant, and absolute jurisdiction over this immense tract was committed to forty men. How King James was ever induced to sign such a charter has remained an unsolved mystery.

A plan of colonizing was now projected on a grand scale. John Smith was appointed admiral of New England for life. The king, notwithstanding the opposition of the House of Commons, issued a proclamation enforcing the provisions of the charter, and everything gave promise of the early settlement of America. Such were the schemes of men to possess and people the Western Continent. Meanwhile, a Power higher than the will of man was working in the same direction. The time had come when, without the knowledge or consent of James

I., without the knowledge or consent of the Council of Plymouth, a permanent settlement should be made on the bleak shores of New England.

The PURITANS! Name of all names in the early history of the West! About the close of the sixteenth century a number of poor dissenters scattered through the North of England, especially in the counties of Nottingham, Lincoln and York, began to join themselves together for the purposes of free religious worship. Politically, they were patriotic subjects of the English king; religiously, they were rebels against the authority of the English Church. Their rebellion, however, only extended to the declaration that every man has a right to discover and apply the truth as revealed in the Scriptures without the interposition of any power other than his own reason and conscience. Such a doctrine was very repugnant to the Church of England. Queen Elizabeth herself declared such teaching to be subversive of the principles on which her monarchy was founded. King James was not more tolerant; and from time to time violent persecutions broke out against the feeble and dispersed Christians of the north.

Despairing of rest in their own country, the Puritans finally determined to go into exile, and to seek in another land the freedom of worship which their own had denied them. They turned their faces toward Holland, made one unsuccessful attempt to get away, were brought back and thrown into prisons. Again they gathered together on a bleak heath in Lincolnshire, and in the spring of 1608 embarked from the mouth of the Humber. Their ship brought them in safety to Amsterdam, where, under the care of their heroic pastor, John Robinson, they passed one winter, and then removed to Leyden. Such was the beginning of their wandering. They took the name of PILGRIMS, and grew content to have no home or resting-place. Privation and exile could be endured when sweetened with liberty.

But the love of native land is a universal passion. The Puritans in Holland did not forget—could not forget—that they were Englishmen. During their ten years of residence at Leyden they did not cease to long for a return to the country which had cast them out. Though ruled by a heartless monarch and a bigoted priesthood, England was their country still. The unfamiliar language of the Dutch grated harshly on their ears. They pined with unrest, conscious of their ability and willingness to do something which should convince even King James of their patriotism and worth.

It was in this condition of mind that about the year 1617 the Puritans began to meditate a removal to the wilds of the New World. There, with honest purpose and prudent zeal, they would extend the dominions of the English king. They would forget the past, and be at peace with their country. Accordingly, John Carver and Robert Cushman were despatched to England to ask permission for the church of Leyden to settle in America. The agents of the London Company and the Council of Plymouth gave some encouragement to the request, but the king and his ministers, especially Lord Bacon, set their faces against any project which might seem to favor heretics. The most that King James would do was to make an informal promise to let the Pilgrims alone in America. Such has always been the despicable attitude of bigotry toward every liberal enterprise.

The Puritans were not discouraged. With or without permission, protected or not protected by the terms of a charter which might at best be violated, they would seek asylum and rest in the Western wilderness. Out of their own resources, and with the help of a few faithful friends, they provided the scanty means of departure and set their faces toward the sea. The Speedwell, a small vessel of sixty tons, was purchased at Amsterdam, and the Mayflower, a larger and more substantial ship, was hired for the voyage. The former was to carry the emigrants from Leyden to Southampton, where they were to be joined by the Mayflower, with another company from London. Assembling at the harbor of Delft, on the River Meuse, fifteen miles south of Leyden, as many of the Pilgrims as could be accommodated went on board the Speedwell. The whole congregation accompanied them to the shore. There Robinson gave them a consoling farewell address, and the blessings and prayers of those who were left behind followed the vessel out of sight.

Both ships came safely to Southampton, and within two weeks the emigrants were ready for the voyage. On the 5th of August, 1620, the vessels left the harbor; but after a few days' sailing the Speedwell was found to be shattered, old and leaky. On this account both ships anchored in the port of Dartmouth, and eight days were spent in making the needed repairs. Again the sails were set; but scarcely had the land receded from sight before the captain of the Speedwell declared his vessel unfit to breast the ocean, and then, to the great grief and discouragement of the emigrants, put back to Plymouth. Here the bad ship was abandoned but the Pilgrims were encouraged and feasted by the citizens, and the more zealous went on board the Mayflower, ready and anxious for a final effort. On the 6th day of September the first colony of New England, numbering one hundred and two souls, saw the shores of Old England grow dim and sink behind the sea.

The Mayflower at Sea.

The voyage was long and perilous. For sixty-three days the ship was buffeted by storms and driven. It had been the intention of the Pilgrims to found their colony in the beautiful country of the Hudson; but the tempest carried them out of their course, and the first land seen was the desolate Cape Cod. On the 9th of November the vessel was anchored in the bay; then a meeting was held on board and the colony organized under a solemn compact. In the charter which they there made for themselves the emigrants declared their loyalty to the English Crown, and covenanted together to live in peace and harmony, with equal rights to all, obedient to just laws made for the common good. Such was the simple but sublime constitution of the oldest New England State. A nobler document is not to be found among the records of the world.[6] To this instrument all the heads of families, forty-one in number, solemnly set their names. An election was held in which all had an equal voice, and John Carver was unanimously chosen governor of the colony.

After two days the boat was lowered, but was found to be half rotten and useless. More than a fortnight of precious time was required to make the needed repairs. Standish, Bradford and a few other hardy spirits got to shore and explored the country; nothing was found but a heap of Indian corn under the snow. By the 6th of December the boat was ready for service, and the governor, with fifteen companions, went ashore. The weather was dreadful. Alternate rains and snow-storms converted the clothes of the Pilgrims into coats-of-mail. All day they wandered about, and then returned to the sea-shore. In the morning they were attacked by the Indians, but escaped to the ship with their lives, cheerful and giving thanks. Then the vessel was steered to the south and west for forty-five miles around the coast of what is now the county of Barnstable. At nightfall of Saturday a storm came on; the rudder was wrenched away, and the poor ship driven, half by accident and half by the skill of the pilot, into a safe haven on the west side of the bay. The next day, being the Sabbath, was spent in religious devotions, and on Monday, the 11th of December, Old Style, 1620, the Pilgrim Fathers landed on the Rock of Plymouth.

It was now the dead of winter. There was an incessant storm of sleet and snow, and the houseless immigrants, already enfeebled by their sufferings, fell a-dying of hunger, cold and exposure. After a few days spent in explorations about the coast, a site was selected near the first landing, some trees were felled, the snow-drifts cleared away, and on the 9th of January the heroic toilers began to build New Plymouth. Every man took on himself the work of making his own house; but the ravages

---

[6] See Appendix, note B.

of disease grew daily worse, strong arms fell powerless, lung-fevers and consumptions wasted every family. At one time only seven men were able to work on the sheds which were building for shelter from the storms; and if an early spring had not brought relief, the colony must have perished to a man. Such were the privations and griefs of that terrible winter when New England began to be.

CHAPTER VIII.

VOYAGES AND SETTLEMENTS OF THE DUTCH.

THE first Dutch settlement in America was made on Manhattan or New York Island. The colony resulted from the voyages and explorations of the illustrious SIR HENRY HUDSON. In the year 1607 this great British seaman was employed by a company of London merchants to sail into the North Atlantic and discover a route eastward or westward to the Indies. He made the voyage in a single ship, passed up the eastern coast of Greenland to a higher point of latitude than ever before attained, turned eastward to Spitzbergen, circumnavigated that island, and then was compelled by the icebergs to return to England. In the next year he renewed his efforts, hoping to find between Spitzbergen and Nova Zembla an open way to the East. By this course he confidently expected to shorten the route to China by at least eight thousand miles. Again the voyage resulted in failure; his employers gave up the enterprise in despair, but his own spirits only rose to a higher determination. When the cautious merchants would furnish no more means, he quitted England and went to Amsterdam. Holland was at this time the foremost maritime nation of the world, and the eminent navigator did not long go begging for patronage in the busy marts of that country. The Dutch East India Company at once furnished him with a ship, a small yacht called the Half Moon, and in April of 1609 he set out on his third voyage to reach the Indies. About the seventy-second parallel of latitude, above the capes of Norway, he turned eastward, but between Lapland and Nova Zembla the ocean was filled with icebergs, and further sailing was impossible. Baffled but not discouraged, he immediately turned his prow toward the shores of America; somewhere between the Chesapeake and the North Pole he would find a passage into the Pacific ocean.

In the month of July Hudson reached Newfoundland, and passing to the coast of Maine, spent some time in repairing his ship, which had been shattered in a storm. Sailing thence southward, he touched at Cape Cod, and by the middle of August found himself as far south as the

Chesapeake. Again he turned to the north, determined to examine the coast more closely, and on the 28th of the month anchored in Delaware Bay. After one day's explorations the voyage was continued along the coast of New Jersey, until, on the 3d of September, the Half Moon came to a safe anchorage in the bay of Sandy Hook. Two days later a landing was effected, the natives flocking in great numbers to the scene, and bringing gifts of corn, wild fruits and oysters. The time until the 9th of the month was spent in sounding the great harbor; on the next day the vessel passed the Narrows, and then entered the noble river which bears the name of Hudson.

To explore the beautiful stream was now the pleasing task. For eight days the Half Moon sailed northward up the river. Such magnificent forests, such beautiful hills, such mountains rising in the distance, such fertile valleys, planted here and there with ripening corn, the Netherlanders had never seen before. On the 19th of September the vessel was moored at what is now the landing of Kinderhook; but an exploring party, still unsatisfied, took to the boats and rowed up the river beyond the site of Albany. After some days they returned to the ship, the moorings were loosed, the vessel dropped down the stream, and on the 4th of October the sails were spread for Holland. On the homeward voyage Hudson, not perhaps without a touch of national pride, put into the harbor of Dartmouth. Thereupon the government of King James, with characteristic illiberality, detained the Half Moon, and claimed the crew as Englishmen. All that Hudson could do was to forward to his employers of the East India Company an account of his successful voyage and of the delightful country which he had visited under the flag of Holland.

Now were the English merchants ready to spend more money to find the north-west passage. In the summer of 1610, a ship, called the Discovery, was given to Hudson; and with a vision of the Indies flitting before his imagination he left England, never to return. He had learned by this time that nowhere between Florida and Maine was there an opening through the continent to the Pacific. The famous pass must now be sought between the Gulf of St. Lawrence and the southern point of Greenland. Steering between Cape Farewell and Labrador, in the track which Frobisher had taken, the vessel came, on the 2d day of August into the mouth of the strait which bears the name of its discoverer. No ship had ever before entered these waters. For a while the way westward was barred with islands; but passing between them, the bay seemed to open, the ocean widened to the right and left, and the route to China was at last revealed. So believed the great captain and his crew; but sailing farther to the west, the inhospitable shores narrowed on the more inhospitable sea, and Hudson found himself environed with the terrors of winter in the frozen gulf of the North. With unfaltering courage he bore up until his provisions were almost exhausted; spring was at hand, and the day of escape had already arrived, when the treacherous crew broke out in mutiny. They seized Hudson and his only son, with seven other faithful sailors, threw them into an open shallop, and cast them off among the icebergs. The fate of the illustrious mariner has never been ascertained.

In the summer of 1610 the Half Moon was liberated at Dartmouth, and returned to Amsterdam. In the same year several ships owned by Dutch merchants sailed to the banks of the Hudson River and engaged in the fur-trade. The traffic was very lucrative, and in the two following years other vessels made frequent and profitable voyages. Early in 1614 an act was passed by the States-General of Holland giving to certain merchants of Amsterdam the exclusive right to trade and establish settlements within the limits of the country explored by Hudson. Under this commission a fleet of five small trading-vessels arrived in the summer of the same year at Manhattan Island. Here some rude huts had already been built by former traders, but now a fort for the defence of the place was erected, and the settlement named New Amsterdam. In the course of the autumn Adrian Block, who commanded one of the ships, sailed through East River into Long Island Sound, made explorations along the coast as far as the mouth of the Connecticut, thence to Narraganset Bay, and even to Cape Cod. Almost at the same time Christianson, another Dutch commander, in the same fleet, sailed up the river from Manhattan to Castle Island, a short distance below the site of Albany, and erected a block-house, which was named Fort Nassau, for a long time the northern outpost of the settlers on the

Hudson. Meanwhile, Cornelius May, the captain of a small vessel called the Fortune, sailed from New Amsterdam and explored the Jersey coast as far south as the Bay of Delaware. Upon these two voyages, one north and the other south from Manhattan Island where the actual settlement was made, Holland set up a feeble claim to the country which was now named NEW NETHERLANDS, extending from Cape Henlopen to Cape Cod—a claim which Great Britain and France treated with derision and contempt. Such were the feeble and inauspicious beginnings of the Dutch colonies in New York and Jersey.

PART III.
COLONIAL HISTORY.
A. D. 1607-1775.

PARENT COLONIES.

CHAPTER IX.

VIRGINIA.—THE FIRST CHARTER.

MANY circumstances impeded the progress of the oldest Virginia colony. The first settlers at Jamestown were idle, improvident, dissolute. Of the one hundred and five men who came with Newport in the spring of 1607 only twelve were common laborers. There were four carpenters in the company, and six or eight masons and blacksmiths, but the lack of mechanics was compensated by a long list of forty-eight gentlemen. If necessity had not soon driven these to the honorable vocations of toil, the colony must have perished. The few married men who joined the expedition had left their families in England. The prospect of planting an American State on the banks of James River was not at all encouraging.

From the first the affairs of the colony were badly managed. King James made out instructions for the organization of the new State, and then, with his usual stupidity, sealed up the parchment in a box which was not to be opened until the arrival of the emigrants in America. The names of the governor and members of the council were thus unknown during the voyage; there was no legitimate authority on shipboard; insubordination and anarchy prevailed among the riotous company. In this state of turbulence and misrule, an absurd suspicion was blown out against Captain John Smith, the best and truest man in the colony. He was accused of making a plot to murder the council, of which he was supposed to be a member, and to make himself monarch of Virginia. An arrest followed, and confinement until the end of the voyage. When at last the colonists reached the site of their future settlement, the king's instructions were unsealed and the names of the seven members of the Inferior Council made known. Then a meeting of that body was held and Edward Wingfield duly elected first governor of Virginia. Smith, who had been set at liberty, was now charged with sedition and excluded from his seat in the council. He demanded to be tried; and when it was found that his jealous enemies could bring nothing but their own suspicions against him, he was acquitted, and finally, through the good offices of Robert Hunt, restored to his place as a member of the corporation.

Captain John Smith.

As soon as the settlement was well begun and the affairs of the colony came into a better condition, the restless Smith, accompanied by Newport and twenty others, ascended and explored James River for forty-five miles. This was the first of those marvelous expeditions which were undertaken and carried out by Smith's enterprise and daring. Just below the falls of the river, at the present site of Richmond, the English explorers came upon the capital of Powhatan, the Indian king. Smith was not greatly impressed with the magnificence of an empire whose chief city was a squalid village of twelve wigwams. The native monarch received the foreigners with formal courtesy and used his authority to moderate the dislike which his subjects manifested at the intrusion. About the last of May the company returned to Jamestown, and fifteen days later Newport embarked for England.

The colonists now for the first time began to realize their situation. They were alone amid the solitudes of the New World. The beauties of the Virginia wilderness were around them, but the terrors of the approaching winter were already present to their imagination. In the latter part of August dreadful diseases broke out in the settlement, and the colony was brought to the verge of ruin. The fort which had been built for the defence of the plantation was filled with the sick and dying. At one time no more than five men were able to go on duty as sentinels. Bartholomew Gosnold, the projector of the colony and one of the best men in the council, died, and before the middle of September one-half of the whole number had been swept off by the terrible malady. If the frosts of autumn had not come to check the ravages of disease, no soul would have been left to tell the story.

Civil dissension was added to the other calamities of the settlement. President Wingfield, an unprincipled man, and his confederate, George Kendall, a member of the council, were detected in embezzling the stores of the colony. Attempting to escape in the company's vessel, they were arrested, impeached and removed from office. Only three councilmen now remained, Ratcliffe, Martin and Smith; the first was chosen president. He was a man who possessed neither ability nor courage, and the affairs of the settlers grew worse and worse. After a few weeks of vacillation and incompetency, he, like his predecessor, was caught in an attempt to abandon the colony, and willingly gave up an office which he could not fill. Only Martin and Smith now remained; the former elected the latter president of Virginia! It was a forlorn piece of business, but very necessary for the public good. In their distress and bitterness there had come to pass among the colonists a remarkable unanimity as to Smith's merits and abilities. The new administration entered upon the discharge of its duties without a particle of opposition.

The new president, though not yet thirty years of age, was a veteran in every kind of valuable human experience. Born an Englishman; trained as a soldier in the wars of Holland; a traveler in France, Italy and Egypt; again a soldier in Hungary; captured by the Turks and sold as a slave; sent from Constantinople to a prison in the Crimea; killing a taskmaster who beat him, and then escaping through the woods of

Russia to Western Europe; going with an army of adventurers against Morocco; finally returning to England and joining the London Company,—he was now called upon by the very enemies who had persecuted and ill-treated him to rescue them and their colony from destruction. A strange and wonderful career! John Smith was altogether the most noted man in the early history of America.

Under the new administration the Jamestown settlement soon began to show signs of vitality and progress. Smith's first care, after the settlers were in a measure restored to health, was to improve the buildings of the plantation. The fortifications of the place were strengthened, dwellings were repaired, a storehouse erected, and everything made ready for the coming winter. The next measure was to secure a supply of provisions from the surrounding country. A plentiful harvest among the Indians had compensated in some degree for the mismanagement and rascality of the former officers of the colony, but to procure corn from the natives was not an easy task. Although ignorant of the Indian language, Smith undertook the hazardous enterprise. Descending James River as far as Hampton Roads, he landed with his five companions, went boldly among the natives, and began to offer them hatchets and copper coins in exchange for corn. The Indians only laughed at the proposal, and then mocked the half-starved foreigners by offering to barter a piece of bread for Smith's sword and musket. Finding that good treatment was only thrown away, the English captain formed the desperate resolution of fighting. He and his men fired a volley among the affrighted savages, who ran yelling into the woods. Going straight to their wigwams, he found an abundant store of corn, but forbade his men to take a grain until the Indians should return to attack them. Sixty or seventy painted warriors, headed by a priest who carried an idol in his arms, soon came out of the forest and made a violent onset. The English not only stood their ground, but made a rush, wounded several of the natives and captured their idol. A parley now ensued; the terrified priest came and humbly begged for his fallen deity, but Smith stood grimly with his musket across the prostrate idol, and would grant no terms until six unarmed Indians had loaded his boat with corn. Then the image was given up, beads and hatchets were liberally distributed among the warriors who ratified the peace by performing a dance of friendship, while Smith and his men rowed up the river with a boat-load of supplies.

John Smith Among the Indians.

There were other causes of rejoicing at Jamestown. The neighboring Indians, made liberal by their own abundance, began to come into the fort with voluntary contributions. The fear of famine passed away. The woods were full of wild turkeys and other game, inviting to the chase as many as delighted in such excitement. Good discipline was maintained in the settlement and friendly relations established with several of the native tribes. Seeing the end of their distresses, the colonists revived in spirit; cheerfulness and hope took the place of melancholy and despair.

As soon as the setting in of winter had made an abandonment of the colony impossible, the president, to whose ardor winter and summer were alike, gave himself freely to the work of exploring the country. With a company of six Englishmen and two Indian guides he began the ascent of the Chickahominy River. It was generally believed by the people of Jamestown that by going up this stream they could reach the Pacific Ocean. Smith knew well enough the absurdity of such an opinion, but humored it because of the opportunity which it gave him to explore new territory. The rest might dig imaginary gold-dust and hunt for the Pacific; he would see the country and map the course of the river.

The company proceeded up the Chickahominy until their barge ran aground in shallow water. Mooring the boat in a place of safety, Smith left four of the Englishmen to guard it, and with the other two and the Indian guides ascended the stream in a canoe. When this smaller craft could go no farther, it was put in charge of the white men, while the captain, with only the savages, proceeded on foot. For twenty miles he continued along the banks of the river, now dwindled to a mere creek winding about the woods and meadows. Meanwhile, the men who were left to protect the barge disobeyed their orders, and wandering into the forest, were attacked by three hundred Indians under the command of their king, Opechancanough, the brother of Powhatan. Three of the Englishmen escaped to the boat, but the fourth, George Cassen by name, was taken prisoner. Him the savages compelled by torture to reveal the whereabouts of Smith. The two men who guarded the canoe were next overtaken and killed. The captain himself was at last discovered, attacked, wounded with an arrow and chased through the woods. The missiles of the barbarians flew around him in a shower, but he compelled the Indian guides to stand between him and his enemies, and every discharge of his musket brought down a savage. He fought like a lion at bay, tied one of the guides to his left arm for a buckler, ran and fired by turns, stumbled into a morass, and was finally overtaken. The savages were still wary of their dangerous antagonist until he laid down his gun, made signs of surrender and was pulled out of the mire.

Without exhibiting the least signs of fear, Smith demanded to see the Indian chief, and on being taken into the presence of that dignitary began to excite his interest and curiosity by showing him a pocket compass and a watch. These mysterious instruments struck the Indians with awe; and profiting by his momentary advantage, the prisoner began to draw figures on the ground, and to give his captors some rude lessons in geography and astronomy. The savages were amazed and listened for hour, but then grew tired, bound their captive to a tree and prepared to shoot him. At the critical moment he flourished his compass in the air as though performing a ceremony, and the Indians forbore to shoot. His sagacity and courage had gained the day, but the more appalling danger of torture was yet to be avoided. The savages, however, were thoroughly superstitious, and became afraid to proceed against him except in the most formal manner. He was regarded by them as an inhabitant of another world whom it was dangerous to touch.

Smith was first taken to the town of Orapax, a few miles north-east of the site of Richmond. Here he found the Indians making great preparations to attack and destroy Jamestown. They invited him to join them and became their leader, but he refused, and then terrified them by describing the cannon and other destructive weapons of the English. He also managed to write a letter to his countrymen at the settlement, telling them of his captivity and their own peril, asking for certain articles, and requesting especially that those bearing the note should be thoroughly frightened before their return. This letter, which seemed to them to have such mysterious power of carrying intelligence to a distance, was not lost on the Indians, who dreaded the writer more than ever. When the warriors bearing the epistle arrived at Jamestown and found everything precisely as Smith had said, their terror and amazement knew no bounds, and as soon as they returned to Orapax all thought of attacking the settlement was at once given up.

The Indians now marched their captive about from village to village, the interest and excitement constantly increasing, until, near the fork of

York River, they came to Pamunkey, the capital of Opechancanough. Here Smith was turned over to the priests, who assembled in their Long House, or judgment-hall, and for three days together danced around him, sang and yelled after the manner of their superstition. The object was to determine by this wild ceremony what their prisoner's fate should be. The decision was against him, and he was condemned to death.

It was necessary that the sanction of the Indian emperor should be given to the sentence, and Smith was now taken twenty-five miles down the river to a town where Powhatan lived in winter. The savage monarch was now sixty years of age, and, to use Smith's own language, looked every inch a king. He received the prisoner with all the rude formalities peculiar to his race. Going to the Long House of the village, the emperor, clad in a robe of raccoon skins, took his seat on a kind of throne prepared for the occasion. His two daughters sat right and left, while files of warriors and women of rank were ranged around the hall. The king solemnly reviewed the cause and confirmed the sentence of death. Two large stones were brought into the hall, Smith was dragged forth bound, and his head put into position to be crushed with a war club. A stalwart painted savage was ordered out of the rank and stood ready for the bloody tragedy. The signal was given, the grim executioner raised his bludgeon, and another moment had decided the fate of both the illustrious captive and his colony. But the peril went by harmless. Matoaka,[7] the eldest daughter of Powhatan, sprang from her seat and rushed between the warrior's uplifted club and the prostrate prisoner. She clasped his head in her arms and held on with the resolution of despair until her father, yielding to her frantic appeals, ordered Smith to be unbound and lifted up. Again he was rescued from a terrible death. There is no reason in the world for doubting the truth of this affecting and romantic story, one of the most marvelous and touching in the history of any nation.

Powhatan, having determined to spare his captive's life, received him into favor. The prisoner should remain in the household of the

---

[7] Powhatan's tribe had a superstition that no one whose real name was unknown could be injured. They therefore told the English falsely that Matoaka's name was Pocahontas.

monarch, making hatchets for the warriors and toys for the king's daughters. By degrees his liberties were enlarged, and it was even agreed soon afterward that he should return to his own people at Jamestown. The conditions of his liberation were that he should send back to Orapax two cannons and a grindstone. Certain warriors were to accompany Smith to the settlement and carry the articles to Powhatan. There should then be peace and friendship between the English and the Red men. The journey was accordingly begun, the company camping at night in the woods, and Smith being in constant peril of his life from the uncertain disposition of the savages. But the colony was reached in safety, the lost captain and his twelve Indian guides being received with great gladness.

Smith's first and chief care was to make a proper impression on the minds of the savages. He had improved the opportunities of his captivity by learning the language of Powhatan's people, and by making himself familiar with their peculiarities and weaknesses—an experience of vast importance to himself and the colony. He now ordered the two cannons which he had promised to give Powhatan to be brought out and loaded to the muzzle with stones. Then, under pretence of teaching the Indians gunnery, he had the pieces discharged among the tree-tops, which were bristling with icicles. There was a terrible crash, and the savages, cowering with fear and amazement, could not be induced to touch the dreadful engines. The barbarous delegation returned to their king with neither guns nor grindstones.

As a matter of fact, the settlers were very little to be dreaded by anybody. Only thirty-eight of them were left alive, and these were frost bitten and half starved. Their only competent leader had been absent for seven weeks in the middle of one of the severest winters known in modern times. The old fears and discontents of the colonists had revived; and when Smith returned to the settlement, he found all hands preparing to escape in the pinnace as soon as the ice should break in the river. With much persuasion and a few wholesome threats he induced the majority to abandon this project, but the factious spirits of the colony, burning with resentment against him and his influence, made a conspiracy to kill him, and he knew not what hour might be his last.

In the midst of these dark days Captain Newport arrived from England. He brought a full store of supplies and one hundred and twenty emigrants. Great was the joy throughout the little plantation; only the president was at heart as much grieved as gladdened, for he saw in the character of the new comers no promise of anything but vexation and disaster. Here were thirty-four gentlemen at the head of the list to begin with then came gold-hunters, jewelers, engravers, adventurers, strollers and vagabonds, many of whom had more business in jail than at Jamestown. To add to Smith's chagrin, this company of worthless creatures had been sent out contrary to his previous protest and injunction. He had urged Newport to bring over only a few industrious mechanics and laborers; but the love of gold among the members of the London Company had prevailed over common sense to send to Virginia another crowd of profligates.

The kind of industry which Smith had encouraged in the colony was now laughed at. As soon as the weather would permit, the new comers and as many of the old settlers as had learned nothing from the past year's experience began to stroll about the country digging for gold. In a bank of sand at the mouth of a small tributary of the James some glittering particles were found, and the whole settlement was ablaze with excitement. Martin and Newport, both members of the council, were carried away with the common fanaticism. The former already in imagination saw himself loaded with wealth and honored with a peerage. The latter, having filled one of his ships with the supposed gold-dust, sent it to England, and then sailed up James River to find the Pacific Ocean! Fourteen weeks of the precious springtime, that ought to have been given to ploughing and planting, were consumed in this stupid nonsense. Even the Indians ridiculed the madness of men who for imaginary grains of gold were wasting their chances for a crop of corn.

In this general folly Smith was quite forgotten; but foreseeing that the evil must soon work its own cure, he kept his patience, and in the mean time busied himself with one of his most brilliant and successful enterprises; this was no less than the exploration of Chesapeake Bay and its tributaries. Accompanied by Dr. Russell and thirteen other comrades who had remained faithful to him, he left Jamestown on the 2d day of

June. He had nothing but an open barge of three tons' burden, but in this he steered boldly out by way of Hampton Roads and Cape Henry as far as Smith's Island. Returning thence around the peninsula which ends with Cape Charles, the survey of the eastern shore of the bay was begun, and continued northward as far as the river Wicomico, in Maryland. From this point the expedition crossed over to the mouth of the Patuxent, and thence coasted northward along the western side to the Patapsco. Here some members of the company became discontented, and insisted on returning to the colony. Smith gave a reluctant consent, but in

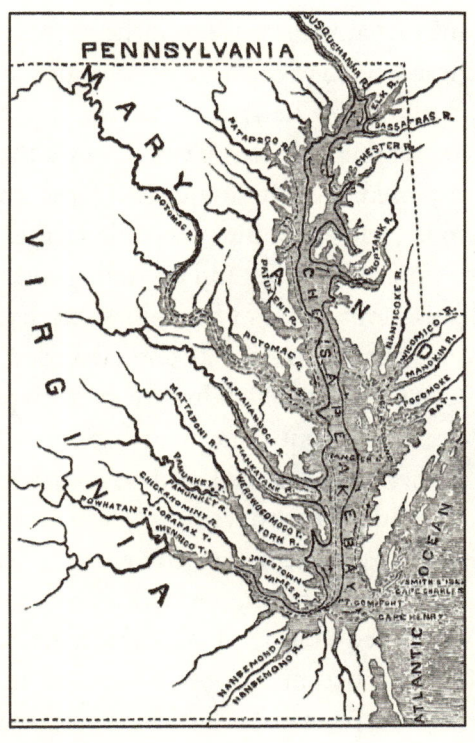

Jamestown and Vicinity. Smith's First Voyage in the Chesapeake ----

steering southward had the good fortune to enter the mouth of the Potomac. The crew were so much pleased with the prospect that they agreed to explore the great river before returning homeward. Accordingly, the barge was steered upstream as far as the falls above Georgetown. The country was much admired; and when the explorers were tired of adventure, they dropped down the river to the bay, and turning southward, reached Jamestown on 21st of July.

After a rest of three days a second voyage was begun. This time the expedition reached the head of the bay, and sailed up the Susquehanna River until the volume of water would float the barge no farther. Here an acquaintance was made with a race of Indians of gigantic stature and fiercer disposition than was known among the natives of Virginia. On the return voyage Smith passed down the bay, exploring every sound and inlet of any note, as far as the mouth of the Rappahannoc; this stream he ascended to the head of navigation, and then, returning by way of the York and Chesapeake Rivers, reached Jamestown on the 7th of September. He had been absent a little more than three months, had explored the winding coast of the great bay for fully three thousand miles, had encountered hostile savages by hundreds and thousands, had been driven hither and thither by storms, once wrecked, once stung by a poisonous fish and brought so near to death that his comrades digged his grave; now he was come back to the colony with a MAP OF THE CHESAPEAKE which he sent by Newport to England, and which is still preserved. Only one man had been lost on the expedition. Richard Fetherstone had died, and was buried on the Rappahannoc.

Within three days after Smith's return to Jamestown he was formally elected president. He entered at once upon the duties of his office, correcting abuses, enforcing the laws and restoring order to the distracted colony. There was a marked change for the better; gold-hunting became unpopular, and the rest of the year was noted as a season of great prosperity. Late in the autumn Newport arrived with seventy additional immigrants, increasing the number to more than two hundred. The health was so good that only seven deaths occurred between September and May of the following year. Excellent discipline was maintained. Every well man was obliged to work six hours a day. New houses were built, new fields fenced in; and all through the winter the sound of axe and saw and hammer gave token of a prosperous and growing village. Such was the condition of affairs in the spring of 1609.

CHAPTER X.

VIRGINIA.—THE SECOND CHARTER.

ON the 23d of May, 1609, King James, without consulting the wishes of his American colonists, revoked their constitution, and granted to the London Company a new charter, by the terms of which the government of Virginia was completely changed. The territory included under the new patent extended from Cape Fear to Sandy Hook, and westward to the Pacific Ocean. The members of the Superior Council were now to be chosen by the stockholders of the company, vacancies were to be filled by the councilors, who were also empowered to elect a governor from their own number.

The council was at once organized in accordance with this charter, and the excellent Lord De La Ware chosen governor for life. With him were joined in authority Sir Thomas Gates, lieutenant-general; Sir George Somers, admiral; Christopher Newport, vice-admiral; Sir Thomas Dale, high marshal; Sir Ferdinand Wainman, master of horse; and other dignitaries of similar sort. Attracted by the influence of these noblemen, a large company of more than five hundred emigrants was speedily collected, and early in June a fleet of nine vessels sailed for America. Lord Delaware did not himself accompany the expedition, but delegated his authority to three commissioners, Somers, Gates and Newport. About the middle of July the ships, then passing the West Indies, were over taken and scattered by a storm. One small vessel was wrecked, and another, having on board the commissioners of Lord Delaware, was driven ashore on one of the Bermuda Islands, where the crew remained until April of the following year; the other seven ships came safely to Jamestown.

But who should now be governor? Captain Smith was at first disposed to give up his office, but in a few days the affairs of the colony were plainly going to ruin, and he was urged by the old settlers and the better class of new-comers to continue in authority. Accordingly, declaring that his powers as president under the old constitution did not cease until some one should arrive from England properly commissioned to supersede him, he kept resolutely to the discharge of his duties, although in daily peril of his life. He arrested Ratcliffe[8] and Archer, put some of the most rebellious brawlers in prison, and then, in order to distract the attention of the rest, planned two new settlements, one, of a hundred and twenty men, under the command of Martin, to be established at Nansemond; the other, of the same number, under Captain West, to form a colony at the falls of the James. Both companies behaved badly. In a few days after their departure troubles arose between West's men and the Indians. The president was sent for in order to settle the difficulty; but finding his efforts unavailing, he returned to Jamestown. On his way down the river, while asleep in the boat, a bag of gunpowder lying near by exploded, burning and tearing his flesh so terribly that in his agony he leaped overboard. Being rescued from the river, he was carried to the he lay for some time racked with fever and tortured with his wounds. Finally, despairing of relief under the imperfect medical treatment which the colony afforded, he decided to return to England. He accordingly delegated his authority to Sir George Percy, a brother of the earl of Northumberland, and about the middle of September, 1609, left the scene of his heroic toils and sufferings, never to return.

There remained at Jamestown a colony of four hundred and ninety persons, well armed, well sheltered and well supplied. But such was the viciousness and profligacy of the greater number, and such the insubordination and want of proper leadership, after Smith's departure, that by the beginning of winter the settlement was face to face with starvation. The Indians became hostile and hovered around the plantations, stragglers were intercepted and murdered, houses were fired at every opportunity, disease returned to add to the desolation, and cold and hunger completed the terrors of a winter which was long remembered with a shudder and called THE STARVING TIME. By the last of March there were only sixty persons alive, and these, if help had not come speedily, could hardly have lived a fortnight.

---

[8] This man's real name was not Ratcliffe, but Sicklemore. He had been president of the colony in 1607, and was an accomplished thief as well as an impostor.

Meanwhile, Sir Thomas Gates and his companions, who had been shipwrecked in the Bermudas, had constructed out of the materials of their old ship, with such additional timber as they could cut from the forest, two small vessels, and set sail for Virginia. They came in full expectation of a joyful greeting from a happy colony. What, therefore, was their disappointment and grief when a few wan, half-starved wretches crawled out of their cabins to beg for bread! Whatever stores the commissioners had brought with them were distributed to the famishing settlers, and Gates assumed control of the government.

But the colonists had now fully determined to abandon for ever a place which promised them nothing but disaster and death. In Vain did the commissioners remonstrate; they were almost driven by the clamors around them to yield to the common will. An agreement was made to sail for Newfoundland; there the remnant of the Virginia colony should be distributed among the fishermen until such time as some friendly ship might carry them back to England.

On the 8th of June Jamestown was abandoned. The disheartened settlers, now grown resentful, were anxious before leaving to burn the town, but Gates defeated this design, and was himself the last man to go on board. Four pinnaces lay at their moorings in the river; embarking in these, the colonists dropped down with the tide, and it seemed as though the enterprise of Raleigh and Gosnold had ended in failure and humiliation.

But Lord Delaware was already on his way to America. Before the escaping settlers had passed out of the mouth of the river, the ships of the noble governor came in sight. Here were additional immigrants, plentiful supplies and promise of better things to come. Would the colonists return? The majority gave a reluctant consent, and before nightfall the fires were again kindled on the hearthstones of the deserted village. The next day was given to religious services; the governor caused his commission to be read, and entered upon the discharge of his duties. The amiability and virtue of his life, no less than the mildness and decision of his administration, endeared him to all and inspired the colony with hope.

Autumn came, and Lord Delaware fell sick. Against his own will, and to the great regret of the colony, he was compelled to return to England.

Having reluctantly delegated his authority to Percy—the same who had been the deputy of Captain Smith—the good Delaware set sail for his own country. It was an event of great discouragement; but fortunately, before a knowledge of the governor's departure reached England, the Superior Council had despatched a new shipload of stores and another company of emigrants, under command of Sir Thomas Dale. The vessel arrived at Jamestown on the 10th of May, and Percy was superseded by the captain, who bore a commission from the council. Dale had been a military officer in the wars of the Netherlands, and he now adopted a system of martial law as the basis of his administration. He was, however, a man so tolerant and just that very little complaint was made on account of his arbitrary method of governing.

One of Dale's first acts was to write to the council in England, requesting that body to send out immediately as large a number of colonists as possible, with an abundance of supplies. For once the council acted promptly; and in the latter part of August, Sir Thomas Gates arrived with a fleet of six ships, having on board three hundred immigrants and a large quantity of stores. There was great thanksgiving in the colony, a fresh enthusiasm was enkindled, and contentment came with a sense of security.

Thus far the property of the settlers at Jamestown had been held in common. The colonists had worked together, and in time of harvest deposited their products in storehouses which were under the control of the governor and council. Now the right of holding private property was recognized. Governor Gates had the lands divided so that each settler should have three acres of his own; every family might cultivate a garden and plant an orchard, the fruits of which no one but the owner was allowed to gather. The benefits of this system of labor were at once apparent. The laborers, as soon as each was permitted to claim the rewards of his own toil, became cheerful and industrious. There were now seven hundred persons in the colony; new plantations were laid out on every side, and new settlements were formed on both banks of the river and at considerable distances from Jamestown. The promise of an American State, so long deferred, seemed at last to be realized.

CHAPTER XI.

VIRGINIA.—THE THIRD CHARTER.

EARLY in the year 1612 the London Company obtained from the king a third patent, by the terms of which the character of the government was entirely changed. The Superior Council was abolished and the powers of that body transferred to the stockholders, who were authorized to hold public meetings, to elect their own officers, to discuss and decide all questions of law and right, and to govern the colony on their own responsibility. The cause of this change was the unprofitableness of the colony as a financial enterprise, and the consequent dissatisfaction of the company with the management of the council. The new patent, although not so intended by the king, was a great step toward a democratic form of government in Virginia.

2. The year 1613 was marked by two important events, both of them resulting from the lawless behavior of Captain Samuel Argall. While absent on an expedition up the Potomac River he learned that Pocahontas, who had had some difficulty with her father's tribe, was residing in that neighborhood. Procuring the help of a treacherous Indian family, the English captain enticed the unsuspecting girl on board his vessel and carried her captive to Jamestown. The authorities of the colony, instead of punishing Argall for this atrocity, aggravated the outrage by demanding that Powhatan should pay a heavy ransom for his daughter's liberation. The old king indignantly refused, and ordered his tribes to prepare for war. Meanwhile, Pocahontas, who seems not to have been greatly grieved on account of her captivity, was converted to the Christian faith and became by baptism a member of the Episcopal Church. She was led to this course of action chiefly by the instruction and persuasion of John Rolfe, a worthy young man of the colony, who after the baptism of the princess sought her in marriage. Powhatan and his chief men gave their consent, and the nuptials were duly celebrated in the spring of the following year. By this means war was averted, and a bond of union established between the Indians and the whites.

3. Two years later Rolfe and his wife went to England, where they were received in the highest circles of society. Captain Smith gave them a letter of introduction to Queen Anne, and many other flattering attentions were bestowed on the modest daughter of the Western wilderness. In the following year, Rolfe made preparations to return to America; but before embarking, Pocahontas fell sick and died. There was left of this marriage a son, who afterward came to Jamestown and was a man of some importance in the affairs of the colony. To him several influential families of Virginians still trace their origin. John Randolph of Roanoke was a grandson of the sixth generation from Pocahontas.

When Captain Argall returned from his expedition up the Potomac, he was sent with an armed vessel to the coast of Maine. The avowed object of the voyage was to protect the English fishermen who frequented the waters between the Bay of Fundy and Cape Cod, but the real purpose was to destroy the colonies of France, if any should be found within the limits of the territory claimed by England. Arriving at his destination, Argall soon found opportunity for the display of his violence and rapacity. The French authorities of Acadia were at this time building a village on Mount Desert Island, near the mouth of the Penobscot. This settlement was the first object of Argall's vengeance. The place was captured, pillaged and burned; part of the inhabitants were put on board a vessel bound for France, and the rest were carried to the Chesapeake. The French colony at the mouth of the St. Croix River next attracted the attention of the English captain, who cannonaded the fort and destroyed every building in the settlement. Passing thence across the bay to Port Royal, Argall burned the deserted hamlet which Poutrincourt and his companions had built there eight years before. On his way back to Virginia he made a descent on the Dutch traders of Manhattan Island, destroyed many of their huts, and compelled the settlers to acknowledge the sovereignty of England. The result of these outrageous proceedings was to confine the French settlements in America to the banks of the St. Lawrence, and to leave a clear coast for the English flag from Nova Scotia to Florida.

In the month of March, 1614, Sir Thomas Gates returned to England, leaving the government in the hands of Dale, whose administration lasted for two years. During this time the laws of the colony were much improved, and, more important still, the colonial industry took an entirely different form. Hitherto the labor of the settlers had been directed to the planting of vineyards and to the manufacture of potash, soap, glass and tar. The managers of the London Company had at last learned that these articles could be produced more cheaply in Europe than in America. They had also discovered that there were certain products peculiar to the New World which might be raised and exported with great profit. Chief among such native products was the plant called tobacco, the use of which had already become fashionable in Spain, England and France. This, then, became the leading staple of the colony, and was even used for money. So entirely did the settlers give themselves to the cultivation of the famous weed that the very streets of Jamestown were ploughed up and planted with it.

It was a great disaster to the people of the colony when Argall was chosen deputy-governor. He was a man who had one virtue, courage; and in all other respects was thoroughly bad. The election occurred in 1617, and through the influence of an unscrupulous faction composed of Argall's friends he was not only selected as Lord Delaware's deputy in America, but was also made an admiral of the English navy. His administration was characterized by fraud, oppression and violence. Neither property nor life was secure against his tyranny and greed. By and by, the news of his proceedings reached England; emigration ceased at once, and the colony became a reproach, until Lord Delaware restored confidence by embarking in person for Virginia. But the worthy nobleman died on the voyage, and Argall continued his exactions and cruelty. In the spring of 1619, he was at last displaced through the influence of Sir Edwyn Sandys, and the excellent Sir George Yeardley appointed to succeed him.

Martial law was now abolished. The act which required each settler to give a part of his labor for the common benefit was also repealed, and thus the people were freed from a kind of colonial servitude. Another action was taken of still greater importance. Governor Yeardley, in accordance with instructions received from the company, divided the plantations along James River into eleven districts, called boroughs, and issued a proclamation to the citizens of each borough to elect two of their own number to take part in the government of the colony. The elections were duly held, and on the 30th of July, 1619, the delegates came together at Jamestown. Here was organized the Virginia HOUSE OF BURGESSES, a colonial legislature, the first popular assembly held in the New World.

The Burgesses had many privileges, but very little power. They might discuss the affairs of the colony, but could not control them; pass laws, but could not enforce them; declare their rights, but could not secure them. Though the governor and council should both concur in the resolutions of the assembly, no law was binding until ratified by the company in England. Only one great benefit was gained—the freedom of debate. Wherever that is recognized, liberty must soon follow.

Wives for the Settlers at Jamestown.

The year 1619 was also marked by the introduction of negro slavery into Virginia. The servants of the people of Jamestown had hitherto been persons of English or German descent, and their term of service had varied from a few months to many years. No perpetual servitude had thus far been recognized, nor is it likely that the English colonists would of themselves have instituted the system of slave labor. In the month of August a Dutch man-of-war sailed up the river to the plantations, and offered by auction twenty Africans. They were purchased by the wealthier class of planters, and made slaves for life. It was, however, nearly a half century from this time before the system of negro slavery became well established in the English colonies.

Twelve years had now passed since the founding of Jamestown. Eighty thousand pounds sterling had been spent by the company in the attempted development of the new State. As a result there were only six hundred men in the colony, and these for the most part were rovers who intended to return to England. Sir Thomas Smith, the treasurer, had managed matters badly. Very few families had emigrated, and society in Virginia was coarse and vicious. In this condition of affairs Smith was superseded by Sir Edwyn Sandys, a man of great prudence and integrity. A reformation of abuses was at once begun and carried out. By his wisdom and liberality the new treasurer succeeded before the end of the summer of 1620 in collecting and sending to America a company of twelve hundred and sixty-one persons. Another measure of still greater importance was equally successful. By the influence of Sandys and his friends, ninety young women of good breeding and modest manners were induced to emigrate to Jamestown. In the following spring sixty others of similar good character came over, and received a hearty welcome.

The statement that the early Virginians bought their wives is absurd. All that was done was this: when Sandys sent the first company of women to America, he charged the colonists with the expense of the voyage—a measure made necessary by the fact that the company was almost bankrupt. An assessment was made according to the number who were brought over, and the rate fixed at a hundred and twenty pounds of tobacco for each passenger—a sum which the settlers cheerfully paid. The many marriages that followed were celebrated in the usual way, and nothing further was thought of the transaction. When the second shipload came, the cost of transportation was reported at a hundred and fifty pounds for each passenger, which was also paid without complaint.

In July of 1621 the London Company, which had now almost run its course, gave to Virginia a code of written laws and frame of government modeled after the English constitution. The terms of the instrument were few and easily understood. The governor of the colony was as hitherto to be appointed by the company, a council to be chosen by the same body, and a house of burgesses, two members from each district, to be elected by the people. In making laws the councilors and burgesses sat together. When a new law was proposed, it was debated, and if passed received the governor's signature, then was transmitted to England and ratified or rejected by the company. The constitution also acknowledged the right of petition and of trial by jury, but the most remarkable and liberal concession was that which gave the burgesses the power of vetoing any objectionable acts of the company.

Governor Yeardley's administration ended in October of 1621. At that time Sir Francis Wyatt arrived, commissioned as governor and bearing the new constitution of Virginia. The colony was found in a very flourishing condition. The settlements extended for a hundred and forty miles along both banks of James River and far into the interior, especially northward toward the Potomac. There remained but one cause of foreboding and alarm. The Indians had seen in all this growth and prosperity the doom of their own race, and had determined to make one desperate effort to destroy their foes before it should be too late. To do this in open war was impossible; necessity and the savage impulse working together suggested treachery as the only means likely to accomplish the result. Circumstances favored the villainous undertaking. Pocahontas was dead. The peaceable and faith-keeping Powhatan had likewise passed away. The ambitious and crafty Opechancanough, who succeeded to his brother's authority in 1618, had ever since been plotting the destruction of the English colony, and the time had come for the bloody tragedy.

The savages carefully concealed their murderous purpose. Until the very day of the massacre they continued on terms of friendship with the English. They came unmolested into the settlements, ate with their victims, borrowed boats and guns, made purchases, and gave not the slightest token of hostility. The attack was planned for the 22d of March, at mid-day. At the fatal hour the work of butchery began. Every hamlet in Virginia was attacked by a band of yelling barbarians. No age, sex or condition awakened an emotion of pity. Men, women and children were indiscriminately slaughtered, until three hundred and forty-seven had perished under the knives and hatchets of the savages.

But Indian treachery was thwarted by Indian faithfulness. What was the chagrin and rage of the warriors to find that Jamestown and the other leading settlements had been warned at the last moment, and were prepared for the onset? A converted Red man, wishing to save an Englishman who had been his friend, went to him on the night before the massacre and revealed the plot. The alarm was spread among the settlements, and thus the greater part of the colony escaped destruction. But the outer plantations were entirely destroyed. The people crowded together on the larger farms about Jamestown, until of the eighty settlements there were only eight remaining. Still, there were sixteen hundred resolute men in the colony; and although gloom and despondency prevailed for a while, the courage of the settlers soon revived, and sorrow gave place to a desire for vengeance.

It was now the turn of the Indians to suffer. Parties of English soldiers scoured the country in every direction, destroying wigwams, burning villages and killing every savage that fell in their way, until the tribes of Opechancanough were driven into the wilderness. The colonists, regaining their confidence and zeal, returned to their deserted farms, and the next year brought such additions that the census showed a population of two thousand five hundred.

Meanwhile, difficulties arose between the corporation and the king. Most of the members of the London Company belonged to the patriot party in England, and the freedom with which they were in the habit of discussing political and governmental matters was very distasteful to the monarch. A meeting of the stockholders, now a numerous body, was held once every three months, and the debates took a wider and still wider range. The liberal character of the Virginia constitution was offensive to King James, who determined by some means to obtain control of the London Company, or else to suppress it altogether. A committee was accordingly appointed to look into the affairs of the corporation and to make a report on its management. The commissioners performed their duty, and reported that the company, in addition to being a hot-bed of political agitation, was unsound in every part, that the treasury was bankrupt, and especially that the government of Virginia was bad and would continue so until a radical change should be made in the constitution of the new State.

Legal proceedings were now instituted by the ministers to ascertain whether the company's charter had not been forfeited. The question came before the judges, who had no difficulty in deciding that the violated patent was null and void. In accordance with this decision, the charter of the corporation was canceled by the king, and in June of 1624 the London Company ceased to exist. But its work had been well done; a torch of liberty had been lighted on the banks of the James which all the gloomy tyranny of after times could not extinguish. The Virginians were not slow to remember and to claim ever afterward the precious rights which were guaranteed in the constitution of 1621. And the other colonies would be satisfied with nothing less than the chartered privileges which were recognized in the laws of the Old Dominion.

CHAPTER XII.

Virginia.—The Royal Government.

A ROYAL government was now established in Virginia. To the colonists themselves the change of authorities was scarcely perceptible. The new administration consisted of a governor and twelve councilors appointed by the crown. The General Assembly of the colony was left undisturbed, and all the rights and privileges of the colonists remained as before. The king's hostility had been directed against the London Company, and not against the State of Virginia; now that the former was destroyed the latter was left unmolested. Governor Wyatt was continued in office; and in making up the new council the king wisely took pains to select the known friends of the colony rather than certain untried partisans of his own court. The Virginians found in the change of government as much cause of gratitude as of grief.

King James of England died in 1625. His son, Charles I., a young, inexperienced and stubborn prince, succeeded to the throne. The new king paid but little attention to the affairs of his American colony, until the commerce in tobacco attracted his notice. Seeing in this product a source of revenue for the crown, he attempted to gain a monopoly of the trade, but the colonial authorities outwitted him and defeated the project. It is worthy of special note that while conferring with the colony on this subject the king recognized the Virginia assembly as a rightfully constituted power. The reply which was finally returned to the king's proposal was signed not only by the governor and council, but by thirty-one of the burgesses.

In 1626 Governor Wyatt retired from office, and Yeardley, the old friend and benefactor of the colonists, was reappointed. The young State was never more prosperous than under this administration, which was terminated by the governor's death, in November of 1627. During the preceding summer a thousand new immigrants had come to swell the population of the growing province.

The council of Virginia had a right, in case of an emergency, to elect a governor. Such an emergency was now present, and Francis West was chosen by the councilors; but as soon as the death of Yeardley was known in England, King Charles commissioned John Harvey to assume the government. He arrived in the autumn of 1629, and from this time until 1635, the colony was distracted with the presence of a most unpopular chief magistrate. He seems to have been disliked on general principles, but the greatest source of dissatisfaction was his partiality to certain speculators and land monopolists who at this time infested Virginia, to the annoyance and injury of the poorer people. There were many old land grants covering districts of territory which were now occupied by actual settlers, and between the holders of the lands and the holders of the titles violent altercations arose. In these disputes the governor became a partisan of the speculators against the people, until the outraged assembly of 1635 passed a resolution that Sir John Harvey be thrust out of office, and Captain West be appointed in his place "until the king's pleasure may be known in this matter." A majority of the councilors sided with the burgesses, and Harvey was obliged to go to England to stand his trial.

King Charles treated the whole affair with contempt. The commissioners appointed by the council of Virginia to conduct Harvey's impeachment were refused a hearing, and he was restored to the governorship of the unwilling colony. He continued in power until the year 1639, when he was superseded by Wyatt, who ruled until the spring of 1642.

And now came the English Revolution. The exactions and tyranny of Charles at last drove his subjects into open rebellion. In January of 1642, the king and his friends left London, and repairing to Nottingham, collected an army of royalists. The capital and southern part of the country remained in the power of Parliament. The High Church party and the adherents of monarchy took sides with the king, while the republicans and dissenters made up the opposing forces. The country was plunged into the horrors of civil war. After a few years of conflict the royal army was routed and dispersed; the king escaped to Scotland, and the leading royalists fled to foreign lands. On the demand of Parliament Charles was given up and brought to trial. The cause was heard, a sentence of death was passed, and on the 30th of January, 1649, the unhappy monarch was beheaded.

Monarchy was now abolished. Oliver Cromwell, the general of the Parliamentary army, was made Lord Protector of the Commonwealth of England. By him the destinies of the nation were controlled until his death, in 1658, when he was succeeded by his son Richard. But the latter, lacking his father's abilities and courage, became alarmed at the dangers that gathered around him, and resigned. For a few months the country was in anarchy, until General Monk, who commanded the English army of the North, came down from Scotland and declared a restoration of the monarchy. The exiled son of Charles I. was called home and proclaimed king, the people acquiesced, Parliament sanctioned the measure, and on the 18th of May, 1660, Charles II. was placed on the throne of England.

These were times full of trouble. Virginia shared in some degree the distractions of the mother-country, yet the evil done to the new State by the conflict in England was less than might have been expected. In the first year of the civil war Sir William Berkeley became governor of the colony, and, with the exception of a brief visit to England in 1645, remained in office for ten years. His administration, notwithstanding the commotions abroad, was noted as a time of rapid growth and development. The laws were greatly improved and made conformable to the English statutes. The old controversies about the lands were satisfactorily settled. Cruel punishments were abolished and the taxes equalized. The general assembly was regularly convened to bear its part in the government, and Virginia was in all essential particulars a free as well as a prosperous State. So rapid was the progress that in 1646 there were twenty thousand people in the colony.

But there were also drawbacks to the prosperity of Virginia. Religious intolerance came with its baleful shadow to disturb the State. The faith of the Episcopal Church was established by law, and dissenting was declared a crime. The Puritans were held in contempt by the people, who charged them with being the destroyers of the peace of England. In March of 1643 a statute was enacted by the assembly declaring that no person who disbelieved the doctrines of the English Church should be allowed to teach publicly or privately, or to preach the gospel, within the limits of Virginia. The few Puritans in the colony were excluded from their places of trust, and some were even driven from their homes. Governor Berkeley, himself a zealous churchman, was a leader in these persecutions, by which all friendly relations with New England were broken off for many years.

A worse calamity befell in a second war with the Indians. Early in 1644, the natives, having forgotten their former punishment, and believing that in the confusion of the civil war there still remained a hope of destroying the English, planned a general massacre. On the 18th of April, at a time when the authorities were somewhat off their guard, the savages fell upon the frontier settlements, and before assistance could be brought murdered three hundred people. Alarmed at their own atrocity, the warriors then fled, but were followed by the English forces and driven into the woods and swamps. The aged Opechancanough was captured, and died a prisoner. The tribes were chastised without mercy, and were soon glad to purchase peace by the cession of large tracts of land.

The Virginians adhered with great firmness to the cause of Charles I. in his war with Parliament, and after his death proclaimed the exiled Charles II. as rightful sovereign of the country. Cromwell and the Parliament were much exasperated at this course of conduct, and measures were at once devised to bring the colony to submission. An ordinance was passed laying heavy restrictions on the commerce of such English colonies as refused to acknowledge the supremacy of Parliament. All foreign ships, especially those of Holland, were forbidden to enter the colonial harbors. In 1651 the noted statute called the Navigation Act was passed, and the trade of the colonies was still more seriously distressed. In this new law it was enacted that the foreign commerce of Virginia, now grown into importance, should be carried on wholly in English vessels, and directed exclusively to English ports.

The Virginians held out, and Cromwell determined to employ force. A war-vessel called the Guinea was sent into the Chesapeake to compel submission, but in the last extreme the Protector showed himself to be just as well as wrathful. There were commissioners on board the frigate authorized to make an offer of peace, and this was gladly accepted. It was seen that the cause of the Stuarts was hopeless. The people of Virginia, although refusing to yield to threats and violence, cheerfully entered into negotiations with Cromwell's delegates, and ended by acknowledging the supreme authority of Parliament. The terms of the settlement were very favorable to popular liberty; the commercial restrictions of the two previous years were removed, and the trade of the colony was made as free as that of England. No taxes might be levied or duties collected except such as were imposed by the general assembly of the State. The freedom of an Englishman was guaranteed to every citizen, and under the control of her own laws Virginia again grew prosperous.

No further difficulty arose during the continuance of the Commonwealth. The Protector was busied with the affairs of Europe, and had neither time nor disposition to interfere in the affairs of a remote colony. The Virginians were thus left free to conduct their government as they would. Even the important matter of choosing a governor was submitted to an election in the House of Burgesses; when so great a power had been once exercised, it was not likely to be relinquished without a struggle. Three governors were chosen in this way, and what was at first only a privilege soon became a right. Special acts of the assembly declared that such a right existed, and that it should be transmitted to posterity.

In 1660, just at the time of the resignation of Richard Cromwell, Samuel Matthews, the last of the three elected governors, died. The burgesses were immediately convened, and an ordinance was passed declaring that the supreme authority of Virginia was resident in the colony, and would continue there until a delegate with proper credentials should arrive from the British government. Having made this declaration, the house elected as governor Sir William Berkeley, who by accepting the office acknowledged the right of the burgesses to choose. The question of recognizing Charles II. as king was debated at the same session, but prudence suggested that the colonial authorities would better await the natural course of events. For the present it was decided to remain faithful to Parliament. Most of the people, no doubt, desired the restoration, but policy forbade any open expressions of such a preference. It would be time enough when monarchy was actually restored.

In May of 1660 Charles II. became king of England. As soon as this event was known in Virginia, Governor Berkeley, forgetting the source of his own authority, and in defiance of all consistency, issued writs in the name of the king for the election of a new assembly. The friends of royalty were delighted with the prospect. The adherents of the Commonwealth were thrust out of office, and the favorites of the king established in their places. Great benefits were expected from the change, and the whole colony was alive with excitement and zeal. But the disappointment of the people was more bitter than their hopes had been extravagant. The Virginians soon found that they had exchanged a republican tyrant with good principles for a monarchial tyrant with bad ones. King Charles II. was the worst monarch of modern times, and the people of Virginia had in him and his government a special cause of grief. The commercial system of the Commonwealth, so far from being abolished, was re-enacted in a more hateful form than ever. The new statute provided that all the colonial commerce, whether exports or imports, should he carried on in English ships, the trade between the colonies was burdened with a heavy tax for the benefit of the government, and tobacco, the staple of Virginia, could be sold nowhere but in England. This odious measure gave to English merchantmen a monopoly of the carrying trade of the colonies, and by destroying competition among the buyers of tobacco robbed the Virginians to that extent of their leading product. Remonstrance was tried in vain. The cold and selfish monarch only sneered at the complaints of his American subjects, and the commercial ordinances were rigorously enforced.

Charles II. seemed to regard the British empire as personal property to be used for the benefit of himself and his courtiers. In order to reward the worthless profligates who thronged his court, he began to grant to them large tracts of land in Virginia. What did it matter that these lands had been redeemed from the wilderness and were covered with orchards and gardens? It was no uncommon thing for an American planter to find that his farm, which had been cultivated for a quarter of a century, was given away to some dissolute flatterer of the royal household. Great distress was occasioned by these iniquitous grants, until finally, in 1673, the king set a limit to his own recklessness by giving away the whole State. Lord Culpepper and the earl of Arlington, two ignoble noblemen, received under the great seal a deed by which was granted to them for thirty one years all the dominion of land and water called Virginia.

Unfortunately, the colonial legislation of these times became as selfish and narrow-minded as the policy of the king was mean. An aristocratic party which had arisen in the colony obtained control of the House of Burgesses, and the new laws rivaled those of England in illiberality. Episcopalianism was again established as the State religion. A proscriptive ordinance was passed against the Baptists, and the peace-loving Quakers were fined, persecuted and imprisoned. Burdensome taxes were laid on personal property and polls; the holders of large estates were exempt and the poorer people afflicted. The salaries of the officers were secured by a permanent duty on tobacco, and, worst of all, the biennial election of burgesses was abolished, so that the members of the existing assembly continued indefinitely in power. For a while Berkeley and his council outdid the tyranny of England.

And then came open resistance. The people were worn out with the governor's exactions, and availed themselves of the first pretext to assert their rights by force of arms. A war with the Susquehanna Indians furnished the occasion for an insurrection. The tribes about the head of Chesapeake Bay and along the Susquehanna had been attacked by the Senecas and driven from their homes. They, in turn, fell upon the English settlers of Maryland, and the banks of the Potomac became the scene of a border war. Virginia and Maryland made common cause against the savages. John Washington, great-grandfather of the first president of the United States, led a company of militia into the enemy's country, and compelled the Susquehannas to sue for peace. Six of their chieftains went into Virginia as ambassadors, and, to the lasting dishonor of the colony, were foully murdered. This atrocity maddened the savages, and a devastating warfare raged along the whole frontier.

Governor Berkeley, not without some show of justice, sided with the Indians. But the colonists remembered only the many acts of treachery and bloodshed of which the red men had before been guilty, and were determined to have revenge. In this division of sentiment among the people, the assembly and the aristocratic party took sides with the governor and favored a peace; while the popular party, disliking Berkeley and hating the Indians, resolved to overthrow him and destroy them at one blow. A leader was found in that remarkable man, Nathaniel Bacon. Young, brave, eloquent, patriotic, full of enthusiasm and energy, he became the soul and life of the popular party. His own farm in the county of Henrico had been pillaged and his tenants murdered by the savages. Exasperated by these injuries, he was the more easily urged by the public voice to accept the dangerous office of leading an insurrection.

Five hundred men rushed to arms and demanded to be led against the Indians. Alarm, excitement and passion prevailed throughout the colony. The patriot forces were organized; and without permission of a government which they had ceased to regard, the march was begun into the enemy's country. Berkeley and the aristocratic faction were enraged at this proceeding, and proclaimed Bacon a traitor. A levy of troops was made for the purpose of dispersing the rebellious militia; but scarcely had Berkeley and his forces left Jamestown when another popular uprising in the lower counties compelled him to return. Affairs were in an uproar. Bacon came home victorious. The old assembly was unceremoniously broken up, and a new one elected on the basis of universal suffrage. Bacon was chosen a member for Henrico, and soon after elected commander-in-chief of the Virginia army. The governor refused to sign his commission, and Bacon appealed to the people; the militia again flew to arms, and Berkeley was compelled to yield. Not only was the commission signed, but a paper drawn up by the burgesses in commendation of Bacon's loyalty, zeal and patriotism received the executive signature and was transmitted to Parliament.

Governor Berkeley and the Insurgents.

Peace returned to the colony. The power of the savages was completely broken. A military force was stationed on the frontier, and a sense of security returned to all the settlements. But Berkeley was petulant, proud and vengeful; and it was only a question of time when the struggle would be renewed. Seizing the first opportunity, the governor left Jamestown and repaired to the county of Gloucester, on the north side of York River. Here be summoned a convention of loyalists, who, contrary to his expectations and wishes, advised moderation and compromise; but the hot-headed old cavalier would yield no jot of his prerogative to what he was pleased to call a rabble, and Bacon was again proclaimed a traitor.

It was evident that there must be fighting. Berkeley and his forces left Gloucester, crossed the Chesapeake Bay, and took station on the eastern shore, in the county of Accomac. Here his troops were organized; the crews of some English ships were joined to his command, and the fleet set sail for Jamestown. The place was taken without much resistance; but when Bacon with a few companies of patriots drew near, the loyal forces deserted and went over to his standard. The governor with his adherents was again obliged to fly, and the capital remained in possession of the people's party. The assembly was about to assume control of the government without the governor, whose flight to Accomac had been declared an abdication, when a rumor arose that an English fleet was approaching for the subjugation of the colonies. The patriot leaders held a council, and it was determined that Jamestown should be burned. Accordingly, in the dusk of the evening the torch was applied, and the only town in Virginia laid in ashes. The leading men set the example by throwing firebrands into their own houses; others caught the spirit of sacrifice; the flames shot up through the shadows of night; and Governor Berkeley and his followers, on board a fleet twenty miles down the river, had tolerably fair warning that the capital of Virginia could not be used for the purposes of despotism.

In this juncture of affairs Bacon fell sick and died. It was an event full of grief and disaster. The patriot party, discouraged by the loss of the heroic chieftain, was easily dispersed. A few feeble efforts were made to revive the cause of the people, but the animating spirit which had controlled and directed until now was gone. The royalists found an able leader in Robert Beverly, and the authority of the governor was rapidly restored throughout the province. The cause of the people and the leader of the people had died together.

Berkeley's vindictive passions were now let loose upon the defeated insurgents. Fines and confiscations became the order of the day. The governor seemed determined to drown the memory of his own wrongs in the woes of his subjects. Twenty-two of the leading patriots were seized and hanged with scarcely time to bid their friends farewell. Thus died Thomas Hansford, the first American who gave his life for freedom. Thus perished Edmund Cheesman, Thomas Wilford and the noble William Drummond, martyrs to liberty. Nor is it certain when the vengeful tyrant would have stayed his hand, had not the assembly met and passed an edict that no more blood should be spilt for past offences. One of the burgesses from the county of Northampton said in the debate that if the governor were let alone he would hang half the country. When Charles II. heard of Berkeley's ferocity, he exclaimed, "The old fool has taken away more lives in that naked country than I for the murder of my father"; and the saying was true.

The history of this insurrection was for a long time recited by Bacon's enemies. Until the present century no one appeared to rescue the leader's name from obloquy. In the light of after times his character will shine with a peculiar lustre. His motives were as exalted as his life was pure, and his virtues as noted as his abilities were great. His ambition was for the public welfare, and his passions were only excited against the enemies of his country.

The consequences of the rebellion were very disastrous. Berkeley and the aristocratic party had now a good excuse for suppressing all liberal sentiments and tendencies. The printing-press was interdicted. Education was discouraged or forbidden. To speak or to write anything against the administration or in defence of the late insurrection was made a crime to be punished by fine or whipping. If the offence should be three times repeated, it was declared to be treason punishable with death. The former tyrannical methods of taxation were revived, and Virginia was left at the mercy of arbitrary rulers.

CHART II.

1600

11. **Gustavus Adolphus the Great.**		89. **Pet**
Grotius.		
Galileo. 18. **The Thirty Years' War** begins.		
Kepler. 48. Peace of Westphalia.		85. Revocation
24-42. **Richelieu.** 43. **Louis XIV.**		87. Habeas
Shakespeare. **Milton.**	**Locke.**	
		88. Seco
Bacon. 49. **Cromwell.**		88. Willi
		of Mary, 94. V
3. James VI. ⎫ 25. **Charles I.** 42. **The Revolution.**	60. The Restoration.	
James I. ⎭	60. **Charles II.**	85. James

:9. Second Charter granted. 42. Berkeley's administration.
: 12. The Third Charter. 44. Indian massacre. 76. Bacon's Rebellion.
: 19. House of Burgesses established. 77. Virginia become
7. : **VIRGINIA** colonized by the **London** 51. First Navigation Act. 84. Royal gov
: Company at Jamestown. :
: 24. Dissolution of the 50.:**NORTH CAROLINA** settled by the **Englis** 83. Seth Soth
: London Company. 63. Grant made to Lord Clarendon.
: 19. Introduction of Slavery. : 85. Sir Joh
:**John Smith,** governor. 65. **Sir John Yeamans,** govern
: 77. Culpepper's reb
: 34.: **MARYLAND** settled by the Catho- 91. M
: lics under **Lord Baltimore.** 75. **Charles Calvert**
: 39. Representative government established. 92. L

38. **Governor Kief.** 64. Taken by the English. 91. Sl
14. :**NEW YORK** settled by the **Dutch.** Berkeley and Carteret. 92.
47. **Stuyvesant.** 70. Lovelace.
25. **Minuits,** governor. 56. New York City founded. 74. Edmu
38. Wilmington settled by the Swedes. 82.:**DELAWA**

23.:**NEW JERSEY** settled by the **Dutch.**
81. First General
29. **NEW HAMPSHIRE** settled. 80. : New Hampshire
27. Boston founded. : as a distinct colony.

30. :**MAINE** settled. : 76. King Philip's defe
20. : **MASSACHUSETTS** settled by the **Puritans** at Plymouth. 84. Massach
30. **Winthrop,** governor. 90. Firs
38. Harvard College founded. 90. Kin
39. First printing-press set up at Cambridge.
92. Wi
exc

36. :**RHODE ISLAND** settled by **Roger Williams.**
: 39. Newport founded. 87. Rhode
: 37. **Pequod War.** 89. The I
30. : **CONNECTICUT** granted to the earl of Warwick.
: 35. Saybrook founded.
:33. Hartford founded. 62. New charter granted.

70. : **SOUTH CAROLIN**
: Locke's Constitution ad
: 86. Arrival

COLONIAL PERIOD
A. D. 1607–1776.

82. : **PENNS**
the Qu
: 92. Pe

CHART II.

COLONIAL PERIOD. A. D. 1607-1776.

1700

the Great.
Charles XII.
War of the Spanish Succession.
Leibnitz.
    13. Peace of Utrecht.
Edict of Nantes.
pus.   15. **Louis XV.**

Revolution.
and Mary, and after the death
liam III.

2. Anne. 14. George I. 27. George II.

           62. Catharine II.
40. **Frederick the Great.**
40. War of the Austrian Succession terminated
   by 48. **Peace of Aix-la-Chapelle.** 89. French
                                      Revolution.
                                       93. Reign
Voltaire.   74. Louis XVI. of Terror.
Dr. Johnson.   Burke.
    65. The Rockingham Ministry.
Newton.   **Chatham.** Pitt.
55. War between France and England. Fox.
    65. **The Stamp Act.**
60. George III.

Proprietary government.   32. **Birth of Washington.**   65. The Virginia Resolutions.
ment re-established.

governor.
   9. Arrival of the German immigrants.

Archdale, governor.
   11. **The Coree War.**
on.   29. Final separation of the Carolinas.
land becomes a royal government.

nel Copley.

ghter, governor.   44. Negro plot. 58. Fall of Louisburg.
etcher. 1. **Cornbury.** 32. **Cosby,** governor. 65. Declaration of Rights.
Bellamont.   54. **French and Indian War.**
Andros.   65. First Colonial Congress assembles at New York.

separated from New York.

Union of East and West Jersey.   **Dr. Benjamin Franklin.**
embly.   38. Royal government established.
United with Massachusetts.   41. New Hampshire finally sepa-
    20. Introduction of tea.   rated from Mass. 67. The tea tax.
                              61. Writs of Assistance.
                              73. **The Boston "Tea Party."**
nd death.
   4. First newspaper.   44. **King George's War.**   75. *Lexington.*
tts loses her charter.
ue of paper money   45. *Louisburg* taken. 74. Boston Port Bill.
William's War.   68. General Gage arrives in Boston.
2. **Queen Anne's War.**
raft 10. First post-office.   59. *Quebec* 75. *Bunker Hill.*
nent.   taken. 70. Tumult in Boston.

nd joined to New York.

ng of the charter.

1. Yale College founded.

ettled by the **English.**
d. 2. Expedition against St. Augustine.
he Huguenots.   29. Royal government established.

                                      76. Independence.
VANIA settled by   55. Braddock's defeat.
rs under **Penn.**   74. Second Congress assem-
oses his commission.   bles at Philadelphia.

        33. **GEORGIA** settled by the **English**
            under **Oglethorpe.**
                52. Royal government established.

In 1675, Lord Culpepper, to whom with Arlington the province had been granted two years previously, obtained the appointment of governor for life. The right of the king was thus by his own act relinquished, and Virginia became a proprietary government. The new executive arrived in 1680 and assumed the duties of his office. His whole administration was characterized by avarice and dishonesty. Regarding Virginia as his personal estate, he treated the Virginians as his tenants and slaves. Every species of extortion was resorted to, until the mutterings of rebellion were again heard throughout the impoverished colony. In 1683, Arlington surrendered his claim to Culpepper, who thus became sole proprietor as well as governor; but before he could proceed to further mischief, his official career was cut short by the act of the king. Charles II., repenting of his own rashness, found in Culpepper's vices and frauds a sufficient excuse to remove him from office and to revoke his patent. In 1684, Virginia again became a royal province, under the government of Lord Howard, of Effingham, who was succeeded by Francis Nicholson, formerly governor of New York. His administration was signalized by the founding of WILLIAM AND MARY COLLEGE, so named in honor of the new sovereigns of England. This, next to Harvard, was the first institution of liberal learning planted in America. Here the boy Jefferson, author of the Declaration of Independence, shall be educated! From these halls, in the famous summer of 1776, shall be sent forth young James Monroe, future President of the United States! After Nicholson's administration, Sir Edmund Andros, recently expelled by the people of Massachusetts, assumed for a while the government of Virginia. The affairs of the colony during the next forty or fifty years are not of sufficient interest and importance to require extended notice in an abridgment of American history. At the outbreak of the French and Indian War, Virginia will show to the world that the labors of Smith, and Gosnold, and Bacon have not been in vain.

CHAPTER XIII.

Massachusetts.—Settlement.

THE spring of 1621 brought a ray of hope to the distressed Pilgrims of New Plymouth. Never was the returning sun more welcome. The fatal winter had swept off one-half of the number. The son of the benevolent Carver was among the first victims of the terrible climate. The governor himself sickened and died, and the broken-hearted wife found rest in the same grave with her husband. But now, with the approach of warm weather, the destroying pestilence was stayed, and the spirits of the survivors revived with the season. Out of the snows of winter, the desolations of disease, and the terrors of death the faith of the Puritan had come forth triumphant.

For a while the colonists were apprehensive of the Indians. In February, Miles Standish was sent out with his soldiers to gather information of the numbers and disposition of the natives. The army of New England consisted of six men besides the general. Deserted wigwams were found here and there; the smoke of camp-fires arose in the distance; savages were occasionally seen in the forest. These fled, however, at the approach of the English, and Standish returned to Plymouth.

A month later the colonists were astonished by the sudden appearance in their midst of a Wampanoag Indian named Samoset. He ran into the village, offered his hand in token of friendship, and bade the strangers welcome. He gave an account of the numbers and strength of the neighboring tribes, and recited the story of a great plague by which, a few years before, the country had been swept of its inhabitants. The present feebleness and desolate condition of the natives had resulted from the fatal malady. Another Indian, by the name of Squanto, who had been carried away by Hunt in 1614, and had learned to speak English, came also to Plymouth, and confirmed what Samoset had said.

By the influence of these two natives friendly relations were at once established with the Wampanoags. Massasoit, the great sachem of the nation, was invited to visit the settlement, and came attended by a few of his warriors. The Pilgrims received him with as much parade and ceremony as the colony could provide; Captain Standish ordered out his soldiers, and Squanto acted as interpreter. Then and there was ratified the first treaty made in New England. The terms were few and simple. There should be peace and friendship between the whites and the red men. No injury should be done by either party to the other. All offenders should be given up to be punished. If the English engaged in war, Massasoit should help them; if the Wampanoags were attacked unjustly, the English should give aid against the common enemy. Mark that word *unjustly*: it contains the essence of Puritanism.

The Treaty Between Governor Carver and Massasoit.

The treaty thus made and ratified remained inviolate for fifty years. Other chiefs followed the example of the great sachem and entered into friendly relations with the colony. Nine of the leading tribes acknowledged the sovereignty of the English king. One Chieftain threatened hostilities, but Standish's army obliged him to beg for mercy. Canonicus, king of the Narragansetts, sent to William Bradford, who had been chosen governor after the death of Carver, a bundle of arrows wrapped in the skin of a rattlesnake; but the undaunted governor stuffed the skin with powder and balls and sent it back to the chief, who did not dare to accept the dangerous challenge. The hostile emblem was borne about from tribe to tribe, until finally it was returned to Plymouth.

The summer of 1621 was unfruitful, and the Pilgrims were brought to the point of starvation. To make their condition still more grievous, a new company of immigrants, without provisions or stores, arrived, and were quartered on the colonists during the fall and winter. For six months together the settlers were obliged to subsist on half allowance. At one time only a few grains of parched corn remained to be distributed, and at another there was absolute destitution. In this state of affairs some English fishing-vessels came to Plymouth and charged the starving colonists two prices for food enough to keep them alive.

The intruding immigrants just mentioned had been sent to America by Thomas Weston, of London, one of the projectors of the colony. They remained with the people of Plymouth until the summer of 1622, then removed to the south side of Boston Harbor and began a new settlement called Weymouth. Instead of working with their might to provide against starvation, they wasted the fall in idleness, and attempted to keep up their stock of provisions by defrauding the Indians. Thus provoked to hostility, the natives formed a plan to destroy the colony; but Massasoit, faithful to his pledges, went to Plymouth and revealed the plot. Standish marched to Weymouth at the head of his regiment, now increased to eight men, attacked the hostile tribe, killed several warriors and carried home the chief's head on a pole. The tender-hearted John Robinson wrote from Leyden: "I would that you had converted some of them before you killed any."

In the following spring most of the Weymouth settlers abandoned the place and returned to England, The summer of 1623 brought a plentiful harvest to the people of the older colony, and there was no longer any danger of starvation. The natives, preferring the chase, became dependent on the settlement for corn, and furnished in exchange an abundance of game. The main body of Pilgrims still tarried at Leyden. Robinson made unwearied efforts to bring his people to America, but the adventurers of London who had managed the enterprise would provide no further means either of money or transportation and now, at the end of the fourth year, there were only a hundred and eighty persons in New England. The managers had expected profitable returns, and were disappointed. They had expended thirty-four thousand dollars; there was neither profit nor the hope of any. Under this discouragement the proprietors made a proposition to sell out their claims to the colonists. The offer was accepted; and in November of 1627 eight of the leading men of Plymouth purchased from the Londoners their entire interest for the sum of nine thousand dollars.

Before this transfer of right was made the colony had been much vexed by the efforts of the managers to thrust on them a minister of the Established Church. Was it not to avoid this very thing that they had come to the wilds of the New World? Should the tyranny of the prelates follow them even across the sea and into the wilderness? There was dissension and strife for a while; the English managers withheld support; oppression was resorted to; the stores intended for the colonists were sold to them at three prices; and they were obliged to borrow money at sixty per cent. But no exactions could break the spirit of the Pilgrims; and the conflict ended with the purchase of whatever rights the London proprietors had in the colony.

The year 1624 was marked by the founding of a settlement at Cape Ann. John White, a Puritan minister of Dorchester, England, collected a small company of emigrants and sent them to America. The colony was established, but after two years of discouragement the cape was abandoned as a place unsuitable, and the company moved farther south to Naumkeag, afterward called Salem. Here a settlement was begun, and in 1628 was made permanent by the arrival of a second colony, in charge of John Endicott, who was chosen governor. In March of the same year the colonists obtained a patent from the Council of Plymouth; and in 1629 Charles I. issued a charter by which the proprietors were incorporated under the name of THE GOVERNOR AND COMPANY OF MASSACHUSETTS BAY IN NEW ENGLAND. In July two hundred additional immigrants arrived, half of whom settled at Plymouth, while the other half removed to a peninsula on the north side of Boston Harbor and laid the foundation of Charlestown.

At the first it had been decided that the charter of the colony should be left in England, and that the governor should reside there also. After further discussion, this decision was reversed, and in September it was decreed that the whole government should be transferred to America, and that the charter, as a pledge of liberty, should be entrusted to the colonists themselves. As soon as this liberal action was made known emigration began on an extensive scale. In the year 1630 about three hundred of the best Puritan families in the kingdom came to New England. Not adventurers, not vagabonds, were these brave people, but virtuous, well-educated, courageous men and women who for conscience' sake left comfortable homes with no expectation of returning. It was not the least of their good fortune to choose a noble leader.

John Winthrop.

If ever a man was worthy to be held in perpetual remembrance, that man was John Winthrop, governor of Massachusetts. Born a royalist, he cherished the principles of republicanism. Himself an Episcopalian, he chose affliction with the Puritans. Surrounded with affluence and comfort, he left all to share the destiny of the persecuted Pilgrims. Calm, prudent and peace able, he joined the zeal of an enthusiast with the sublime faith of a martyr.

A part of the new immigrants settled at Salem; others at Cambridge and Watertown, on Charles River; while others, going farther south, founded Roxbury and Dorchester. The governor, with a few of the leading families, resided for a while at Charlestown, but soon crossed the harbor to the peninsula of Shawmut and laid the foundation of BOSTON, which became henceforth the capital of the colony and the metropolis of New England. With the approach of winter sickness came, and the distress was very great. Many of the new-comers were refined and tender people who could not endure the bitter blasts of Massachusetts Bay. Coarse fare and scanty provisions added to the griefs of disease. Sleet and snow drifted through the cracks of the thin board huts where enfeebled men and delicate women moaned out their lives. Before mid-winter two hundred had perished. A few others, heartsick and despairing, returned to England; but there was heard neither murmur nor repining. Governor Winthrop wrote to his wife: "I like so well to be here that I do not repent my coming."

At a session of the general court of the colony, held in 1631, a law was passed restricting the right of suffrage. It was enacted that none but members of the church should be permitted to vote at the colonial elections. The choice of governor, deputy-governor and assistant councilors was thus placed in the hands of a small minority. Nearly three-fourths of the people were excluded from exercising the rights of freemen. Taxes were levied for the support of the gospel; oaths of obedience to the magistrates were required; attendance on public worship was enforced by law; none but church-members were eligible to offices of trust. It is strange indeed that the very men who had so recently, through perils by sea and land, escaped with only their lives to find religious freedom in another continent, should have begun their career with intolerance and proscription. The only excuse that can be found for the gross inconsistency and injustice of such legislation is that bigotry was the vice of the age rather than of the Puritans.

One manly voice was lifted up against this odious statute. It was the voice of young ROGER WILLIAMS, minister of Salem. To this man belongs the shining honor of being first in America or in Europe to proclaim the full gospel of religious toleration. He declared to his people that the conscience of man may in no wise be bound by the authority of the magistrate; that civil government has only to do with civil matters, such as the collection of taxes, the restraint and punishment of crime, and the protection of all men in the enjoyment of equal rights. For these noble utterances he was obliged to quit the ministry of the church at Salem and retire to Plymouth. Finally, in 1634, he wrote a paper in which the declaration was made that grants of land, though given by the king of England, were invalid until the natives were justly recompensed. This was equivalent to saying that the colonial charter itself was void, and that the people were really living upon the lands of the Indians. Great excitement was occasioned by the publication, and Williams consented that for the sake of public peace the paper should be burned. But he continued to teach his doctrines, saying that compulsory attendance at religious worship, as well as taxation for the support of the ministry, was contrary to the teachings of the gospel. When arraigned for these bad doctrines, he crowned his offences by telling the court that a test of church-membership in a voter or a public officer was as ridiculous as the selection of a doctor of physio or the pilot of a ship on account of his skill in theology.

These assertions raised such a storm in court that Williams was condemned for heresy and banished from the colony. In the dead of winter he left home and became an exile in the desolate forest. For fourteen weeks he wandered on through the snow, sleeping at night on the ground or in a hollow tree, living on parched corn, acorns and roots. He carried with him one precious treasure—a private letter from Governor Winthrop, giving him words of cheer and encouragement. Nor did the Indians fail to show their gratitude to the man who had so nobly defended their rights. In the country of the Wampanoags he was kindly entertained. Massasoit invited him to his cabin at Pokanoket, and Canonicus, king of the Narragansetts, received him as a friend and brother. On the left bank of Blackstone River, near the head of Narragansett Bay, a resting-place was at last found; the exile pitched his tent, and with the opening of spring planted a field and built the first house in the village of Seekonk. Soon the information came that he was still within the territory of Plymouth colony, and another removal became necessary. With five companions who had joined him in banishment, he embarked in a canoe, passed down the river and crossed to the west side of the bay. Here he was safe; his enemies could hunt him no farther. A tract of land was honorably purchased from Canonicus; and in June of 1636, the illustrious founder of Rhode Island laid out the city of PROVIDENCE.

Roger Williams' Reception by the Indians.

Meanwhile, his teachings were bearing fruit in Massachusetts. In 1634 a representative form of government was established against the opposition of the clergy. On election-day the voters, now numbering between three and four hundred, were called together, and the learned Cotton preached powerfully and long against the proposed change. The assembly listened attentively, and then went on with the election. To make the reform complete, a BALLOT-BOX was substituted for the old method of public voting. The restriction on the right of suffrage was the only remaining bar to a perfect system of self-government in New England.

During the next year three thousand new immigrants arrived. It was worth while—so thought the people of England—to come to a country where the principles of freedom were spreading with such rapidity. The new-comers were under the leadership of Hugh Peters and Sir Henry Vane; the former the Puritan pastor of some English exiles at Rotterdam, in Holland, and the latter a young nobleman who afterward played an important part in the history of England. Such was his popularity with the people of Massachusetts, and such his zeal and piety, that in less than a year after his arrival he was chosen governor of the colony.

By this time the settlements around Massachusetts Bay were thickly clustered. Until new homes should be found there was no room for the immigrants who were constantly coming. To enlarge the frontier, to plunge into the wilderness and find new places of abode, became a necessity. One little company of twelve families, led by Simon Willard and Peter Bulkeley, marched through the woods until they came to some open meadows sixteen miles from Boston, and there laid the foundations of Concord. A little later in the same year, another colony of sixty persons left the older settlements and pressed their way westward as far as the Connecticut River. The march itself was a grievous hardship, but greater toils and sufferings were in store for the adventurous company. A dreadful winter overtook them in their new homes but half provided. Some died; others, disheartened, waded back through the dreary untrodden snows and came half famished to Plymouth and Boston; but the rest, with true Puritan heroism, outbraved the winter and triumphed over the pangs of starvation. Spring brought a recompense for hardship: the heroic pioneers crept out of their miserable huts to become the founders of Windsor, HARTFORD and Wethersfield, the oldest towns in the Connecticut valley.

The banishment of Roger Williams, instead of bringing peace, brought strife and dissension to the people of Massachusetts. The ministers were stem and exacting. Every shade of popular belief was closely scrutinized; the slightest departure from orthodox doctrines was met with a charge of heresy, and to be a heretic was to become an outcast. Still, the advocates of free opinion multiplied. The clergy, notwithstanding their great influence among the people, felt insecure.

Religious debates became the order of the day. Every sermon had to pass the ordeal of review and criticism.

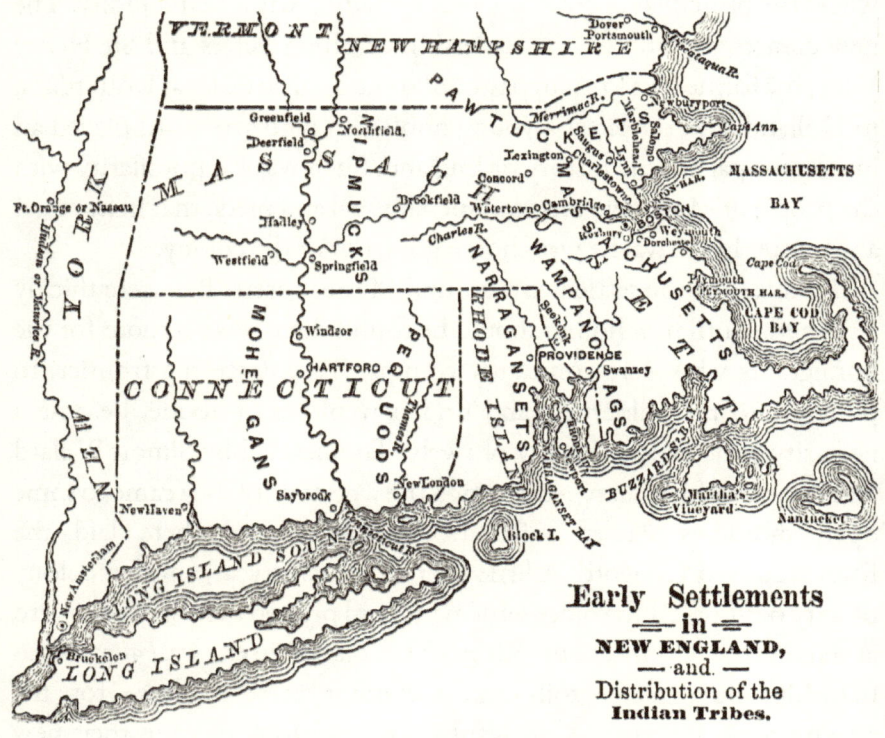

Map of Early Settlements in New England.

Most prominent among those who were said to be "as bad as Roger Williams, or worse," was Mrs. Anne Hutchinson, a woman of genius who had come over in the ship with Sir Henry Vane. She desired the privilege of speaking at the weekly debates, and was refused. Women had no business at these assemblies, said the elders. Indignant at this, she became the champion of her sex, and declared that the ministers who were defrauding women of the gospel were no better than Pharisees. She called meetings of her friends, spoke much in public, and pleaded with great fervor for the full freed of conscience. The liberal doctrines of the exiled Williams were reaffirmed with more power and eloquence than ever. Many of the magistrates were converted to the new beliefs; the governor himself espoused the cause of Mrs. Hutchinson; and a majority of the people of Boston inclined to her opinions.

For a while there was a reign of discord; but as soon as Sir Henry's term of office expired a call was issued for a meeting of the synod of New England. The body convened in August of 1637; a decree was proposed; Mrs. Hutchinson and her friends were declared unfit for the society of Christians, and banished from the territory of Massachusetts. With a large number of friends the exiles wended their way toward the home of Roger Williams. Miantonomoh, a Narragansett chieftain, made them a gift of the beautiful island of Rhode Island; there, in the month of March, 1641, a little republic was established, in whose constitution freedom of conscience was guaranteed and persecution for opinion's sake forbidden.

The year 1636 was an important epoch in the history of Massachusetts. The general court of the colony passed an act appropriating between one and two thousand dollars to found and endow a college. The measure met with popular favor; the Puritans were an educated people, and were quick to appreciate the advantages of learning. New town was selected as the site of the proposed school. Plymouth and Salem gave gifts to help the enterprise; and from villages in the Connecticut valley came contributions of corn and wampum. In 1638, John Harvard, a young minister of Charlestown, died, bequeathing his library and nearly five thousand dollars to the school. To perpetuate the memory of the noble benefactor the new institution was named HARVARD COLLEGE; and in honor of the place where the leading men of Massachusetts had been educated, the name of Newtown was changed to Cambridge. Thus early did the people of New England stamp their approval on the cause of education. In spite of sterile soil and desolate landscapes—in spite of destroying climate and wasting diseases—in spite even of superstition and bigotry—the people who educate will ever be great and free.

The PRINTING-PRESS came also. In 1638, Stephen Daye, an English printer, arrived at Boston, bringing a font of types, and in the following year set up a press at Cambridge. The first American publication was an almanac calculated for New England, and bearing date of 1639. During the next year, Thomas Welde and John Eliot, two ministers of Roxbury, and Richard Mather, of Dorchester, translated the Hebrew Psalms into

English verse, and published their rude work in a volume of three hundred pages—the first book printed on this side of the Atlantic.

The rapid growth of Massachusetts now became a source of alarm to the English government. Those liberal principles of religion and politics which were openly avowed and gloried in by the citizens of the new commonwealth were hateful to Charles I. and his ministers. The archbishop of Canterbury was much offended. Something must be done to check the further growth of the Puritan colonies. The first measure which suggested itself was to stop emigration. For this purpose an edict was issued as early as 1634, but was of no effect. The officers of the government neglected to enforce the law. Four years later, more vigorous measures were adopted. A squadron of eight vessels, ready to sail from London, was detained by the royal authority. Many of the most prominent Puritan families in England were on board of these ships. Historians of high rank have asserted—but without sufficient proof—that John Hampden and Oliver Cromwell were of the number who were turned back by the detention. At all events, it would have been the part of wisdom in King Charles to allow all Puritans to leave his realm as fast as possible. By detaining them in England he only made sure the Revolution, and by so much hastened his own downfall.

CHAPTER XIV.

Massachusetts.—The Union.

NEW ENGLAND was fast becoming a nation. Wellnigh fifty towns and villages dotted the face of the country. Nearly a million of dollars had been spent in settling and developing the new State. Enterprises of all kinds were rife. Manufactures, commerce and the arts were rapidly introduced. William Stephens, a shipbuilder who came with Governor Winthrop to Boston, had already built and launched an American vessel of four hundred tons burden. Before 1640, two hundred and ninety-eight emigrant ships had anchored in Massachusetts Bay. Twenty-one thousand two hundred people, escaping from English intolerance of Church or State, had found home and rest between Plymouth Rock and the Connecticut valley. It is not wonderful that the colonists began to cast about them for better political organization and more ample forms of government.

Many circumstances impelled the colonies to union. First of all, there was the natural desire of men to have a regular and permanent government. England, torn and distracted with civil war, could do nothing for or against her colonies; they must take care of themselves. Here was the western frontier exposed to the hostilities of the Dutch towns on the Hudson; Connecticut alone could not defend herself. Similar trouble was apprehended from the French on the north; the English settlements on the Piscataqua were weak and defenceless. Indian tribes capable of mustering a thousand warriors were likely at any hour to fall upon remote and helpless villages; the prevalence of common interests and the necessities of common defence made a union of some sort indispensable.

The first effort to consolidate the colonies was ineffectual. Two years later, in 1639, the project was renewed, but without success. Again, in 1643, a measure of union was brought forward and finally adopted. By the terms of this compact, Massachusetts, Plymouth, Connecticut and New Haven were joined in a loose confederacy, called THE UNITED

COLONIES OF NEW ENGLAND. The chief authority was conferred upon a general assembly, or congress, composed of two representatives from each colony. These delegates were chosen annually at an election where all the freemen voted by ballot. There was no president other than the speaker of the assembly, and he had no executive powers. Each community retained, as before, its separate local existence; and all subordinate questions of legislation were reserved to the respective colonies. Only matters of general interest—such as Indian affairs, the levying of troops, the raising of revenues, declarations of war and treaties of peace—were submitted to the assembly.

Provision was made for the admission of other colonies into the union, but none were ever admitted. The English settlement on the Piscataqua was rejected because of heterodoxy in religion. The Providence Plantations were refused for similar reasons. Should Roger Williams return to plague an assembly where an approved church-membership was the sole qualification for office? The little island of Rhode Island, with its Jewish republic, also knocked for admission; Anne Hutchinson's commonwealth was informed that Plymouth colony had rightful jurisdiction there, and that heresy was a bar to all petitions.

Until the year 1641 the people of Massachusetts had had no regular code of laws. At a meeting of the assembly in December of this year, Nathaniel Ward brought forward a written instrument which, after mature deliberation, was adopted as the constitution of the State. This fundamental statute was called the BODY OF LIBERTIES, and was ever afterward esteemed as the great charter of colonial freedom. It may be doubted whether any other primitive constitution, either ancient or modern, contains more wisdom than this early code of Massachusetts.

A further modification in the government was effected in 1644. Until this time the representatives of the people had sat and voted in the same hall with the governor and his assistant magistrates. It was now decreed that the two bodies should sit apart, each with its own officers and under its own management. By this measure the people's branch of the legislature was made independent and of equal authority with the governor's council. Thus step by step were the safeguards of liberty established and regular forms of government secured.

The people of Massachusetts were little grieved on account of the English Revolution. It was for them a vindication and a victory. The triumph of Parliament over King Charles was the triumph of Puritanism both in England and America. Massachusetts had no cause to fear so long as the House of Commons was crowded with her friends and patrons. But in the hour of victory the American Puritans showed themselves more magnanimous than those of the mother-country; when Charles I., the enemy of all colonial liberties, was brought to the block, the people of New England, whose fathers had been exiled by *his* father, lamented his tragic fate and preserved the memory of his virtues.

During the supremacy of the Long Parliament several acts were passed which put in peril the interests of Massachusetts, but by a prudent and far-sighted policy all evil results were avoided. Powerful friends, especially Sir Henry Vane, stood up in Parliament and defended the colony against the intrigues of her enemies. Ambassadors, men of age and experience, went often to London to plead for colonial rights. Soon after the abolition of monarchy a statute was made which threatened for a while the complete subversion of the new State. Massachusetts was invited to surrender her charter, to receive a new instrument instead, and to hold courts and issue writs in the name of Parliament. The measure seemed fair enough, but the people of New England were too cautious to stake their all on the fate of a Parliament whose power was already waning. The requisition was never complied with. Cromwell did not insist on the surrender; no one else had power to enforce the act; and Massachusetts retained her charter.

The Protector was the constant friend of the American colonies. Even Virginia, though slighting his authority, found him just as well as severe. The people of New England were his special favorites. To them he was bound by every tie of political and religious sympathy. For more than ten years, when he might have been an oppressor, he continued the benefactor, of the English in America. During his administration the northern colonies were left in the full enjoyment of their coveted rights. In commerce, in the industry of private life, and especially in religion, the people of Massachusetts were as free as the people of England.

In the year 1652, it was decreed by the general court at Boston that the jurisdiction of the province extended as far north as three miles above the most northerly waters of the river Merrimac. This declaration, which was in strict accordance with the charter of the colony, was made for the purpose of annexing Maine to Massachusetts. By this measure the territory of the latter State was extended to Casco Bay. Settlements had been made on the Piscataqua as early as 1626, but had not flourished. Thirteen years later a royal charter was issued to Sir Ferdinand Gorges, a member of the Council of Plymouth, who became proprietor of the province. His cousin, Thomas Gorges, was made deputy-governor. A high-sounding constitution, big enough for an empire, was drawn up, and the little village of Gorgeana, afterward York, became the capital of the kingdom. Meanwhile, in 1630, the Plymouth Council had granted to another corporation sixteen hundred square miles of the territory around Casco Bay, and this claim had been purchased by Rigby, a republican member of Parliament. Between his deputies and those of Gorges violent disputes arose. The villagers of Maine, sympathizing with neither party, and emulous of the growth and prosperity of the southern colonies, laid their grievances before the court at Boston, and the annexation of the province followed.

In July of 1656, the QUAKERS began to arrive at Boston. The first who came were Ann Austin and Mary Fisher. The introduction of the plague would have occasioned less alarm. The two women were caught and searched for marks of witchcraft, their trunks were broken open, their books were burned by the hangman, and they themselves thrown into prison. After several weeks' confinement they were brought forth and banished from the colony. Before the end of the year eight others had been arrested and sent back to England. The delegates of the union were immediately convened, and a rigorous law was passed, excluding all Quakers from the country. Whipping, the loss of one ear and banishment were the penalties for the first offence; after a second conviction the other ear should be cut off; and should the criminal again return, his tongue should be bored through with a red-hot iron.

In 1657, Ann Burden, who had come from London to preach against persecution, was seized and beaten with twenty stripes. Others came, were whipped and exiled. As the law became more cruel and proscriptive, fresh victims rushed forward to brave its terrors. The assembly of the four colonies again convened, and advised the authorities of Massachusetts to pronounce the penalty of death against the fanatical disturbers of the public peace. When the resolutions embodying this advice was put before the assembly, to his everlasting honor, the younger Winthrop, delegate from Connecticut, voted No! Massachusetts accepted the views of the greater number, and the death-penalty was passed by a majority of one vote.

In September of 1659, four persons were arrested and brought to trial under this law. The prisoners were given the option of going into exile or of being hanged. Two of them (Mary Dyar and Nicholas Davis) chose banishment; but the other two (Marmaduke Stephenson and William Robinson) stood firm, denounced the wickedness of the court, and were sentenced to death. Mary Dyar, in whom the love of martyrdom had triumphed over fear, now returned, and was also condemned. On the 27th of October the three were led forth to execution. The men e hanged without mercy; and the woman, after the rope had been adjusted to her neck, was reprieved only to be banished. She was conveyed beyond the limits of the colony, but immediately returned and was executed. William Leddra was next seized, tried and sentenced. As in the case of the others, he was offered perpetual exile instead of death. He refused, and was hanged.

Before the trial of Leddra was concluded, Wenlock Christison, who had already been banished, rushed into the court-room and began to upbraid the judges for shedding the blood of the innocent. When put on his second trial, he spoke boldly in his own defence; but the jury brought in a verdict of guilty, and he was condemned to die. Others, eager for the honor of martyrdom, came forward in crowds, and the jails were filled with voluntary prisoners. But before the day arrived for Christison's execution, the public conscience was aroused; the law was repealed, the prison doors were opened, and Christison, with twenty-seven companions, came forth free. The bloody reign of proscription had ended, but not until four innocent enthusiasts had given their lives for liberty of conscience.

But let a veil be drawn over this sorrowful event. The history of all times is full of scenes of violence and wrong. It could not be expected that an American colony, founded by exiles, pursued with malice and beset with dangers, should be wholly exempt from the shame of evil deeds. The Puritans established a religious rather than a civil commonwealth; whatever put the faith of the people in peril seemed to them more to be dreaded than pestilence or death. To ward off heresy, even by destroying the heretic, seemed only a natural self-defence. A nobler lesson has been learned in the light of better times.

The English Revolution had now run its course. Cromwell was dead. The Commonwealth tottered and fell. Charles II. was restored to the throne of his ancestors. Tidings of the Restoration reached Boston on the 27th of July, 1660. In the same vessel that bore the news came Edward Whalley and William Goffe, two of the judges who had passed sentence of death on Charles I. It was now their turn to save their lives by flight. Governor Endicott received them with courtesy; the agents from the British government came in hot pursuit with orders to arrest them. For a while the fugitives, aided by the people of Boston, baffled the officers, and then escaped to New Haven. Here for many weeks they lay in concealment; not even the Indians would accept the reward which was offered for their apprehension. At last the exiles reached the valley of the Connecticut and found refuge at the village of Hadley where they passed the remainder of their lives. It was in October of this same fatal year that Hugh Peters, the old friend of the colony, the father-in-law of the younger Winthrop, was hanged at London. The noble Sir Henry Vane was hunted down in Holland, surrendered to the English government, condemned and beheaded.

Owing to the partiality of Cromwell, the restrictions on colonial commerce which bore so heavily on Virginia were scarcely felt by Massachusetts. On the restoration of monarchy a severer policy was at once adopted. All vessels not bearing the English flag were forbidden to enter the harbors of New England. A law of exportation was enacted by which all articles produced in the colonies and demanded in England should be shipped to England only. Such articles of American production as the English merchants did not desire might be sold in any of the ports of Europe. The law of importation was equally odious; such articles as were produced in England should not be manufactured in America, and should be bought from England only. Free trade between the colonies was forbidden; and a duty of five per cent, levied for the benefit of the English king, was put on both exports and imports. Human ingenuity could hardly have invented a set of measures better calculated to produce an AMERICAN REVOLUTION.

In 1664, war broke out between England and Holland. It became a part of the English military plans to reduce the Dutch settlements on the Hudson; and for this purpose a fleet was sent to America. But there was another purpose also. Charles II. was anxious to obtain control of the New England colonies, that he might govern them according to the principles of arbitrary power. The chief obstacle to this undertaking was the charter of Massachusetts—an instrument given under the great seal of England, and not easily revoked. To accomplish the same end by other means was now the object of the king; and with this end in view four commissioners were appointed with instructions to go to America, to sit in judgment upon all matters of complaint that might arise in New England, to settle colonial disputes, and to take such other measures as might seem most likely to establish peace and good order in the country. The royal commissioners embarked in the British fleet, and in July arrived at Boston.

They were not wanted at Boston. The people of Massachusetts knew very well that the establishment of this supreme judgeship in their midst was a flagrant violation of their chartered right of self-government. Before the commissioners landed the patent was put into the hands of a committee for safe keeping. A decree of the general court forbade the citizens to answer any summons issued by the royal judges. A powerful letter, full of loyalty and manly protests, was sent directly to the king. The commissioners became disgusted with the treatment which they received at the hands of the refractory colony, and repaired to Maine and New Hampshire. Here they were met with some marks of favor; but their official acts were disregarded and soon forgotten. In Rhode Island the judges were received with great respect, and their decisions accepted as the decisions of the king. The towns of Connecticut were next visited but the people were cold and indifferent, and the commissioners retired. Meanwhile, the English monarch, learning how his grand judges had been treated, sent a message of recall, and before the end of the year they gladly left the country. After a gallant fight, Massachusetts had preserved her liberties. Left in the peaceable enjoyment of her civil rights, she entered upon a new career of prosperity which, for a period of ten years, was marked with no calamity.

CHAPTER XV.

Massachusetts—King Philip's War.

MASSASOIT, the old sachem of the Wampanoags, died in 1662. For forty-one years he had faithfully kept the treaty made by himself with the first settlers at Plymouth. His elder son, Alexander, now became chief of the nation, but died within the year; and the chieftainship descended to the younger brother, PHILIP OF MOUNT HOPE. It was the fate of this brave and able man to lead his people in a final and hopeless struggle against the supremacy of the whites. Causes of war had existed for many years, and the time had come for the conflict.

The unwary natives of New England had sold their lands. The English were the purchasers; the chiefs had signed the deeds; the price had been fairly paid. Year by year the territory of the tribes had narrowed; the old men died, but the deeds remained and the lands could not be recovered. There were at this time in the country east of the Hudson not more than twenty-five thousand Indians; the English had increased to fully twice that number. A new generation had arisen who could not understand the validity of the old titles. The young warriors sighed for the freedom of their fathers' hunting-grounds. They looked with ever-increasing jealousy on the growth of English villages and the spread of English farms. The ring of the foreigner's axe had scared the game out of the forest, and the foreigner's net had scooped the fishes from the red man's river. Of all their ancient domain, the Wampanoags had nothing left but the two narrow peninsulas of Bristol and Tiverton, on the eastern coast of Narragansett Bay.

There were personal grievances also. While Alexander lived he had been arrested, tried by an English jury and imprisoned. He had caught his death-fever in a Boston jail. Another chieftain was apprehended in a similar way; and then the Indian witness who appeared at the trial was murdered for giving testimony. The perpetrators of this crime were seized by the English, convicted and hanged. Perhaps King Philip, if left to himself, would have still sought peace. He was not a rash man, and clearly foresaw the inevitable issue of the struggle. He hesitated, and was affected with great grief when the news came that an Englishman had been killed. But the young men of the tribe were thirsting for bloody revenge, and could no longer be restrained. The women and children were hastily sent across the bay and put under the protection of Canonchet, king of the Narragansetts. On the 24th of June, 1675, the village of Swanzey was attacked; eight Englishmen were killed; and the alarm of war sounded through the colonies.

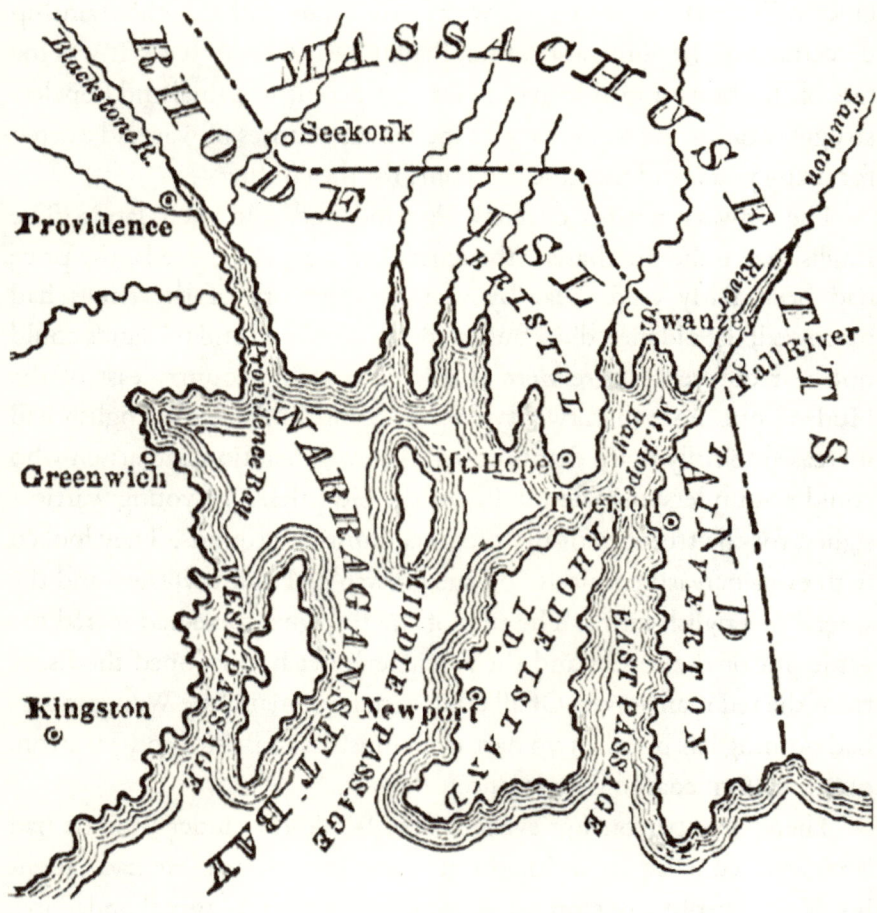

First Scene of King Phillip's War.

Within a week the militia of Plymouth, joined by volunteer companies from Boston, entered the enemy's country. A few Indians were overtaken and killed. The troops marched into the peninsula of

Bristol, reached Mount Hope, and compelled Philip to fly for his life. With a band of fugitives numbering five or six hundred, he escaped to Tiverton, on the eastern side of the bay. Here, a few days afterward, they were attacked; but lying concealed in a swamp, they beat back their assailants with considerable loss. The place was then surrounded and besieged for two weeks; but Philip and his men, when brought to the point of starvation, managed to escape in the night, crossed the bay and fled to the country of the Nipmucks, in Central Massachusetts. Here the king and his warriors became the heralds of a general war. The slumbering hatred of the savages was easily kindled into open hostility. For a whole year the scattered settlements of the frontier became a scene of burning, massacre and desolation.

After Philip's flight from Tiverton, the English forces marched into the country of the Narragansetts. Here the women and children of the Wampanoags had been received and sheltered. The wavering Canonchet was given his choice of peace or war. He cowered before the English muskets and signed a treaty, agreeing that his nation should observe neutrality and deliver up all fugitives from the hostile tribe. Still, it only a question of time when the Narragansetts would break their covenant and espouse the cause of Philip.

The war was now transferred to the Connecticut valley. It had been hoped that the Nipmucks would remain loyal to the English; but the influence of the exiled chieftain prevailed with them to take up arms. As usual with savages, treachery was added to hostility. Captains Wheeler and Hutchinson, with a company of twenty men, were sent to Brookfield to hold a conference with ambassadors from the Nipmuck nation. Instead of preparing for the council, the Indians laid an ambush near the village, and when the English were well surrounded, fired upon them, killing nearly the whole company. A few survivors, escaping to the settlement, gave the alarm, and the people fled to their block-house just in time to save their lives.

For two days the place was assailed with every missile that savage ingenuity could invent. Finally, the house was fired with burning arrows, and the destruction of all seemed certain; but just as the roof began to blaze, the friendly clouds poured down a shower of rain, and the flames were extinguished. Then came reinforcements from Springfield, and the Indians fled. The people of Brookfield now abandoned their homes and sought refuge in the towns along the river. On the 26th of August, a battle was fought in the outskirts of Deerfield. The whites were successful; but a few days afterward the savages succeeded in firing the village, and the greater part of it was burned to the ground. A storehouse containing the recently-gathered harvests was saved, and Captain Lathrop, with a company of eighty picked men, undertook the dangerous task of removing the stores to Hadley. A train of wagons, loaded with wheat and corn and guarded by the soldiers, left Deerfield on the 18th of September, and had proceeded five miles, when they were suddenly surrounded by eight hundred Indians who lay in ambush at the ford of a small creek. The whites fought desperately, and were killed almost to a man. Meanwhile, Captain Mosely, at the head of seventy militia, arrived, and the battle continued, the English retreating until they were reinforced by a band of a hundred and sixty English and Mohegans. The savages were then beaten back with heavy losses. The little stream where this fatal engagement occurred, was henceforth called Bloody Brook.

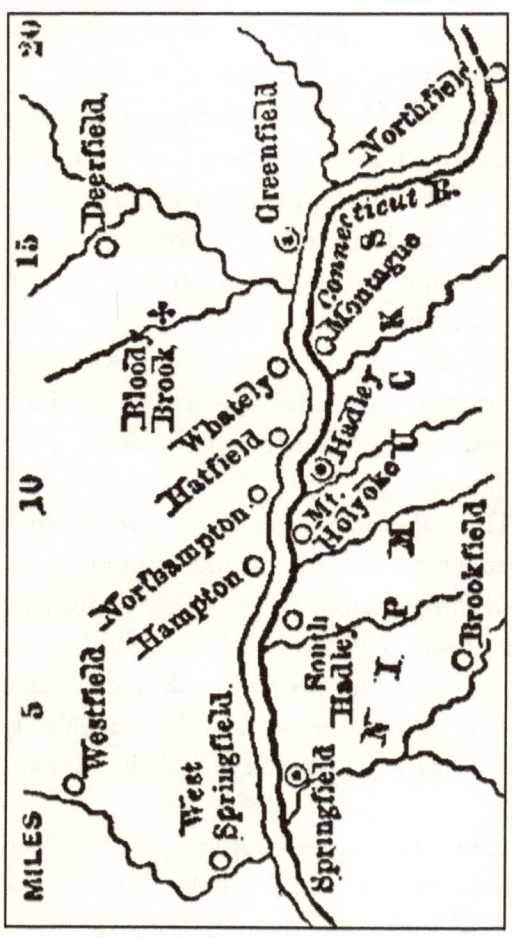

Second Scene of King Phillip's War.

On the same day of the burning of Deerfield, Hadley was attacked while the people were at church. Everything was in confusion, and the barbarians had already begun their work of butchery, when the gray haired General Goffe, who was concealed in the village, rushed forth from his covert, and by rallying and directing the flying people saved them from destruction. After the Indians had been driven into the woods, the aged veteran went back to his hiding-place, and was seen no more. Late in the autumn, a battle was fought at Springfield; the town was assaulted and most of the dwellings burned. Another attack was made on Hadley, and a large part of the village was left in ashes. Hatfield was the next object of savage vengeance; but here the English were found prepared, and the Indians were repulsed with heavy losses. The farms and the weaker settlements were now abandoned, and the people sought shelter in the stronger towns near the river.

Philip, finding that he could do no further harm on the northern frontier, gathered his warriors together and repaired to the Narragansetts. By receiving them, Canonchet openly violated his treaty with the English, but to refuse them was contrary to the savage virtues of his race. To share the dubious fate of Philip was preferred to the longer continuance of a hateful alliance with foreigners. The authorities of Massachusetts immediately declared war against the Narragansett nation, and Rhode Island was invaded by a thousand men under command of Colonel Josiah Winslow. It was the determination to crush the Wampanoags and the Narragansetts at one blow; the manner of defence adopted by the savages favored such an undertaking. In the middle of an immense cedar swamp, a short distance south-west of Kingston, in the county of Washington, the Indians collected to the number of three thousand. Into this place was gathered the whole wealth of the Narragansett nation. A village of wigwams extended over several acres of land that rose out of the surrounding morasses. A fort was built on the island, and fortified with a palisade and a breastwork of felled timber. Here the savages believed themselves secure from assault. The English regiment arrived at the swamp at daybreak on the 19th of December, and struggling through the bogs, reached the fort at noonday. The attack was made immediately. The only entrance to the camp was by means of a fallen tree that lay from an opening in the palisade to the opposite bank of a pond. Over this hazardous passage a brave few sprang forward, but were instantly swept off by the fire of the Indians. Another company, made cautious by the fate of their comrades, crept around the defences, until, finding a point unguarded, they charged straight into the enclosure. The work of death and destruction now began in earnest. The wigwams were set on fire, and the kindling flames swept around the village. The yells of the combatants mingled with the roar of the conflagration. But the superior discipline and valor of the whites soon decided the battle. The Indians, attempting to escape from the burning fort, ran everywhere upon the loaded muskets of the English. A thousand warriors were killed and hundreds more were captured. Nearly all the wounded perished in the flames. There, too, the old men, the women and babes of the nation met the horrors of death by fire. The pride of the Narragansetts had perished in a day. But the victory was dearly purchased; eighty English soldiers, including six captains of the regiment, were killed, and a hundred and fifty others were wounded.

Third Scene of King Phillip's War.

A few of the savages, breaking through the English lines, escaped. Led by Philip, they again repaired to the Nipmucks, and with the opening of spring the war was renewed with more violence than ever. As their fortunes declined the Indians grew desperate; they had nothing more to lose. Around three hundred miles of frontier, extending from Maine to the mouth of the Connecticut, there was massacre and devastation. Lancaster, Medfield, Groton and Marlborough were laid in ashes. Weymouth, within twenty miles of Boston, met the same fate. Everywhere were seen the traces of rapine and murder.

But the end was near at hand. The resources of the savages were wasted, and their numbers grew daily less. In April, Canonchet was overtaken and captured on the banks of the Blackstone. He was offered his life if he would procure a treaty of peace; but the haughty chieftain rejected the proposal with disdain, and was put to death. Philip was still at large, but his company had dwindled to a handful. In the early summer, his wife and son were made prisoners the latter was sold as a slave, and ended his life under the lash of a taskmaster in the Bermudas. The savage monarch was heartbroken now, and cared no longer for his life. Repairing secretly to his old home at Mount Hope, his place of concealment was revealed to the whites. A company of soldiers was sent to surround him. A treacherous Indian guided the party to the spot, and then himself, stealing nearer, took a deadly aim at the breast of his chieftain. The report of a musket rang through the forest, and the painted king of the Wampanoags sprang forward and fell dead.

New England suffered terribly in this war. The expenses and losses of the war amounted to fully five hundred thousand dollars. Thirteen towns and six hundred dwellings lay smouldering in ashes. Almost every family had heard the war-whoop of the savages. Six hundred men, the flower and pride of the country, had fallen in the field. Hundreds of families had been butchered in cold blood. Gray-haired sire, mother and babe had sunk together under the vengeful blow of the red man's gory tomahawk. Now there was peace again. The Indian race was swept out of New England. The tribes beyond the Connecticut came humbly submissive, and pleaded for their lives. The colonists returned to their desolated farms and villages to build new homes in the ashes of old ruins.

Death of King Phillip.

The echo of King Philip's war had hardly died away before the country was involved in troubles of a different sort. It had been expected that the English government would do something to repair the heavy losses which the colonists had sustained; but not so. Instead of help came Edward Randolph, a royal emissary, with authority to collect duties and abridge colonial liberties. Governor Leverett received him coldly, and told him in plain words that not even the king could right fully restrict the freedom of his American subjects; that the people of the colonies had finished the Indian war without a cent of expense to the English treasury, and that they were now fairly entitled to the enjoyment of their chartered rights. After a six weeks' sojourn at Boston, Randolph sailed back to London, bearing to the ministry an exaggerated account of colonial arrogance. The king was already scheming to revoke all the New England charters; Randolph's reception furnished a further pretext for such a course of action.

The next trouble was concerning the jurisdiction of Maine. Sir Ferdinand Gorges, the old proprietor of that province, was now dead; but his heirs had never relinquished their claims to the territory. The people of Maine had meanwhile put themselves under the authority of Massachusetts; but the representatives of Gorges carried the matter before the privy council, and in 1677 a decision was rendered in their favor. Thereupon the Boston government made a proposition to the Gorges family to purchase their claims; the proposition was accepted, and on the 6th of May the heirs signed a deed by which, in consideration of twelve hundred and fifty pounds sterling, the soil and jurisdiction of the province were transferred to Massachusetts.

A similar difficulty arose in regard to New Hampshire. As far back as 1622 the Plymouth council had granted this territory to two of their own number—Gorges, just mentioned, and Captain John Mason. Seven years after the grant was made, Gorges surrendered his claim to Mason, who thus became sole proprietor. But this territory was also covered by the charter of Massachusetts. Mason died; and now, in 1679, his son Robert came forward and claimed the province. This cause was also taken before the ministers, who decided that the title of the younger Mason was valid. To the great disappointment of the people of both provinces, the two governments were arbitrarily separated. The king's policy was now made manifest. A royal government, the first in New England, was immediately established over New Hampshire; Mason nominated Edward Cranfield as governor, the king confirmed the appointment, and received in return one-fifth of all the rents.

But the people took care that the rents should not amount to much. They refused to recognize Cranfield's commission, and thwarted his plans in every way possible. Being in despair, he wrote to the English government that he would esteem it the greatest happiness to return home and leave the unreasonable people of New Hampshire to themselves. The king attributed all this trouble to the influence of Massachusetts. He could not forget how that commonwealth had treated his custom-house officer Randolph. The hostility of the English government to the existing order of things in New England became more bitter than ever. TO carry out his plan of subverting the colonial governments, the king directed his judges to make an inquiry as to whether Massachusetts had not forfeited her charter. The proceedings were protracted until the summer of 1684, when the royal court gave a decision in accordance with the monarch's wishes. The patent was forfeited, said the judges; and the English crown might justly assume entire control of the colony. The plan of the king was thus on the point of realization, but the shadow of death was already at his door. On the 6th of February, 1685, his evil reign of twenty-five years ended with his life.

The new sovereign, James II, immediately adopted his brother's colonial policy. In the next year after his accession, the scheme so long entertained was successfully carried out. The charter of Massachusetts was formally revoked; all the colonies between Nova Scotia and Narragansett Bay were consolidated, and Joseph Dudley appointed president. New England was not prepared for open resistance; the colonial assembly was dissolved by its own act, and the members returned sullenly to their homes. In the winter following, Dudley was superseded by Sir Edmund Andros, who had been appointed royal governor of all New England. His commission ought to have been entitled AN ARTICLE FOR THE DESTRUCTION OF COLONIAL LIBERTY.

If James II. had searched his kingdom, he could hardly have found a tool better fitted to do his will. The scarlet-coated despot landed at Boston on the 20th of December, and at once began the work of demolishing the cherished institutions of the people. Randolph was made chief secretary and censor of the press nothing might be printed without his sanction. Popular representation was abolished. Voting by ballot was prohibited. Town meetings were forbidden. The Church of England was openly encouraged. The public schools were allowed to go to ruin. Men were arrested without warrant of law; and when as prisoners they arose in court to plead the privileges of the great English charter which had stood unquestioned for four hundred and fifty years, they were told that the Great Charter was not made for the perverse people of America. Dudley, who had been continued in office as chief-justice, was in the habit of saying to his packed juries, at the close of each trial: "Now, worthy gentlemen, we expect a good verdict from you to-day;" and the verdicts were rendered accordingly.

Thus did Massachusetts lose her liberty; and Plymouth fared no better. If the stronger colony fell prostrate, what could the weaker do? The despotism of Andros was quickly extended from Cape Cod Bay to the Piscataqua. New Hampshire was next invaded and her civil rights completely overthrown. Rhode Island suffered the same calamity. In May of 1686 her charter was taken away with a writ, and her constitutional rights subverted. Some of the colonists brought forward Indian deeds for their lands; the royal judges replied, with a sneer, that the signature of Massasoit was not worth as much as the scratch of a bear's paw. The seal of Rhode Island was broken, and an irresponsible council appointed to conduct the government. Attended by an armed guard, Andros proceeded to Connecticut. Arriving at Hartford in October of 1687, he found the assembly of the province in session, and demanded the surrender of the colonial charter. The instrument was brought in and laid upon the table. A spirited debate ensued, and continued until evening. When it was about to be decided that the charter should be given up, the lamps were suddenly dashed out. Other lights were brought in; but the charter had disappeared. Joseph Wadsworth, snatching up the precious parchment, bore it off through the darkness and concealed it in a hollow tree, ever afterward remembered with affection as THE CHARTER OAK. But the assembly was overawed and the free government of Connecticut subverted. Thus was the authority of Andros established throughout the country. The people gave vent to their feelings by calling him THE TYRANT OF NEW ENGLAND.

But his dominion ended suddenly. The English Revolution of 1688 was at hand. James II. was driven from his throne and kingdom. The entire system of arbitrary rule which that monarch had established fell with a crash, and Andros with the rest. The news of the revolution and of the accession of William and Mary reached Boston on the 4th of April, 1689. A few days afterward, the governor had occasion to write a note to his colonel of militia, telling him to keep the soldiers under arms, as there was "a general buzzing among the people." On the 18th of the month, the citizens of Charlestown and Boston rose in open rebellion. Andros and his minions, attempting to escape, were seized and marched to prison. The insurrection spread through the country; and before the 10th of May every colony in New England had restored its former liberties.

CHAPTER XVI.

Massachusetts.—War and Witchraft.

In 1689, war was declared between France and England. This conflict, known in American history as King William's War, grew out of the English Revolution of the preceding year. When James II. escaped from his kingdom, he found refuge at the court of Louis XIV of France. The two monarchs were both Catholics, and both held the same despotic theory of government. On this account, and from other considerations, an alliance was made between them, by the terms of which Louis agreed to support James in his effort to recover the English throne. Parliament, meanwhile, had settled the crown on William of Orange. By these means the new sovereign was brought into conflict not only with the exiled James, but also with his confederate, the king of France. The war which thus originated in Europe soon extended to the American colonies of the two nations; New England and New France entered the conflict under the flags of their respective countries.

The struggle began on the north-eastern frontier of New Hampshire. On the 27th of June, a party of Indians in alliance with the French made an attack on Dover. The venerable magistrate of the town, Richard Waldron, now eighty years of age, was inhumanly murdered. Twenty-three others were killed, and twenty-nine dragged of captive into the wilderness.

In August a war-party of a hundred Abenakis embarked in a fleet of canoes, floated out of the mouth of the Penobscot, and steered down the coast to Pemaquid, now Bremen. The inhabitants were taken by surprise; a company of farmers were surrounded in the harvest-field and murdered. The fort was besieged for two days and compelled to surrender. A few of the people escaped into the woods, but the greater number were killed or carried away captive. A month later an alliance was effected between the English and the powerful Mohawks west of the Hudson but the Indians refused to make war upon their countrymen of

Maine. The Dutch settlements of New Netherland, having now passed under the dominion of England, made common cause against the French.

In January of 1690 a regiment of French and Indians left Montreal and directed their march to the south. Crossing the Mohawk River, they arrived on the 8th of February at the village of Schenectady. Lying concealed in the forest until midnight, they stole through the unguarded gates, raised the war-whoop and began the work of death. The town was soon in flames. Sixty people were killed and scalped; the rest, escaping half clad into the darkness, ran sixteen miles through the snow to Albany. The settlement of Salmon Falls, on the Piscataqua, was next attacked and destroyed by a war-party led by the Frenchman Hertel. Joining another company from Quebec, under command of Portneuf, the savages proceeded against the colony at Casco Bay. The English fort at that place was taken and the settlements broken up. Thus far the fortunes of the war had been wholly on the side of the French and their allies.

But New England was now thoroughly aroused. In order to provide the ways and means of war, a colonial congress was convened at New York. Here it was resolved to attempt the conquest of Canada by marching an army by way of Lake Champlain against Montreal. At the same time, Massachusetts was to co-operate with the land forces by sending a fleet by way of the St. Lawrence for the reduction of Quebec. Thirty four vessels, carrying two thousand troops, were accordingly fitted out, and the command given to Sir William Phipps. Proceeding first against Port Royal, he compelled a surrender; the whole of Nova Scotia submitted without a struggle. If the commander had sailed at once against Quebec, that place too would have been forced to capitulate; but vexatious delays retarded the expedition until the middle of October. Meanwhile, an Abenaki Indian had carried the news of the coming armament to Frontenac, governor of Canada; and when the fleet came in sight of the town, the castle of St. Louis was so well garrisoned and provisioned as to bid defiance to the English forces. The opportunity was lost, and it only remained for Phipps to sail back to Boston. To meet the expenses of this unfortunate expedition,

Massachusetts was obliged to issue bills of credit which were made a legal tender in the payment of debt. Such was the origin of PAPER MONEY in America.

Meanwhile, the land forces had proceeded from Albany as far as Lake Champlain. Here dissensions arose among the commanders. Colonel Leisler of New York charged Winthrop of Connecticut with treachery; and the charge was returned that Leisler's commissary had furnished no supplies for the Connecticut soldiers. The quarrel became so violent that the expedition had to be abandoned, and the troops marched gloomily homeward. The great campaign had resulted in complete humiliation.

Sir William Phipps had as little success in civil matters as in the command of a fleet. Shortly after his return from Quebec he was sent as ambassador to England. The objects of his mission were, in the first place, to procure aid from the English government in the further prosecution of the war; and secondly, to secure, if possible, a reissue of the old colonial charter. To the first of these requests the ministers replied that the armies and navies of England could not be spared to take part in a petty Indian war; and the second was met with coldness and refusal. King William was secretly opposed to the liberal provisions of the former charter, and looked with disfavor on the project of renewing it. It is even doubtful whether Phipps himself desired the restoration of the old patent; for when he returned to Boston in the spring of 1692, he bore a new instrument from the king, and a commission as royal governor of the province. By the terms of this new constitution, Plymouth, Maine and Nova Scotia were consolidated with Massachusetts; while New Hampshire, against the protests and petitions of her people, was forcibly separated from the mother colony.

The war still continued, but without decisive results. In 1694, the village of Oyster River, now Durham, was destroyed by a band of savages led by the French captain Villieu. The inhabitants, to the number of ninety-four, were either killed or carried into captivity. Two years later the English fortress at Pemaquid was a second time surrendered to the French and Indians, under command of Baron Castin. The captives were sent to Boston and exchanged for prisoners in the hands of the English. In the following March, the town of Haverhill, on the

Merrimac, was captured under circumstances of special atrocity. Nearly forty persons were butchered in cold blood; only a few were spared for captivity. Among the latter was Mrs. Hannah Dustin. Her child, only a week old, was snatched out of her arms and dashed against a tree. The heartbroken mother, with her nurse and a lad named Leonardson, from Worcester, was taken by the savages to an island in the Merrimac, a short distance above Concord. Here, while their captors, twelve in number, were asleep at night, the three prisoners arose, silently armed themselves with tomahawks, and with one deadly blow after another crushed in the temples of the sleeping savages, until ten of them lay still in death; then, embarking in a canoe, the captives dropped down the river and reached the English settlement in safety. Mrs. Dustin carried home with her the gun and tomahawk of the savage who had destroyed her family, and a bag containing the scalps of her neighbors. It is not often that the mother of a murdered babe has found such ample vengeance.

But the war was already at an end. Early in 1697, commissioners of France and England assembled at the town of Ryswick, in Holland; and on the 10th of the following September, a treaty of peace was concluded. King William was acknowledged as the rightful sovereign of England, and the colonial boundary-lines of the two nations in America were established as before.

Massachusetts had in the mean time been visited with a worse calamity than war. The darkest page in the history of New England is that which bears the record of the SALEM WITCHCRAFT. The same town which fifty-seven years previously had cast out Roger Williams was now to become the scene of the most fatal delusion of modern times. In February of 1692, in that part of Salem afterward called Danvers, a daughter and a niece of Samuel Parris, the minister, were attacked with a nervous disorder which rendered them partially insane. Parris believed, or affected to believe, that the two girls were bewitched, and that Tituba, an Indian maid-servant of the household, was the author of the affliction. He had seen her performing some of the rude ceremonies of her own religion, and this gave color to his suspicions. He tied Tituba, and whipped the ignorant creature until, at his own dictation, she confessed herself a witch. Here, no doubt, the matter would have ended had not other causes existed for the continuance and spread of the miserable delusion.

But Parris had had a quarrel in his church. A part of the congregation desired that George Burroughs, a former minister, should be reinstated, to the exclusion of Parris. Burroughs still lived at Salem; and there was great animosity between the partisans of the former and the present pastor. Burroughs disbelieved in witchcraft, and openly expressed his contempt of the system. Here, then, Parris found an opportunity to turn the confessions of the foolish Indian servant against his enemies, to overwhelm his rival with the superstitions of the community, and perhaps to have him put to death. There is no doubt whatever that the whole murderous scheme originated in the personal malice of Parris.

But there were others ready to aid him. First among these was the celebrated Cotton Mather, minister of Boston. He, being in high repute for wisdom, had recently preached much on the subject of witchcraft, teaching the people that witches were dangerous and ought to be put to death. He thus became the natural confederate of Parris, and the chief author of the terrible scenes that ensued. Sir William Phipps, the royal governor, who had just arrived from England, was a member of Mather's church. Increase Mather, the father of Cotton, had nominated Phipps to his present office. Stoughton, the deputy-governor, who was appointed judge and presided at the trials of the witches, was the tool of Parris and the two Mathers. To these men, more especially to Parris and Mather, must be charged the full infamy of what followed.

By the laws of England witchcraft was punishable with death. The code of Massachusetts was the same as that of the mother-country. In the early history of the colony, one person charged with being a wizard had been arrested at Charlestown, convicted and executed. But with the progress and enlightenment of the people, many had grown bold enough to denounce and despise the baleful superstition. Something, therefore, had to be done to save the tottering fabric of witchcraft from falling into contempt. A special court was accordingly appointed by Governor Phipps to go to Salem and to sit in judgment on the persons accused by Parris. Stoughton was the presiding judge, Parris himself the prosecutor, and Cotton Mather a kind of bishop to decide when the testimony was sufficient to condemn.

On the 21st of March, the horrible proceedings began. Mary Cory was arrested, not indeed for being a witch, but for denying the reality of witchcraft. When brought before the church and court, she denied all guilt, but was convicted and hurried to prison. Sarah Cloyce and Rebecca Nurse, two sisters of the most exemplary lives, were next apprehended as witches. The only witnesses against them were Tituba, her half-witted Indian husband and the simple girl Abigail Williams, the niece of Parris. The victims were sent to prison, protesting their innocence. Giles Cory, a patriarch of eighty years, was next seized; he also was one of those who had opposed Parris. The Indian accuser fell down before Edward Bishop, pretending to be in a fit under satanic influence; the sturdy farmer cured him instantly with a sound flogging, and said that he could restore the rest of the afflicted in the same manner. He and his wife were immediately arrested and condemned. George Burroughs, the rival of Parris, was accused and hurried to prison. And so the work went on, until seventy-five innocent people were locked up in dungeons. Not a solitary partisan of Parris or Mather had been arrested.

In the hope of saving their lives, some of the terrified prisoners now began to confess themselves witches, or bewitched. It was soon found that a confession was almost certain to procure liberation. It became evident that the accused were to be put to death, not for being witches or wizards, but for denying the reality of witchcraft. The special court was already in session; convictions followed fast; the gallows stood waiting for its victims. The truth of Mather's preaching was to be established by hanging whoever denied it; and Parris was to save his pastorate by murdering his rival. When the noble Burroughs mounted the scaffold, he stood composedly and repeated correctly the test-prayer which it was said no wizard could utter. The people broke into sobs and moans, and would have rescued their friend from death; but the tyrant Mather dashed among them on horseback, muttering imprecations, and drove the hangman to his horrid work. Old Giles Cory, seeing that conviction was certain, refused to plead, *and was pressed to death*. Five women were hanged in one day. Between the 10th of June and the 22d of September, twenty victims were hurried to their doom. Fifty-five others had been tortured into the confession of abominable falsehoods. A hundred and fifty lay in prison awaiting their fate. Two hundred were accused or suspected, and ruin seemed to impend over New England. But a reaction at last set in among the people. Notwithstanding the vociferous clamor and denunciations of Mather, the witch tribunals were overthrown. The representative assembly convened early in October, and the hated court which Phipps had appointed to sit at Salem was at once dismissed. The spell was dissolved. The thralldom of the popular mind was broken. Reason shook off the terror that had oppressed it. The prison doors were opened, and the victims of malice and superstition went forth free. In the beginning of the next year a few persons charged with witchcraft were again arraigned and brought before the courts. Some were even convicted, but the conviction went for nothing; not another life was sacrificed to passion and fanaticism.

Most of those who had participated in the terrible deeds of the preceding summer confessed the great wrong which they had done; but confessions could not restore the dead. The bigoted Mather, in a vain attempt to justify himself before the world, wrote a treatise in which he expressed his great thankfulness that so many witches had met their just loom. It is not the least humiliating circumstance of this sad business that Mather's hypocritical and impudent book received the approbation of the president of Harvard College. In all this there is to the American student one consoling reflection—the pages of his country's history will never again be blotted with so dark a stain.

CHAPTER XVII.

MASSACHUSETTS.—WARS OF ANNE AND GEORGE.

THE peace which followed the treaty of Ryswick was of short duration. Within less than four years France and England were again involved in a conflict which, beginning in Europe, soon extended to the American colonies. In the year 1700, Charles II., king of Spain, died, having named as his successor Philip of Anjou, a grandson of Louis XIV. This measure pointed clearly to a union of the crowns of France and Spain. The jealousy of all Europe was aroused; a league was formed between England, Holland and Austria; the archduke Charles of the latter country was put forward by the allied powers as a candidate for the Spanish throne; and war was declared against Louis XIV. for supporting the claims of Philip.

England had against France another cause of offence. In September of 1701, James II., the exiled king of Great Britain, died at the court of Louis, who now, in violation of the treaty of Ryswick, recognized the son of James as the rightful sovereign of England. This action was regarded as an open insult to English nationality. King William led his armies to the field not less to thwart the ambition of France than to save his own crown and kingdom. But the English monarch did not live to carry out his plans. While yet the war was hardly begun, the king fell from his horse, was attacked with fever, and died in May of 1702. Parliament had already settled the crown on Anne, the sister-in-law of William and daughter of James II. The new sovereign adopted the policy of her predecessor. From the circumstance of her reign, the conflict with France, which lasted for nearly thirteen years, is known in history as QUEEN ANNE'S WAR; but a better name is The War of the Spanish Succession.

In America the field of operations was limited to New England and South Carolina. The central colonies were scarcely aware that war existed. The military operations of both parties were conducted in a feeble and desultory manner. The more influential Indian tribes held aloof from the struggle. In August, 1701 the powerful Five Nations, whose dominions south of Lake Ontario and the river St. Lawrence formed a barrier between Canada and New York, made a treaty of neutrality with both the French and the English. The Abenakis of Maine did the same; but the French Jesuits prevailed with the latter to break their compact. The first notice of treachery which the English had, was a fearful massacre. In one day the whole country between the town of Wells and the Bay of Casco was given up to burning and butchery.

In midwinter of 1703-4 the town of Deerfield was destroyed. A war-party of three hundred French and Indians, setting out from Canada, marched on the snow-crust into the Connecticut valley. On the last night of February, the savages lay in the pine forest that surrounded the ill-fated village. Just before, daybreak they rushed from their covert and fired the houses. Forty-seven of the inhabitants were tomahawked. A hundred and twelve were dragged into captivity. The prisoners, many of them women and children, were obliged to march to Canada. The snow lay four feet deep. The poor wretches, haggard with fear and starvation, sank down and died. The deadly hatchet hung ever above the heads of the feeble and the sick. Eunice Williams, the minister's wife, fainted by the wayside; in the presence of her husband and five captive children, her brains were dashed out with a tomahawk. Those who survived to the end of the journey were afterward ransomed and permitted to return to their desolated homes. A daughter of Mr. Williams remained with the savages, grew up among the Mohawks, married a chieftain, and in after years returned in Indian garb to Deerfield. No entreaties could induce her to remain with her friends. The solitude of the woods and the society of her tawny husband had prevailed over the charms of civilization.

In Maine and New Hampshire the war was marked with similar barbarities. Farms were devastated; towns were burned; the inhabitants were murdered or carried to Canada. Prowling bands of savages, led on by French officers, penetrated at times into the heart of Massachusetts. Against the treacherous barbarians and their bloodthirsty leaders there was no security either at home or abroad. Along the desolated frontier ruin prevailed, as in the days of King Philip.

In 1707, the reduction of Port Royal was undertaken by Massachusetts. A fleet, bearing a thousand soldiers, was equipped and sent against the town. But Baron Castin, who commanded the French garrison, conducted the defence with so much skill that the English were obliged to abandon the undertaking. From this costly and disastrous expedition Massachusetts gained nothing but discouragement and debt. Nevertheless, after two years of preparation, the enterprise was renewed; and in 1710 an English and American fleet of thirty-six vessels, having on board four regiments of troops, anchored before Port Royal. The garrison was weak; Subercase, the French commander, had neither talents nor courage; famine came; and after a feeble defence of eleven days, the place surrendered at discretion. By this conquest all of Nova Scotia passed under the dominion of the English. The flag of Great Britain was hoisted over the conquered fortress, and the name of Port Royal gave place to ANNAPOLIS, in honor of Queen Anne.

Vast preparations were now made for the invasion of Canada. A land force under command of General Nicholson was to march against Montreal, while Quebec, the key to the French dominions in America, was to be reduced by an English fleet. For this purpose fifteen men-of-war and forty transports were placed under command of Sir Hovenden Walker. Seven regiments of veterans, selected from the armies of Europe, were added to the colonial forces and sent with the expedition. Before such an armament the defences of Quebec could hardly hold out an hour. But for the utter incompetency of the admiral, success would have been assured.

For six weeks in midsummer the great fleet lay idly in Boston Harbor. Sir Hovenden was getting ready to sail. The Abenaki Indians carried the news leisurely to Quebec; and every day added to the strength of the ramparts. At last, on the 30th of July, when no further excuse could he invented, the ships set sail for the St. Lawrence. At the Bay of Gaspé the admiral thought it necessary to loiter a while; then he busied himself with devising a plan to save his ships from the ice during the next winter: Proceeding slowly up the St. Lawrence, the fleet, on the 22d of August, was enveloped in a thick fog. The wind blew hard from the east. The commander was cautioned to remain on deck, but went quietly to bed. A messenger aroused him just in time to see eight of his best vessels dashed to pieces on the rocks. Eight hundred and eighty-four men went down in the foaming whirlpools. A council of war was held, and all voted that it was impossible to proceed. In a letter to the English government, Walker expressed great gratitude that by the loss of a thousand men the rest had been saved *from freezing to death at Quebec*. The fleet sailed back to England, and the colonial troops were disbanded at Boston.

Meanwhile, the army of General Nicholson had marched against Montreal. But when news arrived of the failure of the fleet, the land expedition was also abandoned. The dallying cowardice of Walker had brought the campaign of 1711 to a shameful end. France had already made overtures for peace. Negotiations were formally begun in the early part of 1712; and on the 11th of April in the following year a treaty was concluded at Utrecht, a town of Holland. By the terms of the settlement, England obtained control of the fisheries of Newfoundland. Labrador, the Bay of Hudson and the whole of Acadia, or Nova Scotia, were ceded to Great Britain. On the 13th of July the chiefs of the hostile Indian tribes met the ambassadors of New England at Portsmouth, and a second treaty was concluded, by which peace was secured throughout the American colonies.

For thirty-one years after the close of Queen Anne's war, Massachusetts was free from hostile invasion. This was not, however, a period of public tranquillity. The people were dissatisfied with the royal government which King William had established, and were at constant variance with their governors. Phipps and his administration had been heartily disliked. Governor Shute was equally unpopular. Burnett, who succeeded him, and Belcher afterward, were only tolerated because they could not be shaken off. The opposition to the royal officers took the form of a controversy about their salaries. The general assembly insisted that the governor and his councilors should be paid in proportion to the importance of their several offices, and for actual service only. But the royal commissions gave to each officer a fixed salary, which was frequently out of all proportion to the services required. After many years of antagonism, the difficulty was finally adjusted with a compromise in which the advantage was wholly on the side of the people. It agreed that the salaries of the governor and his assistants should be annually allowed, and the amount fixed by vote of the assembly. The representatives of popular liberty had once more triumphed over the principles of arbitrary rule.

On the death of Charles VI. of Austria, in 1740, there were two principal claimants to the crown of the empire—Maria Theresa, daughter of the late emperor, and Charles Albert of Bavaria. Each claimant had his party and his army; war followed; and nearly all the nations of Europe were swept into the conflict. As usually happened in such struggles, England and France were arrayed against each other. The contest that ensued is generally known as the War of the Austrian Succession, but in American history is called KING GEORGE'S WAR; for George II. was now king of England.

In America the only important event of the war was the capture of Louisburg, on Cape Breton Island. This place had been fortified at vast expense by the French. Standing at the principal entrance to the gulf and river of St. Lawrence, the fortress was regarded as a key to the Canadian provinces. New England was quick to note that both Newfoundland and Nova Scotia were threatened so long as the French flag floated over Louisburg. Governor Shirley brought the matter before the legislature of Massachusetts, and it was resolved to attempt the capture of the enemy's stronghold.

The other colonies were invited to aid the enterprise. Connecticut responded by sending more than five hundred troops; New Hampshire and Rhode Island each furnished three hundred; a park of artillery was sent from New York; and Pennsylvania contributed a supply of provisions. The force of Massachusetts alone numbered more than three thousand. It only remained to secure the co-operation of the English fleet then cruising in the West Indies. An earnest invitation was sent to Commodore Warren to join his armament with the colonial forces; but having no orders, he declined the request. Everything devolved on the army and navy of New England, but there was no quailing under the responsibility. William Pepperell, of Maine, was appointed commander-in-chief; and on the 4th of April, 1745, the fleet sailed for Cape Breton.

At Canseau, the eastern cape of Nova Scotia, the expedition was detained for sixteen days. The sea was thick with ice-drifts floating from the north. But the delay was fortunate, for in the mean time Commodore Warren had received instructions from England to proceed to Massachusetts and aid Governor Shirley in the contemplated reduction of Cape Breton. Sailing to the north, Warren brought his fleet safely to Canseau on the 23d of April. On the last day of the month the armament, now numbering a hundred vessels, entered the Bay of Gabarus in sight of Louisburg. A landing was effected four miles below the city. On the next day a company of four hundred volunteers, led by William Vaughan, marched across the peninsula and attacked a French battery which had been planted on the shore two miles beyond the town. The French, struck with terror at the impetuosity of the unexpected charge, spiked their guns and fled. Before morning the cannons were re-drilled and turned upon the fortress. An English battery was established on the east side of the harbor, but the sea-walls of Louisburg were so strong that little damage was done by the guns across the bay. An attack in the rear of the town seemed impossible on account of a large swamp which lay in that direction; but the resolute soldiers of New England lashed their heavy guns upon sledges, and dragged them through the marsh to a tract of solid ground within two hundred yards of the enemy's bastions. Notwithstanding the advantage of this position, the walls of the fort stood firm, and the siege progressed slowly.

On the 18th of May a French ship of sixty-four guns, laden with stores for the garrison, was captured by Warren's fleet. The French were greatly discouraged by this event, and the defence grew feeble. The English were correspondingly elated with the prospect of success. On the 26th of the month an effort was made to capture the French battery in the harbor. A company of daring volunteers undertook the hazardous enterprise by night. Embarking in boats, they drew near the island where the battery was planted, but were discovered and repulsed with the loss of a hundred and seventy-six men. It was now determined to carry the town by storm. The assault was set for the 18th of June; but on the day previous the desponding garrison sent out a flag of truce; terms of capitulation were proposed and accepted, and the English flag rose above the conquered fortress.

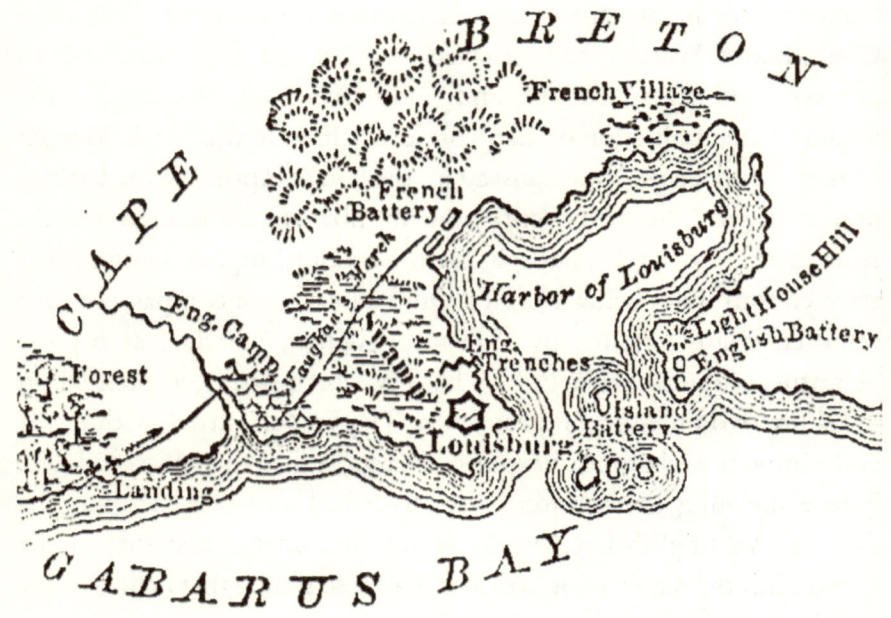

Siege of Louisburg, 1745.

By the terms of this surrender not only Louisburg, but the whole of Cape Breton, was given up to England. The rejoicing at Boston and throughout the colonies was only equaled by the indignation and alarm of the French government. Louisburg must be retaken at all hazards, said the ministers of France. For this purpose a powerful fleet, under command of Duke d'Anville, was sent out in the following year. Before reaching America the duke died of a pestilence. His successor went mad and killed himself. Storms and shipwrecks and disasters drove the ill-fated expedition to utter ruin. The renewal of the enterprise, in 1747, was attended with like misfortune. Commodores Warren and Anson overtook the French squadron and compelled a humiliating surrender.

In 1748, a treaty of peace was concluded at Aix-la-Chapelle, a town of Western Germany. After eight years of devastating warfare, nothing was gained but a mutual restoration of conquests. By the terms of settlement, Cape Breton was surrendered to France. With grief and shame the fishermen and farmers of New England saw the island which had been subdued by their valor restored to their enemies. Of all the disputed boundary-lines between the French and English colonies in

America, not a single one was settled by this treaty. The European nations had exhausted themselves with fighting; what cared they for the welfare of distant and feeble provinces? The real war between France and England for colonial supremacy in the West was yet to be fought. Within six years after the treaty of Aix-la-Chapelle, the two great powers were involved in the final and decisive conflict.

The history of Massachusetts has now been traced through a period of a hundred and thirty years. A few words on THE CHARACTER OF THE PURITANS may be appropriately added. They were in the beginning a vigorous and hardy people, firm-set in the principles of honesty and the practices of virtue. They were sober, industrious, frugal; resolute, zealous and steadfast. They esteemed honor above preferment, and truth more than riches. Loving home and native land, they left both for the sake of freedom; and finding freedom, they cherished it with the zeal and devotion of martyrs. Without influence, they became influential; without encouragement, great. Despised and mocked and hated, they rose above their revilers. In the school of evil fortune they gained the discipline of patience. Suffering without cause brought resignation without despair. Themselves the victims of persecution, they became the founders of a colony—a commonwealth—a nation. They were the children of adversity and the fathers of renown.

The gaze of the Puritan was turned ever to posterity. He believed in the future. His affections and hopes were with the coming ages. For his children he toiled and sacrificed; for them the energies of his life were cheerfully exhausted. The system of free schools is the enduring monument of his love and devotion. The printing-press is his memorial. Almshouses and asylums are the tokens of his care for the unfortunate. With him the outcast found sympathy, and the wanderer a home. He was the earliest champion of civil rights, and the builder of THE UNION.

The fathers of New England have been accused of bigotry. The charge is true: it is the background of the picture. In matters of religion they were intolerant and superstitious. Their religious faith was gloomy and foreboding; Human life was deemed a sad and miserable journey. To be mistaken was to sin. To fail in trifling ceremonies was reckoned a grievous crime. In the shadow of such belief the people became austere and melancholy. Escaping from the splendid formality of the Episcopal Church, they set up a colder and severer form of worship; and the form was made like iron. Dissenters themselves, they could not tolerate the dissent of others. To restrain and punish error seemed right and necessary. Williams and Hutchinson were banished; the Quakers were persecuted and the witches hanged. But Puritanism contained within itself the power to correct its own abuses. Within the austere and gloomy fabric dwelt the very soul and genius of FREE THOUGHT. Under the icebound rigors of the faith flowed a current which no fatalism could congeal, no superstition poison. The heart of a mighty, tumultuous, liberty-loving life throbbed within the cold, stiff body of formalism. A powerful vitality, which no disaster could subdue, no persecution quench, warmed and energized and quickened. The tyranny of Phipps, the malice of Parris, and the bigotry of Mather are far outweighed by the sacrifices of Winthrop, the beneficence of Harvard, and the virtues of Sir Henry Vane. The evils of the system may well be forgotten in the glory of its achievements. Without the Puritans, America would have been a delusion and liberty only a name.

CHAPTER XVIII.

NEW YORK.—SETTLEMENT.

ILLUSTRIOUS Sir Henry Hudson! Indomitable explorer, dauntless cavalier of the ocean! Who so worthy to give a name to the great inland sea of the frozen North as he who gave his life in heroic combat with its terrors? Who so fit to become the father of a colony in the New World as he who braved its perils and revealed its mysteries? And where should the new State be planted unless by the broad haven—broadest and best on the American coast—and among the beautiful hills and landscapes

> Where *The Hudson* came rolling through valleys a-smoke
> From the lands of the Iroquois?

It was the good fortune of the American colonies to be founded by men whose lives, like the setting suns of summer, cast behind them a long and glorious twilight. But for the name and genius of Hudson the province of New Netherland had never been.

For ten years after the founding of New Amsterdam the colony was governed by directors. These officers were appointed and sent out by the Dutch East India Company, in accordance with the charter of that corporation. The settlement on Manhattan Island was as yet only a village of traders. Not until 1623 was an actual colony sent from Holland to New Netherland. Two years previously, the Dutch West India Company had been organized, with the exclusive privilege of planting settlements in America. The charter of this company was granted for a period of twenty-four years with the privilege of renewal; and the territory to be colonized extended from the Strait of Magellan to Hudson's Bay. Manhattan Island, with its cluster of huts, passed at once under the control of the new corporation.

In April of 1623, the ship New Netherland, having on board a colony of thirty families, arrived at New Amsterdam. The colonists, called WALLOONS, were Dutch Protestant refugees from Flanders, in Belgium. They were of the same religious faith with the Huguenots of France, and

Sir Henry Hudson.

came to America to find repose from the persecutions of their own country. Cornelius May was the leader of the company. The greater number of the new immigrants settled with their friends on Manhattan Island; but the captain, with a party of fifty, passing down the coast of New Jersey, entered and explored the Bay of Delaware. Sailing up the bay and river, the company landed on the eastern shore; here, at a point a few miles below Camden, where Timber Creek falls into the Delaware, a site was selected and a block-house built named Fort Nassau. The natives were won over by kindness; and when shortly after the fort was abandoned and the settlers returned to New Amsterdam, the Indians witnessed their departure with affectionate regret. In the same year Joris, another Dutch captain, ascended the Hudson to Castle Island, where, nine years previously, Christianson had built the older Fort Nassau. A flood in the river had swept the island bare. Not deeming it prudent to restore the works in a place likely to be deluged, Joris sailed up stream a short distance and rebuilt the fortress on the present site of Albany. The name of this northern outpost was changed to Fort Orange; and here the eighteen families of Joris's company were permanently settled.

In 1624 civil government began in New Netherland. Cornelius. May was first governor of the colony. His official duties, however, were only such as belonged to the superintendent of a trading-post. In the next year William Verhulst became director of the settlement. Herds of cattle, swine and sheep were brought over from Holland and distributed among the settlers. In January of 1626, Peter Minuit, of Wesel, was regularly appointed by the Dutch West India Company as governor of New Netherland. Until this time the natives had retained the ownership of Manhattan Island; but on Minuit's arrival, in May, an offer of purchase was made and accepted. The whole island, containing more than twenty thousand acres, was sold to the Dutch for twenty-four dollars. The southern point of land was selected as a site for fortifications; there a block-house was built and surrounded with a palisade. New Amsterdam was already a town of thirty houses. In the first year of Minuit's administration were begun the settlements of Wallabout and Brooklyn, on Long Island.

The Dutch of New Amsterdam and the Pilgrims of New Plymouth were early and fast friends. The Puritans themselves had but recently arrived from Holland, and could not forget the kind treatment which they had had in that country. They and the Walloons were alike exiles fleeing from persecution and tyranny. On two occasions, in 1627, a Dutch embassy was sent to Plymouth with an expression of good will. The English were cordially invited to remove without molestation to the more fertile valley of the Connecticut. Governor Bradford replied with words of cheer and sympathy. The Dutch were honestly advised of the claims of England to the country of the Hudson; and the people of New Netherland were cautioned to make good their titles by accepting new deeds from the council of Plymouth. A touch of jealousy was manifested when the Dutch were warned not to send their trading-boats into the Bay of Narragansett.

In 1628 the population of Manhattan numbered two hundred and seventy. The settlers devoted their whole energies to the fur-trade. Every bay, inlet and river between Rhode Island and the Delaware was visited by their vessels. The colony gave promise of rapid development and of great profit to the proprietors. If the houses were rude and thatched with straw, there were energy and thrift within. If only wooden chimneys carried up the smoke, the fires of the hearthstones were kindled with laughter and song. If creaking windmills flung abroad their ungainly arms in the winds of Long Island Sound, it was proof that the people had families to feed and meant to feed them.

The West India Company now came forward with a new and peculiar scheme of colonization. In 1629, the corporation created a CHARTER OF PRIVILEGES, under which a class of proprietors called patroons were authorized to possess and colonize the country. Each patroon might select anywhere in New Netherland a tract of land not more than sixteen miles in length, and of a breadth to be determined by the location. On the banks of a navigable river not more than eight miles might be appropriated by one proprietor. Each district was to be held in fee simple by the patroon, who was empowered to exercise over his estate and its inhabitants the same authority as did the hereditary lords of Europe. The conditions were that the estates should be held as dependencies of Holland; that each patroon should purchase his domain of the Indians; and that he should, within four years from the date of his title, establish on his manor a colony of not less than fifty persons. Education and religion were commended in the charter, but no provision was made for the support of either.

Under the provisions of this instrument five estates were immediately established. Three of them, lying contiguous, embraced a district of twenty-four miles in the valley of the Hudson above and below Fort Orange. The fourth manor was laid out by Michael Pauw on Staten Island; and the fifth, and most important, included the southern half of the present State of Delaware. To this estate a colony was sent out from Holland in the spring of 1631. Samuel Godyn was patroon of the domain, but the immediate management was entrusted to David Peterson de Vries. With a company of thirty immigrants, he reached the entrance to Delaware Bay, and anchored within Cape Henlopen. Landing five miles up the bay, at the mouth of Lewis Creek, the colony selected a site and laid the foundations of Lewistown, the oldest settlement in Delaware.

After a year of successful management, De Vries returned to Holland, leaving the settlement in charge of Gillis Hosset. The latter, a man of no sagacity, soon brought the colony to ruin. An Indian chief who offended him was seized and put to death. The natives, who thus far had treated the strangers with deference and good faith, were aroused to vengeance. Rising suddenly out of an ambuscade upon the terrified colonists, they left not a man alive. The houses and palisades were burned to the ground; nothing but bones and ashes remained to testify of savage passion. When De Vries returned, in December of 1632, he found only the blackened ruins of his flourishing hamlet. He sailed first to Virginia for a cargo of supplies, and thence to New Amsterdam; but before the colony could be re-established, Lord Baltimore had received from the English government a patent which embraced the whole of Delaware; the weaker, though older, claim of the Dutch patroon gave way before the charter of his more powerful rival.

In April of 1633, Minuit was superseded in the government of New Netherland by Wouter van Twiller. Three months previously the Dutch had purchased of the natives the soil around Hartford, and had erected a block-house within the present limits of the city. This was the first fortress built on the Connecticut River; but the Puritans, though professing friendship, were not going to give up the valley without a struggle. In October of the same year an armed vessel, sent out from Plymouth, sailed up the river and openly defied the Dutch commander at Hartford. Passing the fortress, the English proceeded up stream to the mouth of the river Farmington, where they landed and built Fort Windsor. Two years later, by the building of Saybrook, at the mouth of the Connecticut, the English obtained command of the river both above and below the Dutch fort. The block-house at Hartford, being thus cut off, was comparatively useless to the authorities of New Netherland English towns multiplied in the neighborhood; and the Dutch finally surrendered their eastern outpost, to their more powerful rivals.

Four of the leading European nations had now established permanent colonies in America. The fifth to plant an American State was Sweden. As early as 1626, Gustavus Adolphus, the Protestant king of that country and the hero of his age, had formed the design of establishing settlements in the West. For this purpose a company of merchants had been organized, to whose capital the king himself contributed four hundred thousand dollars. The objects had in view were to form a refuge for persecuted Protestants and to extend Swedish commerce. But before his plans of colonization could be carried into effect, Gustavus became involved in the Thirty Years' War, then raging in Germany. The company was disorganized, and the capital wasted in the purchase of military stores. In November of 1632 the Swedish king was killed at the battle of Lützen. For a while it seemed that the plan of colonizing America had ended in failure, but Oxenstiern, the great Swedish minister, took up the work which his master had left unfinished. The charter of the company was renewed, and after four years of preparation the enterprise was brought to a successful issue.

De Vries Revisits His Ruined Settlement.

In the mean time, Peter Minuit, the recent governor of New Netherland, had left the service of Holland and entered that of Sweden. To him was entrusted the management of the first Swedish colony which was sent to America. Late in the year 1637, a company of Swedes and Finns left the harbor of Stockholm, and in the following February arrived in Delaware Bay. Never before had the Northerners beheld so beautiful a land. They called Cape Henlopen the Point of Paradise. The whole country, sweeping around the west side of the bay and up the river to the falls at Trenton, was honorably purchased of the Indians. In memory of native land, the name of NEW SWEDEN was given to this fine territory. The colony landed just below the mouth of the Brandywine, in the northern part of the present State of Delaware. On the left bank of a small tributary, at a point about six miles from the bay, a spot was chosen for the settlement. Here the foundations of a fort were laid, and the immigrants soon provided themselves with houses. The creek and the fort were both named in honor of Christiana, the maiden queen of Sweden.

The colony prospered greatly. By each returning ship letters were borne to Stockholm, describing the loveliness of the country. Immigration became rapid and constant. At one time, in 1640, more than a hundred families, unable to find room on the crowded vessels which were leaving the Swedish capital, were turned back to their homes. The banks of Delaware Bay and River were dotted with pleasant hamlets. On every hand appeared the proofs of well-directed industry. Of all the early settlers in America, none were more cheerful, intelligent and virtuous than the Swedes.

From the first, the authorities of New Amsterdam were jealous of the colony on the Delaware. Sir William Kieft, who had succeeded the incompetent Van Twiller in the governorship, sent an earnest remonstrance to Christiana, warning the settlers of their intrusion on Dutch territory. But the Swedes, giving little heed to the complaints of their neighbors, went on enlarging their borders and strengthening their outposts. Governor Kieft was alarmed and indignant at these aggressions, and as a precautionary measure sent a party to rebuild Fort Nassau, on the old site below Camden. The Swedes, regarding this fortress as a menace to their colony, adopted active measures of defence. Ascending the river to within six miles of the mouth of the Schuylkill, they landed on the island of Tinicum, and built an impregnable fort of hemlock logs. Here, in 1643, Governor Printz established his residence. To Pennsylvania, as well as to Delaware, Sweden contributed the earliest colony.

In 1640, New Netherland became involved in a war with the Indians of Long Island and New Jersey. The natives of the lower Hudson were a weak and unwarlike people; under just treatment they would have faithfully kept the peace. But dishonest traders had maddened them with rum and then defrauded and abused them. Burning with resentment and hate, the savages of the Jersey shore crossed over to Staten Island, laid waste the farms and butchered the inhabitants. New Amsterdam was for a while endangered, but was soon put in a state of defence. A company of militia was organized and sent against the Delawares of New Jersey, but nothing resulted from the expedition. A large bounty was offered for every member of the tribe of the Raritans, and many were hunted to death. On both sides the war degenerated into treachery and murder. Through the mediation of Roger Williams, the great peacemaker of Rhode Island, a truce was obtained, and immediately broken. A chieftain's son, who had been made drunk and robbed, went to the nearest settlement and killed the first Hollander whom he met. Governor Kieft demanded the criminal, but the sachems refused to give him up. They offered to pay a heavy fine for the wrong done, but Kieft would accept nothing less than the life of the murderer.

While the dispute was still unsettled, a party of the terrible Mohawks came down the river to claim and enforce their supremacy over the natives of the coast. The timid Algonquins in the neighborhood of New Amsterdam cowered before the mighty warriors of the North, huddled together on the bank of the Hudson, and begged assistance of the Dutch. Here the vindictive Kieft saw an opportunity of wholesale destruction. A company of soldiers set out secretly from Manhattan, crossed the river and discovered the lair of the Indians. The place was surrounded by night, and the first notice of danger given to the savages was the roar of muskets. Nearly a hundred of the poor wretches were killed before daydawn. Women who shrieked for pity were mangled to death, and children were thrown into the river.

When it was known among the tribes that the Dutch, and not the Mohawks, were the authors of this outrage, the war was renewed with fury. The Indians were in a frenzy. Dividing into small war-parties, they concealed themselves in the woods and swamps; then rose, without a moment's warning, upon defenceless farmhouses, burning and butchering without mercy. At this time that noted woman Mrs. Anne Hutchinson was living with her son-in-law in the valley of the Housatonic. Her house was surrounded and set on fire by the savages; every member of the family except one child was cruelly murdered. Mrs. Hutchinson herself was burned alive.

In 1643, Captain John Underhill, a fugitive from Massachusetts, was appointed to the command of the Dutch forces. At the head of a regiment raised by Governor Kieft he invaded New Jersey, and brought the Delawares into subjection. A decisive battle was fought on Long Island; and at Greenwich, in Western Connecticut, the power of the Indians was finally broken. Again the ambassadors of the Iroquois came forward with proposals for peace. Both parties were anxious to rest from the ruin and devastation of war. On the 30th of August, 1645, a treaty was concluded at Fort Amsterdam.

Nearly all of the bloodshed and sorrow of these five years of war may be charged to Governor Kieft. He was a revengeful and cruel man, whose idea of government was to destroy whatever opposed him. The people had many times desired to make peace with the Indians, but the project had always been defeated by the headstrong passions of the governor. A popular party, headed by the able De Vries, at last grew powerful enough to defy his authority. As soon as the war was ended, petitions for his removal were circulated and signed by the people. Two years after the treaty, the Dutch West India Company revoked his commission and appointed Peter Stuyvesant to succeed him. In 1647, Kieft embarked for Europe; but the heavy-laden merchantman in which he sailed was dashed to pieces by a storm on the coast of Wales, and the guilty governor of New Netherland found a grave in the sea.

CHAPTER XIX.

NEW YORK.—ADMINISTRATION OF STUYVESANT.

THE honest and soldierly PETER STUYVESANT was the last and greatest of the governors of New Netherland. He entered upon his duties on the 11th of May, 1647, and continued in office for more than seventeen years. His first care was to conciliate the Indians. By the wisdom and liberality of his government the wayward red men were reclaimed from hostility and hatred. So intimate and cordial became the relations between the natives and the Dutch that they were suspected of making common cause against the English; even Massachusetts was alarmed lest such an alliance should be formed. But the policy of Governor Stuyvesant was based on nobler principles.

Until now the West India Company had had exclusive control of the commerce of New Netherland. In the first year of the new administration this monopoly was abolished, and regular export duties were substituted. The benefit of the change was at once apparent in the improvement of the Dutch province. In one of the letters written to Stuyvesant by the secretary of the company, the remarkable prediction is made that the commerce of New Amsterdam should cover every ocean and the ships of all nations crowd into her harbor. But for many years the growth of the city was slow. As late as the middle of the century, the better parts of Manhattan Island were still divided among the farmers. Central Park was a forest of oaks and chestnuts.

In 1650, a boundary-line was fixed between New England and New Netherland. The Dutch were fearful lest the English should reach the Hudson and cut off the fur-trade between Fort Orange and New Amsterdam. Governor Stuyvesant met the ambassadors of the Eastern colonies at Hartford, and after much discussion an eastern limit was set to the Dutch possessions. The line there established extended across Long Island north and south, passing through Oyster Bay, and thence to Greenwich, on the other side of the sound. From this point northward the dividing-line was nearly identical with the present boundary of Connecticut on the west. This treaty was ratified by the colonies, by the west India Company and by the states-general of Holland; but the English government treated the matter with indifference and contempt.

Stuyvesant had less to fear from the colony of New Sweden. The people of New Netherland outnumbered the Swedes as ten to one, and the Dutch claim to the country of the Delaware had never been renounced. In 1651, an armament left New Amsterdam, entered the bay and came to anchor at a point on the western shore five miles below the mouth of the Brandywine. On the present site of New Castle, Fort Casimir was built and garrisoned with Dutch soldiers. This act was equivalent to a declaration of war. The Swedish settlement of Christiana was almost in sight of the hostile fortress, and a conflict could hardly be avoided. Rising, the governor of the Swedes, looked on quietly until Fort Casimir was completed, then captured the place by stratagem, overpowered the garrison and hoisted the flag of Sweden.

It was a short-lived triumph. The West India Company were secretly pleased that the Swedes had committed an act of open violence. Orders were at once issued to Stuyvesant to visit the Swedish colonists with vengeance, and to compel their submission or drive them from the Delaware. In September of 1655 the orders of the company were carried out to the letter. The old governor put himself at the head of more than six hundred troops—a number almost equal to the entire population of New Sweden—and sailed to Delaware Bay. Resistance was hopeless. The Dutch forces were landed at New Castle, and the Swedes gave way. Before the 25th of the month every fort belonging to the colony had been forced to capitulate. Governor Rising was captured, but was treated with great respect. Honorable terms were granted to all, and in a few days the authority of New Netherland was established throughout the country. Except a few turbulent spirits who removed to Maryland and Virginia, the submission was universal. After an existence of less than eighteen years, the little State of New Sweden had ceased to be. The American possessions and territorial claims of France, England, Holland, Sweden and Spain will be best understood from an examination of the accompanying map, drawn for the year 1655.

Map IV.
French, English, Dutch, Swedish & Spanish Provinces. A. D. 1655.

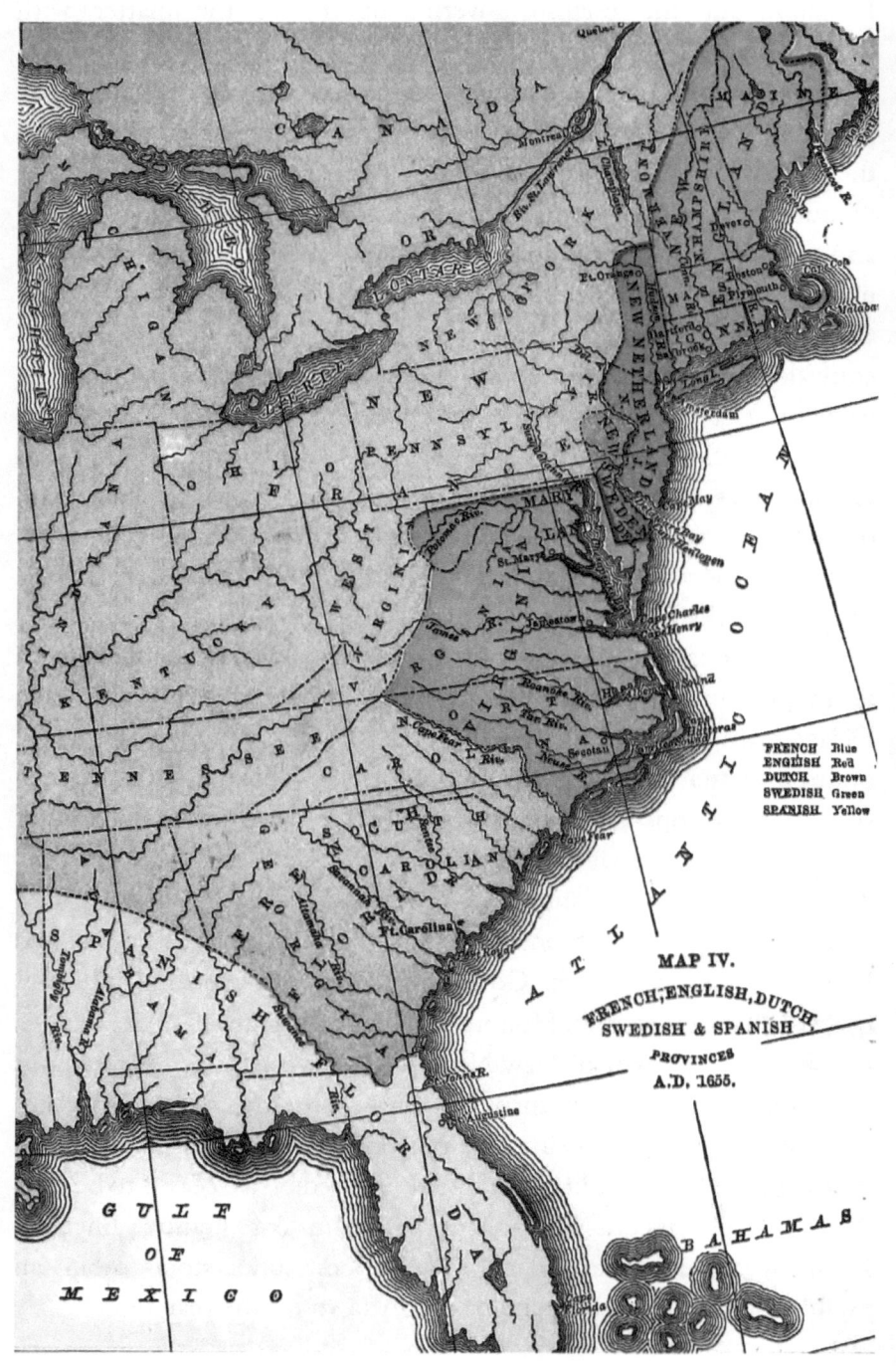

How hardly can the nature of savages be restrained! While Governor Stuyvesant was absent on his expedition against the Swedes, the Algonquin tribes rose in rebellion. The poor creatures were going to take New Amsterdam. In a fleet of sixty-four canoes they appeared before the town, yelling and discharging arrows. What could their puny missiles do against the walls of a European fortress? After paddling about until their rage, but not their hate, was spent, the savages went on shore and began their old work of burning and murder. The return of the Dutch forces from the Delaware induced the sachems to sue for peace, which Stuyvesant granted on better terms than the Indians had deserved. The captives were ransomed, and the treacherous tribes were allowed to go with trifling punishments.

For eight years after the conquest of New Sweden the peace of New Netherland was unbroken. In 1663 the natives of the county of Ulster, on the Hudson, broke out in war. The town of Esopus, now Kingston, was attacked and destroyed. Sixty-five of the inhabitants were either tomahawked or carried into captivity. To punish this outrage a strong force was sent from New Amsterdam. The Indians fled, hoping to find refuge in the woods; but the Dutch soldiers pursued them to their villages, burned their wigwams and killed every warrior who could be overtaken. As winter came on, the humbled tribe began to beg for mercy. In December a truce was granted; and in May of the following year a treaty of peace was concluded.

Governor Stuyvesant had great difficulty in defending his province beyond the Delaware. The queen of Sweden and her ministers at Stockholm still looked fondly to their little American colony, and cherished the hope of recovering the conquered territory. A more dangerous competitor was found in Lord Baltimore, of Maryland, whose patent, given under the great seal of England, covered all the territory between the Chesapeake and Delaware Bay, as far north as the latitude of Philadelphia. Berkeley, of Virginia, also claimed New Sweden as a part of his dominions. Connecticut pushed her settlements westward on Long Island, and purchased all the remaining Indian claims between her western frontier and the Hudson. Massachusetts boldly declared her intention to extend her boundaries to Fort Orange. The indignant Stuyvesant asked the agents of Connecticut where the province of New Netherland could shortly be found; and the agents coolly answered *that they did not know.*

Discord at home added to the governor's embarrassments. For many years the Dutch had witnessed the growth and prosperity of the English colonies. Boston had outgrown New Amsterdam. The schools of Massachusetts and Connecticut flourished; the academy on Manhattan, after a sickly career of two years, was discontinued. In New Netherland heavy taxes were levied for the support of the poor; New England had no poor. Liberty and right were the subjects of debate in every English village; to the Dutch farmers and traders such words had little meaning. The people of New Netherland grew emulous of the progress of their powerful neighbors, and attributed their own abasement to the mismanagement and selfish greed of the West India Company. Without actual disloyalty to Holland, the Dutch came to prefer the laws and customs of England. Under these accumulating troubles the faithful Stuyvesant was wellnigh overwhelmed.

Such was the condition of affairs at the beginning of 1664. England and Holland were at peace. Neither nation had reason to apprehend an act of violence from the other. In all that followed, the arbitrary principles and unscrupulous disposition of the English king were fully manifested. On the 12th of March in this year the duke of York received at the hands of his brother, Charles II., two extensive patents for American territory. The first grant included the district reaching from the Kennebec to the St. Croix River, and the second embraced the whole country between the Connecticut and the Delaware. Without regard to the rights of Holland, in utter contempt of the West India Company, through whose exertions the valley of the Hudson had been peopled, with no respect for the wishes of the Dutch, or even for the voice of his own Parliament, the English monarch in one rash hour despoiled a sister kingdom of a well-earned province.

The duke of York made haste to secure his territory. No time must be left for the states-general to protest against the outrage. An English squadron was immediately equipped, put under command of Richard Nicolls and sent to America. In July the armament reached Boston, and thence proceeded against New Amsterdam. On the 28th of August, the fleet passed the Narrows, and anchored at Gravesend Bay. The English camp was pitched at Brooklyn Ferry; and before the Dutch had recovered from their surprise, the whole of Long Island was subdued. An embassy came over from New Amsterdam. Governor Stuyvesant, ever true to his employers, demanded to know the meaning of

Peter Stuyvesant.

all this hostile array. To receive the surrender of New Netherland was the quiet answer of Nicolls. There must be an immediate acknowledgment of the sovereignty of England. Those who submitted should have the rights of Englishmen those who refused should hear the crash of cannon-balls. The Dutch council of New Amsterdam was immediately convened. It was clear that the burgomasters meant to surrender. The stormy old governor exhorted them to rouse to action and fight; some one replied that the Dutch West India Company was not worth fighting for. Burning with indignation, Stuyvesant snatched up the written proposal of Nicolls and tore it to tatters in the presence of his council. It was all in vain. The brave old man was forced to sign the capitulation; and on the 8th of September, 1664, New Netherland ceased to exist. The English flag was hoisted over the fort and town, and the name of NEW YORK was substituted for New Amsterdam. The surrender of Fort Orange, now named Albany, followed on the 24th and on the 1st of October the Swedish and Dutch settlements on the Delaware capitulated. The conquest was complete. The supremacy of Great Britain in America was finally established. From the north-east corner of Maine to the southern limits of Georgia, every mile of the American coast was under the flag of England.

CHAPTER XX.

New York Under the English.

RICHARD NICOLLS, the first English governor of New York, began his duties by settling the boundaries of his province. It was a work full of trouble and vexation. As early as 1623 the whole of Long Island had been granted to the earl of Stirling. Connecticut also claimed and occupied all that part of the island included in the present county of Suffolk. Against both of these claimants the patent of the duke of York was now to be enforced by his deputy Nicolls. The claim of Stirling was fairly purchased by the governor, but the pretensions of Connecticut were arbitrarily set aside. This action was the source of so much discontent that the duke was constrained to compensate Connecticut by making a favorable change in her south-west boundary-line.

Two months before the conquest of New Netherland by the English, the irregular territory between the Hudson and the Delaware, as far north as a point on the latter river in the latitude of forty-one degrees and forty minutes, was granted to Lord Berkeley and Sir George Carteret. This district, corresponding, except on the northern boundary, with the present State of New Jersey, was now wrested from the jurisdiction of New York, and a separate government established by the proprietors. The country below the Delaware, until recently called New Sweden, but now named THE TERRITORIES, was consolidated with New York and ruled by deputies appointed by the governors of that province. Finally, the new name conferred by Nicolls on his capital was extended to all the country formerly called New Netherland.

At the first the people were deluded with many promises of civil liberty. To secure this, the Dutch, against the passionate appeals of the patriotic Stuyvesant, had voluntarily surrendered themselves to the English government. But it was a poor sort of civil liberty that any province was likely to obtain from one of the Stuart kings of England. The promised right of representation in a general assembly of the people was evaded and withheld. To this was added a greater grief in the annulling of the old titles by which, for half a century, the Dutch farmers had held their lands. The people were obliged to accept new deeds at the hands of the English governor, and to pay him therefor such sums as yielded an immense revenue. The evil done to the province, however, was less than might have been expected from so arbitrary and despotic a government.

In 1667, Nicolls was superseded by Lovelace. With less ability and generosity than his predecessor, he proved a greater tyrant. The bad principles of the system established by the duke of York were now fully developed. The people became dissatisfied and gloomy. Protests against the government and petitions for redress were constantly presented, and constantly rejected with contempt. The discontent was universal. The towns of Southold, Southampton and Easthampton resisted the tax gatherers. The people of Huntington voted that they were robbed of the privileges of Englishmen. The villagers of Jamaica, Flushing and Hempstead passed a resolution that the governor's decree of taxation was contrary to the laws of the English nation. The only attention which Lovelace and his council paid to these resolutions was to declare them scandalous, illegal and seditious, and to order them to be publicly burnt before the town-house of New York. When the Swedes, naturally a quiet and submissive people, resisted the exactions of the government, they were visited with additional severity. "If there is any more murmuring against the taxes, make them so heavy that the people can do nothing but think how to pay them," said Lovelace in his instructions to his deputy.

The Dutch and the English colonists were always friends. Not once in the whole history of the country did they lift the sword against each other. Even while England and Holland were at war, as they were in 1652-54, the American subjects of the two nations remained at peace. Another war followed that act of violence by which, in 1664, the duke of York possessed himself of New Netherland; but the conflict did not extend to America. A third time, in 1672, Charles II. was induced by the king of France to begin a contest with the Dutch government. This time, indeed, the struggle extended to the colonies, and New York was revolutionized, but not by the action of her own people. In 1673 a small squadron was fitted out by Holland and placed under command of the gallant Captain Evertsen. The fleet sailed for America, and arrived before Manhattan on the 30th of July. The governor of New York was absent, and Manning, the deputy-governor, was a coward. The defences of the city were dilapidated, and the people refused to strengthen them. Within four hours after the arrival of the squadron the fort was surrendered. The city capitulated, and the whole province yielded without a struggle. New Jersey and Delaware sent in their submission; the name of New Netherland was revived; and the authority of Holland was restored from Connecticut to Maryland.

The reconquest of New York by the Dutch was only a brief military occupation of the country. The civil authority of Holland was never reestablished. In 1674, Charles II. was obliged by his Parliament to conclude a treaty of peace. There was the usual clause requiring the restoration of all conquests made during the war. New York reverted to the English government, and the rights of the duke were again recognized in the province. To make his authority doubly secure for the future, he obtained from his brother, the king, a new patent confirming the provisions of the former charter. The man who now received the appointment of deputy-governor of New York was none other than Sir Edmund Andros. On the last day of October the Dutch forces were finally withdrawn, and Andros assumed the government.

It was a sad sort of government for the people. The worst practices of Lovelace's administration were revived. The principles of arbitrary rule were openly avowed. Taxes were levied without authority of law, and the appeals and protests of the people were treated with derision. The clamor for a popular legislative assembly had become so great that Andros was on the point of yielding. He even wrote a letter to the duke of York advising that thick-headed prince to grant the people the right of electing a colonial legislature. The duke replied that popular assemblies were seditious and dangerous; that they only fostered discontent and disturbed the peace of the government; and finally, that *he did not see any use for them.* To the people of New York the civil liberty of the New England colonies seemed farther off than ever.

By the terms of his grant the duke of York claimed jurisdiction over all the territory between the Connecticut River and Maryland. To assert and maintain this claim of his master was a part of the deputy governor's business in America. The first effort to extend the duke's territorial rights to the limits of his charter was made in July of 1675. With some armed sloops and a company of soldiers, Andros proceeded to the mouth of the Connecticut in the hope of establishing his jurisdiction. The general assembly of the colony had heard of his coming, and had sent word to Captain Bull, who commanded the fort at Saybrook, to resist Andros in the name of the king. When the latter came in sight and hoisted the flag of England, the same colors were raised within the fortress. The royal governor was permitted to land; but when he began to read his commission, he was ordered in the king's name to desist. Overawed by the threatening looks of the Saybrook militia, Andros retired to his boats and set sail for Long Island.

Notwithstanding the grant of New Jersey to Carteret and Berkeley, the attempt was now made to extend the jurisdiction of New York over the lower province. Andros issued a decree that ships sailing to and from the ports of New Jersey should pay a duty at the custom-house of New York. This tyrannical action was openly resisted. Andros attempted to frighten the assembly of New Jersey into submission, and proceeded so far as to arrest Philip Carteret, the deputy-governor. But it was all of no use. The representatives of the people declared themselves to be under the protection of the Great Charter, which not even the duke of York, or his brother the king, could alter or annul. In August of 1682 the territories beyond the Delaware were granted by the duke to William Penn. This little district, first settled by the Swedes, afterward conquered by the Dutch, then transferred to England on the conquest of New Netherland, was now finally separated from the jurisdiction of New York and joined to Pennsylvania. The governors of the latter province continued to exercise authority over the three counties on the Delaware until the American Revolution.

At the close of Andros's administration, in 1683, Thomas Dongan, a Catholic, became governor of New York. For thirty years the people had been clamoring for a general assembly. Just before Andros left the province, the demand became more vehement than ever. The retiring governor, himself of a despotic disposition, counseled the duke to concede the right of representation to the people. At last James yielded, not so much with the view of extending popular rights, as with the hope of increasing his revenues from the improved condition of his province. Dongan, the new governor, came with full instructions to call an assembly of all the freeholders of New York, by whom certain persons of their own number should be elected to take part in the government. Seventy years had passed since the settlement of Manhattan Island; and now for the first time the people were permitted to choose their own rulers and to frame their own laws.

The first act of the new assembly was to declare that the supreme legislative power of the province resided in the governor, the council and THE PEOPLE. All freeholders were granted the right of suffrage; trial by jury was established; taxes should no more be levied except by consent of the assembly; soldiers should not be quartered on the people; martial law should not exist; no person accepting the general doctrines of religion should be in any wise distressed or persecuted. All the rights and privileges of Massachusetts and Virginia were carefully written by the zealous law-makers of New York in their first charter of liberties.

In July of 1684 an important treaty was concluded at Albany. The governors of New York and Virginia were met in convention by the sachems of the Iroquois, and the terms of a lasting peace were settled. A long war ensued between the Five Nations and the French. The Jesuits of Canada employed every artifice and intrigue to induce the Indians to break their treaty with the English, but all to no purpose; the alliance was faithfully observed. In 1684, and again in 1687, the French invaded the territory of the Iroquois; but the mighty Mohawks and Oneidas drove back their foes with loss and disaster. By the barrier of the friendly Five Nations on the north, the English and Dutch colonies were screened from danger.

In 1685 the duke of York became king of England. It was soon found that even the monarch of a great nation could violate his pledges. King James became the open antagonist of the government which had been established under his own directions. The popular legislature of New York was abrogated. An odious tax was levied by an arbitrary decree.

Printing-presses were forbidden in the province. All the old abuses were revived and made a public boast.

In December of 1686, Edmund Andros became governor of all New England. It was a part of his plan to extend his dominion over New York and New Jersey. To the former province, Francis Nicholson, the lieutenant-general of Andros, was sent as deputy. Dongan was superseded, and until the English Revolution of 1688, New York was ruled as a dependency of New England. When the news of that event and of the accession of William of Orange reached the province, there was a general tumult of rejoicing. The people rose in rebellion against the government of Nicholson, who was glad enough to escape from New York and return to England.

The leader of the insurrection was Jacob Leisler, a captain of the militia. A committee of ten took upon themselves the task of reorganizing the government. Leisler was commissioned to take possession of the fort of New York. Most of the troops in the city, together with five hundred volunteers, proceeded against the fort, which was surrendered without a struggle. The insurgents published a declaration in which they avowed their loyalty to the prince of Orange, their countryman, and expressed their determination to yield immediate obedience to his authority. A provisional government was organized, with Leisler at the head. The provincial councilors, who were friends and adherents of the deposed Nicholson, left the city and repaired to Albany. Here the party who were opposed to the usurpation of Leisler proceeded to organize a second provisional government. Both factions were careful to exercise authority in the name of William and Mary, the new sovereigns of England.

In September of 1689, Milborne, the son-in-law of Leisler, was sent to Albany to demand the surrender of the town and fort. Courtland and Bayard, who were the leaders of the northern faction, opposed the demand with so much vigor that Milborne was obliged to retire without accomplishing his object. Such was the condition of affairs at the beginning of King William's War. How the village of Schenectady was destroyed by the French and Indians, and how an unsuccessful expedition by land and water was planned against Quebec and

Montreal, has been narrated in the history of Massachusetts. Such was the dispiriting effect of these disasters upon the people of Albany and the north that a second effort made by Milborne against the government of the opposing faction was successful; and in the spring of 1690 the authority of Leisler as temporary governor of New York was recognized throughout the province. The summer was spent in fruitless preparations to invade and conquer Canada. The general assembly was convened at the capital; but little was accomplished except a formal recognition of the insurrectionary government of Leisler.

In January of 1691, Richard Ingoldsby arrived at New York. He bore a commission as captain, and brought the intelligence that Colonel Sloughter had been appointed royal governor of the province. Leisler received Ingoldsby with courtesy, and offered him quarters in the city; but the latter, without authority from either the king or the governor, haughtily demanded the surrender of His Majesty's fort. Leisler refused to yield, but expressed his willingness to submit to anyone who bore a commission from King William or Colonel Sloughter. On the 19th of March the governor himself arrived; and Leisler on the same day despatched messengers, tendering his service and submission. The messengers were arrested, and Ingoldsby, the enemy and rival of Leisler, was sent with verbal orders for the surrender of the fort. Leisler foresaw his doom, and hesitated. He wrote a letter to Sloughter, expressing a desire to make a personal surrender of the post to the governor. The letter was unanswered; Ingoldsby pressed his demand; Leisler wavered, capitulated, and with Milborne was seized and hurried to prison.

As soon as the royal government was organized the two prisoners were brought to trial. The charge was rebellion and treason. Dudley, the chief-justice of New England, rendered a decision that Leisler had been a usurper. The prisoners refused to plead, were convicted and sentenced to death. Sloughter, however, determined to know the pleasure of the king before putting the sentence into execution. But the royalist assembly of New York had already come together, and the members were resolved that the prisoners should be hurried to their death. The governor was invited to a banquet; and when heated with strong drink, the death warrant was thrust before him for his signature. He succeeded in affixing his name to the fatal parchment; and almost before the fumes of his drunken revel had passed away, his victims had met their fate. On the 16th of May, Leisler and Milborne were brought from prison, led through a drenching rain to the scaffold and hanged. Within less than a year afterward, their estates, which had been confiscated, were restored to their heirs; and in 1695 the attainder of the families was removed.

The same summer that witnessed the execution of Leisler and Milborne was noted for the renewal of the treaty with the Iroquois. At Albany, Governor Sloughter met the sachems of the Five Nations, and the former terms of fidelity and friendship were reaffirmed. In the following year the valiant Major Schuyler, at the head of the New York militia, joined a war-party of the Iroquois in a successful expedition against the French settlements beyond Lake Champlain. Meanwhile, the assembly of the province had been in session at the capital. Although the representatives were royalists, a resolution was passed against arbitrary taxation, and another which declared the people to be a part of the governing power of the colony. It was not long until one of the governors had occasion to say that the people of New York were growing altogether too big with the privileges of Englishmen.

Soon after his return from Albany, Sloughter's career was cut short by death. He was succeeded in the office of governor by Benjamin Fletcher, a man of bad passions and poor abilities. The new executive arrived in September of 1692. One of the first measures of his administration was to renew the recent treaty with the Iroquois. It was at this time the avowed purpose of the English monarch to place under a common government all the territory between the Connecticut River and Delaware Bay. To further this project, Fletcher was armed with an ample and comprehensive commission. He was made governor of New York, and commander-in-chief not only of the troops of his own province, but also of the militia of Connecticut and New Jersey. In the latter province he met with little opposition; but the Puritans of Hartford resisted so stubbornly that the alarmed and disgusted governor was glad to return to his own capital.

The next effort of the administration was to establish the Episcopal Church in New York. The Dutch and the English colonists of the province were still distinct in nationality; the former, though Calvinists, were not unfriendly to the Episcopal service which the Puritans so heartily despised. In a religious controversy between Fletcher's council and the English, the Dutch, not being partisans of either, looked on with comparative indifference. But when the governor was on the point of succeeding with his measures, the general assembly interposed, passed a decree of toleration, and brought the pretentious Church to a level with the rest. Fletcher gave vent to his indignation by calling his legislators a set of unmannerly and insubordinate boors.

In 1696 the territory of New York was invaded by the French under Frontenac, governor of Canada. The faithful Iroquois made common cause with the colonial forces, and the formidable expedition of the French was turned into confusion. Before the loss could be repaired and a second invasion undertaken, King William's War was ended by the treaty of Ryswick. In the following year, the earl of Bellomont, an Irish nobleman of excellent character and popular sympathies, succeeded Fletcher in the government of New York. His administration of less than four years was the happiest era in the history of the colony. His authority, like that of his predecessor, extended over a part of New England. Massachusetts and New Hampshire were under his jurisdiction, but Connecticut and Rhode Island remained independent. To this period belong the exploits of the famous pirate, Captain William Kidd.

For centuries piracy had been the common vice of the high seas. The nations were just now beginning to take active measures for the suppression of the atrocious crime. The honest and humane Bellomont was one who was anxious to see the end of piratical violence. His commission contained a clause which authorized the arming of a vessel to range the ocean in pursuit of pirates. The ship was to bear the English flag, and was also commissioned as a privateer to prey upon the commerce of the enemies of England. The vessel was owned by a company of distinguished and honorable persons; Governor Bellomont himself was one of the proprietors; and William Kidd received from the English admiralty a commission as captain. The ship sailed from England before Bellomont's departure for New York. Hardly had the earl reached his province when the news came that Kidd himself had turned pirate and become the terror of the seas. For two years he continued his infamous career, then appeared publicly in the streets of Boston, was seized, sent to England, tried, convicted and hanged. What disposition was made of the enormous treasures which the pirate-ship had gathered on the ocean has never been ascertained. It has been thought that the vast hoard of ill-gotten wealth was buried in the sands of Long Island. Governor Bellomont was charged with having shared the booty, but an investigation before the House of Commons showed the accusation to be groundless.

In striking contrast with the virtues and wisdom of Bellomont were the vices and folly of Lord Cornbury, who succeeded him. He arrived at New York in the beginning of May, 1702. A month previously the proprietors of New Jersey had surrendered their rights in the province to the English Crown. All obstacles being thus removed, the two colonies were formally united in one government under the authority of Cornbury. For a period of thirty-six years the territories, though with separate assemblies, continued under the jurisdiction of a single executive.

One of Cornbury's first acts was to forge a clause in his own commission. Desiring to foster the Established Church, and finding nothing to that effect in his instructions, he made instructions for himself. At first the people received him with great favor. The assembly voted two thousand pounds sterling to compensate him for the expenses of his voyage. In order to improve and fortify the Narrows, an additional sum of fifteen hundred pounds was granted. The money was taken out of the treasury, but no improvement was visible at the Narrows. The representatives modestly inquired what had become of their revenues. Lord Cornbury replied that the assembly of New York had no right to ask questions until the queen should give them permission. The old and oft-repeated conflict between personal despotism and popular liberty broke out anew. The people of the province were still divided on the subject of Leisler's insurrection. Cornbury became a violent partisan, favoring the enemies and persecuting the friends of that unfortunate leader; and so from year to year matters grew constantly worse, until between the governor and his people there existed no relation but that of mutual hatred.

In 1708 the civil dissensions of the province reached a climax. Each succeeding assembly resisted more stubbornly the measures of the governor. Time and again the people petitioned for his removal. The councilors selected their own treasurer, refused to vote appropriations, and curtailed Cornbury's revenues until he was impoverished and ruined. Then came Lord Lovelace with a commission from Queen Anne, and the passionate, wretched governor was unceremoniously turned out of office. Left to the mercy of his injured subjects, they arrested him for debt and threw him into prison, where he lay until, by his father's death, he became a peer of England and could be no longer held in confinement.

During the progress of Queen Anne's War the troops of New York cooperated with the army and navy of New England. Eighteen hundred volunteers from the Hudson and the Delaware composed the land forces in the unsuccessful expedition against Montreal in the winter of 1709-10. The provincial army proceeded as far as South River, east of Lake George. Here information was received that the English fleet which was expected to cooperate in the reduction of Quebec had been sent to Portugal; the armament of New England was insufficient of itself to attempt the conquest of the Canadian stronghold; and the troops of New York and New Jersey were obliged to retreat. Again, in 1711, when the incompetent Sir Hovenden Walker was pretending to conduct his fleet up the St. Lawrence, and was in reality only anxious to get away, the army which was to invade Canada by land was furnished by New York. A second time the provincial forces reached Lake George; but the dispiriting news of the disaster to Walker's fleet destroyed all hope of success, and the discouraged soldiers returned to their homes.

Failure and disgrace were not the only distressing circumstances of these campaigns; a heavy debt remained to overshadow the prosperity of New York and to consume her revenues. For many years the resources of the province were exhausted in meeting the extraordinary expenses of Queen Anne's war. In 1713 the treaty of Utrecht put an end to the conflict, and peace returned to the American colonies. In this year the

Tuscaroras of Carolina—a nation of the same race with the Iroquois and Hurons of the North—were defeated and driven from their homes by the Southern colonists. The haughty tribe marched northward, crossed the middle colonies and joined their warlike kinsmen on the St. Lawrence, making the sixth nation in the Iroquois confederacy. Nine years later a great council was held at Albany. There the grand sachems of the Six Nations were met by the governors of New York, Pennsylvania and Virginia. An important commercial treaty was formed, by which the extensive and profitable fur-trade of the Indians, which, until now, had been engrossed by the French, was diverted to the English. In order to secure the full benefits of this arrangement, Governor Burnett of New York hastened to establish a trading-post at Oswego, on the southern shore of Lake Ontario. Five years later a substantial fort was built at the same place and furnished with an English garrison. As late as the middle of the century, Oswego continued to be the only fortified outpost of the English in the entire country drained by the St. Lawrence and its tributaries. The French, meanwhile, had built a strong fort at Niagara, and another at Crown Point, on the western shore of Lake Champlain. The struggle for colonial supremacy between the two nations was already beginning.

The administration of Governor Cosby, who succeeded Burnett in 1732, was a stormy epoch in the history of the colony. The people were in a constant struggle with the royal governors. At this time the contest took the form of a dispute about the freedom of the press. The liberal or democratic party of the province held that a public journal might criticise the acts of the administration and publish views distasteful to the government. The aristocratic party opposed such liberty as a dangerous license, which, if permitted, would soon sap the foundations of all authority. Zenger, an editor of one of the liberal newspapers, published hostile criticisms on the policy of the governor, was seized and put in prison. Great excitement ensued. The people were clamorous for their champion. Andrew Hamilton, a noted lawyer of Philadelphia, went to New York to defend Zenger, who was brought to trial in July of 1735. The charge was libel against the government; the cause was ably argued, and the jury made haste to bring in a verdict of acquittal. The aldermen of the city of New York, in order to testify their appreciation of Hamilton's services in the cause of liberty, made him a present of an elegant gold box, and the people were wild with enthusiasm over their victory.

New York, like Massachusetts, was once visited with a fatal delusion. In the year 1741 occurred what is known as THE NEGRO PLOT. Slavery was permitted in the province, and negroes constituted a large fraction of the population. Several destructive fires had occurred, and it was believed that they had been kindled by incendiaries. The slaves were naturally distrusted; now they became feared and hated. Some degraded women came forward and gave information that the negroes had made a plot to burn the city, kill all who opposed them, and set up one of their own number as governor. The whole story was the essence of absurdity; but the people were alarmed, and were ready to believe anything. The reward of freedom was offered to any slave who would reveal the plot. Many witnesses rushed forward with foolish and contradictory stories; the jails were filled with the accused; and more than thirty of the miserable creatures, with hardly the form of a trial, were convicted and then hanged or burned to death. Others were transported and sold as slaves in foreign lands. As soon as the supposed peril had passed and the excited people regained their senses, it came to be doubted whether the whole shocking affair had not been the result of terror and fanaticism. The verdict of after times has been *that there was no plot at all.*

During the progress of King George's War the territory of New York was several times invaded by the French and Indians. But the invasions were feeble and easily repelled. Except the abandonment of a few villages in the northern part of the State and the destruction of a small amount of exposed property, little harm was done to the province. The alliance of the fierce Mohawks with the English always made the invasion of New York by the French an exploit of more danger than profit. The treaty of Aix-la-Chapelle, concluded in 1748, again brought peace and prosperity to the people.

Notwithstanding the central position of New York, her growth was slow, her development unsteady, and her prospects darkened with much adversity. In population she stood, at the outbreak of the French and

Indian war, but *sixth* in a list of the colonies. Massachusetts, Connecticut, Pennsylvania, Maryland, and Virginia had all outstripped her in the race. But the elements of future renown were nowhere else more abundantly bestowed. Here at the foot of her principal city lay the most convenient and commodious harbor on the Atlantic. A magnificent river—draining the country as far as where, at Onondaga, burned the great council-fire of the Six Nations—rolled down through fruitful valleys to join the waters of the bay. Best of all, the people who inhabited the noble province were ever ready to resist oppression, bold to defend their rights, and zealous in the cause of freedom.

Such is the history of the little colony planted on Manhattan Island. A hundred and thirty years have passed since the first feeble settlements were made; now the great valley of the Hudson is filled with beautiful farms and teeming villages. The Walloons of Flanders and the Puritans of New England have blended into a common people. Discord and contention, though bitter while they lasted, have borne only the peaceful fruit of colonial liberty. There are other and greater struggles through which New York must pass, other burdens to be borne, other calamities to be endured, other fires in which her sons must be tried and purified, before they gain their freedom. But the oldest and greatest of the middle colonies has entered upon a glorious career, and the ample foundations of an EMPIRE STATE are securely laid.

COLONIAL HISTORY.—CONTINUED.

MINOR EASTERN COLONIES.

CHAPTER XXI.

CONNECTICUT.

THE history of Connecticut begins with the year 1630. The first grant of the territory was made by the council of Plymouth to the earl of Warwick; and in March of 1631 the claim was transferred by him to Lord Say-and-Seal, Lord Brooke, John Hampden and others. Before a colony could be planted by the proprietors, the Dutch of New Netherland reached the Connecticut River and built at Hartford their fort, called the House of Good Hope. The people of New Plymouth immediately organized and sent out a force to counteract this movement of their rivals. The territorial claim of the Puritans extended not only over Connecticut, but over New Netherland itself and onward to the west. Should the intruding Dutch colonists of Manhattan be allowed to move eastward and take possession of the finest valley in New England? Certainly not.

The English expedition reached the mouth of the Connecticut and sailed up the river. When the little squadron came opposite the House of Good Hope, the commander of the garrison ordered Captain Holmes, the English officer, to strike his colors; but the order was treated with derision. The Dutch threatened to fire in case the fleet should attempt to pass; but the English defiantly hoisted sails and proceeded up the river. The puny cannons of the House of Good Hope remained cold and silent. At a point just below the mouth of the Farmington, seven miles above Hartford, the Puritans landed and built the block-house of Windsor.

Roger Williams Opposing the Pequot Emissaries.

In October of 1635 a colony of sixty persons left Boston, traversed the forests of Central Massachusetts, and settled at Hartford, Windsor and Wethersfield. Earlier in the same year the younger Winthrop, a man who in all the virtues of a noble life was a worthy rival of his father, the governor of Massachusetts, arrived in New England. He bore a commission from the proprietors of the Western colony to build a fort at the mouth of the Connecticut River, and to prevent the further encroachments of the Dutch. The fortress was hastily completed and the guns mounted just in time to prevent the entrance of a Dutch trading-vessel which appeared at the mouth of the river. Such was the founding of Saybrook, so named in honor of the proprietors, Lords Say-and-Seal and Brooke. Thus was the most important river of New England brought under the dominion of the Puritans; the solitary Dutch settlement at Hartford was cut off from succor and left to dwindle into insignificance.

To the early annals of Connecticut belongs the sad story of THE PEQUOD WAR. The country west of the Thames was more thickly peopled with savages than any other portion of New England. The haughty and warlike Pequods were alone able to muster seven hundred warriors. The whole effective force of the English colonists did not amount to two hundred men. But the superior numbers of the cunning and revengeful savages were more than balanced by the unflinching courage and destructive weapons of the English.

The first act of violence was committed in the year 1633. The crew of a small trading-vessel were ambushed and murdered on the banks of the Connecticut. An Indian embassy went to Boston to apologize for the crime; the nation was forgiven and received in friendship. A treaty was patched up, the Pequods acknowledging the supremacy of the English and promising to become civilized. The Narragansetts, the hereditary enemies of the Pequods, had already yielded to the authority of Massachusetts and promised obedience to her laws. A reconciliation was thus effected between the two hostile races of savages. But as soon as the Pequods were freed from their old fear of the Narragansetts, they began to violate their recent treaty with the English. Oldham, the worthy captain of a trading-vessel, was murdered near Block Island. A company of militia pursued the perpetrators of the outrage and gave them a bloody punishment. All the slumbering hatred and suppressed rage of the nation burst forth, and the war began in earnest.

In this juncture of affairs the Pequods attempted a piece of dangerous diplomacy. A persistent effort was made to induce the Narragansetts and the Mohegans to join in a war of extermination against the English; and the plot was wellnigh successful. But the heroic Roger Williams, faithful in his misfortunes, sent a letter to Sir Henry Vane, governor of Massachusetts, warned him of the impending danger, and volunteered his services to defeat the conspiracy. The governor replied, urging Williams to use his utmost endeavors to thwart the threatened alliance. Embarking alone in a frail canoe, the exile left Providence, which he had founded only a month before, and drifted out into Narragansett Bay. Every moment it seemed that the poor little boat with its lonely passenger would be swallowed up; but his courage and skill as an oarsman at last brought him to the shore in safety. Proceeding at once to the house of Canonicus, king of the Narragansetts, he found the painted and bloody ambassadors of the Pequods already there. For three days and nights, at the deadly peril of his life, he pleaded with Canonicus and Miantonomoh to reject the proposals of the hostile tribe, and to stand fast in their allegiance to the English. His noble efforts were successful; the wavering Narragansetts voted to remain at peace, and the disappointed Pequod chiefs were sent away.

The Mohegans also rejected the proposed alliance. Uncas, the sachem of that nation, not only remained faithful to the whites, but furnished a party of warriors to aid them against the Pequods. In the meantime, repeated acts of violence had roused the colony to vengeance. During the winter of 1636-37 many murders were committed in the neighborhood of Saybrook. In the following April a massacre occurred at Wethersfield, in which nine persons were butchered. On the 1st day of May the three towns of Connecticut declared war. Sixty gallant volunteers—one-third of the whole effective force of the colony—were put under command of Captain John Mason of Hartford. Seventy Mohegans joined the expedition; and the thoughtful Sir Henry Vane sent Captain Under hill with twenty soldiers from Boston.

The descent from Hartford to Saybrook occupied one day. On the 20th of the month the expedition, sailing eastward, passed the mouth of the Thames; here was the principal seat of the Pequod nation. When the savages saw the squadron go by without attempting to land, they set up shouts of exultation, and persuaded themselves that the English were afraid to hazard battle. But the poor natives had sadly mistaken the men with whom they had to deal. The fleet proceeded quietly into Narragansett Bay and anchored in the harbor of Wickford. Here the troops landed and began their march into the country of the Pequods. After one day's advance, Mason reached the cabin of Canonicus and Miantonomoh, sachems of the Narragansetts. Them he attempted to persuade to join him against the common enemy; but the wary chieftains, knowing the prowess of the Pequods, and fearing that the English might be defeated, decided to remain neutral.

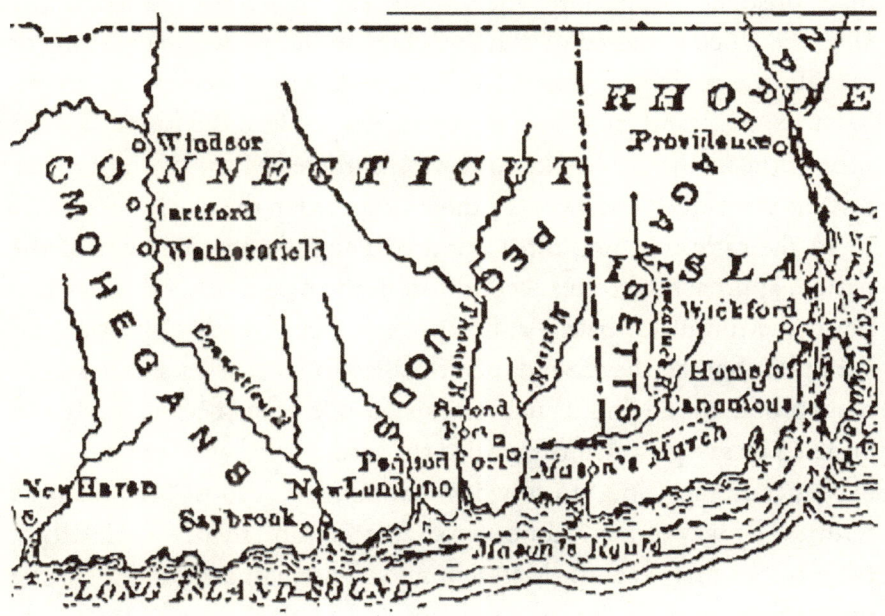

Scene of the Pequod War.

On the evening of the 25th of May the troops of Connecticut came within hearing of the Pequod fort. The unsuspecting warriors spent their last night on earth in uproar and jubilee. At two o'clock in the morning the English soldiers rose suddenly from their places of concealment and rushed forward to the fort. A dog ran howling among the wigwams, and the warriors sprang to arms, only to receive a deadly volley from the English muskets. The fearless assailants leaped over the puny palisades and began the work of death; but the savages rose on every side in such numbers that Mason's men were about to be overwhelmed. "Burn them! burn them!" shouted the dauntless captain, seizing a flaming mat and running to the windward of the cabins. "Burn them!" resounded on every side; and in a few minutes the dry wigwams were one sheet of crackling flame. The English and Mohegans hastily withdrew to the ramparts. The yelling savages found themselves begirt with fire. They ran round and round like wild beasts in a burning circus. If one of the wretched creatures burst through the flames, it was only to meet certain death from a broadsword or a musket-ball. The destruction was complete and awful. Only seven warriors escaped; seven others were made prisoners. Six hundred men, women and children perished, nearly all of them being roasted to death in a hideous heap. Before the rising of the sun the pride and glory of the Pequods had passed away forever. Sassacus, the grand sachem of the tribe, escaped into the forest, fled for protection to the Mohawks, and was murdered. Two of the English soldiers were killed and twenty others wounded in the battle.

In the early morning three hundred Pequods, the remnant of the nation, approached from a second fort in the neighborhood. They had heard the tumult of battle, and supposed their friends victorious. To their utter horror, they found their fortified town in ashes and nearly all their proud tribe lying in one blackened pile of half-burnt flesh and bones. The savage warriors stamped the earth, yelled and tore their hair in desperate rage, and ran howling through the woods. Mason's men returned by way of New London to Saybrook, and thence to Hartford. New troops arrived from Massachusetts. The remnants of the hostile nation were pursued into the swamps and thickets west of Saybrook. Every wigwam of the Pequods was burned, and every field laid waste. The remaining two hundred panting fugitives were hunted to death or captivity. The prisoners were distributed as servants among the Narragansetts and Mohegans; a few were sold as slaves. The first war between the English colonists and the natives had ended in the overthrow and destruction of one of the most powerful tribes of New England. For many years the other nations, when tempted to hostility, remembered the fate of the Pequods.

The final capture of the Pequod fugitives was made at Fairfield, on Long Island Sound, fifty miles south-west from Saybrook. The English thus became better acquainted with the coast west of the mouth of the Connecticut. Some men of Boston were delighted with the beautiful plain between the Wallingford and West Rivers. Here they tarried over winter, building some cabins and exploring the country; such was the founding of NEW HAVEN. Shortly afterward, a Puritan colony from England, under the leadership of Theophilus Eaton and John Davenport, arrived at Boston. Hearing of the beauty of the country on the sound, the new immigrants again set sail, and about the middle of April reached New Haven. On the morning of the first Sabbath after their arrival the colonists assembled for worship under a spreading oak; and Davenport, their minister, preached a touching and appropriate sermon on THE TEMPTATION IN THE WILDERNESS. The next care was to make an honorable purchase of land from the Indians—a policy which was ever afterward faithfully adhered to by the colony. For the first year there was no government except a simple covenant, into which the settlers entered, that all would be obedient to the rules of Scripture.

In June of 1639 the leading men of New Haven held a convention *in a barn*, and formally adopted the Bible as the constitution of the State. Everything was strictly conformed to the religious standard. The government was called the House of Wisdom, of which Eaton, Davenport and five others were the seven Pillars. None but church members were admitted to the rights of citizenship. All offices were to be filled by the votes of the freemen at an annual election. For twenty years consecutively, Mr. Eaton—first and greatest of the pillars—was chosen governor of the colony. Other settlers came, and pleasant villages sprang up on both shores of Long Island Sound.

Civil government began in Connecticut in the year 1639. Until that time the Western colonies had been subject to Massachusetts, and had scarcely thought of independence. But when the soldiers of Hartford returned victorious from the Pequod war, the exulting people began to think of a separate commonwealth. If they could fight their own battles, could they not make their own laws? Delegates from the three towns came together at Hartford, and on the 14th of January a constitution was framed for the colony. The new instrument was one of the most simple and liberal ever adopted. An oath of allegiance to the State was the only qualification of citizenship. No recognition of the English king or of any foreign authority was required. Different religious opinions were alike tolerated and respected. All the officers of the colony were to be chosen by ballot at an annual election. The law-making power was vested in a general assembly, and the representatives were apportioned among the towns according to population. Neither Saybrook nor New Haven adopted this constitution, by which the other colonies in the valley of the Connecticut were united in a common government.

In 1643, Connecticut became a member of the Union of New England. Into this confederacy New Haven was also admitted; and in the next year Saybrook was purchased of George Fenwick, one of the proprietors, and permanently annexed to Connecticut. The anticipated difficulties with the Dutch of New Netherland had made the colonies of the West anxious for a closer union with Massachusetts. The fears of the people were not entirely quieted until 1650, when Governor Stuyvesant met the commissioners of Connecticut at Hartford, and established the western boundary of the province. This measure promised peace; but in 1651 war broke out between England and Holland, and notwithstanding the recent pledges of friendship, New England and New Netherland were wellnigh drawn into the conflict. Stuyvesant was suspected of inciting the Indians against the English; a declaration of war was proposed before the delegates of the united colonies, and was only prevented from passing by the veto of Massachusetts. Left without support, Connecticut and New Haven next sought aid from Cromwell, who entered heartily into the project and sent out a fleet to co-operate with the colonists in the reduction of New Netherland. But while the western towns were busily preparing for war, the news of peace arrived, and hostilities were happily averted.

On the restoration of monarchy in England, Connecticut made haste to recognize King Charles as rightful sovereign. It was as much an act of sound policy as of loyal zeal. The people of the Connecticut valley were eager for a royal charter. They had conquered the Pequods; they had bought the lands of the Mohegans; they had purchased the claims of the earl of Warwick; it only remained to secure all these acquisitions with a patent from the king. The infant republic selected its best and truest man, the scholarly younger Winthrop, and sent him as ambassador to London. He bore with him a charter which had been carefully prepared by the authorities of Hartford; the problem was to induce the king to sign it.

The aged Lord Say-and-Seal, for many years the friend and benefactor of the colony, was now an important officer of the Crown. To him Winthrop delivered a letter, unfolded his plans and appealed for help; and the appeal was not in vain. The earl of Manchester, lord chamberlain to the king, was induced to lend his aid. Winthrop easily obtained an audience with the sovereign, and did not fail to show him a ring which Charles I. had given as a pledge of friendship to Winthrop's grandfather. The little token so moved the wayward monarch's feelings that in a moment of careless magnanimity he signed the colonial charter without the alteration of a letter. Winthrop returned to the rejoicing colony, bearing a patent the most liberal and ample ever granted by an English monarch. The power of governing themselves was conferred on the people without qualification or restriction. Every right of sovereignty and of independence, except the name, was conceded to the new State. The

The Younger Winthrop.

territory included under the charter extended from the bay and river of the Narragansetts westward to the Pacific. The people who had built the House of Wisdom at New Haven now found themselves the unwilling subjects of the new commonwealth of Connecticut.

For fourteen years the excellent Winthrop was annually chosen governor of the colony. Every year added largely to the population and wealth of the province. The civil and religious institutions were the freest and best in New England. Peace reigned; the husbandman was undisturbed in the field, the workman in his shop. Even during King Philip's War, Connecticut was saved from invasion. Not a war-whoop was heard, not a hamlet burned, not a life lost, within her borders. Her soldiers made common cause with their brethren of Massachusetts and Rhode Island; but their own homes were saved from the desolations of war.

In July of 1675, Sir Edmund Andros, the governor of New York, arrived with an armed sloop at the mouth of the Connecticut. Orders were sent to Captain Bull, who commanded the fort at Saybrook, to surrender his post; but the brave captain replied by hoisting the flag of England and assuring the bearer of the message that his master would better retire. Andros, however, landed and came to a parley with the officers of the fort. He began to read his commission, but was ordered to stop. In vain did the arrogant magistrate insist that the dominions of the duke of York extended from the Connecticut to the Delaware. "Connecticut has her own charter, signed by His Gracious Majesty King Charles II.," said Captain Bull. "Leave of your reading, or take the consequences!" The argument prevailed, and the red-coated governor, trembling with rage, was escorted to his boat by a company of Saybrook militia.

In 1686, when Andros was made royal governor of New England, Connecticut was again included in his jurisdiction. The first year of his administration was spent in establishing his authority in Massachusetts, Rhode Island and New Hampshire. In the following October he made his famous visit to Hartford. On the day of his arrival he invaded the provincial assembly while in session, seized the book of minutes, and with his own hand wrote FINIS at the bottom of the page. He demanded the immediate surrender of the colonial charter. Governor Treat pleaded long and earnestly for the preservation of the precious document. Andros was inexorable. The shades of evening fell. Joseph Wadsworth found in the gathering darkness an opportunity to conceal the cherished parchment—a deed which has made his own name and the name of a tree immortal. Two years later, when the government of Andros was over thrown, Connecticut made haste to restore her liberties.

In the autumn of 1693, another attempt was made to subvert the freedom of the colony. Fletcher, the governor of New York, went to Hartford to assume command of the militia of the province. He bore a commission from King William; but by the terms of the charter the right of commanding the troops was vested in the colony itself. The general assembly refused to recognize the authority of Fletcher, who, nevertheless, ordered the soldiers under arms and proceeded to read his commission as colonel. "Beat the drums!" shouted Captain Wadsworth, who stood at the head of the company. "Silence!" said Fletcher; the drums ceased, and the reading began again. "Drum! drum!" cried Wadsworth; and a second time the voice of the reader was drowned in the uproar. "Silence! silence!" shouted the enraged governor. The dauntless Wadsworth stepped before the ranks and said, "Colonel Fletcher, if I am interrupted again, I will let the sunshine through your body in an instant." That ended the controversy. Benjamin Fletcher thought it better to be a living governor of New York than a dead colonel of the Connecticut militia.

"I give these books for the founding of a college in this colony." Such were the words of ten ministers who, in the year 1700, assembled at the village of Branford, a few miles east of New Haven. Each of the worthy fathers, as he uttered the words, deposited a few volumes on the table around which they were sitting; such was the founding of YALE COLLEGE. In 1702 the school was formally opened at Saybrook, where it continued for fifteen years, and was then removed to New Haven. One of the most liberal patrons of the college was Elihu Yale, from whom the famous institution of learning derived its name. Common schools had existed in almost every village of Connecticut since the planting of the colony. The children of the Pilgrims have never forgotten the cause of education.

The half century preceding the French and Indian war was a period of prosperity to all the western districts of New England. Connecticut was especially favored. Almost unbroken peace reigned throughout her borders. The blessings of a free commonwealth were realized in full measure. The farmer reaped his fields in cheerfulness and hope. The mechanic made glad his dusty shop with anecdote and song. The merchant feared no duty, the villager no taxes. Want was unknown and pauperism unheard of. Wealth was little cared for and crime of rare occurrence among a people with whom intelligence and virtue were the only foundations of nobility. With fewer dark pages in her history, less austerity of manners and greater liberality of sentiment, Connecticut had all the lofty purposes and shining virtues of Massachusetts. The visions of Hooker and Haynes, and the dreams of the quiet Winthrop, were more than realized in the happy homes of the Connecticut valley.

CHAPTER XXII.

RHODE ISLAND.

IT was in June of 1636 that the exiled Roger Williams left the country of the Wampanoags and passed down the Seekonk to Narragansett River. His object was to secure a safe retreat beyond the limits of Plymouth colony. He, with his five companions, landed on the western bank, at a place called Moshassuck, purchased the soil of the Narragansett sachems, and laid the foundations of Providence. Other exiles joined the company. New farms were laid out, new fields were ploughed and new houses built; here, at last, was found at PROVIDENCE PLANTATION a refuge for all the distressed and persecuted.

The leader of the new colony was a native of Wales; born in 1606; liberally educated at Cambridge; the pupil of Sir Edward Coke; in after years the friend of Milton; a dissenter; a hater of ceremonies; a disciple of truth in its purest forms; an uncompromising advocate of freedom; exiled *to* Massachusetts, and now exiled *by* Massachusetts, he brought to the banks of the Narragansett the great doctrines of perfect religious liberty and the equal rights of men. If the area of Rhode Island had corresponded with the grandeur of the principles on which she was founded, who could have foretold her destiny?

Roger Williams belonged to that most radical body of dissenters called Anabaptists. By them the validity of infant baptism was denied. Williams himself had been baptized in infancy; but his views in regard to the value of the ceremony had undergone a change during his ministry at Salem. Now that he had freed himself from all foreign authority both of Church and State, he conceived it to be his duty to receive a second baptism. But who should perform the ceremony? Ezekiel Holliman, a layman, was selected for the sacred duty. Williams meekly received the rite at the hands of his friend, and then in turn baptized him and ten other exiles of the colony. Such was the organization of THE FIRST BAPTIST CHURCH in America.

The beginning of civil government in Rhode Island was equally simple and democratic. Mr. Williams was the natural ruler of the little province, but be reserved for himself neither wealth nor privilege. The lands which he purchased from Canonicus and Miantonomoh were freely distributed among the colonists. Only two small fields, to be planted and tilled with his own hands, were kept by the benevolent founder for himself. How different from the grasping avarice of Wingfield and Lord Cornbury! All the powers of the colonial government were entrusted to the people. A simple agreement was made and signed by the settlers that in all matters not affecting the conscience they would yield a cheerful obedience to such rules as the majority might make for the public welfare. In questions of religion the individual conscience should be to every man a guide. When Massachusetts objected that such a democracy would leave nothing for the magistrates to do, Rhode Island answered that magistrates were wellnigh useless.

The new government stood the test of experience. The evil prophecies of its enemies were unfulfilled; instead of predicted turmoil and dissension, Providence Plantation had nothing but peace and quiet. It was found that all religious sects could live together in harmony, and that difference of opinion was not a bar to friendship. All beliefs were welcome at Narragansett Bay. A Buddhist from Japan or a pagan from Madagascar would have been received at Providence and cordially entertained. Miantonomoh, the young sachem of the Narragansetts, loved Roger Williams as a brother. It was the confidence of this chieftain that enabled Williams to notify Massachusetts of the Pequod conspiracy, and then at the hazard of his life to defeat the plans of the hostile nation. This magnanimous act awakened the old affections of his friends at Salem and Plymouth, and an effort was made to recall him and his fellow-exiles from banishment. It was urged that a man of such gracious abilities, so full of patience and charity, could never be dangerous in a State; but his enemies answered that the principles and teachings of Williams would subvert the commonwealth and bring Massachusetts to ruin. The proposal was rejected. The ancient Greeks sometimes recalled their exiled heroes from banishment; the colony of Massachusetts, never.

The Old Stone Tower at Newport.

During the Pequod war of 1637, Rhode Island was protected by the friendly Narragansetts. The territory of this powerful tribe lay between Providence and the country of the Pequods, and there was little fear of an invasion. The next year was noted for the arrival of Mrs. Hutchinson and her friends at the island of Rhode Island. The leaders of the company were John Clarke and William Coddington. It had been their intention to conduct the colony to Long Island, or perhaps to the country of the Delaware. But Roger Williams made haste to welcome them to his province, where no man's conscience might be distressed.

Governor Vane of Massachusetts, sympathizing with the refugees, prevailed with Miantonomoh to make them a gift of Rhode Island. Here, in the early spring of 1638, the colony was planted. The first settlement was made at Portsmouth, in the northern part of the island. Other exiles came to join their friends, and civil government was thought desirable. The Jewish nation furnished the model. William Coddington was chosen judge in the new Israel of Narragansett Bay, and three elders were appointed to assist him in the government. In the following year the title of judge gave way to that of governor, and the administration became more modern in its methods. At the same time a party of colonists removed from Portsmouth, already crowded with exiles, to the south-western part of the island, and laid the foundations of NEWPORT. Hither had come, more than six hundred years before, the hardy adventurers of Iceland. Here had been a favorite haunt of the wayward sea kings of the eleventh century. Here, in sight of the new settlement, stood the old stone tower, the most celebrated monument left by the Norsemen in America.

The island was soon peopled. The want of civil government began to be felt as a serious inconvenience. Mr. Coddington's new Israel had proved an utter failure. In March of 1641 a public meeting was convened the citizens came together on terms of perfect equality, and the task of framing a constitution was undertaken. In three days the instrument was completed. The government was declared to be a "DEMOCRACIE," or government by the people. The supreme authority was lodged with the whole body of freemen in the island; and freemen, in this instance, meant everybody. The vote of the majority should always rule. No soul should be distressed on account of religious doctrine Liberty of conscience, even in the smallest particular, should be universally respected. A seal of State was ordered, having for its design a sheaf of arrows and a motto of AMOR VINCET OMNIA. The little republic of Narragansett Bay was named the Plantation of Rhode Island.

In 1643 was formed the Union of New England. Providence and Rhode Island both pleaded for admission, and both were rejected. The meaning of this illiberal action on the part of the older and more powerful colonies was that the settlements on the Narragansett belonged to the jurisdiction of Plymouth. Alarmed at the prospect of being again put under the dominion of their persecutors, the exiled republicans of Rhode Island determined to appeal to the English government for a charter. Roger Williams was accordingly appointed agent of the two plantations and sent to London. He was cordially received by his old and steadfast friend Sir Henry Vane, now an influential member of Parliament. The plea of Rhode Island was heard with favor; and on the 14th of March in the following year the coveted charter was granted. Great was the rejoicing when the successful ambassador returned to his people. The grateful colonists met their benefactor at Seekonk, and conducted him to Providence with shouts and exultation. Rhode Island had secured her independence.

The first general assembly of the province was convened at Portsmouth, in 1647. The new government was organized in strict accordance with the provisions of the charter. A code of laws was framed; the principles of democracy were reaffirmed, and full religious toleration and freedom of conscience guaranteed to all. A president and subordinate officers were chosen, and Rhode Island began her career as an independent colony.

Once the integrity of the province was endangered. In 1651 William Coddington, who had never been satisfied with the failure of his Jewish commonwealth, succeeded in obtaining from the English council of state a decree by which the island of Rhode Island was separated from the common government. But the zealous protests of John Clarke and Roger Williams, who went a second time to London, prevented the disunion, and the decree of separation was revoked. The grateful people now desired that their magnanimous benefactor should be commissioned by the English council as governor of the province; but the blind gratitude of his friends could not prevail over the wisdom of the prudent leader. He foresaw the danger, and refused the tempting commission. Roger Williams was proof against all the seductions of ambition.

The faithful Clarke remained in England to guard the interests of the colony. It was not long until his services were greatly needed. The restoration of monarchy occurred in 1660. Charles II. came home in triumph from his long exile. Rhode Island had accepted a charter from the Long Parliament; that Parliament had driven Charles I. from his throne, had made war upon him, beaten him in battle, imprisoned him, beheaded him. Was it likely that the son of that monarch would allow a colonial charter issued by the Long Parliament to stand? Would he not with vindictive scorn dash the patent of the little republic out of existence? The people of Rhode Island had hardly the courage to plead for the preservation of their liberty but taking heart, they wrote a loyal petition to the new sovereign, praying for the renewal of their charter. To their infinite delight, and to the wonder of after times, the king listened with favor; Clarendon, the minister, assented; and on the 8th of July, 1663, the charter was reissued. The freedom of the colony was in no wise restricted. All the liberal provisions of the parliamentary patent were revived. Not even an oath of allegiance was required of the people.

On the 24th of November the island of Rhode Island was thronged with people. George Baxter had come with the charter. Opening the box that contained it, he held aloft the precious parchment. There, sure enough, was the signature of King Charles II. There was His Majesty's royal stamp; there was the broad seal of England. The charter was read aloud to the joyful people. The little "democracie" of Rhode Island was safe. The happy colonists were not to blame when they began their letter of thanks as follows: "To King Charles of England, for his high and inestimable—yea, incomparable—favor."

For nearly a quarter of a century Rhode Island prospered. The distresses of King Philip's War were forgotten. Roger Williams grew old and died. At last came Sir Edmund Andros, the enemy of New England. After overthrowing the liberties of Massachusetts, he next demanded the surrender of the charter of Rhode Island. The demand was for a while evaded by Governor Walter Clarke and the colonial assembly. But Andros, not to be thwarted, repaired to Newport, dissolved the government and broke the seal of the colony. Five irresponsible councilors were appointed to control the affairs of the province, and the commonwealth was in ruins.

But the usurpation was as brief as it was shameful. In the spring of 1689 the news was borne to Rhode Island that James II. had abdicated the throne of England, and that Andros and his officers were prisoners at Boston. On May-day the people rushed to Newport and made a proclamation of their gratitude for the great deliverance. Walter Clarke was reelected governor, but was fearful of accepting. Almy was elected, and also declined. Then an old Quaker, named Henry Bull, more than eighty years of age, was chosen. He was one of the founders of the colony. He had known Anne Hutchinson and Roger Williams. Should he, in his gray hairs, through fear and timidity, refuse the post of danger? The old veteran accepted the trust, and spent his last days in restoring the liberties of Rhode Island.

Again the little State around the Bay of Narragansett was prosperous. For more than fifty years the peace of the colony was undisturbed. The principles of the illustrious founder became the principles of the commonwealth. The renown of Rhode Island has not been in vastness of territory, in mighty cities or victorious armies, but in a steadfast devotion to truth, justice and freedom.

CHAPTER XXIII.

NEW HAMPSHIRE.

IN the year 1622 the territory lying between the rivers Merrimac and Kennebec, reaching from the sea to the St. Lawrence, was granted by the council of Plymouth to Sir Ferdinand Gorges and John Mason. The history of New Hampshire begins with the following year. For the proprietors made haste to secure their new domain by actual settlements. In the early spring of 1623 two small companies of colonists were sent out by Mason and Gorges to people their province. The coast of New Hampshire had first been visited by Martin Pring in 1603. Eleven years later the restless Captain Smith explored the spacious harbor at the mouth of the Piscataqua, and spoke with delight of the deep and tranquil waters.

One party of the new immigrants landed at Little Harbor, two miles south of the present site of Portsmouth, and began to build a village. The other party proceeded up stream, entered the Cocheco, and, four miles above the mouth of that tributary, laid the foundations of Dover. With the exception of Plymouth and Weymouth, Portsmouth and Dover are the oldest towns in New England. But the progress of the settlements was slow; for many years the two villages were only fishing-stations. In 1629 the proprietors divided their dominions, Gorges retaining the part north of the Piscataqua, and Mason taking exclusive control of the district between the Piscataqua and the Merrimac. In May of this year, Rev. John Wheelwright, who soon afterward became a leader in the party of Anne Hutchinson, visited the Abenaki chieftains, and purchased their claims to the soil of the whole territory held by Mason; but in the following November, Mason's title was confirmed by a second patent from the council, and the name of the province was changed from Laconia to NEW HAMPSHIRE. Very soon Massachusetts began to urge her chartered rights to the district north of the Merrimac; already the claims to the jurisdiction of the new colony were numerous and conflicting.

In November of 1635, Mason died, and his widow undertook the government of the province. But the expenses of the colony were greater than the revenues; the chief tenants could not be paid for their services; and after a few years of mismanagement the territory was given up to the servants and dependents of the late proprietor. Such was the condition of affairs when Mrs. Hutchinson and her friends were banished from Boston. Wheelwright, who was of the number, now found use for the lands which he had purchased in New Hampshire. When Clarke and Coddington, leading the greater number of the exiles, set out for Rhode Island, Wheelwright, with a small party of friends, repaired to the banks of the Piscataqua. At the head of tide-water on that stream they halted, and founded the village of Exeter. The little colony was declared a republic, established on the principle of equal right and universal toleration.

The proposition to unite New Hampshire with Massachusetts was received with favor by the people of both colonies. The liberal provisions of the Body of Liberties, adopted by the older province in 1641, excited the villagers of the Piscataqua, and made them anxious to join the destinies of the free commonwealth of Massachusetts. A union was immediately proposed; on the 14th of the following April terms of consolidation were agreed on, and New Hampshire, by the act of her own people, was united with the older colony. It is worthy of special notice that the law of Massachusetts restricting the rights of citizenship to church members was not extended over the new province. The people of Portsmouth and Dover belonged to the Church of England, and it was deemed unjust to discriminate against them on account of their religion. New Hampshire was the only colony east of the Hudson not originally founded by the Puritans.

The union continued in force until 1679. In the mean time the heirs of Mason had revived the claim of the old proprietor of the province. The cause had been duly investigated in the courts of England, and in 1677 a decision was reached that the Masonian claims were invalid as to the *civil jurisdiction* of New Hampshire, but valid as to the *soil*—that is, the heirs were the lawful owners, but not the lawful governors, of the territory. It was evident from the character of this decision that King

Charles intended to assert his own right of government over New Hampshire, and at the same time to confer the ownership of the soil upon the representatives of Mason. Nor was the province long left in doubt as to the king's intentions. On the 24th of July, 1679, a decree was published by which New Hampshire was separated from the jurisdiction of Massachusetts and organized as a distinct royal province. The excuse was that the claims of the Masons against the farmers of New Hampshire would have to be determined in colonial courts, and that colonial courts could not be established without the organization of a separate colony. It was clearly foreseen that in such trials the courts of Massachusetts would always decide against the Masons. The purpose of the king became still more apparent when Robert Mason, himself the largest claimant of all, was allowed to nominate a governor for the province: Edward Cranfield was selected for that office.

The people of New Hampshire were greatly excited by the threatened destruction of their liberties. Before Cranfield's arrival the rugged sawyers and lumbermen of the Piscataqua had convened a general assembly at Portsmouth. The first resolution which was passed by the representatives showed the spirit of colonial resistance in full force. "NO act, imposition, law or ordinance," said the sturdy legislators, "shall be valid unless made by the assembly and approved by the people." When the indignant king heard of this resolution, he declared it to be both wicked and absurd. It was not the first time that a monarch and his people had disagreed.

In November of 1682, Cranfield dismissed the popular assembly. Such a despotic act had never before been attempted in New England. The excitement ran high; the governor was openly denounced, and his claims for rents and forfeitures were stubbornly resisted. At Exeter the sheriff was beaten with clubs. The farmers' wives met the tax-gatherers with pailfulls of hot water. At the village of Hampton, Cranfield's deputy was led out of town with a rope round his neck. When the governor ordered out the militia, not a man obeyed the summons. It was in the midst of these broils that Cranfield, unable to collect his rents and vexed out of his wits, wrote to England begging for the privilege of going home. The "unreasonable" people who were all the time caviling at his commission and denying his authority were at length freed from his presence.

An effort was now made to restore New Hampshire to the jurisdiction of Massachusetts; but before this could be done the charter of the latter province had been taken away and Edmund Andros appointed governor of all New England. The colonies north of the Merrimac, seeing that even Massachusetts had been brought to submission, offered no resistance to Andros, but quietly yielded to his authority. Until the English revolution of 1688, and the consequent downfall of Andros, New Hampshire remained under the dominion of the royal governor. But when he was seized and imprisoned by the citizens of Boston, the people of the northern towns also rose in rebellion and reasserted their freedom. A general assembly was convened at Portsmouth in the spring of 1690, and an ordinance was at once passed reannexing New Hampshire to Massachusetts. But in August of 1692 this action was annulled by the English government, and the two provinces were a second time separated against the protests of the people. In 1698, when the earl of Bellomont came out as royal governor of New York, his commission was made to include both Massachusetts and New Hampshire. For a period of forty-two years the two provinces, though retaining their separate legislative assemblies, continued under the authority of a common executive. Not until 1741 was a final separation effected between the colonies north and south of the Merrimac.

Meanwhile, the heirs of Mason, embarrassed with delays and vexed by opposing claimants, had sold to Samuel Allen, of London, their title to New Hampshire. To him, in 1691, the old Masonian patent was transferred. His son-in-law, named Usher, a land speculator of Boston, was appointed deputy governor. The new proprietor made a long and futile effort to enforce his claim to the lands of the province, but was everywhere resisted. Lawsuits were begun in the colonial courts, but no judgments could be obtained against the occupants of lands; all efforts to drive the farmers into the payment of rents or the surrender of their homes were unavailing. For many years the history of New Hampshire contains little else than a record of strife and contention. Finally, Allen died; and in 1715, after a struggle of a quarter of a century, his heirs abandoned their claim in despair. A few years afterward one of the descendants of Mason discovered that the deed which his kinsmen had made to Allen was defective. The original Masonian patent was accordingly revived, and a last effort was made to secure possession of the province, but was all in vain. The colonial government had now grown strong enough to defend the rights of its people, and the younger Masons were obliged to abandon their pretensions. In the final adjustment of this long-standing difficulty the colonial authorities allowed the validity of the Masonian patent as to *the unoccupied portions* of the territory, and the heirs made a formal surrender of their claims to all the rest.

Of all the New England colonies, New Hampshire suffered most from the French and Indian Wars. Her settlements were feeble, and her territory most exposed to savage invasion. In the last year of King Philip's War the suffering along the frontier of the province was very great. Again, in the wars of William, Anne and George, the villages of the northern colony were visited with devastation and ruin. But in the intervals of peace the spirits of the people revived, and the hardy settlers returned to their wasted farms to begin anew the struggle of life. Out of these conflicts and trials came that sturdy and resolute race of pioneers who bore such a heroic part in the greater contests of after years.

Such is the story of the planting, progress, and development of New England. Hither had come, in the beginning, a people of sober habits, frugal lives, and lofty purposes. Before their imagination was one vision—the vision of freedom. And freedom to the men who laid the foundations of civilization in New England meant the breaking off of every species of thralldom. These people came to the New World *to stay*. They voluntarily chose the wilderness with its forests, and snows, and savages. For forests, and snows, and savages were better than luxury with despotism. In Virginia as late as the middle of the eighteenth century many of the planters still locked fondly across the ocean and spoke of England as their "home." Not so with the people whose hamlets were scattered from the Penobscot to the Housatonic. With them the humble cabin in the frozen woods under the desolate sky of winter was a cheerful and sunny "home"—if only FREEDOM was written on the threshold.

COLONIAL HISTORY.—CONTINUED.

MINOR MIDDLE COLONIES.

CHAPTER XXIV.

NEW JERSEY.

THE colonial history of New Jersey properly begins with the founding of Elizabethtown, in 1664. As early as 1618 a feeble trading station had been established at Bergen, west of the Hudson; but forty years elapsed before permanent dwellings were built in that neighborhood. In 1623 the block-house, called Fort Nassau, was erected at the mouth of Timber Creek, on the Delaware; after a few months' occupancy, May and his companions abandoned the place and returned to New Amsterdam. Six years later the southern part of the present State of New Jersey was granted to Godyn and Blomaert, two of the Dutch patroons; but no settlement was made. In 1634 there was not a single European living between Delaware Bay and the fortieth degree of latitude. In 1651 a considerable district, including the site of Elizabethtown, was purchased by Augustine Herman; but still no colony was planted. Seven years afterwards a larger grant, embracing the old trading house at Bergen, was made; and in 1663 a company of Puritans, living on Long Island, obtained permission of Governor Stuyvesant to settle on the banks of the Raritan; but no settlement was effected until after the conquest.

All the territory of New Jersey was included in the grant made by King Charles to his brother the duke of York. Two months before the conquest of New Netherland by the English, that portion of the duke's province lying between the Hudson and the Delaware, extending as far north as forty-one degrees and forty minutes, was assigned by the proprietor to Lord Berkeley and Sir George Carteret. These noblemen were already proprietors of Carolina; but they had adhered to the king's cause during the civil war in England, and were now rewarded with a second American province. Almost immediately after the conquest another company of Puritans made application to Governor Nicolls, and received an extensive grant of land on Newark Bay. The Indian titles were honorably purchased; in the following October a village was begun and named Elizabethtown, in honor of Lady Carteret.

In August of 1665, Philip Carteret, son of Sir George, arrived as governor of the province. At first he was violently opposed by Nicolls of New York, who refused to believe that the duke had divided his territory. But Carteret was armed with a commission, and could not be prevented from taking possession of the new settlements below the Hudson. Elizabethtown was made the capital of the colony; other immigrants arrived from Long Island and settled on the banks of the Passaic; Newark was founded; flourishing hamlets appeared on the shores of the bay as far south as Sandy Hook. In honor of Sir George Carteret, who had been governor of the Isle of Jersey, in the English Channel, his American domain was named NEW JERSEY.

Experience had taught the proprietors wisdom; they had learned that freedom is essential to the prosperity of a colony, and that liberal concessions to the people are better than great outlays of money. Berkeley and Carteret, though royalists themselves, provided for their new State an excellent constitution. Person and property were put under the protection of law. The government was made to consist of a governor, a council and a popular legislative assembly. There should be no taxation unless levied by the representatives of the people. Difference of opinion should be respected, and freedom of conscience guaranteed to every citizen. The proprietors reserved to themselves only the right of annulling objectionable acts of the assembly and of appointing the governor and colonial judges. The lands of the province were distributed to the settlers for a quit-rent of a half penny per acre, not to be paid until 1670.

In 1668 the first general assembly convened at Elizabethtown. Nearly all the representatives were Puritans, and the laws and customs of New England were thus early impressed on the legislation of the colony.

Affairs went well until 1670, when the half-penny quit-rents were due to the proprietors. The colonists, in the mean time, had purchased their lands of the Indians, and also of Governor Nicolls of New York, who still claimed New Jersey as a part of his province. To the settlers, therefore, it seemed that their titles to their farms were good without further payment to Philip Carteret or anybody else. The collection of the rents was accordingly resisted; and the colony became a scene first of strife and then of revolution. In May of 1672 the colonial assembly convened and deposed the governor from office. James Carteret, another son of Sir George, was chosen governor, and Philip returned to England.

In 1673 the Dutch succeeded in retaking New York from the English. For a few months the old province of New Netherland, including the country as far south as the Delaware, was restored to Holland. But in the next year the whole territory was re-ceded by the states-general to England. The duke of York now received from his brother, the king, a second patent for the country between the Connecticut and the Delaware, and at the same time confirmed his former grant of New Jersey to Berkeley and Carteret. Then, in utter disregard of the rights of the two proprietors, the duke appointed Sir Edmund Andros as royal governor of the whole province. Carteret determined to defend his claim against the authority of Andros; but Lord Berkeley, disgusted with the duke's vacillation and dishonesty, sold his interest in New Jersey to John Fenwick, to be held in trust for Edward Byllinge.

In 1675, Philip Carteret returned to America and resumed the government of the province from which he had been expelled. Andros opposed him in every act; claimed New Jersey as a part of his own dominions; kept the colony in an uproar; compelled the ships which came a-trading with the new settlements to pay tribute at New York; and finally arrested Carteret and brought him to his own capital for trial. Meanwhile, Byllinge became embarrassed with debt, and was forced to make an assignment of his property. Gawen Laurie, Nicholas Lucas and William Penn were appointed trustees, and to them Byllinge's interest in New Jersey was assigned for the benefit of his creditors.

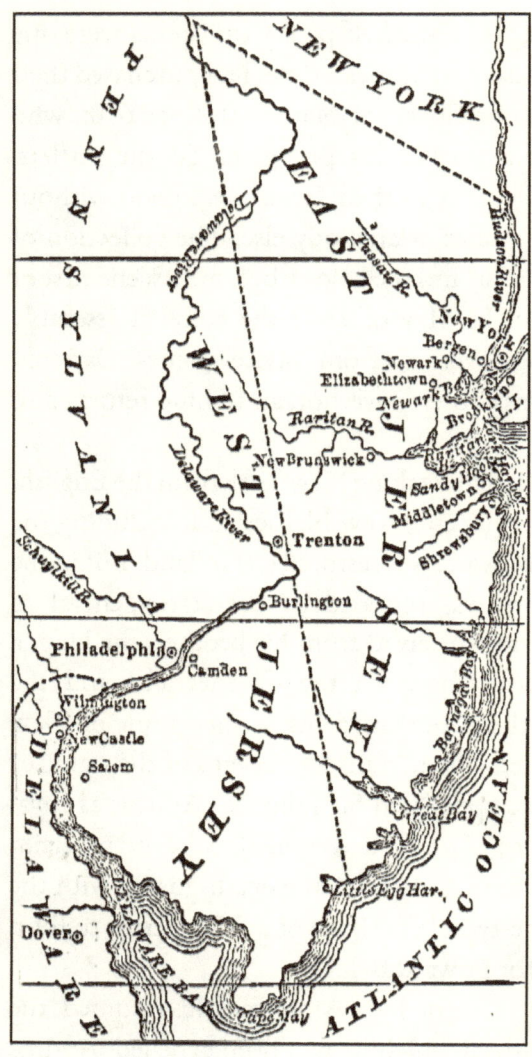

East and West Jersey, 1677.

The assignees were Quakers. Here, then, was an opportunity to establish another asylum for the persecuted, and to found a commonwealth of Friends. Penn and his associates at once applied to Sir George Carteret for a division of the province. That nobleman was both willing and anxious to enter into an arrangement by which his own half of the territory could be freed from all encumbrance. It was accordingly agreed to divide New Jersey so that Carteret's district should be separated from the domain of the Quakers. After much discussion an agreement was reached in the summer of 1676, and a line of division was drawn through the province as follows: Beginning at the southern point of land on the east side of Little Egg Harbor, and running north of north west to a point on the river Delaware in the latitude of forty-one degrees and forty minutes. The territory lying east of this line remained to Sir George as sole proprietor, and was named EAST JERSEY; while that portion lying between the line and the Delaware was called WEST JERSEY, and passed under the exclusive control of Penn and his associates as assignees of Byllinge.

Early in the following March the Quaker proprietors completed and published a body of laws under the, singular title of CONCESSIONS. But the name was significant, for everything was conceded to the people. This first simple code enacted by the Friends in America rivaled the charter of Connecticut in the liberality and purity of its principles. The authors of the instrument accompanied its publication with a general letter addressed to the Quakers of England, recommending the province and inviting immigration.

The invitation was not in vain. Before the end of the year a colony of more than four hundred Friends arrived in the Delaware, and found homes in West Jersey. Only one circumstance clouded the prospects of the new commonwealth of peace. The agent of Andros, governor of New York, was stationed at New Castle, on the western bank of the Delaware, to command the entrance to the river. The Quaker ships were obliged to pay customs before proceeding to their destination. A powerful remonstrance was drawn up by the Friends and sent to England. For once the duke of York listened to reason and agreed to submit his cause to the courts; and for once a decision was rendered in accordance with right and justice. The eminent jurist Sir William Jones decided that the duke had no legal right to collect duties and taxes in the country of the Delaware. All claims to the territory and government of West Jersey were accordingly withdrawn; and the Quaker colonists were left in the enjoyment of independence. The heirs of Sir George Carteret were quick to see that the same decision would free their half of the province from the jurisdiction of Andros. An effort was accordingly made by the proprietors of East Jersey to secure a deed of release from the duke of York. The petition was favorably entertained, the deed issued and the whole territory between the Hudson and the Delaware freed from foreign authority.

In November of 1681, Jennings, the deputy-governor of West Jersey, convened the first general assembly of the province. The men who had so worried the aristocracy of England by wearing their hats in the presence of great men, and by saying *Thee* and *Thou*, now met together to make their own laws. The code was brief and simple. The doctrines of the CONCESSIONS were reaffirmed. Men of all races and of all religions were declared to be equal before the law. No superiority was conceded to rank or title, to wealth or royal birth. Imprisonment for debt was forbidden. The sale of ardent spirits to the Red men was prohibited. Taxes should be voted by the representatives of the people. The lands of the Indians should be acquired by honorable purchase. Finally, a criminal—unless a murderer, a traitor or a thief—might be pardoned by the person against whom the offence was committed.

In 1682, William Penn and eleven other Friends purchased of the heirs of Carteret the province of East Jersey. Robert Barclay, an eminent Quaker of Aberdeen, in Scotland, and author of the book called Barclay's *Apology*, was appointed governor for life. The whole of New Jersey was now under the authority of the Friends. The administration of Barclay, which continued until his death, in 1690, was chiefly noted for a large immigration of Scotch Quakers who left the governor's native country to find freedom in East Jersey. The persecuted Presbyterians of Scotland came to the province in still greater numbers.

On the accession of James II., in 1685, the American colonies from Maine to Delaware were consolidated, and Edmund Andros appointed royal governor. His first year in America was spent in establishing his authority at Boston, Providence and Hartford. Not until 1688 were New York and the two Jerseys brought under his jurisdiction. The short reign of King James was already at an end before Andros could succeed in setting up a despotism on the ruin of colonial liberty. When the news came of the abdication and flight of the English monarch, the governor of New England could do nothing but surrender to the indignant people whom he had wronged and insulted. His arrest and imprisonment was the signal for the restoration popular government in all the colonies over which he had ruled.

But the condition of New Jersey was deplorable. It was almost impossible to tell to whom the jurisdiction of the territory rightfully belonged. So far as the eastern province was concerned, the representatives of Carteret claimed it; the governor of New York claimed it; Penn and his associates claimed it. As to the western province, the heirs of Bylinge claimed it; Lucas, Laurie and Penn claimed it; the governor of New York claimed it. Over all these pretensions stood the paramount claim of the English king. From 1689 to 1692 there was no settled form of government in the territory; and for ten years thereafter the colony was vexed and distracted with the presence of more rulers than any one province could accommodate.

At last self-interest solved the problem. The proprietors came to see that a peaceable possession of the *soil* of the Jerseys was worth more than the uncertain honors of government. A proposition was accordingly made that all the claimants should surrender their rights of civil jurisdiction to the English Crown, retaining only the ownership of the soil. The measure was successfully carried out; and in April of 1702, all proprietary claims being waived in favor of the sovereign, the territory between the Hudson and the Delaware became a royal province.

Penn's Colonists on the Delaware.

New Jersey was now attached to the government of Lord Cornbury of New York. The union of the two colonies, however, extended only to the office of chief magistrate; each province retained its own legislative assembly and a distinct territorial organization. This method of government continued for thirty-six years, and was then terminated by the action of the people. In 1728 the representatives of New Jersey sent a petition to George II., praying for a separation of the two colonies; but the application was at first refused. Ten years later the petition was renewed, and through the influence of Lewis Morris brought to a successful issue. New Jersey was made independent, and Morris himself received a commission as first royal governor of the separated province.

The people of New Jersey were but little disturbed by the successive Indian wars. The native tribes on this part of the American coast were weak and timid. Had it not been for the cruelties of Kieft and the wrongs of other governors of New York, the peace of the middle colonies would never have been broken. The province of New Jersey is specially interesting as being the point where the civilization of New England met and blended with the civilization of the South. Here the institutions, manners and laws of the Pilgrims were first modified by contact with the less rigid habits and opinions of the people who came with Gosnold and Smith. The dividing line between East and West Jersey is also the dividing line between the austere Puritans of Massachusetts and the chivalrous cavaliers of Virginia. Happily, along this dividing line the men of peace, the followers of Penn and Barclay, came and dwelt as if to subdue ill-will and make a UNION possible.

Chapter XXV.

Pennsylvania.

THE Quakers were greatly encouraged with the success of their colonies in West New Jersey. The prospect of establishing on the banks of the Delaware a free State, founded on the principle of universal brotherhood, kindled a new enthusiasm in the mind of William Penn. For more than a quarter of a century the Friends had been buffeted with shameful persecutions. Imprisonment, exile and proscription had been their constant portion, but had not sufficed to abate their zeal or to quench their hopes of the future. The lofty purpose and philanthropic spirit of Penn urged him to find for his afflicted people an asylum of rest. In June of 1680 he went boldly to King Charles, and petitioned for a grant of territory and the privilege of founding a Quaker commonwealth in the New World.

The petition was seconded by powerful friends in Parliament. Lords North and Halifax and the earl of Sunderland favored the proposition, and the duke of York remembered a pledge of assistance which he had given to Penn's father. On the 5th of March, 1681, a charter was granted; the great seal of England, with the signature of Charles II., was affixed; and William Penn became the proprietor of PENNSYLVANIA. The vast domain embraced under the new patent was bounded on the east by the river Delaware, extended north and south over three degrees of latitude, and westward through five degrees of longitude. Only the three counties comprising the present State of Delaware were reserved for the duke of York.

In consideration of this grant, Penn relinquished a claim of sixteen thousand pounds sterling which the British government owed to his father's estate. He declared that his objects were to found a free commonwealth without respect to the color, race or religion of the inhabitants; to subdue the natives with no other weapons than love and justice; to establish a refuge for the people of his own faith; and to enlarge the borders of the British empire. One of the first acts of the great proprietor was to address a letter to the Swedes who might be included within the limits of his province, telling them to be of good cheer, to keep their homes, make their own laws and fear no oppression.

Within a month from the date of his charter, Penn published to the English nation a glowing account of his new country beyond the Delaware, praising the beauty of the scenery and salubrity of the climate, promising freedom of conscience and equal rights, and inviting emigration. There was an immediate and hearty response. In the course of the summer three shiploads of Quaker emigrants left England for the land of promise. William Markham, agent of the proprietor, came as leader of the company and deputy-governor of the province. He was instructed by Penn to rule in accordance with law, to deal justly with all men, and especially to make a league of friendship with the Indians. In October of the same year the anxious proprietor sent a letter directly to the natives of the territory, assuring them of his honest purposes and brotherly affection.

The next care of Penn was to draw up a frame of government for his province. Herein was his great temptation. He had almost exhausted his father's estate in aiding the persecuted Quakers. A stated revenue would be very necessary in conducting his administration. His proprietary rights under the charter were so ample that he might easily reserve for himself large prerogatives and great emoluments in the government. He had before him the option of being a consistent, honest Quaker or a politic, wealthy governor. He chose like a man; right triumphed over riches. The constitution which he framed was liberal almost to a fault; and the people were allowed to adopt or reject it as they might deem proper.

In the mean time, the duke of York had been induced to surrender his claim to the three reserved counties on the Delaware. The whole country on the western bank of the bay and river, from the open ocean below Cape Henlopen to the forty-third degree of north latitude, was now under the dominion of Penn. The summer of 1682 was spent in further preparation. The proprietor wrote a touching letter of farewell to the Friends in England; gathered a large company of emigrants;

embarked for America; and on the 27th of October landed at New Castle, where the people were waiting to receive him.

William Penn.

WILLIAM PENN, the founder of Philadelphia, was born on the 14th of October, 1644. He was the oldest son Sir William Penn of the British navy. At the age of twelve he was sent to the University of Oxford, where he distinguished himself as a student until he was expelled on account of his religious opinions. Afterward he traveled on the Continent; was again a student at Saumur; returned to study law at London; went to Ireland; became a soldier; heard the preaching of Loe and was converted to the Quaker faith. His disappointed and angry father drove him out of doors, but he was not to be turned from his course. He publicly proclaimed the doctrines of the Friends; was arrested and imprisoned for nine months in the Tower of London. Being released, he repeated the offence, and lay for half a year in a dungeon at Newgate. A second time liberated, but despairing of toleration for his people in England, he cast his gaze across the Atlantic. West Jersey was purchased; but the boundary was narrow, and the great-scaled proprietor sought a grander and more beautiful domain. His petition was heard with favor and the charter of Pennsylvania granted by King Charles. Colonists came teeming; and now the Quaker king himself, without pomp or parade, without the discharge of cannon or vainglorious ceremony, was come to New Castle to found a government on the basis of fraternity and peace. It was fitting that he should call the new republic a holy experiment.

As soon as the landing was effected, Penn delivered an affectionate and cheerful address to the crowd of Swedes, Dutch and English who came to greet him. His former pledges of a liberal and just government were publicly renewed, and the people were exhorted to sobriety and honesty. From New Castle the governor ascended the Delaware to Chester; passed the site of Philadelphia; visited the settlements of West New Jersey; and thence traversed East Jersey to Long Island and New York. After spending some time at the capital of his friend, the duke of York, and speaking words of cheer to the Quakers about Brooklyn, he returned to his own province and began his duties as chief magistrate.

Markham, the deputy-governor, had been instructed to establish fraternal relations with the Indians. Before Penn's arrival treaties had been made, lands purchased, and pledges of friendship given between the Friends and the Red men. Now a great conference was appointed with the native chiefs. All the sachems of the Lenni Lenapes and other neighboring tribes were invited to assemble. The council was held on the banks of the Delaware under the open sky. Penn, accompanied by a few unarmed friends, clad in the simple garb of the Quakers, came to the appointed spot and took his station under a venerable elm, now leafless; for it was winter. The chieftains, also unarmed, sat, after the manner of their race, in a semicircle on the ground. It was not Penn's object to purchase lands, to provide for the interests of trade or to make a formal treaty, but rather to assure the untutored children of the woods of his honest purposes and brotherly affection. Standing before them with grave demeanor and speaking by an interpreter, he said: "MY FRIENDS: We have met on the broad pathway of good faith. We are all one flesh and blood. Being brethren, no advantage shall be taken on either side. When disputes arise, we will settle them in council. Between us there shall be nothing but openness and love." The chiefs replied: "While the rivers run and the sun shines we will live in peace with the children of William Penn."

No record was made of the treaty, for none was needed. Its terms were written, not on decaying parchment, but on the living hearts of men. No deed of violence or injustice ever marred the sacred covenant. The Indians vied with the Quakers in keeping unbroken the pledge of perpetual peace. For more than seventy years during which the province remained under the control of the Friends, not a single war-whoop was heard within the borders of Pennsylvania. The Quaker hat and coat proved to be a better defence for the wearer than coat-of-mail and musket.

Philadelphia and Vicinity.

On the 4th of December, 1682, a general convention was held at Chester. The object was to complete the territorial legislation—a work which occupied three days. At the conclusion of the session, Penn delivered an address to the assembly, and then hastened to the Chesapeake to confer with Lord Baltimore about the boundaries of their respective provinces. After a month's absence he returned to Chester and busied himself with drawing a map of his proposed capital. The beautiful neck of land between the Schuylkill and the Delaware was selected and purchased of the Swedes. In February of 1683 the native chestnuts, walnuts and ashes were blazed to indicate the lines of the streets, and PHILADELPHIA—CITY OF BROTHERLY LOVE—was founded. Within a month a general assembly was in session at the new capital. The people were eager that their Charter of Liberties, now to be framed, should be dated at Philadelphia. The work of legislation was begun and a form of government adopted which was essentially a representative democracy. The leading officers were the governor, a council consisting of a limited number of members chosen for three years, and a larger popular assembly, to be annually elected. Penn conceded everything to the people; but the power of vetoing objectionable acts of the council was left in his hands.

The growth of Philadelphia was astonishing. In the summer of 1683 there were only three or four houses. The ground-squirrels still lived in their burrows, and the wild deer ran through the town without alarm. In 1685 the city contained six hundred houses; the schoolmaster had come and the printing-press had begun its work. In another year Philadelphia had outgrown New York. Penn's work of establishing a free State in America had been well and nobly done. In August of 1684 he took an affectionate farewell of his flourishing colony, and sailed for England. Thomas Lloyd was appointed as president during the absence of the proprietor, and five commissioners, members of the provincial council, were chosen to assist in the government.

Nothing occurred to disturb the peace of Pennsylvania until the secession of Delaware in 1691. The three lower counties, which, ever since the arrival of Penn, had been united on terms of equality with the six counties of Pennsylvania, became dissatisfied with some acts of the general assembly and insisted on a separation. The proprietor gave a reluctant consent; Delaware withdrew from the union and received a separate deputy-governor. Such was the condition of affairs after the abdication of King James II.

William Penn was a friend and favorite of the Stuart kings. It was from Charles II. that he had received the charter of Pennsylvania. Now that the royal house was overthrown, he sympathized with the fallen monarch and locked with coldness on the new sovereigns, William and Mary. For some real or supposed adherence to the cause of the exiled James II., Penn was several times arrested and imprisoned. In 1692 his proprietary rights were taken away, and by a royal commission the government of Pennsylvania was transferred to Fletcher of New York. In the following year Delaware shared the same fate; all the provinces between Connecticut and Maryland were consolidated under Fletcher's authority. In the mean time, the suspicions against Penn's loyalty were found to be groundless, and he was restored to his rights as governor of Pennsylvania.

In December of 1699, Penn again visited his American commonwealth, now grown into a State. The prosperity of the province was all that could be desired but the people were somewhat dissatisfied with the forms of government. The lower counties were again embittered against the acts of the assembly. In order to restore peace and harmony, the benevolent proprietor drew up another constitution, more liberal than the first, extending the powers of the people and omitting the objectionable features of the former charter. But Delaware had fallen into chronic discontent, and would not accept the new frame of government. In 1702 the general assemblies of the two provinces were convened apart; and in the following year Delaware and Pennsylvania were finally separated. But the rights of Penn as proprietor of the whole territory remained as before, and a common governor continued to preside over both colonies.

In the winter of 1701, William Penn bade a final adieu to his friends in America and returned to England. He left Pennsylvania in a state of peace and prosperity. Though there was not a single fort within her borders, the province had been secure against invasion. With neither police nor militia, the people went abroad in safety. With no difference in rank, no preference in matters of opinion, and no proscription for religion's sake, the colony flourished and waxed strong. But the English ministers had now formed the design of abolishing all the proprietary governments, with a view to the establishment of royal governments instead. The presence and influence of Penn were especially required in England in order to prevent the success of the ministerial scheme. After much controversy his rights were recognized and secured against encroachment. In the mean time, the affairs of Pennsylvania were administered by the deputy-governors, Andrew Hamilton and John Evans. The latter, a worldly sort of man, not very faithful to the principles of the Friends, greatly troubled the province by purchasing warlike stores, building forts, and attempting to organize a regiment of militia. The assembly entered a strong protest against these proceedings, so irreconcilable with the policy of the Quakers, and in 1708 Evans was removed from office. After him Charles Gookin received a commission as deputy-governor and entered upon his administration in 1709. Soon afterwards Penn was well-nigh overwhelmed by the rascality of his English agent, Ford, who first involved him in debt and then had him imprisoned. From a shameful confinement of many months he finally released, and his old age was brightened by a gleam of prosperity. But the end of his labors was at hand. In July of 1718 the magnanimous founder of Pennsylvania sank to his final rest. His estates, vast and valuable, but much encumbered with debt, were bequeathed to his three sons, John, Thomas and Richard, who thus became proprietors of Pennsylvania. By them, or their deputies, the province was governed until the American Revolution. In the year 1779 the entire claims of the Penn family to the soil and jurisdiction of the State were purchased by the legislature of Pennsylvania for a hundred and thirty thousand pounds sterling.

The colonial history of the State founded by William Penn and the Quakers is one of special interest and pleasure. It is a narrative that recounts the victories of peace and the triumph of the nobler virtues over violence and wrong. It is doubtful whether the history of any other colony in the world is touched with so many traits of innocence and truth. When the nations grow mercenary and the times seem full of fraud, the early annals of Pennsylvania may well be recited as a perpetual protest against the seeming success of evil. "I will found a free colony for all mankind," were the words of William Penn. How well his work was done shall be fitly told when the bells of his capital city shall ring out the first glad notes of AMERICAN INDEPENDENCE.

COLONIAL HISTORY.—CONTINUED.

MINOR SOUTHERN COLONIES.

CHAPTER XXVI.

MARYLAND.

CAPTAIN JOHN SMITH was the first white man to explore the Chesapeake and its tributaries. After him, in 1621, William Clayborne, a resolute and daring English surveyor, was sent out by the London Company to make a map of the country about the head-waters of the bay. By the second charter of Virginia the territory of that province had been extended on the north to the forty-first parallel of latitude. All of the present State of Maryland was included in this enlargement, which also embraced the whole of Delaware and the greater part of New Jersey and Pennsylvania. The ambition of Virginia was greatly excited by the possession of this vast domain; to explore and occupy it was an enterprise of the highest importance.

Clayborne was a member of the council of Virginia, and secretary of state in that colony. In May of 1631 he received a royal commission authorizing him to discover the sources of the Chesapeake Bay, to survey the country as far as the forty-first degree of latitude, to establish a trade with the Indians, and to exercise the right of government over the companions of his voyage. This commission was confirmed by Governor Harvey of Virginia, and in the spring of the following year Clayborne began his important and arduous work. The members of the London Company were already gathering imaginary riches from the immense fur-trade of the Potomac and the Susquehanna.

The enterprise of Clayborne was attended with success. A trading-post was established on Kent Island, and another at the head of the bay, in the vicinity of Havre de Grace. The many rivers that fall into the Chesapeake were again explored and a trade opened with the natives. The limits of Virginia were about to be extended to the borders of New Netherland. But in the mean time a train of circumstances had been prepared in England by which the destiny of several American provinces was completely changed. As in many other instances, religious persecution again contributed to lay the foundation of a new State in the wilderness. And Sir George Calvert, of Yorkshire, was the man who was destined to become the founder. Born in 1580; educated at Oxford; a man of much travel and vast experience; an ardent and devoted Catholic; a friend of humanity; honored with knighthood, and afterward with an Irish peerage and the title of LORD BALTIMORE,—he now in middle life turned aside from the dignities of rank and affluence to devote the energies of his life to the welfare of the oppressed. For the Catholics of England, as well as the dissenting Protestants, were afflicted with many and bitter persecutions.

Lord Baltimore.

Lord Baltimore's first American enterprise was the planting of a Catholic colony in Newfoundland. King James, who was not unfriendly to the Roman Church, had granted him a patent for the southern promontory of the island; and here, in 1623, a refuge was established for distressed Catholics. But in such a place no colony could be successful. The district was narrow, cheerless, desolate. Profitable industry was impossible. French ships hovered around the coast and captured the English fishing boats. It became evident that the settlement must be removed, and Lord Baltimore wisely turned his attention to the sunny country of the Chesapeake.

In 1629 he made a visit to Virginia. The general assembly offered him citizenship on condition that he would take an oath of allegiance; but the oath was of such a sort as no honest Catholic could subscribe to. In vain did Sir George plead for toleration; the assembly was inexorable. It was on the part of the Virginians a short-sighted and ruinous policy. For the London Company had already been dissolved; the king might therefore rightfully regrant that vast territory north of the Potomac which by the terms of the second charter had been given to Virginia. Lord Baltimore left the narrow-minded legislators, returned to London himself drew up a charter for a new State on the Chesapeake, and easily induced his friend, King Charles I., to sign it. The Virginians had saved their religion and lost a province.

The territory embraced by the new patent was bounded by the ocean, by the fortieth parallel of latitude, by a line drawn due south from that parallel to the most western fountain of the Potomac, by the river itself from its source to the bay, and by a line running due east from the mouth of the river to the Atlantic. The domain included the whole of the present States of Maryland and Delaware and a large part of Pennsylvania and New Jersey. Here it was the purpose of the magnanimous proprietor to establish an asylum for all the afflicted of his own faith, and to plant a State on the broad basis of religious toleration and popular liberty. The provisions of the charter were the most liberal and ample which had ever received the sanction of the English government. Christianity was declared to be the religion of the State, but no preference was given to any sect or creed. The lives and property of the colonists were carefully guarded. Free trade was declared to be the law of the province, and arbitrary taxation was forbidden. The rights of the proprietor extended only to the free appointment of the officers of his government. The power of making and amending the laws was conceded to the freemen of the colony or their representatives.

One calamity darkened the prospect. Before the liberal patent could receive the seal of State Sir George Calvert died. His title and estates descended to his son Cecil; and to him, on the 20th of June, 1632, the charter which had been intended for his noble father was finally issued. In honor of Henrietta Maria, daughter of Henry IV. of France and wife of Charles I., the name of MARYLAND was conferred on the new province. Independence of Virginia was guaranteed in the constitution of the colony, and no danger was to be anticipated from the feeble forces of New Netherland. It only remained for the younger Lord Baltimore to raise a company of emigrants and carry out his father's benevolent designs. The work went forward slowly, and it was not until November of 1633 that a colony numbering two hundred persons could be collected. Meanwhile, Cecil Calvert had abandoned the idea of coming in person to America, and had appointed his brother Leonard to accompany the colonists to their destination, and to act as deputy-governor of the new province.

In March of the following year the immigrants arrived at Old Point Comfort. Leonard Calvert bore a letter from King Charles to Governor Harvey of Virginia, commanding him to receive the newcomers with courtesy and favor. The order was complied with; but the Virginians could look only with intense jealousy on a movement which must soon deprive them of the rich fur-trade of the Chesapeake. The colonists proceeded up the bay and entered the Potomac. At the mouth of Piscataway Creek, nearly opposite Mount Vernon, the pinnace was moored, and a cross was set up on an island. On the present site of Fort Washington there was an Indian village whose inhabitants came out to meet the English. A conference was held, and the sachem of the nation told Leonard Calvert in words of dubious meaning that he and his colony *might stay or go just as they pleased*. Considering this answer as a menace, and deeming it imprudent to plant his first settlement so far up the river, Calvert again embarked with his companions, and dropped down stream to the mouth of the St. Mary's, within fifteen miles of the bay. Ascending the estuary for about ten miles, he came to an Indian town. The natives had been beaten in battle by the Susquehannas, and were on the eve of migrating into the interior. The village was already half deserted. With the consent of the Red men, the English moved into the vacant huts. The rest of the town was purchased, with the adjacent territory, the Indians promising to give possession at the opening of the spring. The name of ST. MARY'S was given to this the oldest colony of Maryland, and the name of the river was changed to St. George's.

Calvert treated the natives with great liberality. The consequence was that the settlers had peace and plenty. The Indian women taught the wives of the English how to make corn-bread, and the friendly warriors instructed the colonists in the mysteries of hunting. Game was abundant. The lands adjacent to the village were already under cultivation. The settlers had little to do but to plant their gardens and fields and wait for the coming harvest. There was neither anxiety nor want. The dream of Sir George Calvert was realized. Within six months the colony of St. Mary's had grown into greater prosperity than the settlement at Jamestown had reached in as many years. Best of all, the pledge of civil liberty and religious toleration was redeemed to the letter. Two years before the founding of Rhode Island the Catholics of the Chesapeake had emancipated the human conscience, built an asylum for the distressed, and laid the foundations of a free State.

Within less than a year after the founding of St. Mary's the freemen were convened in a general assembly. In February of 1635 the work of colonial legislation was first begun. The records of this and several succeeding sessions were destroyed in the rebellion of 1645, and not much is known concerning the character of the earliest laws. But it is certain that the province was involved in difficulty. For Clayborne still stood his ground on Kent Island, and openly resisted Lord Baltimore's authority. His settlement on the island was almost as strong as the colony at St. Mary's; and Clayborne, unscrupulous as to the right, and confident in his power, resolved to appeal to arms. In 1637 a bloody skirmish occurred on the banks of the river Wicomico, on the eastern shore of the bay. Several lives were lost, but the insurgents were defeated. Calvert's forces proceeded to Kent Island, overpowered the settlement, and executed one or two persons who had participated in the rebellion.

Clayborne, in the mean time, had escaped into Virginia. The assembly of Maryland demanded the fugitive; but the governor refused, and sent the prisoner to England for trial. The legislators of St. Mary's charged the absent criminal with murder and piracy, tried him, condemned him and confiscated his estates. Clayborne, who was safe in

England, appealed to the king. The cause was heard by a committee of Parliament, and it was decided that the commission of Clayborne, which was only a license to trade in the Chesapeake, had been annulled by the dissolution of the London Company, and that the charter of Lord Baltimore was valid against all opposing claimants. Clayborne, however, was allowed to go at large.

In 1639 a regular representative government was established in Maryland. Hitherto a system of popular democracy had prevailed in the province; each freeman had been allowed a vote in determining the laws. With the growth of the colony it was deemed expedient to substitute the more convenient method of representation. When the delegates came together, a declaration of rights was adopted, and the prerogative of the proprietor more clearly defined. All the broad and liberal principles of the colonial patent were reaffirmed. The powers of the assembly were made coextensive with those of the House of Commons in England. The rights of citizenship were declared to be identical with those of English subjects in the mother country.

The Indians of Maryland and Virginia had now grown jealous of foreign encroachments. Vague rumors of the English Revolution had been borne to the Red men, and they believed themselves able to expel the intruders from the country. In 1642 hostilities were begun on the Potomac, and for two years the province was involved in war. But the settlements of Maryland were few and compact, and no great suffering was occasioned by the onsets of the barbarians. In 1644 the savages agreed to bury the hatchet and to renew the broken pledges of friendship. Hardly, however, had the echo of Indian warfare died away, when the colony was visited with a worse calamity by the return of its old enemy, William Clayborne.

He came to find revenge, and found it. The king was now at war with his subjects, and could give no aid to the proprietor of an American province. Clayborne saw his opportunity, hurried to Maryland, and raised the standard of rebellion. Arriving in the province in 1644, he began to sow the seeds of sedition by telling the restless and lawless spirits of the colony that they were wronged and oppressed by a usurping government. Early in 1645 an insurrection broke out. Companies of desperate men came together, and found in Clayborne a natural leader. The government of Leonard Calvert was overthrown, and the governor obliged to fly for his life. Escaping from the province, he found refuge and protection with Sir William Berkeley of Virginia. Clayborne seized the colonial records of Maryland, and destroyed them. One act of violence followed another. The government was usurped, and for more than a year the colony was under the dominion of the insurgents. Meanwhile, however, Governor Calvert collected his forces, returned to the province, defeated the rebels, and in August of 1646 succeeded in restoring his authority. It marks the mild and humane spirit of the Calverts that those engaged in this unjustifiable insurrection were pardoned by a general amnesty.

The acts of the provincial legislature in 1649 were of special importance. It was enacted in broad terms that no person believing in the fundamental doctrines of Christianity should, on account of his religious opinions or practices, be in any wise distressed within the borders of Maryland. It was declared a finable offence for citizens to apply to each other the opprobrious names used in religious controversy. Freedom of conscience was reiterated with a distinctness that could not be misunderstood. While Massachusetts was attempting by proscription to establish Puritanism as the faith of New England, and while the Episcopalians of Jamestown were endeavoring by exclusive legislation to make the Church of England the Church of Virginia, Maryland was joining with Rhode Island and Connecticut in proclaiming religious freedom. It sometimes happened in those days that Protestants escaping from Protestants found an asylum with the Catholic colonists of the Chesapeake.

In 1650 the legislative body of Maryland was divided into two branches. The upper house consisted of the governor and members of his council appointed by the proprietor. The lower house, or general assembly, was composed of burgesses elected by the people of the province. Again the rights of Lord Baltimore were carefully defined by provincial law. An act was also passed declaring that no taxes should be levied without the consent of the assembly. Such was the condition of affairs in the colony when the commonwealth was established in

England. Parliament was now the supreme power in the mother country, and it could hardly be expected that Lord Baltimore's charter would be allowed to stand.

In 1651 parliamentary commissioners were appointed to come to America and assume control of the colonies bordering on the Chesapeake. Clayborne was a member of the body thus appointed. When the commissioners arrived in Maryland, Stone, the deputy of Lord Baltimore, was deposed from office. A compromise was presently effected between the adherents of the proprietor and the opposing faction; and in June of the following year, Stone, with three members of his council, was permitted to resume the government. In April of 1653 the Long Parliament, by whose authority the commissioners had been appointed, was dissolved. Stone thereupon published a proclamation declaring that the recent interference of Clayborne and his associates had been a rebellious usurpation. Clayborne, enraged at this proclamation, collected a force in Virginia, returned into Maryland, again drove Stone out of office, and entrusted the government to ten commissioners appointed by himself.

The Puritan and republican party in Maryland had now grown sufficiently strong to defy the proprietor and the Catholics. A Protestant assembly was convened at Patuxent in October of 1654. The first act was to acknowledge the supremacy of Cromwell; the next to disfranchise the Catholics and to deprive them of the protection of the laws. The ungrateful representatives seemed to forget that if Lord Baltimore had been equally intolerant not one of them would have had even a residence within the limits of Maryland. It would be difficult to find a more odious piece of legislation than that of the assembly at Patuxent. Of course the Catholic party would not submit to a code by which they were virtually banished from their own province.

Civil war ensued. Governor Stone organized and armed the militia, seized the records of the colony, and marched against the opposing forces. A decisive battle was fought just across the estuary from the present site of Annapolis. The Catholics were defeated, with a loss of men in killed and wounded. Stone himself was taken prisoner, and was only saved from death by the personal friendship of some of the insurgents. Three of the Catholic leaders were tried by a court-martial and executed. Cromwell paid but little attention to these atrocities, and made no effort to sustain the government of Lord Baltimore.

In 1656 Josias Fendall, a weak and impetuous man, was sent out by the proprietor as governor of the province. There was now a Catholic insurrection with Fendall at the head. For two years the government was divided, the Catholics exercising authority at St. Mary's, and the Protestants at Leonardstown. At length, in March of 1658, a compromise was effected; Fendall was acknowledged as governor, and the acts of the recent Protestant assemblies were recognized as valid. A general amnesty was published, and the colony was again at peace.

When the death of Cromwell was announced in Maryland, the provincial authorities were much perplexed. One of four courses might be pursued: Richard Cromwell might be recognized as protector; Charles II. might be proclaimed as king; Lord Baltimore might be acknowledged as hereditary proprietor; colonial independence might be declared. The latter policy was adopted by the assembly. On the 12th of March, 1660; the rights of Lord Baltimore were formally set aside; the provincial council was dissolved, and the whole power of government was assumed by the House of Burgesses. The act of independence was adopted just one day before a similar resolution was passed by the general assembly of Virginia. The population of Maryland had now reached ten thousand.

On the restoration of monarchy the rights of the Baltimores were again recognized, and Philip Calvert was sent out as deputy-governor. In the mean time, Fendall had resigned his trust as agent of the proprietor, and had accepted an election by the people. He was now repaid for his double-dealing with an arrest, a trial and a condemnation on a charge of treason. Nothing saved his life but the clemency of Lord Baltimore, who, with his customary magnanimity, proclaimed a general pardon.

Sir Cecil Calvert died in 1675, and his son Charles, a young man who had inherited the virtues of the illustrious family, succeeded to the estates and title of Baltimore. For sixteen years he exercised the rights of proprietary governor of Maryland. The laws of the province were carefully revised, and the liberal principles of the original charter reaffirmed as the basis of the State. Only once during this period was the happiness of the colony disturbed. When the news arrived of the abdication of King James II., the deputy of Lord Baltimore hesitated to acknowledge the new sovereigns, William and Mary. An absurd rumor was spread abroad that the Catholics had leagued with the Indians for the purpose of destroying the Protestants of Maryland in a general massacre. An opposing force was organized; and in 1689 the Catholic party was compelled to surrender the government. For two years the Protestants held the province, and civil authority was exercised by a body called the Convention of Associates.

On the 1st day of June, 1691, the government of Maryland was revolutionized by the act of King William. The charter of Lord Baltimore was arbitrarily taken away, and a royal governor appointed over the province. Sir Lionel Copley received a commission, and assumed the government in 1692. Every vestige of the old patent was swept away. The Episcopal Church was established by law and supported by taxation. Religious toleration was abolished and the government administered on despotic principles. This condition of affairs continued until 1715, when Queen Anne was induced to restore the heir of Lord Baltimore to the rights of his ancestor. Maryland again became a proprietary government under the authority of the Calverts, and so remained until the Revolutionary war.

The early history of the colony planted by the first Lord Baltimore on the shores of the Chesapeake is full of profitable instruction. In no other American province were the essential vices of intolerance more clearly manifested; in no other did the principle of religious freedom shine with a brighter lustre. Nor will the thoughtful student fail to observe how the severe dogmas of Catholicism were softened down when brought into contact with the ennobling virtues of the Calverts, until over river and bay and shore a mellow light was diffused like a halo shining from the altars of the ancient Church.

CHAPTER XXVII.

NORTH CAROLINA.

THE first effort to colonize North Carolina was made by Sir Walter Raleigh. In 1630 an immense tract lying between the thirtieth and the thirty-sixth parallels of latitude was granted by King Charles to Sir Robert Heath. But neither the proprietor nor his successor, Lord Maltravers, succeeded in planting a colony. After a useless existence of thirty-three years, the patent was revoked by the English sovereign. The only effect of Sir Robert's charter was to perpetuate the name of CAROLINA, which had been given to the country by John Ribault in 1562.

In the year 1622 the country as far south as the river Chowan was explored by Pory, the secretary of Virginia. Twenty years later a company of Virginians obtained leave of the assembly to prosecute discovery on the lower Roanoke and establish a trade with the natives. The first actual settlement was made near the mouth of the Chowan about the year 1651. The country was visited just afterward by Clayborne of Maryland, and in 1661 a company of Puritans from New England passed down the coast, entered the mouth of Cape Fear River, purchased lands of the Indians and established a colony on Oldtown Creek, nearly two hundred miles farther south than any other English settlement. In 1663 Lord Clarendon, General Monk, who was now honored with the title of duke of Albemarle, and six other noblemen, received at the hands of Charles II. a patent for all the country between the thirty-sixth parallel and the river St. John's, in Florida. With this grant the colonial history of North Carolina properly begins.

In the same year a civil government was organized by the settlers on the Chowan. William Drummond was chosen governor, and the name of ALBEMARLE COUNTY COLONY was given to the district bordering on the sound. In 1665 it was found that the settlement was north of the thirty-sixth parallel, and consequently beyond the limits of the province. To remedy this defect the grant was extended on the north to thirty-six degrees and thirty minutes, the present boundary of Virginia, and westward to the Pacific. During the same year the little Puritan colony on Cape Fear River was broken up by the Indians; but scarcely had this been done when the site of the settlement, with thirty-two miles square of the surrounding territory, was purchased by a company of planters from Barbadoes. A new county named CLARENDON was laid out, and Sir John Yeamans elected governor of the colony. The proprietors favored the settlement; immigration was rapid; and within a year eight hundred people had settled along the river.

The work of preparing a frame of government for the new province was assigned to Sir Ashley Cooper, earl of Shaftesbury. The proprietors, not without reason, looked forward to the time when a powerful nation should arise within the borders of their vast domain. To draft a suitable constitution was deemed a work of the greatest importance. Shaftesbury was a brilliant and versatile statesman who had entire confidence in his abilities; but in order to give complete assurance of perfection in the proposed statutes, the philosopher John Locke was employed by Sir Ashley and his associates to prepare the constitution. The legislation of the world furnishes no parallel for the pompous absurdity of Locke's performance.

From March until July of 1669 the philosopher worked away in the preparation of his GRAND MODEL; then the mighty instrument was done, and signed. It contained a hundred and twenty articles, called the "Fundamental Constitutions;" and this was but the beginning of the imperial scheme which was to stand like a colossus over the huts and pastures along the Cape Fear and Chowan Rivers. The empire of Carolina was divided into vast districts of four hundred and eighty thousand acres each. Political rights were made dependent upon hereditary wealth. The offices were put beyond the reach of the people. There were two grand orders of nobility. There were dukes, earls and marquises; knights, lords and esquires; baronial courts, heraldic ceremony, and every sort of feudal nonsense that the human imagination could conceive of. And *this* was the magnificent constitution which a great statesman and a wise philosopher had planned for the government of a few colonists who lived on venison and potatoes and paid their debts with tobacco!

It was one thing to make the grand model, and another thing to get it across the Atlantic. In this the proprietors never succeeded. All attempts to establish the pompous scheme of government ended in necessary failure. The settlers of Albemarle and Clarendon had meanwhile learned to govern themselves after the simple manner of pioneers, and they could but regard the model and its authors with disdainful contempt. After twenty years of fruitless effort, Shaftesbury and his associates folded up their grand constitution and concluded that an empire in the pine forests of North Carolina was impossible.

The soil of Clarendon county was little better than a desert. For a while a trade in staves and furs supplied a profitable industry; but when this traffic was exhausted, the colonists began to remove to other settlements. In 1671, Governor Yeamans was transferred to the colony which had been founded in the previous year at the mouth of Ashley River, and before the year 1690 the whole county of Clarendon was a second time surrendered to the native tribes. The settlement north of Albemarle Sound was more prosperous, but civil dissension greatly retarded the development of the country.

For the proprietors were already busy trying to establish their big institutions in the feeble province. The humble commerce of the colony was burdened with an odious duty. Every pound of the eight hundred hogsheads of tobacco annually produced was taxed a penny for the benefit of the government. There were at this time less than four thousand people in North Carolina, and yet the traffic of these poor settlers with New England alone was so weighed down with duties as to yield an annual revenue of twelve thousand dollars. Miller, the governor, was a harsh and violent man. A gloomy opposition to the proprietary government pervaded the colony; and when, in 1676, large numbers of refugees from Virginia—patriots who had fought in Bacon's rebellion—arrived in the Chowan, the spirit of discontent was kindled into open resistance.

The arrival of a merchant-ship from Boston and an attempt to enforce the revenue laws furnished the occasion and pretext of an insurrection. The vessel evaded the payment of duty, and was declared a smuggler. But the people flew to arms, seized the governor and six members of his council, overturned the existing order of things and established a new government of their own. John Culpepper, the leader of the insurgents, was chosen governor; other officers were elected by the people; and in a few weeks the colony was as tranquil as if Locke's grand model had never been heard of. But in the next year, 1679, the imprisoned Miller and his associates escaped from confinement, and going to London told a dolorous story about their wrongs and sufferings. The English lords of trade took the matter in hand, and it seemed that North Carolina was doomed to punishment.

But the colonists were awake to their interests. Governor Culpepper went boldly to England to defend himself and to justify the rebellion. He was seized, indicted for high treason, tried and acquitted by a jury of Englishmen. It marks a peculiar feature of this cause that the sagacious earl of Shaftesbury came forward at the trial and spoke in defence of the prisoner. But Lord Clarendon was so much vexed at the acquittal of the rebellious governor that he sold his rights as proprietor fit the infamous Seth Sothel. This man in 1680 was sent out by his associates as governor of the province. In crossing the ocean he was captured by a band of pirates, and for three years the colony was saved from his evil presence. At last, in 1683, he arrived in Carolina and began his work, which consisted in oppressing the people and defrauding the proprietors. Cranfield of New Hampshire, Cornbury of New York and Wingfield of Virginia were all respectable men in comparison with Sothel, whose sordid passions have made him notorious as the worst colonial governor that ever plundered an American province. After five years of avaricious tyranny, the base, gold-gathering, justice-despising despot was overthrown in an insurrection. Finding himself a prisoner, and fearing the wrath of the defrauded proprietors more than he feared the indignation of the outraged colonists, he begged to be tried by the assembly of the province. The request was granted, and the culprit escaped with a sentence of disfranchisement and a twelve months' exile from North Carolina.

Sothel was succeeded in the governorship by Ludwell, who arrived in 1689. His administration of six years' duration was a period of peace and contentment. The wrongs of his predecessor were corrected as far as possible by a just and humane chief magistrate. In 1695 came Sir John Archdale, another of the proprietors, the rival of Ludwell in prudence and integrity. Then followed the tranquil administration of Governor Henderson Walker; then, in 1704, the foolish attempt of Robert Daniel to establish the Church of England. In the mean time, the colony had grown strong in population and resources. The country south of the Roanoke began to be dotted with farms and hamlets. Other settlers came from Virginia and Maryland. Quakers came from New England and the Delaware. A band of French Huguenots came in 1707. A hundred families of German refugees, buffeted with war and persecution, left the banks of the Rhine to find a home on the banks of the Neuse. Peasants from Switzerland came and founded New Berne at the mouth of the River Trent.

The Indians of North Carolina had gradually wasted away. Pestilence and strong drink had reduced powerful tribes to a shadow. Some nations were already extinct; others, out of thousands of strong-limbed warriors, had only a dozen men remaining. The lands of the savages had passed to the whites, sometimes by purchase, sometimes by fraud, often by forcible occupation. The natives were jealous and revengeful, but weak. Of all the mighty tribes that had inhabited the Carolinas in the days of Sir Walter Raleigh, only the Corees and the Tuscaroras were still formidable. The time had come when these unhappy nations, like the rest of their race, were doomed to destruction. The conflict which ended, and could only end, in the ruin of the Red men, began in the year 1711.

In September of this year, Lawson, the surveyor-general of North Carolina, ascended the Neuse to explore and map the country. The Indians were alarmed at the threatened encroachment upon their territory. A band of warriors took Lawson prisoner, led him before their council, condemned him and burned him to death. On the night of the 22d, companies of savages rose out of the woods, fell upon the scattered settlements between the Roanoke and Pamlico Sound, and murdered a hundred and thirty persons. Civil dissension prevented the colonial authorities from adopting vigorous measures of defence. The protection of the people and the punishment of the barbarians were left to the neighboring provinces. Spottswood, governor of Virginia, made some unsuccessful efforts to render assistance, and Colonel Barnwell came from South Carolina with a company of militia and a body of friendly Cherokees, Creeks and Catawbas. The savages were driven into their fort in the northern part of Craven county, but could not be dislodged. While affairs were in this condition a treaty of peace was made; but Barnwell's men, on their way homeward, violated the compact, sacked an Indian village and made slaves of the inhabitants. The war was at once renewed.

In September of the next year, while the conflict was yet undecided, the yellow fever broke out in the country south of Pamlico Sound. So dreadful were the ravages of the pestilence that the peninsula was wellnigh swept of its inhabitants. Meanwhile, Colonel James Moore of South Carolina had arrived, in command of a regiment of whites and Indians, and the Tuscaroras were pursued to their principal fort on Cotentnea Creek, in Greene county. This place was besieged until the latter part of March, 1713, and was then carried by assault. Eight hundred warriors were taken prisoners. The power of the hostile nation was broken, but the Tuscarora chieftains were divided in council; some were desirous of peace, and some voted to continue the war. This difference of opinion led to a division of the tribe. Those who wished for peace were permitted to settle in a single community in the county of Hyde. Their hostile brethren, seeing that further resistance would be hopeless, determined to leave the country. In the month of June they abandoned their hunting-grounds made sacred by the traditions of their fathers, marched across Virginia, Maryland and Pennsylvania, reached Northern New York, joined their kinsmen, the Oneidas, and became the sixth nation of the Iroquois confederacy.

Thus far the two Carolinas had continued under a common government. In 1729 a final separation was effected between the provinces north and south of Cape Fear River, and a royal governor appointed over each. In spite of Locke's grand model and the Tuscarora war, in spite of the threatened Spanish invasion of 1744, the northern colony had greatly prospered. The intellectual development of the people had not been as rapid as the growth in numbers and in wealth.

Little attention had been given to questions of religion. There was no minister in the province until 1703. Two years later the first church was built. The first court house was erected in 1722, and the printing-press did not begin its work until 1754. But the people were brave and patriotic. They loved their country, and called it the LAND OF SUMMER. In the farmhouse and the village, along the banks of the rivers and the borders of the primeval forests, the spirit of liberty pervaded every breast. The love of freedom was intense, and hostility to tyranny a universal passion. In the times of Sothel it was said of the North Carolinians that they would not pay tribute *even to Cæsar*.

CHAPTER XXVIII.

SOUTH CAROLINA.

IN January of 1670 the proprietors of Carolina sent out a colony under command of Joseph West and William Sayle. There was at this time not a single European settlement between the mouth of Cape Fear River and the St. John's, in Florida. Here was a beautiful coast of nearly four hundred miles ready to receive the beginnings of civilization. The new emigrants, sailing by way of Barbadoes, steered far to the south, and reached the mainland in the country of the Savannah. The vessels first entered the harbor of Port Royal. It was now a hundred and eight years since John Ribault, on an island in this same harbor, had set up a stone engraved with the lilies of France; now the Englishman had come.

The ships were anchored near the site of Beaufort. But the colonists were dissatisfied with the appearance of the country, and did not go ashore. Sailing northward along the coast for forty miles, they next entered the mouth of Ashley River, and landed where the first high land appeared upon the southern bank. Here were laid the foundations of Old Charleston, so named in honor of King, Charles II. Of this, the oldest town in South Carolina, no trace remains except the line of a ditch which was digged around the fort; a cotton-field occupies the site of the ancient settlement.

Sayle had been commissioned as governor and West as commercial agent of the colony. The settlers had been furnished with a copy of Locke's big constitution, but they had no more use for it than for a dead elephant. Instead of the grand model, a little government was organized on the principles of common sense. Five councilors were elected by the people, and five others appointed by the proprietors. Over this council of ten the governor presided. Twenty delegates, composing a house of representatives, were chosen by the colonists. Within two years the system of popular government was firmly established in the province. Except the prevalence of diseases peculiar to the southern climate, no calamity darkened the prospects of the rising State.

In the beginning of 1671 Governor Sayle died, and West, by common consent, assumed the duties of the vacant office. After the lapse of a few months, Sir John Yeamans, who had been governor of the northern province and was now in Barbadoes, was commissioned by the proprietors as chief magistrate of the southern colony. He brought with him to Ashley River a large cargo of African slaves. From the beginning the colonists had devoted themselves to planting; but the English laborers, unused as yet to the climate, could hardly endure the excessive heats of the sultry fields. To the Caribbee negroes, already accustomed to the burning sun of the tropics, the Carolina summer seemed temperate and pleasant. Thus the labor of the black man was substituted for the labor of the white man, and in less than two years from the founding of the colony the system of slavery was firmly established. In this respect the history of South Carolina is peculiar. Slavery had been introduced into all the American colonies, but everywhere else the introduction had been effected by those who were engaged in the slave-trade. In South Carolina alone was the system adopted as a political and social experiment and with a view to the regular establishment of a laboring class in the State. Governor Yeamans was the first to accept this policy, which soon became the general policy of the province. The importation of negroes went on so rapidly that in a short time they outnumbered the whites as two to one.

Immigration from England did not lag. During the year 1671 a system of cheap rents and liberal bounties was adopted by the proprietors, and the country was rapidly filled with people. A tract of a hundred and fifty acres was granted to everyone who would either immigrate or import a negro. Fertile lands were abundant. Wars and pestilence had almost annihilated the native tribes; whole counties were almost without an occupant. The disasters of one race had prepared the way for the coming of another. Only a few years before this time New Netherland had been conquered by the English. The Dutch were greatly dissatisfied with the government which the duke of York had established over them, and began to leave the country. The proprietors of Carolina sent several ships to New York, loaded them with the industrious but discontented people, and brought them without expense to Charleston. The unoccupied lands west of Ashley River were divided among the Dutch, who formed there a thriving settlement called Jamestown. The fame of the new country reached Holland, and other emigrants left fatherland to join their kinsmen in Carolina. Charles II., who rarely aided a colony, collected a company of Protestant refugees from the South of Europe, and sent them to Carolina to introduce the silk-worm and to begin the cultivation of the grape.

In 1680 the present metropolis of South Carolina was founded. The site of Old Charleston had been hastily and injudiciously selected. The delightful peninsula called Oyster Point, between Ashley and Cooper Rivers, was now chosen as the spot on which to build a city. The erection of thirty dwellings during the first summer gave proof of enterprise; the name of CHARLESTON was a second time bestowed, and the village immediately became the capital of the colony. The unhealthy climate for a while retarded the progress of the new town, but the people were lull of life and enterprise; storehouses and wharves were built, and merchant-ships soon began to throng the commodious harbor.

Injustice provoked an Indian war. Some vagabond Nestoes, whose only offence consisted in strolling through the plantations, were shot. The tribe appealed to the government, and the proprietors showed a willingness to punish the wrongdoers; but the pioneers were determined to fight and the savages were naturally revengeful. Scenes of violence continued along the border, and hostilities began in earnest. In the prosecution of the war the colonists were actuated by a shameful spirit of avarice. The object was not so much to punish or destroy the savages as to take them prisoners. A bounty was offered for every captured Indian, and as fast as the warriors were taken they were sold as slaves for the West Indies. The petty strife Continued for a year, and was then concluded with a treaty of peace. Commissioners were appointed, to whom all complaints and disputes between the natives and the colonists should henceforth be submitted.

South Carolina was favored with rapid immigration, and the immigrants were worthy to become the founders of a great State. The best nations of Europe contributed to people the country between Cape

Fear and the Savannah. England continued to send her colonies. In 1683 Joseph Blake, a brother of the great English admiral, devoted his fortune and the last years of his life to bringing a large company of dissenters from Somersetshire to Charleston. In the same year an Irish colony under Ferguson arrived at Ashley River, and met a hearty welcome. A company of Scotch Presbyterians, ten families in all, led by the excellent Lord Cardross, settled at Port Royal in 1684. The authorities of Charleston claimed jurisdiction there, and the new immigrants reluctantly yielded to the claim. Two years afterward a band of Spanish soldiers arrived from St. Augustine, and the unhappy Scotch exiles were driven from their homes. But intolerant France gave up more of her subjects than did all the other nations.

As early as 1598 Henry IV., king of the French, had published a celebrated proclamation, called the Edict of Nantes, by the terms of which the Huguenots were protected in their rights of religious Worship. Now, after eighty-seven years of toleration, Louis XIV., blinded with bigotry and passion and hoping to make Catholicism universal, revoked the kindly edict, and exposed the Protestants of his kingdom to the long-suppressed rage of their enemies. In order to enforce the decree of revocation the French army was quartered in the towns of the Huguenots, the ports were closed against emigration, and the borders were watched to prevent escape. How foolish are the ways of despotism! In spite of every precaution, five hundred thousand of the best people of France, preferring banishment to religious thraldom, escaped from their country and fled, self-exiled, into foreign lands. The Huguenots were scattered from the Baltic Sea to the Cape of Good Hope, and on the Western continent from Maine to Florida. But of all the American colonies, South Carolina received the greatest number of French refugees within her borders. They were met by the proprietors with a pledge of protection and a promise of citizenship; but neither promise nor pledge was immediately fulfilled, for the colony had not yet determined what should be its laws of naturalization. Both the general assembly and the proprietors claimed the right of fixing the conditions. Until that question could be decided the Huguenots were kept in suspense, and were sometimes unkindly treated by the jealous English settlers. Not until 1697 were all discriminations against the French immigrants removed.

In 1686 came James Colleton as colonial governor. He began his administration with a foolish attempt to establish the mammoth constitution of Locke and Shaftesbury. No wonder that the assembly resisted his authority, and that the people were embittered against him. The rents came due; payment was refused, and the colony was in a state of rebellion. In order to divert attention from himself, Colleton published a proclamation setting forth the danger of a pretended invasion by the Indians and Spaniards. The militia was called out and the province declared under martial law. It was all in vain. The people were only exasperated by the arbitrary proceedings of the governor. Tidings came that James II. had been driven from the throne of England. The popular assembly convened, and William and Mary were proclaimed as sovereigns. In 1690 a decree of impeachment was passed against Colleton, and he was banished from the province.

The people of North Carolina had just performed a similar service for Seth Sothel. Not satisfied with his previous success, he at once repaired to Charleston and assumed the government of the southern colony. To Sothel's other merits were added the qualifications of a first-rate demagogue; he induced the people to acquiesce in his usurpation and to sustain his authority. But his avaricious disposition could not long be held in check. The proprietors disclaimed his acts and after a turbulent rule of two years, he and his government were overthrown. One bright page redeems the record of his administration. In May of 1691 the first general act of enfranchisement was passed in favor of the Huguenots.

Philip Ludwell, who had been collector of customs in Virginia, and since 1689 governor of North Carolina, was now sent to establish order in the southern province. He spent a year in a well-meant effort to administer the government of the proprietors; but the people were fixed in their antagonism to the constitution, and nothing could be accomplished. Ludwell gave up the hopeless task, withdrew from the province, and returned to Virginia. South Carolina had fallen into a condition bordering on anarchy.

Nearly a quarter of a century had elapsed since Locke drafted the grand model. At last the proprietors came to see that the establishment of such a monstrous frame of government over an American colony was impossible. Pride said that the constitution should stand, for the nobility of England had declared it immortal. But self-interest and common sense demanded its abrogation, and the demand prevailed. In April of 1693 the proprietors assembled and voted the boasted model out of existence. It was enacted at the same meeting that since the people of Carolina preferred a simple charter government, their request be granted. The magnificent paper empire of Shaftesbury was swept into oblivion.

Thomas Smith was now appointed governor, but was soon superseded by John Archdale, a distinguished and talented Quaker. Arriving in 1695, he began an administration so just and wise that dissension ceased and the colony entered upon a new career of prosperity. The quit-rents on lands were remitted for four years. The people were given the option of paying their taxes in money or in produce. The Indians were conciliated with kindness and protected against kidnappers. Some native Catholics were ransomed from slavery and sent to their homes in Florida, and the Spanish governor reciprocated the deed with a friendly message. When the old jealousy against the Huguenots asserted itself in the general assembly, the benevolent influence of Archdale procured the passage of a law by which all Christians, except the Catholics, were fully enfranchised; the ungenerous exception was made against the governor's will. It was a real misfortune to the colony when, in 1698, the good governor was recalled to England.

James Moore was next commissioned as chief magistrate. The first important act of his administration was a declaration of hostilities against the Spanish settlement of St. Augustine. Queen Anne's War had broken out. The Spaniards were in alliance with the French against the English. By the antagonism of England and Spain, South Carolina and Florida were brought into conflict. Yet a declaration of war was strongly opposed in the assembly at Charleston, and was only passed by a small majority. It was voted to raise and equip a force of twelve hundred men, and to invade Florida by land and water. The summer of 1702 was spent in preparation, and in September the expeditions departed, the land-forces led by Colonel Daniel and the fleet commanded by the governor.

The English vessels sailed down the coast, entered the St. John's and blocked up the river. Daniel marched overland, reached St. Augustine and captured the town. But the Spaniards withdrew without serious loss into the castle, and bade defiance to the besiegers. Without artillery it was evident that the place could not be taken. Colonel Daniel was despatched with a sloop to Jamaica to procure cannons for the siege; but before his return two Spanish men-of-war appeared at the mouth of the St. John's, and Governor Moore found himself blockaded. His courage was not equal to the occasion. Abandoning his ships, he took to the shore, and collecting his forces hastily retreated into Carolina. Daniel returned and entered the St. John's, but discovered the danger in time to make his escape. The governor's retreat occasioned great dissatisfaction. There were insinuations of cowardice and threats of impeachment, but no formal action was taken against him. The only results of the unfortunate expedition were debt and paper money. In order to meet the heavy expenses of the war, the assembly was obliged to issue bills of credit to the amount of six thousand pounds sterling.

Governor Moore retrieved his reputation by invading the Indian nations south-west of the Savannah. In December of 1705 he left the province at the head of fifty volunteers and a thousand friendly natives. White men had not been seen marching in these woods since the days of De Soto. On the 14th of the month the invaders reached the fortified town of Ayavalla, in the neighborhood of St. Mark's. An attack was made and the church set on fire. A Franciscan monk came out and begged for mercy; but the place was carried by assault, and more than two hundred prisoners were taken, only to be enslaved. On the next day Moore's forces met and defeated a large body of Indians and Spaniards. Five important towns were carried in succession, and the English flag was borne in triumph to the Gulf of Mexico. Communication between the Spanish settlements of Florida and the French posts in Louisiana was entirely cut off.

Meanwhile, the Church of England had been established by law in South Carolina. In the first year of Johnston's administration the High Church party succeeded in getting a majority of one in the colonial assembly, and immediately passed an act disfranchising all the dissenters in the province. An appeal was carried to the proprietors, only to be rejected with contempt. The dissenting party next laid their cause before Parliament, and that body promptly voted that the act of disfranchisement was contrary to the laws of England, and that the proprietors had forfeited their charter. The queen's ministers were authorized to declare the intolerant law null and void. In November of the same year the colonial legislature revoked its own act so far as the disfranchising clause was concerned; but Episcopalianism continued to be the established faith of the province.

The year 1706 was a stirring epoch in the history of South Carolina. A French and Spanish fleet was sent from Havana to capture Charleston and subdue the country. The orders were more easily given than executed. The brave people of the capital flew to arms. Governor Johnson and Colonel William Rhett inspired the volunteers with courage; and when the hostile squadron anchored in the harbor, the city was ready for a stubborn defence. Several times a landing was attempted, but the invaders were everywhere repulsed. At last a French vessel succeeded in getting to shore with eight hundred troops, but they were attacked with fury and driven off with a loss of three hundred in killed and prisoners. The siege was at once abandoned; unaided by the proprietors, South Carolina had made a glorious defence.

In the spring of 1715 war broke out with the Yamassees. As usual with their race, the Indians began hostilities with treachery. At the very time when Captain Nairne was among them as a friendly ambassador, the wily savages rose upon the frontier settlements and committed an atrocious massacre. The people of Port Royal were alarmed just in time to escape in a ship to Charleston. The desperate savages rushed on to within a short distance of the capital. It seemed that the city would be taken and the whole colony driven to destruction. But the brave Charles Craven, governor of the province, rallied the militia of Colleton district, and the blood-stained barbarians were driven back. A vigorous pursuit began, and the savages were pressed to the banks of the Salkehatchie. Here a decisive battle was fought, and the Indians were completely routed. The Yamassees collected their shattered tribe and retired into Florida, where they were received by the Spaniards as friends and confederates.

In 1719 the government of South Carolina was revolutionized. At the close of the war with the Yamassees the assembly petitioned the proprietors to bear a portion of the expense. But the avaricious noble men refused, and would take no measures for the future protection of the colony. The people were greatly burdened with rents and taxes. The lands were monopolized; every act of the assembly which seemed for the public good was vetoed by the proprietors. In the new election every delegate was chosen by the popular party. The 21st of December was training-day in Charleston. On that day James Moore, the new chief magistrate elected by the people, was to be inaugurated. Governor Johnson forbade the military display and tried to prevent the inauguration; but the militia collected in the public square, drums were beaten, flags were flung out on the forts and shipping, and before nightfall the proprietary government of Carolina was overthrown. Governor Moore was duly inaugurated in the name of King George I. A colonial agent was at once sent to England; the cause of the colonists was heard, and the forfeited charter of the proprietors abrogated by act of Parliament.

Francis Nicholson was now commissioned as governor. He had already held the office of chief magistrate in New York, in Virginia, in Maryland and in Nova Scotia. He began a successful administration in South Carolina by concluding treaties of peace and commerce with the Cherokees and the Creeks. But another and final change in colonial affairs was now at hand. In 1729 seven of the eight proprietors of the Carolinas sold their entire claims in the provinces to the king. Lord Carteret, the eighth proprietor, would surrender nothing but his right of jurisdiction, reserving his share in the soil. The sum paid by King George for the two colonies was twenty-two thousand five hundred pounds sterling. Royal governors were appointed, and the affairs of the province were settled on a permanent basis, not to be disturbed for more than forty years.

The people who colonized South Carolina were brave and chivalrous. On the banks of the Santee, the Edisto and the Combahee were gathered some of the best elements of the European nations. The Huguenot, the Scotch Presbyterian, the English dissenter, the loyalist and High Churchman, the Irish adventurer and the Dutch mechanic, composed the powerful material out of which soon grew the beauty and renown of the PALMETTO STATE. Equally with the rugged Puritans of the North, the South Carolinians were lovers of liberty. Without the severe morality and formal manners of the Pilgrims, the people who were once governed by the peaceful Archdale and once led to war by the gallant Craven became the leaders in courtly politeness and high-toned honor between man and man. In the coming struggle for freedom South Carolina will bear a noble and distinguished part; the fame of the patriotic Rhett will be perpetuated by Marion and Sumter.

CHAPTER XXIX.

GEORGIA.

GEORGIA, the thirteenth American colony, was founded in a spirit of pure benevolence. The laws of England permitted imprisonment for debt. Thousands of English laborers, who through misfortune and thoughtless contracts had become indebted to the rich, were annually arrested and thrown into jail. There were desolate and starving families. The miserable condition of the debtor class at last attracted the attention of Parliament. In 1728 a commissioner was appointed, *at his own request*, to look into the state of the poor, to visit the prisons of the kingdom, and to report measures of relief. The work was accomplished, the jails were opened, and the poor victims of debt returned to their homes.

The noble commissioner was not yet satisfied. For the liberated prisoners and their friends were disheartened and disgraced in the country of their birth. Was there no land beyond the sea where debt was not a crime, and where poverty was no disgrace? To provide a refuge for the down-trodden poor of England and the distressed Protestants of other countries, the commissioner now appealed to George II. for the privilege of planting a colony in America. The petition was favorably heard, and on the 9th of June, 1732, a royal charter was issued by which the territory between the Savannah and Altamaha Rivers, and westward from the upper fountains of those rivers to the Pacific, was organized and granted to a corporation for twenty-one years, *to be held in trust for the poor*. In honor of the king, the new province received the name of GEORGIA. But what was the name of that high-souled, unselfish commissioner of Parliament?

James Oglethorpe, the philanthropist. Born a loyalist, educated at Oxford, a High Churchman, a cavalier, a soldier, a member of Parliament, benevolent, generous, full of sympathy, far-sighted, brave as John Smith, chivalrous as De Soto, Oglethorpe gave in middle life the full energies of a vigorous body and a lofty mind to the work of building in the sunny South an asylum for the oppressed of his own and other lands. The magnanimity of the enterprise was heightened by the fact that he did not believe in the equality of men, but only in the right and duty of the strong to protect the weak and sympathize with the lowly. To Oglethorpe, as principal member of the corporation, the leadership of the first colony to be planted on the banks of the Savannah, was naturally entrusted.

James Oglethorpe.

By the middle of November a hundred and twenty emigrants were ready to sail for the New World. Oglethorpe, like the elder Winthrop, determined to share the dangers and hardships of his colony. In January of 1733 the company was welcomed at Charleston. Passing down the coast, the vessels were anchored for a short time at Beaufort, while the governor with a few companions ascended the boundary river of Georgia, and selected as the site of his settlement the high bluff on which now stands the city of Savannah. Here, on the 1st day of February, were laid the foundations of the oldest English town south of the Savannah River. Broad streets were laid out; a public square was reserved in each quarter; a beautiful village of tents and board houses, built among the pine trees, appeared as the capital of a new commonwealth where men were not imprisoned for debt.

Tomo-chichi, chief of the Yamacraws, came from his cabin, half a mile distant, to see his brother Oglethorpe. There was a pleasant conference. "Here is a present for you," said the red man to the white man. The present was a buffalo robe painted on the inside with the head and feathers of an eagle. "The feathers are soft, and signify love; the buffalo skin is the emblem of protection. Therefore love us and protect us," said the old chieftain. Such a plea could not be lost on a man like Oglethorpe. Seeing the advantages of peace, he sent an invitation to the chiefs of the Muskhogees to meet him in a general council at his capital. The conference was held on the 29th of May. Long King, the sachem of Oconas, spoke for all the tribes of his nation. The English were welcomed to the country. Bundles of buckskins, and such other good gifts as savage civilization could offer, were laid down plentifully at the feet of the whites. The governor and his poor but generous colony responded with valuable presents and words of faithful friendship. The fame of Oglethorpe spread far and wide among the Red men. From the distant mountains of Tennessee came the noted chief of the Cherokees to confer with the humane and sweet-tempered governor of Georgia.

The councilors in England who managed the affairs of the new State encouraged emigration with every liberal offer. Swiss peasants left their mountains to find a home on the Savannah. The plaid cloak of the Scotch Highlander was seen among the wigwams of the Muskhogees. From distant Salzburg, afar on the borders of Austria, came a noble colony of German Protestants, singing their way down the Rhine and across the ocean. Oglethorpe met them at Charleston, bade them welcome, led them to Savannah and thence through the woods to a point twenty miles up the river, told them of English rights and the freedom of conscience, and left them to found the village of Ebenezer.

In April of 1734, Governor Oglethorpe made a visit to England. His friend Tomo-chichi went with him, and made the acquaintance of King George. It was said in London that no colony was ever before founded so wisely and well as Georgia. The councilors prohibited the importation of rum. Traffic with the Indians—always a dangerous matter—was either interdicted or regulated by special license. When it came to the question of labor, slavery was positively forbidden. It was said that the introduction of slaves would be fatal to the interests of the English and German laborers for whom the colony had been founded. While the governor was still abroad, the first company of Moravians, numbering nine, and led by the evangelist Spangenberg, arrived at Savannah.

In February of 1736, Oglethorpe himself came back with a new colony of three hundred. Part of these were Moravians, and nearly all were people of deep piety and fervent spirit. First among them—first in zeal and first in the influence which he was destined to exert in after times—was the celebrated John Wesley, the founder of Methodism. Overflowing with religious enthusiasm, he came to Georgia, not as a politician, not as a minister merely, but as an apostle. To lead the people to righteousness, to spread the gospel, to convert the Indians, and to introduce a new type of religion characterized by few forms and much emotion, these were the purposes that thronged his lofty fancy. He was doomed to much disappointment. The mixed people of the new province could not be moulded to his will; and after a residence of less than two years he left the colony with a troubled spirit. His brother, Charles Wesley, came also as a secretary to Governor Oglethorpe; but Charles was a poet, a timid and tender-hearted man who pined with homesickness and gave way under discouragement. But when, in 1738, the famous George Whitefield came, his robust and daring nature proved a match for all the troubles of the wilderness. He preached with fiery eloquence. To build an orphan-house at Savannah he went through all the colonies; and those who heard his voice could hardly refuse him money. Thinking no longer of native land, he found a peaceful grave in New England.

Meanwhile, Oglethorpe was busy with the affairs of his growing province. Anticipating war with Spain, he began to fortify. For the Spaniards were in possession of Florida, and claimed the country as far north as St. Helena Sound. All of Georgia was thus embraced in the Spanish claim. But Oglethorpe had a charter for Georgia as far south as the Altamaha, and he had secured by treaty with the Indians all the territory between that river and the St. Mary's. In 1736 he ascended the Savannah and built a fort at Augusta. On the north bank of the Altamaha, twelve miles from its mouth, Fort Darien was built. On Cumberland Island, at the mouth of the St. Mary's, a fortress was erected and named Fort William. Proceeding down the coast with a company of Highlanders, the daring governor reached the mouth of the St. John's, and on Amelia Island built still another fort, which he named St. George. The river St. John's was claimed from this time forth as the southern boundary of Georgia. To make his preparations complete, the governor again visited England, and was commissioned as brigadier-general, with a command extending over his own province and South Carolina. In October of 1737 he returned to Savannah, bringing with him a regiment of six hundred men. Such were the vigorous measures adopted by Oglethorpe in anticipation of a Spanish war.

Country of the Savannah, 1740.

The war came. It was that conflict known in American history as King George's War. England published her declaration of hostility against Spain in the latter part of October, 1739. In the first week of the following January the impetuous Oglethorpe, at the head of the Georgia militia, made a dash into Florida, and captured two fortified towns of the Spaniards. His plans embraced the conquest of St. Augustine and the entire extinction of Spanish authority north of the Gulf of Mexico. Repairing to Charleston, he induced the assembly to support his measures. By the first of May he found himself in command of six hundred regular troops, four hundred volunteers and a body of Indian auxiliaries. With this force he proceeded at once against St. Augustine. The place was strongly fortified, and the Spanish commandant, Monteano, was a man of ability and courage. The siege continued for five weeks, but ended in disaster to the English. For a while the town was successfully blockaded; but some Spanish galleys, eluding the vigilance of Oglethorpe's squadron, brought a cargo of supplies to the garrison. The Spaniards made a sally, attacked a company of Highlanders, and dispersed them. Sickness prevailed in the English camp. The general himself was enfeebled with fever and excitement, but he held on like a hero. The troops of Carolina, disheartened and despairing of success, left their camp and marched homeward. The English vessels gathered up their crews, abandoned the siege and returned to Frederica. Oglethorpe, yielding only to necessity, collected his men from the trenches and withdrew into Georgia.

The Spaniards now determined to carry the war northward and drive the English beyond the Savannah. The Combahee River should be made the northern boundary of Florida. Preparations began on a vast scale. A powerful fleet of thirty-six vessels, carrying more than three thousand troops, was brought from Cuba, and anchored at St. Augustine. In June of 1742 the squadron passed up the coast to Cumberland Island, and attempted the reduction of Fort William. But Oglethorpe by a daring exploit reinforced the garrison, and then fell back to Frederica. The Spanish vessels followed and came to anchor in the harbor of St. Simon's. From the southern point of the island to Frederica, Oglethorpe had cut a road which at one place lay between a morass and a dense forest. Along this path the Spaniards must pass to attack the town. The English general had only eight hundred men and a few Indian allies. In order to cope with superior numbers, Oglethorpe resorted to stratagem.

Scene in St. Augustine.

A Frenchman had deserted to the Spaniards. To him the English general now wrote a letter *as if to a spy*. A Spanish prisoner in Oglethorpe's hands was liberated and bribed to deliver the letter to the deserter. The Frenchman was advised that two British fleets were coming to America, one to aid Oglethorpe and the other to attack St. Augustine. Let the Spaniards remain on the island but three days longer, and they would be ruined. If the enemy did not make an immediate attack on Frederica, his forces would be captured to a man. Oglethorpe knew very well that the prisoner, instead of delivering this letter to the deserter, would give it to the Spanish commander, and that the Spanish commander could not possibly know whether the communication was the truth or a fiction. This letter was delivered, and the astonished Frenchman was arrested as a spy, but the Spaniards could not tell whether his denial was true or false. There was a council of war in the Spanish camp. Oglethorpe's stratagem was suspected, but could not be proved. Three ships had been seen at sea that day; perhaps these were the first vessels of the approaching British fleets. The Spaniards were utterly perplexed; but it was finally decided to take Oglethorpe's advice, and make the attack on Frederica.

The English general had foreseen that this course would be adopted. He had accordingly advanced his small force from the town to the place where the road passed between the swamp and the forest. Here an ambuscade was formed, and the soldiers lay in wait for the approaching Spaniards. On the 7th of July the enemy's vanguard reached the narrow pass, were fired on from the thicket and driven back in confusion. The main body of the Spanish forces pressed on into the dangerous position where superior numbers were of no advantage. The Highlanders of Oglethorpe's regiment fired with terrible effect from the oak woods by the roadside. The Spaniards stood firm for a while, but were presently driven back with a loss of two hundred men. Not without reason the name of Bloody Marsh was given to this battle-field. Within less than a week the whole Spanish force had re-embarked and sailed for Florida. On the way southward the fleet made a second attack on Fort William. But Captain Stuart, with a garrison of only fifty men, made a vigorous and successful defence The English watched the retreating ships beyond the mouth of the St. John's; before the last of July the great invasion was at an end. The Spanish authorities of Cuba were greatly chagrined at the failure of the expedition. The commander of the squadron was arrested, tried by a court-martial and dismissed from the service.

The commonwealth of Georgia was now firmly established, and the settlements had peace. In 1743, Oglethorpe bade a final adieu to the colony to whose welfare he had given more than ten years of his life. He had never owned a house nor possessed an acre of ground within the limits of his own province. He now departed for England crowned with blessings, and leaving behind him an untarnished fame. James Oglethorpe lived to be nearly a hundred years old; benevolence, integrity and honor were the virtues of his declining years. But the new State which he had founded in the West was not always free from evils.

For the regulations which the councilors for Georgia had adopted were but poorly suited to the wants of the colony. The settlers had not been permitted to hold their lands in fee simple. Agriculture had not flourished. Commerce had not sprung up. The laws of property had been so arranged that estates could descend only to the oldest sons of families. The colonists were poor, and charged their poverty to the fact that slave-labor was forbidden in the province. This became the chief question which agitated the people. The proprietary laws grew more and more unpopular. The statute excluding slavery was not rigidly enforced, and, indeed, could not be enforced, when the people had determined to evade it. Whitefield himself pleaded for the abrogation of the law. Slaves began to be hired, first for short terms of service, then for longer periods, then for a hundred years, which was equivalent to an actual purchase for life. Finally, cargoes of slaves were brought directly from Africa, and the primitive free-labor system of Georgia was revolutionized. Plantations were laid out below the Savannah, and cultivated, as those of South Carolina.

Another and more important change was at hand. It became evident that there could be no progress so long as the original charter remained in force. However benevolent the impulse which had called Georgia into being, the scheme of government had proved a sham. The people were improvident, idle, inexperienced. More than six hundred thousand dollars in parliamentary grants, besides private contributions amounting to nearly ninety thousand dollars, had been fruitlessly expended on the lagging province. In 1752 there were only a few scattered plantations and three inconsiderable villages below the Savannah. The white population amounted, at this time, to seventeen hundred souls; and the blacks numbered about four hundred. The industry of Georgia was at a standstill. The extravagant hopes which the colonial managers had entertained of wine, and silk, and indigo, found no realization in the facts. The annual experts of the colony amounted to less than four thousand dollars; and the prospect for the future was as discouraging as the present condition was gloomy.

At last, however, the new order of things was acknowledged by the councilors of the province. They yielded to necessity. In June of 1752, just twenty years from the granting of the charter, the trustees made a formal surrender of their patent to the king. A royal government was established over the country south of the Savannah, and the people were granted the privileges and freedom of Englishmen. A constitution was drawn up by the British Board of Trade, and Captain John Reynolds was commissioned as royal governor. In October of 1754 he arrived at Savannah and began the work of reorganization. For two years and a half he labored assiduously to extricate the affairs of Georgia from the confusion into which they had fallen; and so successful was his work that at the end of this time the population had reached six thousand. The southern boundary of the province remained to be decided by the issue of the French and Indian War. During the progress of that conflict Georgia was saved from calamity by the prudent administration of Governor Ellis, who secured from the powerful Creek confederacy a new treaty of peace. A barrier was thus interposed between the colony and the hostile nations of the West and North. In the year 1758 the province was divided into eight parishes, and at the same time the Church of England was established by law. Still, for a while, the progress of the colony was not equal to the expectations of its founder. But before the beginning of the Revolution, Georgia, though the feeblest of all the Anglo-American provinces, had become a prosperous and growing State.

Such is the story of the planting by our fathers of the Old Thirteen republics—such the record of their growth and prospects. From the gloomy coast of Labrador, where, two hundred and fifty years before, John Cabot had set up the flag of England and arms of Henry VII., to the sunny waters where Ponce de Leon, looking shoreward, called his cavaliers to gaze on the Land of Flowers,—the dominion of Great Britain had been established. Would that dominion last forever? Would the other nations of Europe ever rally and regain their lost ascendency on the Western continent? Would the ties of kinship, the affinity of language, the bond of a common ancestry, stretching from these sea-shore commonwealths across the Atlantic, bind them in perpetual union with the mother Islands? Would these isolated provinces in America—now so quick to take offence at each other's beliefs and actions, and so easily jealous of each other's power and fame—ever unite in a common cause? ever join to do battle for life and liberty? ever become a Nation? Such were the momentous questions, the problems of destiny, which hung above the colonies at the middle of the eighteenth century—problems which the future could not be long in solving.

The history of these American colonies from their first feeble beginnings is full of interest and instruction. The people who laid the foundations of civilization in the New World were nearly all refugees, exiles, wanderers, pilgrims. They were urged across the ocean by a common impulse, and that impulse was the desire to escape from *some* form of oppression in the Old World. Sometimes it was the oppression of the Church, sometimes of the State, sometimes of society. In the wake of the emigrant ship there was always tyranny. Men loved freedom; to find it they braved the perils of the deep, traversed the solitary forests of Maine, built huts on the bleak shores of New England, entered the Hudson, explored the Jerseys, found shelter in the Chesapeake, met starvation and death on the banks of the James, were buffeted by storms around the capes of Carolina, built towns by the estuaries of the great rivers, made roads through the pine-woods, and carried the dwellings of men to the very margin of the fever-haunted swamps of the South. It is all one story—the story of the human race seeking for liberty.

Marquette and Jolliet Discover the Mississippi.

COLONIAL HISTORY.—CONTINUED.

FRENCH AND INDIAN WAR.

CHAPTER XXX.

Causes.

THE time came when the American colonies began to act together. From the beginning they had been kept apart by prejudice, suspicion and mutual jealousy. But the fathers were now dead, old antagonisms had passed away, a new generation had arisen with kindlier feelings and more charitable sentiments. But it was not so much the growth of a more liberal public opinion as it was *the sense of a common danger* that at last led the colonists to make a united effort. The final struggle between France and England for colonial supremacy in America was at hand. Necessity compelled the English colonies to join in a common cause against a common foe. This is the conflict known as THE FRENCH AND INDIAN WAR; with this great event the separate histories of the colonies are lost in the more general history of the nation. The contest began in 1754, but the causes of the war had existed for many years.

The first and greatest of these causes was *the conflicting territorial claims* of the two nations. England had colonized the sea-coast; France had colonized the interior of the continent. From Maine to Florida the Atlantic shore was spread with English colonies; but there were no inland settlements. The great towns were on the ocean's edge. But the claims of England reached far beyond her colonies. Based on the discoveries of the Cabots, and not limited by actual occupation, those claims extended westward to the Pacific. In making grants of territory the English kings had always proceeded upon the theory that the voyage of Sebastian Cabot had given to England a lawful right to the country from one ocean to the other. Far different, however, were the claims of France; the French had first colonized the valley of the St. Lawrence. Montreal, one of the earliest settlements, is more than five hundred miles from the sea. If the French colonies had been limited to the St. Lawrence and its tributaries, there would have been little danger of a conflict about territorial dominion. But in the latter half of the seventeenth century the French began to push their way westward and southward; first, along the shores of the great lakes, then to the head-waters of the Wabash, the Illinois, the Wisconsin and the St. Croix, then down these streams to the Mississippi, and then to the Gulf of Mexico. The purpose of the French, as manifested in these movements, was no less than to divide the American continent and to take the larger portion, to possess the land for France and for Catholicism. For it was the work of the Jesuit missionaries. So important and marvelous are those early movements of the French in the valley of the Mississippi that a brief account of the leading explorations may here be given.

The zealous Jesuits, purposing to extend the Catholic faith to all lands and nations, set out fearlessly from the older settlements of the St. Lawrence to explore the unknown West, and to convert the barbarous races. In 1641, Charles Raymbault, the first of the French missionary explorers, passed through the northern straits of Lake Huron and entered Lake Superior. In the thirty years that followed, the Jesuits continued their explorations with prodigious activity. Missions were established at various points north of the lakes, and in Michigan, Wisconsin and Illinois. In 1673, Joliet and Marquette passed from the head-waters of Fox River over the watershed to the upper tributaries of the Wisconsin, and thence down that river in a seven days' voyage to the Mississippi. For a full month the canoe of the daring adventurers carried them on toward the sea. They passed the mouth of Arkansas River, and reached the limit of their voyage at the thirty-third parallel of latitude. Turning their boat up stream, they entered the mouth of the Illinois and returned by the site of Chicago into Lake Michigan, and thence to Detroit. But it was not yet known whether the great river discharged its flood of waters into the southern gulf or into the Pacific Ocean.

It remained for ROBERT DE LA SALLE, most illustrious of the French explorers, to solve the problem. This courageous and daring man was living at the outlet of Lake Ontario when the news of Marquette's voyage reached Canada. Fired with the passion of discovery, La Salle built and launched the first ship above Niagara Falls. He sailed westward through Lake Erie and Lake Huron, anchored in Green Bay, crossed Lake Michigan to the mouth of the St. Joseph, ascended that stream with a few companions, traversed the country to the upper Kankakee, and dropped down with the current into the Illinois. Here disasters overtook the expedition, and La Salle was obliged to return on foot to Fort Frontenac, a distance of nearly a thousand miles. During his absence, Father Hennepin, a member of the company, traversed Illinois, and explored the Mississippi as high as the Falls of St. Anthony.

In 1681, La Salle returned to his station on the Illinois, bringing men and supplies. A boat was built and launched, and early in the following year the heroic adventurer, with a few companions, descended the river to its junction with the Mississippi, and was borne by the Father of Waters to the Gulf of Mexico. It was one of the greatest exploits of modern times. The return voyage was successfully accomplished. La Salle reached Quebec, and immediately set sail for France. The kingdom was greatly excited, and vast plans were made for colonizing the valley of the Mississippi. In July of 1684 four ships, bearing two hundred and eighty emigrants, left France. Beaujeu commanded the fleet, and La Salle was leader of the colony. The plan was to enter the gulf, ascend the river, and plant settlements on its banks and tributaries. But Beaujeu was a bad and headstrong captain, and against La Salle's entreaties the squadron was carried out of its course, beyond the mouths of the Mississippi, and into the Bay of Matagorda. Here a landing was effected, but the store-ship, with all its precious freightage, dashed to pieces in a storm. Nevertheless, a colony was established, and Texas became a part of Louisiana.

La Salle made many unsuccessful efforts to rediscover the Mississippi. One misfortune after another followed fast, but the leader's resolute spirit remained tranquil through all calamities. At last, with sixteen companions, he set out to cross the continent to Canada. The march began in January of 1687, and continued for sixty days. The wanderers were already in the basin of the Colorado. Here, on the 2oth of March, while La Salle was at some distance from the camp, two conspirators of the company, hiding in the prairie grass, took a deadly aim at the famous explorer, and shot him dead in his tracks. Only seven of the adventurers succeeded in reaching a French settlement on the Mississippi.

France was not slow to occupy the vast country revealed to her by the activity of the Jesuits. As early as 1688 military posts had been established at Frontenac, at Niagara, at the Straits of Mackinaw, and on the Illinois River. Before the middle of the eighteenth century, permanent settlements had been made by the French on the Maumee, at Detroit, at the mouth of the river St. Joseph, at Green Bay, at Vincennes on the Lower Wabash, on the Mississippi at the mouth of the Kaskaskia, at Fort Rosalie, the present site of Natchez, and on the Gulf of Mexico at the head of the Bay of Biloxi. At this time the only outposts of the English colonies were a small fort at Oswego, on Lake Ontario, and a few scattered cabins in West Virginia. It only remained for France to occupy the valley of Ohio, in order to confine the provinces of Great Britain to the country east of the Alleghanies. To do this became the sole ambition of the French, and to prevent it the stubborn purpose of the English.

A second cause of war existed in the long-standing *national animosity of France and England.* The two nations could hardly remain at peace. The French and the English were of different races, languages and laws. For more than two centuries France had been the leader of the Catholic, and England of the Protestant, powers of Europe. Religious prejudice intensified the natural jealousy of the two nations. Rivalry prevailed on land and sea. When, at the close of the seventeenth century, it was seen that the people of the English colonies outnumbered those of Canada by nearly twenty to one, France was filled with envy. When, by the enterprise of the Jesuit missionaries, the French began to dot the basin of the Mississippi with fortresses, and to monopolize the fur-trade of the Indians, England could not conceal her wrath. It was only a question of time when this unreasonable jealousy would bring on a colonial war.

The third and immediate cause of hostilities was *a conflict between the frontiersmen of the two nations* in attempting to colonize the Ohio valley. The year 1749 witnessed the beginning of difficulties. For some time the strolling traders of Virginia and Pennsylvania had frequented the Indian towns on the upper tributaries of the Ohio. Now the traders of Canada began to visit the same villages, and to compete with the English in the purchase of furs. Virginia, under her ancient charters, claimed the whole country lying between her western borders and the southern shores of Lake Erie. The French fur-gatherers in this district were regarded as intruders not to be tolerated. In order to prevent further encroachment, a number of prominent Virginians joined themselves together in a body called THE OHIO COMPANY, with a view to the immediate occupation of the disputed territory. Robert Dinwiddie, governor of the State, Lawrence and Augustus Washington, and Thomas Lee, president of the Virginia council, were the leading members of the corporation. In March of 1749 the company received from George II. an extensive land-grant covering a tract of five hundred thousand acres, to be located between the Kanawha and the Monongahela, or on the northern bank of the Ohio. The conditions of the grant were that the lands should be held free of rent for ten years, that within seven years a colony of one hundred families should be established in the district, and that the territory should be immediately selected.

But the French were equally active. Before the Ohio Company could send out a colony, the governor of Canada despatched Bienville with three hundred men to explore and occupy the valley of the Ohio. The expedition was successful. Plates of lead bearing French inscriptions were buried here and there on both banks of the river, the region was explored as far west as the towns of the Miamis, the English traders were expelled from the country, and a letter was written to Governor Hamilton of Pennsylvania admonishing him to encroach no farther on the territory of the king of France. This work occupied the summer and fall of 1749. In the mean time, the Ohio Company had equipped an exploring party, and placed it under command of Christopher Gist. In November of 1750 he and his company reached the Ohio opposite the mouth of Beaver Creek. Here the expedition crossed to the northern side, tarried at Logstown, passed down the river through the several Indian confederacies to the Great Miami, and thence to within fifteen miles of the falls at Louisville. Returning on foot through Kentucky, the explorers reached Virginia in the spring of 1751.

This expedition was followed by still more vigorous movements on the part of the French. Descending from their headquarters at Presque Isle, now Eric, on the southern shore of the lake, they built a fortress called Le Bœuf, on French Creek, a tributary of the Alleghany. Proceeding down the stream to its junction with the river, they erected a second fort, named Venango. From this point they advanced against a British post on the Miami, broke up the settlement, made prisoners of the garrison and carried them to Canada. The king of the Miami confederacy, who had assisted the English in defending their outpost, was inhumanly murdered by the Indian allies of the French. About the same time the country south of the Ohio, between the Great Kanawha and the Monongahela, was explored by Gist and a party of armed surveyors, acting under orders of the company. In the summer of 1753 the English opened a road from Will's Creek through the mountains into the Ohio valley, and a colony of eleven families was planted on the Youghiogheny, just west of Laurel Hill. It was impossible that a conflict between the advancing settlements of the two nations could be much longer averted.

The Indian nations were greatly alarmed at the threatening prospect. Solemn councils were held among all the tribes, and the affairs of the race were gravely discussed by the copper-colored orators. From the first the Red men rather favored the English cause, but their allegiance was wavering and uncertain. After the murder of the Miami chieftain their hostility to the French became more decided. When, in the spring of 1753, the news was borne to the council-fires on the Ohio that Du Quesne, the governor of Canada, had despatched a company of twelve hundred men to descend the Alleghany and colonize the country, the jealousy of the natives was kindled into open resistance. The tribes most concerned were the Delawares, the Shawnees, the Miamis and the Mingoes. The chieftain of this confederacy, named Tanacharisson, was called the Half-King from the fact that his subjects, except the Miamis, owed a kind of indefinite allegiance to the Iroquois or Six Nations. By the authority of a great council held at Logstown the Half-King was now sent to Erie to remonstrate with the French commandant against a further invasion of the Indian country. "The land is mine, and I will have it," replied the Frenchman, with derision and contempt. The insulted sachem returned to his nation to lift the hatchet against the enemies of his people. It was at this time that the chiefs of many tribes met Benjamin Franklin at the town of Carlisle, Pennsylvania, and formed a treaty of alliance with the English.

Virginia was now thoroughly aroused. But before proceeding to actual hostilities, Governor Dinwiddie determined to try the effect of a final remonstrance with the French. A paper was accordingly drawn up setting forth the nature and extent of the English claim to the valley of the Ohio, and solemnly warning the authorities of France against further intrusion into that region. It was necessary that this paper should be carried to General St. Pierre, now stationed at Erie as commander of the French forces in the West. Who should be chosen to bear the important parchment to its far-off destination? It was the most serious mission ever yet undertaken in America. A young surveyor, named GEORGE WASHINGTON, was called to perform the perilous duty. Him the governor summoned from his home on the Potomac and commissioned as ambassador, and to him was committed the message which was to be borne from Williamsburg, on York River, through the untrodden wilderness to Presque Isle, on the shore of Lake Erie.

On the last day of October, 1753, Washington set out on his long journey. He was attended by four comrades besides an interpreter and Christopher Gist, the guide. The party arrived without accident at the mouth of Will's Creek, the last important tributary of the Potomac on the north. From this place Washington proceeded through the mountains to the head-waters of the Youghiogheny, and thence down that stream to the site of Pittsburg. The immense importance of this place, lying at the confluence of the two great tributaries of the Ohio, and commanding them both, was at once perceived by the young ambassador, who noted the spot as the site of a fortress. Washington was now conducted across the Alleghany by the chief of the Delawares, and thence twenty miles down the river to Logstown. Here a council was held with the Indians, who renewed their pledges of friendship and fidelity to the English. The emissaries of the French were already in the country trying in every conceivable way to entice the Red men into an alliance; but every proposal was rejected. In the beginning of December, Washington and his party moved northward to the French post at Venango. The officers of the fort took no pains to conceal their purpose; the project of uniting Canada and Louisiana by way of the Ohio valley was openly avowed.

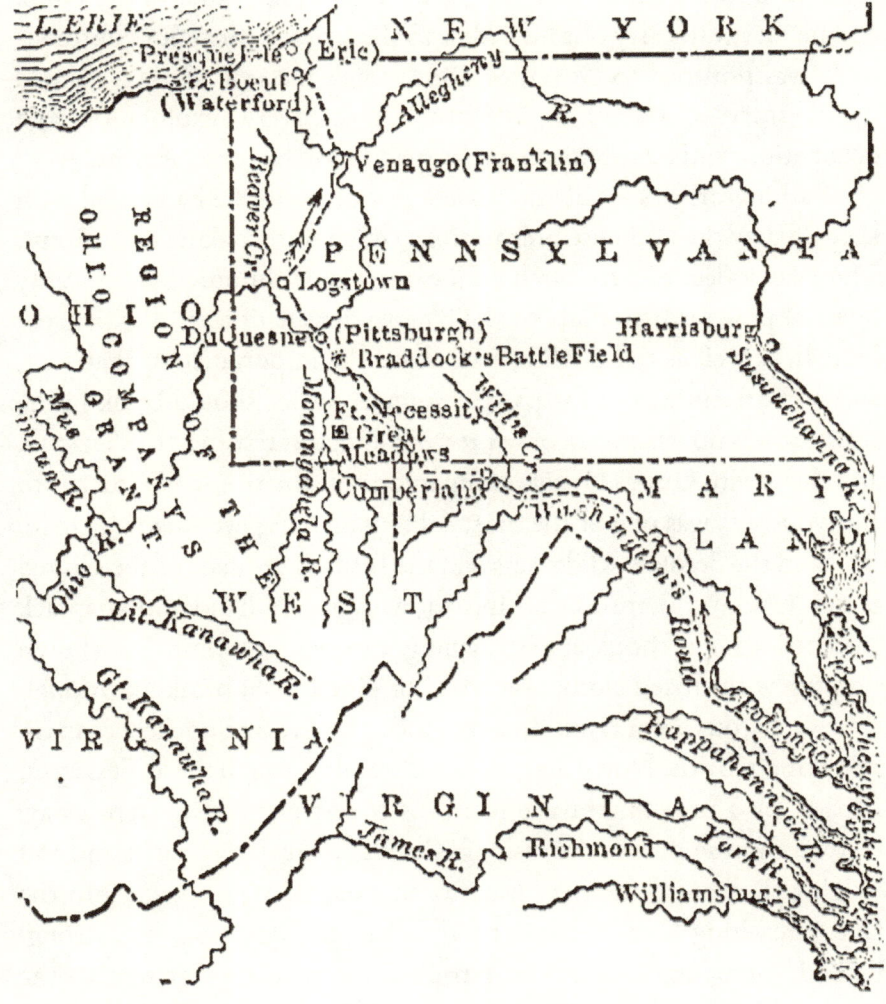

First Scene of the French and Indian War, 1750.

From Venango, Washington set out through the forest to Fort le Bœuf on French Creek, fifty miles above its junction with the Alleghany. This was the last stage in the journey. It was still fourteen miles to Presque Isle; but St. Pierre, the French commander, had come down from that place to superintend the fortifications at Le Bœuf. Here the conference was held. Washington was received with great courtesy, but the general of the French refused to enter into any discussion on the rights of nations. He was acting, he said, under military instructions given by the governor of New France. He had been commanded by his superior officer to eject every Englishman from the valley of the Ohio, and he meant to carry out his orders to the letter. A firm but courteous reply was returned to Governor Dinwiddie's message. France claimed the country of the Ohio in virtue of discovery, exploration and occupation, and her claim should be made good by force of arms.

Washington was kindly dismissed, but not until he had noted with keen anxiety the immense preparations which were making at Le Bœuf. There lay a fleet of fifty birch-bark canoes and a hundred and seventy boats of pine ready to descend the river to the site of Pittsburg. For the French, as well as the English, had noted the importance of that spot, and had determined to fortify it as soon as the ice should break in the rivers. It was now the dead of winter. Washington returned to Venango, and then, with Gist as his sole companion, left the river and struck into the woods. It was one of the most solitary marches ever made by man. There in the desolate wilderness was the future President of the United States. Clad in the robe of an Indian, with gun in hand and knapsack strapped to his shoulders; struggling through interminable snows; sleeping with frozen clothes on a bed of pine-brush; breaking through the treacherous ice of rapid streams; guided by day by a pocket compass, and at night by the North Star, seen at intervals through the leafless trees; fired at by a prowling savage from his covert not fifteen steps away; thrown from a raft into the rushing Alleghany; escaping to an island and lodging there until the river was frozen over; plunging again into the forest; reaching Gist's settlement and then the Potomac,–the strong-limbed young ambassador came back without wound or soar to the capital of Virginia. For his flesh was not made to be torn with bullets or to be eaten by the wolves. The defiant despatch of St. Pierre was laid before Governor Dinwiddie, and the first public service of Washington was accomplished.

In the mean time, the Ohio Company had not been idle. About midwinter a party of thirty-three men had been organized and placed under command of Trent, with orders to proceed at once to the source of the Ohio and erect a fort. The company must have been marching to its destination when Washington returned to Virginia. It was not far from the middle of March, 1754, when Trent's party reached the confluence of the Alleghany and the Monongahela, and built the first rude stockade on the site of Pittsburg.[9] After all the threats and boasting of the French, the English had beaten them and seized the key to the Ohio valley.

But it was a short-lived triumph. As soon as the approaching spring broke the ice-gorges in the Alleghany, the French fleet of boats, already prepared at Venango, came sweeping down the river. It was in vain for Trent with his handful of men to offer resistance. Washington had now been commissioned as lieutenant-colonel, and was stationed at Alexandria to enlist recruits for the Ohio. A regiment of a hundred and fifty men had been enrolled; but it was impossible to bring succor to Trent in time to save the post. On the 17th of April the little band of Englishmen at the head of the Ohio surrendered to the enemy and withdrew from the country. The French immediately occupied the place, felled the forest-trees, built barracks and laid the foundations of FORT DU QUESNE. To recapture this place by force of arms Colonel Washington set out from Will's Creek in the early part of May, 1754. Negotiations had failed; remonstrance had been tried in vain; the possession of the disputed territory was now to be determined by the harsher methods of war.

---

[9] The accounts of this important event are very obscure and unsatisfactory.

CHAPTER XXXI.

CAMPAIGNS OF WASHINGTON AND BRADDOCK.

WASHINGTON now found himself in command of a little army of Virginians. His commission was brief and easily understood: To construct a fort at the source of the Ohio; to destroy whoever opposed him in the work; to capture, kill or repel all who interrupted the progress of the English settlements in that country. In the month of April the young commander left Will's Creek, but the march westward was slow and toilsome. The men were obliged to drag their cannons. The roads were miserable; rain fell in torrents on the tentless soldiers; rivers were bridgeless; provisions insufficient. All the while the faithful Half-King was urging Washington by repeated despatches to hasten to the rescue of the Red men.

On the 26th of May the English regiment reached the Great Meadows. Here Washington was informed that a company of French was on the march to attack him. The enemy had been seen on the Youghiogheny only a few miles distant. A stockade was immediately erected, to which the commander gave the appropriate name of Fort Necessity. Ascertaining from the scouts of the Half-King that the French company in the neighborhood was only a scouting-party, Washington, after conference with the Mingo chiefs, determined to strike the first blow. Two Indians followed the trail of the French, and discovered their hiding place in a rocky ravine. The English advanced cautiously, intending to surprise and capture the whole force; but the French were on the alert, saw the approaching soldiers and, flew to arms. Washington with musket in hand was at the head of his company. "Fire!" was the clear command that rang through the forest, and the first volley of a great war went flying on its mission of death. The engagement was brief and decisive. Jumonville, the leader of the French, and ten of his party were killed, and twenty-one were made prisoners.

A month of precious time was now lost in delays. While Washington at Fort Necessity waited in vain for reinforcements, the French at Fort du Quesne were collecting in great numbers. One small company of volunteers from South Carolina arrived at the English camp; but the captain was an arrogant blockhead who, having a commission from the king, undertook to supersede Washington. The latter, with the Virginians, spent the time of waiting in cutting a road for twenty miles across the rough country in the direction of Fort du Quesne. The Indians were greatly discouraged at the dilatory conduct of the colonies, and the strong war-parties which had been expected to join Washington from the Muskingum and the Miami did not arrive. His whole effective force scarcely numbered four hundred. Learning that the French general De Villiers was approaching with a large body of troops, besides Indian auxiliaries, Washington deemed it prudent to fall back to Fort Necessity. The Carolina captain, who had remained within the fortifications, had done nothing to strengthen the works, although there was the greatest need.

The little fort stood in an open space, midway between two eminences covered with trees. Scarcely were Washington's forces safe within the enclosure, when on the 3d of July the regiment of De Villiers, numbering six hundred, besides the savage allies, came in sight, and surrounded the fort. The French stationed themselves on the eminence, about sixty yards distant from the stockade. From this position they could fire down upon the English with fatal effect. Many of the Indians climbed into the tree-tops, where they were concealed by the thick foliage. For nine hours, during a rain-storm, the assailants poured an incessant shower of balls upon the heroic band in the fort. Thirty of Washington's men were killed, but his tranquil presence encouraged the rest, and the fire of the French was returned with unabated vigor. At length De Villiers, fearing that his ammunition would be exhausted, proposed a parley. Washington, seeing that it would be impossible to hold out much longer, accepted the honorable terms of capitulation which were offered by the French general. On the 4th of July the English garrison, retaining all its accoutrements, marched out of the little fort, so bravely defended, and withdrew from the country. The whole valley of the Ohio remained in undisturbed possession of the French.

Meanwhile, a congress of the American colonies had assembled at Albany. The objects had in view were twofold: first, to renew the treaty with the Iroquois confederacy; and secondly, to stir up the colonial authorities to some sort of concerted action against the French. The Iroquois had wavered from the beginning of the war; the recent reverses of the English had not strengthened the loyalty of the Red men. As to the French aggressions, something must be done speedily, or the flag of England could never be borne into the vast country west of the Alleghanies. The congress was not wanting in abilities of the highest order. No such venerable and dignified body of men had ever before assembled on the American continent. There were Hutchinson of Massachusetts, Hopkins of Rhode Island, Franklin of Pennsylvania, and others scarcely less distinguished. After a few days' consultation, the Iroquois, but half satisfied, renewed their treaty and departed. The chieftains were anxious and uneasy lest, through inactivity and want of union on the part of the colonies, the Six Nations should be left to contend alone with the power of France.

The convention next took up the important question of uniting the colonies in a common government. On the 10th day of July, Benjamin Franklin laid before the commissioners the draft of a federal constitution. His vast and comprehensive mind had realized the true condition and wants of the country; the critical situation of the colonies demanded a central government. How else could revenues be raised, an army be organized and the common welfare be provided for? According to the proposed plan of union, Philadelphia, a central city, was to be the capital. It was urged in behalf of this clause that the delegates of New Hampshire and Georgia, the colonies most remote, could reach the seat of government *in fifteen or twenty days!* Slow-going old patriots! The chief executive of the new confederation was to be a governor-general appointed and supported by the king. The legislative authority was vested in a congress composed of delegates to be chosen triennially by the general assemblies of the respective provinces. Each colony should be represented in proportion to its contributions to the general government, but no colony should have less than two or more than seven representatives in congress. With the governor was lodged the power of appointing all military officers and of vetoing objectionable laws. The appointment of civil officers, the raising of troops, the levying of taxes, the superintendence of Indian affairs, the regulation of commerce, and all the general duties of government, belonged to congress. This body was to convene once a year, to choose its own officers, and to remain in session not longer than six weeks.[10]

Such was the constitution drafted by Franklin and adopted, not without serious opposition, by the commissioners at Albany. It remained for the colonies to ratify or reject the new scheme of government. Copies of the proposed constitution were at one transmitted to the several colonial capitals, and were everywhere received with disfavor; in Connecticut, rejected; in Massachusetts, opposed; in New York, adopted with indifference. The chief objection urged against the instrument was the power of veto given to the governor-general. Nor did the new constitution fare better in the mother country. The English board of trade rejected it with disdain, saying that the froward Americans were trying to make a government of their own. Meanwhile, the French were strengthening their works at Crown Point and Fort Niagara, and rejoicing over their success in Western Pennsylvania.

But the honor of England, no less than the welfare of her colonies, was at stake, and Parliament came to the rescue. It was determined to send a British army to America, to accept the service of such provincial troops as the colonies might furnish, and to protect the frontier against the aggressions of France. As yet there had been no declaration of war. The ministers of the two nations kept assuring each other of peaceable intentions; but Louis XV. took care to send three thousand soldiers to Canada, and the British government ordered General Edward Braddock to proceed to America with two regiments of regulars. Early in 1755 the English armament arrived in the Chesapeake. On the 14th of April Braddock met the governors of all the colonies in a convention at Alexandria. The condition of colonial affairs was fully discussed. It was resolved, since peace existed, not to invade Canada, but to repel the French on the western and northern frontier. The plans of four

---

[10] See Appendix C.

campaigns were accordingly submitted and ratified. Lawrence, the governor of Nova Scotia, was to complete the conquest of that province according to the English notion of boundaries. Johnson of New York was to enroll a force of volunteers and Mohawks in British pay, and to capture the French post at Crown Point. Shirley of Massachusetts was to equip a regiment and drive the enemy from their fortress at Niagara. Last and most important of all, Braddock himself as commander-in-chief was to lead the main body of regulars against Fort da Quesne, retake that post and expel the French from the Ohio valley.

In the latter part of April the British general set out on his march from Alexandria to Will's Creek. The name of the military post at the mouth of this stream was now changed to Fort Cumberland. Braddock's army numbered fully two thousand men. They were nearly all veterans who had seen service in the wars of Europe. A few provincial troops had joined the expedition; two companies of volunteers, led by Colonel Horatio Gates of New York, were among the number. Washington met the army at Fort Cumberland, and became an aid-de-camp of Braddock. The colonies would have assisted with large levies of recruits, had it not been for the nature of the general's authority. It was prescribed in his commission that the provincial captains and colonels *should have no rank* when serving in connection with the British army. So odious was this regulation that Washington had set the example of withdrawing from the service; patriotic motives and the wish of Virginia now induced him to return and to accept a post of responsibility.

On the last day of May the march began from Fort Cumberland. A select force of five hundred men was thrown forward to open the roads in the direction of Fort du Quesne. Sir Peter Halket led the advance, and Braddock followed with the main body. The army, marching in a slender column, was extended for four miles along the narrow and broken road. It was in vain that Washington pointed out the danger of ambuscades and suggested the employment of scouting-parties. Braddock was self-willed, arrogant, proud; thoroughly skilled in the tactics of European warfare, he could not bear to be advised by an inferior. The sagacious Franklin had admonished him to move with caution; but he only replied that it was impossible for savages to make any impression on His

Majesty's regulars. Now, when Washington ventured to repeat the advice, Braddock flew into a passion, strode up and down in his tent, and said that it was high times when Colonel Buckskin could teach a British general how to fight.

On the 19th of June, Braddock put himself at the head of twelve hundred chosen troops and pressed forward more rapidly. Colonel Dunbar was left behind with the remainder of the army. On the 8th of July the van reached the junction of the Youghiogheny and the Monongahela. It was only twelve miles farther to Fort da Quesne, and the French gave up the place as lost. On the next morning the English army advanced along the Monongahela, and at noon crossed to the northern bank just beyond the confluence of Turtle Creek. Still there was no sign of an enemy. Colonel Thomas Gage was leading forward a detachment of three hundred and fifty men. The road was but twelve feet wide; the country uneven and woody. There was a dense undergrowth on either hand; rocks and ravines; a hill on the right and a dry hollow on the left. A few guides were in the advance, and some feeble flanking-parties; in the rear came the general with the main division of the army, the artillery and the baggage. All at once a quick and heavy fire was heard in the front.

France was not going to give up Fort du Quesne without a struggle. For two months the place had been receiving reinforcements; still the garrison was by no means able to cope with Braddock's army. Even the Indians realized the disparity of the contest. It was with great difficulty that, on the night before the battle, the commandant of the fort induced the savages to join in the enterprise of ambuscading the British. At last a force of two hundred and thirty French, led by Beaujeu and Dumas, and a body of six hundred and thirty-seven Indians set out from Du Quesne with a view to harass and annoy the English rather than to face them in a serious battle. It was the purpose of the French, who were entirely familiar with the ground, to lay an ambuscade at a favorable point seven miles distant from the fort. They were just reaching the selected spot and settling into ambush when the flanking-parties of the English came in sight. The French fired; the Indians yelled and slunk into their hiding-places, and the battle began.

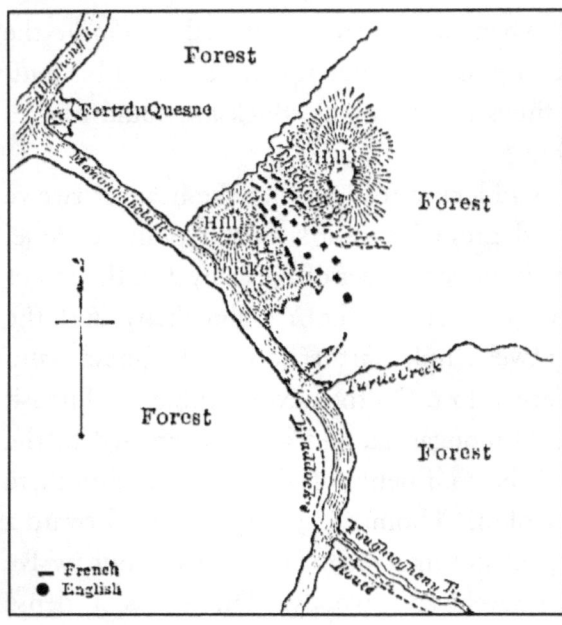
Scene of Braddock's Defeat, 1755.

If Gage had at once thrown forward his forces to the support of the guards, the day could have been saved; but he was confused and undecided. The flanking parties were driven in, leaving their six-pounders in the hands of the enemy. Gage's men wavered, and were mixed in the thickset underwood with a regiment which Braddock had pushed forward to the rescue. The confusion became greater, and there were symptoms of a panic. The men fired constantly, but could see no enemy. Every volley from the hidden foe flew with deadly certainty into the crowded ranks of the English. The rash but brave general rushed to the front and rallied his men with the energy of despair; but it was all in vain. The men stood huddled together like sheep, or fled in terror to the rear. The forest was strewn with the dead; the savages, emboldened by their unexpected success, crept farther and farther along the flanks; and the battle became a rout. Braddock had five horses shot under him; his secretary was killed; both his English aids were disabled; only Washington remained to distribute orders. Out of eighty-two officers twenty-six were killed and thirty-seven wounded. Of the privates seven hundred and fourteen were dead or bleeding with wounds. At last the general received a ball in his right side and sank fainting to the ground. "What shall we do now, colonel?" said he to Washington, who came to his assistance. "Retreat, sir—retreat by all means," replied the young hero, upon whom everything now depended. His own bosom had been for more than two hours a special target for the savages. Two horses had fallen under him, and four times his coat had been torn with balls. A Shawnee chief singled him out and bade his warriors do the same; but their volleys went by harmless. The retreat began at once, and the thirty Virginians, who, with Washington, were all that remained alive, covered the flight of the ruined army. The artillery, provisions, baggage and private papers of the general were left on the field.

Fall of Braddock.

The losses of the French and Indians were slight, amounting to three officers and thirty men killed, and as many others wounded. There was no attempt made at pursuit. The savages fairly reveled in the spoils of the battle-field. They had never known so rich a harvest of scalps and booty. The tawny chiefs returned to Fort du Quesne clad in the laced coats, military boots and cockades of the British officers. The dying Braddock was borne in the train of the fugitives. Once he roused himself to say, "Who would have thought it?" and again, "We shall better know how to deal with them another time." On the evening of the fourth day he died, and was buried by the roadside a mile west of Fort Necessity. When the fugitives reached Dunbar's camp, the confusion was greater than ever. Dunbar was a man of feeble capacity and no courage; pretending to have the orders of the dying general, he proceeded to destroy the remaining artillery, the heavy baggage, and all the public stores, to the value of a hundred thousand pounds. Then followed a precipitate retreat to Fort Cumberland, and then an abandonment of that place for the safer precincts of Philadelphia. It was only the beginning of August, yet Dunbar pleaded the necessity of finding winter quarters for his forces. The great expedition of Braddock had ended in such a disaster as spread consternation and gloom over all the colonies.

CHAPTER XXXII.

Ruin of Acadia.

By the treaty of Utrecht, made in 1713, the province of Acadia, or Nova Scotia, was ceded by France to England. During the following fifty years the colony remained under the dominion of Great Britain, and was ruled by English officers. But the great majority of the people were French, and the English government amounted only to a military occupation of the peninsula. The British colors, floating over Louisburg and Annapolis, and the presence of British garrisons here and there, were the only tokens that this, the oldest French colony in America, had passed under the control of foreigners.

At the time of the cession the population amounted to about three thousand; by the outbreak of the French and Indian War the number had increased to more than sixteen thousand. Lawrence, the deputy-governor of the province, pretended to fear an insurrection. When Braddock and the colonial governors convened at Alexandria, it was urged that something must be done to overawe the French and strengthen the English authority in Acadia. The enterprise of reducing the French peasants to complete humiliation was entrusted to Lawrence, who was to be assisted by a British fleet under Colonel Monckton. On the 20th of May, 1755, the squadron, with three thousand troops, sailed from Boston for the Bay of Fundy.

The Acadian Isthmus, 1755.

The French had but two fortified posts in the province; both of these were on the isthmus which divides Nova Scotia from New Brunswick. The first and most important fortress, named Beau-Sejour, was situated near the mouth of Messagouche Creek, at the head of Chignecto Bay. The other fort, a mere stockade called Gaspereau, was on the north side of the isthmus, at

Bay Verte. De Vergor, the French commandant, had no intimation of approaching danger till the English fleet sailed fearlessly into the bay and anchored before the walls of Beau-Sejour. There was no preparation for defence. On the 3d of June the English forces landed, and on the next day forced their way across the Messagouche. A vigorous siege of four days followed. Fear and confusion reigned among the garrison; no successful resistance could be offered. On the 16th of the month Beau-Sejour capitulated, received an English garrison and took the name of Fort Cumberland. The feeble post at Gaspereau was taken a few days afterward, and named Fort Monckton. Captain Rous was despatched with four vessels to capture the fort at the mouth of the St. John's; but before the fleet could reach its destination, the French reduced the town to ashes and escaped into the interior. In a campaign of less than a month, and with a loss of only twenty men, the English had made themselves masters of the whole country east of the St. Croix.

The War in Acadia was at an end; but what should be done with the people? The French inhabitants still outnumbered the English nearly three to one. Governor Lawrence and Admiral Boscawen, in conference with the chief justice of the province, settled upon the atrocious measure of driving the people into banishment. The first movement was to demand an oath of allegiance which was so framed that the French, as honest Catholics, could not take it. The priests advised the peasants to declare their loyalty, but refuse the oath, which was meant to ensnare their souls. The next step on the part of the English was to accuse the French of treason, and to demand the surrender of all their firearms and boats. To this measure the broken-hearted people also submitted. They even offered to take the oath, but Lawrence declared that, having once refused, they must now take the consequences. The British vessels were made ready, and the work of forcible embarkation began.

The country about the isthmus was covered with peaceful hamlets. These were now laid waste, and the people driven into the larger towns on the coast. Others were induced by artifice and treachery to put themselves into the power of the English. Wherever a sufficient number of the French could be gotten together they were driven on shipboard. They were allowed to take their wives and children and as much property as would not be inconvenient on the vessels. The estates of the province were confiscated, and what could not be appropriated was given to the flames. The wails of thousands of bleeding hearts were wafted to heaven with the smoke of burning homes. At the village of Grand Pre four hundred and eighteen unarmed men were called together and shut up in a church. Then came the wives and children, the old men and the mothers, the sick and the infirm, to share the common fate. The whole company numbered more than nineteen hundred souls. The poor creatures were driven down to the shore, forced into the boats at the point of the bayonet, and carried to the vessels in the bay. As the moaning fugitives cast a last look at their pleasant town, a column of black smoke floating seaward told the story of desolation. More than three thousand of the hapless Acadians were carried away by the British squadron and scattered, helpless, half starved and dying, among the English colonies. The history of civilized nations furnishes no parallel to this wanton and wicked destruction of an inoffensive colony.

The Exile of the Acadians.[11]

---

[11] Longfellow's *Evangeline* is founded on this incident.

CHAPTER XXXIII.

Expeditions of Shirley and Johnson.

The third campaign planned by Braddock at Alexandria was to be conducted by Governor Shirley of Massachusetts. The expedition was to proceed from Albany to Oswego, and thence by water to the mouth of the Niagara. It was known that Fort Niagara was an insignificant post, depending for its defence upon a small ditch, a rotten palisade and a feeble garrison. To capture this place, to obtain command of the river, and to cut off the communications of the French by way of the lakes, were the objects of the campaign. "Fort du Quesne can hardly detain me more than three or four days," said Braddock to Shirley, "and then I will meet you at Niagara."

In the early part of August, Shirley set out at the head of nearly two thousand men. It was the last of the month before he reached Oswego. Here the provincial forces had been ordered to assemble. Four weeks were spent in preparing boats for embarkation. When everything was in readiness, a storm arose; and when the storm abated, the winds blew in the wrong direction. Then came another tempest and another delay; then sickness prevailed in the camp. With the beginning of October Shirley declared the lake to be dangerous for navigation. The Indians deserted the standard of a leader whose skill in war consisted in framing excuses. The fact was that the general, while on the march to Oswego, had learned of the destruction of Braddock's army, and feared that a similar fate might overtake his own. On the 24th of October the greater part of the provincial forces, led by Shirley, marched homeward. Only one result of any importance followed from the campaign—the fort at Oswego was well rebuilt and garrisoned with seven hundred men under Mercer.

Far more important was the expedition entrusted to General William Johnson. The object had in view was to capture the enemy's fortress at Crown Point, and to drive the French from the shores of Lake Champlain. Johnson's army numbered three thousand four hundred men, including a body of friendly Mohawks. The active work of the campaign began early in August, when General Phineas Lyman, at the head of the New England troops, proceeded to the Hudson above Albany, and at a point just below where the river bends abruptly to the west built Fort Edward. Thither in the last days of summer came the commanding general with the main division. The watershed between the Hudson and Lake George is only twelve miles wide. Johnson's army marched across to the head of the lake and laid out a commodious camp. A week was spent in bringing forward the artillery and stores. The soldiers were busy preparing boats for embarkation, and the important matter of fortifying the camp was wholly neglected.

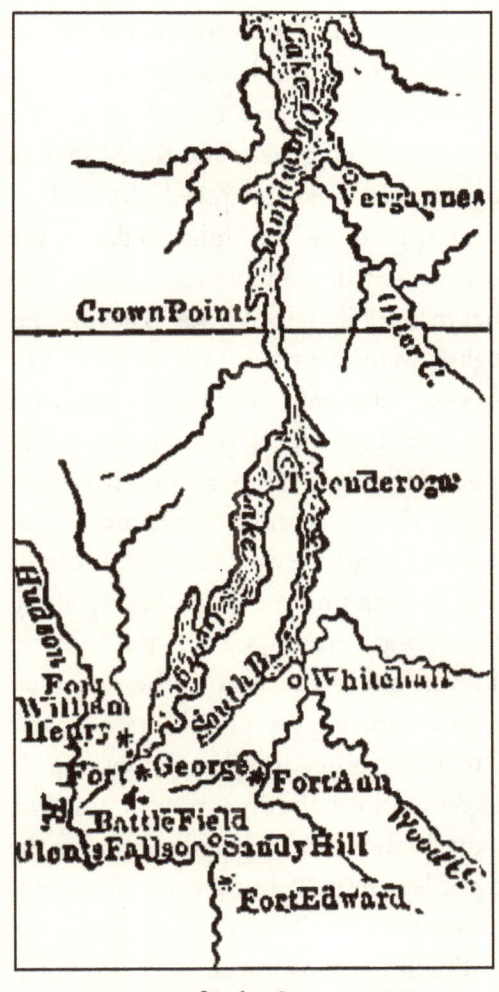

Vicinity of Lake George, 1755.

In the mean time, Dieskau, the daring commandant at Crown Point, determined to anticipate the movements of the English. With a force of fourteen hundred French, Canadians and Indians he sailed up Lake Champlain to South Bay. From this point he marched to the upper springs of Wood Creek, intending to strike to the south, pass the English army and capture Fort Edward before the alarm could be given. But the news was carried to General Johnson; and a force of a thousand men under command of Colonel Williams, accompanied by Hendrick, the gray-haired chieftain of the Mohawks, with two hundred warriors, was sent to the relief of the endangered fort. On the previous night Dieskau's guides had led him out of his course. On the morning of the 8th of September the French general found himself and his army about four miles north of Fort Edward, on the main road from the Hudson to Lake George. Just at this time Colonel Williams's regiment and the Mohawks came in sight, marching toward the fort. Dieskau quickly formed an ambush, and the English were entrapped; but the Indian allies of the French showed themselves to their countrymen, and would not fire. The Canadians and the French poured in a deadly volley; both Williams and Hendrick fell dead, and the English were thrown into confusion. But Colonel Whiting rallied the troops, returned the enemy's fire, and retreated toward the lake. St. Pierre, one of the French generals, was killed.

The noise of battle was heard in Johnson's camp, and preparations were made for a general engagement. There were no entrenchments, but trees were hastily felled for breastworks, and the cannons were brought into position. It was Dieskau's plan to rush into the English camp along with the fugitives whom he was driving before him; but the Indians, afraid of Johnson's guns, would not join in the assault; the Red men retired to a hill at a safe distance. The Canadians were disheartened; and the handful of French regulars made the onset almost unsupported. It was the fiercest battle which had yet been fought on American soil. For five hours the conflict was incessant. In the beginning of the engagement Johnson received a slight wound and left the field; but the troops of New England fought on without a commander. Nearly all of Dieskau's regulars were killed. At last the English troops leaped over the fallen trees, charged across the field, and completed the rout. Three times Dieskau was wounded, but he would not retire. His aids came to bear him off; one was shot dead, and he forbade the others. He ordered his servants to bring him his military dress, and then seated himself on the stump of a tree. A renegade Frenchman belonging to the English army rushed up to make him a prisoner. The wounded general felt for his watch to tender it in token of surrender. The Frenchman, thinking that Dieskau was searching for a pistol, fired, and the brave commander fell, mortally wounded.

The victory, though complete, was dearly purchased. Two hundred and sixteen of the English were killed, and many others wounded. General

Johnson, who had done but little, was greatly praised; Parliament made him a baronet for gaining a victory which the provincials gained for him. Made wiser by the battle, he now constructed on the site of his camp a substantial fort, and named it William Henry. The defences of Fort Edward were strengthened with an additional garrison, and the remainder of the troops returned to their homes. Meanwhile, the French had reinforced Crown Point, and had seized and fortified Ticonderoga. Such was the condition of affairs at the close of 1755.

CHAPTER XXXIV.

Two Years of Disaster.

AFTER the death of Braddock the chief command of the English forces in America was given to Governor Shirley. But no regular military organization had been effected; and the war was carried on in a desultory manner. Braddock had ruined one army; Shirley had scattered another. On Lake George, Johnson had achieved a marked success. In the beginning of 1756, Washington at the head of the Virginian provincials repelled the French and Indians in the valley of the Shenandoah. At the same time the Pennsylvania volunteers, choosing Franklin for their colonel, marched to the banks of the Lehigh, built a fort, and made a successful campaign. In the preceding December, Shirley met the colonial governors at New York and planned the movements for the following year. One expedition, proceeding by way of the Kennebec, was to threaten Quebec. Forts Frontenac, Toronto and Niagara were to be taken. Du Quesne, Detroit and Mackinaw, deprived of their communications, must of course surrender.

In the mean time, after much debate in Parliament, it was decided to consolidate and put under one authority all the military forces in America. The earl of Loudoun received the appointment of commander-in-chief. General Abercrombie was second in rank; and forty British and German officers were commissioned to organize and discipline the colonial army. In the last of April, 1756, Abercrombie, with two battalions of regulars, sailed for New York. Lord Loudoun was to follow with a fleet of transports, bearing the artillery, tents, ammunition and equipage of the expedition. The commander waited a month for his vessels, and then sailed without them. On the 15th of June a man-of-war was despatched to America with a hundred thousand pounds to reimburse the colonies for the expenses of the previous campaigns. At the same time the corps of British officers arrived at New York. Meanwhile, on the 17th of May, Great Britain, after nearly two years of actual hostilities, made an open declaration of war, which was followed by a similar declaration on the part of France.

On the 25th of June, Abercrombie reached Albany. He began his great campaign by surveying the town, digging a ditch and quartering his soldiers with the citizens. In July, Lord Loudoun arrived and assumed the command of the colonial army. The French, meanwhile, profiting by these delays, organized a force of more than five thousand men, crossed Lake Ontario and laid siege to Oswego. The marquis of Montcalm, who had succeeded Dieskau as commander-in-chief, led the expedition. At the mouth of Oswego River there were two forts; the old block-house on the west and the new Fort Ontario on the east. The latter was first attacked. Thirty pieces of cannon were brought to bear on the fortress. After a brave defence of one day, the little garrison abandoned the works and escaped to the old fort across the river. This place was also invested by the French. For two days the English, numbering only fourteen hundred, held out against the besiegers, and then surrendered. A vast amount of ammunition, small arms, accoutrements and provisions fell to the captors. Six vessels of war, three hundred boats, a hundred and twenty cannon and three chests of money were the further fruits of a victory by which France gained the only important outpost of England on the lakes. To please his Indian allies, Montcalm ordered Oswego to be razed to the ground.

During this summer the Delawares, false to their treaty, rose in Western Pennsylvania and almost ruined the country. More than a thousand people were killed or carried into captivity. In August, Colonel John Armstrong, at the head of three hundred volunteers, crossed the Alleghanies, and after a twenty days' march reached the Indian town of Kittaning, forty-five miles north-east from Pittsburg. Lying in concealment until daydawn on the morning of September 8th, the English rose against the savages, and after a desperate battle destroyed them almost to a man. The village was burned and the spirit of the barbarians completely broken. The Americans lost sixteen men. Colonel Armstrong and Captain Hugh Mercer, afterward distinguished in the Revolution, were both severely wounded.

Lord Loudoun continued at Albany. His forces were amply sufficient to capture every stronghold of Canada in the space of six weeks. Instead of marching boldly to the north, he whiled away the summer and fall, talked about an attack from the French, digged ditches, slandered the provincial officers and waited for winter. When the frosts came, he made haste to distribute the colonial troops and to quarter the regulars on the principal towns. The vigilant French, learning what sort of a general they had to cope with, crowded Lake Champlain with boats, strengthened Crown Point and completed a fort at Ticonderoga. With the exception of Armstrong's expedition against the Indians, the year 1756 closed without a single substantial success on the part of the English.

And the year 1757 was equally disastrous. The campaign which was planned by Loudoun was limited to the conquest of Louisburg. Ever since the treaty of Utrecht the French had retained Cape Breton; and the fortress at Louisburg had been made one of the strongest on the continent. On the 20th of June, Lord Loudoun sailed from New York with an army of six thousand regulars. By the first of July he was at Halifax, where he was joined by Admiral Holbourn with a powerful fleet of sixteen men-of-war. There were on board five thousand additional troops fresh from the armies of England. Never was such a use made of a splendid armament. Loudoun landed before Halifax, cleared off a mustering plain, and set his officers to drilling regiments already skilled in every manœuvre of war. To heighten the absurdity, the fields about the city were planted with onions. For it was said that the men might take the scurvy! By and by the news came that the French vessels in the harbor of Louisburg outnumbered by one the ships of the English squadron. To attack a force that seemed superior to his own was not a part of Loudoun's tactics. Ordering the fleet to go cruising around Cape Breton, he immediately embarked with his army, and sailed for New York. Arriving at this place, he proposed to his officers to fortify Long Island in order to defend the continent against an enemy whom he outnumbered four to one.

Meanwhile, the daring Montcalm had made a brilliant campaign in the country of Lake George. With a force of six thousand French and Canadians and seventeen hundred Indians he proceeded up the Sorel, entered Lake Champlain, and reached Ticonderoga. The object of the expedition was to capture and destroy Fort William Henry. The French and the Iroquois, who had now abandoned the cause of the colonies, were fired with enthusiasm. Dragging their artillery and boats across the portage to Lake George, they re-embarked, and on the 3d of August laid siege to the English fort. The place was defended by only five hundred men under the brave Colonel Monro; but there were seventeen hundred additional troops within supporting distance in the adjacent trenches. All this while General Webb was at Fort Edward, but fourteen miles distant, with an army of more than four thousand British regulars. Instead of advancing to the relief of Fort William Henry, Webb held a council to determine if it were not better to retire to Albany, and sent a message to Colonel Monro advising capitulation.

For six days the French pressed the siege with vigor. The ammunition of the garrison was nearly exhausted; half of the guns were burst; nothing remained but to surrender. Honorable terms were granted. The English, retaining their private effects, were released on a pledge not to re-enter the service for eighteen months. A safe escort was promised to Fort Edward. On the 9th of August the French took possession of the fortress. Unfortunately, the Indians procured a quantity of spirits from the English camp. Maddened with intoxication, and in spite of the utmost exertions of Montcalm and his officers, the savages fell upon the prisoners and began a massacre. Thirty of the English were tomahawked and many others dragged away into captivity. The retirement of the garrison to Fort Edward became a panic and a rout.

Such had been the successes of France during the year that the English had not a single hamlet or fortress remaining in the whole basin of the St. Lawrence. Every cabin where English was spoken had been swept out of the Ohio valley. At the close of the year 1757, France possessed twenty times as much American territory as England; and five times as much as England and Spain together. Such had been the imbecility of the English management in America that the flag of Great Britain was brought into disgrace.

CHAPTER XXXV.

Two Years of Successes.

GREAT was the discouragement in England. The duke of Newcastle and his associates in the government were obliged to resign. A new ministry was formed, at the head of which was placed that remarkable man William Pitt, called the Great Commoner. The imbecile Lord Loudoun was deposed from the American army. General Abercrombie was appointed to succeed him; but the main reliance for success was placed, not so much on the commander-in-chief, as on an efficient corps of subordinate officers whom the wisdom of Pitt now directed to America. Admiral Boscawen was put in command of the fleet, consisting of twenty-two ships of the line and fifteen frigates. The able general Amherst was to lead a division. Young Lord Howe, brave and amiable, was next in rank to Abercrombie. The gallant James Wolfe led a brigade. General Forbes held an important command; and Colonel Richard Montgomery was at the head of a regiment.

Three campaigns were planned for 1758. Amherst, acting in conjunction with the fleet, was to capture Louisburg. Lord Howe, under the direction of the commander-in-chief, was to reduce Crown Point and Ticonderoga. The recovery of the Ohio valley was entrusted to General Forbes. On the 28th of May, Amherst, at the head of ten thousand effective men, reached Halifax. In six days more the fleet was anchored in Gabarus Bay. Wolfe put his division into boats, rowed through the surf under fire of the French batteries, and gained the shore without serious loss. The French dismantled their battery and retreated. Wolfe next gained possession of the north-east harbor and planted heavy guns on the cape near the lighthouse. From this position the island battery of the French was soon silenced. Louisburg was fairly invested, and the siege was pressed with great vigor. On the 21st of July three French vessels were burned in the harbor. Two days later, the Prudent, a seventy-four gun ship, was fired and destroyed by the English boats. The town was already a heap of ruins, and the walls of the fortress began to crumble. For a whole week the French soldiers had no place where they could rest in safety; of their fifty-two cannon only twelve remained in position. Further resistance was hopeless. On the 28th of July Louisburg capitulated. Cape Breton and Prince Edward's Island were surrendered to Great Britain. The garrison, together with the marines, in all nearly six thousand men, became prisoners of war and were sent to England. Amherst after his great success abandoned Louisburg, and the fleet took station at Halifax.

Meanwhile, General Abercrombie had not been idle. On the 5th of July an army of fifteen thousand men, led by Lord Howe, reached Lake George and embarked for Ticonderoga. With heavy guns and abundant stores the expedition proceeded to the northern extremity of the lake and landed on the western shore. The country about the French fortress was very unfavorable for military operations. The English proceeded with great difficulty, leaving their artillery behind. Lord Howe led the advance in person. On the morning of the 6th, when the English were nearing the fort, they fell in with the picket line of the French, numbering no more than three hundred. A severe skirmish ensued; the French were overwhelmed, but not until they had inflicted on the English a terrible loss in the death of Lord Howe. The soldiers were stricken with grief, and began a retreat to the landing. Abercrombie was in the rear, but the soul of the expedition had departed.

On the morning of the 8th the English engineer reported falsely that the fortifications of Ticonderoga were flimsy and trifling. Again the army was put in motion and when just beyond the reach of the French guns, the divisions were arranged to carry the place by assault. For more than four hours column after column dashed with great bravery against the breastworks of the enemy, which were found to be strong and well constructed. The defence was made by nearly four thousand French under Montcalm, who, with coat off in the hot July afternoon, was everywhere present encouraging his men. At six o'clock in the evening the English were finally repulsed. The carnage was dreadful, the loss on the side of the assailants amounting in killed and wounded to nineteen hundred and sixteen. In no battle of the Revolution did the British have so large a force engaged or meet so terrible a loss.

The English still outnumbered the French three to one; and they might have easily returned with their artillery and captured the fort. But Abercrombie was not the man to do it. He returned to Fort George, at the head of the lake, and contented himself with sending a force of three thousand men under Colonel Bradstreet against Fort Frontenac. This fortress was situated on the present site of Kingston, at the outlet of Lake Ontario. Marching through the country of the Indians who were still friendly to the English, Bradstreet reached Oswego, embarked his forces, crossed the lake and landed within a mile of Frontenac. The place was feebly defended, and a siege of two days compelled a capitulation. The fortress, so important to the French, was demolished. Forty-six cannon, nine vessels of war and a vast quantity of stores were the fruits of the victory. Except in the waste of life, Bradstreet's success more than counterbalanced the failure of the English at Ticonderoga. The French were everywhere weakened and despairing. In Canada the crops had failed, and there was almost a famine. "Peace, peace, no matter with what boundaries," was the message which the brave Montcalm sent to the French ministry.

Late in the summer, Forbes, at the head of nine thousand men, advanced from Philadelphia against Fort du Quesne. Washington led the Virginia provincials, and Armstrong, who had so distinguished himself at Kittaning, the Pennsylvanians. The main body moved slowly, clearing a broad road and bridging the streams. Washington and the provincials were impatient. Major Grant, more rash than wise, pressed on to within a few miles of Du Quesne. Attempting to lead the French and Indians into an ambuscade, he was himself ambuscaded, and lost a third of his forces. Slowly the main division approached the fort, which was defended by no more than five hundred men. On the 24th of November, Washington with the advance was within ten miles of Du Quesne. During that night the garrison took the alarm, burned the fortress and floated down the Ohio. On the 25th the victorious army marched over the ruined bastions, raised the English flag, and named the place PITTSBURG. The name of the great British minister was justly written over "the gateway of the West."

General Amherst was now promoted to the chief command of the American forces. Parliament cheerfully voted twelve million pounds sterling to carry on the war. The colonies exerted themselves to the utmost. By the beginning of summer, 1759, the British and colonial forces numbered nearly fifty thousand men. The whole population of Canada was only eighty-two thousand; and the entire French army scarcely exceeded seven thousand. Nothing less than the conquest of all Canada would satisfy Pitt's ambition. Three campaigns were planned for the year. General Prideaux was to conduct an expedition against Niagara, capture the fortress and descend the lake to Montreal. Amherst was to lead the main division against Ticonderoga and Crown Point. General Wolfe was to proceed up the St. Lawrence and finish the work by capturing Quebec.

By way of Schenectady and Oswego, Prideaux led his forces to Niagara. On the 10th of July the place was invested. The French general D'Aubry collected from Detroit, Erie, Le Bœuf and Venango a body of twelve hundred men, and marched to the relief of the fort. On the 15th, by the accidental bursting of a mortar, General Prideaux was killed. Sir William Johnson, succeeding to the command, disposed his forces so as to intercept the approaching French. On the morning of the 24th, D'Aubry's army came in sight. A bloody engagement ensued, in which the French were completely routed, leaving their unnumbered dead scattered for miles through the forest. On the next day Niagara capitulated and received an English garrison. The French forces in the town, to the number of six hundred, became prisoners of war. Communication between Canada and Louisiana was for ever broken.

At the same time Amherst was conquering on Lake Champlain. With an army of more than eleven thousand men he proceeded against Ticonderoga. On the 22d of July the English forces were disembarked near the landing-place of Abercrombie. The French did not dare to stand against them. There was a slight skirmish, and then the trenches were deserted. Fort Carillon was given up. On the 26th the French garrison, having partly destroyed the fortifications, abandoned Ticonderoga and retreated to Crown Point. Five days afterward they deserted this place also, and entrenched themselves on Isle-aux-Noix, in the river Sorel. The whole country of Lake Champlain had been recovered without a battle.

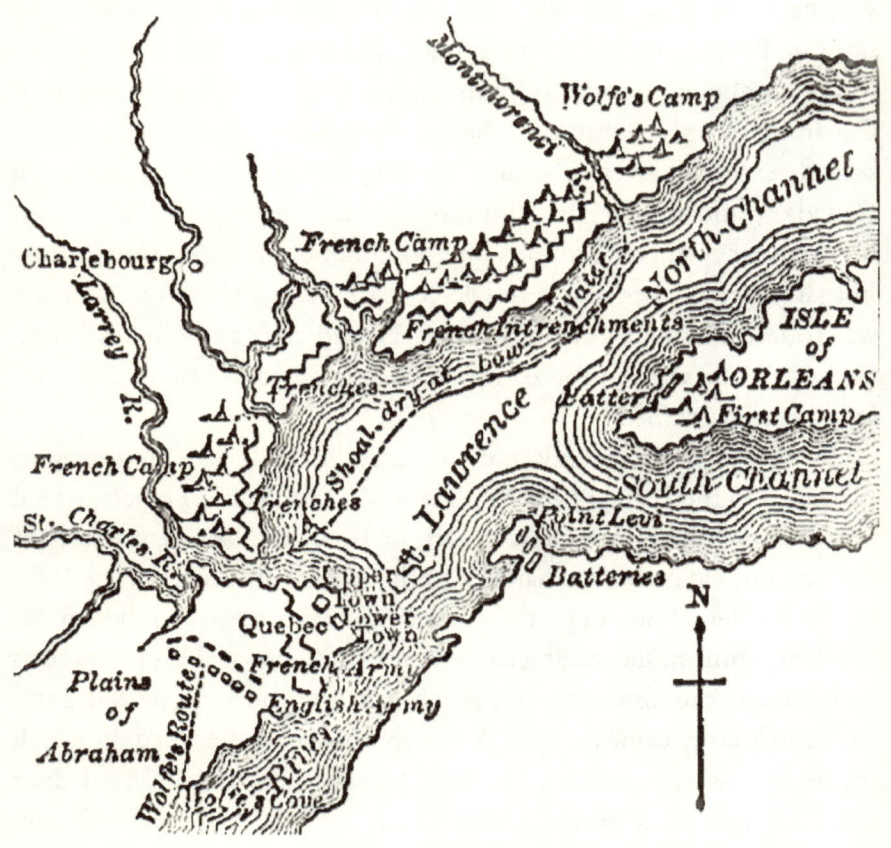

Vicinity of Quebec, 1759.

It remained for General Wolfe to achieve the final victory. As soon as a tardy spring had cleared the St. Lawrence of ice, he began the ascent of the river. His force consisted of nearly eight thousand men, assisted by a fleet of forty-four vessels under command of Admiral Saunders. On the 27th of June the armament arrived without accident at the Isle of Orleans, four miles below Quebec. The English camp was pitched at the upper end of the island. Wolfe's vessels gave him immediate command of the river, and the southern bank was undefended. On the night of the 29th, General Monckton was sent with four battalions to seize Point Levi. The movement was successful, and an English battery was planted opposite the city. From this position the Lower Town was soon reduced to ruins, and the Upper Town much injured; but the fortress seemed impregnable. The French, knowing that it would be impossible to storm the city from the river side, had drawn their line of entrenchment from the northern bank of the St. Lawrence, reaching for five miles from the Montmorenci to the St. Charles. Here Montcalm with ten or twelve thousand French and Canadians awaited the movements of his antagonist.

Wolfe was restless and anxious for battle. On the 9th of July he crossed the north channel, and encamped with his army on the east bank of the Montmorenci. It was determined in a council of war to hazard an engagement. The Montmorenci was fordable when the tide ran out. The attack was planned for July 31st, at the hour of low water. Generals Townshend and Murray were ordered to ford the stream with their two brigades, and at the same time Monckton's regiments of regulars were to cross the St. Lawrence from Point Levi and aid in the assault. The signal was given, and the grenadiers of Murray and Townshend dashed across the Montmorenci; but the boats of Monckton ran aground, and there was considerable delay. The impatient grenadiers, without waiting for orders or support, rushed forward against the French entrenchments, and were driven back with great loss. Before the regulars could be formed in line the battle was decided. Night was approaching; the tide rising; a storm portended and Wolfe, after losing nearly five hundred men, withdrew to his camp.

Disappointment, exposure and fatigue threw the English general into a violent fever, and for many days he was confined to his tent. A council of officers was called, and the indomitable leader proposed a second assault on the French lines. But the proposition was overruled, and it was decided to ascend the St. Lawrence, and if possible gain possession of the Plains of Abraham, in the rear of the city. The camp on the Montmorenci was accordingly broken up, and on the 6th of September the troops and artillery were conveyed to Point Levi. Keeping the French excited with appearances of activity, Wolfe again transferred his army to a point several miles up the river. He then busied himself with a careful examination of the northern bank, in the h0pe of finding some path

General James Wolfe.

among the precipitous cliffs by which to gain the plains. On the 11th he discovered the place called Wolfe's Cove, and decided that here it was possible to make the ascent. Montcalm, deceived by the movements of the fleet, was still in the trenches below the city.

On the night of the 12th of September everything was in readiness. The English silently entered their transports and dropped down the river to the cove. With great difficulty the soldiers clambered up the almost perpendicular precipice; the feeble Canadian guard on the summit was dispersed; and in the gray dawn of morning Wolfe marshaled his army for battle. Montcalm was in amazement when he heard the news. "They are now on the weak side of this unfortunate town," said he; "and we must crush them before mid-day." With great haste the French were brought from the trenches and thrown between Quebec and the advancing English. The battle began with an hour's cannonade; then Montcalm attempted to turn the English flank, but was beaten back. The Canadians and Indians were routed. Then came the weakened battalions of the French; but they were poorly disciplined; the ground was uneven, and Montcalm's lines advanced brokenly. The English reserved their fire until the advancing columns were within forty yards, and then discharged volley after volley. The French wavered and were in confusion. Wolfe, leading the charge, was wounded in the wrist. Again he was struck, but pressed on at the head of his grenadiers. Just at the moment of victory a third ball pierced his breast, and he sank quivering to the earth. "They run, they run!" said the attendant who bent over him. "Who run?" was the feeble response. "The French are flying everywhere," replied the officer. "Do they run already? Then I die happy," said the expiring hero; and his spirit passed away amid the smoke of battle. Monckton was dangerously wounded and borne from the field. Montcalm, still attempting to rally his broken regiments, was struck with a ball, and fell. "Shall I survive?" said he to his surgeon. "But a few hours at most," replied the attendant. "So much the better," replied the heroic Frenchman. "I shall not live to witness the surrender of Quebec."

Further defence of the Canadian stronghold was useless. Five days after the battle the French authorities surrendered to General Townshend, and an English garrison took possession of the citadel. The year 1759 closed with the complete triumph of the English arms. In the following spring France made a great effort to recover her losses. A severe battle was fought a few miles west of Quebec, and the English were driven into the city. But reinforcements came, and the French were beaten back. On the 8th of September, in the same year, Montreal, the last important post of France in the valley of the St. Lawrence, surrendered to General Amherst. Canada had passed under the dominion of England.

In the spring of 1760 the Cherokees of Tennessee rose against the English. Fort Loudoun, in the north-eastern extremity of the State, was besieged by the Red men, and forced to capitulate. Honorable terms were promised to the garrison; but as soon as the surrender was made, the savages fell upon their prisoners and massacred or dragged into captivity the whole company. Colonels Montgomery and Grant were despatched by General Amherst to chastise the Indians. After a vigorous campaign the savages were driven into the mountains and compelled to sue for peace.

The conquest of Canada was the overthrow of the French power in America. It remained, however, for the English authorities to take actual possession of the immense territory bordering on the Great Lakes. At the time of the capture of Montreal this vast domain was held by feeble fortresses, scattered here and there, and garrisoned by detachments of French soldiers. The Marquis of Vaudreuil in surrendering Montreal had stipulated that all the western forts under the control of France should be given up to England. In the fall of 1760 Major Robert Rogers was accordingly despatched by General Amherst, with a company of two hundred provincial rangers, to receive the surrender of the outposts.

By the last of November, Rogers, having ascended the St. Lawrence and passed through Lakes Ontario and Erie, reached Detroit. Over this, the most important of the French posts in the West, the English flag was raised; Forts Miami on the southern shore of Lake Michigan and Ouatanon on the Wabash were also given up without resistance. Rogers then pressed on to take possession of Mackinaw, Green Bay and St. Marie, but was turned back by the storms on Lake Huron; and it was not until the following summer that those remote fortresses were garrisoned by detachments of British soldiers.

No sooner were the English in complete possession of the country than they began by neglect and ill-treatment to excite the dormant passions of the Red men. During the progress of the war the Indians had become completely subordinated by French influence; and the English were hated with all the ferocity of the savage nature. It was not long till there were mutterings of an outbreak. The tribes could not be made to comprehend that Canada had been finally taken from their friends, the French. They confidently expected the day when the king of France should send new armies and expel the detested English. Infatuated with this belief, instigated by the French themselves, and stung by many insults real and imaginary, the warriors began their usual atrocities on the frontiers. In the summer of 1761, the Senecas conspired with the Wyandots to capture Detroit by treachery, and massacre the garrison; and the plot was barely thwarted by Colonel Campbell, the commandant. In the following summer another attempt of a similar sort was discovered and defeated. It was in this condition of affairs that the celebrated Pontiac came forward and organized the most far-reaching and dangerous conspiracy ever known among the Indian tribes of America.

Pontiac was chief of the Ottawas, whose principal seat was the district between Lakes Erie and Michigan. In the somewhat prolonged interval between the conquest of Canada and the treaty of 1763, this sagacious warrior, doubting the possibility of a peace between the rival nations, conceived the design of uniting all the Indian tribes from the Alleghanies to the Mississippi in an overwhelming confederacy, which should upon a given day strike all the English forts upon the frontier a deadly blow, and sweep away in a common ruin every English family west of the mountains. The plot was constructed with the White man's skill and the Red man's cunning. The 7th of May, 1763, was named as the day of destruction. But when the time came the impatient savage tribes were unable to act in per feet concert, and ultimate failure was the consequence, though the immediate result was terribly disastrous.

Pontiac reserved for himself the most difficult task of all—the capture of Detroit. But in the hour of impending doom, woman's love interposed to save the garrison from butchery. An Indian girl of the Ojibwa nation, came to the fort with a pair of moccasins for Major Gladwyn, the commandant, and in parting with him manifested unusual agitation and distress. She was seen to linger at the street corner, and the sentinel summoned her to return to the major's quarters. There, after much persuasion and many assurances of protection, she yielded to his urgent inquiries into the cause of her grief and revealed the plot. When Pontiac's band on the following day attempted to gain the fort by treachery, they found every soldier and citizen under arms and ready to receive them. Then followed a protracted siege, and the savage horde was finally driven off. But in all other quarters the attacks were attended with the most fatal results. On the 16th of May Fort Sandusky was taken and burned, and the garrison butchered by a band of Wyandots. A few days later Fort St. Joseph suffered a similar fate at the hands of the Pottawattamies. On the 29th of the month Fort Mackinaw was taken and its defenders nearly all murdered by the Chippeways. One out post after another was captured and burned, until by the middle of summer every English fort in the West, except Niagara, Fort Pitt and Detroit, had fallen into the hands of the savages. But in the mean time rumors of a treaty between France and England were borne to the Red men; and they, becoming alarmed at their own atrocities, began to sue for peace. The confederacy crumbled into nothing. Every tribe seemed as anxious to avoid the consequences as it had been to take up the hatchet. Pontiac and his band of Ottawas held out for two years longer; then, abandoned by his followers, he fled to the Illinois, among whom he was finally killed in a drunken brawl at the Indian town of Cahokia, opposite St. Louis.

The Revelation of Pontiac's Conspiracy.

For three years after the fall of Montreal the war between France and England lingered on the ocean. The English fleets were everywhere victorious. On the 10th of February, 1763, a treaty of peace was made at Paris. All the French possessions in North America eastward of the Mississippi from its source to the river Iberville, and thence through Lakes Maurepas and Pontchartrain to the Gulf of Mexico, were surrendered to Great Britain. At the same time Spain, with whom England had been at war, ceded East and West Florida to the English Crown. As reciprocal with this provision France was obliged to make a cession to Spain of all that vast territory west of the Mississippi, known as the Province of Louisiana. By the sweeping provisions of this treaty the French king *lost his entire possessions in the New World*. Thus closed the French and Indian War, one of the most important in the history of mankind. By this conflict it was decided that the decaying institutions of the Middle Ages should not prevail in the West; and that the powerful language, laws and liberties of the English race should be planted for ever in the vast domains of the New World.

CHAPTER XXXVI.

CONDITION OF THE COLONIES.

BEFORE entering upon the stirring events of the Revolution, it will be of interest to glance at THE GENERAL CONDITION OF THE AMERICAN COLONIES. There were thirteen of them: four in New England,—Massachusetts, Rhode Island, Connecticut, New Hampshire; four Middle Colonies,—New York, New Jersey, Pennsylvania, Delaware; five Southern,—Virginia, North Carolina, South Carolina, Georgia. All had grown and prospered. The elements of power were everywhere present. A willful, patriotic, and vigorous race of democrats had taken possession of the New World. Institutions unknown in Europe, peculiar to the West, made necessary by the condition and surroundings of the colonies, had sprung up and were taking deep root in American soil.

According to estimates made for the year 1760 the population of the colonies amounted to a million six hundred and ninety-five thousand souls. Of these about three hundred and ten thousand were blacks. Massachusetts was at this period perhaps the strongest colony, having more than two hundred thousand people of European ancestry within her borders. True, Virginia was the most populous, having an aggregate of two hundred and eighty-four thousand inhabitants, but of these one hundred and sixteen thousand were Africans, slaves. Next in strength stood Pennsylvania with a population of nearly two hundred thousand; next Connecticut with her hundred and thirty thousand people; next Maryland with a hundred and four thousand; then New York with eighty-five thousand; New Jersey not quite as many; then South Carolina, and so through the feebler colonies to Georgia, in whose borders were less than five thousand inhabitants, including the negroes.

By the middle of the eighteenth century the people of the American colonies had to a certain extent assumed a national character; but they were still strongly marked with the peculiarities which their ancestors had brought from Europe. In New England, especially in Massachusetts and Connecticut, the principles and practices of Puritanism still held universal sway.

The Old Thirteen Colonies.

On the banks of the Hudson the language, manners, and customs of Holland were almost as prevalent as they had been a hundred years before. By the Delaware the Quakers were gathered in such numbers as to control all legislation, and to prevent serious innovations upon the simple methods of civil and social organization introduced by Penn.

On the northern bank of the Potomac, the youthful Frederick, the sixth Lord Baltimore, a frivolous and dissolute governor, ruled a people who still conformed to the order of things established a hundred and thirty years previously by Sirs George and Cecil Calvert. In Virginia, mother of States and statesmen, the people had all their old peculiarities; a somewhat haughty demeanor; pride of ancestry; fondness for aristocratic sports; hospitality; love of freedom. The North Carolinians were at this epoch the same rugged and insubordinate race of hunters that they had always been. The legislative assembly, in its controversies with Governor Dobbs, manifested all the intractable stubbornness which characterized that body in the days of Seth Sothel. In South Carolina there was much prosperity and happiness. But there, too, popular liberty had been enlarged by the constant encroachment of the legislature upon the royal prerogative. The people, mostly of French descent, were as hot-blooded and jealous of their rights as their ancestors had been in the times of the first immigrations. Of all the American colonies Georgia had at this time least strength and spirit. Under the system of government established at the first the common wealth had languished. Not until 1754, when Governor Reynolds assumed control of the colony, did the affairs of the people on the Savannah begin to flourish. Even afterwards, something of the indigence and want of thrift which had marked the followers of Oglethorpe still prevailed in Georgia. Nevertheless, after making allowance for all these differences of colonial character, a considerable degree of American unity had been attained; inter-colonial relations were well established; and the people were far less antagonistic and sectional than they had been.

In matters of education New England took the lead. Her system of free schools extended everywhere from the Hudson to the Penobscot. Every village furnished facilities for the acquirement of knowledge. So complete and universal were the means of instruction that in the times preceding the Revolution there was not to be found in all New England an adult, born in the country, who could not read and write. Splendid achievement of Puritanism! In the Middle Colonies education was not so general; but in Pennsylvania there was much intelligent activity among the people. Especially in Philadelphia did the illustrious Franklin scatter the light of learning. South of the Potomac educational facilities were irregular and generally designed for the benefit of the wealthier classes. But in some localities the means of enlightenment were well provided; institutions of learning sprang up scarcely inferior to those of the Eastern provinces, or even of Europe. Nor should the private schools of the colonial times be forgotten. Many men—Scottish reformers, Irish liberals, and French patriots—despising the bigotry and intolerance of their countrymen, fled for refuge to the New World, and there by the banks of the Housatonic, the Hudson, the Delaware, the Potomac, the Ashley, and the Savannah, taught the lore of books and the lesson of liberty to the rugged boys of the American wilderness. Among the Southern colonies Virginia led the van in matters of education; while Maryland, the Carolinas, and Georgia lagged behind. Previous to the Revolution nine colleges worthy of the name had been established in the colonies. These were Harvard, William and Mary, Yale, Princeton, King's (now called Columbia), Brown, Queen's (afterwards called Rutgers), Dartmouth, and Hampden and Sydney. In 1764 the first medical college was founded, at Philadelphia.

Of the printing-press, that other great agent and forerunner of civilization, the work was already effective. As early as 1704 the Boston *News-Letter*, first of periodicals in the New World, was published in the city of the Puritans; but fifteen years elapsed before another experiment of the same sort was made. In 1721 the New England *Courant*, a little sheet devoted to free thought and the extinction of rascality, was established at Boston by the two Franklins—James and Benjamin. In 1740 New York had but one periodical, Virginia one, and South Carolina one; and at the close of the French and Indian War, there were no more than ten newspapers published in the colonies. The chief obstacles to such publications were the absence of great cities and the difficulty of communication between distant sections of the country. Boston and Philadelphia had each no more than eighteen thousand inhabitants; New York but twelve thousand. In all Virginia there was not one important town; while as far south as Georgia there was scarcely a considerable village. To reach this widely scattered population with periodical publications was quite impossible. Books were few, and of little value. Some dry volumes of history, theology, and politics were the only stock and store. On the latter subject the publications were sometimes full of pith and spirit. But notwithstanding this barrenness of books and general poverty of the resources of knowledge, it was no unusual thing to find at the foot of the Virginia mountains, in the quiet precincts of Philadelphia, by the banks of the Hudson, or in the valleys of New England, a man of great and solid learning. Such a man was Thomas Jefferson; such were Franklin, and Livingston, and the Adamses—men of profound scholarship, bold in thought, ready with the pen, skillful in argument; studious, witty, and eloquent.

Nothing impeded the progress of the colonies more than the want of thoroughfares and easy communication between the different sections. No general system of post-offices or post-roads had as yet been established; and the people were left in comparative or total ignorance of passing events. No common sentiments could be expressed—no common enthusiasm be kindled in the country—by the slow-going mails and packets. The sea-coast towns and cities found a readier intercourse by means of small sloops plying the Atlantic; but the inland districts were wholly cut off from such advantages. Roads were slowly built from point to point, and lines of travel by coach and wagon were gradually established. To the very beginning of the Revolution the people lived apart, isolated and dependent upon their own resources for life and enjoyment. When in 1766 an express wagon made the trip from New York to Philadelphia in two days, it was considered a marvel of rapidity. Six years later the first stage-coach began to run regularly between Boston and Providence.[12]

Before the Revolution the Americans were for the most part an agricultural people. Within the tide-water line of Virginia the lands were divided into estates, and the planters devoted themselves almost exclusively to the cultivation of tobacco. Farther inland the products were more various: wheat, maize, potatoes; upland cotton, hemp, and

---

[12] It is remarkable to note how tardily the attention of a people will be turned to the building of roads. Thus, for instance, in so old a country as Scotland there were no great thoroughfares constructed until after the Scotch Rebellion of 1745.

flax. In the Carolinas and Georgia the rice crop was most important; after that, indigo, cotton, and some silk; tar, turpentine, and what the hunter and fisherman gathered from the woods and streams. New York, Philadelphia and Boston were then as now the great centers of trade; but commerce was carried on in a slow and awkward manner, wholly unlike the rushing activity of more recent times. Ship-building was one of the most important colonial interests. In the year 1738 no less than forty-one sailing vessels, with an average burden of a hundred and fifty tons, were built and launched at the ship-yards of Boston. New England was the seat of whatever manufacturing interest prevailed in the country. But all enterprise in this direction was checked and impeded by the British Board of Trade, whose stupid and arbitrary restrictions acted as a damper on every kind of colonial thrift. No sooner would some enterprising company of New England men begin the building of a factory than this officious Board would interfere in such a way as to make success impossible. So jealous was the English ministry of American progress! If, previous to the Revolution, any colonial manufacture was successfully established, it was done *against* the will of Great Britain, and in spite of her mean and churlish opposition.

Such were the American colonies—such the people whose budding nationality was now to be exposed to the blasts of war. These people, whose ancestors had been driven into exile by the exactions of European governments and the bigotry of ecclesiastical power, had become the rightful proprietors of the New World. They had fairly won it from savage man and savage nature. They had subdued it and built States within it. They owned it by all the claims of actual possession; by toil and trial; by the ordeal of suffering; by peril privation, and hardship; by the baptism of sorrow and the shedding of blood. No wonder that patriotism was the child of such travail and discipline! No wonder that the men who from mountain. and sky and river, from orchard and valley and forest, from the memories of the past, the aspirations of the present and the hopes of the future, had drank in the spirit of Liberty until their souls were pervaded with her sublime essence,—were now ready when the iron heel of oppression was set upon their cherished rights, to draw the vindictive sword even against the venerable monarchy of England!

PART IV.

REVOLUTION AND CONFEDERATION.
A. D. 1775-1789.

CHAPTER XXXVII.

CAUSES.

THE war of American Independence was an event of vast moment, affecting the destinies of all nations. The question decided by the conflict was this: Whether the English colonies in America, becoming sovereign, should govern themselves or be ruled as dependencies of a European monarchy. The decision was rendered in favor of separation and independence. The result has been the grandest and most promising example of republican government in the history of the world. The struggle was long and distressing, though not characterized by great violence; the combatants were of the same race and spoke a common language. It is of the first importance to understand the causes of the war.

The most general cause of the American Revolution was THE RIGHT OF ARBITRARY GOVERNMENT, claimed by Great Britain and denied by the colonies. So long as this claim was asserted by England only as a theory, the conflict was postponed; when the English government began to enforce the principle in practice, the colonies resisted. The question began to be openly discussed about the time of the treaty of Aix-la-Chapelle, in 1748; and from that period until the beginning of hostilities, in 1775, each year witnessed a renewal of the agitation. But there were also many subordinate causes tending to bring on a conflict.

First of these was *the influence of France*, which was constantly exerted so as to incite a spirit of resistance in the colonies. The French king would never have agreed to the treaty of 1763—by which Canada was ceded to Great Britain—had it not been with the hope of securing American independence. It was the theory of France that by giving up Canada on the north the English colonies would become so strong as to renounce their allegiance to the crown. England feared such a result. More than once it was proposed in Parliament to re-cede Canada to France in order to check the growth of the American States. "There, now!" said a French statesman when the treaty of 1763 was signed; "we have arranged matters for an American rebellion in which England will lose her empire in the West."

Another cause leading to the Revolution was found *in the natural disposition and inherited character of the colonists*. They were, for the most part, republicans in politics and dissenters in religion. The people of England were monarchists and High Churchmen. The colonists had never seen a king. The Atlantic lay between them and the British ministry. Their dealings with the royal officers had been such as to engender a dislike for monarchical institutions. The people of America had not forgotten—could not well forget—the circumstances under which their ancestors had come to the New World. For six generations the colonists had managed their own affairs; and their methods of government were necessarily republican. The experiences of the French and Indian War had shown that Americans were fully able to defend themselves and their country.

The growth of public opinion in the colonies tended to independence. The more advanced thinkers came to believe that a complete separation from England was not only possible, but desirable. As early as 1755, John Adams, then a young school-teacher in Connecticut, wrote in his diary: "In another century all Europe will not be able to subdue us. The only way to keep us from setting up for ourselves is to disunite us." Such opinions were at first expressed only in private, then by hints in pamphlets and newspapers, and at last publicly and everywhere. The mass of the people, however, were slow to accept an idea which seemed so radical and dangerous. Not until the war had actually begun did the majority declare for independence.

Another cause of the conflict with the mother country was found in *the personal character of the king*. George III., who ascended the English throne in 1760, was one of the worst monarchs of modern times. His notions of government were altogether despotic. He was a stubborn, stupid, thick-headed man in whose mind the notion of human rights was entirely wanting. It was impossible for him to conceive of a magnanimous project or to appreciate the value of civil liberty. His reign of sixty years was as odious as it was long. In the management of the British empire he employed only those who were the narrow-minded partisans of his own policy. His ministers were, for the most part, men as incompetent and illiberal as himself. With such a king and such a ministry it was not likely that the descendants of the Pilgrims would get on smoothly.

The more immediate cause of the Revolution was the passage by Parliament of *a number of acts destructive of colonial liberty*. These acts were resisted by the colonies, and the attempt was made by Great Britain to enforce them with the bayonet. The subject of this unjust legislation, which extended over a period of twelve years just preceding the war, was the question of taxation. It is a well-grounded principle of English common law that the people, by their representatives in the House of Commons, have the right of voting whatever taxes and customs are necessary for the support of the kingdom. The American colonists claimed the full rights of Englishmen. With good reason it was urged that the general assemblies of colonies held the same relation to the American people as did the House of Commons to the people of England. The English ministers replied that Parliament, and not the colonial assemblies, was the proper body to vote taxes in any and all parts of the British empire. But we are not represented in Parliament, was the answer of the Americans; the House of Commons may therefore justly assess taxes in England, but not in America. Many of the towns, boroughs and shires in these British isles have no representatives in Parliament, and yet the Parliament taxes them, replied the ministers, now driven to sophistry. If any of your towns, boroughs and shires are not represented in the House of Commons, they *ought* to be, was the American rejoinder; and there the argument ended. Such were the essential points of the controversy. It is now proper to notice the several parliamentary acts which the colonies complained of and resisted.

The first of these was THE IMPORTATION ACT, passed in 1733. This statute was itself a kind of supplement to the old Navigation Act of 1651. By the terms of the newer law exorbitant duties were laid on all the sugar, molasses and rum imported into the colonies. At first the payment of these unreasonable customs was evaded by the merchants, and then the statute was openly set at naught. In 1750 it was further enacted that iron-works should not be erected in America. The manufacture of steel was specially forbidden; and the felling of pines, outside of enclosures, was interdicted. All of these laws were disregarded and denounced by the people of the colonies as being unjust and tyrannical. In 1761 a strenuous effort was made by the ministry to enforce the Importation Act. The colonial courts were authorized to issue to the king's officers a kind of search-warrants, called Writs of Assistance. Armed with this authority, petty constables might enter any and every place, searching for and seizing goods which were suspected of having evaded the duty. At Salem and Boston the greatest excitement prevailed. The application for the writs was resisted before the courts. James Otis, an able and temperate man, pleaded eloquently for colonial rights, and denounced the parliamentary acts as unconstitutional. The address was a masterly defence of the people, and produced a profound sensation throughout the colonies. Already there were hints at resistance by force of arms.

In 1763, and again in the following year, the English ministers undertook to enforce the law requiring the payment of duties on sugar and molasses. The officers of the admiralty were authorized to seize and confiscate all vessels engaged in the unlawful trade. Before the passage of this act was known at Boston, a great town-meeting was held. Samuel Adams was the orator. A powerful argument was produced showing conclusively that under the British constitution taxation and representation were inseparable. Nevertheless, vessels from the English navy were sent to hover around the American harbors. A great number of merchantmen bearing cargoes of sugar and wine were seized; and the colonial trade with the West Indies was almost destroyed.

The year 1764 witnessed the first formal declaration of the purpose of Parliament to tax the colonies. Mr. Grenville was now prime minister.

On the 10th of March a resolution was adopted by the House of Commons declaring that it would be proper to charge certain stamp duties on the American colonies. It was announced that a bill embodying this principle would be prepared by the ministers and presented at the next session of Parliament. In the mean time, the news of the proposed measure was borne to America. Universal excitement and indignation prevailed in the colonies. Political meetings became the Order of the day. Orators were in great demand. The newspapers teemed with arguments against the proposed enactment. Resolutions were passed by the people of almost every town. Formal remonstrances were addressed to the king and the two houses of Parliament. Agents were appointed by the colonies and sent to London in the hope of preventing the passage of the law.

A new turn was now given to the controversy. The French and Indian war had just been concluded with a treaty of peace. Great Britain had incurred a heavy debt. The ministers began to urge that the expenses of the war ought to be borne by the colonies. The Americans replied that England ought to defend her colonies, from motives of humanity; that in the prosecution of the war the colonists had aided Great Britain as much as Great Britain had aided them; that the cession of Canada had amply remunerated England for her losses; that it was not the payment of money which the colonies dreaded, but the surrender of their liberties. It was also added that in case of another war the American States would try to fight their own battles.

Early in March of 1765, the English Parliament, no longer guided by the counsels of Pitt, passed the celebrated STAMP ACT. In the House of Commons the measure received a majority of five to one. In the House of Lords the vote was unanimous. At the time of the passage of the act the king was in a fit of insanity, and could not sign the bill. On the 22d of the month the royal assent was given by a board of commissioners acting for the king. "The sun of American liberty has set," wrote Benjamin Franklin to a friend at home. "Now we must light the lamps of industry and economy." "Be assured," said the friend, in reply, "that we shall light *torches of another sort.*" And the answer reflected the sentiment of the whole country.

The provisions of the Stamp Act were briefly these: Every note, bond, deed, mortgage, lease, license and legal document of whatever sort, required in the colonies, should, after the 1st day of the following November, be executed on paper bearing an English stamp. This stamped paper was to be furnished by the British government; and for each sheet the colonists were required to pay a sum varying, according to the nature of the document, from three pence to six pounds sterling. Every colonial pamphlet, almanac and newspaper was required to be printed on paper of the same sort, the value of the stamps in this case ranging from a half penny to four pence; every advertisement was taxed two shillings. No contract should be of any binding force unless written on paper bearing the royal stamp.

The news of the hateful act swept over America like a thundercloud. The people were at first grief-stricken; then indignant; and then wrathful. Crowds of excited men surged into the towns, and there were some acts of violence. The muffled bells of Philadelphia and Boston rung a funeral peal; and the people said it was the death-knell of liberty. In New York a copy of the Stamp Act was carried through the streets with a death's-head nailed to it, and a placard bearing this inscription: THE FOLLY OF ENGLAND AND THE RUIN OF AMERICA. The general assemblies were at first slow to move; there were many loyalists among the members; and the colonial governors held their offices by appointment of the king. It was hazardous for a provincial legislator to say that an act of the British Parliament was the act of tyrants. But the younger representatives, hot-blooded as well as patriotic, did not hesitate to express their sentiments. In the Virginia House of Burgesses there was a memorable scene.

Patrick Henry, the youngest member of the House, an uneducated mountaineer recently chosen to represent Louisa county, waited for some older delegate to lead the burgesses in opposition to Parliament. But the older members hesitated or went home. Offended at this lukewarmness, Henry in his passionate way snatched a blank-leaf out of an old law book and hastily drew up a series of fiery resolutions, declaring that the Virginians were Englishmen with English rights; that the people of Great Britain had the exclusive privilege of voting their own taxes, and so had the Americans; that the colonists were not bound to yield obedience to any law imposing taxation on them; and that whoever said the contrary was an enemy to the country. The resolutions were at once laid before the house.

A violent debate ensued, in which the patriots had the best of the argument. It was a moment of intense interest. Two future Presidents of the United States were in the audience; Washington occupied his seat as a delegate, and Thomas Jefferson, a young collegian, stood just outside of the railing. The eloquent and audacious Henry bore down all opposition. "Tarquin and Cæsar had each his Brutus," said the indignant orator; "Charles I. had his Cromwell, and George III.—" "Treason!" shouted the speaker. "Treason! treason!" exclaimed the terrified loyalists, springing to their feet."—And George III. may profit by their example," continued Henry; and then added as he took his seat, "If that be treason, make the most of it!" The resolutions were put to the house and carried; but the majorities on some of the votes were small, and the next day, when Henry was absent, the most violent paragraph was reconsidered and expunged: some of the members were greatly frightened at their own audacity. But the resolutions in their entire form had gone before the country as the formal expression of the oldest American commonwealth, and the effect on the other colonies was like the shock of a battery.

Patrick Henry.

Similar resolutions were adopted by the assemblies of New York and Massachusetts—in the latter State before the action of Virginia was known. At Boston, James Otis successfully agitated the question of an

American Congress. It was proposed that each colony, acting without leave of the king, should appoint delegates, who should meet in the following autumn and discuss the affairs of the nation. The proposition was favorably received; nine of the colonies appointed delegates; and on the 7th of October THE FIRST COLONIAL CONGRESS assembled at New York. There were twenty-eight representatives: Timothy Ruggles of Massachusetts was chosen president. After much discussion A DECLARATION OF RIGHTS was adopted setting forth in unmistakable terms that the American colonists, as Englishmen, could not and would not consent to be taxed but by their own representatives. Memorials were also prepared and addressed to the two houses of Parliament. A manly petition, professing loyalty and praying for a more just and humane policy toward his American subjects, was directed to the king.

The 1st of November came. On that day the Stamp Act was to take effect. During the summer great quantities of the stamped paper had been prepared and sent to America. Ten boxes of it were seized by the people of New York and openly destroyed. In Connecticut, the stamp-officer was threatened with hanging. In Boston, houses were destroyed and the stamps given to the winds and flames. Whole cargoes of the obnoxious paper were reshipped to England; and every stamp officer in America was obliged to resign or leave the country. By the 1st of November there were scarcely stamps enough remaining to furnish after times with specimens. The day was kept as a day of mourning. The stores were closed; flags were hung at half mast; the bells were tolled; effigies of the authors and abettors of the Stamp Act were borne about in mockery, and then burned. The people of New Hampshire formed a funeral procession and buried a coffin bearing the inscription of LIBERTY. A cartoon was circulated hinting at union as the remedy for existing evils. The picture represented a snake broken into sections. Each joint was labeled with the initials of a colony the head was marked "N. E." for New England; and the title was *Join or Die!*

At first, legal business was almost entirely suspended. The courthouses were shut up. Society was at a standstill; not even a marriage license could be legally issued. By and by, the people breathed more freely; the offices were opened, and business went on as before; but was *not* transacted with stamped paper. It was at this juncture that the patriotic society known as THE SONS OF LIBERTY was organized. The members were pledged to oppose British tyranny to the utmost, and to defend with their lives the freedom of the colonies. Equally important was the action of the colonial merchants. The importers of New York, Boston and Philadelphia entered into a solemn compact to purchase no more goods of Great Britain until the Stamp Act should be repealed. And the people, applauding the action of their merchants, cheerfully denied themselves of all imported luxuries.

Great was the wrath of the British government when the news of these proceedings was borne across the ocean. But a large party of English tradesmen and manufacturers sided with the colonists. Better still, some of the most eminent statesmen espoused the cause of America. Even Lord Camden in the House of Lords spoke favorably of colonial rights. Before the House of Commons Mr. Pitt delivered a powerful address. "You have," said he, "no right to tax America. I rejoice that America has resisted. Three millions of our fellow-subjects so lost to every sense of virtue as tamely to give up their liberties would be fit instruments to make slaves of the rest." The new Whig prime minister, the marquis of Rockingham, was also a friend of the colonies, and looked with disfavor on the legislation of his predecessor. On the 18th of March, 1766, the Stamp Act was formally repealed. As a kind of balm to soothe the wounded feelings of the Tories—as the adherents of Grenville were now called—a supplemental resolution was added to the repeal declaring that Parliament had the right *to bind the colonies in all cases whatsoever.*

The joy both in England and America was unbounded. The vessels in the river Thames were decked with flags, and the colonial orators spoke to enthusiastic crowds gathered around bonfires. There was a great calm in all the country; but it was only the lull before the coming of a greater storm. A few months after the repeal of the Stamp Act the ministry of Rockingham was dissolved and a new cabinet formed under the leadership of Pitt, who was now made earl of Chatham. Unfortunately, however, the prime minister was for a long time confined by sickness to his home in the country. During his absence, Mr.

Townshend, chancellor of the exchequer, in a moment of unparalleled folly, brought forward a new scheme for taxing America. On the 29th of June 1767, an act was passed imposing a duty on all the glass, paper, painters' colors and tea which should thereafter be imported into the colonies. At the same time a resolution was adopted suspending the powers of the general assembly of New York until that body should vote certain supplies for the royal troops stationed in the province. A more rash and disastrous piece of legislation never was enacted.

All the smothered resentment of the colonies burst out anew. Another agreement not to purchase British goods was immediately entered into by the American merchants. The newspapers were filled with bitter denunciations of Parliament. Early in 1768 the assembly of Massachusetts adopted a circular calling upon the other colonies for assistance in the effort to obtain redress of grievances. The ministers were enraged and required the assembly in the king's name to rescind their action, and to express regret for that "rash and hasty proceeding." Instead of that, the sturdy legislature reaffirmed the resolution by a nearly unanimous vote. Thereupon Governor Bernard dissolved the assembly; but the members would not disperse until they had prepared a list of charges against the governor and requested the king to remove him.

In the month of June fuel was added to the flame. A sloop, charged with attempting to evade the payment of duty, was seized by the customhouse officers. The people rose in a mob; attacked the houses of the officers, and obliged the occupants to seek shelter in Castle William, at the entrance of the harbor. The governor now appealed to the ministers for help; and General Gage, commander-in-chief of the British forces in America, was ordered to bring from Halifax a regiment of regulars and overawe the people. On the 1st of October the troops, seven hundred strong, marched with fixed bayonets into the capital of Massachusetts. The people were maddened by this military invasion of their city. When the governor required the selectmen of Boston to provide quarters for the soldiers, he was met with an absolute refusal; and the troops were quartered in the state-house.

In February of 1769, Parliament advanced another step toward war. The people of Massachusetts were declared rebels, and the governor was directed to arrest those deemed guilty of treason and send them to England for trial. The general assembly met this additional outrage with defiant resolutions. Scenes almost as violent as these were at the same time enacted in Virginia and North Carolina. In the latter State a popular insurrection was suppressed by Governor Tryon; the insurgents, escaping across the mountains, obtained lands of the Cherokees, and became the founders of Tennessee.

Early in 1770 a serious affray occurred in New York. The soldiers wantonly cut down a liberty pole which had stood for several years in the park. A conflict ensued, in which the people came out best; another pole was erected in the northern part of the city. On the 5th of March a more serious difficulty occurred in Boston. An altercation had taken place between a party of citizens and the soldiers. A crowd gathered, surrounded Captain Preston's company of the city guard, hooted at them, and dared them to fire. At length the exasperated soldiers discharged a volley, killing three of the citizens and wounding several others. This outrage, known as the Boston Massacre, created a profound sensation. The city was ablaze with excitement. Several thousand men assembled under arms. Governor Hutchinson came out, promising that justice should be done and trying to appease the multitude. The brave Samuel Adams spoke for the people. An immediate withdrawal of the troops from the city was demanded, and the governor was obliged to yield. Captain Preston and his company were arrested and tried for murder. The prosecution was conducted with great spirit, and two of the offenders were convicted of manslaughter.

On the very day of the Boston massacre, Lord North, who had become prime minister, secured the passage by Parliament of an act repealing all the duties on American imports except that on tea. The exception was made only to show that the right of taxing the colonies was not relinquished. The merchants of New York and Boston at once relaxed their non-importation agreement except so far as it related to tea; to that extent the compact was retained; and the people voluntarily pledged themselves to use no more tea until the duty should be unconditionally repealed. The antagonism toward the mother country was abating somewhat, when in 1772 an act was passed by Parliament requiring that the salaries of the governor and judges of Massachusetts should be paid out of the colonial revenues without consent of the assembly. That body retaliated by a declaration that the parliamentary statute was a violation of the chartered rights of the people, and therefore void. About the same time the Gaspee, a royal schooner which had been annoying the people of Providence, was boarded by a company of patriots and burned.

In 1773 the ministers attempted to enforce the tea-tax by a stratagem. Owing to the duty, the price of tea in the American market had been doubled. But there was no demand for the article; for the people would not buy. As a consequence the warehouses of Great Britain were stored with vast quantities of tea, awaiting shipment to America. Parliament now removed the export duty which had hitherto been charged on tea shipped from England. The price was by so much lowered; and the ministers persuaded themselves that, when the cheaper tea was offered in America, the silly colonists would pay their own import duty without suspicion or complaint.

To carry out this scheme English ships were loaded with tea for the American market. Some of the vessels reached Charleston; the tea was landed, but the people forbade its sale. The chests were stored in mouldy cellars, and the contents ruined. At New York and Philadelphia the ports were closed and the ships forbidden to enter. At Boston the vessels entered the harbor. The tea had been consigned to Governor Hutchinson

Samuel Adams.

and his friends; and special precautions were taken to prevent a failure of the enterprise. But the authorities stubbornly stood their ground, and would not permit the tea to be landed. On the 16th of December the dispute was settled in a memorable manner. There was a great town-meeting at which seven thousand people were assembled. Adams and Quincy spoke to the multitudes. Evening came on, and the meeting was about to adjourn, when a war whoop was heard, and about fifty men disguised as Indians passed the door of the Old South Church. The crowd followed to Griffin's wharf, where the three tea-ships were at anchor. Then everything became quiet. The disguised men quickly boarded the vessels, broke open the three hundred and forty chests of tea that composed the cargoes, and poured the contents into the sea. Such was THE BOSTON TEA-PARTY.

Parliament made haste to find revenge. On the last day of March, 1774, THE BOSTON PORT BILL was passed. It was enacted that no kind of merchandise should any longer be landed or shipped at the wharves of Boston. The custom-house was removed to Salem, but the people of that town refused the benefits which were proffered by the hand of tyranny. The inhabitants of Marblehead tendered the free use of their warehouses to the merchants of Boston. The assembly stood stoutly by the cause of the people. When the news of the passage of the Port Bill reached Virginia, the burgesses at once entered a protest on the journals of the house. When Governor Dunmore ordered the members to their homes, they met in another place, and passed a recommendation for a general congress of the colonies. On the 20th of May the venerated charter of Massachusetts was annulled by act of Parliament. The people were declared rebels; and the governor was ordered to send abroad for trial all persons who should resist the royal officers. The colonial assembly made answer by adopting a resolution that the powers of language were not sufficient to express the impolicy, injustice, in humanity and cruelty of the acts of Parliament.

In September THE SECOND COLONIAL CONGRESS assembled at Philadelphia. Eleven colonies were represented. It was unanimously agreed to sustain Massachusetts in her conflict with a wicked ministry. One address was sent to the king; another to the English nation; and another to the people of Canada. Before adjournment a resolution was adopted recommending the suspension of all commercial intercourse with Great Britain until the wrongs of the colonies should be redressed. Parliament immediately retaliated by ordering General Gage, who had been recently appointed governor of Massachusetts, to reduce the colonists by force. A fleet and an army of ten thousand soldiers were sent to America to aid in the work of subjugation.

In accordance with the governor's orders, Boston Neck was seized and fortified. The military stores in the arsenals at Cambridge and Charlestown were conveyed to Boston; and the general assembly was ordered to disband. Instead of doing so, the members resolved themselves into a provincial congress, and voted to equip an army of twelve thousand men for the defence of the colony. There was no longer any hope of a peaceable adjustment. The mighty arm of Great Britain was stretched out to smite and crush the sons of the Pilgrims. The colonists were few and feeble but they were men of iron wills who had made up their minds to die for liberty. It was now the early spring of 1775, and the day of battle was at hand.

CHAPTER XXXVIII.

The Beginning.

As soon as the intentions of General Gage were manifest, the people of Boston, concealing their ammunition in cart-loads of rubbish, conveyed it to Concord, sixteen miles away. Gage detected the movement, and on the night of the 18th of April despatched a regiment of eight hundred men to destroy the stores. Another purpose of the expedition was to capture John Hancock and Samuel Adams, who were supposed to be hidden at Lexington or Concord. The fact was that they were not hidden anywhere, but were abroad encouraging the people. The plan of the British general was made with great secrecy; but the patriots were on the alert, and discovered the movement.

About midnight the regiment, under command of Colonel Smith and Major Pitcairn, set out for Concord. The people of Boston, Charlestown and Cambridge were roused by the ringing of bells and the firing of cannons. Two hours before, the vigilant Joseph Warren had despatched William Dawes and Paul Revere to ride with all speed to Lexington and to spread the alarm through the country. Against two o'clock in the morning the minute-men were under arms; and a company of a hundred and thirty had, assembled on the common at Lexington. The patriots loaded their guns and stood ready; but no enemy appeared, and it was agreed to separate until the drum-beat should announce the hour of danger. At five o'clock the British van, under command of Pitcairn, came in sight. The provincials to the number of seventy reassembled; Captain Parker was their leader. Pitcairn rode up and exclaimed: "Disperse, ye villains! Throw down your arms, ye rebels, and disperse!" The minute-men stood still; Pitcairn discharged his pistol at them, and with a loud voice cried, "Fire!" The first volley of the Revolution whistled through the air, and sixteen of the patriots, nearly a fourth of the whole number, fell dead or wounded. The rest fired a few random shots, and then dispersed.

The British pressed on to Concord; but the inhabitants had removed the greater part of the stores to a place of safety, and there was but little destruction. Two cannons were spiked, some artillery carriages burned, and a small quantity of ammunition thrown into a mill-pond. While the British were ransacking the town the minute-men began to assemble from all quarters. Attempting to enter the village, the patriots encountered a company of soldiers who were guarding the North Bridge, over Concord River. Here the Americans, for the first time, fired under orders of their officers, and here two British soldiers were killed. The bridge was taken by the provincials, and the enemy began a retreat—first into the town, and then through the town on the road to Lexington. This was the signal for the minute-men to attack the foe from every side. For six miles the battle was kept up along the road. Hidden behind rocks, trees, fences and barns, the patriots poured a constant fire upon the thinned ranks of the retreating enemy. Nothing but good discipline and reinforcements which, under command of Lord Percy, met the fugitives just below Lexington, saved the British from total rout and destruction. The fight continued to the precincts of Charlestown, the militia becoming more and more audacious in their charges. At one time it seemed that the whole British force would be obliged to surrender. Such a result was prevented only by the fear that the fleet would burn the city. The American loss in this the first battle of the war was forty-nine killed, thirty-four wounded and five missing; that of the enemy was two hundred and seventy-three—a greater loss than the English army sustained on the Plains of Abraham.

The battle of Lexington fired the country. Within a few days an army of twenty thousand men had gathered about Boston. A line of entrenchments encompassing the city was drawn from Roxbury to Chelsea. To drive Gage and the British into the sea was the common talk in that tumultuous camp. And the number constantly increased. John Stark came down at the head of the New Hampshire militia. Israel Putnam, with a leather waistcoat on, was helping some men to build stone wall on his farm when the news from Lexington came flying. Hurrying to the nearest town, he found the militia already mustered. Bidding the men follow as soon as possible, he mounted a horse and rode to Cambridge, a distance of a hundred miles, in eighteen hours. Rhode Island sent her quota under the brave Nathaniel Greene. Benedict Arnold came with the provincials of New Haven. Ethan Allen, of Vermont, made war *in the other direction.*

This daring and eccentric man was chosen colonel by a company of two hundred and seventy patriots who had assembled at Bennington. Before the battle of Lexington, the legislature of Connecticut had privately voted a thousand dollars to encourage an expedition against Ticonderoga. To capture this important fortress, with its vast magazine of stores was the object of Allen and the audacious mountaineers of whom he was the leader. Benedict Arnold left Cambridge, and joined the expedition as a private. On the evening of the 9th of May, the force, whose movements had not been discovered, reached the eastern shore of Lake Champlain, opposite Ticonderoga.

Only a few boats could be procured; and when day broke on the following morning, but eighty-three men had succeeded in crossing. With this mere handful—for the rest could not be waited for—Allen, with Arnold by his side, made a dash, and gained the gateway of the fort. The sentinel was driven in, closely followed by the mountaineers, who set up such a shout as few garrisons had ever heard. Allen's men hastily faced the barracks and stood ready to fire; he himself rushed to the quarters of Delaplace, the commandant, and shouted for the incumbent to get up. The startled official thrust out his head. "Surrender this fort instantly," said Allen. "By what authority?" inquired the astounded officer. "In the name of the great Jehovah and the Continental Congress!"[13] said Allen, flourishing his sword. Delaplace had no alternative. The garrison, numbering forty-eight, were made prisoners and sent to Connecticut. A fortress which had cost Great Britain eight million pounds sterling was captured in ten minutes by a company of undisciplined provincials. By this daring exploit a hundred and twenty cannon and vast quantities of military stores fell into the hands of the Americans. Two days afterward Crown Point was also taken without the loss of life.

---

[13] This saying will appear especially amusing when it is remembered that the "Continental Congress" referred to did not convene until about *six hours after Ticonderoga was captured.*

On the 25th of May, Generals Howe, Clinton and Burgoyne arrived at Boston. They brought with them powerful reinforcements from England and Ireland; the British army was augmented to more than ten thousand men. Gage, becoming arrogant, issued a proclamation, branding those in arms as rebels and traitors, offering pardon to all who would submit, but excepting Samuel Adams and John Hancock; these two were to suffer the penalty of treason—provided Gage could inflict it. It was now rumored—and the rumor was well founded—that the British were about to sally out of Boston with the purpose of burning the neighboring towns and devastating the country. The Americans determined to anticipate this movement by seizing and fortifying Bunker Hill, a height which commanded the peninsula of Charlestown.

On the night of the 16th of June the brave Colonel Prescott, grandfather of Prescott the historian, was sent with a thousand men to occupy and entrench the hill. Marching by way of Charlestown Neck, the provincials came about eleven o'clock to the eminence which they were instructed to fortify. Prescott and his engineer Gridley, not liking the position of Bunker Hill, proceeded down the peninsula seven hundred yards to another height, afterward called Breed's Hill. The latter was within easy cannon range of Boston. On this summit a redoubt eight rods square was planned by the engineer; and there, from midnight to day-dawn, the men worked in silence. The British ships in the harbor were so near that the Americans could hear the sentinels on deck repeating the night call, "All is well." The works were not yet completed when morning revealed the new-made redoubt to the astonished British of Boston.

"We must carry those works immediately," said General Gage to his officers. For he saw that Prescott's cannon now commanded the city. As soon as it was light, the ships in the harbor began to cannonade the American position. The British batteries on Copp's Hill also opened a heavy fire. But little damage was done in this way; and the Americans returned only an occasional shot; for their supply of ammunition was very limited. Just after noon a British column of about three thousand veterans, commanded by Generals Howe and Pigot, landed at Morton's Point. The plan was to carry Breed's Hill by assault. The Americans numbered in all about fifteen hundred. They were worn out with toil and hunger; but there was no quailing in the presence of the enemy. During the cannonade Prescott climbed out of the defences and walked leisurely around the parapet in full view of the British officers. Generals Putnam and Warren volunteered as privates, and entered the trenches. At three o'clock in the afternoon Howe ordered his column forward. At the same time every gun in the fleet and batteries was turned upon the American position. Charlestown was wantonly set on fire and four hundred buildings burned. Thousands of eager spectators climbed to the house-tops in Boston and waited to behold the shock of battle. On came the British in a stately and imposing column.

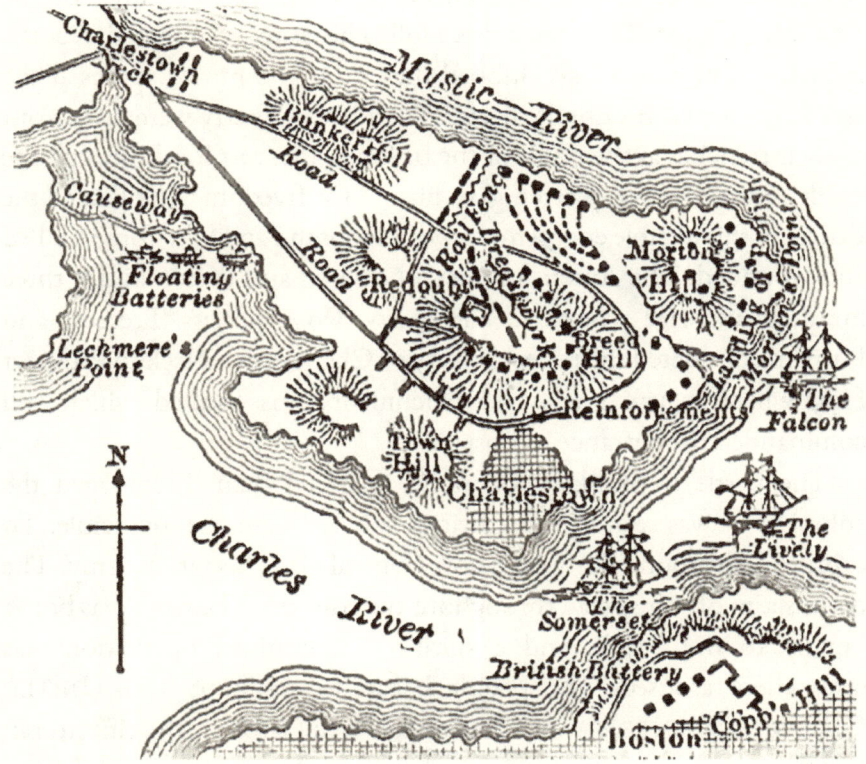

Scene of the Battle of Bunker Hill, 1775.

The Americans reserved their fire until the advancing line was within a hundred and fifty feet. "Fire!" cried Prescott; and instantly from breastwork and redoubt every gun was discharged. The front rank of the

British melted away; there was a recoil, and fifteen minutes after ward a precipitate retreat. Beyond musket range Howe rallied his men and led them to the second charge. Again the American fire was withheld until the enemy was but a few rods distant. Then with steady aim volley after volley was poured upon the charging column until it was broken and a second time driven into flight.

The British officers were now desperate. The vessels of the fleet changed position until the guns were brought to bear upon the inside of the American works. For the third time the assaulting column was put in motion. The British soldiers came on with fixed bayonets up the hillside strewn with the dead and dying. The Americans had but three or four rounds of ammunition remaining. These were expended on the advancing enemy. Then there was a lull. The British clambered over the ramparts. The provincials clubbed their guns and hurled stones at the assailants. It was in vain; the heroic defenders of liberty were driven out of their trenches at the point of the bayonet. Prescott lived through the battle, but the brave Warren gave his life for freedom. The loss of the British in this terrible engagement was a thousand and fifty-four in killed and wounded. The Americans lost a hundred and fifteen killed, three hundred and five wounded, and thirty-two prisoners. Prescott and Putnam conducted the retreat by way of Charlestown Neck to Prospect Hill, where a new line of entrenchments was formed which still commanded the entrance to Boston.

The battle of Bunker Hill rather inspired than discouraged the colonists. It was seen that the British soldiers were not invincible. To capture a few more hills would cost General Gage his whole army. The enthusiasm of war spread throughout the country. The news was borne rapidly to the South, and a spirit of determined opposition was everywhere aroused. The people began to speak of THE UNITED COLONIES OF AMERICA. At Charlotte, North Carolina, the citizens ran together in a hasty convention, and startled the country by making *a declaration of independence*. The British ministers had little dreamed of raising such a storm.

On the day of the capture of Ticonderoga the colonial Congress, which had adjourned in the previous autumn, reassembled at

Philadelphia. Washington was there, and John Adams and Samuel Adams, Franklin and Patrick Henry; Jefferson came soon afterward. A last appeal was addressed to the king of England; and the infatuated monarch was plainly told that the colonists had chosen war in preference to voluntary slavery. Early in the session John Adams made a powerful address, in the course of which he sketched the condition and wants of the country and of the army. The necessity of appointing a commander-in-chief and the qualities requisite in that high officer were dwelt upon; and then the speaker concluded by putting in nomination George Washington of Virginia. As soon as his name was mentioned, Washington arose and withdrew from the hall. For a moment he was overpowered with a sense of the responsibility which was about to be put upon him, and to his friend Patrick Henry he said with tears in his eyes: "I fear that this day will mark the downfall of my reputation." On the 15th of June the nomination was unanimously confirmed by Congress; and the man who had saved the wreck of Braddock's army was called to build a nation.

GEORGE WASHINGTON, descended from the distinguished family of the Wessyngtons in England, was born in Westmoreland county, Virginia, on the 11th of February (Old Style), 1732. At the age of eleven he was left, by the death of his father, to the sole care of a talented and affectionate mother. His education was limited to the common branches of learning, extending only to geometry and trigonometry. Surveying was his favorite study. In his boyhood he was passionately fond of athletic sports and military exercises. As he grew to manhood he was marked above all his companions for the dignity of his manners, the soundness of his judgment and the excellence of his character. At the age of sixteen he was sent by his uncle to survey a tract of land on the South Potomac, and for three years his life was in the wilderness. On reaching his majority he was already more spoken of than any other young man in the colony. The important duties which he performed in the service of the Ohio Company, the beginning of his military career and his noted campaign with Braddock have already been narrated. After the French and Indian War he was a member of the Virginia House of Burgesses; was then chosen a member of the Continental Congress; and was now called by that body to control the destinies of the unorganized mass of men composing the American army. With great dignity he accepted the appointment, refused all compensation beyond his actual expenses, set out with an escort by way of New York, and reached Cambridge fifteen days after the battle of Bunker Hill.

Washington's duties and responsibilities were overwhelming. Congress had voted to raise and equip twenty thousand men, but the means of doing so were not furnished. The colonies had not yet broken their allegiance to the British Crown. For six months Congress stood waiting for the king's answer to its address. The country was sound and patriotic; but its methods of action were irregular and uncertain. Washington had a force of fourteen thousand five hundred men, but they were undisciplined and insubordinate. The revenues and supplies of war were almost wholly wanting. At the time of the battle of Bunker Hill the whole army had but twenty-seven half barrels of powder. The work of organization was at once begun. Four major-generals, one adjutant and eight brigadiers were appointed. The army was arranged in three divisions. The right wing, under General Ward, held Roxbury; the left, commanded by General Charles Lee, rested at Prospect Hill, near Charlestown Neck; the centre, under the immediate direction of the commander-in-chief, lay at Cambridge. Boston was regularly invested, and the siege was pressed with constantly increasing vigor.

During the summer and autumn of 1775, the king's authority was overthrown in all the colonies. The royal governors either espoused the cause of the people, were compelled to resign or were driven off in insurrections. Lord Dunmore, governor of Virginia, seized the public powder. Patrick Henry led the people, and demanded restitution. The governor was overawed, and paid the value of the powder. Fearing further aggression, he went on board a man-of-war, proclaimed freedom to the slaves, raised a force of loyalists, met the provincials at the village of Great Bridge near Norfolk, and was defeated. Obliged to retire from the country, he gratified his vindictive disposition by burning Norfolk.

The American colonies looked to Canada for sympathy and aid. It was believed that the Canadians would make common cause against Great

Britain. In order to encourage such a movement and to secure possession of the Canadian government, an expedition was planned against the towns on the St. Lawrence. Generals Schuyler and Montgomery were placed in command of a division which was to proceed by way of Lake Champlain and the river Sorel to St. John and Montreal. The former fort was reached on the 10th of September, but the Americans, finding the place too strong to be carried by assault, fell back twelve miles to Isle-aux-Noix in the Sorel. This place General Schuyler fortified, and then returned to Ticonderoga for reinforcements. Sickness detained him there, and the whole command devolved on Montgomery. This gallant officer returned to St. John and captured the fortress. Fort Chambly, ten miles farther north, was also taken. Montreal was next invested, and on the 13th of November obliged to capitulate.

Leaving garrisons in the conquered towns, Montgomery proceeded with his regiment, now reduced to three hundred men, against Quebec. This stronghold was already threatened from another quarter. Late in the autumn, Colonel Benedict Arnold set out with a thousand men from Cambridge, passed up the Kennebec and urged his way through the wilderness to the Chaudiere, intending to descend that stream to Point Levi. The march was one of untold hardship and suffering. As winter came on the men were brought to the verge of starvation. The daring leader pressed on in the hope of gathering supplies from some unguarded French village. Before his return the famishing soldiers had killed and devoured every dog that could be found. Then the brave fellows gnawed the roots of trees and ate their moose-skin moccasins until Arnold's return, when the whole force proceeded to Quebec. Morgan, Greene and Meigs, all three noted leaders of the Revolution, and Aaron Burr, one day to become Vice-President of the United States, were in this company of suffering heroes.

Arnold and his men, climbing to the Plains of Abraham, as Wolfe had done sixteen years previously, offered battle. But the English garrison of Quebec remained in their fortifications awaiting an assault which the Americans were not strong enough to make. Conscious of his weakness, Arnold withdrew his men to Point aux Trembles, twenty miles up the river, and there awaited the approach of Montgomery.

When the latter arrived, he assumed command of the whole force, which did not exceed nine hundred effective men. Quebec was defended by greatly superior numbers, well fortified and warmly quartered. For three weeks, with his handful of men, Montgomery besieged the town, and then, relying only on the courageous valor of his men, determined to stake everything on an assault.

It was the last day of December, 1775. Before daybreak the little army was divided into four columns. The first division, under Montgomery, was to pass down the St. Lawrence and attack the Lower Town in the neighborhood of the citadel. The second column, led by Arnold, was to sweep around the city to the north, attack by way of the St. Charles, and join Montgomery in order to storm the Prescott Gate. The other two divisions were to remain in the rear of the Upper Town, making feigned attacks to draw the attention of the garrison. Montgomery's column reached the point from which the charge was to begin. A battery lay just before, and it was thought that the gunners had not discovered the assailants. "Men of New York," said the brave Montgomery, "you will not fear to follow where your general leads! Forward!" There were masses of ice and clouds of blinding snow, and broken ground and the cold gray light of morning. As the Americans were rushing forward, all of a sudden the battery burst forth with a storm of grape-shot. At the first discharge Montgomery and both of his aids fell dead. The column was shattered. The men were heartbroken at the death of their beloved general. They staggered a moment, then fell back, and returned to Wolfe's Cove, above the city.

Arnold, ignorant of what had happened, fought his way into the Lower Town on the north. While leading the charge he was severely wounded and borne to the rear. Captain Morgan, who succeeded him, led his brave band farther and farther along the narrow and dangerous streets until he was overwhelmed and compelled to surrender. Arnold retired with his broken remnant to a point three miles above the city. Reinforcements soon began to arrive; but the smallpox broke out in the camp, and active operations could not be resumed. As soon as the ice disappeared from the St. Lawrence, Quebec was strengthened by the arrival of fresh troops from England. Governor Carleton now began offensive movements; the Americans fell back from post to post, until, by the middle of the following June, Canada was entirely evacuated.

The worst calamity of the whole campaign was the death of General Richard Montgomery. He was one of the noblest of the many noble men who gave their lives in the cause of American liberty. Born of an illustrious Irish family, he became a soldier in his boyhood. He had shared the toils and the triumph of Wolfe. To the enthusiasm of a warm and affectionate nature he joined the highest order of military talents and the virtues of an exalted character. Even in England his death was mentioned with sorrow. New York, his adopted State, claimed his body, brought his remains to her own metropolis and buried them with tears. To after times the Congress of the nation transmitted his fame by erecting a noble monument.

CHAPTER XXXIX.

THE WORK OF '76.

AT last came the king's answer to the appeal of Congress. It was such an answer as George III. and his ministers always made to the petitioners for human rights. The colonies were insulted and spurned; their petition was treated with contempt. The king of England did not know any such a body as the Continental Congress. The first thing necessary was to disband the army and to submit without conditions. Then the monarch would settle all questions with each colony separately. By this offensive and tyrannical answer the day of independence was brought nearer.

Meanwhile, General Howe had succeeded Gage in command of the British troops in Boston. All winter long the city was besieged by Washington. By the middle of February the American army had increased to fourteen thousand men. The country became restless; and Congress urged the commander-in-chief to press the enemy with greater vigor. Washington, knowing the insufficiency of his supplies, and fearing the consequences of rashness more than the charge of inactivity, narrowed his lines, strengthened his works, and waited his opportunity. By the first day of spring, 1776, he felt himself strong enough to risk an assault; the officers of his staff thought otherwise, and a different plan was adopted.

On the north, Boston was commanded by the peninsula of Charlestown on the south, by Dorchester Heights. Since the battle of Bunker Hill the former position had been held by the British; the latter was, as yet, unoccupied. Washington now resolved to take advantage of the enemy's oversight, to seize the Heights and drive Howe out of Boston. A strong entrenching party was prepared and put under command of General Thomas. For two days the attention of the British was drawn by a constant fire from the American batteries. Then, on the night of the 4th of March, the detachment set out under cover of the darkness, passed over Dorchester Neck, and reached the Heights unperceived.

Through the night the Americans worked with an energy rarely equaled. The British, distracted with the cannonade, noticed nothing unusual; and when morning dawned, they could hardly trust their senses. There was a line of formidable entrenchments frowning upon the city; cannon were mounted, and the Americans in force. Howe saw at a glance that he must immediately carry the threatening redoubts or himself abandon Boston. Enraged at being outgeneraled, he ordered Lord Percy to select a column of two thousand four hundred men and storm the American works before nightfall.

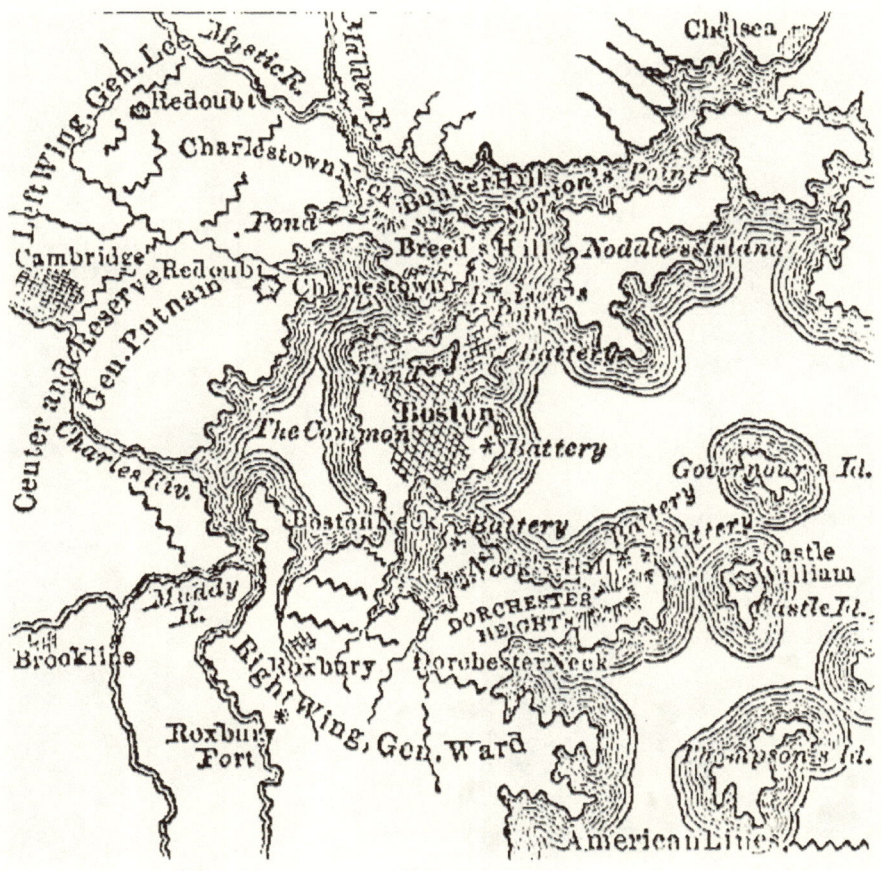

Siege of Boston, 1776.

CHART III.

	1775	76	77	78	79	80	81
	Louis XVI.	Capture of Montreal. Quebec.—Death of Montgomery. 17,000 Hessians hired for the American war. American army evacuates Canada.		Alliance with France. The British ministry offer terms to the Americans.	🏳 Paul Jones' victory.	War between En	
	George III.						
VIRGINIA.		Norfolk burned by Lord Dunmore.		British fleet arrives in Chesapeake Bay.			Richmond
NORTH CAROLINA.						🏳 King's Mountain.	🏳 Gu General Gr
SOUTH CAROLINA.			🏳 Charleston.			🏳 Siege of Charleston. 🏳 Monk's Corner.	🏳 Sanders Cre 🏳 Cowpens 🏳 Camden 🏳 Nine Enta
GEORGIA.				🏳 Savannah.	Sunbury captured by the British. 🏳 Siege of Savannah.		
NEW YORK.		🏳 Ticonderoga. 🏳 Crown Point. New York taken by the British. 🏳 Long Island, 🏳 White Plains. 🏳 Fort Washington.	Arrival of La Fayette. 🏳 Sag Harbor. Fort Edward abandoned. American army arrives at New York. 🏳 Bennington. 🏳 Saratoga, and surrender of Burgoyne.		🏳 Stony Point.	Arnold's treasor André executed	
NEW JERSEY.		🏳 Trenton. 🏳 Princeton.		Winter-quarters at Morristown.		🏳 Springfield.	Mutiny of t Mutiny of t
NEW HAMPSHIRE.			🏳 Hubbardton.				
RHODE ISLAND.				French fleet in Narragansett Bay. 🏳 Quaker Hill.		🏳 Penobscot River.	French fleet arrives
MASSACHUSETTS	🏳 Lexington. 🏳 Bunker Hill.	British evacuate Boston.					
CONNECTICUT.			Tryon's expedition.				A
PENNSYLVANIA.		Washington appointed commander-in-chief. Declaration of Independence. Philadelphia captured. Silas Deane sent to France. 🏳 Brandywine. Dr. Franklin, commissioner to France. 🏳 Germantown.		British evacuate Philadelphia.			Article
MARYLAND.							
DELAWARE.							

REVOLUTION AND CONFEDERATION. A. D. 1775-1789.

82	83	84	85	86	87	88
Retirement of Lord North. Preliminary treaty.						
nd and Holland. Supplemental treaty.						
Siege of Gibraltar. Definitive treaty.						
ned by Arnold.		Washington retires to Mount Vernon.				Virginia ratifies the Constitution.
'orktown.		Virginia cedes the North-western territory to the Government.				
rd.						
e's retreat.						
		The British evacuate Charleston.				South Carolina ratifies the Constitution.
'ix. 'prings.						
		The British evacuate Savannah.				Georgia ratifies the Constitution.
		The British evacuate New York.				
				Decimal currency adopted.		
Dissatisfaction in the army.						New York ratifies the Constitution.
New Jersey line.					New Jersey ratifies the Constitution.	
Pennsylvania line.						
						New Hampshire ratifies the Constitu'n
Newport.						
				Shay's rebellion.		Massachusetts ratifies the Constitution.
		Massachusetts cedes the North-western territory to the Government.				
ld's depredations.						Connecticut ratifes the Constitution.
					Constitutional Convention.	
of Confederation ratified.					Constitution adopted.	
					Constitution ratified.	
		Washington resigns his commission.				Maryland ratifies the Constitution.
				Annapolis Convention.		
						Delaware ratifies the Constitution.

Percy put his men in order and proceeded as far as Castle Island, intending to make the assault in the afternoon. Washington visited the trenches and exhorted his men. It was the anniversary of the Boston Massacre, and the soldiers were eager to avenge the deaths of their countrymen. A battle was momentarily expected; but while Percy delayed, a violent storm arose and rendered the harbor impassable. It continued to blow for a whole day, and the attack could not be made. Before the following morning the Americans had so strengthened and extended their fortifications that all thoughts of an assault were abandoned. Howe found himself reduced to the humiliating extremity of giving up the capital of New England to the rebels.

After some days there was an informal agreement between Washington and the British general that the latter should be allowed to retire from Boston unmolested on condition that the city should not be burned. On the 17th of March the arrangement was consummated, and the whole British army went on board the fleet and sailed out of the harbor. Nearly fifteen hundred loyalists, fearing the vengeance of the patriots, left their homes and fortunes to escape with Howe. The American advance at once entered the city. On the 20th, Washington made a formal entry at the head of the triumphant army. The desolated town, escaping from the calamities of a ten months' siege, broke forth in exultation. The exiled patriots returned by thousands to their homes. The country was wild with delight. From all quarters came votes of thanks and messages of encouragement. Congress ordered a gold medal to be struck in honor of Washington, victorious over an enemy "for the first time put to flight."

The next care of the commander-in-chief was to strengthen the defences of Boston. That done, he repaired with the main division of the army to New York. It was not known to what part of the coast Howe would direct his course; and Washington feared that his antagonist might make a sudden descent in the neighborhood of Long Island. General Lee pressed forward with the Connecticut militia, and reached New York just in time to baffle an attempt of Sir Henry Clinton, whose fleet arrived off Sandy Hook and threatened the city. Clinton next sailed southward, and on the 3d of May was joined by Sir Peter Parker, in command of another fleet, and Lord Cornwallis with two thousand five hundred men. The force was deemed sufficient for any enterprise, and it was determined to capture Charleston.

In the mean time, General Lee had reached the South, and was watching the movements of Clinton. The Carolinians rose in arms and flocked to Charleston. The city was fortified; and a fort, which commanded the entrance to the harbor, was built on Sullivan's Island. On the 4th of June the British squadron came in sight, and a strong detachment was landed on Long Island, a short distance east of Fort Sullivan There was a delay until the 28th of the month; then the British fleet began a furious bombardment of the fortress, which was commanded by Colonel Moultrie. Three men-of-war, attempting to pass the fort, were stranded. Clinton ordered a storming-party to wade the channel between Long Island and Sullivan's Island and carry the works by assault; but the water was too deep to be forded, and Colonel Thompson, who was stationed with a company of riflemen on the opposite bank, drove the British back in confusion. For eight hours the vessels of the fleet poured a tempest of balls upon the fort; but the walls, built of the spongy palmetto, were little injured. The four hundred militiamen who composed the garrison fought like veterans. The republican flag was shot away and thrown out ide of the parapet; Sergeant Jasper leaped down from the wall, recovered the flag and set it in its place again. The fire from the fleet was returned with great spirit; and as evening drew on the British were obliged to retire with a loss of more than two hundred men. Lord Campbell, the royal governor of South Carolina, was killed, and Admiral Parker was severely wounded. The loss of the garrison amounted in killed and wounded to thirty-two. As soon as the British could repair their shattered fleet they abandoned the siege and set sail for New York. In honor of its brave defender the fort on Sullivan's Island was named Fort Moultrie.

During the summer Washington's forces were augmented to about twenty-seven thousand men; but the terms of enlistment were constantly expiring; sickness prevailed in the camp; and the effective force was but little more than half as great as the aggregate. On the other hand, Great Britain was making the vastest preparations. By a treaty with some of the petty German States, seventeen thousand Hessian mercenaries were hired to fight against America. George III. was going to quell his revolted provinces by turning loose upon them a brutal foreign soldiery. Twenty-five thousand additional English troops were levied; an immense squadron was fitted out to aid in the reduction of the colonies, and a million dollars were voted for the extraordinary expenses of the war department.

By these measures the Americans were greatly exasperated. Until now it had been hoped that the difficulty with the mother country could be satisfactorily adjusted without breaking allegiance to the British Crown. The colonists had constantly claimed to be loyal subjects of Great Britain, demanding only the rights and liberties of Englishmen. Now the case seemed hopeless; and the sentiment of disloyalty spread with alarming rapidity. The people urged the general assemblies, and the general assemblies urged Congress, to a more decided assertion of sovereignty. The legislature of Virginia led the way by advising in outspoken terms a declaration of independence. Congress responded by recommending all the colonies to adopt such governments as might best conduce to the happiness and safety of the people. This action was taken early in May, and in the course of the following month nearly all the provinces complied with the recommendation.

Finally, on the 7th of June, 1776, Richard Henry Lee of Virginia offered a resolution in Congress declaring that the United Colonies are, and of right ought to be, free and independent States; that they are absolved from all allegiance to the British Crown; and that all political connection between them and Great Britain is, and ought to be, dissolved. A long and exciting debate ensued. The sentiment of independence gained ground; but there was still strong opposition to the movement. After some days the final consideration of Lee's resolution was postponed until the 1st of July. On the 11th of June a committee, consisting of five members, was appointed to prepare a more elaborate and formal declaration. Mr. Lee had been called home by sickness; and his colleague, Thomas Jefferson, was accordingly made chairman of the committee. The other members were John Adams of Massachusetts, Benjamin Franklin of Pennsylvania, Roger Sherman of Connecticut and

Robert R. Livingston of New York. The special work of preparing the paper was allotted to Jefferson and Adams; the latter deferred to the former, whose vigorous style of writing specially fitted him for the task. The great document was accordingly produced in Jefferson's hand, with a few interlinings by Adams and Franklin.

On the 1st of July, Lee's resolution was taken up, and at the same time the committee's report was laid before Congress. On the next day the original resolution was adopted. During the 3d, the formal declaration was debated with great spirit, and it became evident that the work of the committee would be accepted. The discussion was resumed on the morning of the 4th, and at two o'clock on the afternoon of that memorable day the DECLARATION OF AMERICAN INDEPENDENCE was adopted by a unanimous vote.

All day long the old bellman of the State House had stood in the steeple ready to sound the note of freedom to the city and the nation. The hours went by; the gray-haired veteran in the belfry grew discouraged, and began to say: "They will never do it—they will never do it." Just then the lad who had been stationed below ran out and exclaimed at the top of his voice, "Ring! ring!" And the aged patriot did ring as he had never rung before. The multitudes that thronged the streets caught the signal and answered with shouts of exultation. Swift couriers bore the glad news throughout the land. Everywhere the declaration was received with enthusiastic applause. At Philadelphia the king's arms were torn down from the court-house and burned in the street. At Williamsburg, Charleston and Savannah there were bonfires and illuminations. At Boston the declaration was read in Faneuil Hall, while the cannon from Fort Hill and Dorchester shook the city of the Puritans. At New York the populace pulled down the leaden statue of George III. and cast it into bullets. Washington received the message with joy, and ordered the declaration to be read at the head of each brigade. Former suffering and future peril were alike forgotten in the general rejoicing.

The leading principles of the Declaration of Independence are these: That all men are created equal; that all have a natural right to liberty and the pursuit of happiness; that human governments are instituted for the sole purpose of securing the welfare of the people; that the people have a natural right to alter their government whenever it becomes destructive of liberty; that the government of George III. had become destructive of liberty; that the despotism of the king and his ministers could be shown by a long list of indisputable proofs—and the proofs are given; that time and again the colonies had humbly petitioned for a redress of grievances; that all their petitions had been spurned with derision and contempt; that the king's irrational tyranny over his American subjects was no longer endurable; that an appeal to the sword is preferable to slavery; and that, therefore, the United Colonies of America are, and of right ought to be, free and independent States. To the support of this sublime declaration of principles the members of the Continental Congress mutually pledged their lives, their fortunes and their sacred honor.

On leaving Boston, General Howe sailed to Halifax. There he remained until the middle of June, when he embarked his forces and set sail for Sandy Hook. Early in July he landed a force of nine thousand men on Staten Island. Thither Clinton came from the unsuccessful siege of Charleston, and Admiral Howe, brother of General Howe, from England. The whole British force, now gathered in the vicinity of New York, amounted to fully thirty thousand men. Nearly half of them were the hated Hessians whom the king of Great Britain had hired at thirty-six dollars a head. Washington's army was inferior in numbers, poorly equipped and imperfectly disciplined.

There was some delay in military operations; for Lord Howe, the admiral, had been instructed to try conciliatory measures with the Americans. First, he sent to the American camp an officer with a despatch directed to George Washington, *Esquire*. Of course Washington refused to receive a communication which did not recognize his official position. In a short time Howe sent another message, addressed to George Washington, etc., etc., etc.; and the bearer, who was Howe's adjutant-general, insisted that *and-so-forth* might be translated *General of the American Army*. Washington was the last man in the world to be caught with a subterfuge and the adjutant was sent away. It was already well known that Howe's authority extended only to granting pardons, and to unessential matters about which the

Americans were no longer concerned. Washington therefore replied that since no offence had been committed no pardon was required; that the colonies were now independent, and would defend themselves against all aggression.

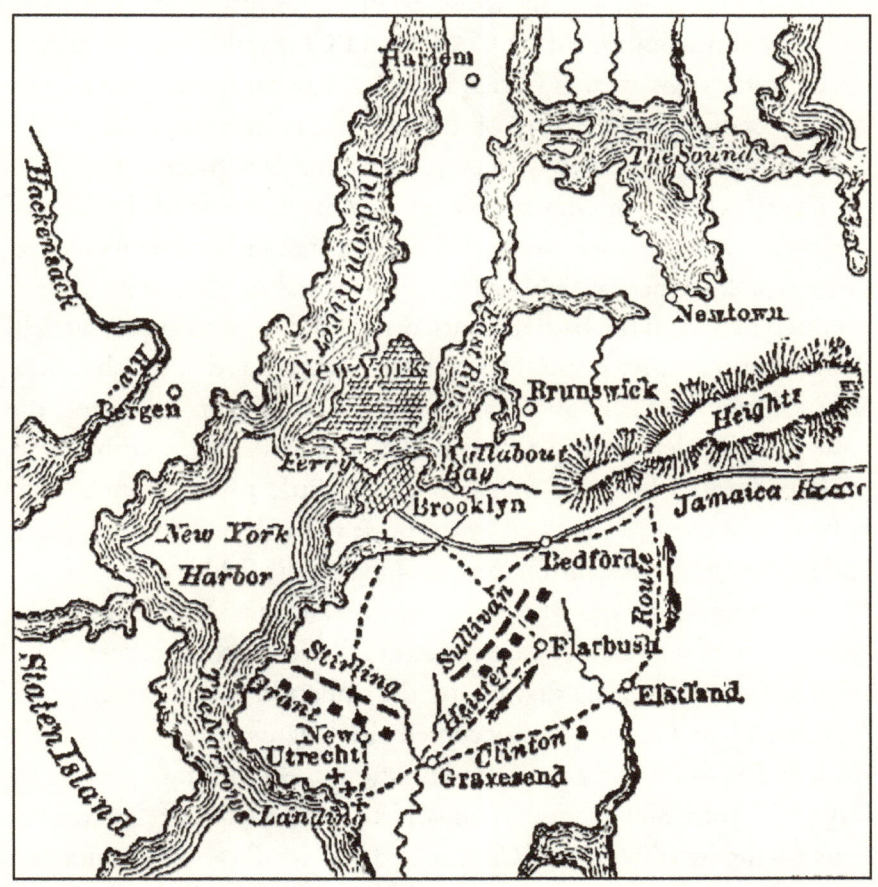

Battle of Long Island, 1776.

Baffled in his efforts, Lord Howe and his brother determined to begin hostilities. On the 22d of August the British, to the number of ten thousand, landed on the south-western coast of Long Island, near the village of New Utrecht. The Americans, about eight thousand strong, commanded by Generals Sullivan and Stirling, were posted in the vicinity of Brooklyn. The advance of the British was planned with great skill. From Gravesend, where Howe's forces were landed, there were three roads to Brooklyn; the British army was accordingly arranged in three divisions. The first column, commanded by General Grant, was to advance by way of Utrecht and the Narrows. The second division, composed of the Hessians, under command of General Heister, was to proceed to Flatbush, and thence to Bedford and Brooklyn. The third and strongest column, led by Clinton and Cornwallis, was to make a circuit to the right as far as Flatland, reach the Jamaica road, and pass by way of Bedford to the rear of the American left wing. All of the movements were executed with perfect ease and fatal precision.

The advance from Gravesend began on the morning of the 27th of August. Grant's division proceeded as far as the hill now embraced in Greenwood Cemetery, where he met General Stirling with fifteen hundred men; and the battle at once began. But in this part of the field there was no decisive result. Heister, in command of the British centre, advanced beyond Flatbush, and engaged the main body of the Americans, under General Sullivan. Here the battle began with a brisk cannonade, in which the Hessians gained little or no ground until Sullivan was suddenly alarmed by the noise of battle on his left and rear, and the battalions of Clinton came rushing on the field.

For General Putnam, who had come over and taken command of the entire force of the island, had, neglectful of Washington's orders, failed to guard the passes on the left of the American army. During the previous night Clinton had occupied the heights above the Jamaica road, and now his force came down, unopposed and unperceived, by way of Bedford. Sullivan found himself surrounded, cutoff, hemmed in between the two divisions of Clinton and Heister. From that moment it was only a question as to what part of the army could be saved from destruction. The men fought desperately, and many broke through the closing lines of the British. The rest were scattered, killed or taken prisoners.

Cornwallis's division pressed on to cut off the retreat of Stirling. At first the British were repulsed, and Stirling began his retreat toward Brooklyn. At Gowanus Creek a number of his men were drowned and many others captured; the rest reached the American lines in safety. Before the battle was ended Washington arrived on the field, and his soul was wrung with anguish at the sight. At first his army seemed ruined; but his resolute and tranquil spirit rose above the disasters of the battle. Generals Stirling, Sullivan and Woodhull were all prisoners in the hands of the enemy. Nearly a thousand patriot soldiers were killed, wounded or missing. It seemed an easy thing for Clinton and Howe to press on and capture all the rest. Yet in a few hours Washington brought together his shattered forces, reorganized his brigades and stood ready for an assault in the trenches back of Brooklyn.

During the 28th, Howe, who was a sluggish, sensual man, ate pudding and waited for a fitter day. On the 29th there was a heavy fog over island and bay and river. Washington, clearly perceiving that he could not hold his position, and that his army was in great peril, resolved to withdraw to New York. The enterprise was extremely hazardous, requiring secrecy, courage and despatch. By eight o'clock on that memorable night every boat and transport that could be obtained was lying at the Brooklyn ferry. There, under cover of the darkness, the embarkation began. Washington personally superintended every movement. All night with muffled oars the boatmen rowed silently back and forth, bearing the patriots to the northern side of the channel. At daylight on the following morning, just as the last boatload was leaving the wharf, the movement was discovered by the British. They rushed into the American entrenchments, and found nothing there except a few worthless guns. After a severe battle which had cost him nearly four hundred men, Howe had gained possession of Long Island–and nothing more. General Greene, who was a competent judge, declared that Washington's retreat was the most masterly he ever read or heard of.

The defeat on Long Island was very disastrous to the American cause. The army was dispirited. As fast as their terms of enlistment expired the troops returned to their homes. Desertions became alarmingly frequent; and it was only by constant exertion that Washington kept his army from disbanding. To add to the peril, the British fleet doubled Long Island and anchored within cannon-shot of New York. Washington, knowing himself unable to defend the city, called a council of war, and it was determined to retire to the Heights of Harlem. On the 15th of September the British landed in force on the east side of Manhattan

Island, about three miles above New York. Thence they extended their lines across the island to the Hudson, and took possession of the city. It was in this juncture of affairs that Howe made overtures of peace to Congress. General Sullivan was paroled and sent to Philadelphia as Howe's agent; but Congress was in no mood to be conciliated. Franklin, on behalf of that body, wrote Howe a letter, telling him many unpalatable truths about what might henceforth be expected from the American colonies.

On the next day after the British gained possession of New York, there was a skirmish between the advance parties of the two armies north of the city. The Americans gained a decided advantage, and the British were driven back with a loss of a hundred men. On the American side the loss included Colonel Knowlton and Major Leitch—two valuable officers—and nearly fifty privates. On the night of the 20th of September a fire broke out in New York and destroyed nearly five hundred buildings. On the 16th of October, while the Americans were still in their entrenchments above the city, Howe embarked his forces, passed into Long Island Sound and landed in the vicinity of Westchester. The object was to get upon the American left flank and cut off communications with the Eastern States. Washington, ever on the alert, detected the movement, put his army in motion and faced the British east of Harlem River. For some days the two generals manœuvred, and on the 28th a battle was brought on at White Plains. Howe began the engagement with a furious cannonade, which was answered with spirit. The Americans were driven from one important position, but immediately reentrenched themselves in another. Night came on; Howe waited for reinforcements, and Washington withdrew to the heights of North Castle. Howe remained for a few days at White Plains, and then returned to New York.

Washington, apprehending that the British would now proceed against Philadelphia, crossed to the west bank of the Hudson and took post with General Greene at Fort Lee. Four thousand men were left at North Castle under command of General Lee. Fort Washington, on Manhattan Island, five miles north of the city, was defended by three thousand men under Colonel Magaw. This fort was a place of great natural and artificial strength. The skill of its construction had attracted the attention of Washington and led to an acquaintance with the engineer, who from that time forth, through the stormy vicissitudes of nearly a quarter of a century, enjoyed the unclouded confidence of his chief; the engineer was ALEXANDER HAMILTON, then a stripling of but twenty years of age.

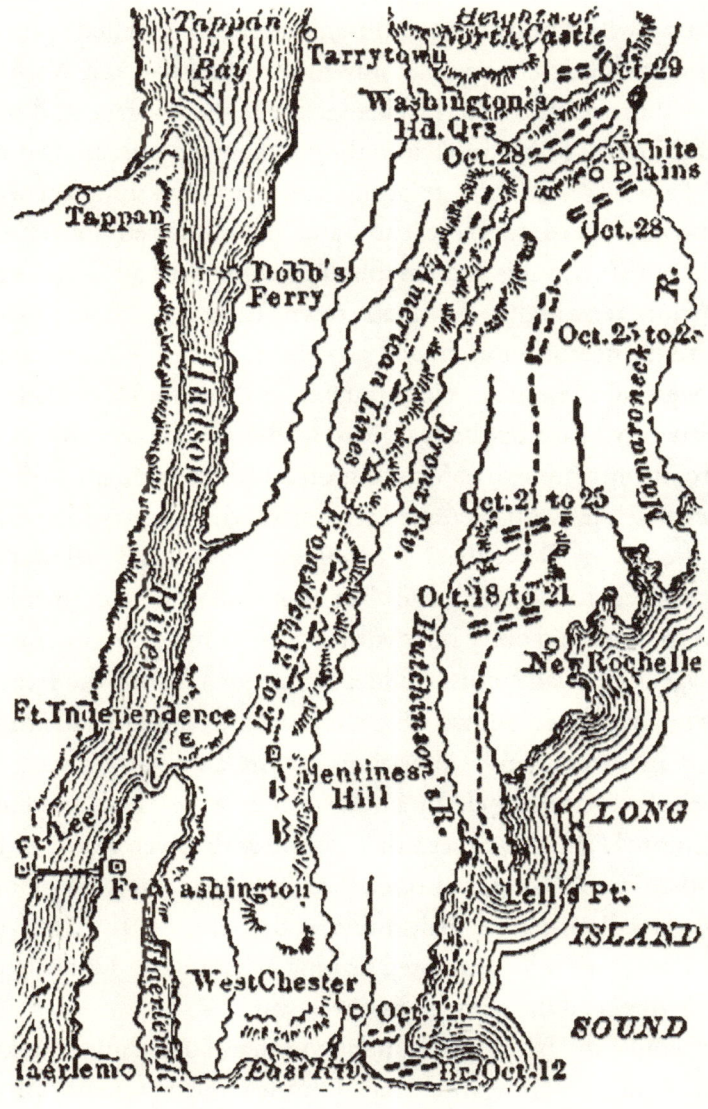

Scene of Operations about New York, 1776.

On the 16th of November the British attacked Fort Washington in overwhelming force. The garrison made a stubborn defence. More than five hundred of the assailants were killed or wounded. But valor could not prevail against superior numbers, and Magaw, after losing a hundred and fifty men, was obliged to capitulate. The garrison, numbering more than two thousand, were made prisoners of war and crowded into the foul jails of New York. Two days after the surrender, Cornwallis crossed the Hudson with a body of six thousand men and marched against Fort Lee. Seeing that a defence would only end in worse disaster, Washington hastily withdrew across the Hackensack. All the baggage and military stores collected in Fort Lee fell into the hands of the British, who at once pressed forward after the retreating Americans. Washington with his army, now reduced to three thousand men, crossed the Passaic to Newark; but Cornwallis and Knyphausen came hard after the fugitives. The patriots retreated to Elizabeth town, thence to New Brunswick, thence to Princeton, and finally to Trenton on the Delaware. The British were all the time in close pursuit, and the music of their bands was frequently heard by the rearguard of the American army. Nothing but the consummate skill of Washington saved the remnant of his forces from destruction. Despair seemed settling on the country like a pall.

On the 8th of December, Washington crossed the Delaware. The British essayed to do the same, but the American commander had secreted or destroyed every boat within seventy miles. In order to effect his passage, Cornwallis must build a bridge, or wait for the freezing of the river. The latter course was chosen; and the British army was stationed in detachments in various towns and villages east of the Delaware. Trenton was held by a body of nearly two thousand Hessians under Colonel Rahl. It was seen that as soon as the river should be frozen the British would march unopposed into Philadelphia. Congress accordingly adjourned to Baltimore; and there, on the 20th of the month, a resolution was adopted arming Washington with dictatorial powers to direct all the operations of the war.

Meanwhile, the British fleet under command of Admiral Parker had left New York for Narragansett Bay. On the same day that Washington crossed the Delaware the islands of Rhode Island, Prudence and

Conanicut were taken; and the American squadron under Commander Hopkins was blockaded in Blackstone River. During his retreat across New Jersey, Washington had sent repeated despatches to General Lee, in command of the detachment at North Castle, to join the main army as soon as possible. Lee was a proud, insubordinate man, and virtually disobeyed his orders. Marching leisurely into New Jersey, he reached Morristown. Here he tarried, and took up his quarters at an inn at Basking Ridge. On the 13th of December, a squad of British cavalry dashed up to the tavern, seized Lee and hurried him off to New York. General Sullivan, who had recently been exchanged, now took command of Lee's division, and hastened to join Washington. Fifteen hundred volunteers from Philadelphia and vicinity were added, making the entire American force a little more than six thousand.

The tide of misfortune turned at last. Washington saw in the disposition of the British forces an opportunity to strike a blow for his disheartened country. The leaders of the enemy were off their guard. They believed that the war was ended. Cornwallis obtained leave of absence, left New Jersey under command of Grant, and made preparations to return to England. The Hessians on the east side of the river were spread out from Trenton to Burlington. Washington conceived the bold design of crossing the Delaware and striking the detachment at Trenton before a concentration of the enemy's forces could be effected. The American army was accordingly arranged in three divisions. The first, under General Cadwallader, was to cross the river at Bristol and attack the British at Burlington. General Ewing with his brigade was to pass over a little below Trenton for the purpose of intercepting the retreat. Washington himself, with Greene and Sullivan and twenty-four hundred men, was to cross nine miles above Trenton, march down the river and assault the town. The movement was planned with the utmost secrecy–the preparations made with prudence and care. Christmas night was selected as the time; for it was known that the Hessians would spend the day in drinking and carousals.

About the 20th of the month, the weather became very cold, and by the evening of the 25th the Delaware was filled with floating ice. Ewing and Cadwallader were both baffled in their efforts to cross the river.

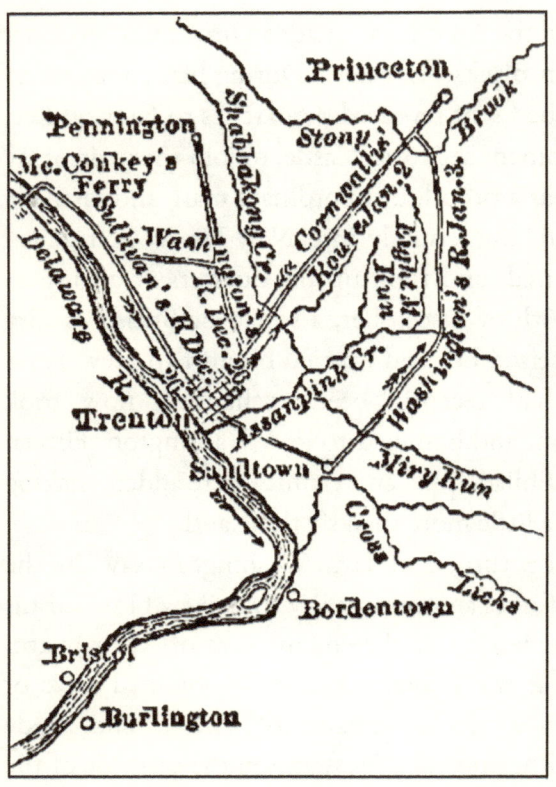
Battle of Trenton and Princeton, 1776-7.

Washington's division succeeded in getting over, but the passage was delayed till three o'clock in the morning. All hope of reaching Trenton before daybreak was at an end; but Washington, believing that the Hessians would sleep late after their revels, divided his army into two columns and pressed forward. One division, led by Sullivan, passed down the river to attack the town on the west; the other, commanded by Washington and Greene, made a circuit to the Princeton road. The movement was entirely successful. At eight o'clock in the morning the American columns came rushing into the village from both directions. The astonished Hessians sprang from their quarters and attempted to form in line. At the first onset Colonel Rahl was mortally wounded. Forty or fifty others fell before the volleys of the patriots. For a few minutes there was confusion, and then a cry for quarter. Nearly a thousand of the dreaded Hessians threw down their arms and begged for mercy. At the first alarm about six hundred light horse and infantry had escaped toward Bordentown. All the rest were made prisoners of war. Before nightfall Washington, with his victorious men and the whole body of captives, was safe on the other side of the Delaware.

The battle of Trenton roused the nation from despondency. Confidence in the commander and hope in the ultimate success of the

American cause were everywhere revived. The militia from the neighboring provinces flocked to the general's standard; and fourteen hundred soldiers, whose term of enlistment now expired, cheerfully re-entered the service. It was at this time that Robert Morris of Philadelphia, the great financier of the Revolution, came forward with his princely fortune to the support of his distressed country. As to Cornwallis, he found it necessary to postpone his visit to England and hasten back to New Jersey.

Three days after his victory, Washington again crossed the Delaware and took post at Trenton. Here all the American detachments in the vicinity were ordered to assemble. To General Heath, in command of the New England militia stationed at Peekskill, on the Hudson, Washington sent orders to move into New Jersey. The British fell back from their outposts on the Delaware and concentrated in great force at Princeton. Cornwallis took command in person, and resolved to attack and overwhelm Washington at Trenton. So closed the year. Ten days previously, Howe only waited for the freezing of the Delaware before taking up his quarters in Philadelphia. Now it was a question whether he would be able to hold a single town in New Jersey.

CHAPTER XL.

OPERATIONS OF '77.

ON the 1st of January, 1777, Washington's army at Trenton numbered about five thousand men. On the next day Cornwallis approached from Princeton with greatly superior forces. The British were exasperated and the Americans resolute. During the afternoon there was severe and constant skirmishing in the fields and along the roads to the east and north of Trenton. As the columns of the enemy pressed on, Washington abandoned the village and took up a stronger position on the south side of Assanpink Creek. The British, attempting to force a passage, were driven back; it was already sunset, and Cornwallis deferred the attack till the morrow.

2. Washington's position was critical in the extreme. To attempt to recross the Delaware was hazardous. To retreat in any direction was to lose all that he had gained by his recent victory. To be beaten in battle was utter ruin. In the great emergency he called a council of war and announced his determination to leave the camp by night, make a circuit to the east, pass the British left flank and strike the detachment at Princeton before his antagonist could discover or impede the movement. Orders were immediately issued for the removal of the baggage to Burlington. In order to deceive the enemy, the camp-fires along the Assanpink were brightly kindled and a guard left to keep them burning through the night. Then the army was put in motion by the circuitous route to Princeton. Everything was done in silence, and the British sentries walked their beats until the morning light showed them a deserted camp. Just then the roar of the American cannon, thirteen miles away, gave Cornwallis notice of how he had been outgeneraled.

At sunrise Washington was entering Princeton. At the same moment the British regiments stationed there were marching out by the Trenton road to reinforce Cornwallis. The Americans met them in the edge of the village, and the battle at once began. The patriots, under General Mercer, posted themselves behind a hedge, and were doing good work with their muskets until the British charged bayonets. Then the militia gave way in confusion, and Mercer, one of the bravest of the brave, received a mortal wound. But the Pennsylvania reserves and regulars were at hand, led by the commander-in-chief. The valor of Washington never shone with brighter lustre. He spurred among his flying men, who rallied at his call. He rode between the hostile lines and reined his horse within thirty yards of the enemy's column. There he stood. From both sides there came a crash of musketry. Washington's aid drew his hat over his eyes that he might not see the chieftain die. The wind tossed up the smoke, and there, unhurt, was the sublime leader of the American armies. The British were already broken and flying, with a loss of four hundred and thirty men in killed, wounded and missing. The loss of the Americans was small; but the gallant Mercer was greatly lamented.

Washington had intended to press on to Brunswick and destroy the enemy's magazines. His men, however, were too much exhausted for the march. The legions of Cornwallis were already in hearing, and there was no time for delay. Washington accordingly withdrew to the north, and on the 5th of January took a strong position at Morristown. Cornwallis hastened to New Brunswick to protect his stores. In a short time the whole of New Jersey north of Newark and Elizabethtown was recovered by the patriots. In all parts of the State the militia rose in arms; straggling parties of the British were cut off, and the outposts of the enemy were kept in constant alarm. The Hessians, whose barbarous invasion and brutal conduct had almost ruined the country, were the special objects of patriot vengeance. Vexed by the perpetual assaults of partisan warfare, Cornwallis gradually contracted his lines, abandoning one post after another, until his whole force was cooped up in New Brunswick and Amboy. The boastful British army that was to have taken Philadelphia now thought only of a safe return to New York.

In the early spring, General Howe despatched a fleet up the Hudson to destroy the American stores at Peekskill. Macdougal, the commandant, finding himself too feeble to make a successful defence, blew up the magazines and retreated. On the 18th of April Cornwallis marched a division out of New Brunswick and surprised General Lincoln, who was stationed at Boundbrook on the Raritan; but the latter made good his retreat with a trifling loss. On the 25th of the same month, General Tryon with a detachment of two thousand men landed on the north shore of Long Island Sound, and proceeded against Danbury, Connecticut. After destroying a large quantity of stores and burning the town the British began a retreat to the coast. Immediately they were attacked on flank and rear by the exasperated patriots, who, led by the aged Wooster and the daring Arnold, made charge after charge on the retreating foe. Before regaining their shipping the British lost more than two hundred men; of the patriots about sixty were killed and wounded. The veteran Wooster, now sixty-eight years of age, fell in this engagement.

A similar expedition, undertaken by the Americans, was more successful. Colonel Meigs, of Connecticut, learning that the British were collecting stores at Sag Harbor, near the eastern extremity of Long Island, gathered two hundred militiamen, and determined to surprise the post. On the night of the 22d of May he embarked his men in whaleboats, crossed the Sound, and reached Sag Harbor just before daydawn on the following morning. The British, numbering a hundred, were overpowered; only four of them escaped; five or six were killed, and the remaining ninety were made prisoners. A gun-ship, ten loaded transports and a vast amount of stores were destroyed by the victorious patriots, who, without the loss of a man, returned to Guilford with their captives. For this gallant deed Colonel Meigs received an elegant sword from Congress.

Washington remained in his camp at Morristown until the latter part of May. Cornwallis was still at New Brunswick, and it was necessary that the American commander should watch the movements of his antagonist. The patriot forces of the North were now concentrated on the Hudson and a large camp, under command of Arnold, was laid out on the Delaware. Both divisions were within supporting distance of Washington, who now broke up his winter-quarters and took an advantageous position at Boundbrook, only ten miles from the British camp. Howe now crossed over from New York, reinforced Cornwallis and threatened an attack upon the American lines; but Washington stood his ground, and Howe pressed forward as far as Somerset Court-

House, in the direction of the Delaware. The movement was only a feint intended to draw Washington from his position; but he was too wary to be deceived, and the British fell back through New Brunswick to Amboy. The American lines were now advanced as far as Quibbletown. While in this position, Howe, on the night of the 25th of June, turned suddenly about and made a furious attack on the American van; but Washington withdrew his forces without serious loss and regained his position at Boundbrook. Again the British retired to Amboy, and on the 30th of the month crossed over to Staten Island. After more than six months of manœuvring and fighting the invading army was fairly driven out of New Jersey.

On the 10th of July a brilliant exploit was performed in Rhode Island. Colonel William Barton, of Providence, learning that Major-General Prescott of the British army was quartered at a farm-house near Newport, apart from his division, determined to capture him. On the night of the 10th of July the daring colonel, with forty volunteers, embarked at Providence, dropped down the bay, and reached the island near Prescott's lodgings. The movement was not discovered. The British sentinel was deceived with a plausible statement, and then threatened with death if he did not remain quiet. The patriots rushed forward, burst open Prescott's door, seized him in bed, and hurried him, half clad, to the boats. The alarm was raised; a squad of cavalry came charging to the water's edge; but the provincials were already paddling out of sight with their prisoner. This lucky exploit gave the Americans an officer of equal rank to exchange for General Lee. Colonel Barton was rewarded with promotion and an elegant sword.

Meanwhile, Congress had returned to Philadelphia. The American government was at this time essentially weak in its structure and inefficient in action. Nevertheless, there was much valuable legislation which tended to strengthen the army and the nation. But the most auspicious sign that gladdened the patriots was the unequivocal sympathy of the French. From the beginning of the contest the people of France had espoused the American cause. Now, after the lapse of two years, their sympathy became more outspoken and enthusiastic. True, the French government would do nothing openly which was calculated to provoke a war with Great Britain. Outwardly the forms and sentiments of peace were preserved between the two nations; but secretly the French rejoiced at British misfortune and applauded the action of the colonies. Soon the Americans came to understand that if money was required France would lend it; if supplies were needed, France would furnish them; if arms were to be purchased, France had arms to sell. During the year 1777 the French partisans of America managed to supply the colonies with more than twenty thousand muskets and a thousand barrels of powder.

At last the republicans of France, displeased with the double-dealing of their government, began to embark for America. Foremost of all came the gallant young MARQUIS OF LA FAYETTE.[14] Though the king withheld permission, though the British minister protested, though family and home and kindred beckoned the youthful nobleman to return, he left all to fight the battle of freedom in another land. Fitting a vessel at his own expense, he eluded the officers, and with the brave De Kalb and a small company of followers reached Georgetown, South Carolina, in April of 1777. He at once entered the patriot army as a volunteer, and in the following July was commissioned as a major-general. Not yet twenty years of age, he clung to Washington as son to father, and through life their friendship was unclouded.

One of the most important events of the whole war was the campaign of Lieutenant-General Burgoyne. This distinguished British officer arrived at Quebec in March of 1777. Superseding Sir Guy Carleton in command of the English forces in Canada, he spent the months of April and May in organizing a powerful army for the invasion of New York. By the beginning of June he had thoroughly equipped a force of ten thousand men, of whom about seven thousand were British and Hessian veterans; the rest were Canadians and Indians. The plan of the campaign embraced a descent upon Albany by way of Lake Champlain, Lake George and the Upper Hudson. From Albany it was Burgoyne's purpose to descend the river to New York and unite his forces with the main division of the British army. By this means New England was to be

---

[14] La Fayette's name was *Gilbert Motier*.

cut off from the Middle and Southern colonies and the whole country placed at the mercy of Howe. That any successful resistance could be offered to the progress of the invading army was little imagined.

On the 1st of June Burgoyne reached St. John's, at the foot of Lake Champlain, and on the 16th proceeded to Crown Point. This place, which was undefended, was occupied by a British garrison; and the main army swept on to Ticonderoga, which was at that time held by three thousand men under General St. Clair. The British soon gained possession of Mount Defiance, and planted a battery seven hundred feet above the American works. Mount Hope was also seized and retreat by way of Lake George cut off. St. Clair, seeing that resistance would be hopeless, abandoned the fort on the night of the 5th of July, and escaped with the garrison by way of Mount Independence and Wood Creek. The British pressed after the fugitives, and overtook them at Hubbardton, a village in Vermont, seventeen miles from Ticonderoga. A sharp engagement ensued, in which the Americans fought so obstinately as to check the pursuit; and then continued their retreat to Fort Edward. On the following day the British reached Whitehall and captured a large quantity of baggage, stores and provisions.

At this time the American army of the North was commanded by General Schuyler, a man whose patriotism was greater than his abilities. His headquarters were at Fort Edward, where he remained until after the arrival of St. Clair. The garrison now numbered between four and five thousand men; but this force was deemed inadequate to hold the place against Burgoyne's army. Schuyler therefore evacuated the post and retreated down the Hudson as far as the islands at the mouth of the Mohawk. Burgoyne came on by way of Fort Ann, which the Americans had demolished, and thence through the woods over obstructed roads to Fort Edward, where he arrived on the 30th of July. Fearing that his supplies would be exhausted before he could reach Albany, the British general now made a halt, and despatched Colonel Baum with five hundred men to seize the provincial stores at Bennington, Vermont. Colonel John Stark rallied the New Hampshire militia, and on the 15th of August met the British a short distance from the village. On the following morning there was a furious battle, in which Baum's force was fairly annihilated. A battalion of Hessians, led by Breymann, arrived on the field, only to be utterly routed by the Americans, who were reinforced by the gallant colonel Warner. The British lost a hundred and forty in killed and wounded, and nearly seven hundred prisoners. The whole country was thrilled by the victory, and the patriots began to rally from all quarters.

A few days after the battle of Bennington, Burgoyne received intelligence of a still greater reverse. At the beginning of the invasion a large force of Canadians, Tories and Indians, commanded by General St. Leger, had been sent by way of Oswego against Fort Schuyler, at the head of navigation on the Mohawk. This important post was held by a small garrison under Colonel Gansevoort. On the 3d of August St. Leger invested the fort, and it seemed that a successful defence was impossible; but the brave General Herkimer rallied the militia of the surrounding country and advanced to the relief of the garrison. When nearing the fort, the patriots fell into an Indian ambuscade, and a terrible hand-to-hand conflict ensued in the woods. Herkimer was defeated with a loss of a hundred and sixty men in killed, wounded and prisoners. The loss of the savages was almost as great. Hardly had the conflict ended when the garrison made a sally, carried everything before them, and then fell back with trophies and prisoners. Already the impetuous and fearless Arnold had volunteered to lead a detachment from the Hudson for the relief of the fort. At his approach the savages plundered the British camp and fled. St. Leger, dismayed at the treachery of the barbarians, raised the siege and retreated. Fort Schuyler was saved and strengthened. Such was the news that was borne to Burgoyne at Fort Edward.

The British general had now lost a month in procuring supplies from Canada. Should he retreat? Ruin and disgrace were in that direction. Should he go forward? More than nine thousand patriot soldiers were in *that* direction. For General Lincoln had arrived with the militia of New England; Washington had sent several detachments from the regular army; Morgan had come with his famous riflemen. Meanwhile, General Gates had superseded Schuyler in command of the northern army. On the 8th of September the American headquarters were advanced to Stillwater. At Bemis's Heights, a short distance north of this place, a strong camp was laid out and fortified under direction of the noted Polish engineer Thaddeus Kosciusko. On the 14th of the month, Burgoyne crossed the Hudson and took post at Saratoga. Until the 18th he advanced his camp a mile each day, when the two armies were face to face and but two miles apart. On the afternoon of the 19th the advance parties of the British attacked the American wings, and a general battle ensued, continuing until nightfall. The conflict, though severe, was indecisive; the Americans retired within their lines, and the British slept under arms on the field. To the patriots, whose numbers were constantly increasing, the result of the battle was equivalent to a victory.

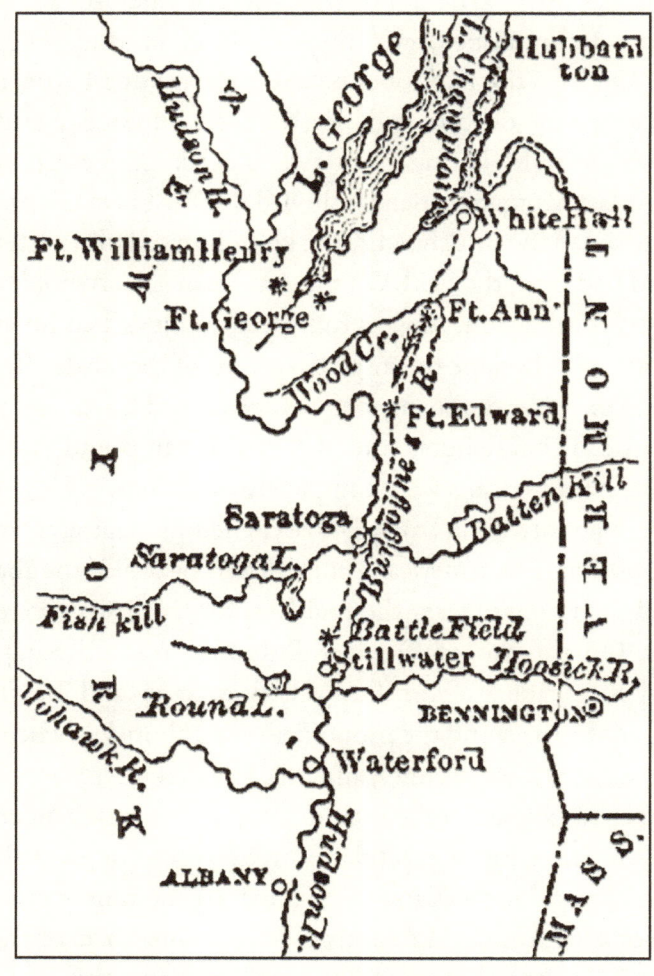

Scene of Burgoyne's Invasion, 1777.

The condition of Burgoyne grew more and more critical. On all sides the lines of Gates were closing around him. His supplies failed; his soldiers were put on partial rations; his Canadian and Indian allies deserted his standard. But the British general was courageous and resolute; he strengthened his defences and flattered his men with the hope that General Clinton, who now commanded the British army in New York, would make a diversion in their favor. The latter did ascend the river as far as Forts Clinton and Montgomery. Both these forts, after an obstinate defence, were carried by assault. Colonel Vaughan was sent on with a thousand men as far as the town of Kingston, which was burned besides the destruction of stores and private property, nothing further was accomplished, and the condition of Burgoyne became desperate. On the 7th of October he hazarded another battle, in which he lost his bravest officers and nearly seven hundred privates. The conflict was terrible, lasting from two o'clock in the afternoon till twilight. At last Morgan's riflemen singled out the brave General Fraser, who commanded the British right, and killed him. His disheartened men turned and fled from the field. On the American side, Arnold, who had resigned his commission, rode at full speed to his old command, and, *without authority*, became the inspiring genius of the battle. He charged like a madman, drove the enemy before him, eluded Gates's aid who was sent to call him back, burst into the British camp and was severely wounded. The Americans were completely victorious.

On the night after the battle Burgoyne led his shattered army to a stronger position. The Americans immediately occupied the abandoned camp, and then pressed after the fugitives; for the British were already retreating. On the 9th of October Burgoyne reached Saratoga and attempted to escape to Fort Edward. But Gates and Lincoln now commanded the river, and the proud Briton was hopelessly hemmed in. He held out to the last extremity, and finally, when there were only three days between his soldiers and starvation, was driven to surrender. On the 17th of October terms of capitulation were agreed on, and the whole army, numbering five thousand seven hundred and ninety-one, became prisoners of war. Among the captives were six members of the British Parliament. A splendid train of brass artillery consisting of forty-two pieces, together with nearly five thousand muskets, and an immense quantity of ammunition and stores, was the further fruit of the victory. The valor of the patriots had fairly eclipsed the warlike renown of Great Britain.

As soon as Burgoyne's invasion was at an end, a large portion of the Victorious army of the North was despatched to the aid of Washington. For, in the mean time, a great campaign had been in progress in the South; and the patriots were sorely pressed. At the beginning of July, Howe had abandoned New Jersey. On the 23d of the same month he sailed with eighteen thousand men to attack Philadelphia by way of the Delaware. Washington, suspecting the object of the expedition, broke up his camp and marched rapidly southward. Off the capes of Virginia Howe learned that the Americans had obstructed the Delaware, so as to prevent the passage of his fleet. He therefore determined to enter the Chesapeake, anchor at the head of the bay and make the attack by land. As soon as Washington obtained information of the enemy's plans, he advanced his headquarters from Philadelphia to Wilmington, and there the American army, numbering between eleven and twelve thousand men, was concentrated. The forces of Howe were vastly superior in numbers and equipments, but Washington hoped by selecting his ground and acting on the defensive to beat back the invaders and save the capital.

On the 25th of August, the British landed at Elk River, in Maryland, and nine days afterward began their march toward Philadelphia. After a council of war and some changes in the arrangement of his forces, Washington selected the left bank of the Brandywine as his line of defence. The left wing of the American army was stationed at Chad's Ford to dispute the passage, while the right wing, under General Sullivan, was extended for three miles up the river. On the 11th of September the British reached the opposite bank and began battle. What seemed to be their principal attack was made by the Hessians under Knyphausen at the ford; and here Wayne's division held the enemy in check. But the onset of Knyphausen was only a feint to keep the Americans engaged until a stronger column of the British, led by Cornwallis and Howe, could march up the south bank of the

Brandywine and cross at a point above the American right. In this way Sullivan, who was not on the alert, allowed himself to be outflanked. Washington was misled by false information; the right wing, though the men under La Fayette and Stirling fought with great courage, was crushed in by Cornwallis; and the day was hopelessly lost.

During the night the defeated patriots retreated to Westchester. Greene brought up the rear in good order; through his efforts and those of the commander-in-chief the army was saved from destruction. The loss of the Americans in killed, wounded and missing amounted to fully a thousand men that of the British to five hundred and eighty-four. The gallant La Fayette was severely wounded; Count Pulaski, a brave Pole who had espoused the patriot cause, so distinguished himself in this engagement that Congress honored him with the rank of brigadier and gave him command of the cavalry. On the day after the battle, Washington continued his retreat to Philadelphia, and then took post at Germantown, a few miles from the city. Undismayed by his reverse, he resolved to risk another engagement. Accordingly, on the 15th of the month, he recrossed the Schuylkill and marched toward the British camp. Twenty miles below Philadelphia he met Howe at Warren's Tavern. For a while the two armies manœuvred, the enemy gaining the better position; then a spirited skirmish ensued, and a great battle was imminent. But just as the conflict was beginning a violent tempest of wind and rain swept over the field. The combatants were deluged, their cartridges soaked, and fighting made impossible. On the next day Howe marched down the Schuylkill; Washington recrossed the river and confronted his antagonist. Howe turned suddenly about and hurried up stream along the right bank in the direction of Reading. Washington, fearing for his stores, pressed forward up the left bank to Pottstown. But the movement of the British westward was only feigned; again Howe wheeled, marched rapidly to the ford above Norristown, crossed the river and hastened to Philadelphia. On the 26th of September the city was entered without opposition, and the main division of the British army encamped at Germantown.

At the approach of Howe, Congress adjourned to Lancaster. On the 27th of September the members met at that place, and again adjourned to York, where they assembled on the 30th and continued to hold their sessions until the British evacuated Philadelphia in the following summer. Washington now made his camp on Skippack Creek, about twenty miles from the city. As soon as Howe found himself safe in the "rebel capital," as he was pleased to call it, he despatched a large division of his army to capture forts Mifflin and Mercer on the Delaware. Germantown was thus considerably weakened, and Washington resolved to attempt a surprise. The same plan of attack which had been so successful at Trenton was again adopted. On the night of the 3d of October the American army, arranged in several divisions, marched silently toward Germantown. The roads were rough, and the different columns reached the British outposts at irregular intervals. The morning was foggy, and the movements of both armies were unsteady and confused. There was much severe fighting, and at one time it seemed that the British would be overwhelmed; but they gained possession of a large stone house and held it. A foolish attempt to dislodge them gave the enemy time to rally. Some strong columns of Americans were kept out of the battle by the inefficiency of their commanders; the tide turned against the patriots, and the day was lost. Of the Americans a hundred and fifty-two were killed, five hundred and twenty-one wounded, and about four hundred missing. Howe reported the British loss at five hundred and thirty-five. The retreat of the Americans was covered by Greene and Pulaski.

On the 22d of October Fort Mercer, on the New Jersey side of the Delaware, seven miles below Philadelphia, was assaulted by twelve hundred Hessians under Count Donop. The garrison, though numbering but four hundred, made a brave and successful resistance. The assault was like that at Bunker Hill. Count Donop received a mortal wound, and nearly four hundred of his men fell before the American entrenchments. At the same time the British fleet, assisted by a land force from Philadelphia, attacked Fort Mifflin on Mud Island, in the Delaware. Here also the assailants met with an obstinate resistance. The assault became a siege, which lasted till the 15th of November. The patriots held out against superior numbers until every gun was dismounted and every palisade demolished. Then at midnight the ruined fortress was set on fire, and the garrison escaped to Fort Mercer. To make a second attack on this place Howe despatched two thousand men under Cornwallis. Washington sent General Greene to succor the fortress; but Cornwallis was strongly reinforced, and the American general would not hazard a battle. On the 20th of November Fort Mercer was abandoned to the British; and thus General Howe obtained undisputed control of the Delaware.

After the battle of Germantown Washington took up his headquarters at Whitemarsh, twelve miles from Philadelphia. Winter was approaching, and the patriots began to suffer for food and clothing. Howe, knowing the distressed condition of the Americans, determined to surprise their camp. On the evening of the 2d of December he held a council of war, and it was decided to march against Washington on the following night. But Lydia Darrah, at whose house the council was held, overheard the plan of the enemies of her country. On the following morning she obtained a passport from Lord Howe, left the city on pretence of *going to mill*, rode rapidly to the American lines, and sent information of the impending attack to Washington. When, on the morning of the 4th, the British approached Whitemarsh they found the cannon mounted and the patriots standing in order of battle. The British general manœuvred for four days, and then marched back to Philadelphia. During the remainder of the winter the city was occupied by nearly twenty thousand English and Hessian soldiers. There they reveled and rioted. Everything that the magazines of Great Britain could furnish was lavished upon the army of invaders who lay warmly housed in the city of Penn. In the patriot camp there was a different scene.

On the 11th of December Washington left his position at Whitemarsh and went into winter-quarters at Valley Forge on the right bank of the Schuylkill. The march thither occupied four days. Thousands of the soldiers were without shoes, and the frozen ground was marked with bloody footprints. The sagacity of Washington had pointed to a strong position for his encampment. To the security of the river and hills the additional security of redoubts and entrenchments was added. Log cabins were built for the soldiers, and everything was done that could be done to secure the comfort of the suffering patriots. But it was a long and dreary winter; moaning and anguish were heard in the camp, and the echo fell heavy on the soul of the commander. These were the darkest days of Washington's life. Congress in a measure abandoned him, the people withheld their sympathies. The brilliant success of the army of the North was unjustly compared with the reverses of the army of the South. Many men high in military and civil station left the great leader unsupported in the hour of his grief; even Samuel Adams, impatient under calamity, withdrew his confidence. There was a miserable conspiracy headed by Gates, Conway and Mifflin. Washington was to be superseded, and Gates or Lee was to be made commander-in-chief. But the alienation was only for a moment; the allegiance of the army remained unshaken, and the nation's confidence in the troubled chieftain became stronger than ever. Still, at the close of 1777, the patriot cause was obscured with clouds and misfortune.

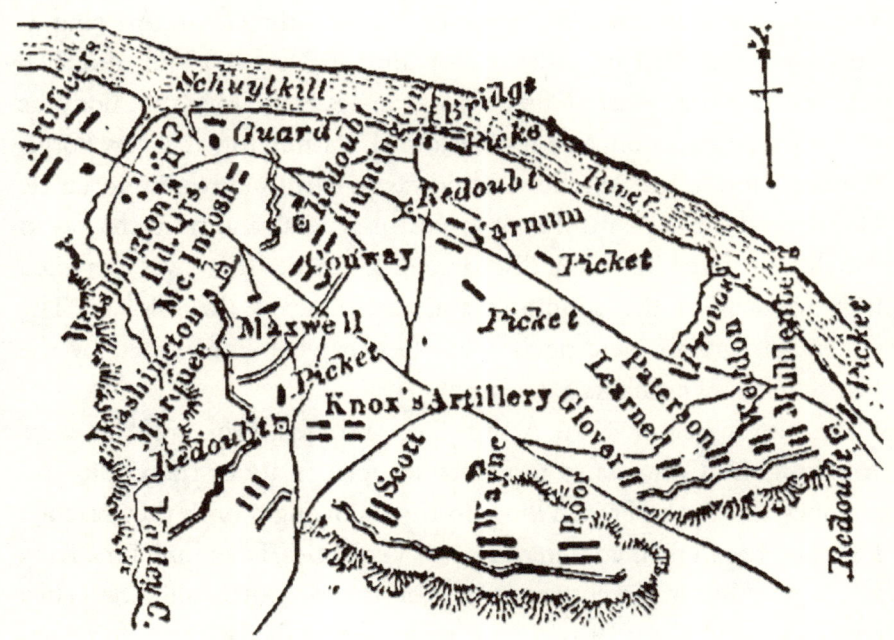

Encapment at Valley Forge, 1777-8.

CHAPTER XLI.

FRANCE TO THE RESCUE.

FOUR months before the declaration of independence, Silas Deane of Connecticut was appointed commissioner to France. His business at the French court was to act as the political and commercial agent of the United Colonies. His first service was to make a secret arrangement with Beaumarchais, a rich French merchant, by which the latter was to supply the Americans with the materials necessary for carrying on the war. The king of France and his prime minister, Vergennes, winked at this proceeding; but the agents of Great Britain were jealous and suspicious, and it was not until the autumn of 1777 that a ship laden with two hundred thousand dollars' worth of arms, ammunition and specie could be sent to America. In that ship came Baron Steuben, a veteran soldier and disciplinarian from the army of Frederic the Great. Arriving at Portsmouth, the baron tarried a short time in New England, and then repaired to York, where Congress was in session. From that body he received a commission, and at once joined Washington at Valley Forge. His accession to the American army was an event of great importance. He received the appointment of inspector-general; and from the day in which he entered upon the discharge of his duties there was a marked improvement in the condition and discipline of the soldiers. The American regulars were never again beaten when confronted by the British in equal numbers.

In November of 1776 Arthur Lee and Benjamin Franklin were appointed by Congress to negotiate an open treaty of friendship and commerce with the French king. In the following month they reached Paris and began their conferences with Vergennes. For a long time King Louis and his minister were wary of the proposed alliance. They cordially hated Great Britain, they rejoiced that the British empire was about to be dismembered, they gave secret encouragement to the colonies to hold out in their rebellion, they loaned money and shipped arms to America; but an open alliance was equivalent to a war with England, and that the French court dreaded.

Now it was that the genius of Dr. Franklin shone with a peculiar lustre. At the gay court of Louis XVI. he stood as the representative of his country. No nation ever had an ambassador of greater wisdom and sagacity. His reputation for learning had preceded him the dignity of his demeanor and the simplicity of his manners added to his fame. Whether as philosopher or diplomatist, no man in that great city of fashion was the equal of the venerable American patriot. His wit and genial humor made him admired; his talents and courtesy commanded respect; his patience and perseverance gave him final success. During the whole of 1777 he remained at Paris and Versailles, availing himself of every opportunity to promote the interests of his country. At last came the news of Burgoyne's surrender. A powerful British army had been subdued by the colonists without aid from abroad. The success of the American arms and the prospect of commercial advantage decided the wavering policy of the king, and in the beginning of winter he made an announcement of his determination to accept an alliance with the colonies. On the 6th of February, 1778, a treaty was concluded; France acknowledged the independence of the United States and entered into relations of reciprocal friendship with the new nation. It was further stipulated that in case England should declare war against France, the Americans and the French should make common cause, and that neither should subscribe to a treaty of peace without the concurrence of the other. In America the news of the new alliance was received with great rejoicing; in England, with vindictive anger.

BENJAMIN FRANKLIN, the author of the first treaty between the United States and a foreign nation, was born in Boston on the 17th of January, 1706. His father was a manufacturer of soap and candles. To this humble vocation the young Benjamin was devoted by his parents; but the walls of a candle-shop were too narrow for his aspiring genius. At the age of twelve he was apprenticed to his brother to learn the art of printing; but the brother beat him, and he ran off to New York. There he found no employment. In 1723 he repaired to Philadelphia, entered a printing-office, and rose to distinction. He visited England; returned;

Benjamin Franklin.

founded the first circulating library in America; became a man of science; edited *Poor Richard's Almanac*; originated the American Philosophical Society; discovered the identity of electricity and lightning; made himself known in both hemispheres; espoused the cause of the patriots; and devoted the unimpaired energies of his old age to perfecting the American Union. The name of Franklin is one of the brightest in the history of any nation.

In May of 1778 Congress ratified the treaty with France. A month before this time a French fleet, commanded by Count d'Estaing, had been despatched to America. The object was to sail into the Delaware and blockade the British squadron at Philadelphia. Both France and Great Britain understood full well that war was inevitable, and each immediately prepared for the conflict. George III. now became willing to treat with his American subjects. Lord North, the prime minister, brought forward two bills in which everything that the colonists had claimed was conceded. The bills were passed by Parliament, and the king assented. Commissioners were sent to America; but Congress informed them that nothing but an express acknowledgment of the independence of the United States would now be accepted. Then the commissioners tried bribery and intrigue; and Congress would hold no further conference with them.

From September of 1777 until the following June the British army remained at Philadelphia. The fleet of Admiral Howe lay in the Delaware. In the spring of 1778, General Howe was superseded by Sir Henry Clinton. When the rumor came that the fleet of D'Estaing was approaching, the English admiral withdrew from the Delaware and sailed for New York. Finally, on the 18th of June, the British army evacuated Philadelphia and retreated across New Jersey. Washington occupied the city, crossed the river, and followed the retreating foe. At Monmouth, eighteen miles south-east of New Brunswick, the British were overtaken. On the morning of the 28th General Lee was ordered to attack the enemy. The first onset was made by the American cavalry under La Fayette; but they were driven back by Cornwallis and Clinton. Lee, who had opposed the battle, and was not anxious for victory, ordered his line to fall back to a stronger position; but the troops mistook the order and began a retreat, the British charging after them. Washington met the fugitives, rallied them, administered a severe rebuke to Lee, and ordered him to the rear. During the rest of the engagement the haughty officer, half treacherous in his principles and practices, remained at a distance, making satirical remarks about the battle. The fight continued till nightfall; the advantage was with the Americans; and Washington, in hope of a complete victory, anxiously waited for the morning. During the night, however, Clinton succeeded in withdrawing his forces from the field, and thus escaped the peril of defeat.

The loss of the Americans in the battle of Monmouth was sixty-seven killed and a hundred and sixty wounded. The British left nearly three hundred dead on the field. On the day after the battle Washington received an insulting letter from Lee demanding an apology for the language which the commander-in-chief had used. Washington replied that the language was warranted by the circumstances. This Lee answered in a still more offensive manner, and was thereupon arrested, tried by a court-martial, and dismissed from his command for twelve months. The brave, rash man never re-entered the service, and did not live to see his country's independence.

The British land and naval forces were now concentrated at New York. Washington followed, crossed the Hudson, and took up his headquarters at White Plains. On the 11th of July Count d'Estaing's fleet arrived off Sandy Hook and attempted to attack the British squadron in the bay but the bar at the entrance prevented the passage of the French vessels. D'Estaing next sailed for Newport, Rhode Island, where the British, commanded by General Pigot, were in strong force. At the same time a division of the American army, led by General Sullivan, proceeded to Providence to co-operate with the French fleet in the attack on Newport. Greene and La Fayette came with reinforcements, and the whole army took post at Tiverton. On the 9th of August Sullivan succeeded in crossing the eastern passage of the bay, and secured a favorable position on the island. A joint attack by land and sea was planned for the following day. On that morning, however, the fleet of Lord Howe, who had left New York in pursuit of the French, came in sight; and D'Estaing, instead of beginning the bombardment of Newport, sailed out to give battle to Howe. Just as the two squadrons were about to begin an engagement a violent storm arose by which the fleets were parted and greatly damaged. D'Estaing repaired to Boston, and Howe returned to New York.

Sullivan laid siege to Newport; but when the French squadron sailed away, he found it necessary to retreat. The British pursued the Americans, and overtook them in the northern part of the island; a battle ensued, and Pigot was repulsed with a loss of two hundred and sixty men. On the following night Sullivan succeeded in reaching the mainland and it was well that he did so; for on the next day General Clinton arrived at Newport with a division of four thousand regulars. The Americans saved themselves by hastily retiring from the neighborhood. Clinton, having sent out a detachment under Colonel Grey to burn the American shipping in Buzzard's Bay, destroy the stores in New Bedford and ravage Martha's Vineyard, returned to New York.

The command of the British naval forces in America was now transferred from Lord Howe to Admiral Byron. Sir Henry Clinton, unable to accomplish anything in honorable warfare, descended to marauding and robbery. Early in October a band of incendiaries, led by Ferguson, burned the American ships at Little Egg Harbor. For several miles inland the country was devastated, houses pillaged, barns burned, patriots murdered. To the preceding July belongs the sad story of the Wyoming massacre. Major John Butler, a tory of Niagara, raised a company of sixteen hundred loyalists, Canadians and Indians, and marched into the valley of Wyoming, county of Luzerne, Pennsylvania. The settlement was defenceless. The fathers and brothers were away in the patriot army. There were some feeble forts on the Susquehanna in the neighborhood of Wilkesbarre, but they were useless without defenders. On the approach of the tories and savages the few militia remaining in the valley, together with the old men and boys, rallied for the defence of their homes. A battle was fought, and the poor patriots were utterly routed. The fugitives fled to the principal fort, which was crowded with women and children. On came the murderous horde, and demanded a surrender. Honorable terms were promised by Butler, and the garrison capitulated. On the 5th of July the gates were opened, and the barbarians entered. Immediately they began to plunder, then to burn, and then to use the hatchet and the scalping-knife. There is no authentic record of the horrible atrocities that followed. The savages divided into parties, scattered through the valley, plundered, robbed, burned, and drove almost every surviving family into the swamps or mountains. In this way George III. would subdue the American colonies.

November witnessed a similar massacre at the village of Cherry Valley, Otsego county, New York. This time the invaders were led by Joseph Brant, the Mohawk sachem, and Walter Butler, a son of Major John Butler. The people of Cherry Valley were driven from their homes; every house in the village was burned; women and children were tomahawked and scalped; and forty miserable sufferers dragged into captivity. To avenge these outrages an expedition was sent against the savages on the Upper Susquehanna; and they in turn were made to feel the terrors of war. In the preceding December the famous Major Clarke had received from Patrick Henry, then governor of Virginia, a commission to proceed against the Indians west of the Alleghanies. The expedition left Pittsburg in the spring of 1778; descended to the mouth of the Ohio; and on the 4th of the following July captured Kaskaskia. Other important posts were taken and in August Vincennes was forced to capitulate.

On the 3d of November Count d'Estaing's fleet sailed from Boston for the West Indies. In December Admiral Byron, in command of the

British squadron, left New York to try the fortunes of war on the ocean. A few days previously, Colonel Campbell, with a force of two thousand men, was sent by General Clinton for the conquest of Georgia. On the 29th of December the expedition reached Savannah. The place was defended by General Robert Howe with a regiment of five hundred and fifty regulars, and three hundred militia. Notwithstanding the superior numbers of the British, Howe determined to risk a battle; but the result was disastrous. The Americans were routed and driven out of the city. Escaping up the river, the defeated patriots crossed into South Carolina and found refuge at Charleston. Such was the only real conquest made by the British during the year 1778. It was now nearly four years since the battle of Concord, and Great Britain had lost vastly more than she had gained in her struggle with the colonies. The city of New York was held by Clinton; Newport was garrisoned by a division under Pigot; the feeble capital of Georgia was conquered; all the rest remained to the patriots.

CHAPTER XLII.

Movements of '79.

THE winter of 1778-79 was passed by the American army at Middlebrook, New Jersey. With the opening of spring there was much discouragement among the soldiers; for they were neither paid nor fed. Only the personal influence of Washington and the patriotism of the camp prevented a mutiny. Clinton opened the campaign with a number of predatory incursions into the surrounding country. In February, Tryon, the old tory governor of New York, a man so savage in his nature that the Indians called him *the Big Wolf*, marched from Kingsbridge with a body of fifteen hundred regulars and tories to destroy the salt works at Horse Neck, Connecticut. General Putnam, who chanced to be in that neighborhood, rallied the militia and made a brave defence. The Americans planted some cannon on the brow of a hill and fought with much spirit until they were outflanked by the British and obliged to fly. It was here that General Putnam, pursued and about to be over taken by a party of dragoons, turned out of the road, spurred his horse down a precipice and escaped.[15] Tryon destroyed the salt-works, plundered and burned the village of West Greenwich and returned to Kingsbridge.

In the latter part of May Clinton himself sailed with an armament up the Hudson to Stony Point. This strong position, commanding the river, had been chosen by Washington as the site of a fort; the Americans were engaged upon the unfinished works when Clinton's squadron came in sight. The feeble garrison, unable to resist the overwhelming numbers of the enemy, escaped from the fortifications. On the 1st of June the British entered, mounted cannon and began to bombard Verplanck's Point, on the other side of the river. Here the patriots made a brave resistance; but the British landed a strong force, surrounded the fort and compelled a surrender. Both Verplanck's and Stony Point were

---

[15] After all, Putnam's exploit was not so marvelous. In 1825 some of General La Fayette's dragoons rode down the same hill for sport.

strongly fortified and garrisoned by the enemy. About the same time Virginia suffered from an incursion of the tories. A vast amount of public and private property was destroyed and several towns, including Norfolk and Portsmouth, were laid in ashes.

In July the ferocious Tryon again distinguished himself. With a force of twenty-six hundred Hessians and tories he sailed to New Haven, captured the city and would have burned it but for fear of the gathering militia. Having set East Haven on fire, the destroyers sailed down the Sound to the beautiful town of Fairfield, which was given to the flames. At Norwalk, while the village was burning and the terrified people flying from their homes, Tryon, on a neighboring hill, sat in a rocking-chair and laughed heartily at the scene. It was not long until these dastardly outrages were made to appear more dastardly by contrast with a heroic exploit of the patriots.

Early in July General Wayne received orders to attempt the recapture of Stony Point. On the 15th of the month he mustered a force of light infantry at a convenient point on the Hudson and marched against the seemingly impregnable fortress. The movement was not discovered by the enemy. At eight o'clock in the evening Wayne halted a mile from the fort and gave orders for the assault. A negro who had learned the countersign went with the advance; the British pickets were deceived, caught and gagged. The Americans advanced in two columns, the first led by Wayne, and the second by the gallant Frenchman, Colonel De Fleury. Everything was done in silence. Muskets were unloaded and bayonets fixed; not a gun was to be fired. The two divisions, attacking from opposite sides, were to meet in the middle of the fort. The assault was made a little after midnight. Within pistol-shot of the sentinels on the height, the Americans were discovered. There was the cry, *To arms!* the rattle of drums, and then the roar of musketry and cannon. The patriots never wavered. The ramparts were sealed; and the British, finding themselves between two closing lines of bayonets, cried out for quarter. Sixty-three of the enemy fell in the struggle; the remaining five hundred and forty-three were made prisoners. Of the Americans only fifteen were killed and eighty-three wounded. In the days that followed the assault Wayne secured the ordnance and stores, valued at more than a hundred and fifty thousand dollars, then destroyed the fort and marched away. On the 20th a division of the British army, arriving at Stony Point, found nothing but a desolated hill. In honor of his brave deed General Wayne received a gold medal from Congress.

Three days after the taking of Stony Point, Major Lee with a company of militia attacked the British garrison at Jersey City. Again the assault was successful, the enemy losing nearly two hundred men. On the 25th of the same month a fleet of thirty-seven vessels, which had been equipped by Massachusetts, was sent against a British post recently established at the mouth of the Penobscot. The enterprise, however, was managed with little skill and less success. On the 13th of August, while the American ships were still besieging the post, they were suddenly attacked and destroyed by a British fleet. In the summer of this year an army of four thousand six hundred men, commanded by Generals Sullivan and James Clinton, was sent against the Indians of the Upper Susquehanna. The atrocities of Wyoming were now fully avenged, and the savages driven to destruction. At Elmira, on the Tioga River, the Indians and tories had fortified themselves; but on the 29th of August they were forced from their stronghold and utterly routed. The whole country between the Susquehanna and the Genesee was wasted by the patriots, who, in the course of the campaign, destroyed forty Indian villages. In the latter part of October Sir Henry Clinton, alarmed by the rumored approach of the French fleet, withdrew the British forces from Rhode Island. The retirement from Newport was made with so much haste that the heavy guns and large quantities of stores were left behind. Such were the leading military movements in the North.

Meanwhile, the war had continued in Georgia and South Carolina; and the patriots had met with many reverses. At the beginning of the year Fort Sunbury, on St. Catherine's Sound, was the only post held by the Americans south of the Savannah. On the 9th of January this fort was captured by a body of British troops from Florida, led by General Prevost. This officer then joined his forces with those of Colonel Campbell, who had just effected the conquest of Savannah, and assumed command of the British army in the South. A force of two thousand regulars and loyalists, commanded by Campbell, was at once despatched against Augusta; for there the republican legislature had assembled after the fall of Savannah. On the 29th of January the British reached their destination, and Augusta fell a prey to the invaders. For a while the whole of Georgia was prostrated before the king's soldiery.

In the mean time, the tories of Western Carolina had risen in arms and were advancing to join the forces of Campbell at Augusta. While marching thither they were attacked and defeated in a canebrake by the patriots under Captain Anderson. On the 14th of February the tories were again overtaken in the country west of Broad River. Colonel Pickens, at the head of the Carolina militia, fell upon them with such fury that the whole force was annihilated. Colonel Boyd, the tory leader, and seventy of his men were killed. Seventy-five others were captured, tried for treason and condemned to death; but only five of the ringleaders were hanged. On receiving intelligence of what had happened, Campbell hastily evacuated Augusta and retreated toward Savannah. The western half of Georgia was recovered more quickly than it had been lost.

While the British were retreating down the river, General Lincoln, who now commanded the American forces in the South, sent General Ashe with a division of two thousand men to intercept the enemy. On the 25th of February the Americans crossed the Savannah and pursued Campbell as far as Brier Creek, forty-five miles below Augusta. The bridge over this stream had been destroyed by the retreating British, and the patriots came to a halt. While they were delayed General Prevost marched with a strong force from Savannah, crossed Brier Creek above the American position, and completely surrounded General Ashe's command. A battle was fought on the 3d of March; the Americans, after losing more than three hundred men in killed, wounded and prisoners, were totally routed and driven into the swamps and river. The remnants of Ashe's army rejoined General Lincoln at Perrysburg. The shock of this defeat again prostrated Georgia, and a royal government was established over the State.

But the Carolinians rallied with great vigor. Within a month General Lincoln was again in the field with a force of more than five thousand men. Still hoping to reconquer Georgia, he advanced up the left bank of the river in the direction of Augusta; but at the same time General

Prevost crossed the Savannah and marched against Charleston. On the 12th of May he summoned the city to surrender, but General Moultrie, who commanded the patriots, was in no humor to do it. Prevost made preparations for a siege; but learning that General Lincoln had turned back to attack him, he made a hasty retreat. The Americans pursued, overtook the enemy at Stono Ferry, ten miles west of Charleston, made an imprudent attack and were repulsed with considerable loss. Before retiring from the State, Prevost succeeded in establishing a post at Beaufort, and then fell back to Savannah. From June until September military operations were almost wholly suspended.

And now came Count d'Estaing with his fleet from the West Indies to Carolina to co-operate with General Lincoln in the reduction of Savannah. Prevost was alarmed, and concentrated his forces for the defence of the city. The storm-winds of the equinox were approaching, and D'Estaing stipulated with the Americans that his fleet should not be long detained on that coast devoid of harbors. On the 12th of September the French, numbering six thousand, effected a landing, and advanced to the siege. Eleven days elapsed before the slow-moving General Lincoln arrived with his forces. Meanwhile, on the 16th of the month, D'Estaing had demanded a surrender; but Prevost, who asked a day for consultation and used it in strengthening his works and in receiving reinforcements from Beaufort, answered with a message of defiance. After Lincoln's arrival the siege was prosecuted with great vigor. The city was bombarded wellnigh to destruction; the people were driven into the cellars, and dared not venture forth on peril of their lives. But the British defences remained unshaken. At last the impatient D'Estaing notified Lincoln that the city must be stormed or the siege abandoned. The former course was preferred. On the 8th of October a conference was held, and it was determined to make the assault at daylight on the following morning.

Accordingly, an hour before sunrise the allies advanced against the redoubts of the British. The attack was made irregularly, but with great vehemence; the defence, with desperate determination. The struggle around the ramparts was brief but furious. At one time it seemed that the works would be carried. The French and the patriots mounted the parapet and planted the flags of Carolina and France. But the emblems of victory, with those who bore them, were hurled into the dust. Here the brave Sergeant Jasper, the hero of Fort Moultrie, fell to rise no more. After an hour of the most gallant fighting, the allied columns were shattered and driven back with fearful losses. D'Estaing was twice wounded. The noble Pulaski was struck with a grape-shot and borne dying from the field. The repulse was complete, humiliating, disastrous. D'Estaing retired with his men on board the fleet and sailed for France. Lincoln with the remnants of his army retreated to Charleston.

While the siege of Savannah was progressing, the American arms were made famous on the ocean. On the 23d of September Paul Jones, cruising off the coast of Scotland with a flotilla of French and American vessels, fell in with a fleet of British merchantmen, conveyed by two men-of-war. The battle that ensued was bloody beyond precedent in naval warfare. For an hour and a half the *Serapis*, a British frigate of forty-four guns, engaged the *Poor Richard*[16] within musket-shot. Then the vessels, both in a sinking condition, were run alongside and lashed together. The marines fought with the fury of madmen until the *Serapis* struck her colors. Jones hastily transferred his men to the conquered ship, and the *Poor Richard* went down. The remaining British vessel was also attacked and captured. So desperate was the engagement that of the three hundred and seventy-five men on board the fleet of Jones three hundred were either killed or wounded.

So closed the year 1779. The colonies were not yet free. The French alliance, which had promised so much, had brought but little benefit. The credit of Congress had sunk almost to nothing; the national treasury was bankrupt. The patriots of the army were poorly fed, and paid only with unkept promises. The disposition of Great Britain was best illustrated in the measures adopted by Parliament for the campaigns of the ensuing year. The levies made by the House of Commons were eighty-five thousand marines and thirty-five thousand additional troops; while the extraordinary expenses of the War Department were set at twenty million pounds sterling.

---

[16] So named in honor of Dr. Franklin's almanac.

CHAPTER XLIII.

Reverses and Treason.

During the year 1780 military operations at the North were, for the most part, suspended. Twice did the British under Knyphausen advance from New York into New Jersey; and twice they were driven back. Early in July Admiral De Ternay arrived at Newport with a French squadron and six thousand land-troops under Count Rochambeau. The Americans were greatly elated at the coming of their allies; but Washington's army was in so destitute a condition that active co-operation was impracticable. In September the commander-in-chief held a conference with Rochambeau, and the plans of future campaigns were in part determined.

In the South there was much activity, and the patriots suffered many reverses. South Carolina was completely overrun with the invading armies. On the 11th of February Admiral Arbuthnot, in command of a British squadron, anchored before Charleston. Sir Henry Clinton and a division of five thousand men from the army in New York were on board the fleet. The plan of the campaign was to subjugate the whole South, beginning with Charleston. The city was defended by fourteen hundred men, under General Lincoln, who began his preparations by fortifying the neck of the peninsula. The British effected a landing a few miles below the harbor, advanced up the right bank of Ashley River, and crossed to the north of the city. A month was spent by Clinton in making cautious approaches toward the American entrenchments. On the 7th of April General Lincoln was reinforced by seven hundred veterans from Virginia. Two days afterward Admiral Arbuthnot, favored by the wind and tide, succeeded in passing Fort Moultrie with his fleet, and anchored within cannon-shot of the city. A summons to surrender was answered by Lincoln with the assurance that Charleston would be defended to the last extremity.

A siege was at once begun, and prosecuted with great vigor. Desiring to keep a way open for retreat, Lincoln sent a body of three hundred men under General Huger to scour the country north of Cooper River and rally the militia. Apprised of this movement, Tarleton with a legion of British cavalry stole upon Huger's forces at Monk's Corner, thirty miles north of Charleston, routed and dispersed the whole company. The city was now fairly hemmed in, and the thunder of two hundred cannon shook the beleaguered ramparts. From the beginning the defence had been hopeless, and every day the condition of the town became more desperate. Finally the fortifications were beaten down, and Clinton made ready to storm the American works; not till then did Lincoln and the civil authorities, dreading the havoc of an assault, agree to capitulate. On the 12th of May the principal city of the South was given up to the British and the men who had so bravely defended it became prisoners of war.

Siege of Charleston, 1780.

A few days before the surrender Tarleton, who was ranging the country to the north and west, surprised and dispersed a body of militia who had gathered on the Santee. After the capture of the city, three expeditions were directed into different sections of the State. The American post at Ninety-Six, a hundred and fifty miles north-west of the capital, was seized. A second detachment of the British invaded the country bordering on the Savannah. Cornwallis with the principal division marched to the north-east, crossed the Santee and captured Georgetown, near the mouth of the Great Pedee. Here he learned that Colonel Buford, with a body of five hundred patriots, who had left North Carolina for the relief of Charleston, was now retreating through the district north of Camden. Tarleton with seven hundred cavalry pressed rapidly across the country, overtook the Americans on the Waxhaw, a tributary of the Catawba, surprised them, and, while negotiations for a surrender were pending, charged upon and massacred nearly the whole company. For this atrocious deed Cornwallis commended Tarleton to the special favor of the British Parliament.

By such means the authority of Great Britain was re-established over South Carolina. As soon as the work was done, Clinton and Arbuthnot, with about half of the British army, sailed for New York. Cornwallis was left with the remainder to hold the conquered territory; for it was the *territory*, and not the *people*, who were conquered. In this condition of affairs, two daring patriot leaders arose to rescue the republican cause. These men, ever afterward famous, were Thomas Sumter and Francis Marion. Under their leadership the militia in the central and western portions of the State, especially on the upper tributaries of Broad River, were rallied, armed and mounted. An audacious partisan warfare was begun, and exposed detachments of the British army were swept off as though an enemy had fallen on them from the skies. At Rocky Mount, on the Wateree, Colonel Sumter burst upon a party of dragoons, who barely saved themselves. On the 6th of August he attacked a large detachment of regulars and tories at Hanging Rock, in Lancaster county, defeated them and retreated. It was in this battle that young Andrew Jackson began his career as a soldier.

The exploits of Sumter were even surpassed by those of Marion. His company consisted at first of twenty men and boys, white and black, half clad and poorly armed. But the number constantly increased, and the

"Ragged Regiment" soon became a terror to the enemy. Every British outpost was in peril. There was no telling when or where the sword of the fearless leader would fall. From the swamps at midnight he and his men would suddenly dart upon the encampments of the enemy, sweeping everything before them. When the British expected Marion in front, he would assail the rearguard with the utmost fury, and then disappear; when they thought him hovering on their flank, he was a hundred miles away. During the whole summer and autumn of 1780 be swept around Cornwallis's positions, cutting his lines of communication and making incessant onsets with an audacity as destructive as it was provoking. In the midst of this wild and lawless warfare, Marion preserved an unblemished reputation. Fifteen years afterward, when he lay on his deathbed, he declared that he had never intentionally wronged any man; and it was truthfully written on his monument that he lived without fear and died without reproach.

After the fall of Charleston, General Gates was appointed to command in the South. With a strong force of regulars and such militia as would join his standard, be advanced across North Carolina, and at the beginning of August reached the southern boundary of the State. Lord Rawdon, who commanded the British posts in the northern parts of South Carolina, called in his detachments and concentrated his forces at Camden. Hither came also Cornwallis with reinforcements from Charleston and Georgetown. The Americans moved forward and took post at Clermont, thirteen miles north-west from Camden. By a singular coincidence Cornwallis and Gates each formed the design of surprising his antagonist in the night. Accordingly, on the evening of the 15th of August, Gates set out for Camden, and at the same time Cornwallis moved toward Clermont. About daydawn the two armies met midway on Sander's Creek. Both generals were surprised, but both made immediate preparations for battle. As soon as it was light the conflict began. Steadiness and courage in all parts of the field would have given the victory to the Americans, but at the first onset the Virginia and Carolina militia broke line, threw their arms away and fled. For a while the Continentals of Maryland and Delaware sustained the battle with great bravery, but at length they were outflanked by Webster's cavalry and driven back. The American officers made heroic efforts to save the day, but all in vain; the retreat became a rout. Baron de Kalb, the friend of La Fayette and fellow-sufferer with Washington at Valley Forge, remained on the field trying to rally his men until he was wounded eleven times and fell in the agony of death. More than a thousand of the Americans were killed, wounded or captured. The shattered remnants continued the retreat to Charlotte, North Carolina, eighty miles distant. The military reputation of Gates, which never had any solid foundation, was blown away like chaff, and he was superseded by General Greene, who, after Washington, was the best officer of the Revolution.

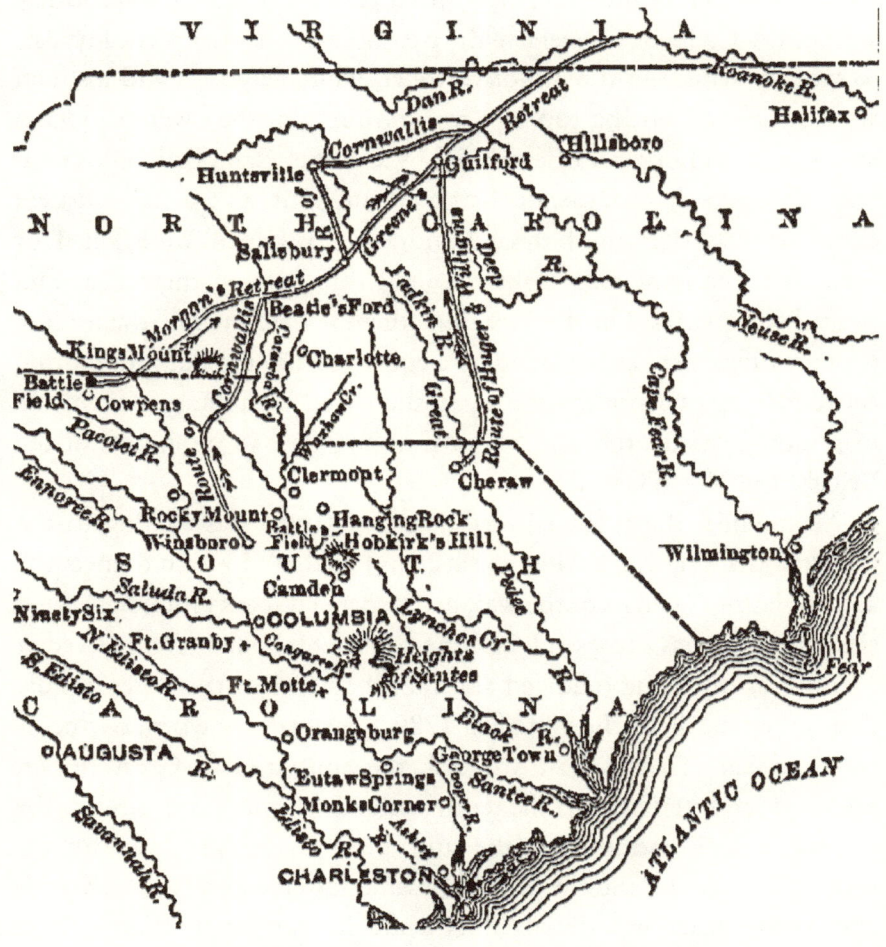

Scene of Operations in the South, 1780, 81.

Cornwallis was again master of South Carolina. A few days after the battle of Sander's Creek, Sumter's corps was overtaken by Tarleton at Fishing Creek, thirty miles north-west from Camden, and completely routed. Only Marion and his troopers remained to harass the victorious enemy. The triumph of the British was marked by cruelty and oppression. Cornwallis visited the patriots with merciless severity, and the ruined State crouched at the feet of the conqueror. On the 8th of September the British advanced from Camden into North Carolina, and on the 25th reached Charlotte, the Americans having retreated to Salisbury. While this movement was in progress, Colonel Ferguson, with a force of eleven hundred regulars and tories, was sent into the country west of the Catawba to overawe the patriots and encourage the loyalists to take up arms. On the 7th of October, while Ferguson and his men were encamped on the top of King's Mountain, they were suddenly attacked by a thousand riflemen led by Colonel Campbell. The camp was surrounded; a desperate battle of an hour and a half ensued; Ferguson was slain, and three hundred of his men were killed or wounded; the remaining eight hundred threw down their arms and begged for quarter. On the morning after the battle ten of the leading tory prisoners were condemned by a court-martial and hanged. During the remaining two months of the year there were no military movements of importance. Georgia and South Carolina were in the power of the British, and North Carolina was invaded.

Meanwhile, the financial credit of the nation was sinking to the lowest ebb. Congress, having no silver and gold with which to meet the accumulating expenses of the war, had resorted to paper money. At first the expedient was successful, and the continental bills were received at par; but as one issue followed another, the value of the notes rapidly diminished, until, by the middle of 1780, they were not worth two cents to the dollar. To aggravate the evil, the emissaries of Great Britain executed counterfeits of the congressional money and sowed the spurious bills broadcast over the land. Business was paralyzed for the want of a currency, and the distress became extreme; but Robert Morris and a few other wealthy patriots came forward with their private fortunes and saved the suffering colonies from ruin. The mothers of

America also lent a helping hand; and the patriot camp was gladdened with many a contribution of food and clothing which woman's sacrificing care had provided.

In the midst of the general gloom the country was shocked by the rumor that Benedict Arnold had turned traitor. And the news, though hardly credible, was true. The brave, rash man, who, on behalf of the patriot cause, had suffered untold hardships and shed his blood on more fields than one, had blotted the record of his heroism with a deed of treason. After the battle of Bemis's Height, in the fall of 1777, Arnold was promoted by Congress to the rank of major-general. Being disabled by his wound, he was made commandant of Philadelphia after the evacuation of the city by the British. Here he married the daughter of a loyalist, and living in the old mansion of William Penn entered upon a career of luxury and extravagance which soon overwhelmed him with debt and bankruptcy. In order to keep up his magnificence, he began system of frauds on the commissary department of the army. His bearing toward the citizens was that of a military despot; the people groaned under his tyranny, and charges were preferred against him by Congress. The cause was finally heard by a court-martial in December of 1779. Arnold was convicted on two of the charges, and, by the order of the court, was mildly reprimanded by Washington.

Professing unbounded patriotism, and seeming to forget the disgrace which his misconduct had brought upon him, Arnold applied for and obtained command of the important fortress of West Point on the Hudson. On the last day of July, 1780, he reached the camp and assumed control of the most valuable arsenal and depot of stores in America. He had already formed the treasonable design of surrendering the fort into the hands of the enemy. For months he had kept up a secret correspondence with Sir Henry Clinton, and now the scheme ripened, on Arnold's part, into an open proposition to betray his country for gold. It was agreed that on a certain day the British fleet should ascend the Hudson, that the garrison should be divided and scattered, and the fortress given up without a struggle.

On the 21st of September Sir Henry Clinton sent Major John André up the river to hold a personal conference with Arnold and make the final arrangements for the surrender. André, through whom the correspondence between Arnold and Clinton had been carried on, was a former acquaintance of Arnold's wife, and now held the post of adjutant-general in the British army. He went to the conference, not as a spy, but wearing full uniform; and it was agreed that the meeting should be held outside of the American lines. About midnight of the 21st he went ashore from the *Vulture*, a sloop of war, and met Arnold in a thicket on the west bank of the river, two miles below Haverstraw. Daydawn approached, and the conspirators were obliged to hide themselves. In doing so they entered the American lines; Arnold gave the password, and André, disguising himself, assumed the character of a spy.

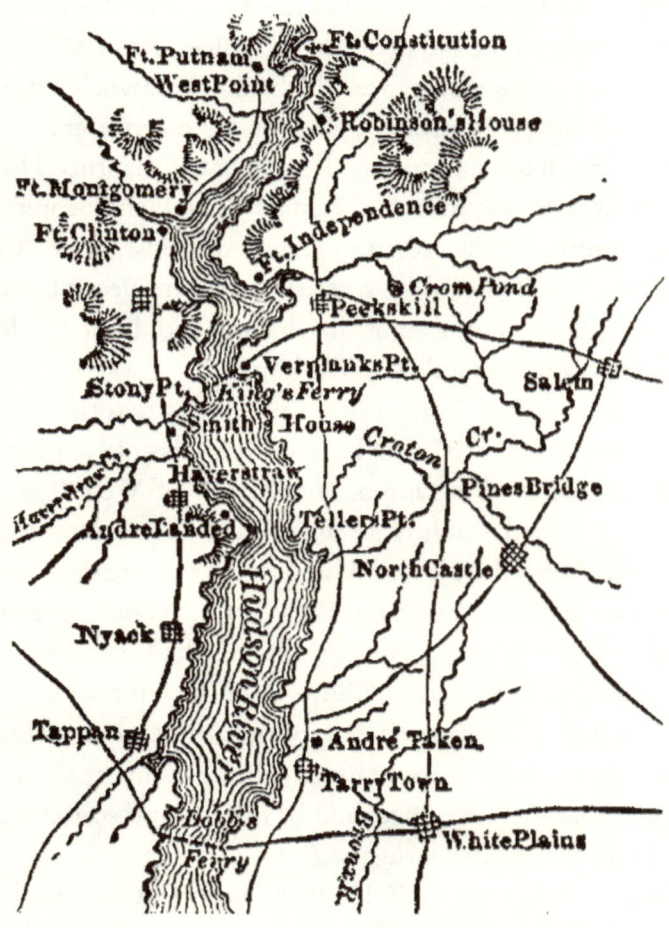

Scene of Arnold's Treason, 1780.

During the next day the traitor and his victim remained concealed at the house of a tory named Smith. Here the awful business was completed. Arnold was to surrender West Point, its garrisons and stores, and to receive for his treachery ten thousand pounds and a commission as brigadier in the British army. All preliminaries being settled, papers containing a full description of West Point, its defences and the best method of attack were made out and given to André, who secreted the dangerous documents in his stockings. During that day an American battery drove the *Vulture* from its moorings in the river; and at nightfall André was obliged to cross to the other side and proceed by land toward New York. He passed the American outposts in safety; but at Tarrytown, twenty-five miles from the city, he was suddenly confronted by three militiamen[17] who stripped him, found his papers, and delivered him to Colonel Jameson at North Castle. Through that officer's amazing stupidity Arnold was at once notified that *John Anderson*—that being the assumed name of André—had been taken with his passport and some papers "of a very dangerous tendency." Arnold, on hearing the news, fled to the river and escaped on board the *Vulture*. André was tried by a court-martial at Tappan, and condemned to death. On the 2d of October he was led to the gallows, and, under the stern code of war, was hanged. Though dying the death of a felon, he met his doom like a brave man, and after times have commiserated his sad fate. Arnold received his *pay*.

In the dark days of December there came a ray of light from Europe. For several years Holland had secretly favored the Americans; now she began negotiations for a commercial treaty similar to that already existing between France and the United States. Great Britain discovered the purposes of the Dutch government; there were angry remonstrances, and then, on the 20th of December, an open declaration of war. Thus the Netherlands were added to the enemies of England; it seemed that George III. and his ministers would have enough to do without further efforts to enforce a stamp-act or levy a tax on tea.

---

[17] John Paulding, David Williams and Isaac van Wart. Congress afterward rewarded them with silver medals and pensions for life.

CHAPTER XLIV.

THE END.

FOR the Americans the year 1781 opened gloomily. The condition of the army was desperate—no food, no pay, no clothing. Even the influence of Washington was not sufficient to quiet the growing discontent of the soldiery. On the first day of January the whole Pennsylvania line, numbering nearly two thousand, mutinied, left their camp at Morristown and marched toward Philadelphia. General Wayne, after trying in vain to prevent the insurrection, went with his men, still hoping to control them. At Princeton they were met by two emissaries from Sir Henry Clinton, and were tempted with offers of money, clothing and release from military service if they would desert the American standard. The mutinous patriots made answer by seizing the British agents and delivering them to General Wayne to be hanged as spies. For this deed the come missioners of Congress, who now arrived, offered the insurgents a large reward, but the reward was indignantly refused. Washington, knowing how shamefully the army had been neglected by Congress, was not unwilling that the mutiny should take its own course. The congressional agents were therefore left to adjust the difficulty with the rebellious troops. But the breach was easily healed; a few liberal concessions on the part of the government sufficed to quiet the mutiny.

About the middle of the same month the New Jersey brigade, stationed at Pompton, revolted. This movement Washington quelled by force. General Robert Howe marched to the camp with five hundred regulars and compelled twelve of the principal mutineers to execute the two leaders of the revolt. From that day order was completely restored. These insurrections had a good rather than a bad effect; Congress was thoroughly alarmed, and immediate provisions were made for the better support of the army. An agent was sent to France to obtain a further loan of money. Robert Morris was appointed secretary of finance; the Bank of North America was organized; and although the outstanding debts of the United States could not be paid, yet all future obligations were promptly met, for Morris and his friends pledged their private fortunes to sustain the credit of the government.

In the North military movements were begun by Arnold. On arriving at New York the traitor had received the promised commission, and was now a brigadier-general in the British army. In the preceding November, Washington and Major Henry Lee formed a plan to capture him. Sergeant John Champe undertook the daring enterprise, deserted to the enemy, entered New York, joined Arnold's company, and with two assistants concerted measures to abduct him from the city and convey him to the American camp. But Arnold suddenly moved his quarters, and the plan was defeated. A month afterward he was given command of a fleet and a land-force of sixteen hundred men, and on the 16th of December left New York to make a descent on the coasts of Virginia.

Early in January the traitor entered James River and began war on his countrymen. His proceedings were marked with much ferocity, but not with the daring which characterized his former exploits. In the vicinity of Richmond a vast quantity of public and private property was destroyed. The country along the river was devastated; and when there was nothing left to excite his cupidity or gratify his revenge, Arnold took up his headquarters in Portsmouth, a few miles south of Hampton Roads. Again Washington planned his capture. The French fleet, anchored at Newport, was ordered to sail for Virginia to cooperate with La Fayette, who was sent in the direction of Portsmouth with a detachment of twelve hundred men. But Admiral Arbuthnot, being apprised of the movement, sailed from New York and drove the French squadron back to Rhode Island. La Fayette, deprived of the expected aid, was forced to abandon the undertaking, and Arnold again escaped.

About the middle of April General Phillips arrived at Portsmouth with a force of two thousand British regulars. Joining his troops with those of Arnold, he assumed command of the whole, and again the fertile districts of Lower Virginia were ravaged with fire and sword. Early in May, Phillips died, and for seven days Arnold held the supreme command of the British forces in Virginia. That was the, height of his treasonable glory. On the 20th of the month Lord Cornwallis arrived at Petersburg and ordered him to begone. Returning to New York, he received from Clinton a second detachment, entered the Sound, landed at New London, in his native State, and captured the town. Fort Griswold, which was defended by Colonel Ledyard with a hundred and fifty militia men, was carried by storm. When Ledyard surrendered, the British officer who received his sword stabbed him to death; it was the signal for a massacre of the garrison, seventy-three of whom were murdered in cold blood; of the remainder, thirty were wounded and the rest made prisoners. With this bloody and ignominious deed the name of Arnold disappears from American history.

Meanwhile, some of the most stirring events of the war had occurred at the South. At the close of the preceding year General Greene had taken command of the American army—which was only the shadow of an army—at Charlotte, North Carolina. Cornwallis had fallen back in the direction of Camden. Greene with great energy reorganized his forces and divided them into an eastern and a western division; the command of the latter was given to General Morgan. In the first days of January this gallant officer was sent into the Spartanburg district of South Carolina to repress the tories and encourage the patriot militia. His success was such as to exasperate Cornwallis, who immediately despatched Colonel Tarleton with his famous cavalry legion to destroy Morgan's forces or drive them out of the State. The Americans, apprised of Tarleton's approach, took a favorable position at the Cowpens, where, on the 17th of January, they were attacked by the British, eleven hundred strong. Tarleton, confident of success, made the onset with impetuosity; but Morgan's men sustained the shock with firmness, and, when the enemy's reserves were called into action, either held their ground or retired in good order. At the crisis of the battle the American cavalry, commanded by Colonel William Washington, made a furious charge and scattered the British dragoons like chaff before them. The rout was complete—the victory decisive. Washington and Tarleton had a personal encounter on the field, and the latter fled with a sword-gash in his hand. His corps was annihilated; ten British officers and ninety privates were killed, and five hundred and twenty-three were captured. Two pieces of artillery, eight hundred muskets and two flags were among the trophies of the battle.

When Cornwallis, who was encamped with his army thirty miles down the Catawba, heard of the disaster to his arms, he made a rapid march up the river to reach the fords in Morgan's rear. But Greene, who had also heard the news, hastened to the camp of Morgan, took command in person and began a hasty retreat. At the same time he sent word to General. Huger, who commanded the eastern division, to fall back toward Charlotte, where it was proposed to form a junction of the two wings of the army. On the 28th of January Morgan's division reached the Catawba and crossed to the northern bank, with prisoners, spoils and baggage. Within two hours the British van arrived at the ford; but it was already sunset, and Cornwallis concluded to wait for the morning; then he would cross and win an easy victory. During the night the clouds opened and poured down torrents; in the morning the river was swollen to a flood. It was many days before the British forced their way across, dispersing the militia on the opposite bank. And now began a second race, this time for the fords of the Yadkin.

The distance was sixty miles and the roads wretched. In two days the Americans reached the river. The crossing was nearly effected, when the British appeared in sight, attacked the rearguard and captured a few wagons; nothing else was injured. That night the Yadkin was made impassable by rains in the mountains, and Cornwallis was again delayed; Greene pressed forward to Guilford Court-House, where he arrived on the 7th of February. The British marched up the Yadkin to the shallow ford at Huntsville, where, on the 9th of the month, they succeeded in crossing. The lines of retreat and pursuit were now parallel, and the two armies were less than twenty-five miles apart. A third time the race began, and again the Americans won it. On the 13th, Greene, with the main division, crossed the Dan into Virginia, and on the following day the American rearguard entered the boats and was safe. The British van was already in sight and the whole army but a few miles distant. Never was a retreat more skillfully conducted. Cornwallis, mortified at his repeated failures, abandoned the pursuit and retired with his army to Hillsborough.

Once in Virginia, Greene was rapidly reinforced. After a few days of recruiting and rest he felt himself strong enough to begin offensive movements. On the 22d of February he recrossed the Dan into North Carolina. Meanwhile, Cornwallis had despatched Tarleton with a body of cavalry into the region between the Haw and Deep Rivers to encourage the tories. Being informed of this movement, Greene sent Colonel Lee into the same district. Three hundred loyalists, already under arms, were marching to join Tarleton. On the route they were intercepted by the American cavalry, whom, supposing them to be British, they saluted with a shout of "Long live the king!" Colonel Lee and his men quietly surrounded the unsuspecting tories, fell upon them as a band of traitors, and killed or captured the entire company.

By the addition of the Virginia militia Greene's army now numbered four thousand four hundred men. Determining to avoid battle no longer, he marched to Guilford Court-House, took a strong position and awaited his antagonist. Cornwallis, accepting the challenge, at once moved forward to the attack. On the 15th of March the two armies met on Greene's chosen ground, and a severe but indecisive battle was fought. The forces of Greene were superior in numbers, and those of Cornwallis in discipline. If the American militia had stood firm, the result would not have been doubtful; but the raw recruits behaved badly, broke line and fled. Confusion ensued; the Americans fought hard, but were eventually driven from the field and forced to retreat for several miles. In killed and wounded the British loss was greatest; but large bodies of the militia returned to their homes, reducing Greene's army to less than three thousand. Nevertheless, to the British the result was equivalent to a defeat.

Cornwallis now boasted, made big proclamations, and then retreated. On the 7th of April he reached the sea-coast at Wilmington, and immediately thereafter proceeded to Virginia. How he arrived at Petersburg, superseded Arnold and sent him out of the State has already been narrated. The British forces in the Carolinas remained under command of Lord Rawdon, who was posted with a strong division at Camden, with him General Greene, after the departure of Cornwallis, was left to contend. The American army was accordingly advanced into South Carolina. A detachment was sent against Fort Watson, on the east bank of the Santee, and the place was obliged to surrender. Greene marched with the main body to Hobkirk's Hill, a short distance north of Camden, posted his men in a strong position and awaited the movements of Rawdon. What that officer would do was not long a question of doubt. On the 25th of April he moved from Camden with his entire force and attacked the American camp. For once General Greene came near being surprised; but his men were swiftly formed for battle; Rawdon's column was badly arranged; and for a while it seemed that the entire British force would be slain or captured. Just at the critical moment, however, some valuable American officers who commanded in the centre were killed; their regiments, becoming confused, fell back; Rawdon saw his advantage, pressed forward, broke the centre, captured the hill, and won the day. The Americans retired from the field, but saved their artillery and bore away the wounded. Again the genius of Greene made defeat seem little less than victory.

On the 10th of May Lord Rawdon evacuated Camden and retired to Eutaw Springs, sixty-five miles above the mouth of the Santee. The British posts at Granby, Orangeburg, Fort Mott and Augusta fell successively into the hands of the patriots. By the 5th of June only Eutaw Springs, Charleston and Ninety-Six remained in possession of the enemy. The latter place was already besieged by General Greene, who, after the battle of Hobkirk's Hill, advanced to Fort Granby, and thence to Ninety-Six. For twenty-seven days the siege was pressed with vigor. The supply of water was cut off from the fort, and the garrison could not have held out more than two days longer; but Lord Rawdon was rapidly approaching with a force of two thousand men; and the Americans, after an unsuccessful assault, were obliged, on the 18th of June, to raise the siege and retreat. Rawdon pursued, but Greene escaped, as usual, and the British, abandoning Ninety-Six, fell back to Orangeburg. Greene, with ceaseless activity, followed the retreating enemy, and would, but for their strength, have assaulted Rawdon's works. Deeming the position impregnable, the American general recrossed the Santee and took his station on the highlands in Sumter district. Here, in the healthful air of the hill-country, he passed the sickly months of summer.

Sumter, Lee and Marion were constantly abroad, traversing the country in all directions, cutting of supplies from the enemy, breaking his lines of communication and smiting the tories right and left. Lord Rawdon now resigned the command of the British forces to Colonel Stuart and went to Charleston. While there he became a principal actor in one of the most shameful scenes of the Revolution. Colonel Isaac Hayne, an eminent patriot who had formerly taken an oath of allegiance to the king, was caught in command of a troop of American cavalry. He was at once taken to Charleston, arraigned before Colonel Balfour, the commandant, hurried through the mockery of a trial and condemned to death. Rawdon gave his sanction, and on the 31st of July Colonel Hayne was hanged. Just men in Europe joined with the patriots of America in denouncing the act as worthy of barbarism.

General Greene.

On the 22d of August General Greene left the heights of the Santee and marched toward Orangeburg. The British decamped at his approach and took post at Eutaw Springs, forty miles below. The Americans pressed after them and overtook them on the 8th of September. One of the fiercest battles of the war ensued; and General Greene was denied a decisive victory only by the bad conduct of some of his men, who, before the field was fairly won, abandoned themselves to eating and drinking in the enemy's camp. Stuart rallied his troops, returned to the charge and regained his position. Greene, after losing five hundred and fifty-five men, gave over the struggle. The British lost in killed and wounded nearly seven hundred, and more than five hundred prisoners. On the day after the battle Stuart hastily retreated to Monk's Corner; Greene followed with his army, and after two months of manœuvring and desultory warfare the British were driven into Charleston. In the mean time, General St. Clair had cleared North Carolina by forcing the enemy to evacuate Wilmington. In the whole country south of Virginia only Charleston and Savannah remained under dominion of the king's army; the latter city was evacuated by the British on the 11th of July, and the former on the 14th of December, 1782. Such was the close of the Revolution in the Carolinas and Georgia.

But the final scene was to be enacted in Virginia. There, in the last days of April, 1781, Cornwallis took command of the British army and began to ravage the country on both banks of the James. In the course of the following two months property, public and private, was destroyed to the value of fifteen million dollars. La Fayette, to whom the defence of the State had been entrusted, was unable to meet Cornwallis in the field, but watched his movements with sleepless vigilance. While the British were in the vicinity of Richmond a detachment under Tarleton proceeded as far west as Charlottesville, where the Virginia legislature was in session. The town was taken, the country devastated, and seven members of the assembly made prisoners. Governor Jefferson escaped only by riding into the mountains.

When there was little left to destroy, Cornwallis marched down the north bank of the James to Green Springs, eight miles above the site of Jamestown. He had received orders from Sir Henry Clinton to descend the river and take such a position on the coast as would keep the army within supporting distance of New York; for Clinton was very apprehensive that Washington and the French would attack him. La Fayette hovered upon the rear of Cornwallis; and on the 6th of July, when it was supposed that the main body of the enemy had crossed the

James, General Wayne, who led the American advance, suddenly attacked the whole British army. Cornwallis was so surprised by the audacious onset that when Wayne, seeing his mistake, made a hasty retreat, no pursuit was attempted. The loss of the two armies was equal, being a hundred and twenty on each side. After the passage of James River, the British marched to Portsmouth, where Arnold had had his headquarters in the previous spring. There Cornwallis would have fortified himself; but the orders of Clinton were otherwise; and in the first days of August the army was again embarked and conveyed to Yorktown, on the southern bank of York River, a few miles above the mouth.

La Fayette quickly advanced into the peninsula and took post but eight miles distant from the British. From this position he sent urgent despatches to Washington, beseeching him to come to Virginia and aid in striking the enemy a fatal blow. A powerful French armament, commanded by Count de Grasse, was hourly expected in the Chesapeake and La Fayette saw at a glance that if a fleet could be anchored in the mouth of York River, cutting off retreat, the doom of Cornwallis would be sealed. During the months of July and August, Washington, from his camp on the Hudson, looked wistfully to the South. But all the while Clinton was kept in feverish alarm by false despatches, written for the purpose of falling into his hands. These intercepted messages indicated that the Americans and French would immediately begin the siege of New York; and for that Clinton made ready. When, in the last days of August, he was informed that Washington had broken up his camp and was already marching with his whole army toward Virginia, the British general would not believe it, but went on preparing for a siege. Washington pressed rapidly forward, paused two days at Mount Vernon, where he had not been for six years, and met La Fayette at Williamsburg. Meanwhile, on the 30th of August, the French fleet, numbering twenty-eight ships of the line, with nearly four thousand troops on board, had reached the Chesapeake and safely anchored in the mouth of York River. Cornwallis, with the British army, was blockaded both by sea and land.

Siege of Yorktown, October, 1781.

To add still further to the strength of the allies, Count de Barras, who commanded the French flotilla at Newport, sailed into the Chesapeake with eight ships of the line and ten transports, bearing cannon for the siege. On the 5th of September the English admiral Graves appeared in the bay, and a naval battle ensued, in which the British ships were so roughly handled that they returned to New York. On the 28th of September the allied armies, superior in numbers and confident of success, encamped around Yorktown. The story of the siege is brief. Tarleton, who occupied Gloucester Point, on the other side of the river, made one spirited sally, but was driven back with severe loss. On the night of the 6th of October the trenches were opened at the distance of six hundred yards from the British works. The cannonade was constant and effective. On the 11th of the month the allies drew their second parallel within three hundred yards of Cornwallis's redoubts. On the night of the 14th the enemy's outer works were carried by storm. At daydawn of the 16th the British made a sortie, only to be hurled back into their entrenchments. On the next day Cornwallis proposed a surrender; on the 18th terms of capitulation were drawn up and signed; and at two o'clock in the afternoon of the 19th Major-General O'Hara—for Cornwallis, feigning sickness, remained in his tent—led the whole British army from the trenches into an open field, where, in the presence of the allied ranks of France and America, seven thousand two hundred and forty-seven English and Hessian soldiers laid down their arms, delivered their standards, and became prisoners of war. Eight hundred and forty sailors were also surrendered. Seventy-five brass and thirty-one iron guns were taken, together with all the accoutrements of the army.

By a swift courier the news was borne to Congress. On the evening of the 23d the messenger rode into Philadelphia. When the sentinels of the city called the hour of ten that night, they added, *"and Cornwallis is taken."* On the morrow Congress assembled, and before that august body the despatch of Washington was read. The members, exulting and weeping for gladness, went in concourse with the citizens to the Dutch Lutheran church and turned the afternoon into a thanksgiving. The note of rejoicing sounded through the length and breadth of the land; for it was seen that the dominion of the Briton in America was forever broken.

After the surrender the conquered army was marched under guard to the barracks of Lancaster. Washington, with the victorious Americans and French, returned to the camps of New Jersey and the Hudson. On the Continent of Europe the news was received with every demonstration of gladness. In England the king and his ministers heard the tidings with mortification and rage; but the English people were either secretly pleased or openly rejoiced. During the fall and winter the ministerial majority in Parliament fell off rapidly; and on the 20th of March, 1782, Lord North and his friends, unable longer to conduct the government, resigned their offices. A new ministry was immediately formed, favorable to America, favorable to freedom, favorable to peace. In the beginning of May the command of the British forces in the United States was transferred from Clinton to Sir Guy Carleton, a man friendly to American interests. The hostile demonstrations of the enemy, now confined to New York and Charleston, ceased; and Washington made no efforts to dislodge the foe, for the war had really ended.

In the summer of 1782 Richard Oswald was sent by Parliament to Paris. The object of his mission was to confer with Franklin and Jay, the ambassadors of the United States, in regard to the terms of peace. Before the discussions were ended, John Adams, arriving from Amsterdam, and Henry Laurens from London, entered into the negotiations. On the 30th of November preliminary articles of peace were agreed to and signed on the part of Great Britain by Oswald, and on behalf of the United States by Franklin, Adams, Jay and Laurens. In the following April the terms were ratified by Congress; but it was not until the 3d of September, 1783, that a final treaty was effected between all the nations that had been at war. On that day the ambassadors of Holland, Spain, England, France and the United States, in a solemn conference at Paris, agreed to and signed the articles of a permanent peace.

The terms of THE TREATY OF 1783 were briefly these: A full and complete recognition of the independence of the United States; the recession by Great Britain of Florida to Spain; the surrender of all the remaining territory east of the Mississippi and south of the great lakes to the United States; the free navigation of the Mississippi and the lakes by American vessels; the concession of mutual rights in the Newfoundland fisheries; and the retention by Great Britain of Canada and Nova Scotia, with the exclusive control of the St. Lawrence.

Early in August Sir Guy Carleton received instructions to evacuate New York city. Three months were spent in making arrangements for this important event. Finally, on the 25th of November, everything was in readiness; the British army was embarked on board the fleet; the sails were spread; the ships stood out to sea; dwindled to white specks on the horizon; disappeared. The Briton was gone. After the struggles and sacrifices of an eight years' war the patriots had achieved the independence of their country. The United States of America took an equal station among the nations of the earth.

Map V. The United States from the Close of the Revolution to the Purchase of Louisiana. 1783-1803.

Map V.
THE UNITED STATES
AT THE
CLOSE OF THE REVOLUTION.
Treaty of 1783.

Nine days after Carleton's departure there was a most affecting scene in the city. Washington assembled his officers and bade them a final adieu. When they were met, the chieftain spoke a few affectionate words to his comrades, who came forward in turn and with tears and sobs which the veterans no longer cared to conceal bade him farewell. Washington then walked to Whitehall, followed by a vast concourse of citizens and soldiers, and thence departed to Annapolis, where Congress was in session. On his way he paused at Philadelphia and made to the proper officers a report of his expenses during the war. The account was in his own handwriting, and covered a total expenditure of seventy-four thousand four hundred and eighty-five dollars—all correct to a cent. The route of the chief from Paulus's Hook to Annapolis was a continuous triumph. The people by hundreds and thousands flocked to the villages and roadsides to see him pass; gray-headed statesmen to speak words of praise; young men to shout with enthusiasm; maidens to strew his way with flowers.

On the 23d of December Washington was introduced to Congress. To that body of patriotic sages he delivered an address full of feeling, wisdom and modesty. Then with that dignity which always marked his conduct he surrendered his commission as commander-in-chief of the American army. General Mifflin, the president of Congress, responded in an eloquent manner, and then the hero retired to his home at Mount Vernon. The man whom, the year before, some disaffected soldiers were going to make king of America, now, by his own act, became a citizen of the Republic.

CHAPTER XLV.

CONFEDERATION AND UNION.

DURING the progress of the Revolution the civil government of the United States was in a deplorable condition. Nothing but the imminent peril of the country had, in the first place, led to the calling of a Continental Congress. And when that body assembled, it had no method of proceeding, no constitution, no power of efficient action. The two great wants of the country were *money* to carry on the war and *a central authority* to direct the war: the former of these was never met; and Washington was made to supply the latter. Whenever Congress would move in the direction of a firmer government, division would spring up, and action would be checked by the remonstrance of jealous colonies. Nevertheless, the more far-seeing statesmen of the times labored constantly to create substantial political institutions.

Foremost of all those who worked for better government was Benjamin Franklin. As early as the times of the French and Indian War he began to agitate the question of a permanent union of the colonies. During the troubled years just preceding the Revolution he brooded over his cherished project, and in 1775 laid before Congress the plan of a perpetual confederation of the States. But the attention of that body was wholly occupied with the stirring events of the day, and Franklin's measure received but little notice. Congress, without any real authority, began to conduct the government, and its legislation was generally accepted by the States. Still, the central authority was only an authority by sufferance, and was liable at any time to be annulled by the caprice of State legislatures.

Under such a system thinking men grew restless. On the 11th of June, 1776, a committee was appointed by Congress to prepare a plan of confederation. After a month the work was completed and laid before the house. Another month was spent in fruitless debates, and then the question was laid over till the following spring. In April of 1777 the discussion was resumed, and continued through the summer. Meanwhile, the power of Great Britain being overthrown, the States had all adopted republican governments, and the sentiment of national union had made considerable headway. Finally, on the 15th of November, a vote was taken in Congress, and the articles of confederation reported by the committee were adopted. The next step was to transmit the articles to the several State legislatures for ratification. The time thus occupied extended to the following June, and then the new frame of government returned to Congress with many amendments. These having been considered and the most serious objections removed, the articles were signed by the delegates of eight States on the 9th of July, 1778. Later in the same month the representatives of Georgia and North Carolina affixed their signatures. In November the delegates of New Jersey, and in the following February those of Delaware, signed the compact. Maryland held aloof; and it was not until March of 1781 that the consent of that commonwealth could be obtained. Thus the Revolution was nearly ended before the new system was finally ratified.

The government of the United States under the articles of confederation was a democratic republic. It presented itself under the form of A LOOSE UNION OF INDEPENDENT COMMONWEALTHS—a confederacy of sovereign States. The executive and legislative powers of the general government were vested in Congress—a body composed of not less than two nor more than seven representatives from each State. But Congress could exercise no other than *delegated powers*; the sovereignty was reserved to the States. The most important of the exclusive privileges of Congress were the right of making war and peace, the regulation of foreign intercourse, the power to receive and send ambassadors, the control of the coinage of money, the settlement of disputed boundaries and the care of the public domain. There was no chief magistrate of the Republic; and no general judiciary was provided for. The consent of nine States was necessary to complete an act of legislation. In voting each State cast a single ballot. The union of the States was declared to be perpetual.

On the day of the ratification of the articles by Maryland the old Congress adjourned, and on the following morning reassembled under the new form of government. From the very first the inadequacy of that government was manifest. To begin with, it contradicted the doctrines of the Declaration of Independence. Congress had but a shadow of authority, and that shadow, instead of proceeding from the people emanated from States which were declared to be sovereign and independent. The first great duty of the new government was to provide for the payment of the war debt, which had now reached the sum of thirty-eight million dollars. Congress could only recommend to the several States the levying of a sufficient tax to meet the indebtedness. Some of the States made the required levy; others were dilatory; others refused. At the very outset the government was balked and thwarted. The serious troubles that attended the disbanding of the army were traceable rather to the inability than to the indisposition of Congress to pay the soldiers. The princely fortune of Robert Morris was exhausted and himself brought to poverty in a vain effort to sustain the credit of the government. For three years after the treaty of peace public affairs were in a condition bordering on chaos. The imperiled state of the Republic was viewed with alarm by the sagacious patriots who had carried the Revolution to a successful issue. It was seen that unless the articles of confederation could be replaced with a better system the nation would go to ruin.

The project of remodeling the government originated at Mount Vernon. In 1785, Washington, in conference with a company of statesmen at his home, advised the calling of a convention to meet at Annapolis in the following year. The proposition was received with favor; and in September of 1786 the representatives of five States assembled. The question of a tariff on imports was discussed; and then the attention of the delegates was turned to a revision of the articles of confederation. Since only a minority of the States were represented in the conference, it was resolved to adjourn until May of the following year, and all the States were urgently requested to send representatives at that time. Congress also invited the several legislatures to appoint delegates to the proposed convention. All of the States except Rhode Island responded to the call and on the second Monday in May, 1787, the representatives assembled at Philadelphia. Washington, who was a delegate from Virginia, was chosen president of the convention. A desultory discussion followed until the 29th of the month, when Edmund Randolph introduced a resolution to set aside the articles of confederation and adopt a new constitution. There was further debate; and then a committee was appointed to revise the articles. Early in September the work was done; the report of the committee was adopted and that report was THE CONSTITUTION OF THE UNITED STATES.[18] At the same time it was resolved to send copies of the new instrument to the several legislatures for ratification or rejection.

While the constitutional convention was in session at Philadelphia the last colonial Congress was sitting in New York. The latter body was in a feeble and distracted condition. Only eight States were represented. It was evident that the old Confederation, under which the colonies had won their freedom, was tottering to its fall. Nevertheless, before the adjournment of Congress, a measure was successfully carried through which was only second in importance to the formation of the constitution. This was the organization of THE NORTH WESTERN TERRITORY. As a preliminary measure this vast domain was ceded to the United States by Virginia, New York Massachusetts, and Connecticut. For the government of the territory an ordinance, drawn up by Mr. Jefferson, was adopted on the 13th of July, 1787. General Arthur St. Clair, then president of Congress, received the appointment of military governor, and in the summer of the following year began his duties with headquarters at Marietta. By the terms of the ordinance it was stipulated

Alexander Hamilton.

---

[18] The Constitution was written by Gouverneur Morris, of Pennsylvania.

that not less than three nor more than five States should be formed out of the great territory thus brought under the dominion of civilization; that the States when organized should be admitted on terms of equality with the original members of the confederation, and that slavery should be prohibited. Out of this noble domain the five great States of Ohio, Indiana, Illinois, Michigan, and Wisconsin were destined in after times to be formed and added to the Union.

On the question of adopting the Constitution the people were divided. It was the first great political agitation in the country. Those who favored the new frame of government were called FEDERALISTS; those who opposed, ANTI-FEDERALISTS or REPUBLICANS. The leaders of the former party were Washington, Jay, Madison, and Hamilton, the latter statesman throwing the whole force of his genius and learning into the controversy. In those able papers called the *Federalist* he and Madison successfully answered every objection of the anti-Federal party. Hamilton was the first and perhaps the greatest expounder of constitutional liberty in America. To him the Republic owes a debt of perpetual gratitude for having established on a firm and enduring basis the true principles of free government.

Under the Constitution of the United States the powers of government are arranged under three heads—LEGISLATIVE, EXECUTIVE, and JUDICIAL. The legislative power is vested in Congress—a body composed of a Senate and a House of Representatives. The members of the Senate are chosen by the legislatures of the several States, and serve for a period of six years. Each State is represented by two Senators. The members of the House of Representatives are elected by the people of the respective States; and each State is entitled to a number of representatives proportionate to the population of that State. The members of this branch are chosen for a term of two years. Congress is the law-making power of the nation; and all legislative questions of a general character are the appropriate subjects of congressional action.

The executive power of the United States is vested in a President, who is chosen for a period of four years by a body of men called the electoral college. The electors composing the college are chosen by the people of the several States; and each State is entitled to a number of electors equal to the number of its representatives and senators in Congress. The duty of the President is to enforce the laws of Congress in accordance with the Constitution. He is commander-in-chief of the armies and navies of the United States. Over the legislation of Congress he has the power of veto; but a two-thirds congressional majority may pass a law without the President's consent. He has the right of appointing cabinet officers and foreign ministers; but all of his appointments must be approved by the Senate. The treaty-making power is also lodged with the President; but here again the concurrence of the Senate is necessary. In case of the death, resignation, or removal of the President, the Vice-President becomes chief magistrate; otherwise his duties are limited to presiding over the Senate.

The judicial power of the United States is vested in a supreme court and in inferior courts established by Congress. The highest judicial officer is the chief-justice. All the judges of the supreme and inferior courts hold their offices during life or good behavior. The jurisdiction of these courts extends to all causes arising under the Constitution, laws, and treaties of the United States. The right of trial by jury is granted in all cases except the impeachment of public officers. Treason against the United States consists only in levying war against them, or in giving aid and comfort to their enemies.

The Constitution further provides that full faith shall be given in all the States to the records of every State; that the citizens of any State shall be entitled to the privileges of citizens in all the States; that new territories may be organized and new States admitted into the Union; that to every State shall be guaranteed a republican form of government; and that the Constitution may be altered or amended whenever the same is proposed by a two-thirds majority of both houses of Congress, and ratified by three-fourths of the legislatures of the several States. In accordance with this last provision fifteen amendments have been made to the Constitution. The most important of these are the articles which guarantee religious freedom; change the method of electing President and Vice-President; abolish Slavery; and forbid the abridgment of suffrage on account of race or color.[19]

---

[19] See Appendix F.

Such was the Constitution adopted, after much debate, for the government of the American people. Would the people ratify it? or had the work been done in vain? The little State of Delaware was first to answer the question. In her convention on the 3d of December, 1787, the voice of the commonwealth was *unanimously* recorded in favor of the new Constitution. Ten days later Pennsylvania gave her decision by a vote of forty-six to twenty-three in favor of ratification. On the 19th of December New Jersey added her approval *by a unanimous vote;* and on the 2d of the following month Georgia did the same. On the 9th of January the Connecticut convention followed, with a vote of a hundred and twenty-eight to forty, in favor of adoption. In Massachusetts the battle was hard fought and barely won. A ballot, taken on the 6th of February, resulted in ratification by the close vote of a hundred and eighty-seven to a hundred and sixty-eight. This really decided the contest. On the 28th of April Maryland rendered her decision by the strong vote of sixty-three to twelve. Next came the ratification of South Carolina by a vote of a hundred and forty-nine to seventy-three. In the New Hampshire convention there was a hard struggle, but the vote for adoption finally stood fifty-seven to forty-six, June 21st, 1788. This was the *ninth State*, and the work was done. For, by its own terms, the new government was to go into operation when nine States should ratify. The great commonwealth of Virginia still hesitated. Washington and Madison were for the Constitution; but Jefferson and Henry were opposed. Not until the 25th of June did her convention declare for adoption, and then only by a vote of eighty-nine to seventy-nine. It was now clear that the new government would be organized, and this fact was brought to bear as a powerful argument in favor of adoption by the convention at Poughkeepsie. The hope that New York city would be the seat of the Federal government also acted as a motive, and a motion to ratify was finally carried, July 27th, 1788. Only Rhode Island and North Carolina persisted in their refusal. But in the latter State a new convention was called, and on the 13th of November, 1789, the Constitution was formally adopted. As to Rhode Island, her pertinacity was in inverse ratio to her importance. At length Providence and Newport seceded from the commonwealth; the question of dividing the teritory between Massachusetts and Connecticut was raised, and the refractory member at last yielded by adopting the Constitution, May 29th, 1790. Then, for the first time, the English-speaking race in the New World was united under a common government—strong enough for safety, liberal enough for freedom.

In accordance with the provisions of the Constitution and a resolution of Congress, the first Wednesday of January, 1789, was named as the time for the election of a chief magistrate. The people had but one voice as to the man who should be honored with that trust. Early in April the ballots of the electors were counted in the presence of Congress, and George Washington was unanimously chosen President and John Adams Vice-President of the United States. On the 14th of the month Washington received notification of his election, and departed for New York. His route thither was a constant triumph. Maryland welcomed him at Georgetown. Philadelphia by her executive council, the trustees of her university, and the officers of the Cincinnati, did him honor. How did the people of Trenton exult in the presence of the hero who twelve years before had fought their battle! There over the bridge of the Assanpink they built a triumphal arch, and girls in white ran before, singing and strewing the way with flowers. At Elizabethtown he was met by the principal officers of the government and welcomed to the capital where he was to become the first chief magistrate of a free and grateful people. With this auspicious event the period of revolution and confederation ends, and the era of nationality in the New Republic is ushered in. Long and glorious be the history of that Republic, bought with the blood of patriots, and consecrated in the sorrows of our fathers!

PART V.

NATIONAL PERIOD.
A. D. 1789-1882.

CHAPTER XLVI.

WASHINGTON'S ADMINISTRATION, 1789-1797.

ON the 30th of April, 1789, Washington was duly inaugurated first President of the United States. The new government was to have gone into operation on the 4th of March, but the event was considerably delayed. The inaugural ceremony was performed on the balcony of the Old City Hall, on the present Site of the Custom-House, in Wall street. Chancellor Livingston of New York administered the oath of office. The streets and house-tops were thronged with people; flags fluttered; cannon boomed from the Battery. As soon as the public ceremony was ended, Washington retired to the Senate chamber and delivered his inaugural address. The organization of the two houses of Congress had already been effected.

Washington.

The new government was embarrassed with many difficulties. The opponents of the Constitution were not yet silenced, and from the beginning they caviled at the measures of the administration. By the treaty of 1783 the free navigation of the Mississippi had been guaranteed. Now the jealous Spaniards of New Orleans hindered the passage of American ships. The people of the West looked to the great river as the natural outlet of their commerce; they must be protected in their rights. On many parts of the frontier the malignant Red men were still at war with the settlers. As to financial credit, the United States had none. In the very beginning of his arduous duties Washington was prostrated with sickness, and the business of government was for many weeks delayed.

Not until September were the first important measures adopted. On the 10th of that month an act was passed by Congress instituting a department of foreign affairs, a treasury department and a department of war. As members of his cabinet Washington nominated Jefferson, Knox and Hamilton; the first as secretary of foreign affairs; the second, of war; and the third, of the treasury. In accordance with the provisions of the Constitution, a supreme court was also organized, John Jay receiving the appointment of first chief-justice. With him were joined as associate justices John Rutledge of South Carolina, James Wilson of Pennsylvania, William Cushing of Massachusetts, John Blair of Virginia, and James Iredell of North Carolina. Edmund Randolph was chosen attorney-general. Many constitutional amendments were now brought forward, and ten of them adopted. By this action on the part of Congress, the objections of North Carolina and Rhode Island were removed and both States ratified the Constitution, the former in November of 1789 and the latter in the following May.

On the 29th of September, 1789, Congress adjourned until the following January, and Washington availed himself of the opportunity thus offered to make a tour of the Eastern States. Accompanied by his secretaries, he set out in his carriage from New York on the 15th of October, and nine days afterward reached Boston. At every point on the route the affection of the people, and especially of the Revolutionary veterans, burst out in unbounded enthusiasm. On reaching Boston the President was welcomed by Governor John Hancock and the selectmen of the city. No pains were spared that could add to the comfort and pleasure of the new nation's chief magistrate. After remaining a week among the scenes associated with his first command of the American army, he proceeded to Portsmouth and thence returned with improved health and peace of mind by way of Hartford to New York.

In the first months of his administration Washington was much vexed about questions of ceremony and etiquette. How should he appear in public? How often? What kind of entertainment should he give? Who should be invited? What title should he bear? And in what manner be introduced? In these matters there was no precedent to guide him; for who had ever held such a station before? He must not, on the one hand, demean himself like a king, surrounded with peers and courtiers, nor, on the other hand, must he degrade his high office by such blunt democratical ceremonies as would render himself ridiculous and the Presidency contemptible. In his embarrassment Washington sought the advice of Adams, Jefferson, Hamilton, and others in regard to a suitable etiquette and ceremonial for the Republican court. Adams in answer would have much ceremony; Jefferson, none at all. The latter said: "I hope that the terms Excellency, Honor, Worship, Esquire, and even Mr. shall shortly and forever disappear from among us." Hamilton's reply favored a mod crate and simple formality; and this view was adopted by Washington as most consistent with the new frame of government. In the mean time Congress had declared that the chief magistrate should have no title other than that of his office; namely, President of the United States. So with ceremonies few and simple the order of affairs in the presidential office was established.

The national debt, however, was the greatest and most threatening question; but the genius of Hamilton triumphed over every difficulty. The indebtedness of the United States, including the revolutionary expenses of the several States, amounted to nearly eighty millions of dollars. Hamilton adopted a broad and honest policy. His plan, which was laid before Congress at the beginning of the second session, proposed that the debt of the United States due to American citizens, as well as the war debt of the individual States, should be assumed by the general government, *and that all should be fully paid.* By this measure the credit of the country was vastly improved, even before actual payment was begun. As a means of augmenting the revenues of the government a duty was laid on the tonnage of merchant-ships, with a discrimination in favor of American vessels; and customs were levied on all imported articles. Hamilton's financial schemes were violently opposed; but his policy prevailed, and the credit of the government was soon firmly established.

The proposition to assume the debts of the States had been coupled with another to fix the seat of government. After much discussion it was agreed to establish the capital for ten years at Philadelphia, and afterward at some suitable locality on the Potomac. The next important measure was the organization of the territory south-west of the Ohio. In the autumn of 1790 a war broke out with the Miami Indians. Fort Washington, on the present site of Cincinnati, had been established as the capital of the North-western Territory; and General St. Clair had received the appointment as governor. The Indians had fairly relinquished their rights to the surrounding country; but other tribes came forward with pretended claims, and went to war to recover their lost possessions. At the close of September, General Harmar, with fourteen hundred troops, set out from Fort Washington to chastise the hostile Miamis. After destroying several villages and wasting the country as far as the Maumee, he divided his army into detachments. Colonel Hardin, who commanded the Kentucky volunteers, was ambuscaded and his forces routed at a village eleven miles from Fort Wayne; and on the 21st of October the main division was defeated with great loss at the Maumee Ford. General Harmar was obliged to abandon the Indian country and retreat to Fort Washington.

In the beginning of 1791 an act was passed by Congress establishing THE BANK OF THE UNITED STATES. The measure originated with the secretary of the treasury, and was violently opposed by Jefferson and the anti-federal party. About the same time Vermont, which had been an independent territory since 1777, adopted the Constitution, and on the 18th of February was admitted into the Union as the fourteenth State. The claim of New York to the jurisdiction of the province had been purchased, two years previously, for thirty thousand dollars. The first census of the United States, completed for the year 1790, Showed that the population of the country had increased to three million nine hundred and twenty-nine thousand souls.

CHART IV.

1789　　　　**93**　　　　**97**　　　　**1801**　　**5**

French Revolution.　　　　**Napoleon Bonaparte.**
　　　　94. Partition of Poland.　97. Pinckney rejected by the French Directory.
　　　　93. Execution of Louis XVI.　　　　4. The great
　　　　93. Fall of the Girondists.　99. Overthrow of the Directory.
　　　　　　　　　　　　99. Napoleon, First Consul.　4. Napoleon,
　　　　93. **Reign of Terror.**　　　　　Bombardment of Copenhagen.　Tr
　　　　　　94. Fall of Robespierre.　1800.　Marengo.　6.
　　　　　　　　　　　　　　　　　　　　　　　　　　　6.
　　　George III.　　96. Great political disturbances in England.　5.

Washington, President.
　　　　　　　　　　　　　　　　　　　　　2. Ohio admitted into th
91. Vermont admitted into
　　the Union.　　　　　　　　　1800. Removal of the seat of governm
89. North Carolina ratifies the Constitution.　　　to Washington, D. C.
　　　　　　　9d. Tennessee admitted into the Union.
90. Rhode Island ratifies the Constitution.　1800. Passage of the Alien and Se
90. Seat of government at Philadelphia.　**John Adams,** President.
　　　　　　　　　　　　　99. Washington dies at Mount Vernon, a.
　　　　　　　　　　　　　98. War with France.
　　　　　　　　　　　　　　　　　　　　　　　4. Hamilton
　　　　94.　Wayne's victory.　　　　　　　　　　　6
　　93. Genet, French minister at Washington.
　　92. Kentucky admitted into the Union. 99. Treaty with France.

Washington re-elected President.
91. St. Clair's defeat.

91. Bank of the United States established.　　**Thomas Jefferson,**
　　　　　　　　　　　　　　　　　　　　　　5. The
　　　　94. Whisky Insurrection.　　　　　　　　　　li
　　　　93. Jay's Treaty.
　　　　　　　　　　　　　　　　　　　　　　　Jeff
John Adams, Vice-President.
　　　　　　　　John Adams re-elected
John Jay, Chief-　　Vice-President.　Thomas Jefferson, Vice-President.
Jefferson, Secretary of State.
Hamilton, Secretary of Treasury.
Knox, Secretary of War.

　　　　　　　　　　　　　　　　　1. Aaron Burr, Vice-Preside
　　　　　　　　　　　　　　　　　1. War with Tripoli.
　　　　　　　　　　　　　　　　　　　　　　　　Geor
　　　　　　　　　　　　　　　　　3. Commodore Pr
　　　　　　　　　　　　　　　　　3. Purchase of Lo

NATIONAL PERIOD — FIRST SECTION.
A. D. 1789–1825.
CHART IV.

NATIONAL PERIOD–FIRST SECTION. A. D. 1789-1825.

	9	13	17	21	1825
8. The rebellion. Treaty of ror. r. Jena. kade of the rlitz.	9. Divorce of Josephi 8. The Peninsular War. 10. Marriage of N to Maria Tilsit. **Orders in Coun** 9. *Wagram.* coast from Brest to the Elbe.	ne 14. **Louis XVIII.** apoleon 12. Invasion of Russia. cil.	14. Deposition of Napoleon. 15. *Wa*terloo, and banishment 15. Treaty of Paris. 15. Rise of the Radical Party in **George IV.** 16. Parliamentary reforms. 15. *Bomb*ardment of Algiers. 15. War with Algiers.	21. Napoleon dies. 24. **Charles X.** of Napoleon. England.	

James Madison, President.
12. Surrender of Mackinaw.
12. Surrender of Detroit.
11. *Tippe*canoe. 14. Hartford Convention.
12. Henry Dearborn appointed commander-in-chief.
20. Maine admitted into the Union.

14. *Capture of York.*
11. *The Pr*esident *and Little Belt.*
Madison re-elected President.
ed in a du el. 12. Second embargo.
r's conspir acy. 12. War declared against Great Britain.
18. The Seminole War.
12. *Fort Dearborn.* 18. Capture of St. Marks and Pensacola.
24. Visit of La Fayette.
George Clinton re-elected Vice-President.
14. Capture and burning of Washington.
12. *Queenstown.* **James Monroe,** President.
ident. 12. *The Constitution and the Guerriere.* **Monroe** re-elected President.
em of patro nage estab- 14. Treaty of Ghent.
in the pub lic offices. 12. *The Wasp and the Frolic.*
12. *The United States and the Macedonian.* 21. Missouri admitted into the Union.
on re-elec ted President.
12. *The Constitution and the Java.*
7. First stea mboat on the Hudson 13. *Frenchtown.* 18. Illinois admitted into the Union.

14. *Fort Mc Henry.*
Daniel Tompkins, Vice-President.
7. Attack on the Chesapeake. 16. Indiana admitted into the Union.
7. Passage of the Embargo Act. 13. *Fort Meigs.* **Tompkins** re-elected Vice-President.
13. *Perry's victo*ry. 19. Alabama admitted into the Union.
linton, Vice-President.
sent to the Mediterranean. 13. *The Thames.*
15. *New Orlea*ns. 21. Rise of the Slavery agitation.
13. *Horseshoe Bend.*
21. The Missouri Compromise.
13. *The Hornet and the Peacock.*
*The Chesapea*ke *and the Shannon.*
12. Louisiana admitted into the Union.
Elbridge Gerry, Vice-President.
13. *The Argus and the Pelican.*
14. *Lundy's Lane.*
17. Mississippi admitted into the Union.
14. *Plattsburg.* 19. Florida ceded to the United States.

After the defeat of Harmar the government adopted more vigorous measures for the repression of Indian hostilities. On the 6th of September, 1791, General St. Clair, with an army of two thousand men, set out from Fort Washington to break the power of the Miami confederacy. On the night of November 3d he reached a point nearly a hundred miles north of Fort Washington, and encamped on one of the upper tributaries of the Wabash, in what is now the south-west angle of Mercer county, Ohio. On the following morning at sunrise his camp was suddenly assailed by more than two thousand warriors, led by Little Turtle and several American renegades who had joined the Indians. After a terrible battle of three hours' duration, St. Clair was completely defeated, with a loss of fully half his men. The fugitive militia retreated precipitately to Fort Washington, where they arrived four days after the battle. The news of the disaster spread gloom and sorrow throughout the land. When the tidings reached Philadelphia the government was for a while in consternation. For once the benignant spirit of Washington gave way to wrath. *"Here,"* said he in a tempest of indignation,—"HERE, in this very room, I took leave of General St. Clair. I wished him success and honor. I said to him, 'You have careful instructions from the secretary of war, and I myself will add one word—*beware of a surprise*. You know how the Indians fight us. BEWARE OF A SURPRISE!' He went off with that, my last warning, ringing in his ears. And yet he has suffered that army to be cut to pieces, hacked, butchered, tomahawked by a surprise,—the very thing I guarded him against! How can he answer to his country? The blood of the slain is upon him,—the curse of widows and orphans!" Mr. Lear, the secretary, in whose presence this storm of wrath burst forth, sat speechless. Presently Washington grew silent. "What I have uttered must not go beyond this room," said he in a manner of great seriousness. Another pause of several minutes ensued, and then he continued in a low and solemn tone: "I looked at the despatches hastily and did not note all the particulars. General St. Clair shall have justice. I will receive him without displeasure,—*he shall have full justice.*" Notwithstanding his exculpation by a committee of Congress, poor St. Clair, overwhelmed with censures and reproaches, resigned his command and was superseded by General Wayne, whom the people had named Mad Anthony.

The population of the Territory of Kentucky had now reached seventy-three thousand. Only seventeen years before, Daniel Boone, the hardy hunter of North Carolina, had settled with his companions at Boonesborough. Harrodsburg and Lexington were founded about the same time. During the Revolution the pioneers were constantly beset by the savages. After the expedition of General Clarke, in 1779, the frontier was more secure; and in the years following the treaty thousands of immigrants came annually. In the mean time, Virginia had relinquished her claim to the territory; and on the 1st of June, 1792, Kentucky was admitted into the Union. At the presidential election, held in the autumn of the same year, Washington was again unanimously chosen; as Vice-President, John Adams was also re-elected.

During Washington's second administration the country was greatly troubled in its relations with foreign governments. Europe was in an uproar. The French Revolution of 1789 was still running its dreadful course. After three years of unparalleled excesses, the Jacobins of France had beheaded the king and abolished the monarchy. Citizen Genet was sent by the new French republic as minister to the United States. On his arrival at Charleston, and on his way to Philadelphia, he was greeted with unbounded enthusiasm. Taking advantage of his popularity, the ambassador began to abuse his authority, fitted out privateers to prey on the commerce of Great Britain, planned expeditions against Louisiana, and, although the President had already issued a proclamation of neutrality, demanded an alliance with the government. Washington and the cabinet firmly refused; and the audacious minister threatened *to appeal to the people.* In this outrageous conduct he was sustained and encouraged by the anti-Federal party, and for a while the government was endangered. But Washington stood unmoved, declared the course of the French minister an insult to the sovereignty of the United States, and demanded his recall. The republican authorities of France heeded the demand, and Genet was superseded by M. Fouchet.

The President was also much embarrassed by dissensions in his cabinet. From the beginning of his first official term the secretaries of state and the treasury had maintained towards each other an attitude of constant hostility. They had gradually become the heads of rival parties in the government. Hamilton's financial measures were attacked with vehement animosity by Jefferson; and the policy of the latter in his relations and duties as secretary of foreign affairs was the subject of much bitter criticism from the former's scathing pen. The breach between the rivals grew wider and wider. Washington's influence was barely sufficient to prevent the breaking up of his cabinet. So great were the abilities and so valuable the experience of the two secretaries that the services of neither could be spared without serious detriment to the government. Both officers were patriots, and both had insisted on Washington's reelection to the Presidency. After that event, however, Jefferson, in January of 1794, resigned his office and retired to private life at Monticello. A year later Hamilton also retired from the cabinet and was succeeded by Oliver Wolcott of Connecticut.

During the summer and autumn of 1794 the country was much disturbed by a difficulty in Western Pennsylvania known as the whisky insurrection. Hoping to improve the revenues of the government, Congress had, three years previously, imposed a tax on all ardent spirits distilled in the United States. While Genet was at Philadelphia, he and his partisans incited the people of the distilling regions to resist the tax-collectors. The disaffected rose in arms. Washington issued two proclamations, warning the insurgents to disperse; but instead of obeying, they fired upon and captured the officers of the government. The President then ordered General Henry Lee to enter the rebellious district with a sufficient force to restore order and enforce the law. When the troops reached the scene of the disturbance, the rioters had already scattered. The insurrection was a political rather than a social outbreak: the anti-Federalists were in a majority in the distilling region, and the whisky-tax was a measure of the Federal party.

Meanwhile, General Wayne had broken the Miami confederacy. In the fall of 1793 he entered the Indian country with a force of three thousand men. Reaching the scene of St. Clair's defeat, he built a stockade named Fort Recovery, and then pressed on to the junction of the Au Glaize and the Maumee, in Williams county, Ohio. Here he built and garrisoned Fort Defiance. Descending the Maumee to the rapids, he sent proposals of peace to the Indians, who were in council but a few miles distant. Little Turtle, more wise than the other chiefs, would have made a treaty; but the majority were for battle. On the 20th of August Wayne marched against the savages, overtook them where the present town of Waynesfield stands, and routed them with terrible losses. The relentless general then compelled the humbled chieftains to purchase peace by ceding to the United States all the territory east of a line drawn from Fort Recovery to the mouth of the Great Miami River. This was the last service of General Wayne. Remaining for a while in the Indian country, he embarked on Lake Erie to return to Philadelphia. In December of 1796 he died on board the vessel, and was buried at Presque Isle.

The conduct of Great Britain toward the United States became as arrogant as that of France was impudent. In November of 1793 George III. issued secret instructions to British privateers to seize all neutral vessels that might be found trading in the French West Indies. The United States had no notification of this high-handed measure; and American commerce to the value of many millions of dollars was swept from the sea by a process differing in nothing from highway robbery. But for the temperate spirit of the government the country would have been at once plunged into war. Prudence prevailed over passion; and in May of 1794 Chief-Justice Jay was sent as envoy extraordinary to demand redress of the British government. Contrary to expectation, his mission was successful; and in the following November an honorable treaty was concluded. The terms of settlement, however, were exceedingly distasteful to the partisans of France in America, and they determined to prevent its ratification. Every argument and motive which ingenuity or prejudice could supply was eagerly paraded before the people to excite their discontent. Public meetings were held and excited orators harangued the multitudes. In New York a copy of the treaty was burned before the governor's mansion. In Philadelphia there was a similar proceeding; and the whole country was in an uproar. Washington, however, believing the treaty to be just in its main provisions, and earnestly desiring that war might be avoided, favored ratification. The majority in the Senate remained unmoved, and finally in the latter part of June, 1795, the terms of settlement were duly ratified, and signed by the President. It was specified in the treaty that Great Britain should make ample reparation for the injuries done by her privateers, and surrender to the United States certain Western posts which until now had been held by English garrisons. Thus was the threatened war averted.

In October of 1795 the boundary between the United States and Louisiana was settled by a treaty with Spain. The latter country at the same time guaranteed to the Americans the free navigation of the Mississippi. Less honorable was the treaty made with the kingdom of Algiers. For a long time Algerine pirates had infested the Mediterranean, preying upon the commerce of civilized nations; and those nations, in order to purchase exemption from such ravages, had adopted the ruinous policy of paying the dey of Algiers an annual tribute. In consideration of the tribute the dey agreed that his pirate ships should confine themselves to the Mediterranean, and should not attack the vessels of such nations as made the payment. Now, however, with the purpose of injuring France, Great Britain winked at an agreement with the dey by which the Algerine sea-robbers were turned loose on the Atlantic. By their depredations American commerce suffered greatly; and the government of the United States was obliged to purchase safety by paying the shameful tribute.

In the summer of 1796, Tennessee, the third new State, was organized and admitted into the Union. Six years previously North Carolina had surrendered her claims to the territory, which at that time contained a population of thirty-five thousand; and within five years the number was more than doubled. The first inhabitants of Tennessee were of that hardy race of pioneers to whom the perils of the wilderness are as nothing provided the wilderness is free. By the addition of the two States south-west of the Ohio more than eighty-three thousand square miles of territory were brought under the dominion of civilization.

Nothing in history is more surprising than the ascendency which Washington, unto the end of his official career, continued to exercise over the minds of his countrymen. In the House of Representatives, during the last two sessions, there had been a clear majority against him and his policy; and yet the House continued its support of his measures. Even the provisions necessary to carry into effect the hated treaty with Great Britain were made by that body, though the vote was close. So powerful were the President's views in determining the actions of the people that Jefferson, writing to Monroe at Paris, said: "Congress has adjourned. You will see by their proceedings the truth of what I always told you, namely, that one man outweighs them all in influence over the people, who support his judgment against their own and that of their representatives. Republicanism resigns the vessel to its pilot."

Washington was solicited to become a candidate for a third election to the presidency; but he would not. His resolution had already been made to end his public career. With the Father of his Country the evening of life drew on, and rest was necessary. Accordingly, in September of 1796, he issued to the people of the United States his Farewell Address—a document crowded with precepts of political wisdom, prudent counsels, and chastened patriotism.[20] As soon as the President's determination was made known the political parties marshaled their forces and put forward their champions, John Adams appearing as the candidate of the Federal, and Thomas Jefferson of the anti-Federal party. Antagonism to the Constitution, which had thus far been the chief question between the parties, now gave place to another issue—whether it was the true policy of the United States to enter into intimate relations with the republic of France. The anti-Federalists said, *Yes!* that all republics have a common end, and that Great Britain was the enemy of them all. The Federalists said, *No!* that the American republic must mark out an independent course among the nations, and avoid all foreign alliances. On that issue Mr. Adams was elected, but Mr. Jefferson, having the next highest number of votes, became Vice-President for according to the old provision of the Constitution, the person who stood second on the list was declared the second officer in the government.

---

[20] See Appendix G

CHAPTER XLVII.

ADAMS'S ADMINISTRATION, 1797-1801.

John Adams.

JOHN ADAMS, second President of the United States, was born in the town of Braintree, Massachusetts, October 19th, 1735. He was a great-grandson of that Henry Adams who, emigrating from Great Britain in 1640, founded in America a family made famous by many illustrious names. Eight sons of the elder Adams settled around Massachusetts Bay, the grandfather of the President in that part of Braintree afterwards called Quincy. The father of John Adams was a Puritan deacon, a selectman of the town, a farmer of small means, and a shoemaker. The son received a classical education, being graduated at the age of twenty from Harvard College. For a while he taught school, but finding that vocation to be, as he expressed it, a school of *affliction*, he turned his attention to the study of law. In this profession he soon became eminent, removed to Boston, engaged with great zeal in the controversy with the mother country, and was quickly recognized as an able leader of public opinion. From this time forth his services were in constant demand both in his native State and in the several colonial Congresses. He was a member of the celebrated committee appointed to draft the Declaration of Independence, and in the debates on that instrument was its chief defender. During the last years of the Revolution he served his country as ambassador to France, Holland, and Great Britain, being the first minister to that country after the recognition of American independence. From this important station he returned in 1788, and was soon afterwards elected Vice-President under the new frame of government. After serving in this office for eight years, he was chosen as the successor of Washington.

On the 4th of March, 1797, President Adams was inaugurated. From the beginning his administration was embarrassed by a powerful and well-organized opposition. Adet, the French minister, made inflammatory appeals to the people, and urged the government to conclude a league with France against Great Britain. When the President and Congress stood firmly on the doctrine of neutrality, the French Directory grew insolent, and began *to demand* an alliance. The treaty which Mr. Jay had concluded with England was especially complained of by the partisans of France. On the 10th of March the Directory issued instructions to French men-of-war to assail the commerce of the United States. Soon afterward Mr. Pinckney, the American minister, was ordered to leave the territory of France.

These proceedings were equivalent to a declaration of war. The President convened Congress in extraordinary session, and measures were devised for repelling the aggressions of the French. Elbridge Gerry and John Marshall were directed to join Mr. Pinckney in a final effort for a peaceable adjustment of the difficulties. But the effort was fruitless. The Directory of France refused to receive the ambassadors except upon condition that they would pledge the payment into the French treasury of a quarter of a million of dollars. Pinckney answered with the declaration that the United States had *millions for defence, but not a cent for tribute.* The envoys were then ordered to leave the country; but Gerry, who was an anti-Federalist, was permitted to remain. These events occupied the summer and fall of 1797.

In the beginning of the next year an act was passed by Congress completing the organization of the army. Washington was called from the retirement of his old age and appointed commander-in-chief. Hamilton was chosen first major-general. A navy of six frigates, besides privateers, had been provided for at the session of the previous year; and a national loan had been authorized. The patriotism of the people was thoroughly aroused; the treaties with France were declared void, and vigorous preparations were made for the impending war. The American frigates put to sea, and in the summer and fall of 1799 did good service for the commerce of the country. Commodore Truxtun, in the ship *Constellation*, won distinguished honors. On the 9th of February, while cruising in the West Indies, he attacked the *Insurgent*, a French man-of-war carrying forty guns and more than four hundred seamen. A desperate engagement ensued; and Truxtun, though inferior in cannons and men, gained a complete victory. A year later he overtook another frigate, called the *Vengeance*, and after a five hours' battle in the night would have captured his antagonist but for a storm and the darkness. These events added greatly to the renown of the American flag.

The organization of the provisional army was soon completed. The commander-in-chief repaired to Philadelphia and remained five weeks with Generals Hamilton and Pinckney, superintending the work. Such measures were taken as were deemed adequate to the defence of the nation, and then Washington retired to Mount Vernon, leaving the greater part of the responsibility to be borne by Hamilton. The news of these warlike proceedings was soon carried to France, and the shrewd Talleyrand, minister of foreign affairs for the French republic, seeing that his dismissal of Mr. Monroe and General Pinckney had given mortal offence to the American people, managed to signify to Vans Murray, ambassador of the United States to Holland, that if President Adams would send *another* minister to Paris he would be cordially received. Murray immediately transmitted this hint to the President, who caught eagerly at this opportunity to extricate the country from apprehended war. On the 18th of February he transmitted a message to the Senate nominating Mr. Murray himself as minister plenipotentiary to the French republic. The nomination was confirmed, and the ambassador was authorized to proceed at once to France. It was also agreed by the Senate that two other persons should be added to the embassy; and Oliver Ellsworth and William R. Davie were accordingly commissioned to proceed to Amsterdam and join Murray in his important mission to the French capital.

Meanwhile, Napoleon Bonaparte had overthrown the Directory of France and made himself first consul of the republic. More wise and politic than his associates in the government, he immediately sought peace with the United States. For he saw clearly enough that the impending war would, if prosecuted, inevitably result in an alliance between America and England—a thing most unfavorable to the interests of France. He was also confident that peaceful overtures on his part would be met with favor. The three American ambassadors—Murray, Ellsworth and Davie—reached Paris, after many delays, in the beginning of March, 1800. Negotiations were at once opened, and, in the following September, were happily terminated with a treaty of peace. In all his relations with the United States Napoleon acted the part of a consistent and honorable ruler.

Before the war-cloud was scattered America was called to mourn the loss of Washington. On the 14th of December, 1799, after an illness of only a day, the venerated chieftain passed from among the living. All hearts were touched with sorrow. The people put on the garb of mourning. Congress went in funeral procession to the German Lutheran church, where General Henry Lee, the personal friend of Washington, delivered a touching and eloquent oration. Throughout the civilized world the memory of the great dead was honored with appropriate ceremonies. To the legions of France the event was announced by Bonaparte, who paid a beautiful tribute to the virtues of "the warrior, the legislator and the citizen without reproach." As the body of Washington was laid in the sepulchre, the voice of partisan malignity that had not hesitated to assail his name was hushed into everlasting silence; and the world with uncovered head agreed with Lord Byron in declaring the illustrious dead to have been among warriors, statesmen and patriots

"–The first, the last, the best,
THE CINCINNATUS OF THE WEST."

The administration of Adams and the eighteenth century drew to a close together. In spite of domestic dissensions and foreign alarms, the new republic was growing strong and influential. The census of 1800 showed that the population of the country, including the black men, had increased to over five millions. The seventy-five post-offices reported by the census of 1790 had been multiplied to nine hundred and three; the experts of the United States had grown from twenty millions to nearly seventy-one millions of dollars. The permanency of the Constitution as the supreme law of the land was now cheerfully recognized. In December of 1800 Congress for the first time assembled in Washington city, the new capital of the nation. Virginia and Maryland had ceded to the United States the District of Columbia, a tract ten miles square lying on both sides of the Potomac; but the part given by Virginia was afterward re-ceded to that State. The city which was designed as the seat of government was laid out in 1792; and in 1800 the population numbered between eight and nine thousand.

With prudent management and unanimity the Federal party might have retained control of the government. But there were dissensions in Mr. Adams's cabinet. Much of the recent legislation of Congress had been unwise and unpopular. The alien law, by which the President was authorized to send out of the country any foreigners whose presence should be considered prejudicial to the interests of the United States, was specially odious. The sedition law, which punished with fine and imprisonment the freedom of speech and of the press when directed abusively against the government, was denounced by the opposition as an act of tyranny. Partisan excitement ran high. Mr. Adams and Mr. Charles C. Pinckney were put forward as the candidates of the Federalists, and Thomas Jefferson and Aaron Burr of the Republicans or Democrats. The latter were triumphant. In the electoral college Jefferson and Burr each received seventy-three votes; Adams, sixty-five; and Pinckney, sixty-four. In order to decide between the Democratic candidates, the election was referred to the House of Representatives. After thirty-five ballotings, the choice fell on Jefferson; and Burr, who was now second on the list, was declared Vice-President. After controlling the government for twelve years, the Federal party passed from power, never to be restored.

CHAPTER XLVIII.

Jefferson's Administration, 1801-1809.

THOMAS JEFFERSON was born in the county of Albemarle, Virginia, on the 2d of April, 1743. Of his ancestry, history has preserved no record other than the name of his father, Colonel Peter Jefferson, a man noted for native abilities and force of character. The son found excellent advantages of early training in the private school of an exiled Scottish clergyman, and afterwards completed his education at William and Mary College. He then entered upon the study of law, and soon rose to distinction. Like his predecessor in the presidential office, he became in his early manhood deeply absorbed in the controversy with the mother country, and by his radical views in the House of Burgesses contributed much to fix forever the sentiments of that body against the arbitrary measures of the English ministry.

Thomas Jefferson.

From the councils of his native State Jefferson was soon called to the councils of the nation. His coming was anxiously awaited in the famous Congress of 1776; for his fame as a thinker and a democrat had preceded him. To *his* pen and brain the almost exclusive authorship of the great Declaration must be awarded. During the struggles of the Revolution he was among the most distinguished and uncompromising of the patriot leaders. After the war was over, he was sent abroad with Adams and Franklin to negotiate treaties of amity and commerce with the European nations, and was then appointed minister plenipotentiary of the new Republic to France. From this high trust he was recalled to become secretary of state under Washington; in 1796 was elected Vice-President, and in 1800 President of the United States. The American decimal system of coinage, the statute for religious freedom, the Declaration of Independence, the University of Virginia, and the presidency of the Union are the immutable foundations of his fame.

At the beginning of his administration Mr. Jefferson transferred the chief offices of the government to members of the Democratic party. This policy had in some measure been adopted by his predecessor; but the principle was now made universal. Such action was justified by the adherents of the President on the ground that the affairs of a republic will be best administered when the officers hold the same political sentiments. One of the first acts of Congress was to abolish the system of internal revenues. The unpopular laws against foreigners and the freedom of the press were also repealed. But the territorial legislation of Jefferson's first term was most important of all.

In the year 1800 a line was drawn through the North-west Territory from the mouth of the Great Miami River to Fort Recovery, and thence to Canada. Two years afterward the country east of this line was erected into the State of Ohio and admitted into the Union. The portion west of the line, embracing the present States of Indiana, Illinois, Wisconsin and a part of Michigan, was organized under the name of THE INDIANA TERRITORY. Vincennes was the capital; and General William Henry Harrison received the appointment of governor. About the same time the organization of THE MISSISSIPPI TERRITORY, extending from the western limits of Georgia to the great river, was completed. Thus another grand and fertile district of a hundred thousand square miles was reclaimed from barbarism.

More important still was the purchase of Louisiana. In 1800 Napoleon had compelled Spain to make secret cession of this vast territory to France. The First Consul then prepared to send an army to New Orleans for the purpose of establishing his authority. But the government of the United States remonstrated against such a proceeding; France was threatened with multiplied wars at home and Bonaparte, seeing the difficulty of maintaining a colonial empire at so great a distance, authorized his minister to dispose of Louisiana by sale. The President appointed Mr. Livingston and James Monroe to negotiate the purchase. On the 30th of April, 1803, the terms of transfer were agreed on by the agents of the two nations; and for the sum of eleven million two hundred and fifty thousand dollars, Louisiana was ceded to the United States.[21] In another convention, which was signed on the same day, it was agreed that the government of the United States should assume the payment of certain debts due from France to American citizens; but the sum thus assumed should not, inclusive of interest, exceed three million seven hundred and fifty thousand dollars. Thus did the vast domain west of the Mississippi, embracing an area of more than a million square miles, pass under the dominion of the United States.

Four nations—France, the United States, Great Britain, and Spain—were concerned in determining the boundaries of the ceded territory. In regard to the eastern limit, all were agreed that it should be the Mississippi from its source to the thirty-first parallel of latitude. On the south-east the boundary claimed by the United States, Great Britain, and France, was the thirty-first parallel from the Mississippi to the Appalachicola, and down that river to the Gulf. From this line, however, Spain dissented, claiming the Iberville and Lakes Maurepas and Pontchartrain as the true limit between Louisiana and her possessions in West Florida; but she was obliged, after fruitlessly protesting, to yield to the decision of her rivals. On the south, by the consent of all, the boundary was the Gulf of Mexico as far west as the mouth of the Sabine. The south-western limit was established along the last named river as far as the thirty-first parallel thence due north to Red River; up that stream to the one-hundredth meridian from Greenwich; thence north again to the Arkansas; thence with that river to the mountains; and thence north

---

[21] Bonaparte accepted in payment six per cent bonds of the United States, payable fifteen years after date. He also agreed not to sell the bonds at such a price as would degrade the credit of the American government.

with the mountain chain to the forty-second parallel of latitude. Thus far all four of the nations were agreed. But the United States, Great Britain, and France—again coinciding—claimed the extension of the boundary along the forty-second parallel to the Pacific Ocean; and to this extension Spain, for several years, refused her assent; but in the treaty of 1819 her objections were formally withdrawn. In fixing the northern boundary only the United States and Great Britain were concerned; and the forty-ninth parallel from the Lake of the Woods to the Pacific was established as the international line.[22]

Inauguration of the Territorial Government Marietta, Ohio.

---

[22] See Map VII. The discussion of the boundaries of Louisiana is thus fully given because of the many statements, needlessly contradictory, which have been made on the subject. Between the years 1803 and 1819 there was some ground for controversy, but since the latter date none whatever–except as to the northern line. For all the facts tending to elucidate the subject, see *American State Papers*; topics: Treaty of Paris, 1763; Definitive Treaty between Great Britain and the United States, 1783; Text of the Louisiana Cession, 1803; Boundary Conventions between the United States and Great Britain, 1818 and 1846; Treaty of Washington, 1819. See also Walker's *Statistical Atlas of the United States*; subject: Areas and Political Divisions, pp. 2 and 3; and the *American Cyclopædia*; article: Louisiana.

The purchase of Louisiana was the greatest event of Jefferson's administration. Out of the southern portion of the new acquisition the TERRITORY OF ORLEANS was organized, with the same limits as the present State of Louisiana; the rest of the vast tract continued to be called THE TERRITORY OF LOUISIANA. The possession of the Mississippi was no longer a matter of dispute. Very justly did Mr. Livingston say to the French minister as they arose from signing the treaty: "We have lived long, but this is the noblest work of our whole lives."

Two years previous to these events John Marshall had been nominated and confirmed as chief-justice of the United States. His appointment marks an epoch in the history of the country. In the colonial times the English constitution and common law had prevailed in America, and judicial decisions were based exclusively on precedents established in English courts. When, in 1789, the new republic was organized, it became necessary to modify to a certain extent the principles of jurisprudence and to adapt them to the altered theory of government. In some measure this great work was undertaken by Chief-Justice Jay; but he was a great statesman rather than a great judge. It remained for Chief-Justice Marshall to establish on a firm and enduring basis the noble structure of American law. For thirty-five years he remained in his high office, bequeathing to after times a great number of valuable decisions, in which the principles of the jurisprudence of the United States are forth with unvarying clearness and invincible logic.

Chief-Justice Marshall.

The Mediterranean pirates still annoyed American merchantmen. All of the Barbary States—as the Moorish kingdoms of Northern Africa are called—had adopted the plan of extorting annual tributes from the European nations. The emperors of Morocco, Algiers and Tripoli became especially arrogant. In 1803 the government of the United States despatched Commodore Preble to the Mediterranean to protect American commerce and punish the hostile powers. The armament proceeded first against Morocco; but the frigate *Philadelphia*, commanded by Captain Bainbridge, was sent directly to Tripoli. When nearing his destination, Bainbridge gave chase to a pirate which fled for safety to the batteries of the harbor. The *Philadelphia*, in close pursuit, ran upon a reef of rocks near the shore, became unmanageable, and was captured by the Tripolitans. The crew and officers were taken; the latter were treated with some respect, but the former were enslaved. The emperor Yusef and his barbarous subjects were greatly elated at their unexpected success.

In the following February Captain Decatur recaptured the *Philadelphia* in a marvelous manner. Sailing from Sicily in a small vessel called the *Intrepid*, he came at nightfall in sight of the harbor of Tripoli, where the *Philadelphia* was moored. The *Intrepid*, being a Moorish ship which the American fleet had captured, was either unseen or unsuspected by the Tripolitans. As darkness settled on the sea, Decatur steered his course into the harbor, slipped alongside of the *Philadelphia*, lashed the two ships together, sprang on deck with his daring crew of only seventy-four men, and killed or drove overboard every Moor on the vessel. In a moment the frigate was fired, for it was the purpose to destroy her; then Decatur and his men, escaping from the flames, returned to the *Intrepid* and sailed out of the harbor amid a storm of balls from the Tripolitan batteries. Not a man of Decatur's gallant band was lost, and only four were wounded.

In the last of July, 1804, Commodore Preble arrived with his fleet at Tripoli and began a blockade and siege which lasted till the following spring. The town was frequently bombarded, and several Moorish vessels were destroyed; but not even the pounding of American cannon-balls was sufficient to bring Yusef to terms. In the meantime, however, it was ascertained that the services of Hamet, Yusef's elder brother, the deposed sovereign of Tripoli, might be secured to aid in reducing the barbarians to submission. Hamet was at this time in Upper Egypt, commanding an army of Mamelukes in a war against the Turks. To him General William Eaton, the American consul at Tunis, was despatched with proposals of an alliance against the usurping Yusef. Hamet eagerly accepted the overture, and furnished General Eaton with a fine body of Arab cavalry and seventy Greek soldiers. With this force the American commander set out from Alexandria on the 5th of March, 1805. He traversed the Desert of Barca for a thousand miles, and on the 25th of April reached Derne, one of Yusef's eastern sea-ports. Yusef himself was already approaching with an army; and General Eaton found it necessary to storm the town. A division of the American fleet arrived in the harbor at the fortunate moment and aided in the work. The place was gallantly carried. The assaulting column was made up of Arab cavalry, Greek infantry, Tripolitan rebels, and American sailors serving on land! The Stars and Stripes never before or since waved over so motley an assemblage! Yusef, alarmed at the dangers which menaced him by sea and land, made hasty overtures for peace. His offers were accepted by Mr. Lear, the American consul-general for the Barbary States; and a treaty was concluded on the 4th of June, 1805.[23] For several years thereafter the flag of the United States was respected in the Mediterranean.

In the summer of 1804 the country was shocked by the intelligence that Vice-President Burr had killed Alexander Hamilton in a duel. As the first term of Mr. Jefferson drew to a close, Burr foresaw that the President would be renominated, and that he himself would *not* be renominated. Still, he had his eye on the presidency, and was determined not to be baffled. He therefore, while holding the office of Vice-President, became a candidate for governor of New York. From that position he would pass to the presidency at the close of Jefferson's second term. But Hamilton's powerful influence in New York prevented Burr's election; and his presidential ambition received a stunning blow. From that day he determined to kill the man whom he

---

[23] It is a matter of astonishment that Lear agreed to pay Yusef sixty thousand dollars for the liberation of American slaves: their liberation ought to have been *compelled*– and might have been if Lear had said so.

pretended to regard as the destroyer of his hopes. He accordingly sought a quarrel with Hamilton; challenged him; met him at Weehawken, opposite New York, on the morning of the 11th of July, and deliberately murdered him; for Hamilton had tried to avoid the challenge, and when face to face with his antagonist refused to fire. Thus under the savage and abominable custom of dueling the brightest intellect in America was put out in darkness.

In the autumn of 1804 Jefferson was re-elected President. For Vice-President George Clinton of New York was chosen in place of Burr. In the following year that part of the North-western Territory called Wayne county was organized under a separate territorial government with the name of MICHIGAN. In the same spring, Captains Lewis and Clarke, acting under orders of the President, set out from the falls of the Missouri River with a party of thirty-five soldiers and hunters to cross the Rocky Mountains and explore Oregon. Not until November did they reach their destination. For two years, through forests of gigantic pines, along the banks of unknown rivers and down to the shores of the Pacific, did they continue their explorations. After wandering among unheard-of tribes of barbarians, encountering grizzly bears more ferocious than Bengal tigers, escaping perils by forest and flood, and traversing a route of six thousand miles, the hardy adventurers, with the loss of but one man, returned to civilization, bringing new ideas of the vast domains of the West.

After the death of Hamilton, Burr fled from popular indignation and sought refuge in the South. At the opening of the next session of Congress he returned to the capital, and presided over the Senate until the expiration of his term of office. Then he delivered his valedictory, went to the West, and, after traveling through several States, took up his residence with an Irish exile named Harman Blannerhassett, who had laid out an estate and built a splendid mansion on an island in the Ohio, just below the mouth of the Muskingum. Here Burr made a wicked and treasonable scheme against the peace and happiness of the country. His plan was to raise a sufficient military force, invade Mexico, wrest that country from the Spaniards, detach the Western and Southern States from the Union, make himself dictator of a South-western empire, and perhaps subvert the government of the United States. For two years he labored to perfect his plans. But his purposes were suspected. In accordance with a proclamation of the President, the military preparations at Blannerhassett's Island were broken up; and in February of 1807 Burr himself was arrested in Alabama and taken to Richmond to be tried on a charge of treason. Chief-Justice Marshall presided at the trial, and Burr conducted his own defence. The verdict was, "Not guilty, for want of sufficient proof." But his escape was so narrow that under an assumed name he fled from the country. Returning a few years afterward, he resumed the practice of law in New York, lived to extreme old age, and died alone in abject poverty.

During Jefferson's second administration the country was constantly agitated by the aggressions of the British navy on American commerce. England and France were engaged in deadly and continuous war. In order to cripple the resources of their enemy, the British authorities struck blow after blow against the trade between France and foreign nations; and Napoleon retaliated with equal energy and vindictiveness against the commerce of Great Britain. The measures adopted by the two powers took the form of blockade—that is, the surrounding of each other's ports with men-of-war to prevent the ingress and egress of neutral ships. By such means the commerce of the United States, which had grown vast and valuable while the European nations were fighting, was greatly injured and distressed.

In May of 1806 England declared the whole coast of France from Brest to the Elbe to be in a state of blockade. Neutral nations had no warning. Many American vessels, approaching the French ports, were seized and condemned as prizes; all this, too, while the harbors of France were not actually, but only declared to be, blockaded. In the following November Bonaparte issued a decree blockading the British isles. Again the unsuspecting merchantmen of the United States were subjected to seizure, this time by the cruisers of France. In January of the next year the government of Great Britain retaliated by an act prohibiting the French coasting-trade. Every one of these measures was in flagrant violations of the laws of nations. The belligerent powers had no right to take such steps toward each other; as to neutral States, their rights were utterly disregarded; and the nation that suffered most was the United States.

In addition to these causes of complaint an old crime against international law had, in the mean time, been revived by the English government, to the great distress of American commerce. At the outbreak of the French and Indian War George II. had issued an edict forbidding the vessels of neutral nations to trade with the colonies of France or the provinces of any other country with which Great Britain might be at war. The offences committed under the authority of this arbitrary decree, which was known as THE RULE OF 1756, had been greatly injurious to the commerce of the colonies, and during Washington's administration had occasioned many complaints and remonstrances. But in June of 1801, in a treaty between Great Britain and Russia, the former government assented to such a modification of the Rule as rendered it comparatively harmless. The effect of this modification was exceedingly beneficial to neutral nations, especially to America. Between the years 1803 and 1806 the foreign carrying trade of the United States was increased nearly fivefold, while that of England fell off in a nearly corresponding ratio. Vexed and mortified at this result, and caring little for justice if the supremacy of the British merchant-marine could be maintained, the ministry, in the summer of 1805, revived the old edict in full force, and impudently asserted that it was *a part of the law of nations!* The result, as had been clearly foreseen by the English lords of trade who contrived the measure, was that American merchantmen trading largely with the dependencies of France and Spain, were driven from the ocean, and the commerce of the United States shrank suddenly into insignificance.

Finally Great Britain aggravated her injustice by a still more arrogant and unwarrantable procedure. The English theory of citizenship is, that whoever is born in England remains through life a subject of the British Empire. The privilege of an Englishman to expatriate himself—that is, the right to go abroad, to throw off his allegiance to the British crown, and to assume the obligations of citizenship in another nation—is absolutely denied. Under this iron rule of "once an Englishman, always an Englishman," the British cruisers were from time to time authorized to search American vessels and to take therefrom all persons suspected of being subjects of Great Britain. One of the chief objects had in view in this iniquitous business was to prevent the emigration of the Irish to the United States. The impulsive sons of the Emerald Isle, hearing of the free institutions and boundless prospects of America, were flocking hither in great numbers, and something must be done to stop the movement. George III. and his advisers therefore marshaled forth their despotic theory of citizenship and set it up like a death's-head at every port of the British Isles. Inasmuch as every Irishman or Scotchman who ventured on board an American vessel would expose himself to the peril of seizure and impressment, it was, with good reason, believed that not many would take the fearful risk. And the apprehensions of the emigrants were well founded; for all those who had the misfortune to be over taken at sea were, without inquiry, impressed as marines in the English navy. To crowd the decks of their men-of-war with unwilling recruits, torn from home and friends, was the end which the British king and ministry were willing to reach at whatever sacrifice of national honor. Finally to these general wrongs was added a special act of violence which kindled the indignation of the Americans to the highest pitch.

On the 22d of June, 1807, a frigate, named the *Chesapeake* which had just sailed out of the bay of the same name, was approached by a British man-of-war, called the *Leopard*. The frigate was hailed; British officers came on board as friends, and then, to the astonishment of Commodore Barron, who commanded the *Chesapeake*, made a demand to search the vessel for deserters. The demand was indignantly refused and the ship cleared for action. But before the guns could be gotten in readiness, the *Leopard* poured in several destructive broadsides and compelled a surrender. Four men were taken from the captured ship, three of whom proved to be American citizens; the fourth, who was an actual deserter, was tried by the British naval officers and hanged. The government of Great Britain disavowed the outrage of the *Leopard*, and promised reparation; but the promise was never fulfilled.

The President at once issued a proclamation forbidding British ships of war to enter the harbors of the United States. Still, there was no reparation; and on the 21st of December Congress passed the celebrated

EMBARGO ACT. By its provisions all American vessels were detained in the ports of the United States. The object was, by cutting of commercial intercourse with France and Great Britain, to compel them to recognize the rights of American neutrality. But the measure was of little avail; and after fourteen months the embargo act was repealed.[24] Meanwhile, in November of 1808, the British government outdid all previous proceedings by issuing an "order in council," prohibiting *all* trade with France and her allies. And Napoleon, not to be outdone, issued his famous "Milan decree," forbidding all commerce with England and her colonies. Between these outrageous acts of foreign nations and the American embargo, the commerce of the United States was well-nigh crushed out of existence.

Robert Fulton.

While the country was distracted with these troubles Robert Fulton was building THE FIRST STEAMBOAT. This event exercised a vast influence on the future development of the nation. It was of the first importance to the people of the inland States that their great rivers should be enlivened with rapid and regular navigation. This, without the application of steam, was impossible; and this Fulton successfully accomplished. Indeed, the steam boat was the harbinger of a new era in civilization. Fulton was an Irishman by descent and a Pennsylvanian by birth. His education was meagre and imperfect. In his boyhood he became a

---

[24] The embargo act was the subject of much ridicule. The opponents of the measure spelling the word backward, called it the *O Grab me* act.

painter of miniatures at Philadelphia. His friends sent him to London to receive instruction from Benjamin West; but his tastes led him to the useful rather than to the fine arts. From London he went to Paris, where he became acquainted with Chancellor Livingston; and there he conceived the project of applying steam to the purposes of navigation. Returning to New York, he began the construction of a steamboat in East River. When the ungainly craft was completed and brought around to the Jersey side of the city, Fulton invited his friends to go on board and enjoy a trip to Albany. It was the 2d of September, 1807. The incredulous crowds stood staring on the shore. The word was given, and the boat did not move. Fulton went below. Again the word was given, and this time *the boat moved.* On the next day the happy company reached Albany. For many years this first rude steamer, called the *Clermont,* plied the Hudson. The old methods of river navigation were revolutionized.

But the inventive genius of Fulton was by no means satisfied with the great achievement. For years his thoughts had been busy with another project which was considered by himself of greater value and importance to the future interests of mankind than the steamboat. His object was to produce some kind of an engine, so destructive to ships as *to banish naval warfare by making it possible for anyone to destroy the most formidable vessels which could be constructed.* Finally his plans were matured, and the result was the invention of that submarine bomb, called THE TORPEDO, which has played so important a part in the bay and river battles of modern times. This terrible machine is as distinctly and certainly the fruit of Fulton's brain as is steam navigation itself; but the result has hardly met the expectations of the inventor. As early as 1804, having completed the invention at Paris, he offered it successively to the governments of France, Holland, and Great Britain; but neither nation would accept the patronage of so dangerous an engine. In England a public demonstration of its destructive effects was given in the presence of British statesmen and men of science.[25] On the 15th of October, in Walmer Roads, within sight of the residence of William Pitt,

---

[25] Colonel Congreve, inventor of the "Congreve Rocket," was present on the occasion.

the Danish brig *Dorothea*, which had been given by the government for that purpose, was blown to atoms on the first trial. But, although the success of the torpedo was manifest, the English ministry refused to accept the invention on the ground that Great Britain, already mistress of the seas, did not need torpedoes, and that their use by other nations would destroy her supremacy. Logic of habitual selfishness! In 1807, and again in 1810, Fulton offered his invention to the United States, and in the latter year received an appropriation of five thousand dollars for further experiments. Such was the terror inspired by the torpedo that, although it was not very successfully used in the war that ensued, the British cruisers were notably shy of the American coast, and many a seaport town was saved from destruction.

Jefferson's administration drew to a close. The territorial area of the United States had been vastly extended. Burr's wicked and dangerous conspiracy had come to naught. Pioneers were pouring into the valley of the Mississippi. Explorers had crossed the mountains of the great West. The woods by the river-shores resounded with the cry of steam. But the foreign relations of the United States were troubled and gloomy. There were forebodings of war. The President, following the example of Washington, declined a third election, and was succeeded in his high office by James Madison of Virginia. For Vice-President George Clinton was re-elected.

CHAPTER XLIX.

MADISON'S ADMINISTRATION, AND WAR OF 1812.

JAMES MADISON, fourth President of the United States, was born at King George, Virginia, on the 16th of March, 1751. He was educated first in a private school and afterwards at Princeton College, where he was graduated at the age of twenty. Devoting himself to the profession of the law, he found time for extensive reading and a profound study of morals, metaphysics, and polite literature. From these pursuits, so congenial to his disposition, his sterling patriotism called him to take an active part in the struggles of the Revolution. In the councils of his own State and afterwards in the Continental Congress his influence was marked and powerful. But of all the patriot leaders Madison had the calmest and least aggressive spirit. Not by oratory and vehemence of passion, but by philosophy and cogent argument, did he mould the opinions of his fellow-men. It was he who, in 1786, secured the passage by the legislature of Virginia of the resolution, suggested by Washington, calling for a convention of the States at Annapolis—a work which resulted in the formation of the Federal Constitution. Afterwards, with Hamilton and Jay, he defended that great instrument in the *Federalist*; but with the new division of parties, his views underwent a change and he joined himself with the Jeffersonian school of statesmen. For eight years he held the office of secretary of state; and on the 4th of March, 1809,

James Madison.

was inaugurated as Jefferson's successor in the presidency. He owed his election to the Democratic party, whose sympathy with France and hostility to the policy of Great Britain were well known. Three days before the new administration came into power, the embargo act was repealed by Congress; but another measure was adopted instead, called the non-intercourse act. By its terms American merchantmen were allowed to go abroad, but were forbidden to trade with Great Britain. Mr. Erskine, the British minister, now gave notice that by the 10th of June the "orders in council," so far as they affected the United States, should be repealed. But the British government disavowed the act of its agent; and the orders stood as before.

In the following spring the emperor of the French issued a decree authorizing the seizure of all American vessels that might approach the ports of France or other harbors held by his troops. But in November of the same year the hostile decree was reversed, and all restrictions on the commerce of the United States were removed. If Great Britain had acted with equal liberality and justice, there would have been no further complaint. But that government, with peculiar obstinacy, adhered to its former measures, and sent ships of war to hover around the American ports and enforce the odious orders issued in the previous years. It was only a question of time when such insolence would lead to retaliation and war.

The affairs of the two nations were fast approaching a crisis. It became more and more apparent that the wrongs perpetrated by Great Britain against the United States would have to be corrected by force of arms. That England, after such a career of arrogance, would now make reparation for the outrages committed by her navy was no longer to be hoped for. The ministry of that same George III. with whom the colonies had struggled in the Revolution still directed the affairs of the kingdom; from him, now grown old and insane, nothing was to be expected. The government of the United States had fallen completely under control of the party which sympathized with France, while the Federal party, from its leaning toward British interests and institutions, grew weaker year by year. The American people, smarting under the insults of Great Britain, had adopted the motto of FREE TRADE AND

SAILORS' RIGHTS, and for that motto they had made up their minds to fight. The elections, held between 1808 and 1811, showed conclusively the drift of public opinion; the sentiment of the country was that war was preferable to further humiliation and disgrace.

In the spring of 1810 the third census of the United States was completed. The population had increased to seven million two hundred and forty thousand souls. The States now numbered seventeen, and several new Territories were preparing for admission into the Union. The resources of the nation were abundant; its institutions deeply rooted and flourishing. But with the rapid march of civilization westward the jealousy of the Red man was aroused, and Indiana Territory was afflicted with an Indian war.

The Shawnees were the leading tribe in the country between the Ohio and the Wabash. Their chief was the famous Tecumtha, a brave and sagacious warrior; and with him was joined his brother Elkswatawa, called the Prophet. The former was a man of real genius; the latter, a vile impostor who pretended to have revelations from the spirit-world. But they both worked together in a common cause; and their plan was to unite all the nations of the North-west Territory in a final effort to beat back the whites. When, therefore, in September of 1809, Governor Harrison met the chiefs of several tribes at Fort Wayne, and honorably purchased the Indian titles to three million acres of land, Tecumtha refused to sign the treaty, and threatened death to those who did. In the year that followed he visited the nations as far south as Tennessee and exhorted them to lay aside their sectional jealousies, in the hope of saving their hunting-grounds.

Governor Harrison from Vincennes, the capital of the Territory, remonstrated with Tecumtha and the Prophet, held several conferences with them, and warned them of what would follow from their proceedings. Still, the leaders insisted that they would have back the lands which had been ceded by the treaty of Fort Wayne. The governor stood firm, sent for a few companies of soldiers and mustered the militia of the Territory. The Indians began to prowl through the Wabash Valley, murdering and stealing. In order to secure the country and enforce the terms of the treaty, Harrison advanced up the river to Terra

Haute, built a fort which received his own name, passed on to Montezuma, where another block-house was built, and then hastened toward the town of the Prophet, at the mouth of the Tippecanoe. When within a few miles of his destination, Harrison was met by Indian ambassadors, who asked for the appointment of a conference on the following day. Their request was granted; and the American army encamped for the night. The place selected was a piece of high ground covered with oaks. Burnet Creek skirted the encampment on the west. Beyond that, as well as to the east of the oak grove, were prairie marshlands covered with tall grass. Before daybreak on the following morning, 7th of November, 1811, the treacherous savages, numbering seven hundred, crept through the marshes, surrounded Harrison's position and burst upon the camp like demons. But the American militia were under arms in a moment, and fighting in the darkness, held the Indians in check until daylight, and then routed them in several vigorous charges. On the next day the Americans burned the Prophet's town and soon afterward returned victorious to Vincennes. Tecumtha was in the South at the time of the battle; when he returned and found his people scattered and subdued, he repaired to Canada and joined the standard of the British.

Meanwhile, the powers of Great Britain and the United States had come into conflict on the ocean. On the 16th of May Commodore Rodgers, cruising in the American frigate *President*, hailed a vessel off the coast of Virginia. Instead of a polite answer, to his salutation, he received a cannon-ball in the mainmast. Other shots followed, and Rodgers responded with a broadside, silencing the enemy's guns. In the morning—for it was already dark—the hostile ship was found to be the British sloop-of-war *Little Belt*. The vessel had been severely though justly punished by the *President*, having eleven men killed and twenty-one wounded. The event produced great excitement throughout the country.

On the 4th of November, 1811, the twelfth Congress of the United States assembled. In the body were many men of marked ability and patriotism. John C. Calhoun of South Carolina now took his seat as a member of the House of Representatives. Henry Clay, already distinguished as a statesman, was chosen speaker. From the first it was seen that war was inevitable. It was impossible for the United States, knowing that more than six thousand American citizens had been impressed into the British navy, to endure, without dishonor, further injury and insolence. Still, many hoped for peace; and the winter passed without decisive measures. The President himself had no disposition and little capacity for war; and his various messages to Congress were marked as the productions of a ruler over-cautious and timid. But not so with the fiery leaders of the Democracy who supported the President's administration; and notwithstanding the opposition of the Federalists, the war-spirit fired the popular heart.

In the mean time a transaction was brought to light which created intense excitement and roused the indignation of the whole country. On the night of the 2d of February, 1812, an Irishman, named John Henry, now a naturalized citizen of the United States, called at the President's mansion and revealed to him the astounding fact that the ministry of Great Britain, cooperating with Sir James Craig, governor of Canada, *had been engaged for some years in a treasonable scheme to destroy the American Union!* Henry bore a letter from Governor Gerry of Massachusetts, and all the documents necessary to prove the truth of his statements. As early as 1808 the attention of the Canadian governor had been called to certain published articles written by Henry against republican governments; and the latter was summoned to Montreal. From him Craig learned of the intense hostility of the Federal party to the administration and of the great distress of New England on account of the Embargo and other restrictions on commerce. These facts were communicated to the British ministry, and Sir James promised Henry an annual salary of five thousand dollars to return to Boston and become the secret agent of England and Canada.

The purpose of the conspirators was to aggravate the popular discontent of New England until the Eastern States should be induced to secede from the Union and join themselves with Canada. But with the repeal of the Embargo and the subsidence of political excitement, Henry found the depravity of his business only equaled by its unprofitableness. The people of Massachusetts were in no humor to be led into a rebellion. Sir James Craig died, and Henry, unsuccessful and unpaid, went, in 1811, to London and presented his claim for thirty thousand pounds to the English ministers. By them he was well received; but the payment of thirty thousand pounds for services which had resulted in nothing was reckoned a serious matter; and Henry was sent back to get whatever remuneration he could from Sir George Prevost, the successor of Craig in the governorship of Canada. Enraged at his treatment, the spy, instead of returning to Montreal, sailed to Boston, and going thence to Washington divulged the whole conspiracy to the President, surrendered his correspondence with Craig, and received therefor fifty thousand dollars out of the secret service fund of the United States. The disclosure of this perfidious business contributed greatly to consolidate public sentiment against Great Britain and to strengthen the hands of the war party in the government.

On the 4th of April, 1812, an act was passed by Congress laying an embargo for ninety days on all British vessels within the jurisdiction of the United States. But Great Britain would not recede from her hostile attitude. One of the ministers declared that it was "an ancient and well-established right" of His Majesty's government to impress British seamen on board of neutral vessels. Before the final decision of England was known, Louisiana, the eighteenth State, was, on the 8th of April, admitted into the Union. The area of the new commonwealth was more than forty-one thousand square miles; and her population, according to the census of 1810, had reached seventy-seven thousand.

On the 4th of June a resolution declaring war against Great Britain was passed by the House of Representatives. On the 17th of the same month the bill received the sanction of the Senate; and two days afterward the President issued his proclamation of war. Vigorous preparations for the impending conflict were made by Congress. It was ordered to raise twenty-five thousand regular troops and fifty thousand volunteers. At the same time the several States were requested to call out a hundred thousand militia for the defence of the coasts and harbors. A national loan of eleven million dollars was authorized. Henry Dearborn of Massachusetts was chosen first major general and commander-in-chief of the army.

Great Britain was already prepared for the conflict. Her armies in Europe were immense and thoroughly equipped. Napoleon just at this time began his famous invasion of Russia, and the allied nations of Western Europe were for a while relieved of their apprehensions. The British navy amounted to no less than a thousand and thirty-six vessels. Of these there were two hundred and fifty-four ships-of-the-line, not one of which carried less than seventy-four guns of large caliber. At various stations on the American coast there were eighty-five war-vessels bearing the English flag, and ready for immediate action. Lake Ontario was commanded by four British brigs carrying an aggregate of sixty guns. The Canadian armies of England amounted to seven thousand five hundred regulars and forty thousand militia. Back of all these forces and armaments stood the seemingly inexhaustible British treasury, with the ambitious young Lord Castlereagh and his associate ministers to disburse it. As to George III., old age and incurable insanity had at last prevailed to displace him from the throne and to make the Prince Regent, George IV., the actual sovereign. In all that appertained to preparation and readiness for the conflict the United States bore no comparison to the powerful foe.

The first movement of the war was made by General William Hull, governor of Michigan Territory. A force of twelve hundred Ohio volunteers, together with three hundred regulars, was organized at Dayton for the purpose of overawing the Indians on the north-western frontier. Hull was also authorized, should circumstances warrant such a course, to invade and conquer Canada. The march began on the 1st of June; and it was a full month before the army, toiling through more than two hundred 1812 miles of forests, reached the western extremity of Lake Erie. Arriving at the Maumee, Hull despatched his baggage, stores and official papers in a boat to Detroit. But the British forces posted at Malden had already been informed of the declaration of hostilities; and Hull's boat with everything on board was captured. Nevertheless, the American army pressed on to Detroit, where early in July the general received despatches informing him of the declaration of war, and directing him to proceed with the invasion of Canada. On the 12th of the month he crossed the Detroit River to Sandwich with the avowed purpose of capturing Malden. And this might easily have been accomplished had not the inefficiency of the general checked the enthusiasm of the army.

Scene of Hull's Campaign, 1812.

Meanwhile, the news came that the American post at Mackinaw had been surprised and captured by the British. This intelligence furnished Hull a good excuse for recrossing the river to Detroit. Here he received intelligence that Major Brush, sent forward by Governor Meigs of Ohio, was approaching with reinforcements and supplies. Major Van Horne was accordingly despatched with a body of troops to meet Brush at the

River Raisin and conduct him safely to Detroit. But Tecumtha, assisted by some British troops, had cut the lines of communication and laid an ambush for Van Horne's forces in the neigborhood of Brownstown. The scheme was successful; Van Horne ran into the trap and was severely defeated. Any kind of energetic movement on Hull's part would have retrieved the disaster; but energy was altogether wanting; and when, three days later, Colonel Miller with another detachment attacked and routed the savages with great loss, he was hastily recalled to Detroit. The officers and men lost all faith in the commander, and there were symptoms of a mutiny.

In the mean time, General Brock, the governor of Upper Canada, arrived at Malden and took command of the British forces. Acting in conjunction with Tecumtha, he crossed the river, and on the 16th of August advanced to the siege of Detroit. The Americans in their trenches outside of the fort were eager for battle, and stood with lighted matches awaiting the order to fire. When the British were within five hundred yards, to the amazement of both armies Hull hoisted a white flag over the fort. There was a brief parley and then a surrender, perhaps the most shameful in the history of the United States. Not only the army in Detroit, but all the forces under Hull's command, became prisoners of war. The whole of Michigan Territory was surrendered to the British. At the capitulation the American officers in rage and despair stamped the ground, broke their swords and tore off their epaulets. The whole country was humiliated at the disgraceful business. The government gave thirty British prisoners in exchange for Hull, and he was brought before a court-martial charged with treason, cowardice and conduct unbecoming an officer. He was convicted on the last two charges, and sentenced to be shot; but the President, having compassion on one who had served the country in the Revolution, pardoned him. After all the discussions that have been had on Hull and his campaign, the best that can be said of him is that he was a patriot and a coward.

About the time of the fall of Detroit, Fort Dearborn, on the present site of Chicago, was invested by an army of Indians. The garrison was feeble, and the commandant proposed a surrender on condition that his men should retire without molestation. This was agreed to; but the savages, finding that the garrison had destroyed the whisky that was in the fort, fell upon the retreating soldiers, killed some of them, and distributed the rest as captives. On the day after the capitulation Fort Dearborn was burned to the ground.

These losses, however, were more than compensated by the brilliant achievements of the young American navy. From the first it became apparent that the war was destined to be a conflict on the sea-coast and the ocean. The United States would act for the most part on the defensive, and Great Britain would rely chiefly upon her navy. The condition of both nations was such as to provoke this sort of warfare. On the one side was the British armament superior to any other in the world, and on the other an exposed sea-coast, a few fortresses, and a navy of almost insignificant proportions. From the beginning, the policy of the American government had been distinctly declared against a standing army and a regular fleet. It was held that a citizen soldiery and an extemporized flotilla would be sufficient for every emergency. A large military establishment, said the defenders of the American system, is enormously expensive and a constant menace to civil liberty. After the Revolution, especially during the administration of Jefferson, the military spirit was discouraged and the defenses of the country fell into decay. In 1808 the whole coast of Maine was defended only by Fort Sumner, at Portland. New Hampshire had but one fortress, a half ruined block-house at Portsmouth. On the coast of Massachusetts four fortifications—one at Cape Ann, one at Salem, one at Marblehead, and Fort Independence in Boston Harbor furnished the only security against attack. In the neighborhood of Newport, Rhode Island, there were six works, some of importance, others insignificant. New London, Connecticut, was defended by Fort Trumbull, a block-house of considerable strength but in bad repair. On Governor's Island, in New York Harbor, stood Fort Jay, which, together with the Battery at the south end of Manhattan and some slight fortifications on Ellis's and Bedloe's Islands, furnished a tolerable protection. The whole coast of New Jersey lay open to invasion. On Mud Island in the Delaware, a short distance below Philadelphia, stood the formidable Fort Mifflin, an old British fort of the Revolution. Not less in strength and importance was

Fort McHenry on the Patapsco, commanding the approach to Baltimore. Annapolis was defended by Fort Severn, then only a group of breast-works. Norfolk, Virginia, relied for protection on a fort of the same name and another work, called Fort Nelson, on the opposite side of Elizabeth River. In Charleston Harbor stood Fort Johnson on James's Islam, Fort Pinckney in front of the city, and Fort Moultrie of Revolutionary fame. Upon these scattered fortifications and the terror inspired by Fulton's torpedoes the Americans must depend for the defense of a coast-line reaching from Passamaquoddy to the St. Mary's.

Such was the attitude and relative strength of the two nations. Great, therefore, was the astonishment of the world when the American sailors, not waiting to be attacked, went forth without a tremor to smite the mistress of the seas. And greater the admiration when a series of brilliant victories declared for the flag of the Republic. During the summer of 1812 the navy of the United States won a just and lasting renown. On the 19th of August the frigate *Constitution*, commanded by Captain Isaac Hull, overtook the British ship-of-war *Guerriere*, off the coast of Massachusetts. Captain Dacres, who commanded the British vessel, had been boasting of his prowess and sending challenges to American vessels to come out and fight; now there was an opportunity to exhibit his valor. The vessels manœuvred for a while, the *Constitution* closing with her antagonist, until at half-pistol shot she poured in a terrible broadside, sweeping the decks of the *Guerriere* and deciding the contest. Dacres, after losing fifteen men killed and sixty-three wounded, struck his colors and surrendered his shattered vessel as a prize. The American loss was seven killed and an equal number wounded. On the following morning the *Guerriere*, being unmanageable, was blown up; and Hull returned to port with his prisoners and spoils.

On the 18th of October the American sloop-of-war *Wasp*, of eighteen guns, under command of Captain Jones, fell in with a fleet of British merchantmen off the coast of Virginia. The squadron was under convoy of the brig *Frolic*, of twenty-two guns, commanded by Captain Whinyates, who put his vessel between the merchantmen and the *Wasp*, and prepared for battle. A terrible engagement ensued, lasting for three-quarters of an hour. Both ships became nearly helpless; but the *Wasp* closed with her foe and delivered a final broadside which completely cleared the deck. The American crew then boarded the *Frolic* and struck the British flag; for not a seaman was left above deck to perform that service. Scarcely had the smoke of the conflict cleared away when the *Poictiers*, a British seventy-four gun ship, bore down upon the scene, captured the *Wasp* and retook the wreck of the *Frolic*. But the fame of Captain Jones's victory was not dimmed by the catastrophe.

Seven days afterward Commodore Decatur, commanding the frigate *United States*, of forty-four guns, attacked the British frigate *Macedonia*, of forty-nine guns. The battle was fought a short distance west of the Canary Islands. After a two hours' engagement, in which the *United States* was but little injured, the *Macedonia* surrendered, with a loss in killed and wounded of more than a hundred men. On the 12th of December the ship *Essex*, commanded by Captain Porter, captured the *Nocton*, a British packet, having on board fifty-five thousand dollars in specie. More important still was the capture of the frigate *Java* by the *Constitution*, now under command of Commodore Bainbridge. On the 29th of December the two vessels met of San Salvador, on the coast of Brazil. A furious battle ensued, continuing for two hours. Every mast was torn from the British ship, and her hull was burst with round shot. The deck was made slippery with the blood of more than two hundred killed and wounded seamen. The vessel was reduced to a wreck before her flag was struck; then the crew and passengers, numbering upward of four hundred, were transferred to the *Constitution*, and the hull of the *Java* was burned at sea. The news of these successive victories roused the enthusiasm of the people to the highest pitch. In the course of the year two hundred and fifty British ships, carrying three thousand sailors, and cargoes of immense value, were captured by the American cruisers. Filled with exultation, the people of the United States saw in these naval triumphs the omens of complete overthrow to the arrogant dominion of Britain on the seas. The nations of Europe heard in astonishment. France was well pleased; for in these humiliations of her great enemy she witnessed the fulfillment of Napoleon's prophecy when, at the cession of Louisiana, he exclaimed with delight: "There! I have this day given to England a maritime rival that will sooner or later humble her pride!" For a while the English themselves were well-nigh paralyzed. The British newspapers burst forth raging and declared that the time-honored flag of England had been disgraced "by a piece of striped bunting flying at the mast heads of a few fir-built frigates, manned by a handful of **** and outlaws!" And the comment, though stated in unpleasant language, was true!

During the summer and autumn of 1812 military operations were active, but not decisive, on the Niagara frontier. The troops in that quarter, consisting of the New York militia, a few regulars, and recruits from other States, were commanded by General Stephen Van Rensselaer. The first movement of the Americans was made against Queenstown, on the Canada side of the river. On the 13th of October a thousand men were embarked in boats and landed on the western shore. They were resisted at the water's edge, and Colonel Solomon Van Rensselaer, the leader, was wounded. The subordinate officers led the charge, and the British batteries on the heights of Queenstown were carried. The enemy's forces were rallied, however, by General Brock, and returning to the charge, were a second time repulsed. General Brock fell mortally wounded. The Americans began to entrench themselves, and orders were sent across the river for the remaining division, twelve hundred strong, to hasten to the rescue. But the American militia on the eastern shore declared that they were there to defend the United States, and not to invade Canada. There they stood all afternoon, while their comrades at Queenstown were surrounded by the British, who came with strong reinforcements from Fort George. The Americans bravely defended themselves until they had lost a hundred and sixty men in killed and wounded, and were then obliged to surrender. General Van Rensselaer, disgusted at the conduct of the New York militia, resigned his command, and was succeeded by General Alexander Smyth of Virginia.

This officer began his career as commander by issuing two proclamations that would have put to shame the bulletins of Bonaparte or Cæsar. He declared that in a few days his standards should be planted in the strongholds of Canada. After crossing Niagara and conquering the British dominions, he would annex them to the United States! His predecessors in command of the army had been popular men, but wholly destitute of skill or experience in the art of war! The soldiers of the "Army of the Center," as he called the militia under his authority, had now a general who would lead them to certain victory! Every man who performed a gallant action should have his name immortalized in the annals of his country! And so on for quantity and style.

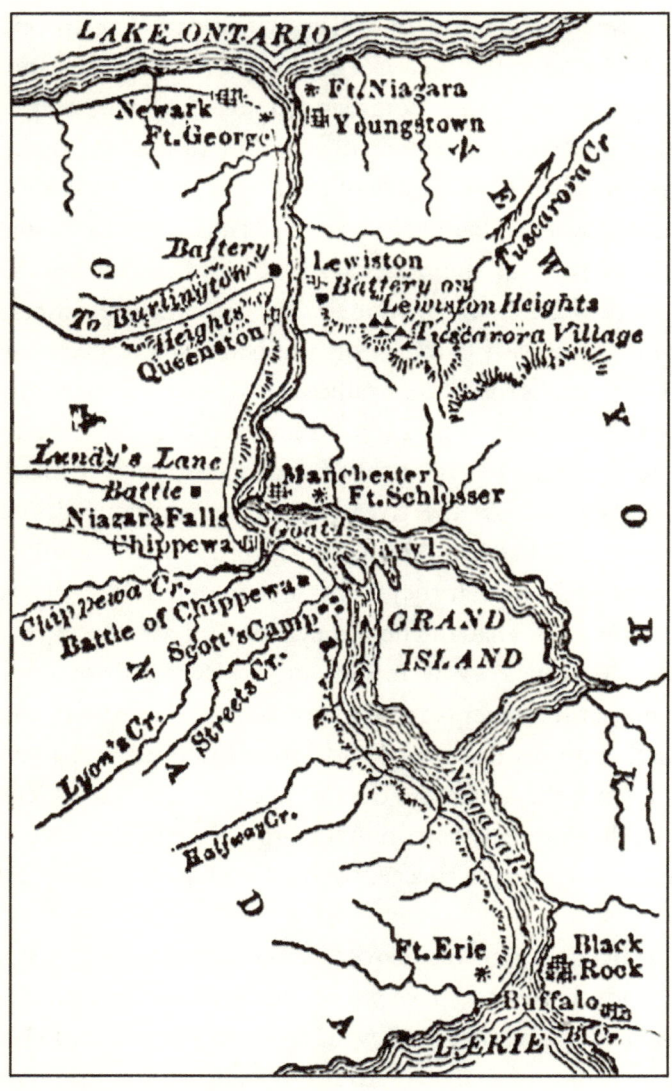

The Niagara Frontier, 1812.

In the mean time the Americans, numbering between four and five thousand, had been rallied at Black Rock, a few miles north of Buffalo. From this point, on the 28th of November, a company was sent across to the Canada shore; but instead of following with a stronger detachment, General Smyth ordered the advance party to return. A few days afterward another crossing was planned, and the Americans were already embarked, when they were commanded to return to winter quarters. The militia became mutinous. Smyth was charged with cowardice and disloyalty, and after three months was deposed from his command. Thus ended the military operations of 1812. In the autumn Madison was re-elected President; the choice for Vice-President fell on Elbridge Gerry of Massachusetts. In the debates at the opening of Congress the policy of the administration was strongly condemned by the opponents of the war; but vigorous measures were adopted for strengthening the army and navy.

CHAPTER L.

WAR OF 1812.—CONTINUED.

IN the beginning of 1813 the American army was organized in three divisions: THE ARMY OF THE NORTH, commanded by General Wade Hampton, to operate in the country of Lake Champlain; THE ARMY OF THE CENTRE, under direction of the commander-in-chief, to resume offensive movements on the Niagara frontier and Lake Ontario; THE ARMY OF THE WEST, under command of General Winchester, who was soon superseded by General Harrison. Early in January the latter division, made up of various detachments of militia from the Western States, moved toward the head of Lake Erie to regain the ground lost by Hull in the previous summer. On the 10th of the month the American advance, composed of eight hundred men under Winchester, reached the rapids of the Maumee. A body of British and Indians was posted at Frenchtown, on the river Raisin, thirty miles from Winchester's camp. A detachment of Americans pressed forward, attacked the enemy, captured the town, encamped there, and on the 20th of the month were joined by Winchester with the main division.

Two days afterward the Americans were suddenly assaulted by a force of a thousand five hundred British and Indians under command of General Proctor. A severe battle was fought, each party losing nearly three hundred men. The British were checked, and for a while the issue was doubtful; but General Winchester, having been taken by the enemy, advised his forces to capitulate under a pledge of protection given by Proctor and his subordinates. As soon as the surrender was made the British general set off at a rapid rate to return to Malden. The American wounded *were left to the mercy of the savages*, who at once began their work with tomahawk and scalping—knife and torch. The two houses into which most of the wounded had been crowded were fired, while the painted barbarians stood around and hurled back into the flames whoever attempted to escape. The rest of the prisoners were dragged away through untold sufferings to Detroit, where they were ransomed at an enormous price. This shameful campaign has fixed on the name of Proctor the indelible stain of infamy.

General Harrison, on hearing the fate of Winchester's division, fell back from the Maumee, but soon returned and built Fort Meigs. Here he remained until the 1st of May, when he was besieged by a force of two thousand British and savages, led by Proctor and Tecumtha. Meanwhile, General Clay with twelve hundred Kentuckians advanced to the relief of the fort. The besiegers were attacked in turn, and at the same time the besieged made a successful sally. But for the mistake of Colonel Dudley, who allowed his detachment to be cut off and captured, the British would have been completely routed. Again the American prisoners were treated with savage cruelty until Tecumtha, *not* Proctor, interfered to save them. In a few days the Indians deserted in large numbers, and Proctor, be coming alarmed, abandoned the siege, and on the 9th of May retreated to Malden.

For nearly three months active operations were suspended. In the latter part of July, Proctor and Tecumtha with a force of nearly four thousand men returned to Fort Meigs, now commanded by General Clay. For several days the British general beat about the American position, attempting to draw out the garrison. Failing in that, he filed off with about half his forces and attacked Fort Stephenson, at Lower Sandusky. This place was defended by a hundred and sixty men under command of Colonel Croghan, a stripling but twenty-one years of age. But he exhibited the skill and bravery of a veteran. To the enemy's summons, accompanied with a threat of massacre in case of refusal, he answered that the fort should be held as long as there was a man left alive within it. For a while the British cannonaded the ramparts without much effect, and on the 2d of August advanced to carry the place by storm. Croghan filled his only gun with slugs and grape-shot, and masked it in such a position as to rake the ditch from end to end. The British, believing the fort to be silenced, crowded into the fatal trench, and were swept away almost to a man. The repulse was complete. Proctor, fearing the approach of Harrison, raised the siege and returned to Malden.

At this time the waters of Lake Erie were commanded by a British squadron of six vessels carrying sixty -three guns. It was seen that a successful invasion of Canada could only be made by first gaining control of the lake. This serious undertaking was imposed on Commodore Oliver H. Perry of Rhode Island—a young man not twenty-eight years old who had never been in a naval battle. His antagonist, Commodore Barclay, was a veteran from the sea-service of Europe. With indefatigable energy Perry directed the construction of nine ships, carrying fifty-four guns, and was soon afloat on the lake. On the 10th of September the two fleets met a short distance north-west of Put-in Bay. Careful directions had been given by both commanders for the impending battle; both were resolved on victory. The fight was begun by the American squadron, Perry's flag-ship, the *Lawrence*, leading the attack. His principal antagonist was the *Detroit*, under the immediate command of Barclay. The British guns, being longer, had the wider range, and were better served. The *Lawrence* was ruined; nearly all the cannon were dismounted, masts torn away, sailors killed.

Between the other ships the battle was proceeding in a desultory way without much damage; but Barclay's flag-ship was almost as nearly wrecked as the *Lawrence*. Perceiving with quick eye how the battle stood, the dauntless Perry, himself unhurt, put on his uniform, seized his banner, got overboard into an open boat, passed within pistol-shot of the enemy's ships, a storm of balls flying around him, and transferred his flag to the *Niagara*. A shout went up from the American fleet; it was the signal of victory. With the powerful *Niagara* still uninjured by the battle, Perry bore down upon the enemy's line, drove right through the midst, discharging terrible broadsides right and left. In fifteen minutes the work was done; the British fleet was helpless. Perry with a touch of pride returned to the bloody deck of the *Lawrence*, and there received the surrender. And then he sent to General Harrison this famous despatch: "We have met the enemy, and they are ours—two ships, two brigs, one schooner and one sloop."

This victory gave the Americans full control of Lake Erie. Both Proctor and Harrison awaited the result. If Barclay should win, Proctor would invade Ohio; if Perry should prove victorious, Harrison would conquer Canada. For the Americans the way was now opened. On the 27th of September Harrison's army was embarked at Sandusky Bay and landed near Malden. The disheartened British retreated to Sandwich, the Americans following hard after. From the latter place Proctor continued his retreat to the river Thames, and there faced about to fight. The battlefield was well chosen by the British, whose lines extended from the river to a swamp, Here, on the 5th of October, they were attacked by the Americans led by Harrison and General Shelby, governor of Kentucky. In the beginning of the battle, Proctor, being a coward, ran. The British regulars sustained the attack with firmness, and were only broken when furiously charged by the Kentuckians under Colonel Richard M. Johnson. When that part of the field was won, the Americans wheeled against the Indians, who, to the number of fifteen hundred, lay hidden in the swamp to the west. Here the battle raged fiercely. Tecumtha had staked all on the issue. For a while his war-whoop sounded above the din of the conflict. Presently his voice was heard no longer, for the great chieftain had fallen. At the same time Colonel Johnson was borne away severely wounded. The savages, appalled by the death of their leader, fled in despair. The victory was complete. So ended the campaign in the West. The Indian confederacy was broken to pieces. All that Hull had lost was regained. Michigan was recovered. Ohio no longer feared invasion. Perry swept Lake Erie with his fleet. Canada was prostrated before the victorious army of Harrison.

Meanwhile, the Creeks of Alabama, kinsmen of the Shawnees, had taken up arms. In the latter part of August, Fort Mims, forty miles north of Mobile, was surprised by the savages, who appeased their thirst for blood with the murder of nearly four hundred people; not a woman or child was spared, and but few of the men in the fort escaped. The news of the massacre spread consternation throughout the Southwest. The governors of Tennessee, Georgia and Mississippi Territory made immediate preparations for invading the country of the Creeks. The Tennesseeans, under command of General Jackson, were first to the rescue. A detachment of nine hundred men, led by General Coffee, reached the Indian town of Tallushatchee, attacked it, burned it, left not an Indian alive. On the 8th of November a battle was fought at Talladega, east of the Coosa, and the savages were defeated with severe losses. In the latter part of the same month another fight occurred at

Autosse, on the south bank of the Tallapoosa, and again the Indians were routed.

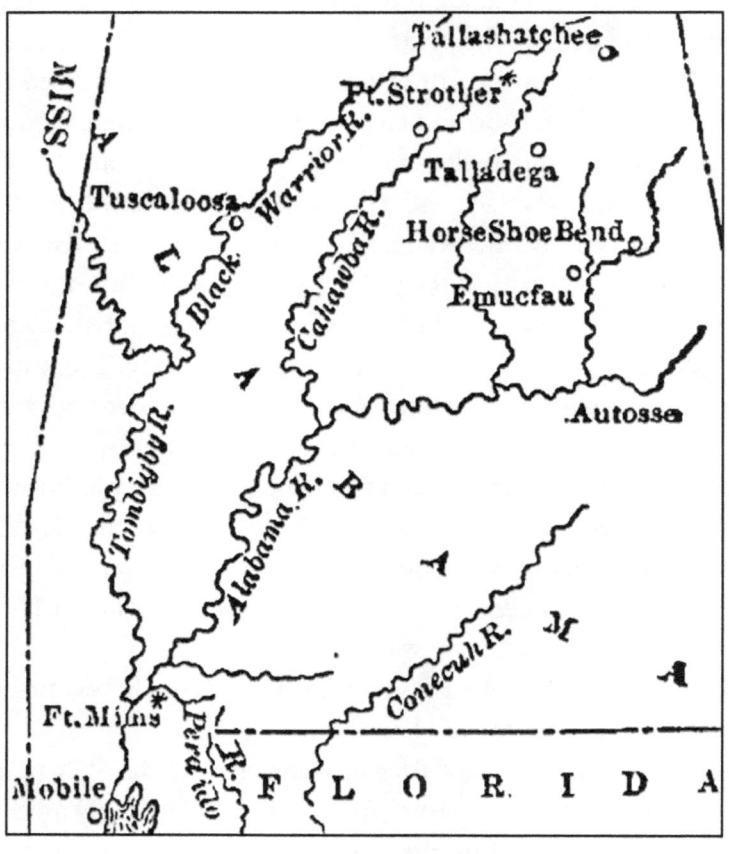

Scene of the Creek War, 1813-14.

During the winter Jackson's troops, unprovided and starving, became mutinous and were going home. But the general set the example of living on acorns; then rode before the rebellious line and threatened with death the first mutineer who stirred. And no man stirred. On the 22d of January, 1814, the battle of Emucfau was fought on the west bank of the Tallapoosa. The valor of the Tennesseeans again gave them the victory. At Tohopeka, called by the whites the Horseshoe Bend, the Creeks made their final stand. Here the Tallapoosa winds westward and northward, enclosing a large tract of land in the form of a peninsula with a narrow neck. This position the Indians had fortified with more than their usual skill. The whites, led by General Coffee, surrounded the place, so as to prevent escape by crossing the river. On the 27th of March, the main body of whites under General Jackson stormed the breastworks and drove the Indians into the bend. There, huddled together without the possibility of escape, a thousand Creek warriors, with the women and children of the tribe, met their doom. The desperate Red men asked no quarter, and none was given. The few chiefs who were still abroad sent in their submission; the spirit of the nation was completely broken.

On the 25th of April, 1813, General Dearborn, commanding the Army of the Centre, embarked his forces at Sackett's Harbor, near the eastern extremity of Lake Ontario. The object of the expedition was to capture Toronto, the capital of Upper Canada. Here was the most important depot of supplies in British America. The American fleet under Commodore Chauncey had already obtained the mastery of the lake, so that Dearborn's passage was unopposed. On the 27th of the month a force of seventeen hundred men, commanded by General Pike, was landed within two miles of Toronto. At the water's edge they were met by the British. The Americans drove the enemy for a mile and a half, stormed a battery, and rushed forward to carry the main defences. At that moment the British magazine blew up with terrific violence. The assaulting column was covered with the debris of the explosion. Two hundred men were killed or wounded. General Pike was fatally injured, but lived long enough to hear the shout of victory; for the Americans, first shocked and then maddened by the calamity, made a furious charge and drove the British out of the town. General Sheaffe with a body of regulars escaped; the rest were taken prisoners. Property to the value of a half million dollars was secured to the victors.

While this movement was taking place the enemy made a descent on Sackett's Harbor. By the withdrawal of the American forces that post had been left exposed. The British succeeded in destroying a quantity of stores; but General Brown rallied the militia, and drove back the assailants with considerable loss. Meanwhile, the victorious troops at Toronto had re-embarked and crossed the lake to the mouth of the Niagara. On the 27th of May the Americans, led by Generals Chandler and Winder, crossed the river and stormed Fort George, on the Canada shore. The British hastily destroyed their posts along the Niagara and retreated to Burlington Bay, at the western extremity of the lake. The Americans, pursuing them thither, were attacked in the night, but succeeded in repulsing the enemy with loss.

During the months of summer military operations on the frontier were suspended. After the battle of the Thames, General Harrison had transferred his forces to Buffalo, and then resigned his commission. On account of old age and ill health General Dearborn also withdrew from the service, and was succeeded by General Wilkinson. The next campaign, which was planned by General Armstrong, secretary of war, embraced the conquest of Montreal. For this purpose the Army of the Centre, under Wilkinson, was ordered to join the Army of the North at some convenient point on the St. Lawrence. The enterprise was attended with many difficulties and not a few delays. Not until the 5th of November did a force of seven thousand men, embarking from the mouth of French Creek, twenty miles north of Sackett's Harbor, sail down the St. Lawrence for the conquest of Montreal. Parties of British, Canadians and Indians, gathering on the northern bank of the river, constantly impeded the progress of the expedition. General Brown was landed with a considerable force to disperse these bands or drive the enemy into the interior. On the 11th of the month a severe battle was fought at a place called Chrysler's Field. Neither party gained a victory, but the advantage remained with the British. The Americans, having lost nearly three hundred men in the fight, passed down the river to St. Regis, on the southern shore, where the forces of General Hampton were expected from Plattsburg to form a junction with Wilkinson's command. But Hampton did not stir; and the project of attacking Montreal had to be abandoned. The Americans then went into winter quarters at Fort Covington, at the fork of Salmon River, nine miles from St. Regis.

In the mean time, the British on the Niagara frontier rallied and advanced against Fort George. General McClure, the commandant, abandoned the place on the approach of the enemy, but before retreating burned the Canadian town of Newark. It cost the people of Northern New York dearly; for the British and Indians crossed the river, captured Fort Niagara, and fired the villages of Youngstown, Lewiston and Manchester. On next to the last day of the year Black Rock and Buffalo were laid in ashes.

In the sea-fights of 1813 victory generally declared for the British. During the year both nations wasted much blood and treasure on the ocean. Off the coast of Demarara, on the 24th of February, the sloop-of-war *Hornet*, commanded by Captain James Lawrence, fell in with the British brig *Peacock*. The ships were equally matched. A terrible battle of fifteen minutes ensued, and the *Peacock*, already sinking, struck her colors. While the Americans were trying to transfer the conquered crew the ocean yawned and the brig sank out of sight. Nine British sailors and three of Lawrence's men were sucked down in the whirlpool.

On returning to Boston the command of the *Chesapeake*—one of the best frigates in the American navy—was given to Lawrence, and again he put to sea. Before sailing he received a challenge from Captain Broke, of the British frigate *Shannon*, to come out and fight him. Lawrence ought not to have accepted the banter; for his equipments were incomplete and his crew ill assorted, sick and half mutinous. But he was young, and the favorite of the nation; fired with applause, he went unhesitatingly to meet his foe. Eastward from Cape Ann the two vessels met on the first day of June. The battle was obstinate, brief, dreadful. In a short time every officer who could direct the movements of the *Chesapeake* was either killed or wounded. The brave young Lawrence was struck with a musket-ball, and fell dying on the bloody deck. As they bore him down the hatchway he gave in feeble voice his last heroic order—ever afterward the motto of the American sailor—"DON'T GIVE UP THE SHIP!" The British were already leaping on deck, and the flag of England was hoisted over the shattered vessel. Both ships were charnel-houses; but the *Shannon* was still able to tow her prize into the harbor of Halifax. There the bodies of Lawrence and Ludlow, second in command, were tenderly and honorably buried by the British.

The next important naval battle was fought on the 14th of August between the American brig *Argus* and the British *Pelican*. The former vessel had made a daring cruise about the coasts of England, capturing more than twenty ships. Herself overtaken by the *Pelican*, she was obliged, after a severe conflict, to surrender. On the 5th of September another British brig, the *Boxer*, cruising off the coast of Maine, was overhauled and captured by the American *Enterprise*, commanded by Captain Burrows. The fight raged for three-quarters of an hour, when the *Boxer* surrendered. Captain Blyth, the British commander, was killed; and the gallant Burrows received a mortal wound. The bodies of both officers were taken to Portland and buried side by side with military honors. All summer long Captain Porter in the frigate *Essex* cruised in the South Atlantic and Pacific Oceans. For five months he was the terror of British merchantmen in those broad waters. On the 28th of the following March, while the *Essex* was lying in the harbor of Valparaiso, she was beset, contrary to the law of nations, by two powerful British vessels, the *Phœbe* and the *Cherub*. The *Essex* had been crippled by a storm, and was anchored in neutral waters in that condition Captain Porter fought his two antagonists until nearly all of his men were killed or wounded; then struck his colors and surrendered. Notwithstanding the losses sustained by the American navy, privateers continued to scour the ocean and capture British vessels.

From honorable warfare the naval officers of England stooped to marauding along the sea-shore. Early in the year a squadron entered Delaware Bay and anchored before Lewistown. A requisition on the inhabitants to supply the fleet with provisions was met with a brave refusal. A threat to burn the town was answered with a message of defiance. A bombardment of twenty-four hours' duration followed; the houses were much injured, and the people fled, carrying their property to places of safety. Other British men-of-war entered the Chesapeake and burned several villages on the shores of the bay. At the town of Hampton, just above the Roads, the soldiers and marines perpetrated such outrages as covered their memory with shame. Commodore Hardy, to whom the blockade of the New England harbors had been assigned, behaved with more humanity; even the Americans recognized and praised his honorable conduct. The year 1813 closed without decisive results.

CHAPTER LI.

THE CAMPAIGNS OF '14.

IN the spring of 1814 another invasion of Canada was planned. The Niagara frontier was the scene of operations; but there was much delay in bringing the scattered detachments of General Wilkinson's army into proper position. Not until the 3d of July did Generals Scott and Ripley, at the head of three thousand men, cross the Niagara from Black Rock to Fort Erie. This post, garrisoned by two hundred British, surrendered without a battle. On the following day the Americans advanced down the river-bank in the direction of Chippewa village. Before reaching that place, however, they were met by the British army, led by General Riall. On the evening of the 5th a severe battle was fought on the plain just south of Chippewa River. The Americans, led on by Generals Scott and Ripley and the gallant Major Jessup, won the day; but their loss amounted to three hundred and thirty-eight men. The British veterans, after more than five hundred of their number had fallen, were driven into their entrenchments.

General Riall retreated first to Queenstown and afterward to Burlington Heights. General Scott, commanding the American right, was detached to watch the movements of the enemy. On the evening of the 25th of July he found himself suddenly confronted by Riall's army, strongly posted on the high grounds in sight of Niagara Falls. Here was fought the hardest battle of the war. A man less courageous and self-confident than Scott would have retreated; but with extraordinary daring he held his own until reinforced by the other divisions of the army. The British reserves were also rapidly brought into action. Twilight faded into darkness, and still the battle was undecided. A detachment of Americans, getting upon the British rear, captured General Riall and his entire staff. Still the contest raged. The key to the enemy's position was a high ground crowned with a battery. Calling Colonel James Miller to his side and pointing to the hill, General Brown said, "Colonel, take your regiment and storm that battery." "I'LL TRY,

SIR," was the answer of the gallant officer; and he *did* take it, and held it against three desperate assaults of the British. In the last charge General Drummond, who led, was wounded, and the royal army, numbering fully five thousand, was driven from the field with a loss of eight hundred and seventy-eight men. The Americans engaged in the battle numbered about four thousand; their loss in killed, wounded and missing was more than eight hundred.

After this battle of Niagara, or Lundy's Lane, as it is sometimes called, General Ripley took command of the American forces; for Generals Brown and Scott were both wounded. It was deemed prudent to fall back to Fort Erie. To that place General Gaines crossed over from Buffalo, and being the senior officer, assumed command of the army. Very soon General Drummond received reinforcements, moved forward, and on the 4th of August invested Fort Erie. The siege continued for ten days, and then the British attempted to storm the works, but were driven back with severe losses. But the enemy was reinforced and the siege resumed. A regular and destructive bombardment was kept up by the British, and was answered by the Americans with equal energy. On the 28th of August General Gaines was injured by the explosion of a shell and obliged to relinquish his command. General Brown, though still suffering from the wound received at Niagara, was again called to direct the defences of the fort. On the 17th of September a sortie was ordered, and the advanced works of the British were gallantly carried. At the same time news arrived that the American general Izard was approaching from Plattsburg with strong reinforcements. Alarmed at the threatening aspect of affairs, the British raised the siege and retreated to Fort George. On the 5th of November Fort Erie was evacuated and destroyed by the Americans, who then recrossed the Niagara and went into winter quarters at Black Rock and Buffalo. So ended the warm the country between Lakes Erie and Ontario.

The winter of 1813-14 was passed by the Army of the North at French Mills, afterward called Fort Covington. In the latter part of February General Wilkinson advanced his forces to Plattsburg, and in the following month began an invasion of Canada. At La Colle, on the west bank of the Sorel, he encountered a force of the enemy, made an imprudent attack and was defeated. Falling back to Plattsburg, he was superseded by General Izard. How that officer marched to the relief of General Brown at Fort Erie has already been narrated. The remaining division of the northern army, fifteen hundred strong, was left under command of General Macomb at Plattsburg. At this time the American flotilla on Lake Champlain was commanded by Commodore MacDonough. For the purpose of destroying this fleet and obtaining control of the lake, the British general Prevost advanced into Northern New York at the head of fourteen thousand men, and at the same time ordered Commodore Downie to ascend the Sorel with his fleet.

The invading army reached Plattsburg without opposition. Commodore MacDonough's squadron lay in the bay. On the 6th of September General Macomb retired with his small but courageous army to the south bank of the Saranac, which skirted the village. On came the British, entered the town, and attempted to cross the river, but were driven back. For four days they renewed their efforts; the Americans had torn up the bridges, and a passage could not be effected. The British fleet was now ready for action, and a general battle by land and water was planned for the 11th. Prevost's army, arranged in three columns, was to sweep across the Saranac and carry Macomb's position, while Downie's powerful flotilla was to bear down on MacDonough. The naval battle began first, and was obstinately fought for two hours and a half. At the end of that time Downie and many of his officers had been killed; the heavier British vessels were disabled and obliged to strike their colors. The smaller ships escaped; for the American brigs were so badly crippled that pursuit could not be made. Nevertheless, the victory on the lake was complete and glorious. The news was carried ashore, where the Americans were bravely contesting the passage of the river against overwhelming numbers. At one ford the British column succeeded in crossing; but the tidings from the lake fired the militia with ardor; they made a rush, and the enemy was driven back. Prevost, after losing nearly two thousand five hundred men and squandering two and a half million dollars in a fruitless campaign, retired precipitately to Canada. The ministry of England, made wise by the disasters of this invasion, began to devise measures looking to peace.

In the country of the Chesapeake the scenes of the previous year were renewed by the British. Late in the summer Admiral Cochrane arrived off the coast of Virginia with an armament of twenty-one vessels. General Ross with an army of four thousand veterans, freed from service in Europe, came with the fleet. The American squadron, commanded by Commodore Barney, was unable to oppose so powerful a force. The enemy's flotilla entered the Chesapeake with the purpose of attacking Washington and Baltimore. The larger division of the British fleet sailed into the Patuxent, and on the 19th of August the forces of General Ross were landed at the town of Benedict. Commodore Barney was obliged to blow up his vessels and take to the shore. From Benedict the British advanced against Washington. At Bladensburg, six miles north east of the capital, they were met, on the 24th of the month, by the militia and the marines under Barney. Here a battle was fought. The undisciplined militia behaved badly. Barney's seamen were overpowered by the British, and himself taken prisoner. The news of the defeat was rapidly borne to Washington. The President, the cabinet officers and the people betook themselves to flight, and Ross marched unopposed into the city. He had been ordered by his superiors to use the torch, and the work of destruction was accordingly begun. All the public buildings except the Patent Office were burned. The beautiful but unfinished Capitol and the President's house were left a mass of blackened ruins. Many private edifices were also destroyed; but General Ross, himself a humane man, did less than he was ordered to do.[26]

Five days after the capture of Washington, a portion of the British fleet, ascending the Potomac, reached Alexandria. The inhabitants of that town, in order to avoid the fate of the capital, purchased the forbearance of the enemy by the surrender of twenty-one ships, sixteen thousand barrels of flour and a thousand hogsheads of tobacco. Baltimore redeemed herself more bravely. Against that city, after the

---

[26] An excuse for this outrageous barbarism was found in the previous conduct of the Americans, who, at Toronto and other places on the Canadian frontier, had behaved but little better.

capture of Washington, General Ross proceeded with his army and fleet. Meanwhile, the militia, to the number of ten thousand, had gathered under command of General Samuel Smith, a Revolutionary veteran. On the 12th of September the British were landed at North Point, at the mouth of the Patapsco and the fleet began the ascent of the river. The land-forces, after marching about halfway to Baltimore, were met by the Americans under General Stricker. A skirmish ensued in which General Ross was killed but Colonel Brooks assumed command of the invading army, and the march continued. When approaching the city, the British came upon the American lines and were brought to a halt by a severe cannonade. General Stricker, however, ordered his men to fall back to a second line of defences, from which they gave the enemy a permanent check.

Meanwhile, the British squadron had ascended the Patapsco and begun the bombardment of Fort McHenry, at the entrance to the harbor. From sunrise of the 13th until after midnight the guns of the fleet poured a tempest of shot and shells upon the fortress.[27] At the end of that time the soldiers of the garrison were as full of spirit and the works as strong as at the beginning. It was plain that the British had undertaken more than they could accomplish. Disheartened and baffled, they ceased to fire. The land-forces retired from before the American entrenchments and re-embarked. The siege of Baltimore was at an end.

During the summer of 1814 two expeditions were made against the British and Indians of the North-west. In May a force of two hundred men ascended the Mississippi from St. Louis and took post at Prairie du Chien, a short distance above the mouth of the Wisconsin. The object was to overawe the hostile Winnebagoes and Chippewas by establishing an outpost in their territory. But before the fort was well begun a force of six hundred Canadians and Indians invested the place, and on the 17th of July compelled the detachment to surrender. The more important expedition was directed against the British fortress and depot

---

[27] During the night of the bombardment Francis S. Key, detained on board a British ship and watching the American flag over Fort McHenry—seen at intervals by the glare of rockets and the flash of cannon—composed *The Star-Spangled Banner*.

of stores at Mackinaw. A regiment of six hundred men, commanded by Colonel Croghan, famous for his heroism at Sandusky, marched northward in midsummer from Detroit. Some vessels of Perry's fleet accompanied the land forces as a convoy; but the movement was slow, and Mackinaw was not reached until the 4th of August. Finding the defences of the place too high and strong to be injured by his guns Croghan ordered an assault, which was made with spirit, but repulsed. The enterprise was then abandoned, with no further injury to the British than the destruction of some supplies and shipping in Georgian Bay.

New England did not escape the ravages of war. On the 9th and loth of August the village of Stonington, in the south-eastern corner of Connecticut, was bombarded by Commodore Hardy; but the British, attempting to land, were beaten back by the militia. The fisheries of the New England coast were for the most part broken up. The salt-works at Cape Cod escaped only by the payment of heavy ransoms. All the principal harbors from Maine to Delaware were under a rigorous blockade, and the foreign commerce of the Eastern States was totally destroyed. The beacons in the lighthouses were allowed to burn out, and a general gloom settled over the country.

From the beginning many of the people of New England had opposed the war. Their interests centred in ships and factories; the former were captured at sea, and the latter came to a stand-still. Industry was paralyzed. The members of the Federal party cried out against the continuance of the contest. The legislature of Massachusetts advised the calling of a convention. The other Eastern States responded to the call; and on the 14th of December the delegates assembled at Hartford. The objects of the convention were not very clearly expressed; but opposition to the war and the policy of the administration was the leading principle. The leaders of the Democratic party, who supported the war-policy of the government, did not hesitate to say that the purposes of the assembly were disloyal and treasonable. Be that as it may, the convention ruined the Federal party. After remaining in session with closed doors for nearly three weeks, the delegates published an address more moderate and just than had been expected; and then adjourned. But little hope of political preferment remained for those who participated in the Hartford convention.

During the progress of the war the Spanish authorities of Florida sympathized with the British. In the month of August a detachment of the enemy's fleet was allowed by the commandant of Pensacola to use that post for the purpose of fitting out an expedition against Fort Bowyer, commanding the entrance to the bay of Mobile. On the 15th of September the latter post was attacked, but the assailants were driven off. General Jackson, who at that time commanded the American forces in the South, remonstrated with the Spaniards against this violation of neutrality, but received no satisfaction. Jackson, whose way it was to mete out summary justice to offenders, marched a force against Pensacola, stormed the town and drove the British out of Florida. This was the beginning of the last campaign of the war.

After the taking of Pensacola, General Jackson returned to his headquarters at Mobile. There he learned that the British were making formidable preparations for the conquest of Louisiana. Repairing at once to New Orleans, he assumed control of the city, declared martial law, mustered the militia, and adopted the most vigorous measures for repelling the invasion. From La Fitte, chief of a band of smugglers in the Bay of Barataria, he obtained information of the enemy's plans. The British army, numbering twelve thousand, came in a fleet of fifty vessels from Jamaica. Sir Edward Packenham, brother-in-law of the duke of Wellington, was commander of the invading forces. On the 10th of December the squadron entered the outlet of Lake Borgne, sixty miles north-east of New Orleans. Four days afterward a flotilla of gun-boats which had been placed to guard the lake was captured by the British, but not until a severe loss had been inflicted on the enemy.

On the 22d of the month Packenham's advance reached the Mississippi nine miles below the city. A detachment was sent to the western bank of the river, but this operation was checked by a counter movement on the part of the Americans. On the night of the 23d General Jackson sent a schooner down the Mississippi to bombard the British camp, while at the same time he and General Coffee advanced with two thousand Tennessee riflemen to attack Packenham's camp in front. After a bloody assault Jackson was obliged to retire, the enemy losing most in the engagement. On the following day Jackson fell back and took a strong position along the canal, four miles below the city. Packenham advanced, and on the 28th cannonaded the American position with but little effect. On New Year's day the attack was renewed. The heavy guns of the British had now been brought into position; but the Americans easily held their ground, and the enemy was again driven back. Packenham now made arrangements to read his whole army in a grand assault on the American lines.

Jackson was ready. Earthworks had been constructed, and a long line or cotton-bales and sand-bags thrown up for protection. On the morning of the memorable 8th of January the British moved forward. They went to a terrible fate. The battle began with the light of early morning, and was ended before nine o'clock. Packenham hurled column after column against the American position, and column after column was smitten with irretrievable ruin. Jackson's men, behind their breastworks, were almost entirely secure from the enemy's fire, while every discharge of the Tennessee and Kentucky rifles told with awful effect on the exposed veterans of England. Packenham, trying to rally his men, was killed; General Gibbs, second in command, was mortally wounded. General Keene fell disabled; only General Lambert was left to call the shattered fragments of the army from the field. Never was there in a great battle such disparity of losses. Of the British fully seven hundred were killed, fourteen hundred wounded, and five hundred taken prisoners. The American loss amounted to *eight killed and thirteen wounded.*

After the battle Jackson granted a truce for the burial of the British dead. That done, General Lambert recalled the detachment from the west bank of the river and retired with his ruined army into Lake Borgne. At Fort Bowyer he received the news of peace. Jackson marched into New Orleans with his victorious army, and was received with unbounded enthusiasm. Such, so far as operations by land were concerned, was the close of the war. On the ocean hostilities lingered until spring. On the 20th of February the American frigate *Constitution*, cruising of Cape St. Vincent, caught sight of two hostile vessels, gave chase, and after a severe fight captured them. They proved to be British brigs—the *Cyane*, of thirty-six guns, and the *Levant*, of eighteen. On the

23d of March the American *Hornet*, commanded by Captain Biddle ended the conflict by capturing the British *Penguin* off the coast of Brazil.

Already a treaty of peace had been made and ratified. Both nations had long desired such a result. In the summer of 1814 American commissioners were sent to Ghent, in Belgium, and were there met by Lord Gambier, Henry Goulburn and William Adams, ambassadors of Great Britain. The agents of the United States were John Quincy Adams, James A. Bayard, Henry Clay, Jonathan Russell and Albert Gallatin. Several months were spent in negotiations; and on the 24th of December, 1814, a treaty was agreed to and signed. In England the news was received with deep satisfaction; in the United States, with a delight bordering on madness. Before the terms of settlement could be known, the people broke forth in universal jubilee. Nobody stopped to inquire whether the treaty was good or bad, honorable or dishonorable. The Federalists found abundant reason for rejoicing that a war which they had persistently opposed as impolitic and unjust, was at an end. The Democrats sent up a double huzza, shouting first for Jackson's victory and afterward for peace. Nor could the country well be blamed for rejoicing that a conflict which had cost the United States a thousand six hundred and eighty-three vessels and more than eighteen thousand sailors, was ended. The war-cloud rolled away like an incubus from the public mind. The long blockaded, half-rotten shipping of New England was decked with flags and streamers, and *in one day* the dock-yards were ringing with the sound of saw and hammer. On the 18th of February the treaty was ratified by the Senate of the United States, and peace was publicly proclaimed. It was in the interim between the conclusion of the treaty and the reception of the news in the United States that the battle of New Orleans was fought. A telegraph would have saved all that bloodshed.

There never was a more absurd treaty than that of Ghent. Its only significance was that Great Britain and the United States, having been at war, agreed to be at peace. Not one of the distinctive issues to decide which the war had been undertaken was settled or even mentioned. Of the impressment of American seamen not a word was said. The wrongs done to the commerce of the United States were not referred to. The rights of neutral nations were left as undetermined as before. Of "free trade and sailors' rights," which had been the battle cry of the American navy, no mention was made. The principal articles of the compact were devoted to the settlement of unimportant boundaries and the possession of some petty islands in the Bay of Passamaquoddy. There is little doubt, however, that at the time of the treaty Great Britain gave the United States a private assurance that impressment and the other wrongs complained of by the Americans should be practiced no more. For the space of sixty years vessels bearing the flag of the United States have been secure from such insults as caused the war of 1812. Another advantage gained by America was the recognition of her naval power. It was no longer doubtful that American sailors were the peers in valor and patriotism of any seamen in the world. It was no small triumph for the Republic that her flag should henceforth be honored on every ocean.

At the close of the conflict the country was burdened with a debt of a hundred million dollars. The monetary affairs of the nation were in a deplorable condition. The charter of the Bank of the United States expired in 1811, and in the following years the other banks of the country were obliged to suspend specie payment. The people were thus deprived of the currency necessary for the transaction of business. Domestic commerce was paralyzed by the want of money, and foreign trade destroyed by the enemy's fleet. In the year after the close of the war a bill was passed by Congress to recharter the Bank of the United States. The measure being objectionable, the President interposed his veto; but in the following session the bill was again passed in an amended form. The capital was fixed at thirty-five million dollars. The central banking-house was established at Philadelphia, and branches were authorized at various other cities. On the 4th of March, 1817, the new financial institution went into operation; and the business and credit of the country were thereby greatly improved. Meanwhile, the United States had been engaged in a foreign war.

During the conflict with Great Britain the Algerine pirates renewed their depredations on American commerce. As soon as the treaty of Ghent was concluded the government of the United States ordered Commodore Decatur, commanding a fleet of nine vessels, to proceed to the

Mediterranean and chastise the Barbary sea-robbers into submission. On the 17th of June, Decatur, cruising near Gibraltar, fell in with the principal frigate of the Algerine squadron, and after a severe fight of twenty minutes compelled the Moorish ship to surrender. Thirty of the piratical crew, including the admiral, were killed, and more than four hundred taken prisoners. On the 19th Decatur captured another frigate bearing twenty guns and a hundred and eight men. A few days afterward he sailed into the Bay of Algiers, and dictated to the humbled and terrified dey the terms of a treaty. The Moorish emperor was obliged to release his American prisoners without ransom, to relinquish all claims to tribute, and to give a pledge that his ships should trouble American merchantmen no more. Decatur next sailed against Tunis and Tripoli, compelled both of these states to give pledges of good conduct, and to pay large sums for former violations of international law. From that day until the present the Barbary powers have had a wholesome dread of the American flag.

The close of Madison's troubled administration was signalized by the admission of Indiana—the smallest of the Western States—into the Union. The new commonwealth, admitted in December, 1816, came with an area of nearly thirty-four thousand square miles, and a population of ninety-eight thousand. About the same time was founded the Colonization Society of the United States. Many of the most distinguished men in America became members of the association, the object of which was to provide somewhere in the world a refuge for free persons of color. Liberia, on the western coast of Africa, was finally selected as the seat of the proposed colony. A republican form of government was established there, and immigrants arrived in sufficient numbers to found a flourishing negro State. The capital was named Monrovia, in honor of James Monroe, who, in the fall of 1816, was elected as Madison's successor in the presidency. At the same time Daniel D. Tompkins of New York was chosen Vice-President.

CHAPTER LII.

Monroe's Administration.

IN its political principles the new administration was Democratic. The policy of Madison was adopted by his successor. But the stormy times of Madison gave place to many years of almost unbroken peace. The new President was a native of Virginia; a man of great talents and accomplishments. He had been a Revolutionary soldier, a member of the House of Representatives; a senator; governor of Virginia; envoy to France; minister to England; secretary of state under Madison. The members of the new cabinet were—John Quincy Adams, secretary of state; William H. Crawford, secretary of the treasury; John C. Calhoun, secretary of war; William Wirt, attorney-general. The animosities and party strifes of the previous years were in a measure forgotten. Statesmen of all parties devoted their energies to the payment of the national debt. It was a herculean task; but commerce revived; the government was economically administered; population increased; wealth flowed in; and in a few years the debt was honestly paid.

In the first summer of Monroe's administration the attention of the United States was directed to the little kingdom of Hayti in the northern part of St. Domingo. Christophe, the sovereign of the country, was anxious to secure from America a recognition of Haytian independence; for he feared that Louis XVIII., the restored Bourbon king of France, would reclaim Hayti as a part of the French empire. The President met the overtures of Christophe with favor, and an agent was sent out in the frigate *Congress* to conclude a treaty of commerce with the kingdom. But the Haytian authorities refused to negotiate with an agent who was not regularly accredited as a minister to an independent state; and the mission resulted in failure and disappointment.

In September of the same year an important treaty was concluded with the Indian nations of what was formerly the Northwestern Territory. The tribes mostly concerned were the Wyandots, Delawares,

Senecas, and Shawnees; but the Chippewas, Ottawas, and Pottawattamies were also interested in the treaty. The subject discussed was the cession, by purchase and otherwise, of various tracts of land, mostly in Ohio. The Indian title to about four millions of acres, embracing the valley of the Maumee, was extinguished by the payment to the tribes concerned of fourteen thousand dollars in cash. Besides this, the Delawares were to receive an annuity of five hundred dollars; while to the Wyandots, Senecas, Shawnees and Ottawas was guaranteed the payment of ten thousand dollars annually forever. The Chippewas and Pottawattamies received an annuity of three thousand three hundred dollars for fifteen years. A reservation of certain tracts, amounting in the aggregate to about three hundred thousand acres, was made by the Red men with the approval of the government. For it was believed that the Indians, living in small districts surrounded with American farms and villages, would abandon barbarism for the habits of civilized life. But the sequel proved that the men of the woods had no aptitude for such a change.

In December of 1817 the western portion of Mississippi Territory was organized as the State of Mississippi and admitted into the Union. The new State contained an area of forty-seven thousand square miles, and a population of sixty-five thousand souls. At the same time the attention of the government was called to a nest of buccaneers who had established themselves on Amelia Island, off the north-eastern coast of Florida. One Gregor McGregor, acting under a commission from the revolutionary authorities of New Granada and Venezuela, had put himself at the head of a band of adventurers, gathered mostly from Charleston and Savannah, and fortified the island as a rendezvous of slave-traders and South American privateers. It was thought by the audacious rascals that the well-known sympathy of the United States for the Spanish American republics south of the Isthmus of Darien would protect them from attack. They accordingly proclaimed a blockade of St. Augustine and proceeded with their business as though there was no civilized power in the world. But the Federal government took a different view of the matter. An armament was sent against the pirates, and the lawless establishment was broken up. Another rendezvous of the same sort, on the island of Galveston, off the coast of Texas, was also suppressed.

In the first year of Monroe's administration the question of internal improvements began to be much agitated. The territorial vastness of the country made it necessary to devise suitable means of communication between the distant parts. Without railroads and canals it was evident that the products of the great interior could never reach a market. Had Congress a right to vote money to make the needed improvements? Jefferson and Madison had both answered the question in the negative. Monroe held similar views; and a majority of Congress voted against the proposed appropriations. In one instance, however, a bill was passed appropriating the means necessary for the construction of a national road across the Alleghanies, from Cumberland to Wheeling. The question of internal improvements was then referred to the several States; and New York took the lead by constructing a splendid canal from Buffalo to Albany, a distance of three hundred and sixty-three miles. The cost of this important work was more than seven and a half million dollars, and the eight years of Monroe's administration were occupied in completing it.

In the latter part of 1817 the Seminole Indians on the frontiers of Georgia and Alabama became hostile. Some bad negroes and treacherous Creeks joined the savages in their depredations. General Gaines, commandant of a post on Flint River, was sent into the Seminole country, but after destroying a few villages his forces were found in adequate to conquer the Red men. General Jackson was then ordered to collect from the adjacent States a sufficient army and reduce the Seminoles to submission. Instead of following his directions, that stern and self-willed man mustered a thousand riflemen from West Tennessee, and in the spring of 1818 overran the hostile country with little opposition. The Indians were afraid to fight the man whom they had named the Big Knife.

While engaged in this expedition against the Seminoles, Jackson entered Florida and took possession of the Spanish post at St. Mark's. He deemed it necessary to do so in order to succeed in suppressing the savages. The Spanish troops stationed at St. Mark's were removed to

Pensacola; and two Englishmen, named Arbuthnot and Ambrister, who fell into Jackson's hands, were charged with inciting the Seminoles to insurrection, tried by a court-martial, and hanged. Jackson then advanced against Pensacola, captured the town, besieged and took the fortress of Barancas, at the entrance to the bay, and sent the Spanish authorities to Havana. These summary proceedings excited much comment throughout the country. The enemies of General Jackson condemned him in unmeasured terms; but the President and Congress justified his deeds. A resolution of censure, introduced into the House of Representatives, was voted down by a large majority. The king of Spain complained much; but his complaint was unheeded. Seeing that the defence of such a province would cost more than it was worth, the Spanish monarch then proposed to cede the territory to the United States. For this purpose negotiations were opened at Washington City; and on the 22d of February, 1819, a treaty was concluded by which East and West Florida and the outlying islands were surrendered to the American government. In consideration of the cession the United States agreed to relinquish all claim to the territory of Texas and to pay to American citizens, for depredations committed by Spanish vessels, a sum not exceeding five million dollars. By the same treaty the eastern boundary of Mexico was fixed at the River Sabine.

The year 1819 was noted for a great financial crisis—the first of many that have occurred to disturb and distress the country. With the reorganization of the Bank of the United States in 1817, the improved facilities for credit gave rise to many extravagant speculations, generally conceived in dishonesty and carried on by fraud. The great branch bank at Baltimore was especially infested by a band of unscrupulous speculators who succeeded, in connivance with the officers, in withdrawing from the institution fully two millions of dollars beyond its securities. President Cheves, however, of the superior Board of Directors, adopted a policy which exposed the prevailing rascality, and by putting an end to the system of unlimited credits, gradually restored the business of the country to a firmer basis. But, for the time being, financial affairs were thrown into confusion; and the Bank of the United States itself was barely saved from suspension and bankruptcy.

Monroe's administration was noted for the great number of new members which were added to the Union. In 1818, Illinois, the twenty-first State, embracing an area of more than fifty-five thousand square miles, was organized and admitted. The population of the new commonwealth was forty-seven thousand. In December of the following year Alabama was added, with a population of a hundred and twenty-five thousand, and an area of nearly fifty-one thousand square miles. About the same time Arkansas Territory was organized out of the southern portion of the Territory of Missouri. Early in 1820 the province of Maine, which had been under the jurisdiction of Massachusetts since 1652, was separated from that government and admitted into the Union. At the time of admission the population of the new State had reached two hundred and ninety eight thousand; and its territory embraced nearly thirty-two thousand square miles. In August of 1821 the great State of Missouri, with an area of sixty-seven thousand square miles, and a population of seventy-four thousand, was admitted as the twenty-fourth member of the Union; but the admission was attended with a political agitation so violent as to threaten the peace of the country.

The bill to organize Missouri as a territory was brought forward in February of 1819. The institution of slavery had already been planted there, and the question was raised in Congress whether the new State should be admitted with the existing system of labor, or whether by congressional action slave-holding should be prohibited. On motion of James Tallmadge of New York a clause was inserted in the territorial bill forbidding any further introduction of slaves into Missouri and granting freedom to all slave-children on reaching the age of twenty-five. The bill as thus amended became the organic law of the territory. A few days afterwards when Arkansas was presented for territorial organization, John W. Taylor of New York moved the insertion of a clause similar to that in the Missouri bill; but the proposed amendment was voted down after a hot debate. Taylor then made a motion that hereafter, in the organization of territories out of the Louisiana purchase, slavery should be interdicted in all that part north of the parallel of thirty-six degrees and thirty minutes. This proposition was also lost after a very excited discussion. Meanwhile, Tallmadge's amendment to the Missouri bill was defeated in the Senate, and as a consequence both the new territories were organized *without restrictions in the matter of slavery.*

When the bill to admit Missouri as a State was finally, in January of 1820, brought before Congress, the measure was opposed by those who had desired the exclusion of slavery. But at that time the new Free State of Maine was asking for admission into the Union; and those who favored slavery in Missouri determined to exclude Maine unless Missouri should also be admitted. After another angry debate, which lasted till the 16th of February, the bill coupling the two new States together was actually passed; and then Senator Thomas of Illinois made a motion that henceforth and forever slavery should be excluded from all that part of the Louisiana cession—Missouri excepted—lying north of the parallel of thirty-six degrees and thirty minutes. Such was the celebrated MISSOURI COMPROMISE, one of the most important acts of American legislation—a measure chiefly supported by the genius, and carried through Congress by the persistent efforts, of Henry Clay. The principal conditions of the plan were these: *first*, the admission of Missouri as a slave-holding State; *secondly*, the division of the rest of the Louisiana purchase by the parallel of thirty-six degrees and thirty minutes; *thirdly*, the admission of new States, to be formed out of the territory south of that line, with or without slavery, as the people might determine; *fourthly*, the prohibition of slavery in all the new States to be organized out of territory north of the dividing-line. By this compromise the slavery agitation was allayed until 1849.

Meanwhile, the country had measurably recovered from the effects of the late war. With peace and plenty the resources of the nation were rapidly augmented. Toward the close of his term the President's administration grew into high favor with the people; and in the fall of 1820 he was re-elected with great unanimity. As Vice-President, Mr. Tompkins was also chosen for a second term. Scarcely had the excitement over the admission of Missouri subsided when the attention of the government was called to an alarming system of piracy which had sprung up in the West Indies. Early in 1822 the American frigate *Congress*, accompanied with eight smaller vessels, was sent thither; and in the course of the year more than twenty piratical ships were captured. In the following summer Commodore Porter was despatched with a larger fleet to cruise about Cuba and the neighboring islands. Such was his vigilance that the retreats of the sea-robbers were completely broken up; not a pirate was left afloat.

At this time the countries of South America were disturbed with many revolutions. From the days of Pizarro these states had been dependencies of European monarchies. Now they declared their independence, and struggled to maintain it by force of arms. The people of the United States, having achieved their own liberty, naturally sympathized with the patriots of the South. Mr. Clay urged upon the government the duty of giving official recognition to the South American republics. At last his views prevailed; and in March of 1822 a bill was passed by Congress recognizing the new states as sovereign nations. In the following year this action was followed up by the President with a vigorous message, in which he declared that for the future *the American continents were not to be considered as subjects for colonization by any European power.* This famous declaration constitutes what has ever since been known in the politics and diplomacy of the United States as THE MONROE DOCTRINE—a doctrine by which the entire Western hemisphere is consecrated to free institutions.

Great was the joy of the American people in the summer of 1824. The venerated La Fayette, now aged and gray, returned once more to visit the land for whose freedom he had shed his blood. The honored patriots who had

La Fayette.

fought by his side came forth to greet him. The younger heroes crowded around him. In every city, and on every battle-field which he visited, he was surrounded by a throng of shouting freemen. His journey through the country was a triumph. It was a solemn and sacred moment when he stood alone by the grave of Washington. Over the dust of the great dead the patriot of France paid the homage of his tears. In September of 1825 he bade a final adieu to the people who had made him their guest, and then sailed for his native land. At his departure, the frigate *Brandywine*—a name significant for *him*—was prepared to bear him away. While Liberty remains to cheer the West, the name of La Fayette shall be hallowed.

Before the departure of the illustrious Frenchman another presidential election had been held. It was a time of great excitement and much division of sentiment. Four candidates were presented for the suffrages of the people. There was an appearance of sectionalism in the canvass. John Quincy Adams was put forward as the candidate of the East; William H. Crawford of Georgia as the choice of the South; Henry Clay and Andrew Jackson as the favorites of the West. Neither candidate received a majority of the electoral votes, and for the second time in the history of the government the choice of President was referred to the House of Representatives. By that body Mr. Adams was duly elected. For Vice President, John C. Calhoun of South Carolina had been chosen by the electoral college.

CHAPTER LIII.

ADAMS'S ADMINISTRATION, 1825-1829.

THE new President was inaugurated on the 4th of March, 1825. He was a man of the highest attainments in literature and statesmanship. At the age of eleven years he accompanied his father, John Adams, to Europe. At Paris and Amsterdam and St. Petersburg the son continued his studies, and at the same time became acquainted with the manners and politics of the Old World. The vast opportunities of his youth were improved to the fullest extent. In his riper years he served his country as ambassador to the Netherlands, Portugal, Prussia, Russia and England. Such were his abilities in the field of diplomacy as to elicit from Washington the extraordinary praise of being the ablest minister of which America could boast. His life, from 1794 till 1817, was devoted almost wholly to diplomatical services at the various European capitals. At that critical period when the relations of the United States with foreign nations were as yet not well established, his genius secured the adoption of treaty after treaty in which the interests of his country were guarded with patriotic vigilance. In 1806 he was honored with the professorship of Rhetoric and Belles-Lettres at Harvard College of which he was an alumnus. He had also held the office of United States senator from Massachusetts; and on the accession of Monroe to the presidency was chosen secretary of state. To the presidential chair he brought the wisdom of mature years, great experience and unusual ability.

The new administration was an epoch of peace and prosperity in the country; but the spirit of party manifested itself with much violence. The adherents of General Jackson and Mr. Crawford united in opposition to the policy of the President; and there was a want of unanimity between the different departments of the government. In the Senate the political friends of Mr. Adams were in a minority, and their majority in the lower House only lasted for one session. In his inaugural address the President strongly advocated the doctrine of internal improvements; but the adverse views of Congress prevented his recommendations from being adopted.

For a quarter of a century a difficulty had existed between the government of the United States and Georgia in respect to the lands held in that State by the Creek Indians. When, in 1802, Georgia relinquished her claim to Mississippi Territory, the general government agreed to purchase and surrender to the State all the Creek lands lying within her own borders. This pledge on the part of the United States had never been fulfilled, and Georgia complained of bad faith. The difficulty became alarming; but finally, in March of 1826, a treaty was concluded between the Creek chiefs and the President, by which a cession of all their lands in Georgia was obtained. At the same time the Creeks agreed to remove to a new home beyond the Mississippi.

On the 4th of July, 1826—just fifty years to a day after the Declaration of Independence—the venerable John Adams, second President of the United States, and his successor, Thomas Jefferson, both died. Both had lifted their voices for freedom in the early and perilous days of the Revolution. One had written and both had signed the great Declaration. Both had lived to see their country's independence. Both had served that country in its highest official station. Both had reached extreme old age: Adams was ninety; Jefferson, eighty-two. Now, while the cannon were booming for the fiftieth birthday of the nation, the gray and honored patriots passed, almost at the same hour, from among the living.

In the following September, William Morgan, a resident of Western New York, having threatened to publish the secrets of the Masonic fraternity, of which he was a member, suddenly disappeared from his home, and was never heard of afterward. The Masons fell under the suspicion of having abducted and murdered him. A great clamor was raised against them in New York, and the excitement extended to other parts of the country. The issue between the Masons and their enemies became a political one, and many eminent men were embroiled in the controversy. For several years the anti-Masonic party exercised a considerable influence in the elections of the country. De Witt Clinton, one of the most prominent and valuable statesmen of New York, had to suffer much, in loss of reputation, from his membership in the order. His last days were clouded with the odium which for the time being attached to the Masonic name.

CHART V.

1825	29	33	37
Frederick William III.			
27. Acknowledgment of the independence of Greece.			40.
Charles X.	30. French Revolution and election of		37. Attempted capture
28. Abolition of the "Test Act."	**Louis Philippe.**		
	30. Polish Revolution.		39. Supp
	31. Fall of Warsaw.		40.
	32. Passage of the Great Reform bill by Parliament.		
George IV.	30. **William IV.**		37. **Victoria.**

John Q. Adams, President.
25. Controversy concerning the lands of the Creek Indians.   37. Michigan admitt

        Andrew Jackson, President.
                              36. Arkansas admitted into t

                       The Black Hawk War.

                            Jackson re-elected President.
26. John Adams d. July 4.
26. Thomas Jefferson d. July 4.
                              35. Seminole War.

                                                       Martin Van B
John C. Calhoun, Vice-President.
                         32. The bill to recharter the United States Bank vetoed
        28. Great political excitement throughout the country.   37. Failure of the S

                              35. Removal of the Cherokees.
                                                      40.
                    Calhoun re-elected Vice-President.
                    32. Great tariff excitement.
                    32. The doctrine of nullification declared by South Caroli
                    32. Proclamation by the President.
                        Martin Van Buren, Vice-President.
                          33. Passage of Mr. Clay's Compromise bill.

                                                         Richard M. J

                            33. Removal of Government funds from the
                                            37. Financial crisis.

                              San Antonio taken by the Texans.
                                  36.   *The Alamo.*
                                36.: **TEXAS INDEPENDEN**
NATIONAL PERIOD — SECOND SECTION
A.D. 1825–1853.   38. **Lamar,** P
CHART V.   36.:   *San Jacinto.*

                            MEXICO.
                            Santa Anna, President.   38. Vera Cruz b
                                  36. The "Central Republic"
                                             37. Bustamente, P

NATIONAL PERIOD–SECOND SECTION. A. D. 1825-1853.

41

:derick William IV.
Jadrid by Don Carlos.
on of the Carlists in Spain.
body of Napoleon returned to France.

nto the Union.
43. The Dorr rebellion in Rhode Island.
44. First telegraph line in the United States.

1. The Webster-Ashburton treaty.

en, President.
the President.
reasury bill.

William H. Harrison, President.
(Died April 4, 1841.)
age of the Treasury bill.
1. Treasury bill repealed.
1. Passage of the Bankrupt law.
1. Veto of the United States Bank, and resignation of the President's Cabinet.

ison, Vice-President.
d States bank.

John Tyler, Vice-President, and President from April, 1841.

. Houston, President.
ent.

. Santa Anna, President.
ed by the French.
red.
ent.

45

46. Election of Pius IX.
48. Revolution in France.
48. A republic proclaimed.
48. Louis Napoleon Bonaparte elected President.

James K. Polk, President.
45. Florida admitted into the Union.
46. Iowa admitted into the Union.
46. The north-western boundary fixed at 49°.
46. General Taylor ordered to the Rio Grande.
46. Congress declares war against Mexico.
46. 🏳 *Palo Alto*.
46. 🏳 *Resaca de la Palma*.
46. 🏳 *Capture of Matamoras*.
46. 🏳 *Monterey*.

George M. Dallas, Vice-President.
48. Discovery of gold in California.

47. 🏳 *Buena Vista*.
47. 🏳 *Vera Cruz*.
47. 🏳 *Cerro Gordo*.
47. 🏳 *Contreras*.
47. 🏳 *Molino del Rey*.
47. 🏳 *Chapultepec*.
47. 🏳 *Fall of Mexico*.
48. Treaty of peace with Mexico.
45. Texas admitted into the Union.

49

48. Outbreak of the Hungarian Revolution.

Zachary Taylor, President.
(Died July 9, 1850.)

54. Treaty with Japan.

Millard Fillmore, Vice-President, and President from July, 1850.

51. The Fugitive Slave law passed.
50. Utah erected into a Territorial government.
49. New Mexico erected into a Territorial government.

50. The "Omnibus Bill" passed.
50. California admitted into the Union.

53

52. Fall of Kossuth and the Hungarian cause.
52. Louis Napoleon, President for ten years.
52. Louis Napoleon, Emperor.
54. The Crimean War.

Fr'nklin Pierce, [President.

54. Treaty with Japan.
54. Passage of the Kansas and Nebraska bill.
54. The Missouri Compromise repealed.
54. Troubles in Kansas.

W. R. King, Vice-Pres.

In the congressional debates of 1828 the question of the tariff was much discussed. By a tariff is understood a duty levied on imported goods. The object of the same is twofold: first, to produce a revenue for the government; and secondly, to raise the price of the article on which the duty is laid, in order that the domestic manufacturer of the thing taxed may be able to compete with the foreign producer. When the duty is levied for the latter purpose, it is called a *protective tariff*. Whether it is sound policy for a nation to have protective duties is a question which has been much debated in all civilized countries. Mr. Adams and his friends decided in favor of a tariff; and in 1828 the duties on fabrics made of wool, cotton, linen and silk, and those on articles manufactured of iron, lead, etc., were much increased. The object of such legislation was to stimulate the manufacturing interests of the country. The question of the tariff has always been a sectional issue. The people of the Eastern and Middle States, where factories abound, have favored protective duties; while in the agricultural regions of the South and West such duties have been opposed.

The administration of John Quincy Adams was the beginning of a new epoch in the history of the United States. The Revolutionary sages had gradually fallen out of the ranks of leadership; and the influences of the Revolution were not any longer distinctly felt in the decision of national questions. Even the war of 1812, with its bitter party antagonisms, its defeats and victories, and its absurd ending, was fading out of memory. New dispositions and tastes arose among the people; new issues confronted the public; new methods prevailed in the halls of legislation. Old party lines could no longer be traced, old party names were reduced to a jargon. Already the United States had surpassed in growth and development the sanguine expectations of the fathers. But the conflicting opinions and interests of the nation, reflected in the stormy debates of Congress, gave cause for constant anxiety and alarm.

With the fall of 1828 came another presidential election. The contest was specially exciting. Mr. Adams, supported by Mr. Clay, the secretary of state, was put forward for re-election. In accordance with an understanding which had existed for several years, General Jackson appeared as the candidate of the opposition. In the previous election

Jackson had received more electoral votes than Adams; but disregarding the popular preference, the House of Representatives had chosen the latter. Now the people were determined to have their way; and Jackson was triumphantly elected, receiving a hundred and seventy-eight electoral votes against eighty-three to his opponent. As soon as the election was over, the excitement—as usual in such cases—abated; and the thoughts of the people were turned to other subjects.

CHAPTER LIV.

Jackson's Administration, 1829-1837.

THE new President was a native of North Carolina, born on the Waxhaw, March 15th, 1767. His belligerent nature broke out in boyhood, and his mother's plan of devoting him to the ministry was hopelessly defeated. At the age of thirteen he was under arms and witnessed Sumter's defeat at Hanging Rock. He was captured by the British, maltreated, and left to die of smallpox; but his mother secured his release from prison and his life was saved. After the Revolution he began the study of law, and at the age of twenty-one went to Nashville. In 1796 he was elected to the House of Representatives from the new State of Tennessee.

Andrew Jackson.

Here his turbulent and willful disposition manifested itself in full force. During the next year he was promoted to the Senate, where he remained a year, *without making a speech or casting a vote*. He then resigned his seat and returned home. His subsequent career is a part of the history of the country, more particularly of the South-west with which section his name was identified. He came to the presidential office as a military hero. But he was more than that: a man of great native powers and inflexible honesty. His talents were strong but unpolished; his integrity unassailable; his will like iron. He was one of those men for whom no toils are too arduous, no responsibility too great. His personal character was strongly impressed upon his administration. Believing that the public affairs would be best conducted by such means, he removed nearly seven hundred office-holders, and appointed in their stead his own political friends. In defence of such a course the precedent established by Mr. Jefferson was pleaded.

In his first annual message the President took strong grounds against rechartering the Bank of the United States. Believing that institution to be both inexpedient and unconstitutional, he recommended that the old charter should be allowed to expire by its own limitation in 1836. But the influence of the bank, with its many branches, was very great; and in 1832 a bill to recharter was brought before Congress and passed. To this measure the President opposed his veto; and since a two-thirds majority in favor of the bill could not be secured, the proposition to grant a new charter failed, and the bank ceased by the original limitation.

It was in the early part of Jackson's administration that the partisan elements of the country, which for some years had been whirling about in a chaotic condition, was resolved into the two great factions of *Whig* and *Democratic*—a form which remained as the established order in politics for a quarter of a century. The old Federal party, under whose auspices the government was organized, had lost control of national affairs on the retirement of John Adams from the presidency. Still the party lingered, opposed the war of 1812, and became odious from its connection with the Hartford Convention. In 1820 only enough of the old organization remained to be severely handled in the great debates on the Missouri Compromise. Then followed, during Monroe's second term, what is known in American political history as THE ERA OF GOOD FEELING. Partisanship seemed ready to expire. On the other side, the line of political descent had begun with the anti-Federalists who after opposing the National constitution and the administrative policy of Washington and Adams, became under the name of *Republicans* the champions of France as against Great Britain. But this name was soon exchanged for that of *Democrats*; and under that title the party came into power with the administration of Jefferson. Then followed the administrations of Madison, Monroe, and John Quincy Adams under the same political banner. But in the case of Adams the new forces were already at work. When Jackson became President his arbitrary measures alarmed the country and drove all the elements of the opposition into a compact phalanx under the leadership of Clay and Webster. To this new party organization the name of *Whig* was given—a name taken from the old Scotch Covenanters and English republicans of the seventeenth century, worn by the patriots of the American Revolution to distinguish them from the Tories, and now adopted as the permanent title of the opponents of Jeffersonian Democracy.

Daniel Webster.

The reopening of the tariff question occasioned great excitement in Congress and throughout the country. In the session of 1831-32 additional duties were levied upon manufactured goods imported from abroad. By this act the manufacturing districts were again favored at the expense of the agricultural States. South Carolina was specially offended. A great convention of her people was held, and it was resolved that the tariff-law of Congress was unconstitutional, and therefore null and void. Open resistance was threatened in case the officers of the government should attempt to collect the revenues in the harbor of Charleston. In the United States Senate the right of a State, under certain circumstances, to nullify an act of Congress was boldly proclaimed. On that issue occurred the famous debate between the eloquent Colonel Hayne, senator from South Carolina, and Daniel Webster of Massachusetts, per traps the greatest master of American oratory. The former appeared as the champion of State rights, and the latter as the advocate of constitutional supremacy.

But the question was not decided by debate. The President took the matter in hand and issued a proclamation denying the right of any State to nullify the laws of Congress. But Mr. Calhoun, the Vice President, resigned his office to accept a seat in the Senate, where he might better defend the doctrines of his State. The President, having warned the people of South Carolina against pursuing those doctrines further, ordered a body of troops under General Scott to proceed to Charleston, and also sent thither a man-of-war. At this display of force the leaders of the nullifying party quailed and receded from their position. Bloodshed was happily avoided; and in the following spring the excitement was allayed by a compromise. Mr. Clay brought forward and secured the passage of a bill providing for a gradual reduction of the duties complained of until, at the end of ten years, they should reach the standard demanded by the South.

In the spring of 1832 the Sac, Fox and Winnebago Indians of Wisconsin Territory began a war. They were incited and led by the famous chief Black Hawk, who, like many great sachems before him, believed in the possibility of an Indian confederacy sufficiently powerful to beat back the whites. The lands of the Sacs and Foxes lying in the Rock River country of Illinois, had been purchased by the government twenty-five years previously. The Indians, however, remained in the ceded territory, since there was no occasion for immediate occupation by the whites. When at last, after a quarter of a century, the Indians were required to give possession, they caviled at the old treaty, and refused to comply. The government insisted that the Red men should fulfill their contract, and hostilities began on the frontier. The governor of Illinois called out the militia, and General Scott was sent with nine companies of artillery to Chicago. At that place his force was overtaken with the cholera, and he was prevented from co-operating with the troops of General Atkinson. The latter, however, waged a vigorous campaign against the Indians, defeated them in several actions, and made Black Hawk prisoner. The captive chieftain was taken to Washington and the great cities of the East, where his understanding was opened as to the power of the nation against which he had been foolish enough to lift his hatchet. Returning to his own people, he advised them that resistance was hopeless. The warriors then abandoned the disputed lands and retired into Iowa.

Land of the Seminoles.

Difficulties also arose with the Cherokees of Georgia. These were the most civilized and humane of all the Indian nations. They had adopted the manners of the whites. They had pleasant farms, goodly towns, schools, printing-presses, a written code of laws. The government of the United States had given to Georgia a pledge to purchase the Cherokee lands for the benefit of the State. The pledge was not fulfilled; the authorities of Georgia grew tired of waiting for the removal of the Indians; and the legislature passed a statute by which the government of the Red men was abrogated and the laws of the State extended over the Indian domain. With singular illiberality, it was at the same time enacted that the Cherokees and Creeks should not have the use of the State courts or the protection of the laws. This code, however, was declared unconstitutional by the supreme court of the United States. The Indians then appealed to the President for help; but he refused to interpose between them and the laws of Georgia. He also recommended the removal of the Cherokees to lands beyond the Mississippi and with this end in view, THE INDIAN TERRITORY was organized in the year 1834. The Indians yielded with great reluctance. More than five million dollars were paid them for their lands; but still they clung to their homes. At last General Scott was ordered to remove them to the new territory, using force if necessary to accomplish the work. The years 1837-38 were occupied with the final transfer of the Cherokees to their homes in the West.

More serious still was the conflict with the Seminoles of Florida. The trouble arose from an attempt on the part of the government to remove the tribe to a new domain beyond the Mississippi. Hostilities began in 1835 and continued for four years. The chief of the Seminoles was Osceola, a half-breed of great talents and audacity. He and Micanopy, another chieftain, denied the validity of a former treaty by which the Seminole lands had been ceded to the government. So haughty was the bearing of Osceola that General Thompson, the agent of the government in Florida arrested him and put him in irons. The red warrior dissembled his purpose, gave his assent to the old treaty, and was liberated. As might have been foreseen, he immediately entered into a conspiracy to slaughter the whites and devastate the country.

At this time the interior of Florida was held by General Clinch, who had his headquarters at Fort Drane, seventy-five miles south-west from St. Augustine. The post was considered in danger; and Major Dade with a hundred and seventeen men was despatched from Fort Brooke, at the head of Tampa Bay, to reinforce General Clinch. After marching about half the distance, Dade's forces fell into an ambuscade, and were all massacred except one man who was left alive under a heap of the dead. On the same day Osceola, with a band of warriors, prowling around Fort King, on the Ocklawaha, surrounded a storehouse where General Thompson was dining with a company of friends. The savages poured in a murderous fire, and then rushed forward and scalped the dead before the garrison of the fort, only two hundred and fifty yards away, could bring assistance. General Thompson's body was pierced by fifteen balls; and four of his nine companions were killed.

On the 31st of December General Clinch fought a battle with the Indians on the banks of the Withlacoochie. The savages were repulsed, but Clinch thought it prudent to retreat to Fort Drane. In the following February General Scott took command of the American forces in Florida. On the 29th of the same month General Gaines, who was advancing from the West with a force of a thousand men for the relief of Fort Drane, was attacked near the battle-field where Clinch had fought. The Seminoles made a furious onset, but were repulsed with severe losses. In May some straggling Creeks who still remained in the country began hostilities; but they were soon subdued and compelled to seek their reservation beyond the Mississippi. In October of 1896 Governor Call of Florida marched with a force of two thousand men against the Indians of the interior. A division of his army overtook the enemy in the Wahoo Swamp, a short distance from the scene of Dade's massacre. A battle ensued, and the Indians were driven into the Everglades with considerable losses. Soon afterward another engagement was fought on nearly the same ground; and again the savages were beaten, though not decisively. The remainder of the history of the Seminole War belongs to the following administration.

In the mean time the President had given a final quietus to the Bank of the United States. After vetoing the bill to recharter that institution, he conceived that the surplus funds which had accumulated in its vaults would be better distributed among the States. He had no warrant of law for such a step; but believing himself to be in the right, he did not hesitate to take the responsibility. Accordingly, in October of 1833, he ordered the accumulated funds of the great bank, amounting to about ten million dollars, to be distributed among certain State banks designated for that purpose. This action on the part of the President was denounced by the opposition as a measure of incalculable mischief—unwarranted, arbitrary, dangerous. In the Senate a powerful coalition, headed by Calhoun, Clay, and Webster, was formed against the President; and the new officers, who had been appointed to carry out his measures, were rejected. A resolution censuring his conduct was then introduced and carried; but a similar proposition failed in the House of Representatives. For a while there was a general cry of indignation, and it seemed that the administration would be overwhelmed; but the President, ever as fearless as he was self-willed and stubborn, held on his course, unmoved by the clamor. The resolution of censure stood upon the journal of the Senate for four years and was then expunged from the record through the influence of Senator Thomas H. Benton of Missouri. The financial panic of 1836-7, following soon after the removal of the funds, was attributed by the opponents of the administration to the President's arbitrary action and the prospective destruction of the national bank. To these strictures the adherents of his own party replied that the financial distress of the country was attributable to the bank itself, which was declared to be an institution too powerful and despotic to exist in a free government. The President was but little concerned with the excitement: he had just entered on his second term, with Martin Van Buren for Vice-President instead of Mr. Calhoun.

The New Patent-Office at Washington.

In 1834 the strong will of the chief magistrate was brought into conflict with France. The American government held an old claim against that country for damages done to the commerce of the United States in the wars of Napoleon. In 1831 the French king had agreed to pay five million dollars for the alleged injuries; but the dilatory government of France postponed and neglected the payment until the President, becoming wrathful, recommended to Congress to make reprisals on French commerce, and at the same time directed the American minister at Paris to demand his passports and come home.

These measures had the desired effect, and the indemnity was promptly paid. The government of Portugal was brought to terms in a similar manner.

The country, though flourishing, was not without calamities. Several eminent statesmen fell by the hand of death. On the 4th of July, 1831, ex-President Monroe passed-away. Like Jefferson and Adams, he sank to rest amid the rejoicings of the national anniversary. In the following year Charles Carroll of Carrollton, the last surviving signer of the Declaration of Independence, died at the age of ninety-six. A short time afterward Philip Freneau, the poet of the Revolution, departed from the land of the living. The patriot bard had reached the age of eighty. On the 24th of June, 1833, John Randolph of Roanoke died in Philadelphia. He was a man admired for his talents, dreaded for his wit and sarcasm, and respected for his integrity as a statesman. In 1835 Chief-Justice Marshall breathed his last, at the age of fourscore years; and in the next year ex-President Madison, worn with the toils of eighty-five years, passed away. To these losses of life must be added two great disasters to property. On the 16th of December, 1835, a fire broke out in the lower part of New York City and laid thirty acres of buildings in ashes. Five hundred and twenty-nine houses and property valued at eighteen million dollars were consumed. Just one year afterward the Patent Office and Post-Office at Washington were destroyed in the same manner. But upon the ruins of these valuable buildings, more noble and imposing structures were soon erected.

Jackson's administration was signalized by the addition of two new States. In June of 1836 Arkansas was admitted, with an area of fifty-two thousand square miles, and a population of seventy thousand. In January of the following year Michigan Territory was organized as a State and added to the Union. The new common wealth brought a population of a hundred and fifty-seven thousand, and an area of fifty-six thousand square miles. The administration was already within two months of its close. The President, following the example of Washington, issued a patriotic farewell address. The dangers of discord and sectionalism among the States were set forth with all the masculine energy of the Jacksonian dialect. The people of the United States were again solemnly warned, as they had been by the Father of his Country, against the baleful influence of demagogues. The horrors of disunion were portrayed in the strongest colors; and people of every rank and section were exhorted to maintain and defend the American Union as they would the last fortress of human liberty. This was the last of those remarkable public papers contributed by Andrew Jackson to the history of his country. Already, in the autumn of the previous year, Martin Van Buren had been elected President. The opposing candidate was General Harrison of Ohio, who received the support of the new Whig party. As to the vice-presidency, no one secured a majority in the electoral college, and the choice devolved on the Senate. By that body Colonel Richard M. Johnson of Kentucky was duly elected.

CHAPTER LV.

Van Buren's Administration, 1837-1841.

MARTIN VAN BUREN, eighth President of the United States was born at Kinderhook, New York, on the 5th of December, 1782. After receiving a limited education he became a student of law, and before reaching his majority was recognized as an influential democratic politician. In his thirtieth year he was elected to the Senate of his native State; and six years afterwards, by supplanting De Witt Clinton, became the recognized leader of the Democracy in New York. In 1821, and again in 1827, he was chosen United States Senator; but in the following year he resigned his office to accept the governorship of his native State. He also, in 1831, resigned his place as secretary of State in the first cabinet of President Jackson, and was appointed minister to England. But when, in December of the same year, his nomination was submitted to the Senate the influence of Vice-President Calhoun assisted by the Whig leaders, Clay and Webster, procured the rejection of the appointment. Mr. Van Buren returned from his unfulfilled mission; became the candidate for the vice-presidency, and was elected in the fall of 1832. Four years later he was called by the voice of the powerful party to which he be longed, to succeed General Jackson in the highest office of the nation.

One of the first duties of the new administration was to finish the Seminole War. In the beginning of 1837 the command of the army in Florida was transferred from General Scott to General Jessup. In the following fall Osceola came to the American camp with a flag of truce; but he was suspected of treachery, seized, and sent a prisoner to Fort Moultrie, where he died in 1838. The Seminoles, though disheartened by the loss of their chief, continued the war. In December Colonel Zachary Taylor, with a force of over a thousand men, marched into the Everglades of Florida, determined to fight the savages in their lairs. After unparalleled sufferings he overtook them, on Christmas day, near Lake Okeechobee. A hard battle was fought, and the Indians were defeated, but not until a hundred and thirty-nine of the whites had fallen. For more than a year Taylor continued to hunt the Red men through the swamps. In 1839 the chiefs sent in their submission and signed a treaty; but their removal to the West was made with much reluctance and delay.

In the first year of Van Buren's administration the country was afflicted with a monetary panic of the most serious character. The preceding years had been a time of great prosperity. The national debt was entirely liquidated, and a surplus of nearly forty million dollars had accumulated in the treasury of the United States. By act of Congress this vast sum had been distributed among the several States. Owing to the abundance of money, speculations of all sorts grew rife. The credit system pervaded every department of business. The banks of the country were suddenly multiplied to nearly seven hundred. Vast issues of irredeemable paper money stimulated the speculative spirit and increased the opportunities for fraud.

The bills of these unsound banks were receivable at the land-offices; and settlers and speculators made a rush to secure the public lands while money was plentiful. Seeing that in receiving such an unsound currency in exchange for the national domain the government was likely to be defrauded out of millions, President Jackson had issued an order called THE SPECIE CIRCULAR, by which the land-agents were directed hence forth to receive nothing but coin in payment for the lands. The effects of this circular came upon the nation in the first year of Van Buren's administration. The interests of the government had been secured by Jackson's vigilance; but the business of the country was prostrated by the shock. The banks suspended specie payment. Mercantile houses failed; and disaster swept through every avenue of trade. During the months of March and April, 1837, the failures in New York and New Orleans amounted to about a hundred and fifty million dollars. A committee of business men from the former city besought the President to rescind the specie circular and to call a special session of Congress. The former request was refused and the latter complied with; but not until the executive was driven by the distresses of the country.

When Congress convened in the following September, several measures of relief were brought forward. A bill authorizing the issue of treasury notes, not to exceed ten millions of dollars, was passed as a temporary expedient. More important by far was the measure proposed by the President and brought before Congress under the name of THE INDEPENDENT TREASURY BILL. By the provisions of this remarkable project the public funds of the nation were to be kept on deposit in a treasury to be established for that special purpose. It was argued by Mr. Van Buren and his friends that the surplus money of the country would drift into the independent treasury and lodge there; and that by this means the speculative mania would be effectually checked; for extensive speculations could not be carried on without an abundant currency. It was in the nature of the President's plan to separate the business of the United States from the general business of the country.

The independent treasury bill was passed by the Senate, but defeated in the House of Representatives. But in the following regular session of Congress the bill was again brought forward and adopted. In the mean time, the business of the country had in a measure revived. During the year 1838 most of the banks resumed specie payments. Commercial affairs assumed their wonted aspect; but trade was less vigorous than before. Enterprises of all kinds languished, and the people were greatly disheartened. Discontent prevailed; and the administration was blamed with everything.

In the latter part of 1837 there was an insurrection in Canada. A portion of the people, dissatisfied with the British government, broke out in revolt and attempted to establish their independence. The insurgents found much sympathy and encouragement in the United States, especially in New York. From that State a party of seven hundred men, taking arms, seized and fortified Navy Island, in the Niagara River. The loyalists of Canada attempted to capture the place, and failed. They succeeded, however, in firing the *Caroline*, the supply-ship of the adventurers, cut her moorings, and sent the burning vessel over Niagara Falls. These events created considerable excitement, and the peaceful relations of the United States and Great Britain were endangered. But the President issued a proclamation of neutrality, forbidding interference with the affairs of Canada; and General Wool was sent to the Niagara frontier with a sufficient force to quell the disturbance and punish the disturbers. The New York insurgents on Navy Island were obliged to surrender, and order was soon restored.

Hardly had the excitement attendant upon the Canadian troubles subsided, before the question was raised as to Van Buren's successor in the presidency. The canvass began early and in a very bitter spirit. The measures of the administration had been of such a nature as to call forth the fiercest political controversy. The Whigs, animated with the hope of victory, met in national convention on the 4th of December, 1839, and again nominated General Harrison as their leader in the coming contest. On the Democratic side Mr. Van Buren had no competitor; but the unanimity of his party could hardly compensate for his misfortunes and blunders. The canvass was the most exciting in the political history of the country. The President was blamed with every thing. The financial distress was laid at his door. Extravagance, bribery, corruption—every thing bad was charged upon him. Men of business advertised to pay six dollars a barrel for flour if Harrison should be elected; three dollars a barrel if Van Buren should be successful. The Whig orators tossed about the luckless administration through all the figures and forms of speech; and the President himself was shot at with every sort of dart that partisan wit and malice could invent. The enthusiasm in the ranks of the opposition rose higher and higher; and the result was the defeat of the Democrats in every State except Alabama, Arkansas, Illinois, Missouri, New Hampshire, Virginia, and South Carolina. The electoral votes of these States—numbering sixty—were given to Van Buren; and the remainder, amounting to two hundred and thirty-four, were cast for General Harrison. After controlling the destinies of the government for nearly forty years, the Democratic party was temporarily routed. For Vice-President, John Tyler of Virginia was chosen.

In the last year of Van Buren's administration was completed the sixth census of the United States. The tables were, as usual, replete with the evidences of growth and progress. The national revenues for the year 1840 amounted to nearly twenty millions of dollars. During the last ten years the center of population had moved westward along the thirty-ninth parallel of latitude from the South Fork of the Potomac to Clarksburg, West Virginia—a distance of fifty-five miles. The area of the

United States now actually inhabited, amounted to eight hundred and seven thousand square miles, being an increase in ten years of twenty-seven and six-tenths per cent. The frontier line, circumscribing the population, passed through Michigan, Wisconsin, Iowa, and the western borders of Missouri, Arkansas, and Louisiana—a distance of three thousand three hundred miles. The population had reached the aggregate of seventeen million souls, being an increase since 1830 of more than six millions. It was found from the tables that eleven-twelfths of the people lived outside of the larger cities and towns, showing the strong preponderance of the agricultural over the manufacturing and commercial interest. One of the most interesting lessons of the census was found in the fact that the wonderful growth of the United States was in *extent and area*, and not in *accumulation*—in the *spread* of civilization rather than in *intensity*. For, since 1830, the average population of the country had not increased by so much as *one person to the square mile!*

The administration of Van Buren has generally been reckoned as unsuccessful and inglorious. But he and his times were unfortunate rather than bad. He was the victim of all the evils which followed hard upon the relaxation of the Jacksonian methods of government. He had neither the will nor the disposition to rule as his predecessor had done; nor were the people and their representatives any longer in the humor to suffer that sort of government. The period was unheroic: it was the ebb-tide between the belligerent excitements of 1832 and the war with Mexico. The financial panic added opprobrium to the popular estimate of imbecility in the government. "The administration of Van Buren," said a bitter satirist, "is like a parenthesis: it may be read in a low tone of voice or altogether omitted *without injuring the sense!*" But the satire lacked one essential quality–truth.

CHAPTER LVI.

ADMINISTRATIONS OF HARRISON AND TYLER, 1841-1845.

THE new President was a Virginian by birth, and the adopted son of Robert Morris, the financier of the Revolution. He was a graduate of Hampden-Sidney College, and afterward a student of medicine. Attracted by the military life, he entered the army of St. Clair; was rapidly promoted; became lieutenant-governor and then governor of Indiana Territory, which office he filled with great ability. His military career in the North-west has already been narrated. He was inaugurated President on the 4th of March, 1841, and began his duties by issuing a call for a special session of Congress to consider "sundry important matters connected with the finances of the country." An able cabinet was organized, at the head of which was Daniel Webster as secretary of state. Everything promised well for the new Whig administration; but before Congress could convene, the venerable President, bending under the weight of sixty-eight years, fell sick, and died just one month after his inauguration. It was the first time that such a calamity had befallen the American people. Profound and universal grief was manifested at the sad event. On the 6th of April Mr. Tyler took the oath of office, and became President of the United States.

He was a statesman of considerable distinction; a native of Virginia a graduate of William and Mary College. At an early age he left the profession of law to enter public life; was chosen a member of Congress; and in 1825 was elected governor of Virginia. From that position he was sent to the Senate of the United States; and now at the age of fifty-one was called to the presidency. He had been put upon the ticket with General Harrison through motives of expediency; for although a Whig in political principles, he was *known to be hostile to the United States Bank.* And this hostility was soon to be manifested in a remarkable manner.

The special session of Congress continued from May till September. One of the first measures proposed and carried was the repeal of the independent treasury bill. A general bankrupt law was then brought forward and passed, by which a great number of insolvent business men were relieved from the disabilities of debt. The next measure—a favorite scheme of the Whigs—was the rechartering of the bank of the United States. The old charter had expired in 1836; but the bank had continued in operation under the authority of the State of Pennsylvania. Now a bill to recharter was brought forward and passed. The President interposed his veto. Again the bill was presented, in a modified form, and received the assent of both Houses, only to be rejected by the executive. By this action a final rupture was produced between the President and the party which had elected him. The indignant Whigs, baffled by a want of a two-thirds majority in Congress, turned upon him with storms of invective. All the members of the cabinet except Mr. Webster resigned; and he retained his place only because of a pending difficulty with Great Britain.

The difficulty was in the nature of a dispute about the north-eastern boundary of the United States. The territorial limit of the country in that direction, not having been clearly defined by the treaty of 1783, had been one of the points under discussion by the commissioners at Ghent in 1814. But like other matters presented for adjudication before that polite and easily satisfied congress, the boundary question had been postponed rather than settled. It was then agreed, however, to refer the establishment of the entire line between the United States and Canada to the decision of three commissioners to be jointly constituted by the two governments. The first of these bodies accomplished its work successfully by awarding to the United States the islands in the Bay of Passamaquoddy. The third commission also performed its duty by establishing the true boundary line from the intersection of the forty-fifth parallel of latitude with the River St. Lawrence to the western point of Lake Huron. To the second commission was assigned the more difficult task of settling the boundary from the Atlantic to the St. Lawrence; and this work they failed to accomplish. For nearly twenty-five years the limit of the United States on the northeast remained in controversy; and at times the difficulty became so serious as to endanger the peace of the two nations. Finally the whole matter at issue was referred to Lord Ashburton, acting on the part of Great Britain, and Mr. Webster, the American Secretary of State. After an able discussion of all the points in dispute, the boundary was definitely established as follows: From the mouth of the River St. Croix ascending that stream to its western fountain; from that fountain due north to the St. John's; thence with that river to its source on the watershed between the Atlantic and the St. Lawrence; thence in a southwesterly direction along the crest of the highlands to the northwestern source of the Connecticut; and down that stream to and along the forty-fifth parallel to the St. Lawrence. The work of the commissioners extended also to the establishment of the boundary from the western point of Lake Huron through Lake Superior to the northwestern extremity of the Lake of Woods, thence—confirming the treaty of October, 1818,—southward to the forty-ninth parallel of latitude, and thence with that parallel to the Rocky Mountains. This important settlement, known as THE WEBSTER-ASHBURTON TREATY, was completed on the 9th of August, 1842, and was ratified by the Senate on the 20th of the same month.

In the next year the country was vexed with a domestic trouble. For nearly two centuries the government of Rhode Island had been administered under a charter granted by Charles II. By the terms of that ancient instrument the right of suffrage was restricted to those who held a certain amount of property. There were other clauses repugnant to the spirit of republicanism; and a proposition was made to change the constitution of the State. On that issue the people of Rhode Island were nearly unanimous; but in respect to the *manner* of abrogating the old charter there was a serious division. One faction, called the "law and order party," proceeding in accordance with the former constitution, chose Samuel W. King as governor. The other faction, called the "suffrage party," acting in an irregular way, elected Thomas W. Dorr. In May of 1842 both parties met and organized their rival governments.

The "law and order party" now undertook to suppress the faction of Dorr. The latter resisted and made an attempt to capture the State arsenal. But the militia, under the direction of King's officers, drove the assailants away. A month later the adherents of Dorr again appeared in arms, but were dispersed by the troops of the United States. Dorr fled from Rhode Island; returned soon afterward, was caught, tried for treason, convicted, and sentenced to imprisonment for life. He was then offered pardon on condition of taking an oath of allegiance. This he stubbornly refused to do; and in June of 1845 obtained his liberty without conditions.

Bunker Hill Monument.

The year 1842 was noted for the completion of THE BUNKER HILL MONUMENT. No enterprise of a similar character had, in the whole history of the country, called forth so much patriotic enthusiasm. The foundation of the noble structure was laid on the 17th of June, 1825, the corner-stone being put into its place by the venerable La Fayette. Daniel Webster, then young in years and fame, delivered the oration of the day, while two hundred Revolutionary veterans—forty of them survivors of the battle fought on that hill-crest just fifty years before—gathered with the throng to hear him. But the work of erection went on slowly. More than a hundred and fifty thousand dollars were expended, and seventeen years lapsed before the grand shaft—commemorative of the heroes living and dead—was finished. At last the work was done, and the mighty column of Quincy granite, thirty-one feet square at the base and two hundred and twenty-one feet in height, stood out sublimely against the clouds and sky. It was deemed fitting, however, to postpone the dedication until the next anniversary of the battle; and preparations were made accordingly. On the 17th of June, 1843, an immense multitude of people—including most of the Revolutionary soldiers who had not yet fallen—gathered from all parts of the Republic to witness the imposing ceremony. Mr. Webster, now full of years and honors, was chosen to deliver the address of dedication—a duty which he performed in a manner so touching and eloquent as to add new luster to his fame as an orator. The celebration was concluded with a public dinner given in Faneuil Hall, the cradle of American liberty.

In the latter part of Tyler's administration the State of New York was the scene of a serious social disturbance. Until the year 1840 the descendants of Van Rensselaer, one of the old Dutch patroons of New Netherland, had held a claim on certain lands in the counties of Rensselaer, Columbia and Delaware. In liquidation of this claim they had continued to receive from the farmers certain trifling rents. At last the farmers grew tired of the payment, and rebelled. From 1840 until 1844 the question was frequently discussed in the New York legislature; but no satisfactory settlement was reached. In the latter year the anti-rent party became so bold as to coat with tar and feathers those of their fellow-tenants who made the payments. Officers were sent to apprehend the rioters; and them they killed. Time and again the authorities of the State were invoked to quell the disturbers; and the question in dispute has never been permanently settled.

Of a different sort was the difficulty with the Mormons, who now began to play a part in the history of the country. Under the leadership of their prophet, Joseph Smith, they made their first important settlement in Jackson county, Missouri. Here their numbers increased to fully fifteen hundred; and they began to say that the great West to be their inheritance. Not liking their neighbors or their practices, the people of Missouri determined to be rid of them. As soon as opportunity offered, the militia was called out, and the Mormons were obliged to leave the State. In the spring of 1839 they crossed the Mississippi into Illinois, and on a high bluff overlooking the river laid out a city which they called Nauvoo, meaning *the Beautiful*. Here they built a splendid temple. Other Mormons from different parts of the Union and from Europe came to join the community, until the number was swelled to ten thousand. Again popular suspicion was aroused against them. Under the administration of Smith, laws were enacted contrary to the statute of Illinois. The people charged the Mormons with the commission of certain thefts and murders; and it was believed that the courts in the neighborhood of Nauvoo would be powerless to convict the criminals.

In the midst of much excitement Smith and his brother were arrested, taken to Carthage, and lodged in jail. On the 27th of June, 1844, a mob gathered, broke open the jail doors and killed the prisoners. During the rest of the summer there were many scenes of violence. In 1845 the charter of Nauvoo was annulled by the legislature of Illinois. Most of the Mormons gave up in despair and resolved to exile themselves beyond the limits of civilization. In 1846 they began their march to the far West. In September Nauvoo was cannonaded for three days, and the remnant of inhabitants driven to join their companions at Council Bluffs. Thence they dragged themselves wearily westward; crossed the Rocky Mountains; reached the basin of the Great Salt Lake, and founded Utah Territory.

Meanwhile, a great agitation had arisen in the country in regard to the republic of Texas. From 1821 to 1836 this vast territory lying between Louisiana and Mexico, had been a province of the latter country. For a long time it had been the policy of Spain and Mexico to keep Texas uninhabited, in order that the vigorous race of Americans might not encroach on the Mexican borders. At last, however, a large land grant was made to Moses Austin of Connecticut, on condition that he would settle three hundred American families within the limits of his domain. Afterward the grant was confirmed to his son Stephen, with the privilege of establishing five hundred additional families of immigrants. Thus the foundation of Texas was laid by people of the English race.

Owing to the oppressive policy adopted by Mexico, the Texans, in the year 1835, raised the standard of rebellion. Many adventurers and some heroes from the United States flocked to their aid. In the first battle, fought at Gonzales, a thousand Mexicans were defeated by a Texan force numbering five hundred. On the 6th of March, 1836, a Texan fort, called the Alamo, was surrounded by a Mexican army of eight thousand, commanded by President Santa Anna. The feeble garrison was overpowered and massacred under circumstances of great atrocity. The daring David Crocket, an ex-congressman of Tennessee, and a famous hunter, was one of the victims of the butchery. In the next month was fought the decisive battle of San Jacinto, which gave to Texas her freedom. The independence of the new State was acknowledged by the United States, Great Britain and France.

As soon as the people of Texas had thrown off the Mexican yoke they asked to be admitted into the Union. At first the proposition was declined by President Van Buren, who feared a war with Mexico. In the last year of Tyler's administration the question of annexation was again agitated. The population of Texas had increased to more than two hundred thousand souls. The territory embraced an area of two hundred and thirty-seven thousand square miles—a domain more than five times as large as the State of Pennsylvania. It was like annexing an empire. The proposition to admit Texas into the Union was the great question on which the

Professor Morse.

people divided in the presidential election of 1844. The annexation was favored by the Democrats and opposed by the Whigs. The parties were equally matched in strength; and the contest surpassed in excitement anything which had been known in American politics. James K. Polk of Tennessee was put forward as the Democratic candidate, while the Whigs chose their favorite leader, Henry Clay. The former was elected, and the hope of the latter to reach the presidency was forever eclipsed. For Vice-President, George M. Dallas of Pennsylvania was chosen.

The convention by which Mr. Polk was nominated was held at Baltimore. On the 29th of May, 1844, the news of the nomination was sent to Washington by THE MAGNETIC TELEGRAPH. It was the first despatch ever so transmitted; and the event marks an era in the history of civilization. The inventor of the telegraph, which has proved so great a blessing to mankind, was Professor Samuel F. B. Morse of Massachusetts. The magnetic principle on which the invention depends had been known since 1774 but Professor Morse was the first to apply that principle for the benefit of men. He began his experiments in 1832: and five years afterward succeeded in obtaining a patent on his invention. Then followed another long delay; and it was not until the last day of the session in 1843 that he procured from Congress an appropriation of thirty thousand dollars. With that appropriation was constructed between Baltimore and Washington the first telegraphic line in the world. Perhaps no other invention has exercised a more beneficent influence on the welfare and happiness of the human race.

When Congress convened in December of 1844, the proposition to admit Texas into the Union was formally brought forward. During the winter the question was frequently debated; and on the 1st of March—only three days before Tyler's retirement from the presidency—the bill of annexation was adopted. The President immediately gave his assent; and the LONE STAR took its place in the constellation of the States. On the day before the inauguration of Mr. Polk bills for the admission of Florida and Iowa were also signed; but the latter State—the twenty-ninth member of the American Union—was not formally admitted until the following year.

CHAPTER LVII.

POLK'S ADMINISTRATION, AND THE MEXICAN WAR, 1845-1849.

PRESIDENT POLK was a native of North Carolina. In boyhood he removed with his father to Tennessee; entered the legislature of the State; and was then elected to Congress, where he served as member or speaker for fourteen years. In 1839 he was chosen governor of Tennessee, and from that position was called, at the early age of forty-nine, to the presidential chair. At the head of the new cabinet was placed James Buchanan of Pennsylvania. It was an office requiring high abilities; for the threatening question with Mexico came at once to a crisis. As soon as the resolution to annex Texas was adopted by Congress, Almonte, the Mexican minister at Washington, demanded his passports and left the country.

On the 4th of July, 1845, the Texan legislature ratified the act of annexation; and the union was completed. Knowing the warlike determination of Mexico, the authorities of Texas sent an immediate and urgent request to the President to despatch an army for their protection. Accordingly, General Zachary Taylor was ordered to march from Camp Jessup, in Western Louisiana, and occupy Texas. The real question at issue between that State and Mexico was concerning boundaries. The foundation of the difficulty had been laid as early as the Mexican revolution of 1821. By that event Mexico had achieved her independence of Spain, and in rearranging her civil administration had united Coahuila and Texas—the two frontier States east of the Rio Grande—under one provincial government. Such was the condition of affairs at the time of the Texan rebellion of 1836. Texas, being successful in her struggle with Mexico, naturally claimed that her own independence carried with it the independence of Coahuila, and that, therefore, the territory of the latter province became an integral part of the new Texan republic. This theory the joint legislature of Texas and Coahuila made haste to put into statutory form by a resolution of December 19th, 1836. Mexico, however, insisted that Texas only, and not Coahuila, had revolted against her authority, and that, therefore, the latter province, was still rightfully a part of the Mexican dominions. Thus it came to pass that Texas—now a State in the American Union—claimed the Rio Grande as her western limit, while Mexico was determined to have the Nueces as the separating line. The territory between the two rivers was in dispute. The government of the United States made a proposal to settle the controversy by negotiation, but the authorities of Mexico scornfully refused. This refusal was construed by the Americans as a virtual acknowledgment that the Mexicans were in the wrong, and that the Rio Grande might justly be claimed as the boundary. Instructions were accordingly sent to General Taylor to advance his army as near to that river as circumstances would warrant. Under these orders he moved forward to Corpus Christi, at the mouth of the Nueces, established a camp, and by the beginning of November, 1845, had concentrated a force of between four and five thousand men.

Texas and Coahuila, 1845.

In the following January General Taylor was ordered to advance to the Rio Grande. It was known that the Mexican government had resolved not to receive the American ambassador sent thither to negotiate a settlement. It had also transpired that an army of Mexicans was gathering in the northern part of the country for the invasion of Texas, or, at any rate, for the occupation of the disputed territory. On the 8th of March the American army began the advance from Corpus Christi to Point Isabel, on the gulf. At that place General Taylor established a dépôt of supplies, and then pressed forward to the Rio Grande. Arriving at the river a few miles above the mouth, he took his station opposite Matamoras and hastily erected a fortress, afterward named Fort Brown.

Scene of Taylor's Campaign, 1846-47.

On the 26th of April, General Arista, who had arrived at Matamoras on the previous day and assumed command of the Mexican forces on the frontier, notified General Taylor that hostilities had begun. On the same day a company of American dragoons, commanded by Captain Thornton, was attacked by a body of Mexicans, *east of the Rio Grande*, and after losing sixteen men in killed and wounded, was obliged to surrender. This was the first bloodshed of the war. At the same time large bodies of Mexicans—marauders, infantry, and cavalry—crossed the Rio Grande be low Fort Brown and threatened the American lines of communication. General Taylor, alarmed lest the Mexicans should make a circuit and capture the stores at Point Isabel, hastened to that place and strengthened the defences. The fort opposite Matamoras was left under the command of Major Brown with a garrison of three hundred men. The withdrawal of the American general with the greater part of his forces was witnessed by the Mexicans in Matamoras, who, mistaking the movement for a retreat inspired by fear, were in great jubilation. *The Republican Monitor*, a Mexican newspaper of Matamoras, published on the following day a flaming editorial, declaring that the cowardly invaders of Mexico had fled like a gang of poltroons to the sea-coast and were using every exertion to get out of the country before the thunderbolt of Mexican vengeance should smite them. Arista himself was confident that the Americans, becoming alarmed at their exposed position, had shrunk from the conflict and that it was only necessary for him to bombard Fort Brown in order to end the war.

As soon as his supplies at Point Isabel were deemed secure, General Taylor set out with a provision-train and an army of more than two thousand men to return to Fort Brown. Meanwhile, the Mexicans to the number of six thousand had crossed the Rio Grande and taken a strong position at Palo Alto, directly in Taylor's route. At noon on the 8th of May the Americans came in sight and immediately joined battle. After a severe engagement of five hours' duration the Mexicans were driven from the field, with the loss of a hundred men. The American artillery was served with signal effect; while the fighting of the enemy was clumsy and ineffectual. Only four Americans were killed and forty wounded;

but among the former was the gallant and much-lamented Major Ringgold of the artillery.

On the following day General Taylor resumed his march in the direction of Fort Brown. When within three miles of that place, he again came upon the Mexicans, who had rallied in full force to dispute his advance. They had selected for their second battle-field a place called Resaca de la Palma. Here an old river-bed, dry and overgrown with cactus, crossed the road leading to the fort. The enemy's artillery was well posted and better served than on the previous day. The American lines were severely galled until the brave Captain May with his regiment of dragoons charged through a storm of grape-shot, rode over the Mexican batteries, sabred the gunners, and captured La Vega, the commanding general. The Mexicans, abandoning their guns and flinging away their accoutrements, fled in a general rout. Before nightfall they had put the Rio Grande between themselves and the invincible Americans. On reaching Fort Brown, General Taylor found that during his absence the place had been constantly bombarded by the guns of Matamoras. But a brave defence had been made, which cost, with other losses and suffering, the life of Major Brown, the commandant. Such was the beginning of a war in which Mexico experienced a long list of humiliating defeats.

When the news of the battles on the Rio Grande was borne through the Union, the war spirit was everywhere aroused. Party dissensions were hushed into silence. The President, in a message to Congress, notified that body that the lawless soldiery of Mexico had shed the blood of American citizens on American soil. On the 11th of May, 1846, Congress promptly responded with a declaration that war already existed by the act of the Mexican government. The President was authorized to accept the services of fifty thousand volunteers, and ten million dollars were placed at his disposal. War meetings were held in all parts of the country, and within a few weeks nearly three hundred thousand men rushed forward to enter the ranks. A grand invasion of Mexico was planned by General Scott. The American forces were organized in three divisions: THE ARMY OF THE WEST, under General Kearney, to cross the Rocky Mountains and conquer the northern

Mexican provinces; THE ARMY OF THE CENTRE, under General Scott as commander-in-chief, to march from the gulf coast into the heart of the enemy's country; THE ARMY OF OCCUPATION, commanded by General Taylor, to subdue and hold the districts on the Rio Grande.

The work of mustering the American troops was entrusted to General Wool. By the middle of summer he succeeded in despatching to General Taylor a force of nine thousand men. He then established his camp at San Antonio, Texas, and from that point prepared the gathering recruits for the field. Meanwhile, Taylor had resumed active operations on the Rio Grande. Ten days after the battle of Resaca de la Palma he crossed from Fort Brown and captured Matamoras. Soon afterward he began his march up the right bank of the river and into the interior. The Mexicans, grown wary of their antagonist, fell back and took post at the fortified town of Monterey. To capture that place was the next object of the campaign; but the American army was feeble in numbers, and General Taylor was obliged to tarry near the Rio Grande until the latter part of August. By that time reinforcements had arrived, increasing his numbers to six thousand six hundred. With this force the march against Monterey was begun; and on the 19th of September the town, defended by fully ten thousand troops, under command of Ampudia, was reached and invested.

The siege was pressed with great vigor. On the 21st of the month several assaults were made, in which the Americans, led by General Worth, carried the fortified heights in the rear of the town. In that part of the defences only the bishop's palace—a strong building of stone—remained; and this was taken by storm on the following day. On the morning of the 23d the city was successfully assaulted in front by Generals Quitman and Butler. In the face of a tremendous cannonade and an incessant tempest of musket-balls discharged from the house-tops and alleys, the American storming-parties charged resistlessly into the town. They reached the Grand Plaza, or public square. They hoisted the victorious flag of the Union. They turned upon the buildings where the Mexicans were concealed; broke open the doors; charged up dark stair ways to the flat roofs of the houses; and drove the terrified enemy to an ignominious surrender. The honors of war were granted to

Ampudia, who evacuated the city and retired toward the capital. The storming of Monterey was a signal victory, gained against great superiority of numbers and advantage of position.

After the capitulation General Taylor received notice that overtures of peace were about to be made by the Mexican government. He therefore agreed to an armistice of eight weeks, during which time neither party should renew hostilities. In reality the Mexicans had no thought of peace. They employed the whole interval in warlike preparations. The famous general Santa Anna was called home from his exile at Havana to take the presidency of the country. In the course of the autumn a Mexican army of twenty thousand men was raised and sent into the field. In the mean time, the armistice had expired; and General Taylor, acting under orders of the War Department, again moved forward. On the 15th of November, the town of Saltillo, seventy miles south-west from Monterey, was captured by the American advance under General Worth. In the following month, Victoria, a city in the province of Tamaulipas, was taken by the command of General Patterson. To that place General Butler advanced from Monterey on the march against Tampico, on the river Panuco. At Victoria, however, he learned that Tampico had already capitulated to Captain Conner, commander of an American flotilla. Meanwhile, General Wool, advancing with strong reinforcements from San Antonio, entered Mexico, and took a position within supporting distance of Monterey. It was at this juncture that General Scott arrived and assumed the command of the American forces.

The Army of the West had not been idle. In June of 1846 General Kearney set out from Fort Leavenworth, on the Missouri, for the conquest of New Mexico and California. After a long and wearisome march he reached Santa Fé, and on the 18th of August captured and garrisoned the city. The whole of New Mexico submitted without further resistance. With a body of four hundred dragoons Kearney then continued his march toward the Pacific coast. At the distance of three hundred miles from Santa Fé he was met by the famous Kit Carson, who brought intelligence from the far West that California had already been subdued. Kearney accordingly sent back three-fourths of his forces, and with a party of only a hundred men made his way to the Pacific. On that far-off coast stirring events had happened.

Fremont on the Rocky Mountains.

For four years Colonel John C. Fremont had been exploring the country west of the Rocky Mountains. He had hoisted the American flag on the highest peak of the great range, and then directed his route by Salt Lake to Oregon. Turning southward into California, he received despatches informing him of the impending war with Mexico. Determined to strike a blow for his country, he urged the people of California, many of whom were Americans, to declare their independence. The hardy frontiersmen of the Sacramento valley flocked to his standard; and a campaign was at once begun to overthrow the Mexican authority. In several petty engagements the Americans were victorious over greatly superior numbers. Meanwhile, Commodore Sloat, commanding an American fleet, had captured the town of Monterey, on the coast, eighty miles south of San Francisco. A few days afterward Commodore Stockton took command of the Pacific squadron and made himself master of San Diego. Hearing of these events, Fremont raised the flag of the United States instead of the flag of California, and joined the naval commanders in a successful movement against Los Angelos, which was taken without opposition. Before the end of summer the whole of the vast province was subdued. In November General Kearney arrived with his company and joined Fremont and Stockton. About a month later the Mexicans rose in rebellion, but were defeated on the 8th of January, 1847, in the decisive battle of San Gabriel, by which the authority of the United States was completely established. A country large enough for an empire had been conquered by a handful of resolute men.

In the mean time, Colonel Doniphan, who had been left by Kearney in command of New Mexico, had made one of the most brilliant movements of the war. With a body of seven hundred fearless men he began a march through the enemy's country from Santa Fé to Saltillo, a distance of more than eight hundred miles. Reaching the Rio Grande on Christmas day, he fought and gained the battle of Bracito; then, crossing the river, captured El Paso, and in two months pressed his way to within twenty miles of Chihuahua. On the banks of Sacramento Creek he met the Mexicans in overwhelming numbers, and on the 28th of February completely routed them. He then marched unopposed into Chihuahua—a city of more than forty thousand inhabitants—and finally reached the division of General Wool in safety.

As soon as General Scott arrived in Mexico he ordered a large part of the Army of Occupation to join him on the gulf for the conquest of the capital. By the withdrawal of these troops from the divisions of Taylor and Wool these officers were left in a very exposed and critical condition for Santa Anna was rapidly advancing against them with an army of twenty thousand men. To resist this tremendous array General Taylor was able to concentrate at Saltillo a force numbering not more than six thousand; and after putting sufficient garrisons in that town and Monterey, his effective forces amounted to but four thousand eight hundred. With this small but resolute army he marched boldly out to meet the Mexican host. A favorable battle-ground was chosen at Buena Vista, four miles south of Saltillo. Here Taylor posted his troops and awaited the enemy.

On the 22d of February the Mexicans, twenty thousand strong, came pouring through the gorges and over the hills from the direction of San

Luis Potosi. Santa Anna demanded a surrender, and was met with defiance. On the morning of the 23d the battle began with an effort to outflank the American position on the right; but the attempt was thwarted by the troops of Illinois. A heavy column was then thrown against the centre, only to be shattered and driven back by Captain Washington's artillery. The Mexicans next fell in great force upon the American left flank, where the second regiment of Indianians, acting under a mistaken order, gave way, putting the army in great peril. But the troops of Mississippi and Kentucky were rallied to the breach; the men of Illinois and Indiana came bravely to the support; and again the enemy was hurled back. In the crisis of the battle the Mexicans made a furious and final charge upon Captain Bragg's battery; but the gunners stood at their posts undaunted, and the columns of lancers were scattered with terrible volleys of grape-shot. A charge of American cavalry, though made at the sacrifice of many lives, added to the discomfiture of the foe. Against tremendous odds the field was fairly won. On the night after the battle the Mexicans, having lost nearly two thousand men, made a precipitate retreat. The American loss was also severe, amounting, in killed, wounded and missing, to seven hundred and forty-six. This was the last of General Taylor's battles. He soon afterward returned to the United States, where he was received with great enthusiasm.

On the 9th of March, 1847, General Scott began the last campaign of the war. With a force of twelve thousand men he landed to the south of Vera Cruz, and in three days the investment of the city was completed. Trenches were opened at the distance of eight hundred yards; and on the morning of the 22d the cannonade was begun. On the water side Vera Cruz was defended by the celebrated castle of San Juan d'Ulloa, erected by Spain in the early part of the seventeenth century, at the cost of four million dollars. For four days an incessant storm of shot and shell from the fleet of Commodore Conner and the land-batteries of Scott was poured upon the doomed castle and town. Life and property were swept into a common ruin. An assault was already planned, when the humbled authorities of the city proposed capitulation. On the night of the 27th terms of surrender were signed, and two days afterward the American flag floated over Vera Cruz.

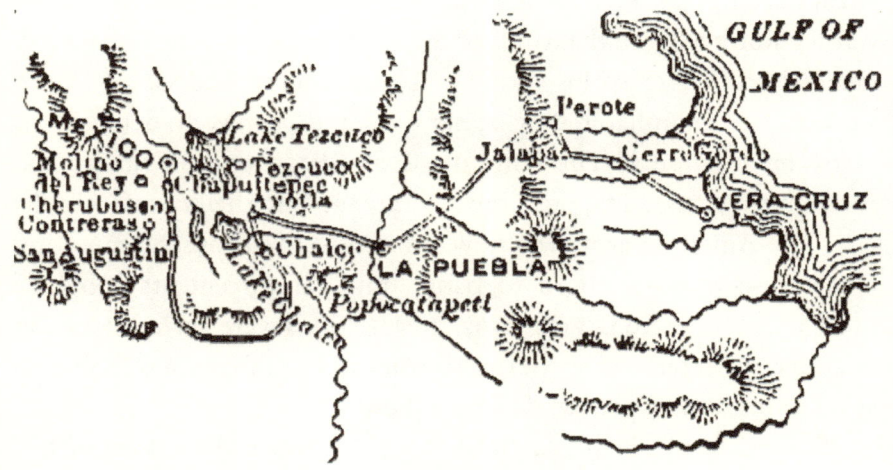

Scene of Scott's Campaign, 1847.

The route from the gulf to the capital was now open. On the 8th of April General Twiggs, in command of the American advance set out on the road to Jalapa. The main division, led by General Scott in person, followed immediately. For several days there was no serious opposition; but on the 12th of the month Twiggs came upon Santa Anna, who, with an army of fifteen thousand men, had taken possession of the heights and rocky pass of Cerro Gordo. The position, though seemingly impregnable, must be carried, or further advance was impossible. On the morning of the 18th the American army was arranged for an assault which, according to all the rules of war, promised only disaster and ruin. But to the troops of the United States nothing now seemed too arduous, no deed too full of peril. Before noonday every position of the Mexicans had been successfully stormed and themselves driven into a precipitate rout. Nearly three thousand prisoners were taken, together with forty-three pieces of bronze artillery, five thousand muskets and accoutrements enough to supply an army. The American loss amounted to four hundred and thirty-one, that of the enemy to fully a thousand. Santa Anna escaped with his life, but left behind his private papers and *wooden leg*.

On the next day the victorious army entered Jalapa. On the 22d the strong castle of Perote, crowning a peak of the Cordilleras, was taken without resistance. Here another park of artillery and a vast amount of warlike stores fell into the hands of the Americans. Turning southward, General Scott next led his army against the ancient and sacred city of Puebla. Though inhabited by eighty thousand people, no defence was made or attempted. The handful of invaders marched unopposed through the gates, and on the 15th of May took up their quarters in the city. The American army was now reduced to five thousand men, and General Scott was obliged to pause until reinforcements could be brought forward from Vera Cruz. Negotiations were again opened in the hope of peace; but the Mexican authorities, stubborn and foolhardy as at the beginning, preferred to fight it out.

By the 7th of August General Scott had received reinforcements, swelling his numbers to nearly eleven thousand. Leaving a small garrison in Puebla, he again began his march upon the capital. The route now lay over the summit of the Cordilleras. At the passes of the mountains resistance had been expected; but the advance was unopposed, and the army swept through to look down on THE VALLEY OF MEXICO. Never before had the American soldiery beheld such a scene. Clear to the horizon stretched a most living landscape of green fields, villages and lakes—a picture too beautiful to be torn with the dread enginery of war.

The army pressed on to Ayotla, only fifteen miles from the capital. Thus far General Scott had followed the great national road from Vera Cruz to Mexico; but now, owing to the many fortifications and dangerous passes in front, it was deemed advisable to change the route. From Ayotla, therefore, the army wheeled to the south, around Lake Chalco, and thence westward to San Augustine. From this place it was but ten miles to the capital. The city could be approached only by causeways leading across marshes and the beds of bygone lakes. At the ends of these causeways were massive gates strongly defended. To the left of the line of march were the almost inaccessible positions of Contreras, San Antonio and Molino del Rey. Directly in front, beyond the marshes and closer to the city, were the powerful defences of Churubusco and Chapultepec, the latter a castle of great strength. These various positions were held by Santa Anna with a force of more than thirty thousand Mexicans. That General Scott, with an army not one-third as great in numbers, could take the city seemed an impossibility. But he was resolved to do it.

On the 19th of August the divisions of Generals Pillow and Twiggs were ordered to storm the Mexican position at Contreras. About nightfall the line of communications between that place and Santa Anna's reserves was cut, and in the darkness of the following midnight an assaulting column, led by General Persifer F. Smith, moved against the enemy's camp. The attack was made at sunrise, and in seventeen minutes six thousand Mexicans, commanded by General Valencia, were driven in utter rout from their fortifications. The American storming-party numbered less than four thousand. This was the *first* victory of that memorable 20th of August. A few hours afterward General Worth advanced against San Antonio, compelled an evacuation and routed the flying garrison. This was the *second* victory. Almost at the same time General Pillow led a column against one of the heights of Churubusco where the enemy had concentrated in great force. After a terrible assault the position was carried and the Mexicans scattered like chaff. This was the *third* triumph. The division of General Twiggs added a *fourth* victory by storming and holding another height of Churubusco, while the *fifth* and last was achieved by Generals Shields and Pierce, who defeated Santa Anna, coming to reinforce his garrisons. The whole Mexican army was hurled back upon the remaining fortification of Chapultepec.

On the morning after the battles the Mexican authorities sent out a proposition to negotiate. It was only a ruse to gain time, for the terms proposed by them were such as conquerors would have dictated to the vanquished. General Scott, who did not consider his army vanquished, rejected the proposals with scorn, rested his men until the 7th of September, and then renewed hostilities. On the next morning General Worth was ordered to take Molino del Rey and Casa de Mata, the western defences of Chapultepec. These positions were held by fourteen thousand Mexicans; but the Americans, after losing a fourth of their number in the desperate onset, were again victorious. The guns were next brought to bear on Chapultepec itself, and on the 13th of the month that frowning citadel was carried by storm. Through the San Cosme and Belen gates the conquering army swept resistlessly, and at nightfall the soldiers of the Union were in the suburbs of Mexico.

General Winfield Scott.

In the darkness of that night Santa Anna and the officers of the government fled from the city; but not until they had turned loose two thousand convicts to fire upon the American army. On the following morning, before day dawn, forth came a deputation from the city to beg for mercy. This time the messengers *were in earnest*; but General Scott, weary of trifling, turned them away with contempt. "Forward!" was the order that rang along the American lines at sun rise. The war-worn regiments swept into the beautiful streets of the famous city, and at seven o'clock the flag of the United States floated over the halls of the Montezumas. So ended one of the most brilliant campaigns known in modern history.

On leaving his conquered capital Santa Anna, with his usual treachery, turned about to attack the American hospitals at Puebla. Here about eighteen hundred sick men had been left in charge of Colonel Childs. For several days a gallant resistance was made by the feeble garrison, until General Lane, on his march to the capital, fell upon the besiegers and scattered them. It was the closing stroke of the war—a contest in which the Americans, few in number and in a far-distant, densely-peopled country, had gained every victory.

The military power of Mexico was now completely broken. Santa Anna was a fugitive. It only remained to determine the conditions of peace. In the winter of 1847-48 American ambassadors met the Mexican Congress, in session at Guadalupe Hidalgo, and on the 2d of February a treaty was concluded between the two nations. The compact was ratified by both governments, and on the 4th of the following July President Polk made a proclamation of peace. By the terms of settlement the boundary line between Mexico and the United States was fixed as follows: The Rio Grande from its mouth to the southern limit of New Mexico; thence westward along the southern and northward along the western boundary of that territory to the river Gila; thence down that river to the Colorado; thence westward to the Pacific. The whole of New Mexico and Upper California was relinquished to the United States. Mexico guaranteed the free navigation of the Gulf of California, and the river Colorado from its mouth to the confluence of the Gila. In consideration of these territorial acquisitions and privileges the United States agreed to surrender all places held by military occupation in Mexico, to pay into the treasury of that country fifteen million dollars, and to assume all debts due from the Mexican government to American citizens, said debts not to exceed three million five hundred thousand dollars. Thus at last was the territory of the United States Spread out in one broad belt from ocean to ocean.

In the mean time the troublesome and alarming question of THE OREGON BOUNDARY was finally disposed of. For more than a quarter of a century the territorial limit of the United States on the northwest had been a matter of controversy between the Federal government and Great Britain. By the terms of the convention of 1818 the international line had been carried westward from the northwestern extremity of the Lake of the Woods along the forty-ninth parallel to the crest of the Rocky Mountains; but from that point to the Pacific no agreement could be reached. As early as 1807, and again in 1818 1nd 1826, the United States had formally claimed the parallel of fifty-four degrees and forty minutes; but this boundary Great Britain refused to accept. By a convention, held in August of 1827, it was agreed by the representatives of the two powers that the territory lying between the forty-ninth parallel—which, according to the English theory, was the true international line—and the parallel of fifty-four degrees and forty minutes should remain open indefinitely and impartially for the joint occupancy of British and American citizens. By this action the difficulty was postponed for sixteen years; but thoughtful statesmen of both nations became alarmed that a question of such magnitude should remain unsettled, and negotiations were renewed. In 1843 the minister resident of the United States in London again proposed the parallel of fifty-four degrees and forty minutes, but the proposition was rejected. In the next year the British ambassador at Washington again suggested the forty-ninth degree of latitude as the true boundary; but to this the government of the United States refused to accede. Then came the war with Mexico and with it the prospective extension of territory on the southwest. The views of the administration in regard to the northwestern boundary became less stringent; and finally, in a convention of the two powers held on the 15th of June, 1846, the question was definitely settled by a treaty. Every point of the long-standing controversy was decided in favor of Great Britain. The forty-ninth parallel was established as the international boundary from the summit of the Rocky Mountains to the middle of the channel which separates the continent from Vancouver's Island; thence southerly through the middle of said channel and of Fuca's Straits to the Pacific. Vancouver's Island itself was awarded to Great Britain; and the free navigation of the Columbia River was guaranteed to the Hudson Bay Company and other British subjects on the same conditions as those imposed on citizens of the United States. The treaty was by no means so favorable as might have been expected, and by many it was denounced as actually dishonorable to the Federal government. It is certain that better terms might have been demanded and obtained.[28]

A few days after the signing of the treaty of peace with Mexico an event occurred in California which spread excitement through the

---

[28] Such was the indignation of the opponents of this treaty—especially of the leaders of the Whig party—that the political battle-cry of *"Fifty-four Forty or Fight!"* became almost as popular a motto as *"Free Trade and Sailors' Rights"* had been in the War of 1812.

civilized world. A laborer, employed by Captain Sutter to cut a millrace on the American fork of the Sacramento River, discovered some pieces of gold in the sand where he was digging. With further search other particles were found. The news spread as if borne on the wind. From all quarters adventurers came flocking. Other explorations led to further revelations of the precious metal. For a while there seemed no end to the discoveries. Straggling gold-hunters sometimes picked up in a few hours the value of five hundred dollars. The intelligence went flying through the States to the Atlantic, and then to the ends of the world. Men thousands of miles away were crazed with excitement. Workshops were shut up, business houses abandoned, fertile farms left tenantless, offices deserted. Though the overland routes to California were scarcely yet discovered, thousands of our eager adventurers started on the long, long journey. Before the end of 1850 San Francisco had grown from a miserable village of huts to a city of fifteen thousand inhabitants. By the close of 1852 the territory had a population of more than a quarter of a million. The importance of the gold mines of California, whose richness is not yet exhausted, can hardly be overestimated.

The Smithsonian Institution.

Overland to California, 1849. (Pass of the Sierras.)

In April of 1846, Congress passed an act organizing THE SMITHSONIAN INSTITUTION at Washington City. Twenty-two years previously an eminent English chemist and philanthropist named James Smithson[29] had died at Genoa, bequeathing on certain conditions a large sum of money to the United States. In the fall of 1838, by the death of

---

[29] Until after his graduation at Oxford in 1786, this remarkable man was known by the name of *James Lewis Macie*. Afterward, of his own accord, he chose the name of his reputed father, Hugh Smithson, duke of Northumberland.

Smithson's nephew, the proceeds of the estate, amounting to five hundred and fifteen thousand dollars, were secured by the agent of the national government and deposited in the mint. It had been provided in the will that the bequest should be used for the establishment at Washington of an institution *for the increase and diffusion of knowledge among men.* To carry out the great design of the testator a plan of organization, prepared by John Quincy Adams, was laid before Congress and after some modifications adopted.

In the act of establishment it was provided that the institution contemplated by Mr. Smithson should be named in his honor "The Smithsonian Institution"; that the same should be under the immediate control of a Board of Regents composed of the President, Vice-President, judges of the Supreme Court, and other principal officers of the government; that the entire Smithsonian fund, amounting with accrued interest to six hundred and fifty-five thousand dollars, should be loaned forever to the United States at six per cent.; that out of the proceeds, together with congressional appropriations and private gifts, buildings should be provided suitable to contain a museum of natural history, a cabinet of minerals, a chemical laboratory, a gallery of art, and a library. Professor Joseph Henry of Princeton College was chosen secretary of the institution, and the plan of organization was speedily and successfully carried out. The result has been the establishment in the United States of one of the most beneficent institutions known in the history of mankind. The Smithsonian *Contributions to Knowledge* already amount to eighteen volumes quarto; and the future is destined to yield still richer results in widening the boundaries of human thought and increasing the happiness of men.

In the first summer of President Polk's administration the country was called to mourn the death of General Jackson. The veteran warrior and statesman lived to the age of seventy-eight, and died at his home, called the Hermitage, in Tennessee. On the 23d of February, 1848, ex-President John Quincy Adams died at the city of Washington. At the time of his decease he was a member of the House of Representatives. He was struck with paralysis in the very seat from which he had so many times electrified the nation with his eloquence.

In 1848 Wisconsin, the last of the five great States formed from the North-western Territory, was admitted into the Union. The new commonwealth came with a population of two hundred and fifty thousand and an area of nearly fifty-four thousand square miles. By establishing the St. Croix instead of the Mississippi as the western boundary of the State, Wisconsin lost a considerable district rightfully belonging to her territory.

Near the close of Polk's administration an important addition was made to the President's cabinet by the establishment of THE DEPARTMENT OF THE INTERIOR. To the three original departments of the government, as organized during the administration of Washington, had already been added the offices of Postmaster-General and Secretary of the Navy. The Attorney-General had also come to be recognized as a regular member of the cabinet. With the grown and development of the nation it was found that the duties belonging to the departments of state and the treasury had become so manifold as to require the establishment of a separate office. A certain part of these duties were accordingly detached, and the new "Home Department"—afterwards called Department of the Interior—was constituted by act of Congress. In the beginning of the next administration the new secretaryship was assigned to General Thomas Ewing of Ohio.

Another presidential election was at hand. Three well-known candidates were presented for the suffrages of the people. General Lewis Cass of Michigan was nominated by the Democrats, and General Zachary Taylor by the Whigs. As the candidate of the new Free-Soil party, ex-President Martin Van Buren was put forward. The rise of this new party was traceable to a question concerning the territory acquired by the Mexican War. In 1846 David Wilmot of Pennsylvania brought before Congress a bill *to prohibit slavery* in all the territory which might be secured by treaty with Mexico. The bill was defeated; but the advocates of the measure, which was called the WILMOT PROVISO, formed themselves into a party, and in June of 1848 nominated Mr. Van Buren for the presidency. The real contest, however, lay between Generals Cass and Taylor. The position of the two leading parties on the question of slavery in the new territories was as yet not clearly defined, and the election was left to turn on the personal popularity of the candidates. The memory of his recent victories in Mexico made General Taylor the favorite with the people, and he was elected by a large majority. As Vice-President, Millard Fillmore of New York was chosen. So closed the agitated but not inglorious administration of President Polk.

CHAPTER LVIII.

ADMINISTRATIONS OF TAYLOR AND FILLMORE, 1849-1853.

THE new President was a Virginian by birth, a Kentuckian by breeding, a soldier by profession. In 1808 he left the farm to accept a commission in the army. During the war of 1812 he distinguished himself in the Northwest, especially in defending Fort Harrison against the Red men. In the Seminole War he bore a conspicuous part, but earned his greatest renown in Mexico. His reputation, though strictly military, was enviable, and his character above reproach. His administration began with a violent agitation on the question of slavery in the territories; California, the El Dorado of the West, was the origin of the dispute.

President Taylor.

In his first message President Taylor expressed his sympathy with the Californians, and advised them to form a State government preparatory to admission into the Union. The advice was promptly accepted. A convention of delegates was held at Monterey in September of 1849. A constitution *prohibiting slavery* was framed, submitted to the people, and adopted with but little opposition. Peter H. Burnet was elected governor of the Territory; members of a general assembly were chosen; and on the 20th of December, 1849, the new government was organized at San Jose. At the same time a petition in the usual form was forwarded to Congress asking for the admission of California as a State.

The presentation of the petition was the signal for a bitter controversy. As in the case of the admission of Missouri, the members of Congress, and to a great extent the people, were sectionally divided. But now the position of the parties was reversed; the proposition to admit the new State was favored by the representatives of the North and opposed by those of the South. The ground of the opposition was that with the extension of the Missouri Compromise line to the Pacific the right to introduce slavery into California was guaranteed by the general government, and that therefore the proposed constitution of the State ought to be rejected. The reply of the North was that the argument could apply only to a *part* of the new State, that the Missouri Compromise had respect only to the Louisiana purchase, and that the people of California had framed their constitution in their own way. Such was the issue; and the debates grew more and more violent, until the stability of the Union was seriously endangered.

Other exciting questions added fuel to the controversy. Texas claimed New Mexico as a part of her territory, and the claim was resisted by the people of Santa Fé, who desired a separate government. The people of the South complained bitterly that fugitive slaves, escaping from their masters, were aided and encouraged in the North. The opponents of slavery demanded the abolition of the slave-trade in the District of Columbia. Along the whole line of controversy there was a spirit of suspicion, recrimination and anger.

The illustrious Henry Clay appeared as a peacemaker. In the spring of 1850 he was appointed chairman of a committee of thirteen, to whom all the questions under discussion were referred. On the 9th of May he brought forward, as a compromise covering all the points in dispute, THE OMNIBUS BILL, of which the provisions were as follows: *First*, the admission of California as a free State; *second*, the formation of new States, not exceeding four in number, out of the territory of Texas, said States to permit or exclude slavery as the people should determine; *third*, the organization of territorial governments for New Mexico and Utah, without conditions on the question of slavery; *fourth*, the establishment of the present boundary between Texas and New Mexico, and the payment to the former for surrendering the latter the sum of ten million dollars from the national treasury; *fifth*, the enactment of a more rigorous law for the recovery of fugitive slaves; *sixth*, the abolition of the slave trade in the District of Columbia.

When the Omnibus Bill was laid before Congress, the debates began anew, and seemed likely to be interminable. While the discussion was at its height and the issue still undecided, President Taylor fell sick, and died on the 9th of July, 1850. In accordance with the provisions of the constitution, Mr. Fillmore at once took the oath of office and entered upon the duties of the presidency. A new cabinet was formed, with Daniel Webster at the head as secretary of state. Notwithstanding the death of the chief magistrate, the government moved on without disturbance.

Henry Clay.

The compromise proposed by Mr. Clay and sustained by his eloquence was at length approved by Congress. On the 18th of September the last clause was adopted, and the whole received the immediate sanction of the President. The excitement in the country rapidly abated, and the distracting controversy seemed at an end. Such was the last, and perhaps the greatest, of those pacific measures originated and carried through Congress by the genius of Henry Clay. He shortly afterward bade adieu to the Senate, and sought at his beloved Ashland a brief rest from the arduous cares of public life.

The passage of the Omnibus Bill brought a *political quiet*; but the *moral convictions* of very few men were altered by its provisions. Public opinion remained as before: in the North, a general, indefinite, but growing hostility to slavery; in the South, a fixed and resolute purpose to defend and extend that institution. To the President, whose party was in the ascendency in most of the Free States, the measure was fatal; for although his cabinet had advised him to sign the bill, the Whigs were at heart opposed to the fugitive slave law, and when he gave his assent they turned coldly from him. In the Whig National convention, two years afterwards, although the policy of the President was approved and the compromise measures ratified by a vote of two hundred and twenty-seven against sixty, not twenty Northern votes could be obtained for his renomination. Thus do political parties punish their leaders for hesitating to espouse a principle which the parties themselves are afraid to avow.

The year 1850 was marked by a lawless attempt on the part of some American adventurers to gain possession of Cuba. It was thought that the people of that island were anxious to throw off the Spanish yoke and to annex themselves to the United States. In order to encourage such a movement, General Lopez organized an expedition in the South, and on the 19th of May, 1850, effected a landing at Cardenas, a port of Cuba. But there was no uprising in his favor; neither Cubans nor Spanish soldiers joined his standard, and he was obliged to seek safety by returning to Florida. Renewing the attempt in the following year, he and his band of four hundred and eighty men were attacked, defeated and captured by an overwhelming force of Spaniards. Lopez and the ringleaders were taken to Havana, tried, condemned and executed.

The first annual message of the President was a document of great ability. Among the many important measures pressed upon the attention of Congress were the following: a system of cheap and uniform postage; the establishment, in connection with the Department of the Interior, of a Bureau of Agriculture; liberal appropriations for the improvement of rivers and harbors; the building of a national asylum for disabled and destitute seamen; a permanent tariff with specific duties on imports and discrimination in favor of American manufactures; the opening of communication between the Mississippi and the Pacific coast; a settlement of the land difficulties in California; an act for the retirement of supernumerary officers of the army and navy; and a board of commissioners to adjust the claims of private citizens against the government of the United States. Only two of these important recommendations—the asylum for sailors and the settlement of the land claims in California—were carried into effect. For the President's party were in a minority in Congress; and the majority refused or neglected to approve his measures.

In 1852 a serious trouble arose with England. By the terms of former treaties the coast-fisheries of Newfoundland belonged exclusively to Great Britain. But outside of a line drawn three miles from the shore American fisherman enjoyed equal rights and privileges. Now the dispute arose as to whether the line should be drawn from one headland to another so as to give all the bays and inlets to England, or whether it should be made to conform to the irregularities of the coast. Under the latter construction American fishing-vessels would have equal claims in the bays and harbors; but this privilege was denied by Great Britain, and the quarrel rose to such a height that both nations sent men-of-war to the contested waters. But reason triumphed over passion, and in 1854 the difficulty was happily settled by negotiation; the right to take fish in any of the bays of the British possessions was conceded to American fishermen.

During the summer of 1852 the celebrated Hungarian patriot Louis Kossuth made the tour of the United States. Austria and Russia had united against his native land and overthrown her liberties. He came to plead the cause of Hungary before the American people, and to obtain such aid as might be privately furnished to his oppressed countrymen. Every-where he was received with expressions of sympathy and good-will. His mission was successful, though the long-established policy of the United States forbade the government to interfere on behalf of the Hungarian patriots.

About this time the attention of the American people was directed in a special manner to explorations in the Arctic Ocean. In 1845 Sir John Franklin, one of the bravest of English seamen, went on a voyage of discovery to the extreme North. He believed in the possibility of passing through an open polar sea into the Pacific. Years went by, and no tidings came from the daring sailor. It was only known that he had passed the country of Esquimaux. Other expeditions were despatched in search, but returned without success. Henry Grinnell, a wealthy merchant of New York, fitted out several vessels at his own expense, put them under command of Lieutenant De Haven, and sent them to the North; but in vain. The government came to Mr. Grinnell's aid. In 1853 a new Arctic squadron was equipped; the command of which was given to Dr. Elisha Kent Kane; but the expedition, though rich in scientific results, returned without the discovery of Franklin.

During the administrations of Taylor and Fillmore the country was called to mourn the loss of many distinguished men. On the 31st of March, 1850, Senator John C. Calhoun of South Carolina passed away. His death was much lamented, especially in his own State, to whose interests he had devoted the energies of his life. His earnestness and zeal and powers of debate have placed him in the front rank of American orators. At the age of sixty-eight he fell from his place like a scarred oak of the forest never to rise again. Then followed the death of the President; and then, on the 28th of June, 1852, Henry Clay, having fought his last battle, sank to rest. On the 24th of the following October the illustrious Daniel Webster died at his home at Marshfield, Massachusetts. The place of secretary of State, made vacant by his death, was conferred on Edward Everett.

John C. Calhoun.

In Europe the news of Lopez's ridiculous invasion of Cuba created great excitement. Notwithstanding a distinct disavowal of the whole proceeding on the part of the Federal government, notwithstanding the immediate dismissal of the officer at New Orleans who had allowed the expedition of Lopez to escape from that port,—the governments of Great Britain and France affected to believe that the covert aim and purpose of the United States was to acquire Cuba by conquest. Acting upon this presumption the British and French ministers proposed to the American government to enter into a *Tripartite Treaty*—so called—in which each of the contracting nations was to disclaim then and forever all intention of possessing Cuba. To this proposal Mr. Everett replied in one of the most masterly State papers on record. Great Britain and France were informed that the annexation of Cuba was regarded by the United States as a measure hazardous and impolitic; that entire good faith would be kept with Spain and with all nations; but that the Federal government did not recognize in any European power the right to meddle with affairs purely American, and that, in accordance with the doctrine set forth by President Monroe, any such interference would be resented as an affront to the sovereignty of the United States.

As Fillmore's administration drew to a close the political parties again marshaled their forces. Franklin Pierce of New Hampshire appeared as the candidate of the Democratic party, and General Winfield Scott as the choice of the Whigs. The question at issue before the country was the Compromise Act of 1850. But the parties, instead of being divided, were for once agreed as to the wisdom of that measure. Both the Whig and Democratic platforms stoutly reaffirmed the justice of the Omnibus Bill, by which the dissensions of the country had been quieted. A third party arose, however, whose members, both Whigs and Democrats, doubted the wisdom of the compromise of 1850, and declared that all the Territories of the United States ought to be free. John P. Hale of New Hampshire was put forward as the candidate of this Free Soil party. Mr. Pierce was elected by a large majority, and William R. King of Alabama was chosen Vice-President.

CHAPTER LIX.

Pierce's Administration, 1853-1857.

THE new chief magistrate was a native of New Hampshire, a graduate of Bowdoin College, a lawyer, a politician, a general in the Mexican War, a statesman of considerable abilities. Mr. King, the Vice-President, had for a long time represented Alabama in the Senate of the United States. On account of failing health he was sojourning in the island of Cuba at the time of the inauguration, and there he received the oath of office. Growing still more feeble, he returned to his own State, where he died on the 18th of April, 1853. As secretary of state under the new administration William L. Marcy of New York was chosen.

In the summer of 1853 the first corps of engineers was sent out by the government to explore the route for A PACIFIC RAILROAD. The enterprise was at first regarded as visionary, then believed in as possible, and finally undertaken and accomplished. In the same year that marked the beginning of the project the disputed boundary between New Mexico and Chihuahua was satisfactorily settled. The maps on which the former treaties with Mexico had been based were found to be erroneous. Santa Anna, who had again become president of the Mexican republic, attempted to take advantage of the error, and sent an army to occupy the territory between the true and the false boundary. This action was resisted by the authorities of New Mexico and the United States, and a second Mexican war seemed imminent. The difficulty was adjusted, however, by the purchase of the doubtful claim of Mexico. This transaction, known as THE GADSDEN PURCHASE, led to the erection of the new Territory of Arizona.

The first year of Pierce's administration was signalized by the opening of intercourse between the United States and the great empire of Japan. Hitherto the Japanese ports had been closed against the vessels of Christian nations. In order to remove this foolish and injurious restriction Commodore Perry, a son of Oliver H. Perry of the war of 1812, sailed with his squadron into the Bay of Yeddo. When warned to depart, he explained to the Japanese officers the sincere desire of the United States to enter into a commercial treaty with the emperor. After much delay and hesitancy consent was obtained to hold an interview with that august personage. Accordingly, on the 14th of July, the commodore with his officers obtained an audience with the dusky monarch of the East, and presented a letter from the President of the United States. Still the government of Japan was wary of accepting the proposition, and it was not until the spring of 1854 that a treaty could be concluded. The privileges of commerce were thus conceded to American merchant vessels, and two ports of entry were designated for their use.

On the very day of Commodore Perry's introduction to the emperor of Japan the Crystal Palace was opened in the city of New York for the second WORLD'S FAIR. The palace itself was a marvel in architecture, being built exclusively of iron and glass. Thousands of specimens of the arts and manufactures of all civilized nations were put on exhibition within the spacious building. The enterprise and inventive genius of the whole country were quickened into a new life by the beautiful and instructive display. International exhibitions are among the happiest fruits of an enlightened age.

During the administration of Pierce the country was frequently disturbed by the filibustering expeditions of General William Walker into Central America. This audacious and unscrupulous adventurer began his operations in 1853 by escaping with a band of followers from the port of San Francisco and making a descent on La Paz in Lower California. In the spring of 1854 he marched overland with a hundred men and raised the standard of revolt in the state of Sonora; but the company was dispersed and himself made prisoner. In May of the same year he was tried by the authorities of San Francisco and acquitted. But not satisfied with his previous experience, he again raised a band of sixty-two followers and proceeded to Central America. Being joined by a regiment of natives he fought and gained a battle at Rivas, on the 29th of June, 1855. In a second battle at Virgin Bay he was also successful. Fighting continued until the following summer when his influence had become so powerful that he was elected president of Nicaraugua. Then came a change in his fortunes. A great insurrection ensued; and the other Central American states, assisted by the Vanderbilt steam-ship company, whose rights he had violated, combined against him and on the 1st of May, 1857, he was again made prisoner. But in a short time he was foot-loose at New Orleans, where he organized a third company of adventurers—men who had everything to gain and nothing to lose—and on the 25th of November succeeded in reaching Punta Arenas, Nicaraugua.

Within less than a month, however, he was again obliged to surrender to Commodore Paulding of the United States navy. For a while the great filibuster was a prisoner at New York; but getting his liberty, he continued his scheming, and in June of 1860 a third time reached Central America at the head of a considerable force. This time the descent was made at Truxillo, Honduras. But the president of that state, assisted by a British man-of-war, soon overpowered and captured the whole band. On the 3d of September Walker was tried by a court-martial at Truxillo, condemned, and shot. The courage with which he met his fate has half redeemed his forfeited fame and left after times in doubt whether he shall be called fanatic or hero.[30]

To this period also belongs the history of what is known in American diplomacy as THE MARTIN KOSZTA AFFAIR. Martin Koszta was a leader in the Hungarian revolt against Austria, in 1849. After the rebellion was suppressed he fled to Turkey whence he was demanded by the Austrian government as a refugee and traitor. The Turkish authorities, however, refused to give him up but agreed that he should be sent into exile to some foreign land never to return. Koszta chose the United States as his asylum, came hither, and took out partial but not complete papers of naturalization. In 1854 he returned to Turkey, contrary—as it was alleged—to his former promise. At the city of Smyrna he received a passport from the American consul residing there, and went ashore. But the Austrian consul at Smyrna, hearing of Koszta's arrival and having no power to arrest him on shore, induced some bandits to seize him and throw him into the water of the bay where a boat in waiting picked him

---

[30] It will be observed that the narrative of Walker's exploits and end, extends nearly to the conclusion of Buchanan's administration.

up and carried him on board an Austrian frigate. The American officials immediately demanded his release, which was refused. Thereupon Captain Duncan Ingraham, commanding the American sloop of war *St. Louis*, loaded his guns, pointed them at the Austrian vessel, and was about to make hot work, when it was agreed by all parties that Koszta should be put in charge of the French government until his nationality should be decided. In this condition of affairs the question was given over for discussion to Baron Hülseman—the Austrian minister at Washington—and William L. Marcy, the American secretary of state. The correspondence was one of the ablest on record and extended, before its termination, to almost every question affecting naturalization and citizenship, and indeed to many other important topics of international law. Mr. Marcy was completely triumphant in his argument and Koszta was remanded to the United States. Of so much importance is *the life of one man*, when it involves the great question of human rights.

In the years 1853-54, the peaceable relations of the United States and Spain were again endangered by Cuban difficulties. President Pierce believed that owing to the financial embarrassment of the Spanish government, Cuba might now be purchased at a reasonable price and annexed to the United States. The delicate business of negotiating was intrusted at first to Mr. Soule, the American minister at Madrid. But afterwards James Buchanan and John Y. Mason were added to the mission. A convention of the ambassadors of the various governments concerned was held at Ostend, and an important instrument was there drawn up–chiefly by Mr. Buchanan—known as THE OSTEND MANIFESTO. The document was chiefly devoted to an elaborate statement of the arguments in favor of the purchase and annexation of Cuba by the United States, as a measure of sound wisdom to both the Spanish and American governments. But nothing of practical importance resulted from the embassy or the manifesto.

And now the great domain lying west of Minnesota, Iowa and Missouri was to be organized into territorial governments. Already into these vast regions the tide of immigration was pouring, and it became necessary to provide for the future. In January of 1854, Senator Stephen

A. Douglas of Illinois brought before the Senate of the United States a proposition to organize the territories of Kansas and Nebraska. In the bill reported for this purpose a clause was inserted providing that the people of the two Territories, in forming their constitutions, *should decide for themselves* whether the new States should be free or slaveholding. This was a virtual repeal of the Missouri Compromise, for both the new territories lay north of the parallel of thirty-six degrees and thirty minutes. Thus by a single stroke the old settlement of the slavery question was to be undone. From January until May, Mr. Douglas's report, known as THE KANSAS-NEBRASKA BILL, was debated in Congress. All the bitter sectional antagonisms of the past were aroused in full force. The bill was violently opposed by a majority of the representatives from the East and North; but the minority, uniting with the congressmen of the South, enabled Douglas to carry his measure through Congress, and in May of 1854 the bill received the sanction of the President.

Kansas itself now became a battle-field for the contending parties. Whether the new State should admit slavery now depended upon the vote of the people. Wherefore both factions made a rush for the territory in order to secure a majority. Kansas was soon filled with an agitated mass of people, thousands of whom had been sent thither to *vote*. An election held in November of 1854 resulted in the choice of a pro-slavery delegate to Congress, and in the general territorial election of the following year the same party was triumphant. The State Legislature thus chosen assembled at Lecompton, organized the government and framed a constitution permitting slavery. The Free Soil party, declaring the general election to have been illegal on account of fraudulent voting, assembled in convention at Topeka, framed a constitution excluding slavery, and organized a rival government. Civil war broke out between the factions. From the autumn of 1855 until the following summer the Territory was the scene of constant turmoil and violence. On the 3d of September the President appointed John W. Geary of Pennsylvania military governor of Kansas, with full powers to restore order and punish lawlessness. On his arrival the hostile parties were quieted and peace restored. But the agitation in the Territory had already extended to all parts of the Union, and became the issue on which the people divided in the presidential election of 1856.

The parties made ready for the contest. James Buchanan of Pennsylvania was nominated as the Democratic candidate. By planting himself on a platform of principles in which the doctrines of the Kansas-Nebraska Bill were distinctly reaffirmed, he was able to secure a heavy vote both North and South. For many Northern Democrats, though opposed to slavery, held firmly to the opinion that the people of every Territory ought to have the right to decide the question for themselves. As the candidate of the Free Soil or People's party, John C. Fremont of California was brought forward. The exclusion of slavery from all the Territories of the United States by congressional action was the distinctive principle of the Free Soil platform. Meanwhile, an American or Know-Nothing party had arisen in the country, the leaders of which, anxious to ignore the slavery question and to restrict foreign influences in the nation, nominated Millard Fillmore for the presidency. But the slavery question could not be put aside; on that issue the people were really divided. A large majority decided in favor of Mr. Buchanan for the presidency, while the choice for the vice-presidency fell on John C. Breckinridge of Kentucky.

CHAPTER LX.

Buchanan's Administration, 1857-1861.

JAMES BUCHANAN was a native of Pennsylvania, born on the 13th of April, 1791, educated for the profession of law. In 1831 he was appointed minister to Russia, was afterward elected to the Senate of the United States, and from that position was called to the office of secretary of state under President Polk. In 1853 he received the appointment of minister to Great Britain, and resided at London until his nomination for the presidency. As secretary of state in the new cabinet, General Lewis Cass of Michigan was chosen.

A few days after the inauguration of the new chief magistrate, the Supreme Court of the United States delivered the celebrated opinion known in American history as THE DRED SCOTT DECISION. Dred Scott, a negro, had been held as a slave by Dr. Emerson of Missouri, a surgeon in the United States army. On the removal of Emerson to Rock Island, Illinois, and afterwards, in 1836, to Fort Snelling, Minnesota, Scott was taken along; and at the latter place he and a negro woman, who had been bought by the surgeon, were married. Two children were born of the marriage, and then the whole family were taken back to St. Louis and sold. Dred thereupon brought suit for his freedom. The cause was heard in the circuit and supreme courts of Missouri, and, in May of 1854, was appealed to the Supreme Court of the United States. After a delay of nearly three years a decision was finally reached in March of 1857. Chief-Justice Taney, speaking for the court, decided that negroes, whether free or slave, *were not citizens of the United States, and that they could not become such by any process known to the Constitution;* that under the laws of the United States a negro could neither sue nor be sued, and that therefore the court had no jurisdiction of Dred Scott's cause; that a slave was to be regarded in the light of a personal chattel, and that he might be removed from place to place by his owner as any other piece of property; that the Constitution gave to every slave-holder the right of removing to or through any State or Territory with his slaves, and of returning at his will with them to a State where slavery was recognized by law; and that therefore the Missouri Compromise of 1820, as well as the compromise measures of 1850, was unconstitutional and void. In these opinions six of the associate justices of the supreme bench—Wayne, Nelson, Grier, Daniel, Campbell, and Catron—concurred; while two associates—Judges McLean and Curtis—dissented. The decision of the majority, which was accepted as the opinion of the court, gave great satisfaction to the ultra slave-holding sentiments of the South, but excited in the North thousands of indignant comments and much bitter opposition.

In the first year of Buchanan's administration there was a Mormon rebellion in Utah. The difficulty arose from an attempt to extend the judicial system of the United States over the Territory. Thus far Brigham Young, the Mormon governor, had had his own way of administering justice. The community of Mormons was organized on a plan very different from that existing in other Territories, and many usages had grown up in Utah which were repugnant to the laws of the country. When, therefore, a Federal judge was sent to preside in the Territory, he was resisted, insulted and driven violently from the seat of justice. The other officials of the Federal government were also expelled, and the Territory became the scene of a reign of terror. The Mormons, however, attempted a justification of their conduct on the ground that the character of the United States officers had been so low and vicious as to command no respect. But the excuse was deemed insufficient, and Brigham Young was superseded in the governorship by Alfred Cumming, superintendent of Indian affairs on the Upper Missouri. Judge Delana Eckels of Indiana was appointed chief-justice of the Territory; and an army of two thousand five hundred men was organized and despatched to Utah to put down lawlessness by force.

But Young and the Mormon elders were in no humor to give up their authority without a struggle. The approaching American army was denounced as a horde of barbarians, and preparations were made for resistance. In September of 1857 the national forces reached the Territory; and on the 6th of October a company of Mormon rangers made good the threats of Young by attacking and destroying most of the supply trains of the army. Winter came on, and the Federal forces, under command of Colonel Albert Sidney Johnston, were obliged to find quarters on Black's Fork, near Fort Bridges. Meanwhile, however, the President had despatched Thomas L. Kane of Pennsylvania with conciliatory letters to the Mormons. Going by way of California, he reached Utah in the spring of 1858, and in a short time succeeded in bringing about a good understanding between Governor Cumming and the insurgents. In the latter part of May, Governor Powell of Kentucky and Major McCulloch of Texas arrived at the quarters of the army, bearing from the President a proclamation of pardon to all who would submit to the national authority. The passions of the Mormons had by this time somewhat subsided and they accepted the overture. In the fall of 1858 the army proceeded to Salt Lake City, but was soon afterwards quartered at Camp Floyd, forty miles distant. The Federal forces remained at this place until order was entirely restored, and in May of 1860 were withdrawn from the Territory.

Early in 1858 an American vessel, while innocently exploring the Paraguay River, in South America, was fired on by a jealous garrison. When reparation for the insult was demanded, none was given, and the government of the United States was obliged to send out a fleet to obtain satisfaction. A commissioner was sent with the squadron who was empowered to offer liberal terms of settlement for the injury. The authorities of Paraguay quailed before the American flag, and suitable apologies were made for the wrong which had been committed.

The 5th of August, 1858, was a memorable day in the history of the world. On that day was completed the laying OF THE FIRST TELEGRAPHIC CABLE across the Atlantic Ocean. The successful accomplishment of this great work was due in a large measure to the energy and genius of Cyrus W. Field, a wealthy merchant of New York. The cable, one thousand six hundred and forty miles in length, was stretched from Trinity Bay, Newfoundland, to Valentia Bay, Ireland. Telegraphic communication was thus established between the Old World and the New, and the fraternal greetings of peaceful nations were for the first time transmitted through the depths of the sea.

In 1858 Minnesota was added to the Union. The area of the new State was a little more than eighty-one thousand square miles, and its

General Sam Houston.

population at the date of admission a hundred and fifty thousand souls. In the next year Oregon, the thirty-third State, was admitted, with a population of forty-eight thousand, and an area of eighty thousand square miles. On the 4th of the preceding March General Sam Houston of Texas bade adieu to the Senate of the United States and retired to private life. His career had been marked by the strangest vicissitudes. He was a Virginian by birth, but his youth was hardened among the mountains of Tennessee. He gained a military fame in the Seminole War, then rose to political distinction, and was elected governor of his adopted State. Overshadowed with a domestic calamity, he suddenly resigned his office, left his home, and exiled himself among the Cherokees, by whom he was made a chief. Afterward he went to Texas, joined the patriots, and became a leading spirit in the struggle for independence. It was he who commanded in the decisive battle of San Jacinto; he who became first president of Texas, and also her first representative in the Senate of the United States. Through all the misfortunes, dangers and trials of his life his character stood like adamant.

In the fall of 1859 the people of the United States were called to mourn the death of WASHINGTON IRVING, THE PRINCE OF AMERICAN LETTERS. For full fifty years the powers of his sublime genius had been unremittingly devoted to the great work of creating for his native land a literature that should adorn and glorify his own and after ages. On both sides of the Atlantic, in every civilized country, his name had become familiar as a household word. He it was first of all, who wrung from the reluctant and proscriptive reviews of England and Scotland an acknowledgment of the power and originality of American genius. The literature of the New World was no longer a scoff and a by-word when Murray, the bookseller of London, was obliged to pay for the manuscript of "Bracebridge Hall"—which he had not yet seen—the sum of a thousand guineas. Except Sir Walter Scott and Lord Byron no other author of Irving's times received such a munificent reward for his labor—no other was so much praised and loved. Whether as humorist or writer of prose fiction, historian or biographer, his name ranks among the noblest and brightest of the world. When the petty revolutions of society and the bloody conflicts of the battle field are forgotten, the monument which the affections of his countrymen have reared to the memory of the illustrious Irving shall stand unshaken and untarnished, transmitting to all after times the record of his virtues and achievements.

Washington Irving.

From the beginning the new administration had stormy times. The slavery question continued to vex the nation. The Dred Scott Decision, to which the President had looked as a measure calculated to allay the excitement, had only added fuel to the flame. In some of the Free States the opposition rose so high that PERSONAL LIBERTY BILLS were passed, the object of which was to defeat the execution of the Fugitive Slave law. In the fall of 1859 the excitement was still further increased by the mad attempt of John Brown of Kansas to excite a general insurrection among the slaves. With a party of twenty-one men as daring as himself, he made a sudden descent on the United States arsenal at Harper's Ferry, captured the place, and held his ground for nearly two days. The national troops and the militia of Virginia were called out in order to suppress the revolt. Thirteen of Brown's men were killed, two made their escape, and the rest were captured. The leader and his six companions were given over to the authorities of Virginia, tried, condemned and hanged. In Kansas the old controversy still continued, but the Free Soil party gained ground so rapidly as to make it certain that slavery would be interdicted from the State. All these facts and events tended to widen the breach between the people of the North and the South. Such was the alarming condition of affairs when the time arrived for holding the nineteenth presidential election.

The canvass was one of intense excitement. Four candidates were presented. The choice of the People's party—now called Republican was Abraham Lincoln of Illinois. The platform of principles adopted by this party again declared opposition to the extension of slavery to be the vital issue. In the month of April the Democratic convention assembled at Charleston. The delegates were divided on the question of slavery, and after much debating the party was disrupted. The Southern delegates, unable to obtain a distinct expression of their views in the platform of principles, and seeing that the Northern wing was determined to nominate Mr. Douglas—the great defender of popular sovereignty—withdrew from the convention. The rest continued in session, balloted for a while for a candidate, and on the 3d of May adjourned to Baltimore, where the delegates, reassembling on the 18th of June, chose Douglas as their standard-bearer in the approaching canvass. The seceding delegates adjourned first to Richmond, and afterwards to Baltimore, where they met on the 28th of June and nominated John C. Breckinridge of Kentucky. The American party—now known as Constitutional Unionists—chose John Bell of Tennessee as their candidate. The contest resulted in the election of Mr. Lincoln. He received the electoral votes of all the Northern States except those of New Jersey, which were divided between himself and his two opponents. The support of the Southern States was for the most part given to Breckinridge. The States of Virginia, Kentucky, and Tennessee cast their ballots, thirty-nine in number, for Mr. Bell. Mr. Douglas received a large popular but small electoral vote, his supporters being scattered through all the States without the concentration necessary to carry any. Thus after controlling the destinies of the Republic for sixty years, with only the temporary overthrow of 1840, the Democratic party was broken into fragments and driven from the field.

The result of the election had been anticipated. The leaders of the South had openly declared that the choice of Lincoln would be regarded as a just cause for the dissolution of the Union. The Republicans of the populous North crowded to the polls, and their favorite was chosen. As to the government, it was under the control of the Douglas Democracy; but a majority of the cabinet and a large number of senators and representatives in Congress were supporters of Mr. Breckinridge and the advocates of disunion as a justifiable measure. It was now evident that with the incoming of the new administration all the departments of the government would pass under the control of the Republican party. The times were full of passion, animosity and rashness. It was seen that disunion was now possible, and that the possibility would shortly be removed. The attitude of the President favored the measure. He was not himself a disunionist. He denied the right of a State to secede; but at the same time he declared himself not armed with the constitutional power necessary to prevent secession by force. The interval, therefore, between the presidential election in November of 1860 and the inauguration of the following spring was seized by the leaders of the South as the opportune moment for dissolving the Union.

The actual work of secession began in South Carolina. On the 17th of December, 1860, a convention assembled at Charleston, and after three days of deliberation passed a resolution that the union hitherto existing between South Carolina and the other States, under the name of the United States of America, was dissolved. It was a step of fearful importance. The action was contagious. The sentiment of disunion spread with great rapidity. The cotton-growing States were almost unanimous in support of the measure. By the 1st of February, 1861, six other States—Mississippi, Florida, Alabama, Georgia, Louisiana and Texas—had passed ordinances of secession and withdrawn from the Union. Nearly all of the senators and representatives of those States, following the action of their constituents, resigned their seats in Congress and gave themselves to the disunion cause.

In the secession conventions there was but little opposition to the movement. In some instances a considerable minority vote was cast. A few of the speakers boldly denounced disunion as bad in principle and ruinous in its results. The course of Alexander H. Stephens, afterward Vice-President of the Confederate States, was peculiar. In the convention of Georgia he undertook the task of preventing the secession of his State. He delivered a long and powerful oration in which he defended the theory of secession, advocated the doctrine of State sovereignty, declared his intention of abiding by the decision of the convention, but at the same time spoke against secession, on the ground that *the measure was impolitic, unwise, disastrous*. Not a few prominent men at the South, held similar views; but the opposite opinion prevailed, and secession was accomplished.

Alexander H. Stephens

On the 4th of February, 1861, delegates from six of the seceded States assembled at Montgomery, Alabama, and formed a new government, under the name of THE CONFEDERATE STATES OF AMERICA. On the 8th of the month the government was organized by the election of Jefferson Davis of Mississippi as provisional President, and Alexander H. Stephens as Vice-President. On the same day of the meeting of the

Confederate Congress, at Montgomery, a peace conference assembled at Washington. Delegates from twenty-one States were present; certain amendments to the Constitution were proposed and laid before Congress for adoption, but that body gave little heed to the measures suggested, and the conference adjourned without practical results.

The country seemed on the verge of ruin. The national government was for the time being paralyzed. The army was stationed in detachments on remote frontiers. The fleet was scattered in distant seas. The President was distracted with hesitancy and the adverse counsels of his friends. With the exception of Forts Sumter and Moultrie in Charleston Harbor, Fort Pickens near Pensacola, and Fortress Monroe in the Chesapeake, all the important posts in the seceded States had been seized by the Confederate authorities, even before the organization of their government. All this while the local warfare in Kansas had continued; but the Free State party had at last gained the ascendency, and the early admission of the new commonwealth, with two additional Republican senators, was foreseen. Early in January the President made a feeble attempt to reinforce and provision the garrison of Fort Sumter. The steamer *Star of the West* was sent with men and supplies, but in approaching the harbor of Charleston was fired on by a Confederate battery and compelled to return. Thus in gloom and grief, and the upheavals of revolution, the administration of Buchanan drew to a close. Such was the dreadful condition of affairs that it was deemed prudent for the new President to approach the capital without recognition. For the first time in the history of the nation the chief magistrate of the republic slipped into Washington city by night.

CHAPTER LXI.
LINCOLN'S ADMINISTRATION, AND THE CIVIL WAR, 1861-1865.

ABRAHAM LINCOLN, sixteenth President of the United States, was a native of Kentucky, born in the county of Larue, on the 12th of February, 1809. His ancestors had emigrated thither from Rockingham County, Virginia: both father and mother were Virginians by birth. The childhood of the future President was passed in utter obscurity. In 1816 his father removed to Spencer County, Indiana—just then admitted into the Union—and built a cabin in the woods near the present village of Gentryville. Here was the scene of Lincoln's boyhood—a constant struggle with poverty, hardship, and toil. At the age of sixteen we find him managing a ferry across the Ohio, at the mouth of Anderson Creek—a service for which he was paid *six dollars per month*. In his youth he received in the aggregate about one year of schooling, which was all he ever had in the way of education. In the year of his majority he removed with his father's family to the north fork of the Sangamon, ten miles west of Decatur, Illinois. Here another log-house was built and a small farm cleared and fenced; and here Abraham Lincoln began for himself the hard battle of life.

> The uncleared forest, the unbroken soil,
>   The iron bark that turns the lumberer's axe,
> The rapid that o'erbears the boatman's toil,
>   The prairie, hiding the mazed wanderer's tracks,
>
> The ambushed Indian, and the prowling bear;—
>   Such were the needs that helped his youth to train—
> Rough culture!—but such trees large fruit may bear,
>   If but their stocks be of right girth and grain!

After serving as a flatboatman on the Mississippi, Lincoln returned to New Salem, twenty miles from Springfield, and became a clerk in a country store. Then, as captain of a company of volunteers, he served in the Black Hawk war. From 1833 to 1836 he was engaged in

Abraham Lincoln.

merchandising, but a dissolute partner brought him to bankruptcy. Turning his attention to the practice of the law, for which profession he had always had a liking, he gradually gained the attention of his fellow-men and soon rose to distinction. His peculiar power—manifested at all periods of his life—of seizing the most difficult thought and presenting it in such quaint and homely phrase as to make the truth appreciable by all men, made him a natural leader of the people. As candidate for the office of United States senator from Illinois he first revealed to the nation, in his great debates with Senator Douglas, the full scope and originality of his genius. Now, at the age of fifty-two, he found laid upon him such a burden of care and responsibility as had not been borne by any ruler of modern times. On the occasion of his inauguration he delivered a long and thoughtful address, declaring his fixed purpose to uphold the Constitution, enforce the laws, and preserve the integrity of the Union.

The new cabinet was organized with William H. Seward of New York as secretary of state. Salmon P. Chase of Ohio was chosen secretary of the treasury, and Simon Cameron secretary of war; but he, in the following January, was succeeded in office by Edwin M. Stanton. The secretaryship of the navy was conferred on Gideon Welles. In his inaugural address and first official papers the President indicated the policy of the new administration by declaring his purpose to repossess the forts, arsenals and public property which had been seized by the

Confederate authorities. It was with this purpose that the first military preparations were made. In the mean time, on the 12th of March, an effort was made by commissioners of the seceded States to obtain from the national government a recognition of their independence; but the negotiations were unsuccessful. Then followed a second attempt on the part of the government to reinforce the garrison of Fort Sumter; and with that came the beginning of actual hostilities.

The defences of Charleston Harbor were held by Major Robert Anderson. His entire force amounted to seventy-nine men. Owing to the weakness of his garrison, he deemed it prudent to evacuate Fort Moultrie and retire to Sumter. Meanwhile, Confederate volunteers had flocked to the city, and powerful batteries had been built about the harbor. When it became known that the Federal government would reinforce the forts, the authorities of the Confederate States determined to anticipate the movement by compelling Anderson to surrender. Accordingly, on the 11th of April, General P. T. Beauregard, commandant of Charleston, sent a flag to Fort Sumter, demanding an evacuation. Major Anderson replied that he should hold the fortress and defend his flag. On the following morning, at half-past four o'clock, the first gun was fired from a Confederate battery. A terrific bombardment of thirty-four hours' duration followed; the fort was reduced to ruins, set on fire, and obliged to capitulate. The honors of war were granted to Anderson and his men, who had made a brave and obstinate resistance. Although the cannonade had been long continued and severe, no lives were lost either in the fort or on the shore. Thus the defences of Charleston Harbor were secured by the Confederates.

The news of this startling event went through the country like a flame of fire. There had been some expectation of violence, but the actual shock came like a clap of thunder. The people of the towns poured into the streets and the country folk flocked to the villages to gather the tidings and to comment on the coming conflict. Gray-haired men talked gravely of the deed that was done, and prophesied of its consequences. Public opinion in both the North and the South was rapidly consolidated. Three days after the fall of Sumter President Lincoln issued a call for seventy-five thousand volunteers to serve three months in the overthrow of the secession movement. Two days later Virginia seceded from the Union. On May 6th Arkansas followed the example, and then North Carolina on the 20th of the same month. In Tennessee—especially in East Tennessee—there was a powerful Opposition to disunion, and it was not until the 8th of June that a secession ordinance could be passed. In Missouri, as will presently be seen, the movement resulted in civil war, while in Kentucky the authorities issued a proclamation of neutrality. The people of Maryland were divided into hostile parties, the disunion sentiment being largely prevalent.

On the 19th of April, when the first regiments of Massachusetts volunteers were passing through Baltimore on their way to Washington, they were fired upon by the citizens, and three men killed. This was the first bloodshed of the war. On the day before this event a body of Confederate soldiers advanced against the armory of the United States at Harper's Ferry. The officer in command hastily destroyed a portion of the vast magazine collected there, and then escaped into Pennsylvania. On the 20th of the month another company of Virginians assailed the great navy yard at Norfolk. The officers commanding fired the buildings and ships, spiked the cannon and withdrew their forces. Most of the guns and many of the vessels were afterward recovered by the Confederates, the property thus captured amounting to fully ten millions of dollars. So rapidly was Virginia filled with volunteers and troops from the South that, for a while, Washington city was in danger of being taken. But the capital was soon secured from immediate danger; and on the 3d of May the President issued another call for soldiers. This time the number was set at eighty-three thousand, and the term of service at three years or during the war. Lieutenant-General Winfield Scott was made commander-in-chief. As many war ships as could be provided were sent to blockade the Southern ports. On every side were heard the notes of preparation. In the seceded States there was boundless and incessant activity. Already the Southern Congress had adjourned from Montgomery, to meet on the 20th of July at Richmond, which was chosen as the capital of the Confederacy. To that place had already come Mr. Davis and the officers of his cabinet, for the purpose of directing the affairs of the government and the army. So stood the antagonistic powers in the beginning of June, 1861. It was now evident to all men (how slow they had been to believe it!) that a great war, perhaps the greatest in modern times, was impending over the nation. It is appropriate to look briefly into THE CAUSES of the approaching conflict.

CHAPTER LXII.

Causes.

THE first and most general cause of the civil war in the United States was *the different construction put upon the national Constitution by the people of the North and the South.* A difference of opinion had always existed as to how that instrument was to be understood. The question at issue was as to the relation between the States and the general government. One party held that under the Constitution the Union of the States is indissoluble; that the sovereignty of the nation is lodged in the central government; that the States are subordinate; that the acts of Congress, until they are repealed or pronounced unconstitutional by the supreme court, are binding on the States; that the highest allegiance of the citizen is due to the general government, and not to his own State; and that all attempts at nullification and disunion are in their nature disloyal and treasonable. The other party held that the national Constitution is a compact between sovereign States; that for certain reasons the Union may be dissolved; that the sovereignty of the nation is lodged in the individual States, and not in the central government; that Congress can exercise no other than delegated powers; that a State feeling aggrieved may annul an act of Congress; that the highest allegiance of the citizen is due to his own State, and afterward to the general government; and that acts of nullification and disunion are justifiable, revolutionary and honorable.

Here was an issue in its consequences the most fearful that ever disturbed a nation. It struck right into the vitals of the government. It threatened with each renewal of the agitation to undo the whole civil structure of the United States. For a long time the parties who disputed about the meaning of the Constitution were scattered in various sections. In the earlier history of the country the doctrine of State sovereignty was most advocated in New England. With the rise of the tariff question the position of parties changed. Since the tariff—a congressional measure—favored the Eastern States at the expense of the

South, it came to pass naturally that the people of New England passed over to the advocacy of national sovereignty, while the people of the South took up the doctrine of State rights. Thus it happened that as early as 1831 the right of nullifying an act of Congress was openly advocated in South Carolina, and thus also it happened that the belief in State sovereignty became more prevalent in the South than in the North. These facts tended powerfully to produce sectional parties and to bring them into conflict.

A second general cause of the civil war was *the different system of labor in the North and in the South.* In the former section the laborers were freemen, citizens, voters; in the latter, bondmen, property, slaves. In the South the theory was that the capital of a country should own the labor; in the North that both labor and capital are free. In the beginning all the colonies had been slaveholding. In the Eastern and Middle States the system of slave-labor was gradually abolished, being unprofitable. In the five great States formed out of the North-western Territory slavery was excluded by the original compact under which that Territory was organized. Thus there came to be a dividing line drawn through the Union east and west. It was evident, therefore, that whenever the question of slavery was agitated a sectional division would arise between the parties, and that disunion and war would be threatened. The danger arising from this source was increased and the discord between the sections aggravated by several subordinate causes.

The first of these was the invention of THE COTTON GIN. In 1793, Eli Whitney, a young collegian of Massachusetts, went to Georgia, and resided with the family of Mrs. Greene, widow of General Greene, of the Revolution. While there his attention was directed to the tedious and difficult process of picking cotton by hand—that is, separating the seed from the fibre. So slow was the process that the production of upland cotton was nearly profitless. The industry of the cotton-growing States was paralyzed by the tediousness of preparing the product for the market. Mr. Whitney undertook to remove the difficulty, and succeeded in inventing a gin which astonished the beholder by the rapidity and excellence of its work. From being profitless, cotton became the most profitable of all the staples. The industry of the South was revolutionized. Before the civil war it was estimated that Whitney's gin had added a thousand millions of dollars to the revenues of the Southern States. The American crop had grown to be seven-eighths of all the cotton produced in the world. Just in proportion to the increased profitableness of cotton slave-labor became important, slaves valuable and the system of slavery a fixed and deep-rooted institution.

From this time onward there was constant danger that the slavery question would so embitter the politics and legislation of the country as to bring about disunion. The danger of such a result was fully manifested in THE MISSOURI AGITATION of 1820-21. Threats of dissolving the Union were freely made in both the North and the South—in the North, because of the proposed enlargement of the domain of slavery; in the South, because of the proposed rejection of Missouri as a slave-holding State. When the Missouri Compromise was enacted, it was the hope of Mr. Clay and his fellow-statesmen to save the Union by removing for ever the slavery question from the politics of the country. In that they succeeded for a while.

Next came THE NULLIFICATION ACTS of South Carolina. And these, too, turned upon the institution of slavery and the profitableness of cotton. The Southern States had become cotton-producing; the Eastern States had given themselves to manufacturing. The tariff measures favored manufactures at the expense of producers. Mr. Calhoun and his friends proposed to remedy the evil complained of by annulling the laws of Congress. His measures failed; but another compromise was found necessary in order to allay the animosities which had been awakened.

THE ANNEXATION OF TEXAS, with the consequent enlargement of the domain of slavery, led to a renewal of the agitation. Those who opposed the Mexican War did so, not so much because of the injustice of the conflict as because of the fact that thereby slavery would be extended. Then, at the close of the war, came another enormous acquisition of territory. Whether the same should be made into free or slave-holding States was the question next agitated. This controversy led to the passage of THE OMNIBUS BILL, by which again for a brief period the excitement was allayed.

CHART VI.

1857	61	65

Frederick William IV.

60. Treaty of Peace between China and England.

Napoleon III.

61. **William I.**

Victoria.

62. Death of **Prince Albert**, the Consort.

58. Mutiny in the East India army.

JAMES BUCHANAN, President. **ABRAHAM LINCOLN**, President.
John C. Breckinridge, V.-Pres. **Hannibal Hamlin**, Vice-President.
61. The "Star of the West" fired upon.
61. Ten of the Southern States secede.

57. The Dred Scott decision.
61. *Fall of Fort Sumter.*
61. The President calls for 75,000 volunteers.
61. The Confederate Congress at Montgomery.
57. Personal Liberty Bill.
61. The President calls for 500,000 men
61. *Bull Run.*
  Ball's Bluff.
57. The Mormon rebellion in Utah.
62. *Mill Spring.*
61. Mason and Slidell captured.
61. **Kansas** admitted into the Union.
58. The first Atlantic Telegraph Cable.
62. *Fort Donelson.*
  Pittsburg Landing.
62. *The Monitor and Merrimac.*
58. **Minnesota** admitted into the Union.
62. *Murfreesborough.*
  Front Royal and Port Republic.
62. *Fair Oaks.*
  Seven Days' battles.
62. *Antietam.*

60. Walker's filibustering schemes defeated.
63. **The Emancipation Proclamation.**
63. *Siege of Vicksburg.*
58. The great campaign of Mr. Lincoln and Senator Douglas.
63. *Chickamauga.*
63. *Lookout Mountain.*
  Missionary Ridge.
63. **West Virginia** admitted into the Union.
63. *Siege of Knoxville.*
58. Troubles with Paraguay.
63. *Morgan's raid.*
63. *Chancellorsville.*
59. Washington Irving died, aged 76.
63. Lee invades Pennsylvania.
63. *Gettysburg.*
63. The President orders a draft for 200,000 troops.
64. The President calls for 300,000 men.
60. The Japanese Commission in the United States.
64. *Dalton, Resaca.*
  Dallas, Kenesaw.
64. *Siege of Atlanta.*
60. Disruption of the Democratic Party at Charleston.
64. *Franklin.*
  Nashville.
64. Sherman's march.
60. Population, 31,443,231.
64. *Fort McAllister.*
  Petersburg.
64. *Mobile Bay.*
  Fort Fisher.
60. Defeat of the Democratic Party.
64. *The Alabama and Kearsarge.*
64. *The Wilderness.*
  Cold Harbor.
64. **LINCOLN** re-elected.
60. South Carolina secedes.
65. *Five Forks.*
  Lee's surrender.
65. Lincoln assassinated.

67. War between ... and A
67. Hanover ab
68. Fc
65. Fenian troubles in Ireland.
68. Pr

66. The Atlantic Cable l

65. Reconstruction of the seceded
ANDREW JOHNSON, Pres
65. **Amnesty Proclamation**

66. Tennessee re-admit

67. Purchase of

68. I
68. T
68. A

68. G

Disturbed condition of affairs in Mexico.
62. French invasion of Mexico.
64. **Maximilian** elected Emperor.
67. The Frenc
67. **Maximil**

NATIONAL PERIOD – THIRD SECTION, A. D. 1857-1877.

69	73	77	1880

en Prussia ria.
ed by Prussia.
tion of a North German Confederati

71. Beginning of

71. *Sedan.*

71. Downfall of N

72.

e of the Reform Bill.
70. Disestablishment of the
71. Bill forbidding
72. Popu

72. **King William** proclaimed Emperor.
the **Franco-Prussian War.**
on.
73. The Irish University Bill defeated.
74. Overthrow of the Gladstone ministry.
74. **Disraeli,** Prime Minister.
apoleon III.
Siege of Paris;
Treaty of Peace.
Irish Church.
the sale of Commissions.
lation of the United Kingdom, 31,465,480.

ULYSSES S. GRANT, President.
Schuyler Colfax, Vice-President.
9. The Pacific Railroad completed.
9. Edwin M. Stanton died, aged 55.

70. The Fifteenth Amendment adopted.
70. Robert E. Lee died, aged 63.
70. Admiral Farragut died, aged 69.
70. Virginia, Mississippi, and Texas re-admitted into the Union.
70. Population, 38,558,371.

RUTHERFORD B. HAYES, President.
William A. Wheeler, Vice-President.

76. **The Sioux War.**
76. The Custer Massacre.
77. The disputed Presidency is settled by a Joint High Commission.

s undertaken by the President.
after April 15, 1865.

ito the Union.

ia.

ament of President Johnson.
teenth Amendment adopted.
as, Alabama, Georgia, Florida, Louisiana, North Carolina, and South Carolina re-admitted into the Union.

71. Burning of Chicago.

onetary panic in New York City.

72. The **Alabama Claims** settled.
72. William H. Seward died, aged 71.
72. **GRANT** re-elected.

Henry Wilson, Vice-President. Died November 22, 1875.

72. Horace Greeley died, aged 61.
72. General George G. Meade died, aged 57.
72. Great fire in Boston.
72. Boundary dispute between the United States and Great Britain settled.

73. **Modoc War.**
73. The Credit Mobilier investigation.
73. Chief-Justice Chase died, aged 65.
73. Great financial crisis.

74. Charles Sumner died, aged 63.

76. **Colorado** admitted into the Union.
76. **Centennial Celebration** at Phil'a.

CHART VI.

NATIONAL PERIOD — THIRD SECTION,
A. D. 1857—1877.

withdrawn.
cuted at Queretaro.

In 1854 THE KANSAS-NEBRASKA bill was passed. Thereby the Missouri Compromise was repealed and the whole question opened anew. Meanwhile, the character and the civilization of the Northern and the Southern people had become quite different. In population and wealth the North had far outgrown the South. In the struggle for territorial dominion the North had gained a considerable advantage. In 1860 the division of the Democratic party made certain the election of Mr. Lincoln by the votes of the Northern States. The people of the South were exasperated at the choice of a chief-magistrate whom they regarded as indifferent to their welfare and hostile to their interests.

The third general cause of the civil war was *the want of intercourse between the people of the North and the South.* The great railroads and thoroughfares ran east and west. Emigration flowed from the East to the West. Between the North and the South there was little travel or interchange of opinion. From want of acquaintance the people, without intending it, became estranged, jealous, suspicious. They misjudged each other's motives. They misrepresented each other's beliefs and purposes. They suspected each other of dishonesty and ill-will. Before the outbreak of the war the people of the two sections looked upon each other almost in the light of different nationalities.

A fourth cause was found in *the publication of sectional books.* During the twenty years preceding the war many works were published, both in the North and the South, whose popularity depended wholly on the animosity existing between the two sections. Such books were generally filled with ridicule and falsehood. The manners and customs, language and beliefs, of one section were held up to the contempt and scorn of the people of the other section. The minds of all classes, especially of the young, were thus prejudiced and poisoned. In the North the belief was fostered that the South was given up to inhumanity, ignorance and barbarism, while in the South the opinion prevailed that the Northern people were a selfish race of mean, cold-blooded Yankees.

The evil influence of demagogues may be cited as the fifth general cause of the war. It is the misfortune of republican governments that they many times fall under the leadership of bad men. In the United States the demagogue has enjoyed special opportunities for mischief, and the people have suffered in proportion. From 1850 to 1860 American statesmanship and patriotism were at a low ebb. Many ambitious and scheming men had come to the front, taken control of the political parties and proclaimed themselves the leaders of public opinion. Their purposes were wholly selfish. The welfare and peace of the country were put aside as of no value. In order to gain power and keep it many unprincipled men in the South were anxious to destroy the Union, while the demagogues of the North were willing to *abuse* the Union in order to accomplish their own bad purposes. Such, in brief, were the causes which led to the civil war, one of the most terrible conflicts of modern times.

CHAPTER LXIII.

FIRST YEAR OF THE WAR.

ON the 24th of May the Union army crossed the Potomac from Washington city to Alexandria. At this time Fortress Monroe, at the mouth of James River, was held by twelve thousand men, under command of General B. F. Butler. At Bethel Church, in the immediate vicinity, was stationed a detachment of Confederates commanded by General Magruder. On the 10th of June a body of Union troops was sent to dislodge them, but was repulsed with considerable loss. Meanwhile the conquest of West Virginia had been undertaken by General George B. M'Clellan.

Scene Operations in West Virginia, 1861.

In the last days of May General T. A. Morris moved forward from Parkers burg to Grafton with a force of Ohio and Indiana troops, and on the 3d of June came upon the Confederates stationed at Philippi. After a brief engagement the Federals were successful; the Confederates retreated toward the mountains. General McClellan now arrived, took command in person, and on the 11th of July gained a victory at Rich Mountain. General Garnett, the Confederate commander, fell back with his forces to Carrick's Ford, on Cheat River, made a stand, was again defeated and himself killed in the battle. On the 10th of August General Floyd, commanding a detachment of Confederates at Carnifex Ferry, on Gauley River, was attacked by General Rosecrans and obliged to retreat. On the 14th of September a division of Confederates under General Robert E. Lee was beaten in an engagement at Cheat Mountain—an action which completed the restoration of Federal authority in West Virginia. In the mean time, other movements of vast importance had taken place.

In the beginning of June General Robert Patterson marched from Chambersburg with the intention of recapturing Harper's Ferry. On the 11th of the month a division of the army commanded by Colonel Lewis Wallace made a sudden and successful onset upon a detachment of Confederates stationed at Romney. Patterson then crossed the Potomac with the main body, entered the Shenandoah Valley, and pressed back the Confederate forces to Winchester. Thus far there had been only petty engagements, skirmishes and marching. The time had now come when the first great battle of the war was to be fought.

After the Union successes in West Virginia the main body of the Confederates, under command of General Beauregard, was concentrated at Manassas Junction, on the Orange Railroad, twenty-seven miles west of Alexandria. Another large force, commanded by General Joseph E. Johnston, was within supporting distance in the Shenandoah Valley. The Union army at Alexandria was commanded by General Irwin McDowell, while General Patterson was stationed in front of Johnston to watch his movements and prevent his forming a junction with Beauregard. On the 16th of July the national army moved forward. Two days afterward an unimportant engagement took place between Centreville and Bull Run.

The Unionists then pressed on, and on the morning of the 21st came upon the Confederate army, strongly posted between Bull Run and Manassas Junction. A general battle ensued, continuing with great severity until noonday. At that hour the advantage was with McDowell, and it seemed not unlikely that the Confederates would suffer a complete defeat. But in the crisis of the battle General Johnston arrived with nearly six thousand fresh troops from the Shenandoah Valley. The tide of victory turned immediately, and in a short time McDowell's whole army was hurled back in utter rout and confusion. A ruinous panic spread through the defeated host. Soldiers and citizens, regulars and volunteers, horsemen and footmen, rolled back in a disorganized mass into the defences of Washington. The Union loss in killed, wounded and prisoners amounted to two thousand nine hundred and fifty-two; that of the Confederates to two thousand and fifty.

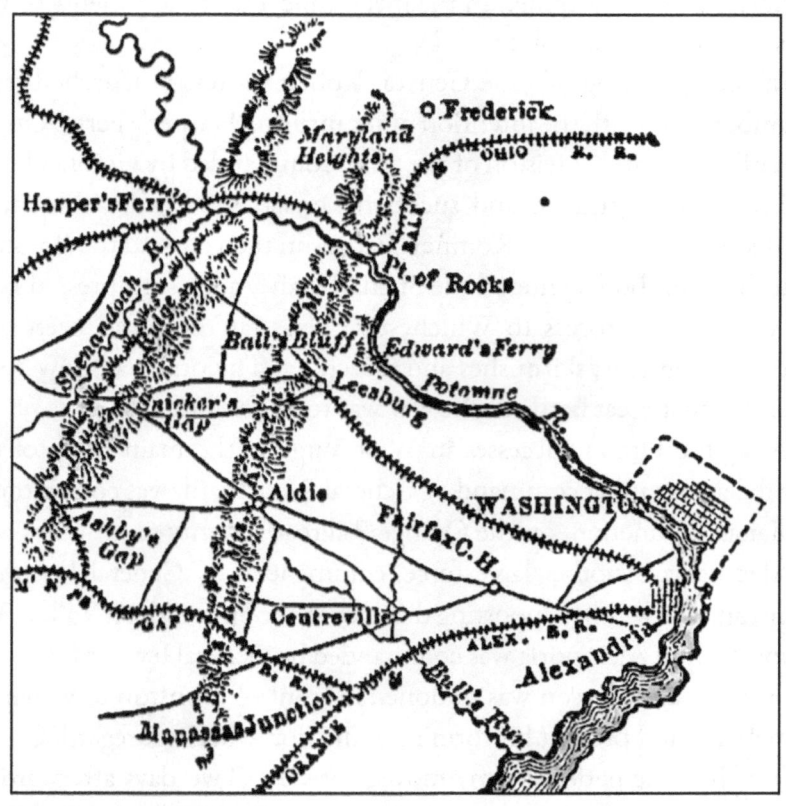

Vicinity of Manassas Junction, 1861.

Great was the humiliation of the North, and greater the rejoicing of the South. For a while the Federal government was more concerned about its own safety than about the conquest of Richmond. In that city, on the day before the battle, the new Confederate government was organized. In the Southern Congress and cabinet were many men of distinguished abilities. Jefferson Davis, the President, was a far-sighted man, of wide experience in the affairs of state, and considerable reputation as a soldier. He had led the troops of Mississippi in the Mexican War, had served in both houses of the national Congress, and as a member of President Pierce's cabinet. His talents, decision of character and ardent advocacy of State rights had made him a natural leader of the South.

The next military movements were made in Missouri. That commonwealth, though slaveholding, still retained its place in the Union. A convention, called by Governor Jackson in accordance with an act of the legislature, had in the previous March refused to pass an ordinance of secession. The disunionists, however, were numerous and powerful; the governor favored their cause, and the State became a battle-field for the contending parties. Both Federal and Confederate camps were organized, and hostilities began in several places. By capturing the United States arsenal at Liberty, in Clay county, the Confederates obtained a considerable supply of arms and ammunition. By the formation of Camp Jackson, near St. Louis, the arsenal in that city was also endangered bubby the vigilance of Captain Nathaniel Lyon the arms and stores were sent up the river to Alton,

Jefferson Davis.

and thence to Springfield. Camp Jackson was soon afterward broken up by the exertions of the same officer.

The lead-mines in the south-west part of the State became an object of great importance to the Confederates, who, in order to secure them, hurried up large bodies of troops from Arkansas and Texas. On the 17th of June Lyon encountered Governor Jackson with a Confederate force at Booneville, and gained a decided advantage. On the 5th of July the Unionists, led by Colonel Franz Sigel, were again successful in a severe engagement with the governor at Carthage. On the 10th of August the hardest battle thus far fought in the West occurred at Wilson's Creek, a short distance south of Springfield. General Lyon made a daring but rash attack on a much superior force of Confederates under command of Generals McCullough and Price. The Federals at first gained the field against heavy odds, but General Lyon was killed, and his men retreated under direction of Sigel.

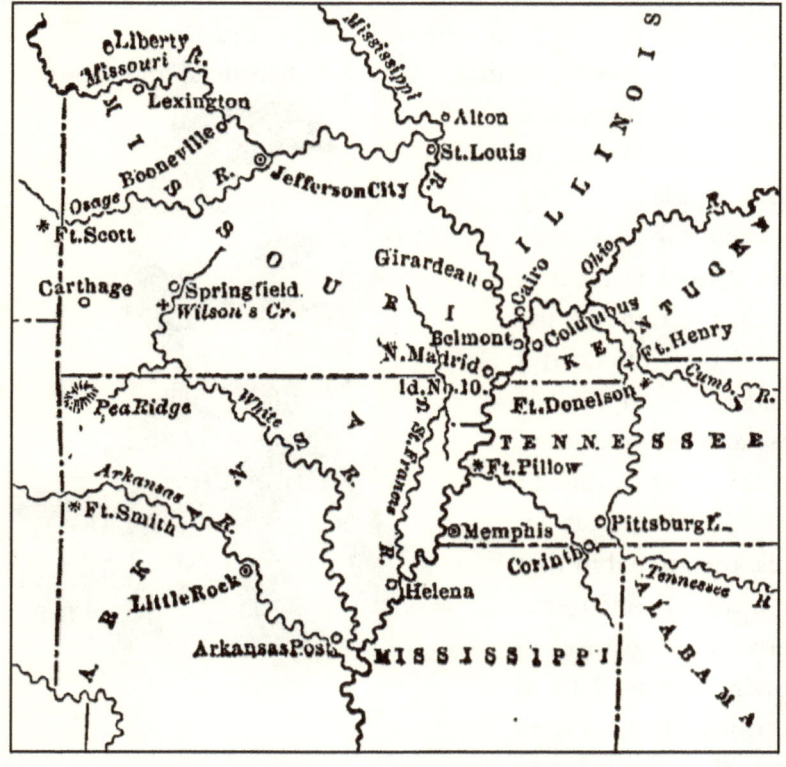

Scene of Operations in the South-West, 1861.

General Price now pressed northward across the State to Lexington, on the Missouri River. This place was defended by a force of Federals two thousand six hundred strong, commanded by Colonel Mulligan. A stubborn defence was made by the garrison, but Mulligan was soon obliged to capitulate. Price then turned southward, and on the 16th of October Lexington was retaken by the Federals. General John C. Fremont, who had been appointed to the command of the Union forces in Missouri, followed the Confederates as far as Springfield, and was on the eve of making an attack, when he was superseded by General Hunter. The latter, after retreating to St. Louis, was in turn superseded by General Halleck on the 18th of November. It was now Price's turn to fall back toward Arkansas. The only remaining movement of importance was at Belmont, on the Mississippi.

The Confederate general Polk, acting under orders of his government, had, notwithstanding that State's neutrality, entered Kentucky with an army, and had captured the town of Columbus. Batteries planted here commanded the Mississippi. The Confederates gathered in force at Belmont, on the opposite bank. In order to dislodge them Colonel Ulysses S. Grant, with a brigade of three thousand Illinois troops, was sent by way of Cairo into Missouri. On the 7th of November he made a vigorous and successful attack on the Confederate camp; but General Polk sent reinforcements across the river, the guns of Columbus were brought to bear on the Union position, and Grant was obliged to retreat.

The rout at Bull Run had the effect to quicken the energies of the North, and troops were rapidly hurried to Washington. The aged General Scott, unable to bear the burden resting upon him, retired from active duty, and General McClellan was called from West Virginia to take command of the Army of the Potomac. By the middle of October his forces had increased to a hundred and fifty thousand men. On the 21st of that month a brigade, numbering nearly two thousand, was thrown across the Potomac at Ball's Bluff. Without proper support or means of retreat, the Federals were attacked by a strong force of Confederates under General Evans, driven to the river, their leader, Colonel Baker, killed, and the whole force routed with terrible loss. Fully eight hundred of Baker's men were killed, wounded or taken prisoners.

During the summer of 1861 the Federal government sent to sea several important naval expeditions. One of these, commanded by Commodore Stringham and General Butler, proceeded to the North Carolina coast, and on the 29th of August captured the forts at Hatteras Inlet. On the 7th of November a second armament, under command of Commodore Dupont and General Thomas W. Sherman, entered the harbor of Port Royal, and captured Forts Walker and Beauregard. Hilton Head, a point most advantageous for military operations against Charleston and Savannah, thus fell into the power of the Federals. Around the whole coast the blockade became so rigorous that commerce and communication between the Confederate States and foreign nations were almost wholly cut off. In this juncture of affairs a difficulty arose which brought the United States and Great Britain to the very verge of war.

The Confederate government had appointed James M. Mason and John Slidell, formerly senators of the United States, to go abroad as ambassadors from the Confederate States to France and England. The envoys went on board a blockade runner, and escaping from Charleston Harbor, reached Havana in safety. At that port they took passage on the British mail steamer *Trent*, and sailed for Europe. On the 8th of November the vessel was overtaken by the United States frigate *San Jacinto*, commanded by Captain Wilkes. The *Trent* was hailed and boarded; the two ambassadors and their secretaries were seized, transferred to the *San Jacinto*, carried to Boston, and imprisoned. The *Trent* proceeded on her way to England; the story of the insult to the British flag was told, and the whole kingdom burst out in a blaze of wrath.

At first the people of the United States loudly applauded Captain Wilkes, and the government was disposed to defend his action. Had such a course been taken, war would have been inevitable. The country was saved from the peril by the adroit and far-reaching diplomacy of William H. Seward, the secretary of state. When Great Britain demanded reparation for the insult and the immediate liberation of the prisoners, he replied in a mild, cautious and very able paper. It was conceded that the seizure of Mason and Slidell was not justifiable according to the law of nations. A suitable apology was made for the wrong done, the Confederate ambassadors were liberated, put on board a vessel and sent to their destination. This action of the secretary was both just and politic. The peril of war went by, and Great Britain was committed to a policy in regard to the rights of neutral flags which she had hitherto denied and which the United States had always contended for. So ended the first year of the civil war.

William H. Seward.

CHAPTER LXIV.

CAMPAIGNS OF '62.

THE Federal forces now numbered about four hundred and fifty thousand men. Of these nearly two hundred thousand, under command of General McClellan, were encamped in the vicinity of Washington. Another army, commanded by General Buell, was stationed at Louisville, Kentucky, and it was in this department that the first military movements of the year were made. On the 9th of January Colonel Humphrey Marshall, commanding a force of Confederates on Big Sandy River, in Eastern Kentucky, was attacked and defeated by a body of Unionists, led by Colonel Garfield. Ten days later another and more important battle was fought at Mill Spring, in the same section of the State. The Confederates were commanded by Generals Crittenden and Zollicoffer, and the Federals by General George H. Thomas. After a hot engagement, in which both sides lost heavily, the Confederates suffered a defeat which was rendered more severe by the loss of Zollicoffer, who fell in the battle.

The next operations were on the Tennessee and the Cumberland. The former river was commanded at the southern border of Kentucky by Fort Henry, and the latter by the more important Fort Donelson, ten miles south of the Tennessee line. At the beginning of the year the capture of both these places was planned by General Halleck. Early in February Commodore Foote was sent up the Tennessee with a flotilla of gunboats, and at the same time General Grant was ordered to move forward and co-operate in an attack on Fort Henry. Before the land-forces were well into position the flotilla compelled the evacuation of the fort, the Confederates escaping to Donelson. Eighty-three prisoners and a large amount of stores were captured.

The Federal gunboats now dropped down the Tennessee, took on supplies at Cairo, and then ascended the Cumberland. Grant pressed on from Fort Henry, and as soon as the flotilla arrived began the siege of Fort Donelson. The defences were strong, and well manned by more than ten thousand Confederates, under General Buckner. Grant's entire force numbered nearly thirty thousand. On the 14th of February the gunboats were driven back with considerable loss, Commodore Foote being among the wounded. On the next day the garrison, hoping to break through Grant's lines, made a sally, but met a severe repulse. On the 16th Buckner was obliged to surrender. His army of ten thousand men became prisoners of war, and all the magazines, stores and guns of the fort fell into the hands of the Federals. It was the first decided victory which had been won by the national arms. The immediate result of the capture was the evacuation of Kentucky and the capital of Tennessee by the Confederates.

After his success at Fort Donelson General Grant ascended the Tennessee as far as Pittsburg Landing. In the beginning of April a camp was established at Shiloh Church, a short distance from the river; and here on the morning of the 6th, the Union army was suddenly attacked by the Confederates, led by Generals Albert S. Johnston and Beauregard. The onset was at first successful. All day long the battle raged with tremendous slaughter on both sides. The Federals were forced back to the river, and but for the protection of the gunboats would have been driven to destruction. Night fell on the scene with the conflict undecided, but in this desperate crisis General Buell arrived from Nashville with strong reinforcements. On the following morning General Grant assumed the General Johnston had been killed in the battle, and Beauregard, on whom the command devolved, was obliged to retreat to Corinth. The losses in killed, wounded and missing in this dreadful conflict were more than ten thousand on each side. There had never before been such a harvest of death in the New World.

Events of importance were also taking place on the Mississippi. When the Confederates evacuated Columbus, Kentucky, they proceeded to Island Number Ten, a few miles below, and built strong fortifications commanding the river. On the western shore was the town of New Madrid, which was held by a Confederate force from Missouri. Against this place General Pope advanced with a body of Western troops, while Commodore Foote descended the Mississippi with his flotilla to attack the forts on the island. Pope was entirely successful in his movement, and gained possession of New Madrid. The land-forces then co-operated with the gunboats, and for twenty-three days Island Number Ten was vigorously bombarded. On the 7th of April, when the Confederates could hold out no longer, they attempted to escape; but Pope had cut off retreat, and the entire garrison, numbering about five thousand, was captured. The Mississippi was thus opened as far down as Memphis, and that city was taken by the fleet of Commodore Davis on the 6th of the following June.

In the beginning of the year General Curtis had pushed forward through Missouri, entered Arkansas and taken position at Pea Ridge, among the mountains in the north-western angle of the State. Here he was attacked on the 6th of March by an army of more than twenty thousand Confederates and Indians, under command of Generals McCulloch, McIntosh and Pike. After a hard-fought battle, which lasted for two days, the Federals were victorious. McCulloch and McIntosh were both killed and their men obliged to retreat toward Texas; but the Union losses were most severe, and the battle was barren of results.

On the next day after the conflict at Pea Ridge an event occurred at Fortress Monroe which came near changing the character of naval warfare. Captain John Ericsson of New York had invented and built a peculiar war-vessel with a single round tower of iron exposed above the water-line. Meanwhile, the Confederates had raised the United States frigate *Merrimac*, one of the sunken ships at the Norfolk navy yard, and had plated the sides with an impenetrable mail of iron. This done, the vessel was sent to attack the Union fleet at Fortress Monroe. Reaching that place on the 8th of March, the *Merrimac*, now called the *Virginia*, began the work of destruction, and before sunset two valuable vessels, the *Cumberland* and the *Congress*, were sent to the bottom. During the night, however, Ericsson's strange ship, called the *Monitor*, arrived from New York, and on the following morning the two iron-clad monsters turned their terrible enginery upon each other. After fighting for five hours, the *Virginia* was obliged to give up the contest and to return badly damaged to Norfolk. Such was the excitement produced by this novel sea-fight that for a while the whole energies of the navy department were devoted to building *monitors*.

Early in 1862 a strong land and naval force, commanded by General Ambrose E. Burnside and Commodore Goldsborough, was sent against the Confederate garrison of Roanoke Island. On the 8th of February the squadron reached its destination; the fortifications on the island were attacked and carried, and the garrisons, nearly three thousand strong, taken prisoners. Burnside next proceeded against Newbern, North Carolina, and on the 14th of March captured the city after four hours of severe fighting. Proceeding southward, he reached the harbor of Beaufort, carried Fort Macon, at the entrance, and on the 25th of April took possession of the town.

On the 11th of the same month Fort Pulaski, commanding the mouth of the Savannah River, surrendered to General Gillmore. By this important capture the chief emporium of Georgia was effectually blockaded. But these reverses of the Confederates were trifling in comparison with that which they sustained in the loss of the city of New Orleans. Early in April a powerful squadron, commanded by General Butler and Admiral Farragut, entered the Mississippi and proceeded as far as Forts Jackson and St. Philip, thirty miles above the gulf. The guns of these forts, standing on opposite shores, completely commanded the river, and obstructions had been placed in the channel. The forty five vessels comprising the Federal fleet were brought into position, and a furious bombardment of the forts was begun. From the 18th to the 24th of April the fight continued without cessation. At the end of that time the forts were but little injured, and Farragut undertook the hazardous enterprise of running past the batteries. In this he succeeded, breaking the chain across the river and overpowering the Confederate fleet above the obstructions. On the next day he reached New Orleans with a portion of his fleet, and took possession of the city. General Butler became commandant, and the fortifications were manned with fifteen thousand Federal soldiers. Three days afterward Forts Jackson and St. Philip surrendered to Admiral Porter, who had remained below and prosecuted the siege. The control of the Lower Mississippi and the metropolis of the South was thus recovered by the Federal government.

The Confederates were not going to give up Kentucky without a struggle. From East Tennessee they invaded the State in two strong divisions, the one led by General Kirby Smith and the other by General Bragg. On the 30th of August Smith's army reached Richmond, attacked a force of Federals stationed there, and routed them with heavy losses. Lexington was taken, and then Frankfort; and Cincinnati was saved from capture only by the extraordinary exertions of General Wallace. Meanwhile, the army of General Bragg had advanced from Chattanooga to Mumfordsville, where, on the 17th of September, he captured a Federal division of four thousand five hundred men. From this point the Confederate general pressed on toward Louisville, and would have taken the city but for a forced march of General Buell from Tennessee. The latter arrived with his army only one day ahead of Bragg, but that one day gave the Unionists the advantage, and the Confederates were turned back. From the North came reinforcements for Buell's army, swelling his numbers to a hundred thousand. In the beginning of October he again took the field, the Confederates slowly retiring to Perryville. At this place, on the 8th of October, Bragg was overtaken, and a severe but indecisive battle was fought. The retreat was then continued to East Tennessee, the Confederates sweeping out of Kentucky a train of four thousand wagons laden with the spoils of the campaign.

In September there were some stirring events in Mississippi. On the 19th of the month a hard battle was fought at Iuka between a Federal army, commanded by Generals Rosecrans and Grant, and a Confederate force, under General Price. The latter was defeated, losing, in addition to his killed and wounded, nearly a thousand prisoners. General Rosecrans now took post at Corinth with twenty thousand men, while General Grant, with the remainder of the Federal forces, proceeded to Jackson, Tennessee. Perceiving this division of the army, the Confederate generals Van Dorn and Price turned about to recapture Corinth. Advancing for that purpose, they came on the 3d of October upon the Federal defences. Another obstinately contested battle ensued, which ended, after two days' fighting and heavy losses on both sides, in the re pulse of the Confederates.

In the mean time, General Grant had removed his headquarters from Jackson to La Grange. His purpose was to co-operate with General Sherman, then at Memphis, in an effort to capture Vicksburg. The movement promised to be successful, but on the 20th of December General Van Dorn succeeded in cutting Grant's line of supplies at Holly Springs, and obliged him to retreat. On the same day General Sherman, with a powerful armament, dropped down the river from Memphis. Proceeding as far as the Yazoo, he effected a landing, and on the 29th of the month made an unsuccessful attack on the Confederates at Chickasaw Bayou. The assault was exceedingly disastrous to the Federals, who lost in killed, wounded and prisoners more than three thousand men. The enterprise was at once abandoned, and the defeated army returned to the fleet of gunboats in the Mississippi.

The closing conflict of this year's operations in the West was the great battle of Murfreesborough. After his successful defence of Corinth General Rosecrans was transferred to the command of the Army of the Cumberland. Late in the fall he made his headquarters at Nashville, and there collected a powerful army. Meanwhile,

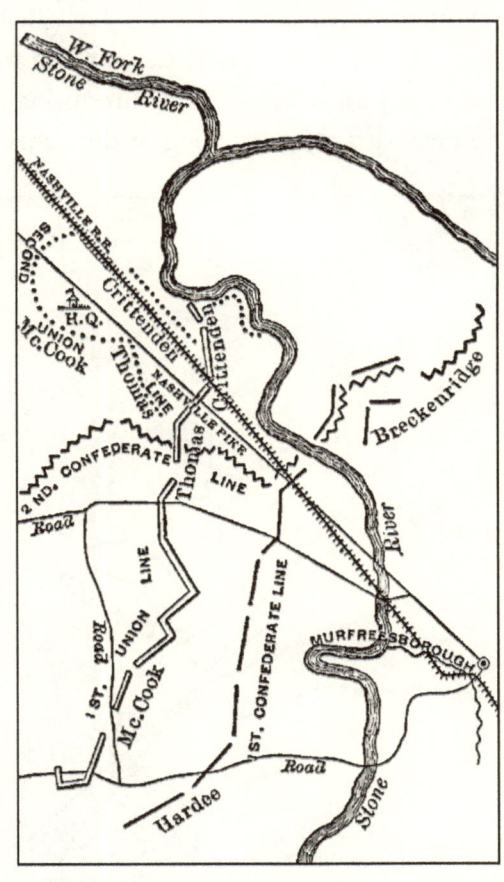

Battle of Mufreesborough, Dec. 31st, 1862.

General Bragg, on his retirement from Kentucky, had thrown his forces into Murfreesborough. Thus the two generals found themselves face to face, and but thirty miles apart. Late in December Rosecrans moved forward to attack his antagonist, and on the evening of the 30th came upon the Confederates strongly posted on Stone's River, a short distance north-west of Murfreesborough. During the night preparations were made on both sides for the impending battle. The plan of attack adopted by the Federal commander contemplated the massing of his forces on the left in such numbers as to crush the Confederate right wing under Breckinridge before assistance could be brought from the west side of the river. Bragg's plan of battle was the exact counterpart of that adopted by Rosecrans. Before daylight the Confederates were heavily massed under Hardee on the left and in the early morning the battle began by a furious and unexpected charge on McCook who commanded the right wing of the Federals. McCook's outcry for help was at first unheeded by Rosecrans, who did not realize the real nature of the Confederate onset. After a terrible struggle which lasted until noonday the Union right was shattered to fragments and driven from the field. The brunt of the battle now fell upon General Thomas, who commanded the Federal right center; and he, too, after desperate fighting, was obliged to fall back to a new position. Here, however, he rallied his forces and held his ground until General Rosecrans readjusted his whole line of battle. While this work was going on, the Confederates were barely prevented from a complete and overwhelming triumph by the almost unparalleled heroism of the division of

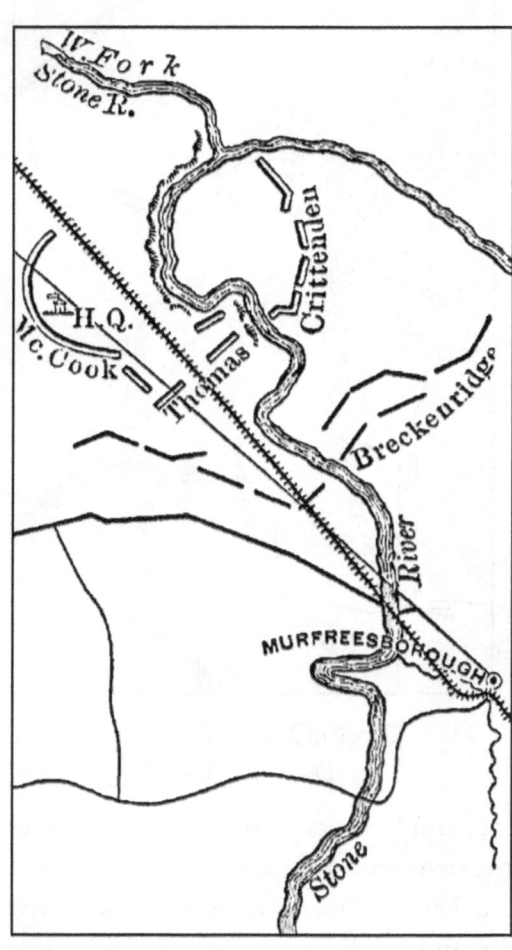

Battle of Mufreesborough,
Jan. 2nd, 1868.

General William B. Hazen. With only thirteen hundred men he stayed the oncoming tide of victorious assailants until the Federal lines were completely restored. At nightfall more than seven thousand Union soldiers were missing from the ranks.

But General Rosecrans, though defeated, was by no means disposed to abandon the contest. During the night after the battle, a council of war was held and complete preparations were made for renewing the struggle on the morrow. On New Year's morning General Bragg found his antagonist strongly posted, with shortened lines, and manifest disposition for battle. The Confederate commander grew cautious; and the day was spent in indecisive skirmishing and artillery firing at long range. Early on the morning of the 2d, the conflict broke out afresh on the east side of Stone's River, and for some hours there was terrific cannonading in that quarter. At three o'clock in the afternoon the Confederates were massed against the Union left, and the Nationals were driven across the river by the shock. But at this juncture the Federal artillery, advantageously posted on the hills west of the stream, opened a murderous fire on the assailing columns. At the same time, the discomfited Federals, rallying to the charge, turned upon their pursuers and in one tremendous onset drove them from the field with the slaughter of thousands. General Bragg had lost the prize. During the night he withdrew his broken and exhausted columns through Murfreesborough and retreated in the direction of Tullahoma. The Union loss in the two battles was a thousand five hundred and thirty-three killed, seven thousand two hundred and forty-five wounded, and nearly three thousand prisoners; that of the Confederates amounted in killed, wounded, and prisoners to between ten and eleven thousand men.

In Virginia the campaigns of 1862 were even more grand and destructive than those in the West. The first stirring scenes of the year were enacted in the Shenandoah Valley. Desiring to occupy this important district, the Federal government sent forward a strong division under General Banks, who pressed his way southward, and in the last days of March occupied the town of Harrisonburg. In order to counteract this movement, the gallant Stonewall Jackson was sent with a force of twenty thousand men to pass the Blue Ridge and cut off Banks's retreat. At Front Royal, on the Shenandoah, just before the gap in the Mountains, the Confederates fell upon a body of Federals, routed them, captured their guns and all the military stores in the town. Banks succeeded, however, in passing with his main division to Strasburg. There he learned of the disaster at Front Royal, and immediately began his retreat down the valley. Jackson pursued him hotly, and it was only by the utmost exertions that the Federals gained the northern bank of the Potomac.

The Confederate leader, though completely victorious, now found himself in great peril. For General Fremont, at the head of a strong force of fresh troops, had been sent into the valley to intercept the retreat of the Confederates. It was now Jackson's time to save his army. With the utmost celerity he sped up the valley, and succeeded in reaching Cross Keys before Fremont could attack him. Even then the battle was so little decisive that Jackson pressed on to Port Republic, attacked the division of General Shields, defeated it, and then retired from the scene of his brilliant campaign to join in the defense of Richmond.

On the 10th of March the grand army of the Potomac, numbering nearly two hundred thousand men, under command of General McClellan, set out from the camps about Washington to capture the Confederate capital. The advance proceeded as far as Manassas Junction, the Confederates falling back and forming a new line of defences on the Rappahannock. At this stage of the campaign McClellan, changing his plan, embarked a hundred and twenty thousand of his men for Fortress Monroe, intending from that point to march up the peninsula between the James and the York. By the 4th of April the transfer of troops was completed, and the Union army left Fortress Monroe for Yorktown. This place was garrisoned by ten thousand Confederates under General Magruder; and yet with so small a force McClellan's advance was delayed for a whole month. When at last, on the 4th of May, Yorktown was taken by siege, the Federal army pressed forward to Williamsburg, where the Confederates made a stand, but were defeated with severe losses. Four days afterward, in an engagement at West Point, at the confluence of the Mattapony and

Pamunkey, the Confederates were again overpowered and driven back. The way to Richmond was now open as far as the Chickahominy, ten miles north of the city. The Union army reached that stream without further resistance, and crossed at Bottom's Bridge.

Scene of Campaign in Virginia, Maryland and Pennsylvania, 1862.

Meanwhile, General Wool, the commandant of Fortress Monroe, had not been idle. On the 10th of May he led an expedition against Norfolk and captured the town; for the Confederate garrison had been withdrawn to aid in the defence of Richmond. On the next day the celebrated iron-clad *Virginia* was blown up to save her from capture by the Federals. The James River was thus opened for the ingress of national transports laden with supplies for the Army of the Potomac. That army, now advanced toward Richmond, and when but seven miles from the city was attacked on the 31st of May by the Confederates at a place called Fair Oaks or Seven Pines. Here for a part of two days the battle raged with great fury. At last the Confederates were driven back; but McClellan's victory was by no means decisive. The Confederate loss was largest, amounting to nearly eight thousand in killed and wounded; that of the Federals was more than five thousand. Among the severely wounded was General Joseph E. Johnston, the commander-in-chief of the Confederates. Two days after the battle his place was filled by the appointment of General Robert E. Lee, a man of military genius, who, until its final downfall, remained the chief stay of the Confederacy.

In the lull that followed the battle of Fair Oaks, McClellan formed the design of changing his base of supplies from the White House, on the Pamunkey, to some suitable point on the James. The movement was one of the utmost hazard, and before it was fairly begun General Lee, on the 25th of June, swooped down on the right wing of the Union army at Oak Grove, and a hard-

General Robert E. Lee.

fought battle ensued without decisive results. On the next day another dreadful engagement occurred at Mechanicsville, and this time the Federals won the field. But on the following morning Lee renewed the struggle at. Gaines's Mill, and came out victorious. On the 28th there was but little fighting. On the 29th McClellan's retreating army was twice attacked—in the morning at Savage's Station and in the afternoon in the White Oak Swamp—but the divisions defending the rearguard kept the Confederates at bay. On the 30th was fought the desperate but indecisive battle of Glendale or Frazier's Farm. On that night the Federal army reached Malvern Hill, on the north bank of the James, twelve miles below Richmond. Although this position was protected by the Federal gunboats in the river, General Lee determined to carry the place by storm. Accordingly, on the morning of the 1st of July the whole Confederate army rushed forward to the assault. All day long the furious struggle for the possession of the high grounds continued. Not until nine o'clock at night did Lee's shattered columns fall back exhausted. *For seven days* the terrific roar of battle had been heard almost without cessation. No such dreadful scenes had ever before been enacted on the American continent.

Although victorious on Malvern Hill, General McClellan, instead of advancing at once on Richmond, chose a less hazardous movement, and on the 2d of July retired with his army to Harrison's Landing, a few miles down the river. The great campaign was really at an end. The Federal army had lost more than fifteen thousand men, and the capture of Richmond, the great object for which the expedition had been undertaken, seemed further off than ever. The losses of the Confederates had been heavier than those of the Union army, but all the moral effect of a great victory remained with the exultant South.

General Lee, perceiving that Richmond was no longer endangered, immediately formed the de sign of invading Maryland and capturing the Federal capital. The Union troops between Richmond and Washington, numbering in the aggregate about fifty thousand, were under command of General John Pope. They were scattered in detachments from Fredericksburg to Winchester and Harper's Ferry. Lee moved northward about the middle of August, and on the 20th of the month Pope, concentrating his forces as rapidly as possible, put the

Rappahannock between his army and the advancing Confederates. Meanwhile General Banks, while attempting to form a junction with Pope, was attacked by Stonewall Jackson at Cedar Mountain, where nothing but desperate fighting saved the Federals from complete rout.

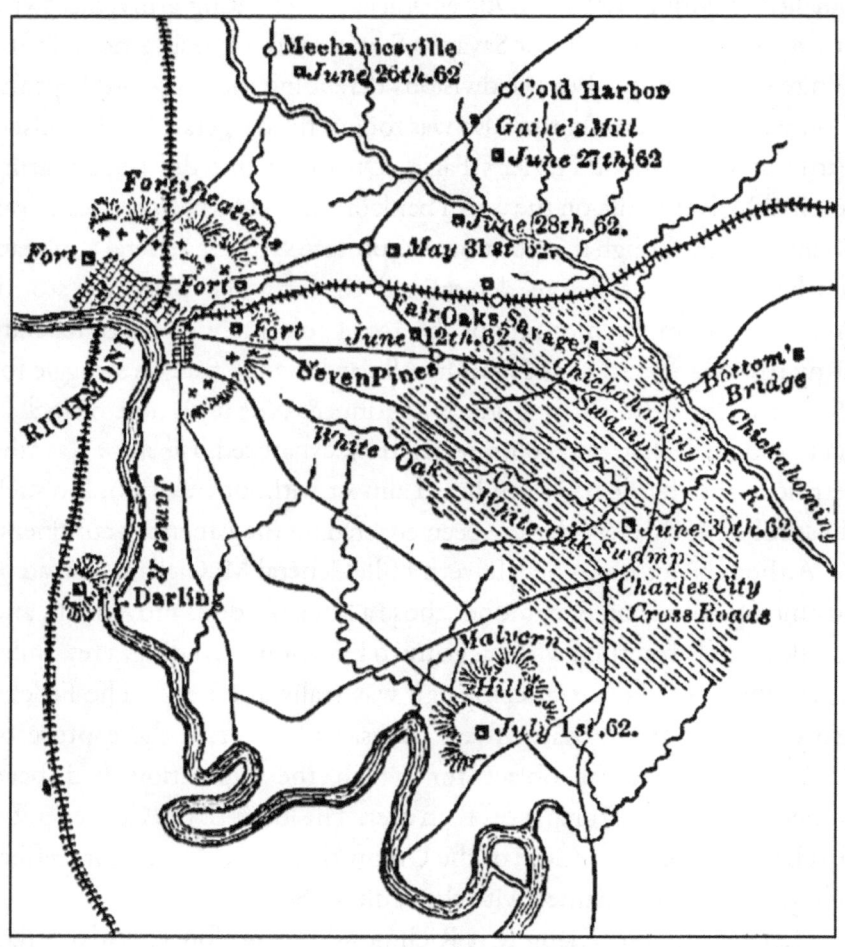

Vicinity of Richmond, 1862.

No sooner had Pope gotten his forces well in hand than Jackson shot by with his division on a flank movement, reached Manassas Junction, and made large captures of men and stores. Pope with great audacity threw his army between the two divisions of the Confederates, hoping to crush Jackson before Lee could come to the rescue. On August 28th and 29th there was terrible but undecisive fighting at Manassas

Junction, the old Bull Run battle-ground, and Centreville. At one time it seemed that Lee's army would be completely defeated; but Pope's reinforcements were purposely delayed by General Porter, and on the 31st of the month the Confederates bore down on the Union army at Chantilly, fought all day, and won a victory. Generals Stevens and Kearney were among the thousands of brave men who fell in this battle. On that night Pope withdrew his shattered columns as rapidly as possible, and found safety within the defences of Washington. His wish to be relieved of his command was immediately complied with; his forces, known as the Army of Virginia, were consolidated with the Army of the Potomac, which had now been recalled from the peninsula below Richmond; and General McClellan was placed in supreme command of all the divisions about Washington.

General Lee prosecuted his invasion of Maryland. Passing up the right bank of the Potomac, he crossed to Point of Rocks, and on the 6th of September captured Frederick. On the 10th Hagerstown was taken, and on the 15th a division of the Confederate army, led by Stonewall Jackson came upon Harper's Ferry and frightened Colonel Miles into surrender by which the garrison, nearly twelve thousand strong, became prisoners of war. On the previous day there was a hard-fought engagement at South Mountain, in which the Federals, led by Hatch and Doubleday, were victorious. McClellan's whole army was now in the immediate rear of Lee, who, on the night of the 14th, fell back to Antietam Creek, and took a strong position in the vicinity of Sharpsburg. On the morning of the 15th there was some sharp but desultory fighting between the Union and Confederate cavalry. During the afternoon the Federal advance, coming in on the Sharpsburg road from Keedysville, received the opening salutes of the Confederate guns on the Antietam. But nightfall came without a serious conflict. On the following morning there was great activity of preparation in both armies. Later in the day the corps of General Hooker, who commanded on the Federal right, was thrown across the stream which separated the combatants and brought into a favorable position for action. In this quarter of the field the Confederate left under General Hood was assaulted and driven back a half mile in the direction of Sharpsburg. The rest of the day was spent in an irregular cannonade. During the night General Mansfield's corps crossed the Antietam on the north bridge and joined Hooker.

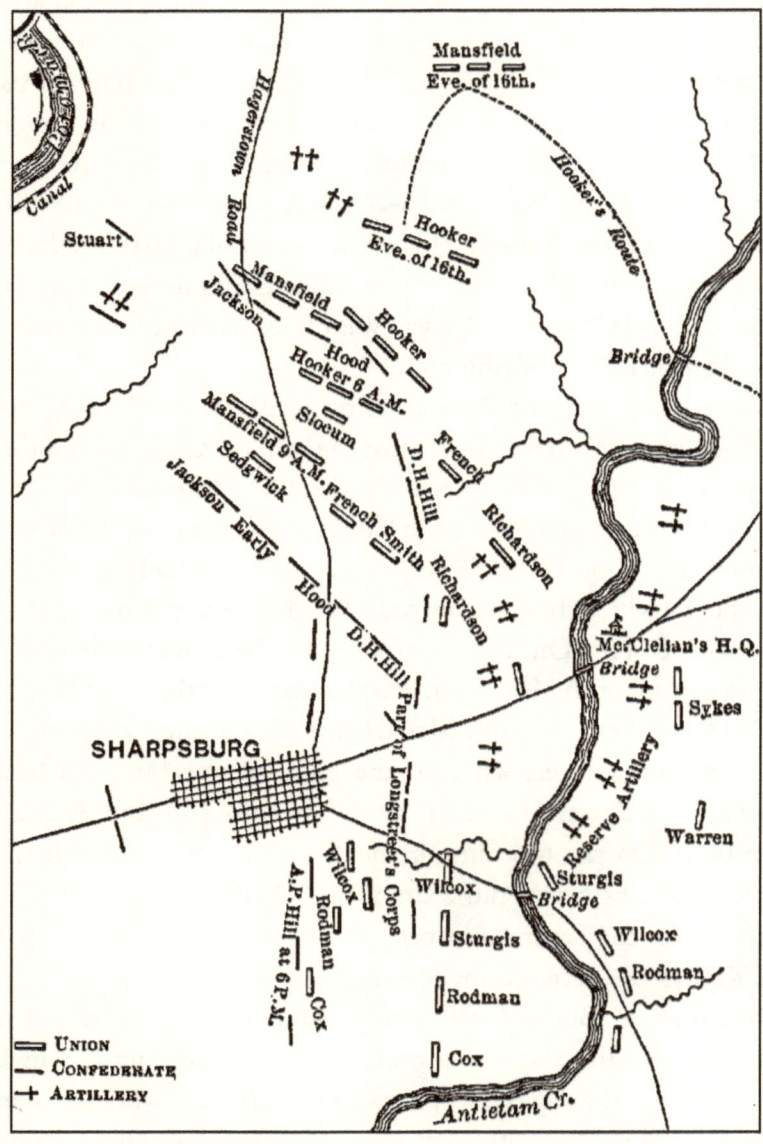

The Battle of Antietam, September 17, '62.

On the morning of the 17th both commanders had their armies well into position, the Federals being strongest in numbers and the

Confederates having the advantage of an unfordable stream in their front. It was of the first importance that General McClellan should gain and hold the four stone bridges by which only his forces could be thrown to the other side. General Burnside, who was ordered to take the lower bridge, cross over, and attack the division of A. P. Hill, encountered unexpected delays and was greatly retarded in his movements. On the right, Hooker renewed the battle at sunrise, and until late in the afternoon the conflict raged with almost unabated fury. Here fell the veteran General Mans field and thousands of his comrades. Meanwhile Burnside had forced the lower crossing and carried the battle far up in the direction of Sharpsburg. But the Confederates being reinforced from other parts of the field made a rally, and the Federals were driven back nearly to the Antietam. It was only by terrible fighting that General Burnside succeeded in holding his position on the west bank of the stream. But on the approach of darkness the greater part of the Union army had gained a safe lodgment between the creek and Sharpsburg.

Nevertheless, the Confederate forces occupied nearly the same ground in the morning; and it seemed that the final struggle was reserved for the morrow. On that day, however, General McClellan acted on the defensive. Two strong divisions of reinforcements, under Generals Humphreys and Couch, arrived, and it was resolved to renew the attack on the following morning. But in the mean time, General Lee had taken advantage of the delay, withdrawn his shattered legions from their position, and recrossed the Potomac into Virginia. The great conflict which had cost each army more than ten thousand men had ended in a drawn battle in which there is little to be praised except the heroism of the soldiery. To the Confederates, however, the result was almost as disastrous as defeat. The promised uprising of the people of Maryland in behalf of the Confederate cause did not occur and General Lee was obliged to give up a fruitless and hopeless invasion which, in the short space of a month, had cost him nearly thirty thousand men. On the other side, the expectations which had been inspired by the movements and despatches of the Union commander previous to the battle had been sorely disappointed.

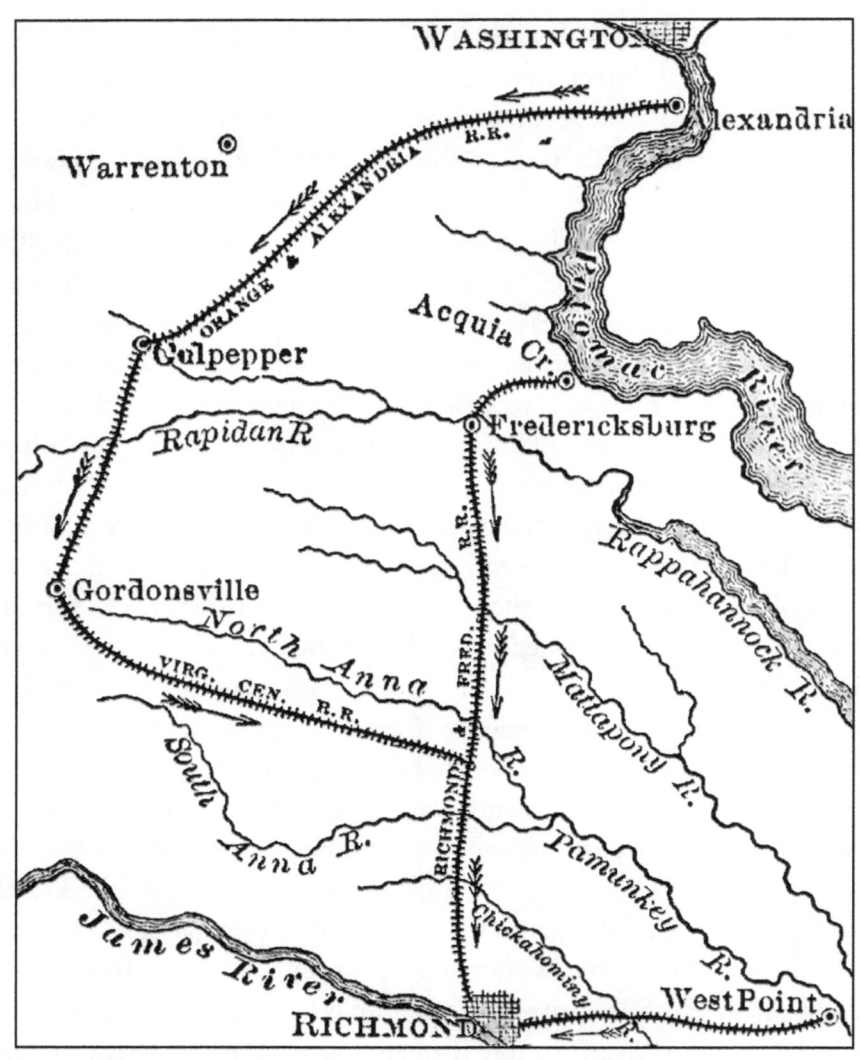

The Proposed Routes from Washington to Richmond, 1862.

On the 26th of October, General McClellan, following the retreating Confederates, again entered Virginia, and reached Rectortown. It was the purpose of the Federal government that the Army of the Potomac should, before the approach of winter, be thrown forward in a second attempt against Richmond. The Union commander still preferred to advance by the route which he had taken the previous spring, making his base of supplies at West Point on the Pamunkey. But this plan was open to the objection that Washington city would thereby be again uncovered and exposed to a counter movement on the part of the Confederates. Yielding to the protest of the President and his cabinet, McClellan altered his plans and chose Alexandria on the Potomac as his base of operations. From this point it was proposed to advance on the Confederate capital by way of the Orange Railroad through Culpepper to Gordonsville, and thence by the Virginia Central to its junction with the line reaching from Fredericksburg to Richmond. The month of October was wasted with delays, and November was well begun before the Federal general with his army of a hundred and twenty thousand men, announced himself ready for the forward movement. On the 7th of the month, just as the Union commander was about to begin the campaign, he was superseded and his command transferred to General Burnside. Right or wrong, the President at last reached the decision that General McClellan was a man over-cautious and slow—too prudent and too much absorbed in preliminaries to lead the armies of the Republic to victory.

General Burnside immediately changed the plan of the proposed campaign. It was decided to form a new base of supplies at the mouth of Acquia Creek, fifty-five miles below Washington and from that point to force a way by battle southward through Fredericksburg. But again movements were much delayed, and that, too, when everything depended on celerity. The pontoons, which were necessary for the crossing of the Rappahannock, were not forthcoming, and a fortnight was lost in preparations. General Lee found abundant time to gather his legions and occupy the heights in the vicinity of Fredericksburg. It was not a part of his plan to dispute the passage of the river but to allow the Federals to cross over and then beat them back from his entrenchments. On the 11th of December the Union army was brought into position on the east bank of the Rappahannock. The divisions lay from the village of Falmouth to a point opposite the mouth of the Massaponax, about three miles below. In front of the corps of General Franklin, who commanded the Federal left wing, the pontoons were successfully laid and the crossing of the river was effected without serious opposition. But opposite Fredericksburg, where the divisions of Generals Sumner and Hooker, who held the Union center and right, were to cross, the work of laying the bridges was hindered by the Confederate sharpshooters lying concealed in the town. General Burnside ordered the Federal guns to be turned in that direction, and in a short time Fredericksburg was battered and burned into ruins. Some Union regiments were next ferried over in boats, and the Confederate picket lines were driven back to the heights. The bridges were completed, and by nightfall of the 12th the army had been transferred to the western side of the river.

On the morning of the 13th the battle began on the left where Franklin's division encountered the corps of Stonewall Jackson. A gallant charge was made by General Meade and a gap was made in the Confederate lines; but no reinforcements were sent forward; the Confederates rallied, and the Federals were driven back with a loss of three thousand seven hundred men. Jackson's loss was almost as great, and in this part of the field neither side might claim a decisive victory. Not so in the center and on the right. Here a portion of General Sumner's men were ordered forward against the Confederates securely and impregnably posted on Marye's Hill. They were mowed down by thousands and hurled back in disdain, while the defenders of the heights hardly lost a man. Time and again the assault was recklessly renewed. A part of Hooker's gallant troops, led by General Humphreys, came forward; charged with unloaded guns; and in fifteen minutes one-half of the four thousand brave fellows went down in death. Night came and ended the useless carnage. General Burnside would have renewed the battle; but his division commanders finally dissuaded him and on the night of the 15th the Federal army was silently withdrawn across the Rappahannock. The Union losses in this terrible conflict amounted to a thousand five hundred killed, nine thousand one hundred wounded, and sixteen hundred and fifty prisoners and missing. The Confederates lost in killed five hundred and ninety-five, four thousand and sixty-one wounded, and six hundred and fifty-three missing and prisoners. Of all the important movements of the war only that of Fredericksburg was undertaken with *no* probability of success. Under the plan of the battle—if plan it might be called, nothing could be reasonably expected but repulse, rout, and ruin. Thus in gloom and disaster to the Federal cause ended the great campaign of 1862.

CHAPTER LXV.

THE WORK OF '63.

THE war had now grown to enormous proportions. The Confederate States were draining every resource of men and means in order to support their armies. The superior energies of the North, though by no means exhausted, were greatly taxed. In the previous year, on the day after the battle of Malvern Hill, President Lincoln had issued a call for three hundred thousand additional troops. During the exciting days of Pope's retreat from the Rappahannock he sent forth another call for three hundred thousand, and to that was added a requisition for a draft of three hundred thousand more. Most of these enormous demands were promptly met, and it became evident that in respect to resources the Federal government was vastly superior to the Confederacy.

On the 1st day of January, 1863, the President issued one of the most important documents of modern times: THE EMANCIPATION PROCLAMATION.[31] The war had been begun with no well-defined intention on the part of the government to free the slaves of the South. But the President and the Republican party looked with disfavor on the institution of slavery; during the progress of the war the sentiment of abolition had grown with great rapidity in the North and when at last it became a military necessity to strike a blow at the labor-system of the Southern States, the step was taken with but little hesitancy or opposition. Thus, after an existence of two hundred and forty-four years, the institution of African slavery in the United States was swept away.

The military movements of the new year began on the Mississippi. After his defeat at Chickasaw Bayou, General Sherman laid a plan for the capture of Arkansas Post, on the Arkansas River. In the first days of January an expedition set out for that purpose, the land-forces being commanded by General McClernand, and the flotilla by Admiral

---

[31] See Appendix H.

Porter. Entering the Arkansas, the Union forces reached their destination on the 10th of the month, fought a hard battle with the Confederates, gained a victory, and on the next day received the surrender of the post with nearly five thousand prisoners. After this success the expedition returned to the vicinity of Vicksburg, in order to co-operate with General Grant in a second effort to capture that stronghold of the Confederacy.

Again the Union forces were collected at Memphis, and embarked on the Mississippi. A landing was effected at the Yazoo; but the capture of the city from that direction was decided to be impracticable. The first three months of the year were spent by General Grant in beating about the bayous, swamps and hills around Vicksburg, in the hope of getting a position in the rear of the town. A canal was cut across a bend in the river with a view to turning the channel of the Mississippi and opening a passage for the gunboats. But a flood in the river washed the works away, and the enterprise ended in failure. Then another canal was begun, only to be abandoned. Finally, in the first days of April, it was determined at all hazards to run the fleet past the Vicksburg batteries. Accordingly, on the night of the 16th, the boats were made ready and silently dropped down the river. All of a sudden the guns burst forth with terrible discharges of shot and shell, pelting the passing steamers; but they went by with comparatively little damage, and found a safe position below the city.

Elated with the successful passage of his fleet, General Grant now marched his land-forces down the right bank of the Mississippi and formed a junction with the squadron. On the 30th of April he crossed the river at Bruinsburg, and on the following day fought and defeated the Confederates at Port Gibson. The evacuation of Grand Gulf, at the mouth of the Big Black River, followed immediately afterward. The Union army now swept around to the rear of Vicksburg. On the morning of the 12th a strong Confederate force was encountered at Raymond, and after a severe engagement was repulsed. Pressing on toward Jackson, the capital of Mississippi, General Grant's right wing, under Sherman and McPherson, met the advance of General Johnston's division coming to reinforce the garrison of Vicksburg. Here, on the

14th of the month, a decisive battle was fought; the Confederates were beaten, and the city of Jackson captured. The communications of Vicksburg were now cut off, and General Pemberton was obliged to repel the Federals or suffer a siege. Sallying forth with the greater part of his forces, he met the Union army on the 16th at Champion Hills, on Baker's Creek. In the battle that followed, as well as in a conflict at the Black River Bridge on the 17th, Grant was again victorious, and Pemberton retired with his disheartened troops within the defences of Vicksburg.

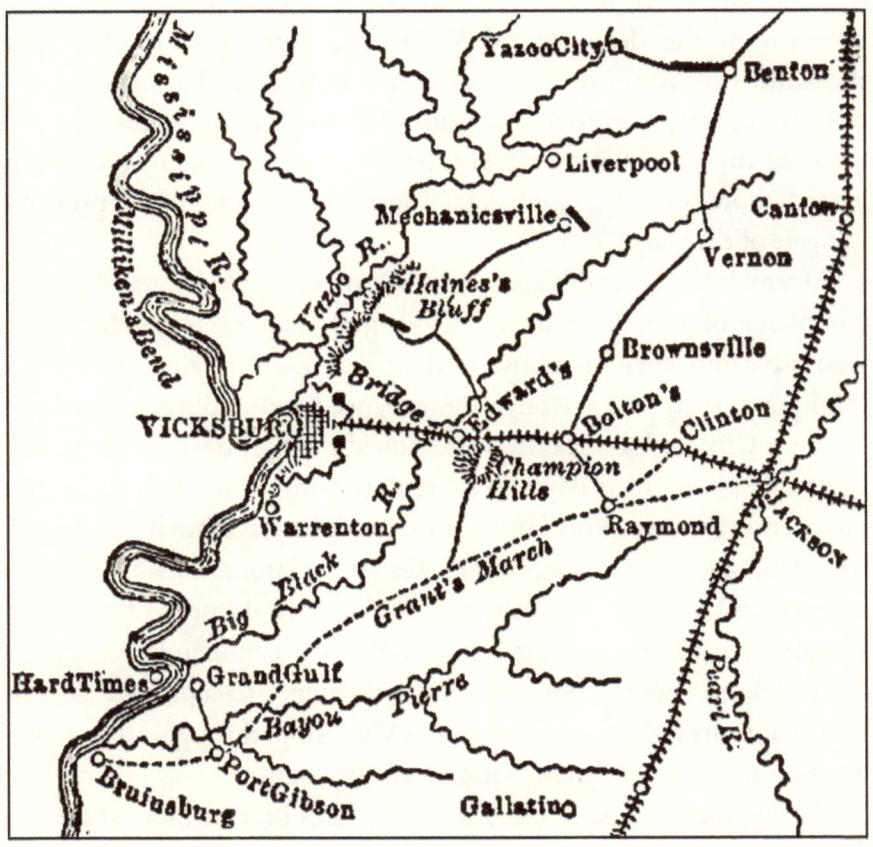

Vicksburg and Vicinity, 1863.

The investment of the city was rapidly completed. Believing that the Confederate works could be carried by storm, General Grant, on the 19th of May, ordered an assault, which resulted in a repulse with terrible losses. Three days afterward the attempt was renewed, but the assailants were again hurled back with a still greater destruction of life. The Union loss in these two unsuccessful assaults amounted to nearly three thousand men. Finding that Vicksburg could not be taken by storm, General Grant began a regular siege, and pressed it with ever-increasing severity. Admiral Porter got his gunboats into position and bombarded the unfortunate town incessantly. Reinforcements swelled the Union ranks. On the other hand, the garrison of the city was in a starving condition. Still, Pemberton held out for more than a month and it was not until the 4th of July that he was driven to surrender. By the act of capitulation the defenders of Vicksburg, numbering nearly thirty thousand, became prisoners of war. Thousands of small-arms, hundreds of cannon, vast quantities of ammunition and warlike stores were the fruits of this great Union victory, by which the national government gained more and the Confederacy lost more than in any previous struggle of the war.

Meanwhile, General Banks, who had superseded General Butler in command of the department of the gulf, had been conducting a vigorous campaign on the Lower Mississippi. Early in January, from his headquarters at Baton Rouge, he advanced into Louisiana, reached Brashear City, and shortly afterward gained a victory over a Confederate force at a place called Bayou Teche. Returning to the Mississippi, he moved northward to Port Hudson, invested the place and began a siege. The beleaguered garrison, under General Gardner, made a brave defence; and it was not until the 8th of July, when the news of the fall of Vicksburg was borne to Port Hudson, that the commandant, with his force of more than six thousand men, was obliged to capitulate. By this important surrender the control of the Mississippi throughout its whole length was recovered by the National government.

During the progress of the war cavalry raids became more and more frequent. Of this nature was Stonewall Jackson's campaign down the Shenandoah valley in the summer of 1862. Later in the same year, just after the battle of Antietam, the Confederate General Stuart, with a troop of eighteen hundred cavalrymen, made a dash into Pennsylvania, reached Chambersburg, captured the town, made a complete circuit of the Army of the Potomac, and returned in safety to Virginia. Just before the investment of Vicksburg, Colonel Benjamin Grierson, of the Sixth Illinois Cavalry, struck out with his command from La Grange, Tennessee, entered Mississippi, traversed the State to the east of Jackson, cut the rail roads, destroyed property, and after a rapid course of more than eight hundred miles gained the river at Baton Rouge. By these raids the border country of both sections was kept in perpetual agitation and alarm.

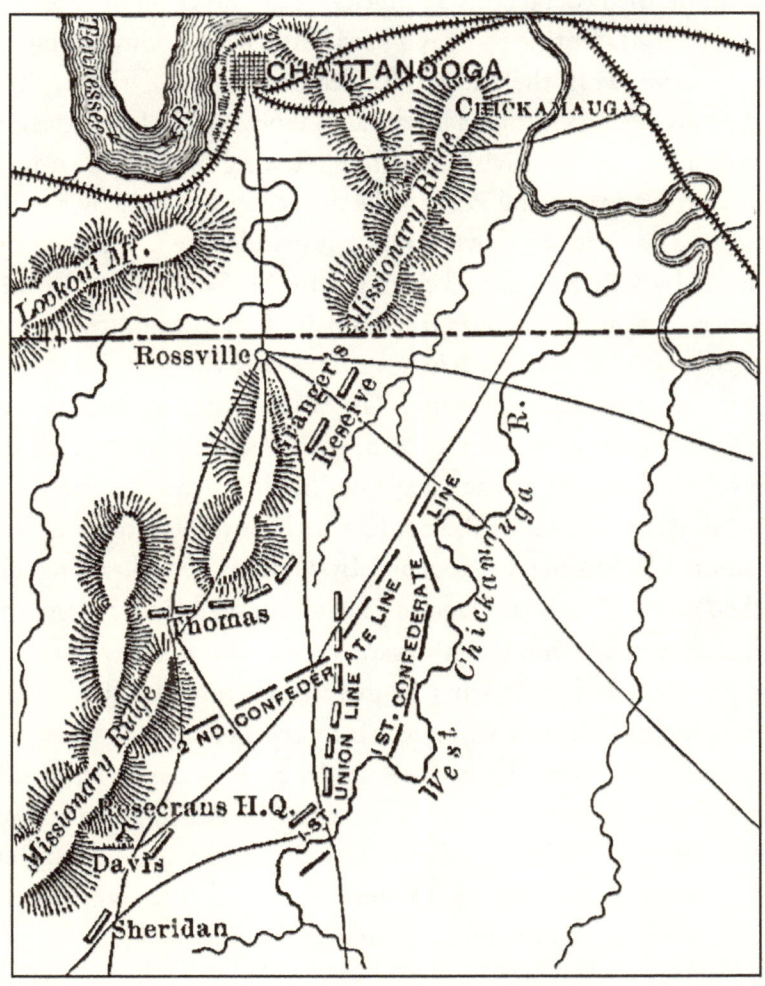

Battle of Chickamauga, Sept. 19, 20, 1863

For a while after the battle of Murfreesborough Rosecrans remained inactive. Late in the spring Colonel Streight's command went on a raid into Georgia, met the division of the Confederate general Forrest, was surrounded and captured. In the latter part of June, Rosecrans by a series of flank movements succeeded in crowding General Bragg out of Tennessee into Georgia. The union general followed his antagonist and took post at Chattanooga, on the left bank of the Tennessee. During the summer months General Bragg was heavily reinforced by Johnston from Mississippi, and Longstreet from Virginia. On the 19th of September he turned upon the Federal army at Chickamauga Creek, in the north-west angle of Georgia. During this day a hard battle was fought, but night fell on the scene with the victory undecided. During the night the Confederates were reinforced by the arrival of General Longstreet, who was stationed with his division on the left wing of Bragg's army. The right was given to General Polk, while the center was held by Ewell and Johnston. The Federal left wing was commanded by General Thomas, the center by Crittenden, and the right by McCook. The plan of the Confederate commander was to crush the Union line, force his way through a gap in Missionary Ridge, capture Rossville and Chattanooga, and annihilate Rosecrans's army. The battle began at half past eight o'clock on the morning of the 20th, the Confederates moving on in powerful masses, and the Federals holding their ground with unflinching courage. After the conflict had continued for some hours, the national battle-line was opened by General Wood, acting under mistaken orders. The Confederate general, seeing his advantage, thrust forward a heavy column into the gap, cut the Union army in two, and drove the shattered right wing in utter rout from the field. General Thomas, with a desperate firmness hardly equaled in the annals of war, held the left until nightfall, and then, under cover of darkness, withdrew into Chattanooga, where the defeated army of Rosecrans had already found shelter. The Union losses in this dreadful battle amounted in killed, wounded and missing to nearly nineteen thousand, and the Confederate loss was even more appalling.

General Bragg at once pressed forward to besiege Chattanooga. The Federal lines of communication were cut off, and for a while the army of Rosecrans was in danger of being annihilated. But General Hooker arrived with two corps from the Army of the Potomac, opened the

Tennessee River, and brought relief to the besieged. At the same time General Grant, being promoted to the chief command of the Western armies, assumed the direction of affairs at Chattanooga. General Sherman also arrived with his division, so strengthening the Army of the Cumberland that offensive operations were at once renewed. The left wing of the Confederate army now rested on Lookout Mountain, and the right on Missionary Ridge. A position seemingly more impregnable could hardly be conceived of. General Bragg was not only confident of his ability to hold his lines against any advance of the Federals but even contemplated the storming of Chattanooga. On the 20th of November he gave notice to General Grant to remove all non-combatants as the town was about to be bombarded; but no attention was paid to the despatch.

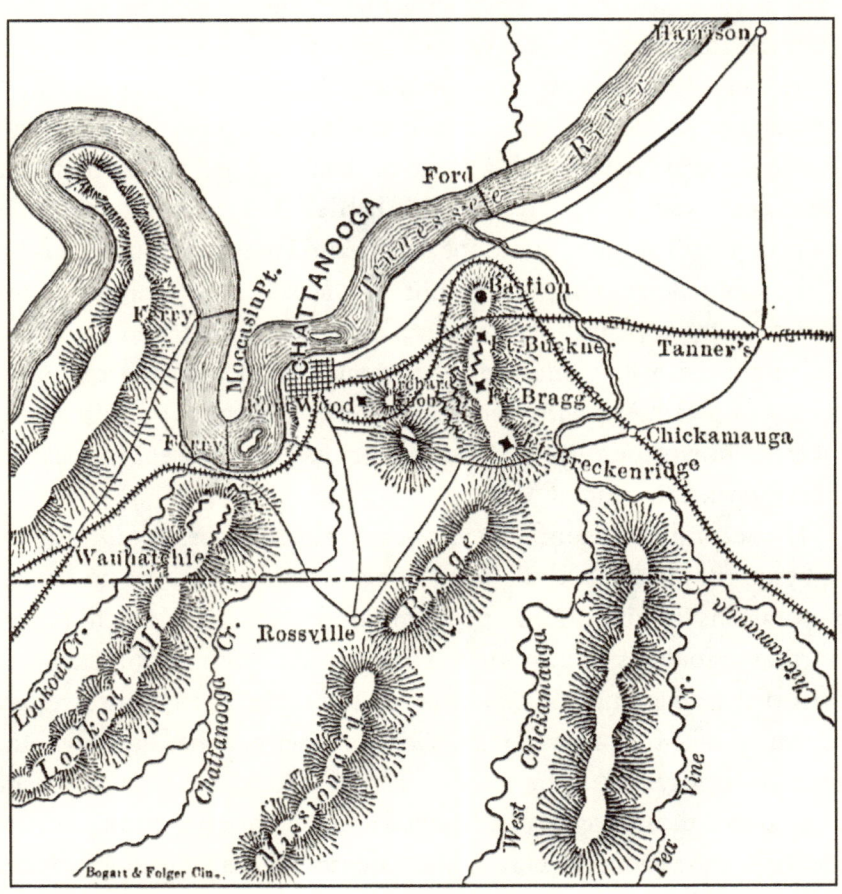

Lookout Mountain and Missionary Ridge, Nov. 23-25, 1863.

On the 23d General Hooker threw his corps across the river below Chattanooga and gained a footing at the mouth of Lookout Creek facing the mountain. From this position the assault was made on the following morning. Hooker was supported by the divisions of Generals Geary and Osterhaus, and the remainder of the Union army was kept in a state of activity in order to prevent the reinforcement of Lookout from Missionary Ridge. A dense fog hung like a hood over the mountain, effectually concealing the movements of the Federals. The charge began between eight and nine o'clock, and in the space of two hours the ranges of Confederate rifle-pits among the foot-hills had been successfully carried. It had been General Hooker's purpose to pause when this work should be accomplished, but the enthusiasm of his army rose to such a pitch as to suggest the still greater achievement of carrying the whole Confederate position. Taking advantage of the fog and the spirit of his soldiers Hooker again gave the command to charge; and up the almost inaccessible slopes of the mountain the troops sprang forward with resistless energy. It was such a scene of dauntless heroism as has rarely been portrayed in the records of battle. The charging columns, struggling against the obstacles of nature and facing the murderous fire of the Confederate guns, could not be checked. The Union flag was carried to the top; and before two o'clock in the afternoon Lookout Mountain, with its cloud-capped summit overlooking the town and river, was swarming with Federal soldiers. The routed Confederates retreated down the eastern slope and across the intervening hills and valleys in the direction of Missionary Ridge.

The second great conflict was reserved for the morrow. During the night of the 24th General Bragg concentrated his forces and made preparations to defend his position to the last. On the following morning Hooker's victorious troops poured down from Lookout, crossed the Chattanooga, and renewed the battle at the southwestern extremity of Missionary Ridge. General Sherman had already built pontoon bridges over the Tennessee and Chickamauga, thrown his corps across those streams, and gained a lodgment on the northeastern declivity of the Ridge. General Thomas, commanding the Union center, lay with his impatient soldiers, on the southern and eastern slopes of

Orchard Knob, awaiting the result of Sherman's and Hooker's onsets. At two o'clock in the afternoon orders were given by General Grant for an assault along the whole line. And the command was instantly obeyed. The thrilling scene of Lookout Mountain was again enacted. The Federal soldiers charged to the summit of Missionary Ridge and the Confederates were driven into a disastrous rout. During the night General Bragg withdrew his shattered columns and retreated in the direction of Ringgold, Georgia. The Federal losses in the two great battles amounted to seven hundred and fifty-seven killed, four thousand five hundred and twenty-nine wounded, and three hundred and thirty missing; the loss of the Confederates in killed, wounded and prisoners reached considerably beyond ten thousand. The results of the conflict were so decisive as to put an end to the war in Tennessee until it was renewed by Hood at Franklin and Nashville in the winter of 1864.

In the mean time, General Burnside was making an effort to hold East Tennessee. On the 1st of September he arrived with his command at Knoxville, where he was received by the people with lively satisfaction. After the battle of Chickamauga, General Longstreet was sent into East Tennessee to counteract the movements of the Unionists. On his march to Knoxville he overtook and captured several small detachments of Federal troops, then invested the town and began a siege. On the 29th of November the Confederates made an attempt to carry Knoxville by storm, but were repulsed with heavy losses. After the retreat of Bragg from Chattanooga, General Sherman marched to the relief of Burnside; but before he could reach Knoxville, Longstreet raised the siege and retreated into Virginia.

In the early part of 1863 the Confederates, led by Generals Marmaduke and Price, resumed activity in Arkansas and Southern Missouri. On the 8th of January they made an attack on Springfield, but were repulsed with considerable losses. Three days afterward, at the town of Hartsville, a battle was fought with a similar result. On the 26th of April, General Marmaduke attacked the post at Cape Girardeau, on the Mississippi, but the garrison succeeded in driving the Confederates away. On the day of the surrender of Vicksburg the Confederate general Holmes, with a force of nearly eight thousand men, made an attack on

Helena, Arkansas, but was repulsed with a loss of one-fifth of his men. On the 13th of August the town of Lawrence, Kansas, was sacked and burned, and a hundred and forty persons killed by a band of desperate fellows led by a chieftain called Quantrell. On the 10th of September the Federal general Steele reached Little Rock, the capital of Arkansas, captured the city and restored the national authority in the State.

To the summer of this year belongs the story of General John Morgan's great raid through Kentucky into Indiana and Ohio. His starting-point was Sparta, Tennessee; the number of his forces three thousand. Pushing northward through Kentucky, he gathered strength, reached the Ohio at Brandenburg, crossed into Indiana, and began his march to the north and east. He was resisted at Corydon and other points by bodies of home-guards, and hotly pursued by a force under General Hobson: Morgan crossed into Ohio at Harrison, made a circuit to the north of Cincinnati, and attempted to recross the river. But the Ohio was now guarded by gunboats, and the raiders were driven back. With numbers constantly diminishing the Confederate leader pressed on, fighting and flying, until he came near the town of New Lisbon, where he was surrounded and captured by the brigade of General Shackelford. For nearly four months Morgan was held as a prisoner; then making his escape, he fled to Kentucky, and finally reached Richmond.

The year 1863 was marked by some movements of importance on the sea-coast. On the 1st of January General Marmaduke, by a brilliant exploit, captured Galveston, Texas. By this means the Confederates secured a port of entry, of which they were greatly in need in the Southwest. On the 7th of April Admiral Dupont, with a powerful fleet of iron clads, made an attempt to capture Charleston, but the squadron was driven back much damaged. In the last days of June the siege of the city begun anew by a strong land-force, under command of General Q. A. Gillmore, assisted by the fleet under Admiral Dahlgren. The Federal army first effected a lodgment on Folly Island, and soon afterward on the south end of Morris Island, where batteries were planted bearing upon Fort Sumter in the channel and Fort Wagner and Battery Gregg at the northern extremity of the island. After the bombardment had continued for some time, General Gillmore, on the 18th of July, made an attempt to carry Fort Wagner by assault, but was repulsed with a loss of more than fifteen hundred men. The siege then progressed until the night of the 6th of September, when the Confederates evacuated the fort and Battery Gregg, and retired to Charleston. Gillmore thus obtained a position within four miles of the city, and brought his guns to bear on the wharves and buildings of the lower town. Meanwhile, the walls of Fort Sumter on the side next to Morris Island had been pounded into powder by the land-batteries and guns of the monitors. The harbor and city, however, still remained under control of the Confederates, the only gain of the Federals being the establishment of a blockade so complete as to seal up the port of Charleston.

During the spring and summer of 1863 the Army of the Potomac was engaged in several desperate conflicts. After his fatal repulse at Fredericksburg General Burnside was superseded by General Joseph Hooker, who, in the latter part of April, moved forward with his army in full force, crossed the Rappahannock and the Rapidan, and reached Chancellorsville. Here, on the evening of the 2d of May, he was attacked by the veteran Army of Northern Virginia, led by Lee and Jackson. The latter general, with extraordinary daring, put himself at the head of a division of twenty-five thousand men, filed off from the battle-field, outflanked the Union army, burst like a thunder-cloud upon the right wing, and swept everything to destruction. But it was the last of Stonewall's battles. As night came on, with ruin impending over the Federal army, the brave Confederate leader, riding through the gathering darkness, received a volley *from his own lines*, and fell mortally wounded. He lingered a week, and died at Guinea Station, leaving a gap in the Confederate ranks which no other man could fill.

On the morning of the 3d the battle was furiously renewed. General Sedgwick, attempting to reinforce Hooker from Fredericksburg, was defeated and driven across the Rappahannock. The main army was crowded between Chancellorsville and the river, where it remained in the utmost peril until the evening of the 5th, when General Hooker succeeded in withdrawing his forces to the northern bank. The Union losses in these terrible battles amounted in killed, wounded and prisoners to about seventeen thousand; that of the Confederates was less by five thousand. Taken altogether, the campaign was the most disastrous of any in which the Federal army had yet been engaged.

The defeat of General Hooker was to some extent mitigated by the successful cavalry raid of General Stoneman. On the 29th of April he crossed the Rappahannock with a body of ten thousand men, tore up the Virginia Central Railroad, dashed on to the Chickahominy, cut General Lee's communications, swept around within a few miles of Richmond, and on the 8th of May recrossed the Rappahannock in safety. At the same time, General Peck, the Federal commandant of Suffolk, on the Nansemond, was successfully resisting a siege conducted by General Longstreet. The Confederates retreated from before the town on the very day of the Union disaster at Chancellorsville.

Stonewall Jackson.[32]

---

[32] The true name of this remarkable man was *Thomas Jonathan* Jackson. In the beginning of the battle of Bull Run, when the Confederates in one part of the field were routed and flying, General Bee, pointing to an immovable column of men, cried out, "Here is Jackson, standing like *a stone wall!*" From that day the man at the head of that column was called *Stonewall* Jackson.

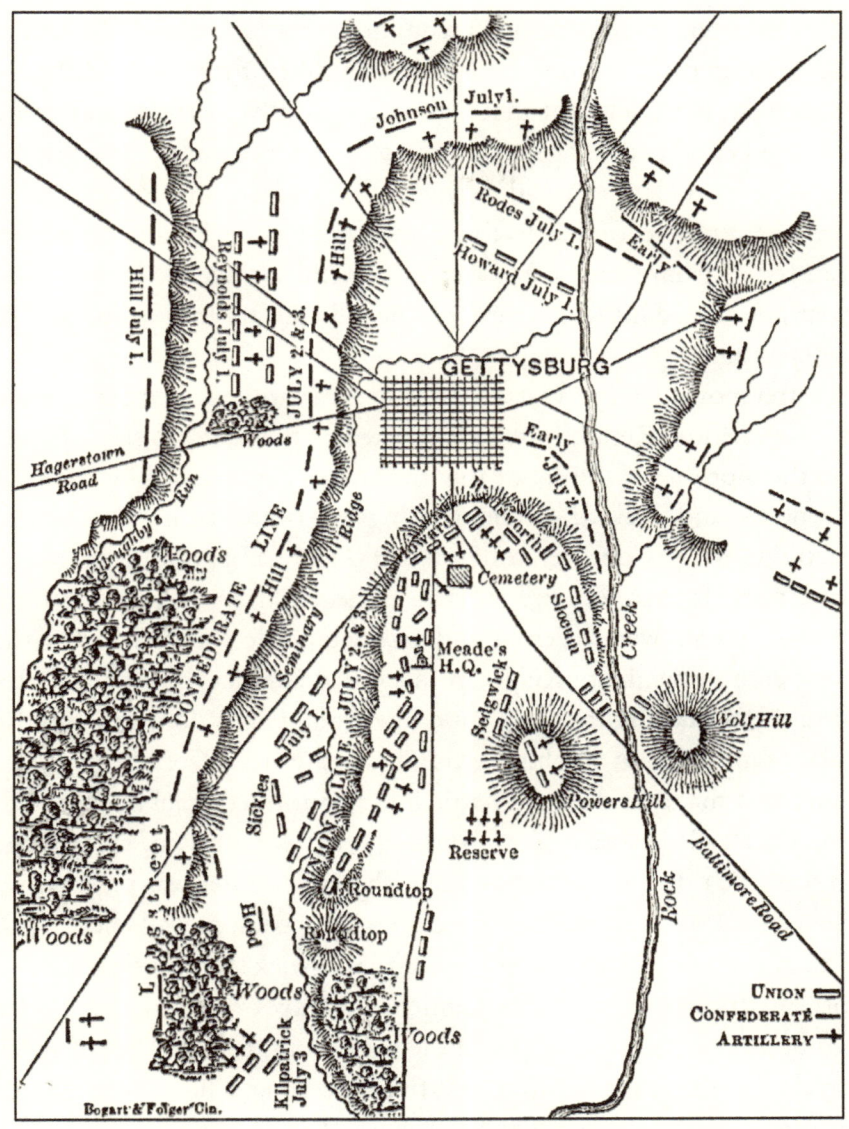

Battle of Gettysburg, July 1, 2, 3, 1863.

Elated with his success on the Rappahannock, General Lee determined to carry the war into Maryland and Pennsylvania. In the first week of June he moved forward with his whole army, crossed the Potomac, and captured Hagerstown. On the 22d of June the invaders entered Chambersburg, and then pressed on through Carlisle to within a few miles of Harrisburg. The militia of Pennsylvania was called out, and volunteers came pouring in from other States. General Hooker, at the head of the Army of the Potomac, pushed forward to strike his antagonist. It was evident that a great and decisive battle was at hand. General Lee, abandoning his purpose of invasion, rapidly concentrated his forces near Gettysburg, the capital of Adams County, Pennsylvania. On the very eve of battle the command of the Union army was transferred from General Hooker to General George G. Meade, who hastily advanced his forces through the hill-country in the direction of Gettysburg.

After more than two years of indecisive warfare it seemed that the fate of the American Republic was to be staked on the issue of a single battle. On the morning of the 1st of July the Union advance, led by Generals Reynolds and Buford, while moving westward from Gettysburg, encountered the Confederate division of General Hill, coming up on the road from Hagerstown; and the struggle began. In the afternoon strong reinforcements were received and a severe battle was fought for the possession of Seminary Ridge. In this initial conflict the Confederates were victorious, driving the Union line from its position, through the village, and back to the high grounds southward. Here at nightfall a stand was made, and a new battle-line was formed reaching from an eminence called Round Top, where the left wing rested, around the crest of the ridges to Cemetery Hill, where the center was posted, and thence to Wolf Hill on Rock Creek. To this position, well-chosen and strong, the whole Union army, except Sedgwick's corps, was hurried forward during the night. The Confederate forces were all brought into position on Seminary Ridge and the high grounds to the left of Rock Creek, forming a semi-circle about five miles long. The cavalry of both armies hung upon the flanks, doing effective service but hardly participating in the main conflict of the center.

On the morning of July 2d, the corps of General Longstreet on the Confederate right moved forward impetuously and attacked the Union left under Sickles. The struggle in this part of the field was for the possession of Great and Little Round Top and after terrible fighting, which lasted until six o'clock in the evening, these strong positions remained in the hands of the Federals. In the center a similar conflict, lasting for the greater part of the day, ensued for the possession of Cemetery Hill. Here, too, notwithstanding the desperate assaults of the Confederates, the integrity of the National line was preserved till nightfall. On the right the Confederate onset was more successful, and the Union right under General Slocum was somewhat shattered. But at ten o'clock at night, when the fighting ceased, it was found that the position of the two armies had not been materially changed by a conflict which had left forty thousand dead and wounded men on the field of battle.

Under cover of the darkness both generals made arrangements to renew the struggle on the morrow, but when morning came both were loath to begin. For each felt that this day's action must be decisive. General Meade had some advantage in the fact that Lee, in in order to continue his invasion, must carry the Union position or retreat. The whole forenoon of the 3d was spent in preparations. At midday there was a lull. Then burst forth the fiercest cannonade ever known on the American continent. Until after two o'clock the hills were shaken with the thunders of more than two hundred heavy guns. The Confederate artillerymen concentrated their fire on the Union center at Cemetery Hill which became a scene of indescribable uproar and death. Then came the crisis. The cannonade ceased. A Confederate column, nearly three miles long, headed by the Virginians under General Pickett, made a final and desperate charge on the Union centre. But the onset was in vain, and the brave men who made it were mowed down with terrible slaughter. The victory remained with the national army, and Lee was obliged to turn back with his shattered legions to the Potomac. The entire Confederate loss in this the greatest battle of the war was nearly thirty thousand; that of the Federals in killed, wounded and missing, twenty-three thousand a hundred and eighty-six. General Lee withdrew his forces into Virginia, and the Union army resumed its old position on the Potomac and the Rappahannock. Such were the more important military movements of 1863.

During this year the administration of President Lincoln was beset with many difficulties. The war-debt of the nation was piling up mountains high. The last calls for volunteers had not been fully met. The anti-war party of the North had grown more bold, and openly denounced the measures of the government. On the 3d of March THE CONSCRIPTION ACT was passed by Congress, and two months afterward the President ordered a general draft of three hundred thousand men. All able bodied citizens between the ages of twenty and forty-five years were subject to the requisition. The measure was bitterly denounced by the opponents of the war, and in many places the draft-officers were forcibly resisted. On the 13th of July, in the city of New York, a vast mob rose in arms, demolished the buildings which were occupied by the provost marshals, burned the colored orphan asylum, attacked the police, and killed about a hundred people, most of whom were negroes. For three days the authorities of the city were set at defiance. On the second day of the reign of terror Governor Seymour arrived and addressed the mob in a mild-mannered way, promising that the draft should be suspended, and advising the rioters to disperse; but they gave little heed to his mellow admonition, and went on with the work of destruction. General Wool, commander of the military district of New York, then took the matter in hand; but the troops at his disposal were at first unable to overawe the insurgents. Some volunteer regiments, however, came trooping home from Gettysburg the Metropolitan police companies were compactly organized; and the combined forces soon crushed the insurrection with a strong hand. After the fall of Vicksburg and the retreat of Lee from Pennsylvania, there were fewer acts of domestic violence. Nevertheless, the anti-war spirit in some parts of the North ran so high that on the 19th of August President Lincoln issued a proclamation suspending the privileges of the writ of *habeas corpus* throughout the Union.

As a means of procuring soldiers the draft amounted to nothing; only about fifty thousand men were thus directly obtained. But volunteering was greatly quickened by the measure, and the employment of substitutes soon filled the ranks of the army. Such, however, were the terrible losses by battle and disease and the expiration of enlistments that in October the President issued another call for three hundred thousand men. At the same time it was provided that any delinquency in meeting the demand would be supplied by a draft in the following January. By these active measures the columns of the Union army were made more powerful than ever. In the armies of the South, on the other hand, there were already symptoms of exhaustion, and the most rigorous conscription was necessary to fill the thinned but still courageous ranks of the Confederacy. It was on the 2oth of June in this year that West Virginia, separated from the Old Dominion, was organized and admitted as the thirty-fifth State of the Union.

CHAPTER LXVI.

THE CLOSING CONFLICTS.

AS in the previous year, the military movements of 1864 began in the West. In the beginning of February General Sherman left Vicksburg with the purpose of destroying the railroad connections of Eastern Mississippi. Marching toward Alabama, he reached Meridian on the 15th of the month. Here, where the railroad from Mobile to Corinth intersects the line from Vicksburg to Montgomery, the tracks were torn up for a distance of a hundred and fifty miles. Bridges were burned, locomotives and cars destroyed, vast quantities of cotton and corn given to the flames. At Meridian General Sherman expected the arrival of a strong force of Federal cavalry which had been sent out from Memphis, under command of General Smith. The latter advanced into Mississippi, but was met, a hundred miles north of Meridian, by the cavalry of Forrest, and driven back to Memphis. Disappointed of the expected junction of his forces, General Sherman retraced his course to Vicksburg. Forrest continued his raid northward, entered Tennessee, and on the 24th of March captured Union City. Pressing on, he reached Paducah, Kentucky, made an assault on Fort Anderson, in the suburbs of the town, but was repulsed with a loss of three hundred men. Turning back into Tennessee, he came upon Fort Pillow, on the Mississippi, seventy miles above Memphis. The place was defended by five hundred and sixty soldiers, about half of whom were negroes. Forrest, having gained the outer defences, demanded a surrender, but was refused. He then ordered an assault, and carried the fort by storm.

To the spring of 1864 belongs the story of THE RED RIVER EXPEDITION, conducted by General Banks. The object had in view was the capture of Shreveport, the seat of the Confederate government of Louisiana. A strong land-force was to march up Red River, supported by fleet of gunboats, under command of Admiral Porter. The army was composed of three divisions: the first, from Vicksburg, numbering ten thousand, commanded by General Smith; the second, from New

Orleans, led by General Banks in person; the third, from Little Rock, under command of General Steele. In the beginning of March Smith's division moved forward to Red River, and was joined by Porter with the fleet. On the 14th of the same month the advance reached Fort de Russy, which was taken by assault. The Confederates retreated up the river to Alexandria, and on the 16th that city was occupied by the Federals. Three days afterward Natchitoches was captured; but here the road turned from the river, and further co-operation between the gunboats and the army was impossible. The flotilla proceeded up stream toward Shreveport, and the land-forces whirled off in a circuit to the left.

On the 8th of April, when the advanced brigades were approaching the town of Mansfield, they were suddenly attacked by the Confederates in full force and advantageously posted. After a short and bloody engagement, the Federals were completely routed. The victors made a vigorous pursuit as far as Pleasant Hill, where they were met on the next day by the main body of the Union army. The battle was renewed with great spirit, and the Federals were barely saved from ruin by the hard fighting of the division of General Smith, who covered the retreat to the river. Nearly three thousand men, twenty pieces of artillery and the supply-trains of the Federal army were lost in these disastrous battles. With great difficulty the flotilla descended the river from the direction of Shreveport; for the Confederates had now planted batteries on the banks. When the Federals had retreated as far as Alexandria, they were again brought to a standstill; the river had fallen to so low a stage that the gunboats could not pass the rapids. The squadron was finally saved from its peril by the skill of Colonel Bailey of Wisconsin, who constructed a dam across the river, raising the water so that the vessels could be floated over. The whole expedition returned as rapidly as possible to the Mississippi. General Steele had, in the mean time, made an advance from Little Rock to aid in the reduction of Shreveport; but learning of the Federal defeats, he withdrew after several severe engagements. To the national government the Red River expedition was a source of much shame and mortification. General Banks was relieved of his command, and General Canby was appointed to succeed him.

On the 2d of March, 1864, General Grant was appointed commander-in-chief of all the armies of the United States. The high grade of *lieutenant-general* was revived by act of Congress, and conferred upon him. No less than seven hundred thousand Union soldiers were now to move at his command. The first month after his appointment was spent in planning the great campaigns of the year. These were two in number. The Army of the Potomac, under command of Meade and the general-in-chief, was to advance upon Richmond, still defended by the Army of Northern Virginia, under Lee. General Sherman, commanding the army at Chattanooga, now numbering a hundred thousand men, was to march against Atlanta, which was defended by the Confederates, under General Johnston. To these two great movements all other military operations were to be subordinate.

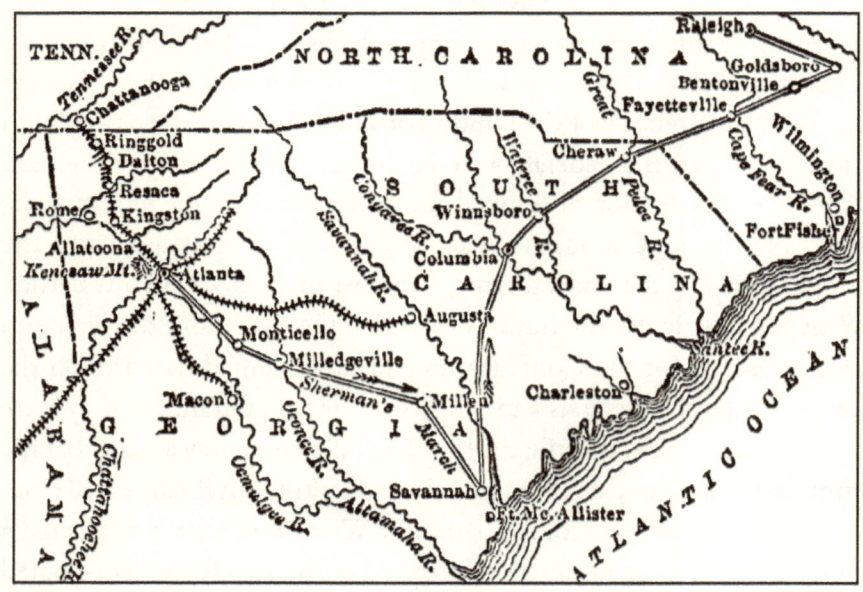

Sherman's Campaign, 1864.

On the 7th of May General Sherman moved forward from Chattanooga. At Dalton he was confronted by the Confederate army, sixty thousand strong. After some manœuvring and fighting, he succeeded in turning Johnston's flank, and obliged him to fall back to Resaca. After two hard battles on the 14th and 15th of May, this place was also carried, and the Confederates retreated by way of Calhoun and Kingston to Dallas. Here, on the 28th, Johnston made a second stand, entrenched himself and fought, but was again outnumbered, outflanked, and compelled to fall back to Lost Mountain. From this position he was forced on the 17th of June, after three days of desultory fighting. The next stand of the Confederates was made on the Great and Little Kenesaw Mountains. From this line on the 22d of June the division of General Hood made a fierce attack upon the Union centre, but was repulsed with heavy losses. Five days afterward General Sherman attempted to carry the Great Kenesaw by storm. The assault was made with great audacity, but ended in a dreadful repulse and a loss of three thousand men. Sherman, undismayed by his reverse, resumed his former tactics, outflanked his antagonist, and on the 3d of July compelled him to retreat across the Chattahoochee. By the 10th of the month the whole Confederate army had retired within the defences of Atlanta.

This stronghold of the Confederacy was at once besieged. Here were the great machine-shops, foundries, car-works and dépôts of supplies upon the possession of which so much depended. At the very beginning of the siege the cautious and skillful General Johnston was superseded by the rash but daring General J. B. Hood. It was the policy of the latter to *fight* at whatever hazard. On the 20th, 22d and 28th of July he made three desperate assaults on the Union lines around Atlanta, but was repulsed with dreadful losses in each engagement. It was in the beginning of the second of these battles that the brave General James B. McPherson, the pride of the Union army, was killed while reconnoitring the Confederate lines. In the three conflicts the Confederates lost more men than Johnston had lost in all his masterly retreating and fighting between Chattanooga and Atlanta. For more than a month the siege was pressed with great vigor. At last, by an incautious movement, Hood separated his army; Sherman thrust a column between the two divisions; and the immediate evacuation of Atlanta followed. On the 2d of September the Union army marched into the captured city. Since leaving Chattanooga General Sherman had lost fully thirty thousand men; and the Confederate losses were even greater.

General Thomas.

By retiring from Atlanta Hood saved his army. It was now his policy to strike northward into Tennessee, and thus compel Sherman to evacuate Georgia. But the latter had no notion of losing his vantage ground and after following Hood north of the Chattahoochee, he turned back to Atlanta. The Confederate general now swept up through Northern Alabama, crossed the Tennessee at Florence and advanced on Nashville. Meanwhile, General Thomas, with the Army of the Cumberland, had been detached from Sherman's army at Atlanta and sent northward to confront Hood in Tennessee. General Schofield, who commanded the Federal forces in the southern part of the State, fell back before the Confederates and took post at Franklin, eighteen miles south of Nashville. Here, on the 30th of November, he was attacked by Hood's legions, and after a hard-fought battle held them in check till nightfall, when he escaped across the river and retreated within the defences of Nashville. At this place all of General Thomas's forces were rapidly concentrated. A line of entrenchments was drawn around the city on the south. Hood came on, confident of victory, and prepared to begin the siege by blockading the Cumberland; but before the work was fairly begun, General Thomas, on the 15th of December, moved from his works, fell upon the Confederate army, and routed it with a loss, in killed, wounded and prisoners, of more than twenty-five thousand men. For many days of freezing weather Hood's shattered columns were pursued, until at last they found refuge in Alabama. The Confederate army was ruined, and the rash general who had led it to destruction was relieved of his command.

On the 14th of November General Sherman burned Atlanta and began his famous MARCH TO THE SEA. His army of veterans numbered sixty thousand men. Believing that Hood's army would be destroyed in Tennessee, and knowing that no Confederate force could with stand him in front, he cut his communications with the North, abandoned his base of supplies, and struck out boldly for the sea-coast, more than two hundred and fifty miles away. As had been foreseen, the Confederates could offer no successful resistance. The Union army swept on through Macon and Milledgeville; reached the Ogeechee and crossed in safety; captured Gibson and Waynesborough; and on the 10th of December arrived in the vicinity of Savannah. On the 13th Fort McAllister, below the city, was carried by storm by the division of General Hazen. On the night of the 20th General Hardee, the Confederate commandant, escaped from Savannah with fifteen thousand men and retreated to Charleston. On the following morning the national advance entered, and on the 22d General Sherman made his headquarters in the city. On his march from Atlanta he had lost only five hundred and sixty-seven men.

The month of January, 1865, was spent by the Union army at Savannah. On the 1st of February General Sherman, having garrisoned the city, began his march against Columbia, the capital of South Carolina. To the Confederates the further progress of the invasion through the swamps and morasses of the State had seemed impossible. Now that the veteran legions were again in motion, alarm and terror pervaded the country. Governor Magarth had already summoned to the field every white man in the State between the ages of sixteen and sixty; but the requisition was comparatively

General Sherman.

ineffectual. Nevertheless, the Confederates formed a line of defence along the Salkhatchie and prepared to dispute Sherman's march northward. It was all in vain. The passages of the river were forced and on the 11th of the month the Confederate lines of communication between Charleston and Augusta were cut off. On the next day Orangeburg was taken by the Seventeenth Corps. On the 14th the fords and bridges of the Congaree were carried and the State road opened in the direction of Columbia. The several divisions pressed rapidly forward; bridges were thrown across the Broad and Saluda Rivers, and the capital lay at the mercy of the conquerors. On the morning of the 17th Mayor Goodwyn and a committee of the common council came out in carriages and the city was formally surrendered.

As soon as it became certain that Columbia must fall into the hands of the Federals, General Hardee, the commandant of Charleston, determined to abandon that city also, and to join Generals Beauregard and Johnston in North Carolina. Accordingly, on the day of the capture of the capital, guards were detailed to destroy all the ware houses, stores of cotton, and depots of supplies in Charleston. The torch was applied, the flames raged, and consternation spread throughout the city. The great depot of the Northwestern Railway, where a large quantity of powder was stored, caught fire, blew up with terrific violence, and buried two hundred people in the ruins. Not until four squares in the best part of the city were laid in ashes was the conflagration checked. During the same night General Hardee with his fourteen thousand troops escaped from desolate Charleston and made his way northward. On the morning of the 18th the news was borne to the National forces on James's and Morris Islands. During the forenoon the Stars and Stripes were again raised over Forts Sumter, Ripley, and Pinckney. Mayor Macbeth surrendered the city to a company which was sent up from Morris Island. The work of saving whatever might be rescued from the flames was at once begun, the citizens and the Federal soldiers working together. By strenuous exertions the principal arsenal was saved; a dépôt of rice was also preserved and its contents distributed to the poor. Colonel Stewart L. Woodford of the One Hundred and Twenty-seventh New York was appointed military governor; and relations, more friendly than might have been expected, were soon established between the soldiery and the citizens.

After destroying the arsenals, machine shops, and founderies of Columbia General Sherman immediately renewed his march northward in the direction of Charlotte, North Carolina. The army swept on without opposition as far as Winnsboro, where a junction was effected with the Twentieth Corps under Slocum. Crossing the Great Pedee at Cheraw, the Union commander pressed on towards Fayetteville where he arrived without serious hindrance, and on the 11th of March took possession of the town. Three days before the campaign had been rendered exciting by a dashing fight between Hampton's and Kilpatrick's cavalry. The former officer was defending the rear of Hardee's column on the retreat from Charleston when the latter, resolving to intercept him, cut through the Confederate lines. But early the next morning Kilpatrick was surprised in his quarters, attacked, and rented, himself barely escaping on foot into a swamp. Here, however, he suddenly rallied his forces, turned on the Confederates and scattered them in a brilliant charge. Hampton, not less resolute than his antagonist, now made a rally and returned to the onset. But Kilpatrick held his ground until he was reinforced by a division of the Twentieth Corps under General Mitchell, when the Confederates were finally driven back. The Union cavalry then proceeded without further molestation to Fayetteville where Sherman's forces were concentrated on the 11th of March.

General Johnston had now been recalled to the command of the Confederate forces, and the advance of the Union forces began to be seriously opposed. At Averasborough, on Cape Fear River, a short distance north of Fayetteville, General Hardee made a stand, but was repulsed with considerable loss. When, on the 19th of March, General Sherman was incautiously approaching Bentonsville, he was suddenly attacked by the ever-vigilant Johnston, and for a while the Union army, after all its marches and victories, was in danger of destruction. But the tremendous fighting of General Jefferson C. Davis's division saved the day, and on the 21st Sherman entered Goldsborough unopposed. Here he was reinforced by a strong column from Newbern under General

Schofield, and another from Wilmington commanded by General Terry. The Federal army now turned to the north-west, and on the 13th of April entered Raleigh. This was the end of the great march; and here, thirteen days after his arrival, General Sherman received the surrender of Johnston's army.

Admiral Farragut.

While these great and decisive events were taking place in the Carolinas, the famous cavalry raid of General Stoneman was in progress. About the middle of March he set out from Knoxville with a force of six thousand men, crossed the mountains, captured Wilkesboro, and forced his way across the Yadkin at Jonesville. It had been the original purpose of the raid that Stoneman should make a diversion in favor of Sherman by striking into the western districts of South Carolina; but that commander, by the celerity of his movements, had already reached Goldsboro in the North State, and was in no need of help. Stoneman's movement therefore became an independent expedition, the general object being the destruction of public property, the capture of Confederate stores, and the tearing up of railroads. Turning to the north, the troopers traversed the western end of North Carolina and entered Carroll county, Virginia. At Wytheville the railroad was torn up, and then the whole line was destroyed from the bridge over New River to within four miles of Lynchburg. Christiansburg was captured and the track of the railway 0bliterated for ninety miles. Turning first to Jacksonville and then southward, the expedition next struck and destroyed the North

Carolina Railroad between Danville and Greensboro. The track in the direction of Salisbury was also torn up, and the factories at Salem burned. The Union prisoners at Salisbury were removed by the Confederates in time to prevent their liberation; but the town was captured and a vast store of ammunition, arms, provision, clothing, and cotton fell into the hands of the raiders. Finally, on the 19th of April, a division under Major Moderwell reached the great bridge where the South Carolina Rail road crosses the Catawba River. This magnificent structure, eleven hundred and fifty feet in length, was set on fire and completely destroyed. After a fight with Ferguson's Confederate cavalry, the Federals turned back to Dallas, where all the divisions were concentrated,—and the raid was at an end. During the progress of the expedition six thousand prisoners, forty-six pieces of artillery; and immense quantities of small arms had fallen into the hands of Stoneman's men: the amount of property destroyed and the damage otherwise done to the tottering Confederacy could not be estimated.

Meanwhile, events of even greater importance had occurred on the gulf and the Atlantic coast. In the beginning of August, 1864, Admiral Farragut bore down with a powerful squadron upon the defences of Mobile. The entrance to the harbor of this city was commanded on the left by Fort Gaines, and on the right by Fort Morgan. The harbor itself was defended by a Confederate fleet and the monster iron-clad ram *Tennessee*. On the 5th of August Farragut prepared for battle and ran past the forts into the harbor. In order to direct the movements of his vessels, the brave old admiral mounted to the maintop of his flag-ship, the *Hartford*, lashed himself to the rigging, and from that high perch gave his commands during the battle. One of the Union ships struck a torpedo and went to the bottom. The rest attacked and dispersed the Confederate squadron; but just as the bay seemed won the terrible *Tennessee* came down at full speed to strike and sink the *Hartford*. The latter avoided the blow; and then followed one of the fiercest conflicts of the war. The Union iron-clads closed around their black antagonist and battered her with their beaks and fifteen-inch bolts of iron until she surrendered. Two days afterward Fort Gaines was taken; and on the 23d of the month Fort Morgan was obliged to capitulate. The port of Mobile was effectually sealed up.

Not less important to the Union cause was the capture of Fort Fisher. This powerful fortress commanded the entrance to Cape Fear River and Wilmington—the last sea-port held by the Confederates. In December Admiral Porter was sent with the most powerful American squadron ever afloat to besiege and take the fort. General Butler, with a land-force of six thousand five hundred men, accompanied the expedition. On the 24th of the month the bombardment began, and the troops were sent ashore with orders to carry the works by storm. When General Weitzel, who led the column, came near enough to the fort to reconnoitre, he decided that an assault could only end with the destruction of his army. General Butler held the same opinion, and the enterprise was abandoned. Admiral Porter remained before Fort Fisher with his fleet, and General Butler returned with the land-forces to Fortress Monroe. Early in January the same troops were sent back to Wilmington, under command of General Terry. The siege was at once renewed by the army and the fleet, and on the 15th of the month Fort Fisher was taken by storm.

In the previous October the control of Albemarle Sound had been secured by a daring exploit of Lieutenant Cushing of the Federal navy. These waters were commanded by a tremendous iron ram called the *Albemarle*. In order to destroy the dreaded vessel a number of daring volunteers, led by Cushing, embarked in a small steamer, and on the night of the 27th of October entered the Roanoke. The ram was discovered lying at the harbor of Plymouth. Cautiously approaching, the lieutenant with his own hands sank a terrible torpedo under the Confederate ship, exploded it, and left the ram a ruin. The adventure cost the lives or capture of all of Cushing's party except himself and one other, who escaped. A few days afterward the town of Plymouth was taken by the Federals.

During the progress of the war the commerce of the United States had suffered dreadfully from the attacks of Confederate cruisers. As early as 1861 the Southern Congress had granted commissions to privateers but neutral nations would not allow such vessels to bring prizes into their ports, and the Privateering Act was of little direct benefit to the Confederacy. But the commerce of the United States was greatly injured. The first Confederate ship sent out was the *Savannah*, which was captured on the same day that she escaped from Charleston. In June of 1861 the *Sumter*, commanded by Captain Semmes, ran the blockade at New Orleans, and for seven months did fearful work with the Union merchantmen. But in February of 1862 Semmes was chased into the harbor of Gibraltar, where he was obliged to sell his vessel and discharge his crew. In the previous October the *Nashville* ran out from Charleston, went to England, and returned with a cargo worth three millions of dollars. In March of 1863 she was sunk by a Union iron-clad in the mouth of the Savannah River.

The ports of the Southern States were now so closely blockaded that war-vessels could no longer be sent abroad. In this emergency the Confederates turned to the ship-yards of Great Britain, and from that vantage-ground began to build and equip their cruisers. In spite of the remonstrances of the United States, the British government connived at this proceeding; and here was laid the foundation of a difficulty which afterward cost the treasury of England fifteen millions of dollars. In the harbor of Liverpool the *Florida* was fitted out; and going to sea in the summer of 1862, she succeeded in running into Mobile Bay. Escaping in the following January, she destroyed fifteen merchantmen, was captured in the harbor of Bahia, Brazil, and brought into Hampton Roads, where an accidental collision sent her to the bottom. The Georgia, the *Olustee*, the *Shenandoah* and the *Chickamauga*, all built at the ship-yards of Glasgow, Scotland, escaped to sea and made great havoc with the merchant-ships of the United States. At the capture of Fort Fisher the *Chickamauga* and another cruiser called the *Tallahassee* were blown up by the Confederates. The *Georgia* was captured in 1863, and the *Shenandoah* continued abroad until the close of the war.

Most destructive of all the Confederate vessels was the famous *Alabama*, built at Liverpool. Her commander was Captain Raphael Semmes, the same who had cruised in the *Sumter*. A majority of the crew of the Alabama were British subjects; her armament was entirely British;

and whenever occasion required, the British flag was carried. In her whole career, involving the destruction of sixty-six vessels and a loss of ten million dollars to the merchant service of the United States, she never entered a Confederate port, but continued abroad, capturing and burning. Early in the summer of 1864 Semmes entered the harbor of Cherbourg, France, and was there discovered by Captain Winslow, commander of the steamer *Kearsarge*. The French government gave the Confederate captain orders to leave the port, and on the 19th of June he went out to give his antagonist battle. Seven miles from the shore the two ships closed for the death-struggle; and after a desperate battle of an hour's duration, the *Alabama* was shattered and sunk. Semmes and a part of his officers and crew were picked up by the English yacht *Deerhound* and carried to Southampton.

After the great battle of Gettysburg, the Confederate army under General Lee was withdrawn into the Shenandoah valley. The Union cavalry, led by General Gregg, pressed after him and at Shepherdstown gained some advantage over the division of Fitzhugh Lee. Meade himself, at the head of the Army of the Potomac, entered Virginia near Berlin and moved southward through Lovettsville to Warrenton. The Blue Ridge was again interposed between the two armies. It was the policy of the Union commander to preoccupy and hold the passes of the mountains and to strike his antagonist a fatal blow when he should attempt to return to Richmond. But Lee's movements were marked with his usual caution and sagacity. Making a feint of crowding his army through Manassas Gap, he succeeded in drawing thither the bulk of the Federal forces, and then by a rapid march southward gained Front Royal and Chester Gap, swept through the pass, and reached Culpepper in safety. General Meade, disappointed in his expectations of a battle, advanced his army and took up a position on the Rappahannock.

In the lull that ensued from July till September of 1863, both generals were much weakened by the withdrawal of large numbers of their troops to take part in the struggles of the Southwest. From Lee's army Longstreet's whole corps had been detached for the aid of Bragg who was hard pressed by Rosecrans, in Tennessee. General Meade, learning of the weakened condition of his foe, crossed the Rappahannock, pressed him back to the south bank of the Rapidan and himself occupied Culpepper. Soon, however, Howard's and Slocum's corps were withdrawn from the Army of the Potomac, and Meade was in turn obliged to act on the defensive. But his ranks were soon filled with reinforcements and the middle of October found him planning a forward movement. Lee, however, had already assumed the offensive and by skillful manœuvers had again thrown his army on the Union flank. Then began the old race for the Potomac, and in that the Federals were successful, reaching Bristow Station and taking up a strong position on the Heights of Centreville. Lee in turn fell back and the two great armies at last came to rest for the winter, the one at Culpepper and the other on the Upper Rappahannock.

In the following spring no movements of importance occurred until the beginning of the campaign of the Army of the Potomac, now commanded by Generals Grant and Meade; and this, which may well be considered as one of the great campaigns of history, has been reserved for the closing narrative of the war. On the night of the 3d of May, 1864, the national camp at Culpepper was broken up, and the march on Richmond was begun. In three successive summers the Union army had been beaten back from that metropolis of the Confederacy. Now a hundred and forty thousand men, led by the lieutenant-general, were to begin the final struggle with the veterans of Lee. On the first day of the advance Grant crossed the Rapidan and entered the Wilderness, a country of oak woods and thickets west of Chancellorsville. He was immediately confronted and attacked by the Confederate army. During the 5th, 6th and 7th of the month the fighting continued incessantly with terrible losses on both sides; but the results were indecisive. Lee retired within his intrenchments, and Grant made a flank movement on the left in the direction of Spottsylvania Court-house. Here followed, from the morning of the 9th till the night of the 12th, one of the bloodiest struggles of the war. The Federals gained some ground and captured the division of General Stewart; but the losses of Lee, who fought on the defensive, were less dreadful than those of his antagonist.

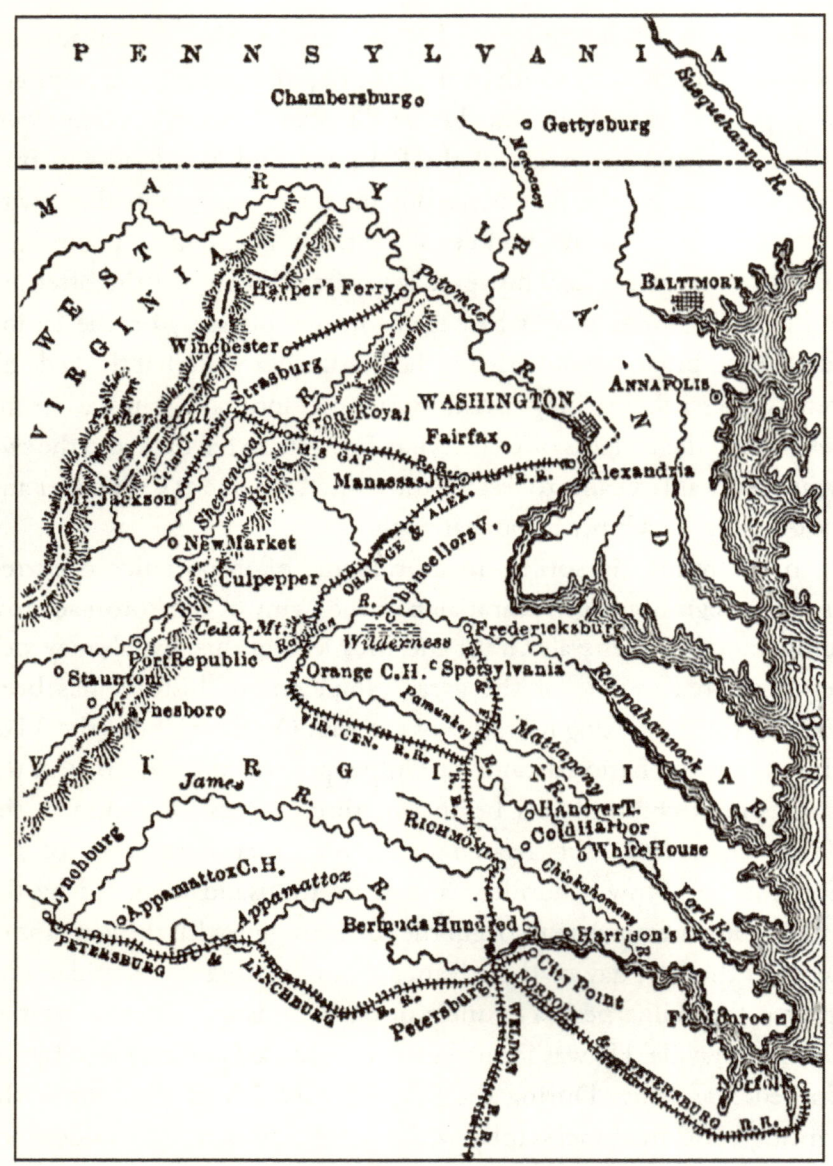

Operations in Virginia, '64, and '65.

After the battle of Spottsylvania, Grant again moved to the left, crossed the Pamunkey to Hanovertown, and came to a place called Cold Harbor, twelve miles north-east of Richmond. Here, on the 1st of June, he attacked the Confederates, strongly posted, but was repulsed with heavy losses. On the morning of the 3d the assault was renewed, and in the brief space of half an hour nearly ten thousand Union soldiers fell dead or wounded before the Confederate entrenchments. The repulse of the Federals was complete, but they held their lines as firmly as ever. Since the beginning of the campaign the losses of the Army of the Potomac, including the corps of Burnside, had reached the enormous aggregate of sixty thousand. During the same period the Confederates had lost in killed, wounded and prisoners about thirty-five thousand men.

General Grant now changed his base to James River with a view to the capture of Petersburg and the conquest of Richmond from the south-east. General Butler had already moved with a strong division from Fortress Monroe, and on the 5th of May had taken Bermuda Hundred and City Point, at the mouth of the Appomattox. Advancing against Petersburg, he was met on the 16th by the corps of General Beauregard and driven back to his position at Bermuda Hundred, where he was obliged to entrench himself and act on the defensive. Here, on the 15th of June, he was joined by General Grant's whole army, and the combined forces moved against Petersburg. On the 17th and 18th several assaults were made on the Confederate entrenchments, but the works could not be carried. Lee's army was hurried within the defences, and in the latter part of June Petersburg was regularly besieged.

Meanwhile, movements of great importance were taking place in the Shenandoah valley. When General Grant moved forward from the Rapidan, he sent General Sigel up the valley with a force of eight thousand men. While the latter was advancing southward he was met at New Market, fifty miles above Winchester, by an army of Confederate cavalry, under General Breckinridge. On the 15th of May Sigel was attacked and routed, and the command of his flying forces was transferred to General Hunter. Deeming the valley cleared, Breckinridge returned to Richmond, whereupon Hunter faced about, marched toward Lynchburg, came upon the Confederates at Piedmont, and gained a signal victory. From this place be advanced with his own forces and the cavalry troops of General Averill against Lynchburg; but finding that he had run into peril, he was obliged to retreat across the mountains into West Virginia. By this movement the valley of the Shenandoah was again exposed to an invasion by the Confederates.

In the hope of compelling Grant to raise the siege of Petersburg, Lee immediately despatched General Early with orders to cross the Blue Ridge, sweep down the valley, invade Maryland and threaten Washington city. With a force of twenty thousand men Early began his movement northward, and on the 5th of July crossed the Potomac. On the 9th he met the division of General Wallace on the Monocacy, and defeated him with serious losses. But the check given to the Confederates by the battle saved Washington and Baltimore from capture. After dashing up within gunshot of these cities, Early ordered a retreat, and on the 12th his forces recrossed the Potomac with vast quantities of plunder.

General Wright, who was sent in pursuit of Early's army, followed him as far as Winchester, and there, on the 24th of July, defeated a portion of his forces. But Early wheeled upon his antagonist, and the Union troops were in turn driven across the Potomac. Following up his advantage, the Confederate general next invaded Pennsylvania, burned Chambersburg, and returned into the valley laden with spoils. Seeing the necessity of putting an end to these devastating raids, General Grant in the beginning of August appointed General Philip H. Sheridan to the command of the consolidated army on the Upper Potomac. The troops thus placed at Sheridan's disposal numbered nearly forty thousand, and with these he at once moved up the valley. On the 19th of September he came upon Early's army at Winchester, attacked and routed him in a hard-fought battle. On the 22d he overtook the defeated army at Fisher's Hill, assaulted Early in his entrenchments, and gained another complete victory.

In accordance with orders given by the commander-in-chief, Sheridan now turned about to ravage the valley. The ruinous work was fearfully well done; and what with torch and axe and sword, there was nothing left between the Blue Ridge and the Alleghanies worth fighting for. Maddened by this destruction and stung by his defeats, the veteran Early rallied his shattered forces, gathered reinforcements, and again entered the valley. Sheridan had posted his army in a strong position on Cedar Creek, a short distance from Strasburg, and feeling secure, had gone to Washington. On the morning of the 19th of October Early cautiously approached the Union camp, surprised it, burst in, carried the position, captured the artillery, and sent the routed troops flying in confusion to ward Winchester. The Confederates pursued as far as Middletown, and there, believing the victory complete, paused to eat and rest. On the previous night Sheridan had returned to Winchester, and was now coming to rejoin his army. On his way he heard the sound of battle, rode twelve miles at full speed, met the panic-struck fugitives, rallied them with a word, turned upon the astonished Confederates, and gained one of the most signal victories of the war. Early's army was disorganized and ruined. Such was the end of the strife in the valley of the Shenandoah.

All fall and winter long, General Grant pressed the siege of Petersburg with varying success. On the 30th of July a mine was exploded under one of the forts. An assaulting column sprang forward to carry the works, gained some of the defences, but was finally repulsed with heavy losses. On the 18th of August a division of the Union army seized the Weldon Railroad and held it against several desperate assaults, in which each army lost thousands of men. On the 28th of September Battery Harrison, on the right bank of the James, was stormed by the Federals, and on the next day General Paine's brigade of colored soldiers carried a powerful redoubt on Spring Hill. On the 27th of October there was a hard-fought battle on the Boydton road, south of Petersburg and then the army went into quarters for the winter.

Late in February the struggle began anew. On the 27th of the month General Sheridan, who had moved from the Shenandoah, gained a victory over the forces of General Early at Waynesborough, and then joined the commander-in-chief at Petersburg. On the 1st of April a severe battle was fought at Five Forks, on the Southside Railroad, in which the Confederates were defeated with a loss of six thousand prisoners. On the next day Grant ordered a general assault on the lines of Petersburg, and the works were carried. On that night the army of General Lee and the members of the Confederate government fled from Richmond; and on the following morning that city, as well as Petersburg, was entered by the Federal army. The warehouses of the ill-fated Confederate capital were fired by the retreating soldiers, and the better part of the city was reduced to ruins.

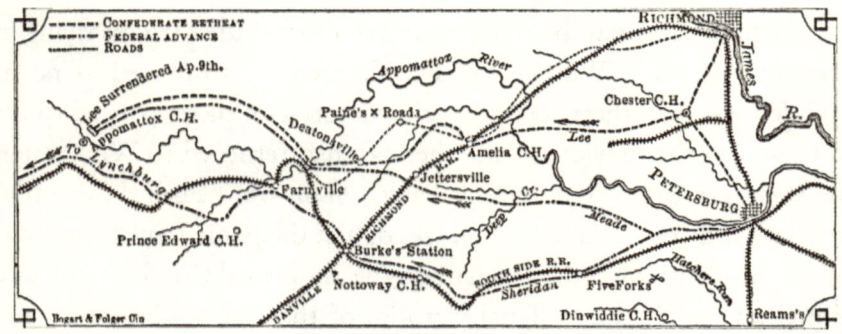

Petersburg, Richmond, Appomattox, 1865.

The strife lasted but a few days longer. General Lee retreated as rapidly as possible to the south-west, hoping to join the army of General Johnston from Carolina. The Confederates, flying from Petersburg, joined those on the retreat from Richmond at Amelia Court House. To this place General Lee had ordered his supply-trains; but the officer having the same in charge, had foolishly mistaken his orders *and driven the train on in the direction of Danville*. Nearly one-half of the Confederate army, now growing hopeless, had to be dispersed to gather supplies by foraging. The 4th and 5th of April—days precious to the sinking heart of Lee—were consumed with the delay. The victorious Federals were pressing on in full pursuit; and on the morning of the 6th nearly the whole Union army was at Jettersville, on the Danville railroad, ready to strike the Confederates at Amelia. Sheridan pressed on by the left flank in the direction of Deatonsville. Ord came up with his division by way of the South Side Railroad to Burke's Station. Lee fell back to the west from Amelia Court House and reached Deatonsville where a severe battle was fought, in which Ewell's division six thousand strong was overwhelmed and captured by Sheridan. The main army of the Confederates, however, gained the Appomattox at Farmville, crossed to the northern bank, and burned the bridges. Lee now endeavored to interpose the river as a barrier between himself and his relentless pursuers; but it was all in vain. Hoping against hope, he made a desperate effort to hold the line of the Lynchburg Railroad, but the vigilant Sheridan was there before him. On the 7th of April a slight success in battle gave a momentary encouragement to the exhausted army; but the flame of hope was blown out as soon as kindled. On that day General Grant, now at Farmville, addressed a note to the Confederate commander expressing a desire that the further effusion of blood might be saved by the surrender of the Confederate army. To this General Lee replied by declaring his desire for peace but adding that the occasion for the surrender of the Army of Northern Virginia had not arrived. On the morning of the 9th, however, when it became known that the left wing of the Union army had se cured the line of the Lynchburg Railroad—when the wreck of Long street's veterans, attempting to continue the retreat, were confronted and driven back by Sheridan—then the iron-souled Confederate leader, seeing the utter uselessness of a further struggle, sent General Grant 21 note asking for a meeting preliminary to a surrender. The Union commander immediately complied with the request. At two o'clock in the afternoon of Palm Sunday, the 9th of April, 1865, the two great generals met each other in the parlor of William McLean at Appomattox Court House. There the terms of surrender were discussed and settled. It was agreed that General Grant should put his proposition in the form of a military note to which General Lee should return a formal answer. The Union commander accordingly drew up and presented the following memorandum:

APPOMATTOX COURT HOUSE, VA., *April* 9, 1865.

GENERAL: In accordance with the substance of my letter to you of the 8th instant, I propose to receive the surrender of the Army of Northern Virginia on the following terms, to-wit: Rolls of all the officers and men to be made in duplicate; one copy to be given to an officer to be designated by me, the other to be retained by such other officer or officers as you may designate. The officers to give their individual paroles not to take up arms against the Government of the United States until properly exchanged; and each company or regimental commander to sign a like parole for the men of their commands. The arms, artillery, and public property, to be parked, and stacked, and turned over to the officers appointed by me to receive them. This will not: embrace the side-arms of the officers nor their private horses or baggage. This done, each officer and man will be allowed to return to his home, not to be disturbed by United States authority so long as they observe their paroles and the laws in force where they reside.

U. S. GRANT, Lieutenant-General.

To this memorandum General Lee responded as follows:

HEAD-QUARTERS, ARMY OF NORTHERN VIRGINIA, *April 9, 1865.*

GENERAL: I received your letter of this date, containing the terms of the surrender of the Army of Northern Virginia, as proposed by you. As they are substantially the same as those expressed in your letter of the 8th instant, they are accepted. I will proceed to designate the proper officers to carry the stipulations into effect.

R. E. LEE, *General.*

Thus the work was done! How the army of General Johnston was surrendered at Raleigh a few days later has already been narrated. After four dreadful years of bloodshed, devastation, and sorrow, THE CIVIL WAR IN THE UNITED STATES WAS AT AN END.

The Federal authority was rapidly extended over the Southern States. After the surrender of Lee and Johnston, there was no further hope of reorganizing the Confederacy. Mr. Davis and his cabinet escaped to Danville, and there for a few days kept up the forms of government. From that place they fled into North Carolina and were scattered. The ex-President with a few friends continued his flight through South Carolina into Georgia, and encamped near the village of Irwinsville, where, on the 10th of May, he was captured by General Wilson's cavalry. He was conveyed as a prisoner to Fortress Monroe, and kept in confinement until May of 1867, when he was taken to Richmond to be tried on a charge of treason. He was admitted to bail; and his cause, after remaining untried for a year and a half, was finally dismissed.

At the presidential election in the autumn preceding the downfall of the Confederacy, Mr. Lincoln was chosen for a second term. As Vice-President, Andrew Johnson of Tennessee was elected in place of Mr. Hamlin. The opposing candidates, supported by the Democratic party, were General George B. McClellan and George H. Pendleton of Ohio. Mr. Lincoln's majority was very heavy, General McClellan carrying only the States of Kentucky, Delaware and New Jersey. In the summer preceding the election the people of Nevada framed a constitution, in accordance with an act of Congress, and on the 31st of October the new commonwealth was proclaimed as the thirty-sixth State of the Union. The gold and silver mines of Nevada were developed with such rapidity that they soon surpassed those of California in their yield of the precious metals.

At the outbreak of the civil war the financial credit of the United States had sunk to a very low ebb. By the organization of the army and navy the expenses of the government were at once swelled to an enormous aggregate. The price of gold and silver advanced so rapidly that the redemption of bank-notes in coin soon became impossible; and on the 30th of December, 1861, the banks of New York, and afterward those of the whole country, suspended specie payments. Mr. Chase, the secretary of the treasury, first sought relief by issuing TREASURY NOTES, receivable as money and bearing seven and three-tenths per cent. interest. This expedient was temporarily successful, but by the beginning of 1862 the expenses of the government had risen to more than a million of dollars daily.

To meet these tremendous demands other measures had to be adopted. Congress accordingly made haste to provide AN INTERNAL REVENUE. This was made up from two general sources: first, *a tax on manufactures, incomes and salaries*; second, *a stamp-duty on all legal documents*. The next measure was the issuance by the treasury of a hundred and fifty millions of dollars in non-interest-bearing LEGAL TENDER NOTES of the United States, to be used as money. These are the notes called *Greenbacks*. The third great measure adopted by the government was the sale of UNITED STATES BONDS. These were made redeemable at any time after five and under twenty years from date, and were from that fact called *Five-Twenties*. The interest upon them was fixed at six per cent., payable semi-annually in gold. Another important series of bonds, called *Ten-Forties*, was afterward issued, being redeemable by the government at any time between ten and forty years from date. In the next place, Congress passed an act providing for the establishment of NATIONAL BANKS. The private banks of the country had been obliged to suspend operations, and the people were greatly distressed for want of money. To meet this demand it was provided that new banks might be established, using national bonds, instead of gold and silver, as a basis of their circulation. The currency of these banks was furnished and the redemption of the same guaranteed by the treasury of the United States. By these measures the means for prosecuting the war were provided. At the end of the conflict the national debt had reached the astounding sum of nearly three thousand millions of dollars.

On the 4th of March, 1865, President Lincoln was inaugurated for his second term. A month afterward the military power of the Confederacy was broken. Three days after the evacuation of Richmond by Lee's army the President visited that city, conferred with the authorities, and then returned to Washington. On the evening of the 14th of April he attended Ford's theatre with his wife and a party of friends. As the play drew near its close a disreputable actor, named John Wilkes Booth, stole unnoticed into the President's box, leveled a pistol at his head, and shot him through the brain. Mr. Lincoln fell forward in his seat, was borne from the building, lingered in an unconscious state until the following morning, and died. It was the greatest tragedy of modern times—the most wicked, atrocious and diabolical murder known in American history. The assassin leaped out of the box upon the stage, escaped into the darkness, and fled. At the same hour another murderer, named Lewis Payne Powell, burst into the bed-chamber of Secretary Seward, sprang upon the couch of the sick man, stabbed him nigh unto death, and made his escape into the night. The city was wild with alarm and excitement. It was clear that a plot had been made to assassinate the leading members of the government. Troops of cavalry and the police of Washington departed in all directions to hunt down the conspirators. On the 26th of April Booth was found concealed in a barn south of Fredericksburg. Refusing to surrender, he was shot by Sergeant Boston Corbett, and then dragged forth from the burning building to die. Powell was caught, convicted and hanged. His fellow-conspirators, David E. Herrold and Geo. A. Atzerott, together with Mrs. Mary E. Surratt, at whose house the plot was formed, were also condemned and executed. Michael O'Laughlin, Dr. Samuel A. Mudd, and Samuel Arnold were sentenced to imprisonment for life, and Edward Spangler for a term of six years.

So ended in darkness, but not in shame, the career of Abraham Lincoln. He was one of the most remarkable men of any age or country—a man in whom the qualities of genius and common sense were strangely mingled. He was prudent, far-sighted and resolute; thoughtful, calm and just; patient, tender-hearted and great. The manner of his death consecrated his memory. From city to city, in one vast funeral procession, the mourning people followed his remains to their last resting-place at Springfield. From all nations rose the voice of sympathy and shame—sympathy for his death, shame for the dark crime that caused it.

> He had been born a destined work to do,
>   And lived to do it; four long-suffering years—
> Ill-fate, ill-feeling, ill-report lived through—
>   And then he heard the hisses change to cheers,
>
> The taunts to tribute, the abuse to praise
>   And took them both with his unwavering mood;
> But as he came on light from darkest days,
>   And seemed to touch the goal from where he stood,
>
> A felon hand, between that goal and him,
>   Reached from behind his head, a trigger prest,
> And those perplexed and patient eyes were dim,
>   Those gaunt long-laboring limbs were laid to rest!
>
> The words of mercy were upon his lips,
>   Forgiveness in his heart and on his pen,
> When this vile murderer brought swift eclipse
>   To thoughts of peace on earth, good-will to men.
>
> The Old World and the New, from sea to sea,
>   Utter one voice of sympathy and shame!

Sore heart, so stopped when it at last beat free,
  Sad life, cut short just as its triumph came!

A deed accurst! Strokes have been struck before
  By the assassin's hand, whereof men doubt
If more of horror or disgrace they bore;
  But thy foul crime, like Cain's stands darkly out!

Vile hand! that branded murder on a strife,
  What e'er its grounds, stoutly and nobly striven,
And with the martyr's crown crownest a life
  With much to praise, little to be forgiven![33]

---

[33] These verses are from the London Punch of May 6th, 1865. For years that paper had caricatured Mr. Lincoln and ridiculed the National government; but now that the deed was done, the British heart reacted and spoke out for humanity.

CHAPTER LXVII.

Johnson's Administration, 1865-1869.

On the day after the assassination of Mr. Lincoln, Andrew Johnson took the oath of office, and became President of the United States. He was a native of North Carolina, born in Raleigh, on the 29th of December, 1808. With no advantages of education, he passed his boyhood in poverty and neglect. In 1826 he removed with his mother to Tennessee and settled at Greenville. Here he was married to an intelligent lady who taught him to write and cipher. Here by dint of native talent, force of will, and strength of character, he first earned the applause of his fellow-men. Here, through toil and hardship, he rose to distinction, and after holding minor offices was elected to Congress. As a member of the United States Senate in 1860-61 he opposed secession with all his zeal, even after the legislature had declared Tennessee out of the Union. On the 4th of March, 1862, he was appointed military governor of that State, and entered upon his duties at Nashville. He began his administration and carried out his measures with all the vigor and vehemence of his nature. There was no quailing or spirit of compromise. His life was many times in peril; but he fed on danger and grew strong under the onsets of his enemies. He held the office of governor until 1864, when he was nominated for the vice-presidency in place of Mr. Hamlin. Now, by the tragic death of the President, he was suddenly called to assume the responsibilities of chief magistrate. In his first congressional message before shadowed a policy of great severity towards the civil and military leaders of the overthrown Confederacy.

On the 1st of February, 1865, Congress adopted an amendment to the Constitution by which slavery was abolished and forbidden in all the States and Territories of the Union. By the 18th of the following December the amendment had been ratified by the legislatures of twenty seven States, and was duly proclaimed as a part of the Constitution. The emancipation proclamation had been issued as a military measure; now the doctrines and results of that instrument were recognized and incorporated in the fundamental law of the land.

On the 29th of May THE AMNESTY PROCLAMATION was issued by President Johnson. By its provisions a general pardon was extended to all persons—except those specified in certain classes—who had participated in the organization and defence of the Confederacy. The condition of the pardon was that those receiving it should take an oath of allegiance to the United States. The excepted persons might also be pardoned on Special application to the President. During the summer of 1865 the great armies were disbanded, and the victors and vanquished returned to their homes to resume the work of peace.

The finances of the nation were in an alarming condition. The war-debt went on increasing until the beginning of 1866, and it was only by the most herculean exertions that national bankruptcy could be warded off. The yearly interest on the debt had grown to a hundred and thirty three million dollars in gold. The expenses of the government had reached the aggregate of two hundred millions of dollars annually. But the augmented revenues of the nation proved sufficient to meet these enormous outlays, and at last the debt began to be slowly diminished. On the 5th of December, 1865, a resolution was passed in the House of Representatives pledging the faith of the United States to the full payment of the national indebtedness, both principal and interest.

During the civil war the emperor Napoleon III. interfered in the affairs of Mexico, and succeeded, by overawing the people with a French army, in setting up an empire. In the early part of 1864 the crown of Mexico was conferred on Maximilian, the archduke of Austria, who established his government and sustained it with French and Austrian soldiers. But the Mexican president Juarez headed a revolution against the usurping emperor; the government of the United States rebuked France for having violated the Monroe doctrine; Napoleon, becoming alarmed, withdrew his army; and Maximilian was overthrown. Flying from Mexico to Queretaro, he was there besieged and taken prisoner. On the 13th of June, 1867, he was tried by court-martial and condemned to be shot; and six days afterward the sentence was carried into execution.

The scheme of Napoleon, who had hoped to profit by the civil war and gain a foothold in the New World, was thus justly brought to shame and contempt.

After a few weeks of successful operation the first Atlantic telegraph, laid by Mr. Field in 1858, had ceased to work. The friends of the enterprise were greatly disheartened. Not so with Mr. Field, who continued both in Europe and America to advocate the claims of his measure and to plead for assistance. He made fifty voyages across the Atlantic, and finally secured sufficient capital to begin the laying of a second cable. The work began from the coast of Ireland in the summer of 1865. When the steamer *Great Eastern* had proceeded more than twelve hundred miles on her way to America, the cable parted and was lost. Mr. Field held on to his enterprise. Six millions of dollars had been spent in unsuccessful attempts, but still he persevered. In July of 1866 a third cable, two thousand miles in length, was coiled in the *Great Eastern*, and again the vessel started on her way. This time the work was completely successful. After twelve years of unremitting effort Mr. Field received a gold medal from the Congress of his country, and the plaudits of all civilized nations.

By an act of Congress, passed on the 1st of November, 1864, THE POSTAL MONEY-ORDER SYSTEM was established in the United States. The design of the measure was to secure a safe and convenient method of transferring small sums of money through the mails. The money-order is divided into two parts—the *order proper* and the *advice*. From the order, which is received and transmitted by the purchaser, the name of the payee is omitted. In the advice, which is sent by the post-master of the issuing office to the post-master of the paying office, the name of the payee is inserted. The advice and the order receive the same stamp and number, and being transmitted separately, constitute an almost perfect check against loss, robbery, and fraud. The largest sum which may be transmitted in one order is fifty dollars, though larger amounts may be sent in separate orders. The amount charged for issuing is trifling, varying with the value of the order, and the security is perhaps as great as human sagacity can provide. Notwithstanding the invaluable benefits of the system, it was at first received with little favor. In 1870 there were two thousand and seventy-six post-offices from which money-orders were issued. During that year the orders numbered a million six hundred and seventy-one thousand two hundred and fifty-three; and the amount transmitted was above thirty-four millions of dollars. On the 1st of October, 1875, the number of money-offices in operation was three thousand six hundred and ninety-six; the number of orders issued during the fiscal year ending on the 30th of June amounted to five millions six thousand three hundred and twenty-three; the amount of money sent to more than seventy-seven millions of dollars. Of all the orders issued during that year only twenty-seven were paid to persons not entitled to receive them. Such have been the advantages of the system as to require its extension to foreign lands. Postal conventions have already been held and arrangements completed for the exchange of money-orders with Switzerland, Great Britain and Ireland and Germany. The requirements of civilization will no doubt soon demand a similar compact with every enlightened nation.

The administration of President Johnson is noted as the time when the Territories of the United States assumed their final form. The vast domains west of the Mississippi were now reduced to proper limits and organized with a view to early admission into the Union as States. A large part of the work was accomplished during the administration of President Lincoln. In March of 1861 the Territory of Dakota, with an area of a hundred and fifty thousand square miles, was detached from Nebraska on the north, and given a distinct territorial organization. In February of 1863 Arizona, with an area of a hundred and thirteen thousand square miles, was separated from New Mexico on the west and organized as an independent Territory. On the 3d of March in the same year Idaho was organized out of portions of Dakota, Nebraska and Washington Territories; and on the 26th of May, 1864, Montana, with an area of a hundred and forty-six thousand square miles, was cut off from the eastern part of Idaho. By this measure the area of the latter Territory was reduced to eighty-six thousand square miles. On the 1st of March, 1867, the Territory of Nebraska, reduced to its present area of seventy six thousand miles, was admitted into the Union as the thirty-seventh State. Finally, on the 25th of July, 1868, the Territory of

Wyoming, with an area of ninety-eight thousand square miles, was organized out of portions of Dakota, Idaho and Utah. Thus were the Territories of the great West reduced to their present limits as represented in the accompanying map.

The year 1867 was signalized by THE PURCHASE OF ALASKA. Two years previously the territory had been explored by a corps of scientific men with a view of establishing telegraphic communication with Asia by way of Behring Strait. The report of the exploration showed that Alaska was by no means the worthless country it had been supposed to be. It was found that the coast-fisheries were of very great value, and that the forests of white pine and yellow cedar were among the finest in the world. Negotiations for the purchase of the peninsula were at once opened, and on the 30th of March, 1867, a treaty was concluded by which, for the sum of seven million two hundred thousand dollars, Russia ceded Alaska to the United States. The territory thus added to the domains of the Republic embraced an area of five hundred and eighty thousand square miles, and a population of twenty-nine thousand souls.

Very soon after his accession to the chief magistracy a serious disagreement arose between the President and Congress. The difficulty grew out of the great question of reorganizing the Southern States. The particular point in dispute was as to the relation which those States had sustained to the Federal Union during the civil war. The President held that the ordinances of secession were in their very nature null and void, and that therefore the seceded States *had never been out of the Union.* The majority in Congress held that the acts of secession were illegal and unconstitutional, but that the seceded States had been by those acts actually detached from the Union, and that special legislation and special guarantees were necessary in order to restore them to their former relations under the government. Such was the real foundation of the difficulty by which the question of reconstructing the Southern States was so seriously embarrassed.

Map VI.

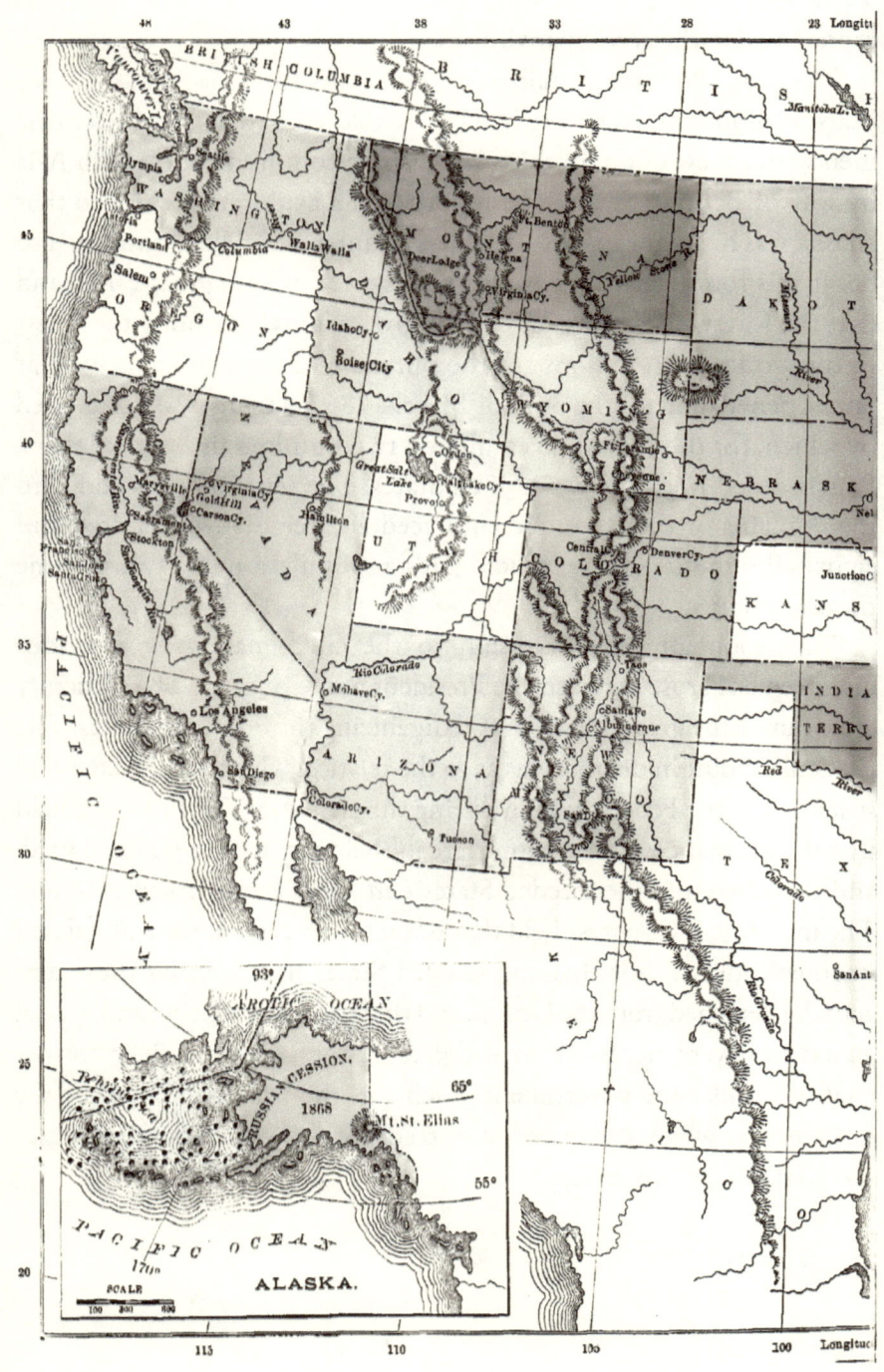

United States. 1877.

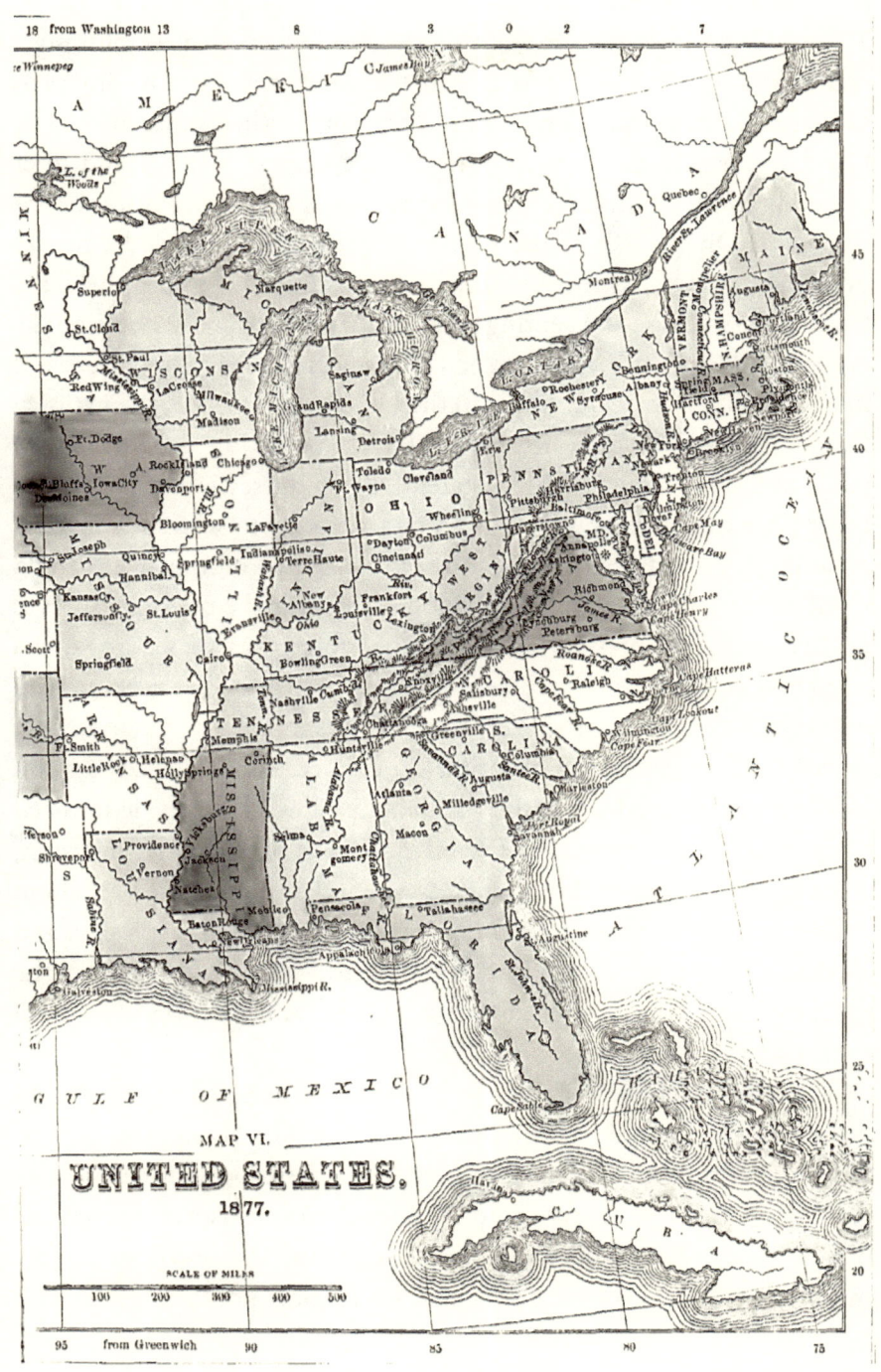

In the summer of 1865 measures of reconstruction were begun by the President in accordance with his own views. On the 9th of May a proclamation was issued for the restoration of Virginia to the Union. Twenty days afterward another proclamation was issued establishing a provisional government over South Carolina; and at brief intervals similar measures were adopted in respect to the other States of the late Confederacy. On the 24th of June all restrictions on trade and inter course with the Southern States were removed by proclamation of the President. On the 7th of the following September a second amnesty proclamation was issued, by which all persons who had upheld the Confederate cause—excepting the leaders—were unconditionally pardoned. Meanwhile, the State of Tennessee had been reorganized, and in 1866 was restored to its place in the Union. Meanwhile, the national Congress was pursuing its own line of policy in regard to the reconstruction of the Southern States. During the session of 1865-66, a committee of fifteen was appointed by that body to whom all matters appertaining to the reorganization of the States of the overthrown Confederacy should be referred. Soon afterwards the celebrated CIVIL RIGHTS BILL was passed, the object of which was to secure to the freedmen of the South the full exercise of citizenship. The measure was opposed and vetoed by the President, but was immediately repassed by a two-thirds congressional majority. On the occasion of the celebration of Washington's birthday at the Capital, the bill was severely denounced by the President in a speech delivered in front of the executive mansion; and the position assumed by Congress was declared to be a new rebellion against the government of the United States. In subsequent speeches and messages the same sentiment was reiterated, and the attitude of the executive and legislative departments became constantly more unfriendly.

In the summer of 1866 a call was issued for a national convention to be held in Philadelphia on the 14th of August. The objects had in view were not very clearly defined; but it was understood that the general condition of the country would be considered, measures of national policy discussed, and all the political elements, in opposition to the majority in Congress be consolidated into a new political party, with which the President's name would be associated in leadership. At the appointed time delegates from all the States and territories were present; many members of the Republican party took part in the movement, and the convention was not lacking in enthusiasm. Still, the meeting exercised but very little permanent influence on the affairs of the country.

Soon afterwards the President made another effort to rally public opinion in favor of his policy. In the latter part of August he set out from Washington, accompanied by Secretaries Seward, Welles, and Randall, General Grant, Admiral Farragut, and other prominent officials, to make a tour of the Northern States. The ostensible object had in view was that the President should be present at the laying of the corner stone of a monument to Senator Douglas at Chicago. Departing from the Capital, the presidential party passed through Philadelphia, New York, and Albany, and after taking part in the ceremonies at Chicago, returned by way of St. Louis, Indianapolis, Louisville, Cincinnati, and Pittsburg. At all the principal towns and cities through which he passed, the President spoke freely to the crowds in defence of his own policy and in denunciation of that of Congress. The whole journey was a scene of intense excitement and partisan animosity. The general effect of the President's course was disastrous to him and his political adherents; for in the elections of the following autumn the measures of Congress were sustained and the members reelected by increased popular majorities. Nevertheless, the result of the election had very little effect in altering the President's views or softening his feelings towards the legislative department of the government.

By degrees the affairs of the administration grew critical. When Congress convened in December of 1866 the policy of the President was severely condemned. The congressional committee, appointed at the session of the previous year, now brought forward a report embodying a full plan of reorganizing the Southern States. After much discussion the measures proposed by the committee were adopted by Congress, and the work of reconstruction was begun. As the first condition for the readmission of a State into the Union, it was enacted that the people of the same, by their legislative assembly or otherwise, should ratify the fourteenth amendment to the constitution which declared the citizenship of all persons born or naturalized in the United States. In furtherance of this policy Congress, at the same session, passed an act requiring that in the national territories the elective franchise should be granted without distinction of race or color, before such territories should be admitted into the Union. A similar measure was adopted in respect to the District of Columbia, forbidding the further restriction of the right of suffrage to white men. To all of these acts President Johnson opposed his veto; but in every case his objection was overcome by the two-thirds majority in Congress.

Concerning the reorganization of the Southern States, the real question at issue was as to whether a *civil* or a *military* method of reconstruction ought to be adopted. From the beginning, the President had urged the superiority of the civil process. But in Congress the opposite opinion prevailed, and the views of the majority were rather intensified by the hostility of the executive. On the 2d of March 1867, an act was passed by which the ten seceded States were divided into five military districts, each district to be under the control of a governor appointed by the President. After appointing the commanders required by this law, the chief magistrate asked the opinion of Mr. Stanbery, his attorney-general, as to the validity of the congressional measures of reconstruction. An answer was returned that most of the acts were null and void; and the President accordingly issued to the military commanders an order which measurably nullified the whole proceeding. But Congress passed a supplemental act declaring the meaning of the previous law, and the process of reorganization was continued under the congressional plan. The work, however, was greatly retarded by the distracted counsels of the government and the chaotic condition of affairs in the South. But in due time the States of Arkansas, Alabama, Georgia, Florida, Louisiana, North Carolina, and South Carolina were reconstructed, and in the months of June and July, 1868, readmitted into the Union. In every case, however, the readmission was effected against the protest, and over the veto of the President.

In the mean time, a difficulty had arisen in the President's cabinet which led to his impeachment. On the 21st of February, 1868, he notified Edwin M. Stanton, secretary of war, of his dismissal from office. The act was regarded by Congress as a usurpation of authority and a violation of law on the part of the President. The reconstruction difficulties had already broken off all friendly relations between the two Houses and the executive. Accordingly, on the 3d of March, articles of impeachment were agreed to by the House of Representatives, in accordance with the forms of the Constitution, and the cause was immediately remanded to the Senate for trial. Proceedings began before that body on the 23d of March and continued until the 26th of May, when the President was acquitted. But his escape was very narrow; a two-thirds majority was required to convict, *and but one vote was wanting.* Chief-Justice Salmon P. Chase, one of the most eminent of American statesmen and jurists, presided over this remarkable trial.

Chief-Justice Chase.

The time for holding another presidential election was already at hand. General Ulysses S. Grant was nominated by the Republicans, and Horatio Seymour of New York by the Democrats. The canvass was attended with great excitement. The people were still agitated, by the recent strife through which the nation had passed, and the questions most discussed by the political speakers were those arising out of the civil war. The principles advocated by the majority in Congress furnished the basis of the Republican platform of 1868, and on that platform General Grant was chosen by a very large electoral majority. The votes of twenty-six States, amounting, in the aggregate, to two hundred and fourteen ballots, were cast in his favor, while his competitor received only the eighty votes of the remaining eleven States. Of the popular vote, however, Mr. Seymour obtained two million seven hundred and three thousand six hundred, against three million thirteen thousand one hundred and eighty-eight given to General Grant. At the same election, the choice for the vice-presidency fell on Schuyler Colfax of Indiana.

CHAPTER LXVIII.

Grant's Administration, 1869-1877.

ULYSSES S. GRANT, eighteenth President of the United States, is a native of Ohio, born at Point Pleasant, in that State, April 27th, 1822. At the age of seventeen he entered the United States Military Academy at West Point, and graduated in 1843. He served with distinction and was promoted for gallantry in the Mexican war; but his first national reputation was won by the capture of Forts Henry and Donelson in 1862. From that time he rapidly rose in rank, and in March, 1864, received the appointment of lieutenant-general and commander-in-chief of the Union army. His subsequent career at the head of that army has already been narrated. At the close of the war his reputation, though strictly military, was very great; and his being involved

President Grant.

in the imbroglio between President Johnson and Congress rather heightened than diminished the estimation in which he was held by the people of the North. Before the Republican convention, held at Chicago on the 21st of May, 1868, he had no competitor, and was unanimously nominated on the first ballot. On the day following his inauguration as President, he sent in to the Senate the following nominations for cabinet officers: For secretary of state, Elihu B. Washburne of Illinois; for secretary of the treasury, Alexander T. Stewart of New York; for secretary of the interior, Jacob D. Cox of Ohio; for secretary of the navy, Adolph E. Borie of Pennsylvania; for secretary of war, John M. Schofield of Illinois; for postmaster general, John A. J. Creswell of Maryland; for attorney-general, E. R. Hoar of Massachusetts. These nominations were at once confirmed; but it was soon discovered that Mr. Stewart, being engaged in commerce, was ineligible, and George S. Boutwell of Massachusetts was appointed in his stead. Mr. Washburne also gave up his office to accept the position of minister to France; and the vacant secretaryship was given to Hamilton Fish of New York.

The first event by which the new administration was signalized was the completion of the Pacific Railroad. This vast enterprise was projected as early as 1853; but ten years elapsed before the work of construction was actually begun. The first division of the road extended from Omaha, Nebraska, to Ogden, Utah, a distance of a thousand and thirty-two miles. The western division, called the Central Pacific Railroad, reached from Ogden to San Francisco, a distance of eight hundred and eighty-two miles. On the 10th of May, 1869, the great work was completed with appropriate ceremonies.

Before the inauguration of President Grant two additional amendments to the Constitution had been adopted by Congress. The first of these, known as the Fourteenth Amendment, extended the right of citizenship to all persons born or naturalized in the United States, and declared the validity of the public debt. This amendment was submitted in 1867, was ratified by three-fourths of the States, and in the following year became a part of the Constitution. A few weeks before the expiration of Mr. Johnson's term the Fifteenth Amendment was adopted by Congress, providing that the right of citizens of the United States to vote shall not be denied or abridged on account of race, color or previous condition of servitude. This clause, which was intended to confer the right of suffrage on the emancipated black men of the South, was also submitted to the States, received the sanction of three-fourths of the legislatures, and on the 30th of March, 1870, was proclaimed by the President as a part of the Constitution.

In the autumn of 1869 occurred the most extraordinary monetary excitement ever known in the United States, or perhaps in the world. A company of unscrupulous speculators in New York city, headed by

Jay Gould and James Fisk, jr., succeeded in producing what is known as a "corner" in the gold market and brought the business interests of the metropolis to the verge of ruin. During the civil war the credit of the government had declined to such an extent that at one time a dollar in gold was worth two hundred and eighty six cents in paper currency. But after the restoration of the national authority the value of paper money appreciated, and in the fall of 1869 the ratio of gold to the greenback dollar had fallen to about one hundred and thirty to one hundred. There were at this time, in the banks of New York, fifteen million dollars in gold coin and in the sub-treasury of the United States a hundred millions more. The plan of Gould and Fisk was to get control by purchase of the greater part of the fifteen millions, to prevent the secretary of the treasury from selling any part of the hundred millions under his authority, then—having control of the market—to advance the price of gold to a fabulous figure, sell out all which they held themselves, and retire from the field of slaughtered fortunes with their accumulated millions of spoils! Having carefully arranged all the preliminaries, the conspirators, on the 13th of September, began their work of purchasing gold, at the same time constantly advancing the price. By the 22d of the month, they had succeeded in putting up the rate to a hundred and forty. On the next day the price rose to a hundred and forty-four. The members of the conspiracy now boldly avowed their determination to advance the rate to two hundred, and it seemed that on the morrow they would put their threat into execution. On the morning of the 24th, known as BLACK FRIDAY, the bidding in the gold-room began with intense excitement. The brokers of Fisk and Gould advanced the price to a hundred and fifty, a hundred and fifty-five, and finally to a hundred and sixty, at which figure they were obliged to purchase several millions by a company of merchants who had banded themselves together with the determination to fight the gold-gamblers to the last. Just at this moment came a despatch that Secretary Boutwell had ordered a sale of four millions from the sub-treasury! There was an instantaneous panic. The price of gold went down twenty per cent. in less than as many minutes! The speculators were blown away in an uproar; but they managed, by accumulated frauds and corruptions, *to carry off with them more than eleven million dollars as the fruits of their nefarious game!* Several months elapsed before the business of the country recovered from the effects of the shock.

In the first three months of 1870 the work of reorganizing the Southern States was completed. On the 24th of January the senators and representatives of Virginia were formally readmitted to their seats in Congress, and the Old Dominion once more took her place in the Union. On the 23d of February a like action was taken in regard to Mississippi; and on the 30th of March the work was finished by the readmission of Texas, the last of the seceded States. For the first time since the outbreak of the civil war the voice of all the States was heard in the councils of the nation.

In this year was completed the ninth census of the United States. It was a work of vast importance, and the results presented were of the most encouraging character. Notwithstanding the ravages of war, the last decade had been a period of wonderful growth and progress. During that time the population had increased from thirty-one million four hundred and forty-three thousand to thirty-eight million five hundred and eighty-seven thousand souls. The centre of population had now moved westward into the great State of Ohio, and rested at a point fifty miles east of Cincinnati. The national debt, though still enormous, was rapidly falling off. The products of the United States had grown to a vast aggregate; even the cotton crop of the South was regaining much of its former importance. American manufactures were competing with those of England in the markets of the world. The Union now embraced thirty-seven States and eleven Territories.[34] From the narrow limits of the thirteen original colonies, with their four hundred and twenty-one thousand square miles of territory, the national domain had spread to the vast area of three million six hundred and four thousand square miles. Few things, indeed, have been more marvelous than the territorial growth of the United States. The purchase of Louisiana more than doubled the geographical area of the nation; the several Mexican

---

[34] Including the Indian Territory and Alaska.

acquisitions were only second in importance; while the recent Russian cession alone was greater in extent than the original thirteen States. The nature of this territorial development will be best understood from an examination of the accompanying map.

In January of 1871 President Grant appointed Senator Wade of Ohio, Professor White of New York and Dr. Samuel Howe of Massachusetts as a board of commissioners to visit Santo Domingo and report upon the desirability of annexing that island to the United States. The question of annexation had been agitated for several years, and the measure was earnestly favored by the President. After three months spent abroad, the commissioners returned and reported in favor of the proposed annexation; but the proposal was met with violent opposition in Congress, and defeated.

The claim of the United States against the British government for damages done to American commerce by Confederate cruisers during the civil war still remained unsettled. These cruisers had been built and equipped in English ports and with the knowledge of the English government. Such a proceeding was in plain violation of the law of nations, even if the independence of the Confederate States had been recognized. Time and again Mr. Seward remonstrated with the British authorities, but without effect. After the war Great Britain became alarmed at her own conduct, and grew anxious for a settlement of the difficulty. On the 27th of February, 1871, a joint high commission, composed of five British and five American statesmen, assembled at Washington city. From the fact that the cruiser *Alabama* had done most of the injury complained of, the claims of the United States were called THE ALABAMA CLAIMS. After much discussion, the commissioners framed a treaty, known as the Treaty of Washington, by which it was agreed that all claims of either nation against the other should be submitted to a board of arbitration to be appointed by friendly nations. Such a court was formed, and in the summer of 1872 convened at Geneva, Switzerland. The cause of the two nations was impartially heard, and on the 14th of September decided in favor of the United States. Great Britain was obliged, for the wrongs which she had done, to pay into the Federal treasury fifteen million five hundred thousand dollars.

Map VII.

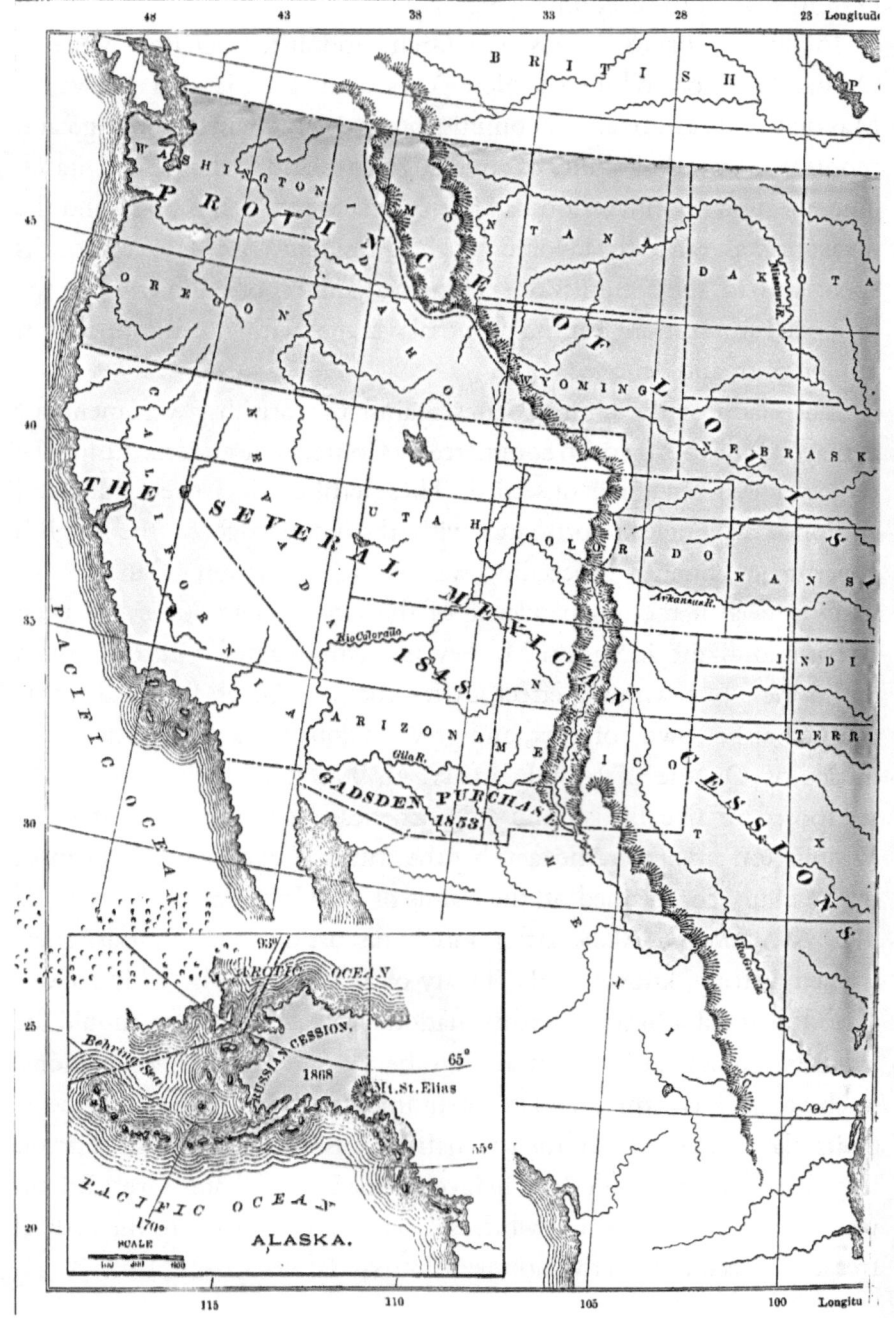

Showing the Territorial Growth of the United States.
1780 to 1877.

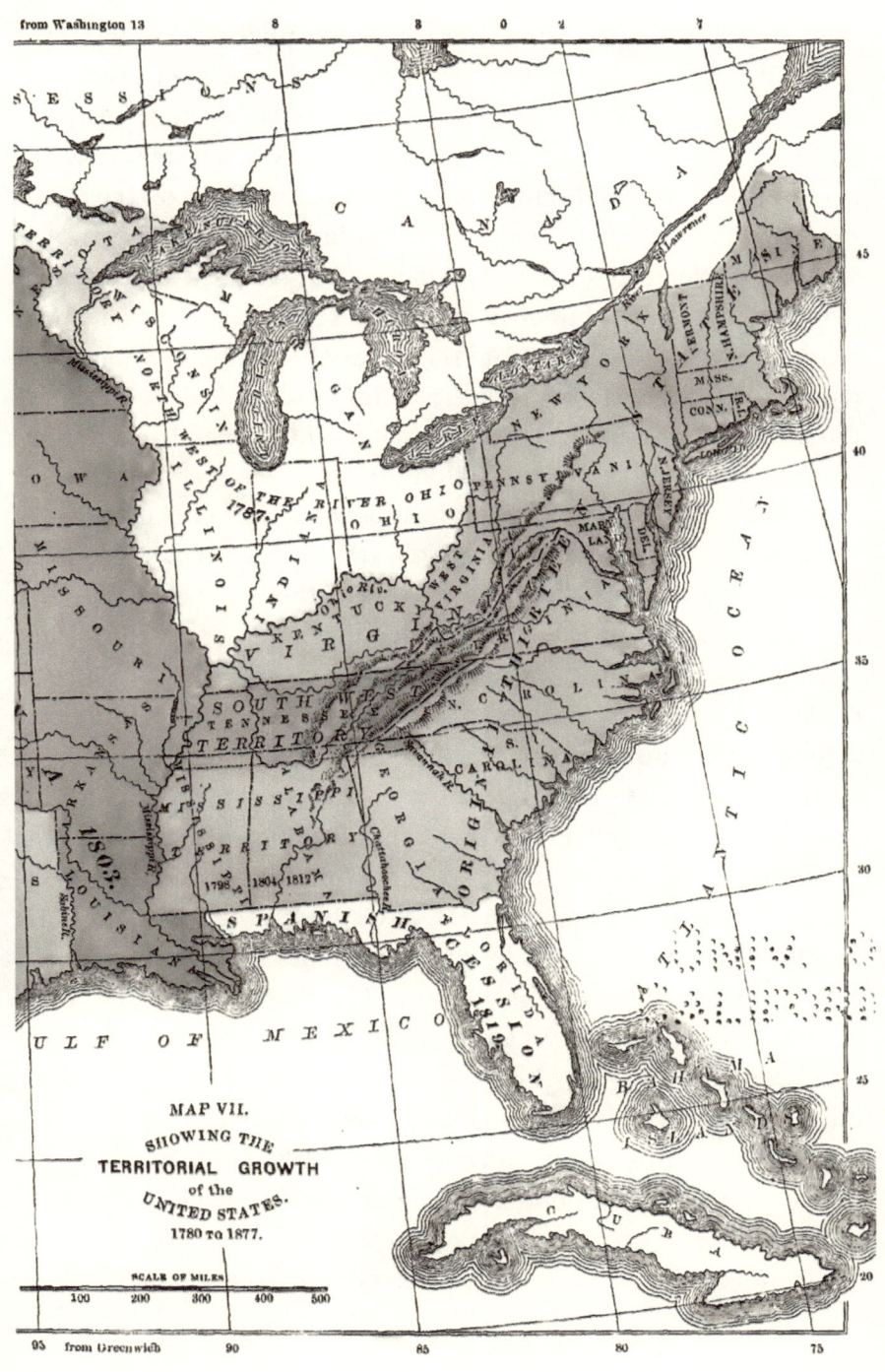

During the year 1871, there were laid and put into operation in the United States no less than *seven thousand six hundred and seventy miles of railroad!* There is perhaps no fact in the history of the world which exhibits so marvelous a development of the physical resources of a nation. Ere the mutterings of the civil war, with its untold destruction of life and treasure, had died away in the distance, the recuperative power, enterprise, and genius of the American people were revealed, as never before, in establishing and extending the lines of travel and commerce. In 1830 there were but twenty-three miles of railway track in the New World. In 1840 the lines in the United States had been extended to two thousand eight hundred and eighteen miles. Ten years later there were nine thousand and twenty one miles of track. According to the reports for 1860, the railroads of the country had reached the enormous extent of thirty thousand six hundred and thirty-five miles; and in the next ten years, embracing the period of the civil war, *the amount was nearly doubled.* Such is the triumphant power of free institutions—the victory of free enterprise, free industry, free thought. There stands the fact! Let the adherents of the Old World's methods, the eulogists of the past, take it and read it. Wherever the human race pants for a larger activity a more glorious exercise of its energies, let the story be told how the United States, just emerged from the furnace of war, smarting with wounds, and burdened with an enormous debt, built in a single year more than twice as many miles of railroad as Spain, ridden with her precedents of kingcraft and priestcraft, has *ever* built in her whole career.

The year 1871 is noted in American history for the burning of Chicago. On the evening of the 8th of October a fire broke out in De Keven street, and was driven by a high wind into the lumber-yards and wooden houses of the neighborhood. The flames leaped the South Branch of the Chicago River and spread with great rapidity through the business parts of the city. All day long the deluge of fire rolled on, crossed the main channel of the river, and swept into a blackened ruin the whole district between the North Branch and the lake as far northward as Lincoln Park. The area burned over was two thousand one hundred acres, or three and a third square miles. Nearly two hundred lives were lost in the conflagration, and the property destroyed amounted to about two hundred millions of dollars. No such a terrible devastation had been witnessed since the burning of Moscow in 1812. In the extent of the district burned over, the Chicago fire stands first, in the amount of property destroyed second, and in the suffering occasioned third, among the great conflagrations of the world.

On the 21st of October, 1872, was settled the only remaining dispute concerning the boundaries of the United States. By the terms of the treaty of 1846 it was stipulated that the North-western boundary line, running westward along the forty-ninth parallel of latitude, should extend to the middle of the channel which separates the continent from Vancouver's Island, and thence southerly *through the middle of said channel* and of Fuca's Straits to the Pacific. But what was "the middle of said channel"? for there were several channels. The British government claimed the Straits of Rosario to be the true line intended by the treaty, while the United States would have the Canal de Haro. So the question stood for a quarter of a century, and was then referred for settlement to the arbitration of William I., Emperor of Germany. That monarch heard the cause, decided in favor of the United States, and the Canal de Haro became the international boundary.

As the first official term of President Grant drew to a close the political parties made ready for the twenty-second presidential election. Many parts of the chief magistrate's policy had been made the subjects of criticism and controversy. The congressional plan of reconstructing the Southern States had prevailed, and with that plan the President was in accord. But the reconstruction measures had been unfavorably received in

Horace Greeley.

the South. The elevation of the negro race to the full rights of citizenship was regarded with apprehension. Owing to the disorganization of civil government in the Southern States, an opportunity was given in certain districts for bad men to band themselves together in lawlessness. The military spirit was still rife in the country, and the issues of the civil war were rediscussed, sometimes with much bitterness. On these issues the people divided in the election of 1872. The Republicans renominated General Grant for the presidency. For the vice-presidency Mr. Colfax declined a renomination, and was succeeded by Henry Wilson of Massachusetts. As the standard bearer of the Liberal Republican and Democratic parties Horace Greeley, editor of the New York *Tribune*, was nominated. This was the last act in that remarkable man's career. For more than thirty years he had been an acknowledged leader of public opinion in America. He had discussed with vehement energy and enthusiasm almost every question in which the people of the United States have any interest. After a lifetime of untiring industry he was now, at the age of sixty-one called to the forefront of political strife. The canvass was one of wild excitement and bitter denunciations. Mr. Greeley was overwhelmingly beaten, and died in less than a month after the election. In his death the nation lost a great philanthropist and journalism its brightest light.

A few days after the presidential election the city of Boston was visited by a conflagration only second in its ravages to that of Chicago in the previous year. On the evening of the 9th of November a fire broke out on the corner of Kingston and Summer streets, spread to the north east, and continued with almost unabated fury until the morning of the 11th. The best portion of the city, embracing some of the finest blocks in the United States, was laid in ashes. The burnt district covered an area of sixty-five acres. Eight hundred buildings, property to the value of eighty million dollars, and fifteen lives were lost by the conflagration.

In the spring of 1872 an order had been issued to Superintendent Odeneal to remove the Modoc Indians from their lands on the southern shore of Lake Klamath, Oregon, to a new reservation. The Indians, who had been greatly mistreated by former agents of the government, refused to go; and in the following November a body of troops was sent to force them into compliance. The Modocs resisted, kept up the war during the winter, and then retreated into an almost inaccessible volcanic region called the lava-beds. Here, in the spring of 1873, the Indians were surrounded, but not subdued. On the 11th of April a conference was held between them and six members of the peace commission; but in the midst of the council the treacherous savages rose upon the kind-hearted men who sat beside them and murdered General Canby and Dr. Thomas in cold blood. Mr. Meacham, another member of the commission, was shot and stabbed, but escaped with his life. The Modocs were then besieged and bombarded in their stronghold; but it was the 1st of June before General Davis with a force of regulars could compel Captain Jack and his murderous band to surrender. The chiefs were tried by court martial and executed in the following October.

In the early part of 1873 a difficulty arose in Louisiana which threatened the peace of the country. Owing to the existence of double election-boards two sets of presidential electors had been chosen in the previous autumn. At the same time two governors—William P. Kellogg and John McEnery—were elected; and rival legislatures were also returned by the hostile boards. Two State governments were accordingly organized, and for a while the commonwealth was in a condition bordering on anarchy. The dispute was referred to the Federal government, and the President decided in favor of Governor Kellogg and his party. The rival government was accordingly disbanded; but on the 14th of September, 1874, a large party, opposed to the administration of Kellogg and led by D. B. Penn, who had been returned as lieutenant-governor with McEnery, rose in arms and took possession of the State-house. Governor Kellogg fled to the custom-house and appealed to the President for help. The latter immediately ordered the adherents of Penn to disperse, and a body of national troops was sent to New Orleans to enforce the proclamation. On the assembling of the legislature in the following December the difficulty broke out more violently than ever, and the soldiery was again called in to settle the dispute.

About the beginning of President Grant's second term, the country was greatly agitated by what was known as THE CREDIT MOBILIER

INVESTIGATION in Congress. The Credit Mobilier of America was a joint stock company organized in 1863 for the purpose of facilitating the construction of public works. In 1867 another company which had undertaken to build the Pacific Railroad purchased the charter of the Credit Mobilier, and the capital was increased to three million seven hundred and fifty thousand dollars. Owing to the profitableness of the work in which the company was engaged, the stock rose rapidly in value and enormous dividends were paid to the shareholders. In 1872 a lawsuit in Pennsylvania developed the startling fact that much of the stock of the Credit Mobilier *was owned by members of Congress*. A suspicion that those members had voted corruptly in the legislation affecting the Pacific Railroad at once seized the public mind and led to a congressional investigation, in the course of which many scandalous transactions were brought to light, and the faith of the people in the integrity of their servants greatly shaken.

In the autumn of 1873 occurred one of the most disastrous financial panics known in the history of the United States. The alarm was given by the failure of the great banking-house of Jay Cooke Company of Philadelphia. Other failures followed in rapid succession. Depositors everywhere hurried to the banks and withdrew their money and securities. Business was suddenly paralyzed, and many months elapsed before confidence was sufficiently restored to enable merchants and bankers to engage in the usual transactions of trade. The primary cause of the panic was the fluctuation in the volume and value of the national currency. Out of this had arisen a wild spirit of speculation which sapped the foundations of business, destroyed financial confidence, and ended in disaster.

Not the least of the evil results of the great monetary disturbance was the check given to THE NORTHERN PACIFIC RAILROAD. As early as 1864 a company had been organized under a congressional charter to construct a railway from Lake Superior to Puget Sound. The work also contemplated the running of a branch road, two hundred miles in length, down the valley of the Columbia River to Portland, Oregon. Large subsidies were granted to the company by Congress, and other favorable legislation was expected. In 1870 the work of construction was begun and carried westward from Duluth, Minnesota. Jay Cooke's banking-house made heavy loans to the company, accepting as security the bonds of the road; for it was confidently expected that such legislation would be obtained as should secure the success of the enterprise and bring the bonds to par. In this condition of affairs the Credit Mobilier scandal was blown before the country; and no Congress would have dared to vote further subsidies to a railroad enterprise. Jay Cooke's securities became comparatively worthless; then followed the failures and the panic. The work of constructing the road was arrested by the financial distress of the country, and has since been pushed forward but slowly and with great difficulty. In 1875 the section of four hundred and fifty miles, extending from Duluth to Bismarck, Dakota, had been put in operation and another section, a hundred and five miles in length, between Kalama and Tacoma, in Washington Territory, had also been completed. Meanwhile, the attention of the country was turned to the Texas and Pacific line, which had been projected from Shreveport, Louisiana, and Texarkana, Arkansas, by way of El Paso to San Diego, California—a distance from Shreveport of a thousand five hundred and fourteen miles. In 1875 the main line had been carried westward a hundred and eighty-nine miles to Dallas, Texas, while the line from Texarkana had progressed seventy-five miles towards El Paso.

On the 4th of March, 1875, the Territory of Colorado was authorized by Congress to form a State constitution. On the 1st of July, in the following year, the instrument thus provided for, was ratified by the people a month later, the President issued his proclamation, and "the Centennial State" took her place in the Union. The new commonwealth embraced an area of a hundred and four thousand five hundred square miles, and a population of forty-two thousand souls. Public attention was directed to the territory by the discovery of gold, in the year 1852. Silver was discovered about the same time, and in the winter of 1858-9, the first colony of miners was established on Clear Creek and in Gilpin County. The entire yield of gold up to the time of the admission of the State was estimated at more than seventy millions of dollars. Until 1859, Colorado constituted a part of Kansas; but in that year a convention was held at Denver, and in 1861 a distinct territorial organization was effected. Since 1870, immigration has been rapid and constant.

The last years of the history of the Republic have been noted for the number of public men who have fallen by the hand of death. In December of 1869, Edwin M. Stanton, secretary of war under President Lincoln, and more recently justice of the supreme court of the United States, died. In 1870 General Robert E. Lee, president of Washington and Lee University, General George H. Thomas and Admiral Farragut passed away. In 1872 William H. Seward, Professor Morse, Horace Greeley and General Meade were all called from the scene of their earthly labors. On the 7th of May, 1873, Chief-Justice Chase fell under a stroke of paralysis at the home of his daughter in New York City; and on the 11th of March in the following year, Senator Charles Sumner of Massachusetts died at Washington. He was a native of Boston; born in 1811; liberally educated at Harvard College. At the age of thirty-five he entered the arena of public life, and in 1850 succeeded Daniel Webster in the Senate of the United States. This position he retained until the time of his death, speaking much and powerfully on all the great questions that agitated the nation. His last days were spent in considering the interests and welfare of that country to whose service he had given the lifelong energies of his genius. On the 22d of November, 1875, Vice President Henry Wilson, whose health had been gradually failing since his inauguration, sank under a stroke of paralysis and died at Washington city. Like Roger Sherman, he had risen from the

Charles Sumner.

shoemaker's bench to the highest honors of his country. Without the learning of Seward and Sumner—without the diplomatic skill of the one or the oratorical fame of the other—he nevertheless possessed those great abilities and sterling merits which will transmit his name to after times on the roll of patriot statesmen.

Independence Hall, 1876.

As the Centennial of American Independence drew near, the people made ready to celebrate the great event with appropriate ceremonies. A hundred years of national prosperity—though not unclouded by ominous shadows and not unhurt by the devastations of war—had swept away, and at last the dawn of the centennial morning was rising in the eastern sky. It was not to be supposed that the thoughtful and patriotic of the land would allow so lustrous an epoch to go by without impressing upon the present generation the lesson of the past and the hope of the future. As early as 1866, a proposition was made by Professor John L. Campbell of Wabash College, that steps should be taken looking to the proper celebration of the great national anniversary. About the same time the question of an international exhibition in honor of our independence, was agitated by the Honorable John Bigelow, a former minister of the United States to France. A correspondence was soon afterward begun and carried on by the Honorable Morton McMichael, Mayor of Philadelphia, Senator Henry S. Lane of Indiana, M. R. Muckle of Pennsylvania, and General Charles B. Norton, who had served as a commissioner of the United States at the *Exposition Internationale* of 1867. To these men, more than to others perhaps, must be awarded the honor of having originated the Centennial Exposition. But it is hardly to be supposed that the American people would have failed, from the want of leaders or any other circumstance, to mark with an imposing display the hundredth year of the Republic.

Such was the origin of the movement; but the development of the project was discouraged for a while with considerable opposition and much lukewarmness. The whole scheme was a vision of enthusiasm, a Quixotical dream,—said the critics and objectors. No such an enterprise could be carried through except under the patronage of the Government, and the Government had no right to make appropriations merely to preserve an old reminiscence. We had had enough of the Fourth of July already. Besides,—said the wits and caricaturists,—the other nations would present a ludicrous figure in helping us to celebrate the anniversary of a rebellion which they had tried to crush a hundred years ago. Victoria was expected—so said they—to send over commissioners to heap contumely and contempt on the grave of her grandfather! No nation of Europe would consent to its own stultification by joining in the jubilee of republicanism. Besides all this caviling, it was foreseen that Philadelphia would quite certainly be selected as the scene of the proposed display, and on that account a good deal of local jealousy was excited in the other principal cities of the Union. Nevertheless, the advocates of the enterprise continued to urge the feasibility and propriety of the exposition; the more enlightened newspapers of the country lent their influence, and the popular voice soon declared in favor of the measure.

As early as the beginning of 1870, the general plan and principal features of the celebration had been determined in the minds of its projectors. As to the *form* of the display, an International Exposition of Arts and Industries was decided on; as to the *scene*, the city of Philadelphia, hallowed by a thousand Revolutionary memories, was selected; as to the *time*, from the 19th of April to the 19th of October, 1876. The first organized body to give aid and encouragement to the enterprise was the Franklin Institute of Philadelphia. Through the influence of that patriotic organization, a Centennial Commission, consisting of seven members appointed by the city council, was constituted, with John L. Shoemaker as chairman. Shortly afterwards a resolution was adopted by the Legislature of Pennsylvania, invoking the aid of Congress in behalf of the proposed celebration; and on the 3d of March, 1871, a bill was passed by the House of Representatives, which became the basis of all subsequent proceedings relating to the Centennial.

In this bill it was provided that an exhibition of American and Foreign arts, products and manufactures should be held under the auspices of the Government of the United States, in the city of Philadelphia, in 1876; that a Centennial Commission, consisting of one member and one alternate from each State and Territory, should be appointed by the President; that to this board of commissioners should be referred the entire management and responsibility of the enterprise; that the members of the board should receive no compensation; that the United States should not be liable for any of the expenses of the exposition; and that the President, when officially informed that suitable buildings had been erected and adequate provisions made for the proposed exhibition, should make proclamation of that fact to the people of the United States and to all foreign nations. During the year 1871, the Centennial Commission was constituted in accordance with the act of Congress. On the 4th of March, 1872, the members assembled at Philadelphia and effected a permanent organization by the election of General Joseph R. Hawley of Connecticut as President. Orestes Cleveland of New Jersey, John D. Creigh of California, Robert Lowry of Iowa, Robert Mallory of Kentucky, Thomas H. Coldwell of Tennessee, John McNeill of Missouri, and William Gurney of South Carolina, were chosen as the seven vice presidents of the organization. As secretary, Professor John L. Campbell of Indiana was elected. The important office of director-general was conferred on Alfred T. Goshorn of Ohio; and as counselor and solicitor John L. Shoemaker of Pennsylvania was chosen.

General Joseph R. Hawley.

The question of money next engaged the attention of the managers. How to provide the funds necessary for carrying forward so vast an enterprise became a source of much discussion and no little anxiety. The positive refusal of the government to become responsible for any part of the expenses of the Exhibition added to the embarrassment; for it was now seen that private resources and the good will of the people must furnish the entire sum necessary for the success of the enterprise. Several measures were accordingly adopted by the Centennial Commission looking to the creation of a treasury. By an act of Congress, passed on the 1st of June, 1872, provision was made for the organization of a Centennial Board of Finance, to which the whole monetary management of the Exposition should be entrusted. This board was organized by the election of John Welsh of Philadelphia as president. William Sellers and John S. Barbour were chosen vice-presidents. The office of secretary and treasurer was conferred on Frederick Fraley; that of auditor, on H. S. Lansing; and that of financial agent, on William Bigler. The board was authorized to issue stock in shares of ten dollars each, the whole number of shares thus issued not to exceed one million. It was also provided that a series of Centennial Memorial Medals should be struck at the mint of the United States, and that the sale of such medals should be under the exclusive control of the Board of Finance. The medals were elegantly executed in several styles and sizes—of gilt, silver, and bronze—furnishing for after ages an impressive token of the American Republic in its hundredth year.

Careful estimates, made by the Centennial Commission and the Board of Finance, placed the entire expense of the Exposition at *eight million five hundred thousand dollars.* Of this sum about two and a half millions were raised by the sale of stock—a work which was at first entrusted to the banks of the country and afterward to a Bureau of Revenue established for that purpose. Long before this amount was secured, however, the legislature of Pennsylvania made a glorious record for that State by appropriating one million dollars for the Exhibition. The "City of Brotherly Love" did better still by voting the sum of one million five hundred thousand dollars. The people of New York City made a contribution of a quarter of a million. The State of New Jersey gave a hundred thousand dollars; New Hampshire, Connecticut, and Delaware, ten thousand dollars each. But notwithstanding these magnificent contributions, the aggregate sum fell far short of the estimates; and the Centennial Commission—in the face of the former illiberal action of Congress—resolved to make a second appeal to that body for help. A bill was accordingly prepared, asking for an appropriation of three million dollars from the national treasury; but on the 6th of May, 1874, the bill was decisively defeated—an act well calculated to bring the American name into contempt and shame.[35] The managers of the Exposition were again thrown back upon the people for sympathy and aid.

---

[35] After times may be astonished to know that the empire of Japan cheerfully contributed six hundred thousand dollars to the success of the American Centennial after the Congress or the United States had twice refused to vote a cent.

Centennial Medal.— Obverse.   Centennial Medal.— Reverse.

Meanwhile, the sale of stock and of medals, as well as other enterprises for the increase of the Centennial funds, was going on successfully. The Exposition gained constantly in public favor. Even in the Far West, Centennial orators traveled through the country districts, stirring up the enthusiasm of the people. The public Free Schools, by exhibitions and excursions, contributed their part towards the success of the great celebration. In June of 1874, the President of the United States extended a cordial invitation to all the civilized nations of the world to participate in an International Exhibition of Arts, Manufactures, and Products of the Soil and Mine, to be held in the city of Philadelphia in 1876, in honor of the one hundredth anniversary of American Independence. By and by, the contagion spread even to Congress, and that body passed an act appropriating five hundred and five thousand dollars for the erection of a Centennial Building in honor of the United States and for the illustration of the functions and resources of the American Government in times of peace and of war. The legislatures of several of the States also became interested in the enterprise, and made appropriations—ranging from five thousand to fifty thousand dollars—for the purpose of erecting State Buildings on the Exhibition grounds, the sum thus contributed amounting to nearly a half million dollars. Finally, as the success of the Exposition became more and more assured, the patriotism of the people and the clamors of the press *drove* the national Congress into an appropriation of a million five hundred thousand dollars to supply the deficit which was still reported by the Board of Finance. Such were the principal measures by which the Centennial fund was finally secured.

One of the first matters to which the attention of the Centennial Commission was directed, was the selection of suitable grounds for holding the Exposition. But that problem was soon solved in the most satisfactory manner. By the act of March 3d, 1871, it was decided by Congress that the Exhibition should be held within the corporate limits of Philadelphia. The authorities of that city, throwing their whole energies into the enterprise, at once proffered to the commissioners the free use of Fairmount Park, one of the largest and most magnificent in the world. This beautiful tract, presenting every variety of surface, well wooded and well watered, extends on both sides of the Schuylkill for more than seven miles, and along the banks of the Wissahickon for nearly the same distance. The entire park embraces two thousand seven hundred and forty acres, and presents to the eye every thing that is lovely and refreshing in woodland scenery, beautified and adorned by the hand of art. The portion of the grounds more particularly set apart for the purposes of the Exposition, including an area of four hundred and fifty acres, lies on the right bank of the Schuylkill, below Belmont, and was formerly known as the old Lansdowne Estate.

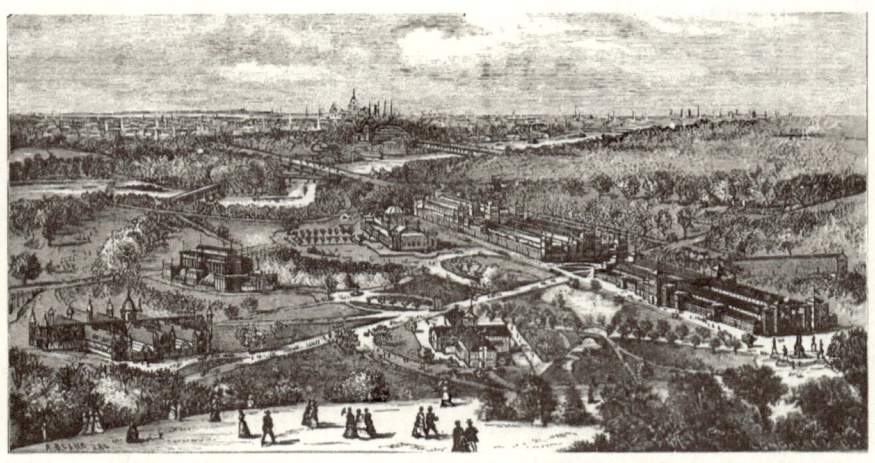

The Centennial Grounds and Buildings.

The formal transfer of the grounds to the Centennial Commission was made on the 4th of July, 1873. An immense throng of citizens and strangers gathered in the park to witness the ceremonies. The address of presentation was made by the Honorable Morton McMichael of Philadelphia, and the response by General Hawley, president of the Commission. The dedicatory oration was then delivered by Governor Hartranft of Pennsylvania, who, after reciting the congressional acts and various other measures upon which the Centennial enterprise had thus far proceeded, continued in the following eloquent manner:

"We have assembled here to dedicate a portion of this beautiful park to the uses of a great International Exhibition, which is to commemorate the anniversary of our country's birth. Upon the threshold of the century to expire in 1876, thirteen poor and feeble colonies, with no common ties other than their love of liberty and hatred of oppression, declared their independence. These Thirteen Colonies, with their offspring, now increased in number to thirty-seven, stretch their empire across a continent, and afford the grandest exhibition of a nation's progress in the world's history. In all the wondrous changes wrought in the nineteenth century, none are so wondrous and conspicuous as the industrial, moral, and physical growth of this our native land. With those powerful auxiliaries, steam and the telegraph—both of which our country gave to mankind—we are striding with majestic steps toward a dominion unrivaled by any other nation on the face of the earth. Let us, then, from every State—north, south, east, and west—bring to this great city, the consecrated place where our liberty was born, the evidences of our culture, the proofs of our skill, and our vast and varied resources, that the world may have a glimpse of our enlargement, industry, wealth, and power. To the myriads who will gather here, let us accord a welcome which shall be in keeping with the dignity and magnitude of our country. Here, too, let our own people gather, garnering new and fresh ideas from a survey of the world's arts and industries; and let us dedicate ourselves to a higher civilization, to more extensive fields of development, to more liberal and more widely diffused education, to the purification of our institutions, and to the preservation of that liberty which is the foundation-stone of our prosperity and happiness."

Governor Hartranft was followed by George M. Robeson, secretary of the navy, who read a proclamation by the President of the United States; and then the General Regulations for the government of the Exposition were announced as follows:

I. The International Exhibition of 1876 will be held in Fair mount Park, in the city of Philadelphia, in the year 1876.

II. The date of opening the Exhibition will be April 19th, 1876, and of closing will be October 19th, 1876.

III. A cordial invitation is hereby extended to every nation of the earth to be represented by its arts, industries, progress, and development.

IV. A formal acceptance of this invitation is requested previous to March 4th, 1874.

V. Each nation accepting this invitation is requested to appoint a Commission, through which all matters pertaining to its own interests shall be conducted. For the purpose of convenient intercourse and satisfactory supervision, it is especially desired that one member of every such Commission be designated to reside at Philadelphia until the close of the Exposition.

VI. The privileges of exhibitors can be granted only to citizens of countries whose governments have formally accepted the invitation to be represented, and have appointed the aforementioned Commission; and all communications must be made through the Governmental Commissions.

VII. Applications for space within the Exposition buildings, or in the adjacent buildings and grounds under the control of the Centennial Commission, must be made previous to March 4th, 1875.

VIII. Full diagrams of the buildings and grounds will be furnished to the Commissioners of the different nations which shall accept the invitation to participate.

IX. All articles intended for exhibition, in order to secure proper position and classification, must be in Philadelphia on or before January 1st, 1876.

X. Acts of Congress pertaining to custom-house regulations, duties, etc., together with all special regulations adopted by the Centennial Commission in reference to transportation, allotment of space, classification, motive power, insurance, police rules, and other matters necessary to the proper display and preservation of materials,—will be promptly communicated to the accredited representatives of the several governments cooperating in the Exposition.

On the day after the dedication of the grounds in Fairmount Park, a copy of the President's proclamation, already mentioned, was transmitted to each of the foreign ministers resident at Washington. At the same time, the American secretary of state notified the ministers that the proposed display was intended as an International Exhibition of Arts, Manufactures, and Products of the Soil and Mine; that the special design of the Exposition was to commemorate the Declaration of the Independence of the United States; that another prime object was to furnish to all nations an opportunity for mutual improvement and a higher culture in beholding the products of each other's civilization that the President of the United States indulged the hope that all the diplomatic representatives of foreign nations would bring the Exposition and its objects to the attention of the people of their respective countries; and that the Exhibition might greatly conduce to the establishment and perpetuation of international friendship and good will. These official communications were cordially received by the foreign ministers and by the governments which they represented. The President's invitations were quickly accepted; and before the expiration of the allotted time, the following nations had notified the American Government of their desire and intention to participate in the Exposition: The Argentine Confederation, Austria, Belgium, Bolivia, Brazil, Chili, China, Denmark, Ecuador, Egypt, France (including Algeria), German Empire Great Britain and her Colonies, Greece, Guatemala, Hawaii, Hayti, Honduras, Italy, Japan, Liberia, Mexico, Netherlands, Nicaragua, Norway, Orange Free State, Persia, Peru, Portugal, Russia, Siam, Spain, Sweden, Switzerland, Tunis, Turkey, United States of Colombia, Venezuela.

One of the earliest and most difficult of the subjects which engaged the attention of the Centennial Commission was the proper analysis and classification of the materials to be exhibited. Until this question was settled it could not be known what buildings to erect or how to erect them. Nor could the various nations know in advance how to select and arrange their products so as to come into proper competition with each other, until a General Classification should be prepared and reported. It was foreseen, moreover, that a mistake in this regard would be in a great measure fatal to the success of the Exposition, as a bad classification would be sure to result in heaping up in the Centennial buildings a vast and chaotic mass of materials which nobody could appreciate or understand. In this important work of classification the Commissioners—considering the magnitude and novelty of the task imposed upon them—succeeded admirably. It was decided to arrange all of the materials which should be presented for exhibition in ten great classes or departments, the names of which should suggest, even to the common beholder, the particular object on display. The following was the General Classification adopted by the Commission:

I. RAW MATERIALS; Mineral, Vegetable, and Animal.

II. MATERIALS AND MANUFACTURES USED FOR FOOD OR IN THE ARTS; the results of Extractive or Combining Processes.

III. TEXTILE AND FELTED FABRICS; Apparel, Costumes, and Personal Ornaments.

IV. FURNITURE AND MANUFACTURES OF GENERAL USE IN CONSTRUCTION AND IN DWELLINGS;

V. TOOLS, IMPLEMENTS, MACHINES, AND PROCESSES.

VI. MOTORS AND TRANSPORTATION.

VII. APPARATUS AND METHODS FOR THE INCREASE AND DIFFUSION OR KNOWLEDGE.

VIII. ENGINEERING; Public Works, Architecture, etc.

IX. PLASTIC AND GRAPHIC ARTS.

X. OBJECTS ILLUSTRATING EFFORTS FOR THE IMPROVEMENT OF THE PHYSICAL, INTELLECTUAL, AND MORAL CONDITION OF MAN.

Each of these general departments was divided and subdivided until a proper classification of all the materials about to be exhibited was secured.

To erect buildings suitable in character and capacity—buildings illustrative of the taste, equal to the enterprise, and worthy of the genius of the American people—was the next great duty devolved upon the Centennial Commission. Here success was necessary. To succeed was to elicit the admiration of every people; to fail was to fail ingloriously. The reputation of the United States was at stake. For the foremost men of all the world, the savants of Europe and Asia—art critics, wits, and journalists; statesmen, poets, and philosophers; admirers of the beautiful, keen-scented satirists, and dislikers of republicanism out of every clime under heaven—were sure to gaze upon and criticise whatever should be built in Fairmount Park, and to carry abroad the story of our honor or our disgrace. Grand and imposing structures would add to the dignity of the great occasion. Mean and insignificant buildings would insure a mean and insignificant exhibition, and that, in its turn, would produce among all nations a contemptuous estimate of the American people and their institutions.

After much deliberation, the Centennial Commission determined upon the erection of five principal buildings, the name and character of each to be determined by the nature of the materials therein to be displayed. The first of these, called THE MAIN BUILDING, was designed with special reference to the exhibition of Products of the Mine, Workmanship in the Metals, Manufactures in general, Educational and Scientific displays. The second building—called THE MEMORIAL HALL, or ART GALLERY—was planned for the exhibition of the Fine Arts in all their various branches and modifications—Sculpture, Painting, Engraving, Lithography, Photography, Industrial and Architectural Designs, Decorations, and Mosaics. The third principal building was named MACHINERY HALL, and was designed for the display of Machines of every pattern and purpose known to man—Motors, Generators of Power, Pneumatic and Hydraulic Apparatuses, Railway Engirery, and Contrivances for Aerial and Water Transportation. The fourth edifice projected by the Commissioners was called AGRICULTURAL HALL, and was planned for the exhibition of all Tree and Forest Products, Fruits of every grade and description, Agricultural Products proper, Land and Marine Animals including the Apparatus used in the Care and Culture of the same, Animal and Vegetable Products, Textile Materials, Implements and Processes peculiar to Agriculture, Farm Engineering, Tillage and General Management of Field, Forest, and Homestead. The fifth and last building, called HORTICULTURAL HALL, was designed for the proper display of Ornamental Trees, Shrubs, and Flowers—Hot-houses, Conservatories, Graperies; Tools, Accessories, Designs, Construction, and Management of Gardens. Such was the general plan under which the principal edifices of Fairmount Park were begun.

On the 4th of July, 1874, the foundations of Memorial Hall were laid with appropriate ceremonies. In the following September, work was begun on the Main Building, and was steadily carried forward during the whole of the next year and until the beginning of February, 1876, when the immense structure was completed. Machinery Hall was built between the months of January and October, 1875. On the 1st of May, in the same year, the foundations of Horticultural Hall were laid, and the building was brought to completion April 1st, 1876. Agricultural Hall was not begun until September of 1875, but the work was carried forward so rapidly that the edifice was completed by the middle of the following April. Meanwhile, the work on THE GOVERNMENT BUILDING, the construction of which had been provided for by the congressional act of March 3d, 1875, was pressed to completion early in 1876. Moreover, it had become apparent to the Commissioners that the space provided in Memorial Hall would by no means accommodate the immense exhibition of Fine Arts which was now confidently expected; and an ART ANNEX was accordingly planned and built. It was also found from the rapidly accumulating applications for space that the Main Building itself would be filled to overflowing; and two Annexes—the principal one for carriages and the other for the display of the Minerals of the United States—were accordingly added to that immense structure.

Other buildings—illustrative of various interests and enterprises brought together from the ends of the earth—were rapidly planned and constructed. A WOMAN'S PAVILION, projected and carried to completion by an organization called the Women's Centennial Executive Committee, was begun in the middle of October, 1875, and finished in the following January. The building was designed for the special exhibition of whatever woman's skill, patience and genius have produced, and are producing, in the way of handicraft, invention, decorations, letters, and art. Next came the several States and Territories, selecting grounds and constructing a series of STATE BUILDINGS, commemorative of the spirit and illustrating the resources of the respective commonwealths of the Union. Nearly all the foreign nations participating in the Exposition made haste to erect, for their own convenience and for the honor of native land elegant GOVERNMENT BUILDINGS—French, Spanish, or British—which became a kind of head-quarters and rendezvous for the several nationalities. Then came model dwellings and Bazaars, School houses and Restaurants, Judges' Halls and model Factories, Newspaper Buildings and Ticket Offices,—until the Centennial grounds (capacious as they were) were filled with—shall it be called a city?—the most imposing, spacious, and ornate ever seen in the world. A more complete description of some of those grand structures will here be appropriate.

The first and largest of them all was the Main Building, situated immediately east of the intersection of Belmont and Elm Avenues. The edifice was in the form of a parallelogram, having a length from east to west of eighteen hundred and eighty feet,[36] and a breadth from north to south of four hundred and sixty-four feet. The building throughout its greater extent was one story high, the main cornice being forty-five feet from the ground. The general height within was seventy feet, rising to ninety feet under the principal arcades. From each of the four corners of the building rose a rectangular tower forty-eight feet square and seventy-five feet high. Over the central portion of the main structure a raised roof one hundred and eighty-four feet square was likewise surmounted at the corners by four towers a hundred and twenty feet in height. In the middle of the two sides, looking north and south, were the principal projections, four hundred and sixteen feet in length. The corresponding projections at the ends were two hundred and sixteen feet long, and extended, the western in the direction of Machinery Hall, and the eastern towards the city. In these four projections were placed the main entrances to the building; that on the east facing the carriage-ways to the city; the southern receiving passengers from the street-cars and the dépôt of the Pennsylvania Railway; the western being rather an exit to other

---

[36] Eighteen hundred and seventy-six feet (the Centennial number) in the clear.

parts of the grounds than an entrance proper; and the northern facing Memorial Hall and the Schuylkill.

Main Exposition Building.

In the ground-plan of this immense building a central nave or avenue, a hundred and twenty feet in width, traversed the main diameter to the distance of eighteen hundred and thirty-two feet. Parallel with this, two side aisles a hundred feet wide, and of the same length with the principal nave, divided the spaces between the same and the sides of the building. These three main avenues were intersected at right angles by cross aisles forty-eight feet in width, dividing the whole area of the floor into blocks or squares, with spacious avenues entirely around them. The principal nave and its parallel aisles were likewise intersected by the main and two subordinate transepts, dividing the central space of the ground-floor into nine great squares, free from columnar support, and embracing an area of over a hundred and seventy-three thousand square feet. The entire area of the ground floor was eight hundred and seventy-two thousand three hundred and twenty square feet; of the floors in the projections, thirty-seven thousand three hundred and forty-four feet; of the tower floors, twenty-six thousand three hundred and forty-four feet;—making an aggregate area of nine hundred and thirty-six thousand and eight square feet, or *twenty-one and forty-seven hundredths acres!* The ground-floor proper covered a space of a little more than twenty acres.[37]

---

[37] A comparison of the leading Centennial buildings (in respect of dimensions) with other famous edifices may prove of interest.

The building was chiefly of iron and glass, and contained a mass of material unprecedented in the history of architecture. The outer walls were carried up in brick-work to the height of seven feet from the foundations, which consisted of stone piers of the most substantial masonry. Above the brick-work the panels between the columns of support were occupied with glazed sash, sections of which were movable for purposes of ventilation. The roof was of tin, laid solidly on boards of pine; and the exterior ornaments—abounding on all the corners, angles, and towers—were of galvanized iron. The columns of interior support—numbering six hundred and seventy-two, and ranging from twenty-three to one hundred and twenty-five feet in length—were of rolled iron, and had an aggregate weight of two million two hundred thousand pounds. The roof trusses and girders were of the same material, and weighed about five million pounds. No less than seven million feet of lumber were used in the construction of the building. The water and drainage pipes—laid for the most part underneath the floor—were four miles in length. Light—whether streaming through acres of stained and fretted glass by day, or blazing from thousands of gas-jets and burnished reflectors by night—was equally and abundantly distributed. Hydrants—everywhere and ever full—promised security against the destroyer.

NAME OF STRUCTURE.		AREA OF GROUND-FLOOR.		
Main Exposition Building,	872,320	Square feet,	20.02	Acres.
Machinery Hall,	558,440	----"-----"	12.82	"
Agricultural Hall,	442,800	----"-----"	10.16	"
Memorial Hall,	73,912	----"-----"	1.76	"
The Louvre (including the court),	309,888	----"-----"	1.69	"
St. Peter's,	273,927	----"-----"	7.11	"
The Capitol,	261,348	----"-----"	6.28	"
The Coliseum,	245,340	----"-----"	6.00	"
St. Paul's,	142,500	----"-----"	5.63	"
Cathedral of Milan,	139,968	----"-----"	3.27	"
Tuileries,	108,864	----"-----"	3.21	"
Westminster,	103,733	----"-----"	2.50	"
St. Sophia,	82,600	----"-----"	2.38	"
St. Stephen's,	81,420	----"-----"	1.89	"
Notre Dame,	56.160	----"-----"	1.27	"

Such were the principal features of the largest, if not the most imposing, edifice in the world. The general effect, notwithstanding the immense size of the building, was especially airy and pleasing. Happy proportions and the regularity of irregularity reduced the apparent dimensions of the mammoth pavilion till the vision was nowhere oppressed with a sense of cumbrous outlines or heaviness of structure. In practical adaptation to the purposes for which it was designed, the building was all that could be desired; and in its effect upon that sense—call it by what name you will—which takes cognizance of the sublime and beautiful, there was small room for caviling and criticism. From the great towers and observatories, rising grandly above the roof, the eye of the beholder, sweeping around the horizon, drank in without fatigue the historic outline of the surrounding country and the midsummer glories of Fairmount Park. Here wound the Schuylkill. Yonder was Laurel Hill, where Elisha Kent Kane sleeps in an uninscribed grave on the rocky hillside. No need of epitaphs for such as him! Farther on there came a glimpse of Germantown, where through the fogs and desolations of that forbidding October day-dawn a hundred years ago the greatest man of all history, at the head of his ragged and half-starved army, struggled against the foe. Here to the east, spreading away from the very feet of the beholder to the distant rolling Delaware, and right and left to the skirts of the horizon, slumbered under the summer sun the old City of Penn, where in those same heroic days, now gliding dreamily into the shadows of the past, Adams and Jefferson and Franklin did the bravest deed in the civil history of the human race. Such were the thrilling associations which clustered around the great Centennial Building. Only one melancholy reflection arose to trouble the soul of the beholder: the grand edifice was designed only as a *temporary* structure—meant to subserve the fleeting purposes of the International Exhibition.

The building second in importance, though not in size, among the Centennial structures, was the Memorial Hall, or Art Gallery. It stands upon a broad terrace in the Lansdowne Plateau at the distance of two hundred and fifty feet from the north projection of the Main Building, and a hundred and sixteen feet above the level of the Schuylkill. The structure is of iron, granite, and glass, and is in that modern style of architecture called the *Renaissance*. The building is in the form of a rectangular parallelogram, and is three hundred and sixty-five feet in length, two hundred and ten feet wide, and fifty-nine feet in height above a twelve-foot basement of stone. The dome, also rectangular in form, rises a hundred and fifty feet above the terrace, and is surmounted with a colossal bell bearing a magnificent statue of the goddess America, cast in zinc, twenty-three and a half feet in height, and weighing six thousand pounds. At the four corners of the base of the dome are seated other statues representing the four quarters of the globe. The floor of the main hall below has an area of more than a half acre, and is capable of accommodating eight thousand spectators at one time. In its architectural elements the building embraces hints derived from many styles, some of which—as, for instance, the arcades—date back as far as the villas of Ancient Rome; but the general effect is that of unity, elegance, and grandeur.

Memorial Hall.

The Centennial surroundings of Memorial Hall were appropriate and striking. Before the main entrance and on either hand were stationed two colossal bronze pegasi curbed by the Muses. On the south-west angle of the terrace a group of statuary, also in bronze, represented the firing of a mortar and the flight of the shell, watched by the men of the battery; while on the southeast angle a corresponding group depicted a dying lioness, surrounded by her whelps and guarded by her lord.

Opposite the main entrances of the edifice the terrace was ascended by flights of stone steps, spacious and grand; and the beholder, when for the first time he reached the plateau, found himself face to face with an edifice among the most novel and beautiful in the New World. As he stood midway between the site of the Main Building and Memorial Hall, he saw, on the one hand, a mammoth structure designed for the exhibition of all things practical, utilitarian, and profitable among the products of thought and application; and, on the other, a temple fit for the repose and revelation of all things ideal, beautiful, and sublime among the trophies of human genius.

The Art Gallery was built at a cost of a million five hundred thousand dollars. The funds for this purpose were the joint contribution of Philadelphia and the State of Pennsylvania. The building was designed as a *permanent* structure, affording for present time a suitable gallery for the Fine Art display of the International Exhibition, and, in its final purpose, becoming a national memorial of the Centennial year. After the close of the Exposition, the edifice was converted, according to the purpose of its founders, into a receptacle for the Pennsylvania Museum of Industrial Art,—an institution similar to that of South Kensington, in London. When the other structures, many in purpose and fashion, which the Centennial celebration had caused to spring up in Fairmount Park, were struck from their foundations—disappearing even as they came, like an exhalation of the night,—Memorial Hall, with its higher purpose and destiny, was happily preserved for after ages as an enduring monument of the artistic taste and patriotism of the American people.

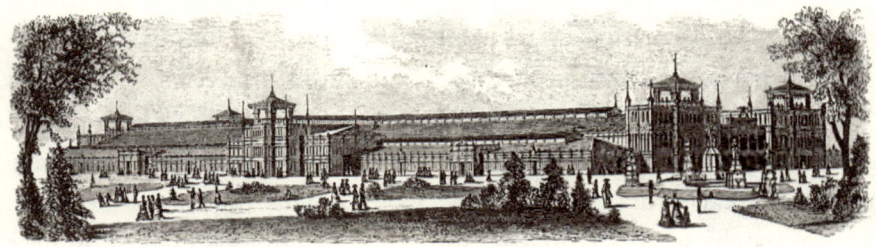

Maschinery Hall.

In its general plan and outline Machinery Hall was similar to the Main Exposition Building, and only second thereto in dimensions. The ground-plan was a rectangular parallelogram fourteen hundred and two feet in length, and three hundred and sixty feet in width. On the south side the central transept of the main hall projected into an Annex, two hundred and eight feet in depth by two hundred and ten feet in breadth. On the north the front of the principal structure was on a right line with the corresponding front of the Main Building, and the two edifices were separated by an intervening space or promenade of only five hundred and forty-two feet; so that, glancing from the east end of the Main Building to the western extreme of Machinery Hall, the eye swept along an almost unbroken front line *more than seventy-two hundredths of a mile in length!* The principal materials used in the construction of Machinery Hall were iron and glass. The piers of the foundation were of stone, and the supporting columns, for the most part, of wood. The main cornice without was forty feet from the ground, and the general height within was seventy feet. The building was painted in a pleasing tint of purplish blue, relieved by various hues of contrasted colors. At the four corners and over the main side-entrances stood the towers, a hundred feet in height, breaking up in some measure the otherwise monotonous outline of the building. In the north-east tower was hung the famous chime of bells, thirteen in number, weighing twenty-one thousand pounds,—many-tongued and clamorous with the silver music which they flung out upon the air in honor of the Old Thirteen States. Over the central gallery a royal bald-eagle looked down upon the great clock which calmly marked the hours of the Centennial summer.

Machinery Hall could hardly be called a thing of beauty: it was too long and low for that;—but if adaptability to the purposes for which it was designed be a criterion, the structure was by no means wanting in taste. American civilization is the civilization of utility, invention, and mechanism. The engine is the emblem, and *Quæ Prosunt Omnibus* the motto, over the doorway of our temple. On the porches and architrave of what great structure might the emblem and the motto be more appropriately set than on the arches of Machinery Hall? For here Invention was queen, and Utility her minister of state. Here was the realm where Thought had the mastery over Matter—the empire of wheels and pistons, where Steam was the Mother of Motion.—All this and more was foreshadowed and provided for in the grand structure designed by the Centennial Commission for the display of machinery.

Agricultural Hall.

The fourth principal building of the Exposition grounds was Agricultural Hall, situated on the eastern side of Belmont Avenue, and beyond the valley of the same name. The ground-plan of the edifice presented a central nave eight hundred and twenty feet in length, and one hundred and twenty-five feet wide. This principal aisle was crossed at right angles by a main and two subordinate transepts–the former one hundred feet, and the latter eighty feet, in width. The projections of these transepts formed two courts on either side of the main structure, which, together with the four spaces similarly formed at the corners of the building, were enclosed with fronts and roofs,–whereby the edifice was extended into an immense parallelogram eight hundred and twenty feet long, and five hundred and forty feet in width. The entire area thus embraced in the ground-floor was *ten and three-tenths acres.*

As to its style, Agricultural Hall had a touch of Gothicism—suggested by the Howe truss-arches of the nave and transepts—in its construction. Over the bisection of the central avenue and the main transept, rose an elegant cupola surmounted by a weather-vane. The entrances were ornamental, and at each side were handsome turrets. The roofs were pointed, stained a greenish tint, and flecked with sky lights. The body of the building was composed of wood, iron, and glass, and was painted brown. The general effect was pleasing, and a bird's-eye view revealed in the edifice and its surroundings a picturesqueness hardly discoverable in any other of the Exposition structures. This building, being devoted to the general purposes of an agricultural display, had the necessary concomitant of yards for the exhibition of all the domestic fowls and animals. The entire cost of Agricultural Hall was nearly two hundred and sixty thousand dollars. The building was a temporary structure, and at the close of the Exposition was taken down and removed from the Park.

In the erection of Horticultural Hall—fifth and smallest of the main Exhibition edifices—the Centennial committees displayed their liking for the Moors. For the building is Arabesque in its architecture. The twelfth century furnishes the model, and the nineteenth does the work. As to situation, Horticultural Hall stands on the Lansdowne Terrace, north of the valley, overlooking the Schuylkill. As to materials,—iron, glass, and wood. As to dimensions,—three hundred and eighty-three feet long, one hundred and ninety-three feet broad, and sixty-nine feet to the top of the lantern. As to cost,—three hundred thousand dollars. As to purpose,—a temple of flowers. As to destiny,—a permanent ornament of Fairmount Park. For the city of Philadelphia contributed the funds for the building, and decided that it should stand in spite of the general demolition and temple-crushing which prevailed at the close of the Exposition.

Next among the notable structures of the Exhibition grounds was that building provided for by the Congressional act of March 3d, 1875, and called the United States Government Building. It stood on Belmont Avenue, northward from Machinery Hall. The ground plan was a cross, with the main stem four hundred and eighty feet, and the transept three hundred and forty feet, in length. In the central part, the building was two stories in height. Over the bisection of the nave and transept rose an octagonal dome, surmounted by a flag-staff. The edifice was elegantly painted, the prevailing color being brown. The roof was black, the dome in imitation of wood, and all the ceilings blue. The walls within were divided into panels, in each of which was laid off a diamond-shaped space containing in its center an emblem representing some department or function of the Government. The general effect of the building was that of airiness and ease—hardly to have been expected in an edifice so strongly and heavily built.

Horticultural Hall.

The Woman's Pavilion, already mentioned, was located at the western end of the Horticultural section of the grounds, and was one of the most beautiful of the Centennial buildings. The structure was of wood and glass. Here again the ground-plan was a cross, each of the arms being a hundred and ninety-two feet long, and sixty-four feet in width. The end of each transept was adorned with an elegant porch; and the spaces in the corners—formed by the four projections of the building—were converted into four minor pavilions, and made an integral part of the main hall. Within, there were in all only four columns of support, the roof resting mainly upon the outside walls. The whole interior was painted in delicate tints of blue, the color without being gray. The central part of the building, surmounted by a lantern bearing a cupola, rose to the height of ninety feet. The ground-floor embraced an area of nearly seven-tenths of an acre.

The British Government Building, generally called "St. George's House," stood on George's Hill, and was the head-quarters of the British commissioners. The edifice, embracing in the ground-plan an area of twenty-two hundred and fifty square feet, was in the style of architecture prevalent in the times of Queen Elizabeth. The roof was composed of red tiles; and the fixtures, furniture, and decorations were all after models which were fashionable at the close of the sixteenth century. The building, which was two stories high, was very handsome—even elegant—in its general appearance, recalling forcibly to mind the most brilliant and romantic period in English history. St. George's House was designed for the accommodation not only of the commissioners from the home empire of Great Britain, but also for the use and comfort of the agents from the British colonial possessions in different parts of the world.

Department of Public Comfort.

The Building of the French Government was located eastward from Memorial Hall. The ground-plan was a parallelogram sixty feet long by forty feet in width. The structure was composed of brick, iron, and glass, and in its general aspect was not unworthy to express the interest felt by the authorities of the Third Republic in the American Centennial. The building was designed to subserve the double purpose of a home for the French Commission and of a hall for the display of models representing the public works of France.

The Building of the German Empire was an edifice still more spacious and imposing. It was located east of Belmont Avenue, near the head of the Lansdowne Valley. The structure was an imitation of stone, in the style of the *Renaissance*. The area of the ground-plan was thirty-four hundred and forty-four square feet, being a parallelogram. The main portico and principal hall were very beautiful, and the walls and ceilings were ornamented with frescos in the best style of art. Here were the head-quarters of the Imperial German Commission, and here also was a suite of reception-rooms for the accommodation of strangers and visitors from the different parts of Father-Land.

The single word "ESPANA" over the portal of an elegant frame structure standing on George's Hill, told the beholder that he was at the entrance to the Government Building of Spain. The edifice was of wood, was two stories in height, and eighty by one hundred feet in dimensions. As in the case of the other structures erected by foreign governments, the Spanish Building was intended primarily for the accommodation of the Centennial Commissioners from Spain, and as a place of assembly for Spaniards and their friends who may be present at the Exposition. The secondary design was that of a suitable hall for the display of models and drawings representing the more important public works, fortifications, historical buildings, etc., of Spain.

The Kingdom of Sweden made a unique contribution to the Centennial grounds in the way of a Model School-house. The building was constructed and furnished in Sweden according to the pattern commonly employed in the better class of the national High Schools. The structure was of native wood, unpainted, but brought to a high degree of luster by skillful polishing. The furniture, apparatus, and text-books displayed within, were excellent in their respective kinds; and the building in its entirety was fully worthy of the ten thousand encomiums which were pronounced upon it.

As already mentioned the different States of the Union—excepting Maine, Virginia, North Carolina, South Carolina, Georgia, Florida, Alabama, Louisiana, Texas, Kentucky, Minnesota, and Oregon—erected buildings on the Centennial grounds, commemorative of the history, public spirit, and resources of the respective commonwealths. These structures varied greatly in their style, expensiveness, and proportions—according to the liberality or parsimony of the several State authorities. The buildings of New York, New Jersey, Pennsylvania, Ohio, and Kansas were perhaps superior to any others of this class in elegance of design and structure. Of similar sort was the splendid Educational Hall of Pennsylvania, designed for the display, by models and model-work, of all the methods and products of education in the Keystone State.

Woman's Pavillion.

Of private structures the grounds were full. There was a commodious and valuable edifice situated at the intersection of the Agricultural Avenue with that of the Republic, called the Department of Public Comfort—a name significant of its design. An elegant building, devoted to the displays of the Singer Sewing Machine Company, stood on the southern declivity of the Lansdowne Valley, north of the Art Gallery. Southward from Machinery Hall a Shoe and Leather Building had been erected, the design of which was to illustrate the various processes and products of that important branch of manufacture. The Building of the Centennial Photographic Association was located on the east side of Belmont Avenue, and was a spacious edifice where all the processes of photography were illustrated. Several of the leading newspapers of the country had buildings of limited size, where their respective publications were advertised and offered for sale. Then came the restaurants, cafés, and bazaars, varying in their sort from common-place and mediocrity to a high degree of elegance and luxury.—An extended description of structures of this grade and fashion would hardly be appropriate in an abridged history of the great Exhibition.

This account of the Exposition buildings can not be better concluded than by a brief reference to the unexpected and extraordinary part which the Empire of Japan had taken in the Centennial. The Japanese buildings—two in number—though neither elaborate in their style nor expensive in construction, were far more elegant, tasteful, and commodious than had been anticipated. The Japanese Dwelling stood on George's Hill, north of the Spanish Government Building; and the oriental edifice *was the better of the two!* Spain, whose immortal navigator of the fifteenth century "gave a New World to Castile and Leon," did obeisance at the American Centennial to the dusky Island Empire of the Far Pacific! The Bazaar of these progressive foreigners was located near the Building of Public Comfort, and extended around three sides of a court. The edifice was of carved wood, built without nails, low in elevation, covered with tiles. The grounds were laid off in the style of a Japanese garden, and were surrounded with a quaint fence of interwoven bamboo. These buildings, however, creditable as they were, by no means did justice to the enterprise and wit of the men who had them in charge. The people of the Western Nations have felt a keen surprise at the intelligence, public spirit, and progress manifested by the Japanese at the Centennial Exhibition.

Such were the buildings erected for the great occasion. And the time drew near when they were to fulfill their purpose. On the 5th of January, 1876, the formal reception of articles for the Exposition was begun. From that time forth the work of setting in proper array the almost infinite variety of materials which came pouring in from all quarters of the world, was pressed with the utmost expedition by the Centennial Commissioners. A branch track of the Pennsylvania Railway was laid to the very portals of the great halls, and every measure was adopted by the managers which could facilitate the delivery and arrangement of the articles of display. Still, there were delays, foreseen and unforeseen; and it became apparent that a brief postponement of the formal opening of the Exhibition would be necessary. The anniversary of the battle of Lexington had been fixed upon as a suitable time for the inaugural ceremonies; but the work lagged, and the Commissioners reluctantly changed the date of opening to the 10th of May, and of closing to the 10th of November.

Meanwhile, on the 13th of October, 1875, A SYSTEM OF AWARDS had been adopted by the Centennial Commission. The members of that body—availing themselves of past experience, and improving upon the imperfect methods employed by the managers of the International Expositions of Paris and Vienna—presented the following General Scheme:

I. Awards shall be based upon Written Reports, attested by the signatures of their authors.

II. Two hundred Judges shall be appointed to make such reports, one-half of whom shall be foreigners, and one-half citizens of the United States. They shall be selected for their known qualifications and character, and shall be experts in the departments to which they shall be respectively assigned. The foreign members of this body shall be appointed by the commissioners of each country, and in conformity with the distribution and allotment to each, which will be hereafter announced. The judges from the United States shall be appointed by the Centennial Commission.

III. The sum of one thousand dollars will be paid to each commissioned judge, for personal expenses.

IV. Reports and awards shall be based upon Merit. The elements of merit shall be held to include considerations relating to originality, invention, discovery, utility, quality, skill, workmanship, fitness for the purposes intended, adaptation to public wants, economy, and cost.

V. Each report shall be delivered to the Centennial Commission as soon as completed, for final award and publication.

VI. Awards shall be finally decreed by the United States Centennial Commission, in compliance with the act of Congress, and shall consist of a Diploma, with a uniform bronze Medal, and a special Report of the judges on the subject of the award.

VII. Each exhibitor shall have the right to reproduce and publish the report awarded to him, but the United States Centennial Commission reserves the right to publish and dispose of all reports in the manner it thinks best for public information, and also to embody and distribute the reports as records of the Exhibition.

The day of opening came. Philadelphia was thronged with strangers from all parts of the world. Every line of travel contributed its multitude. The morning of the 10th of May broke heavily with clouds and rain. But patriotism made gloom impossible in the Quaker City, and enthusiasm supplied the place of sunshine. A thousand flags fluttered in every street, and more than ten times ten thousand people, cheering as they went, pressed their way towards Fairmount Park. A military escort, four thousand strong, conducted the President of the United States to the Centennial grounds. For it was he who should declare the formal opening of the Exposition. The notables of many nations had already preceded him to the scene of the ceremonies. The great open space—traversed by the Avenue of the Republic—between the Main Building and Memorial Hall, had been prepared for the inauguration. There had assembled the Supreme Court of the United States, members of the Cabinet and the American Congress, the governors of many of the States, distinguished officers of the army and navy, the ministers from foreign countries, Dom Pedro II. of Brazil and his queen, illustrious civilians, statesmen and diplomatists, noblemen with titles and greater men without them,—to witness the imposing pageant.

At the appointed hour the splendid orchestra, led by Theodore Thomas, burst forth with the national airs of the various countries participating in the Exhibition. Soon the President ascended the platform and was seated, with the Brazilian Emperor and Empress on his right. Then followed Wagner's celebrated *Centennial Inauguration March*, composed for the occasion. Matthew Simpson, bishop of the Methodist Episcopal Church, then offered an eloquent and fervent prayer, which was followed by the singing of John G. Whittier *Centennial Hymn*. When the strains had died away, the Honorable John Welsh, chairman of the Board of Finance, arose and made a formal presentation of the buildings and grounds to General Hawley, president of the Centennial Commission. The latter, in an appropriate manner, accepted the trust; and then followed the singing of Sidney Lanier's

Centennial Cantata. General Hawley next delivered an address, recounting briefly the things accomplished by the Centennial Commission, and in the name thereof presenting to the President of the United States THE INTERNATIONAL EXHIBITION OF 1876. The President—most famous of all American chief-magistrates for *not* delivering orations—replied to General Hawley in the following well-chosen address:—

Inaugural Ceremonies of the Centennial Exhibition

"MY COUNTRYMEN: It has been thought appropriate, upon this Centennial occasion, to bring together in Philadelphia, for popular inspection, specimens of our attainments in the Industrial and Fine arts, and in literature, science, and philosophy, as well as in the great business of agriculture and commerce. That we may the more thoroughly appreciate the excellencies and deficiencies of our achievements, and also give emphatic expression to our earnest desire to cultivate the friendship of our fellow-members of this great family of nations, the enlightened agricultural, commercial, and manufacturing people of the world have been invited to send hither corresponding specimens of their skill to exhibit on equal terms, in friendly competition with our own.—For so doing we render them our hearty thanks.

"The beauty and utility of the contributions will this day be submitted to your inspection. We are glad to know that a view of specimens of the skill of all nations will afford you unalloyed pleasure, as well as yield to you a valuable practical knowledge of so many of the remarkable results of the wonderful skill existing in enlightened communities.

"One hundred years ago our country was new, and but partially settled. Our necessities have compelled us chiefly to expend our means and time in felling forests, subduing prairies, building dwellings, factories, ships, docks, warehouses, roads, canals, and machinery. Most of our schools, churches, libraries, and asylums have been established within a hundred years. Burdened with these great primal works of necessity, which could not be delayed, we yet have done what this Exhibition will show in the direction of rivaling older and more advanced nations in law, medicine, and theology; in science, literature, philosophy, and the fine arts. Whilst proud of what we have done, we regret that we have not done more. Our achievements have been great enough, however, to make it easy for our people to acknowledge superior merit wherever found.

"And now, fellow-citizens, I hope a careful examination of what is about to be exhibited to you will not only inspire you with a profound respect for the skill and taste of our friends from other nations, but also satisfy you with the attainments made by our own people during the past one hundred years. I invoke your generous cooperation with the worthy Commissioners, to secure a brilliant success to this International Exhibition, and to make the stay of our foreign visitors—to whom we extend a hearty welcome—both profitable and pleasant to them.

"I DECLARE THE INTERNATIONAL EXHIBITION NOW OPEN."

When the President's brief oration was concluded, the National ensign was flung out as a signal from the great flag-staff of the Main Building; the banners of foreign nations were immediately unfurled; cheers rent the air; a salute of a hundred guns from the battery on George's Hill answered to the shout. Memorial Hall, the Main, Building, and Machinery Hall were now thrown open to receive the procession of invited guests—four thousand in number, and first to behold the handiwork of the nations.

General Grant and Major Alfred T. Goshorn, the able and indefatigable Director-General of the Exhibition, led the way from the Main Building, and down the great aisle of Machinery Hall to the center, where a special work had been reserved for the President and the Brazilian Emperor. This honorable duty was to open the valves of the mighty Corliss Engine, whose tremendous pistons were to start into life and motion the in finite machinery of the hall. At twenty minutes past one o'clock, the signal was given by George H. Corliss, the maker of the iron giant. The President and the Emperor, standing upon the raised platform, opened the valves; the ponderous fly-wheel started on its tireless rounds, and the multitudinous engines of the hall began their varied work.— The Centennial Exhibition was fairly inaugurated under the most auspicious omens.

Alfred T. Goshorn.

Such was the beginning. Into the spacious and beautiful park, into the great buildings provided by national wealth and patriotism, had come the products of all lands and the people of all climes. Never before in the history of the world had so many of the fruits of human genius been brought together—never before had so rich a display of the handiwork and skill of man been made. What, therefore, of the Exposition itself? How did it impress the imagination of the beholder? How enlarge his faculties and increase his fund of knowledge? In what way conduce to a higher standard of civilization? For that was the object aimed at.

The first effect of the great Exposition upon the mind of the beholder was *a sense of alarm and bewilderment at the extent of the display.* At the very beginning, he despaired of realizing the exhibition on account of its vast proportions. On ascending from the valley of the Schuylkill to the Lansdowne Plateau, a vision rose upon him possessing every element of intellectual interest, from the simple beauty of the green sward and flower-gardens at his feet, to the stately magnificence of the Main Building and the grandeur of Memorial Hall. Here wound the long asphaltum boulevards, thronged, but not crowded, with ten thousand strangers. Beyond lay a landscape of sloping hill-sides, lakes, forest, and fountains. The entire space, though a most living picture, was noiseless, airy, and clean—a field of many colors, full of sunshine, foliage, and flags. For the banners of all nations waved everywhere.

Entering under the eastern arches of the Main Building, the visitor, rallying from his first surprises, began a work which he should never accomplish—that of examining in detail the exhibits of the great hall. From the gallery overhead floated down upon him the melodious and far-reaching harmonies of the mammoth Hastings organ with its twenty-seven hundred pipes and its twelve hundred and eighty square feet of front. Ascending to the gallery, the observer found himself face to face with the splendid educational display of the State of Massachusetts—best of its kind at the Exposition—embracing the finest of the plans, models, and methods employed in the schools of the Old Bay Commonwealth. Turning about and glancing to the west, down the long avenues, the full vision of the Exhibition burst upon him. There on the ground-floor lay the magnificent "courts," or hollow squares, into which the space had been divided—each of these courts an exposition in itself. Afar to the right, where the main transept ended in the north projection of the building, the gallery was occupied with the great Roosevelt organ with its electric echo and hydraulic engine. In the corresponding gallery, at the south end of the transept, were the fine educational displays of Maine, New Hampshire, Rhode Island, Connecticut, New Jersey, Maryland, Tennessee, Ohio, Indiana, Illinois, Michigan, Wisconsin, Minnesota, and Iowa. In the gallery at the western end of the main avenue—dimly seen at the distance of thirty-five hundredths of a mile—was placed the exhibit of the American Society of Civil Engineers, the display consisting of models, drawings, and photographs peculiar to engineering art.

Descending to the main floor, the observer found himself in a world of wonders. Near the eastern entrance was the fine exhibit made by American stationers, and south of this the splendid book display, representing the superb work done by all the great publishing houses of the country. Further westward was the department allotted to the Yale Lock Manufacturers for the exhibition of their model post-offices. Next came the large section set apart for the dis play of American silks, woolens, and cotton goods-fabrics rivaling the richest products of European and Oriental factories. And the carpet pavilion—also American—with its patterns, delicate, novel, luxurious, merited equal praise for the splendor of its treasures. Nor did the cutlery of the United States, which was exhibited above the sections allotted to textile fabrics, suffer by comparison with the finest corresponding products of British skill.

View in the Main Exhibition Building.

Among the southeastern squares was likewise set the display of American pottery and porcelain. Nearby stood a collection of granite monuments, and in the same vicinity a splendid exhibit of iron and steel, chiefly from the furnaces and works of Pittsburgh. More attractive still was the great display of American watches, made by the Waltham

Company of Massachusetts and the Elgin of Illinois. Beyond the main aisle, to the north, bristled batteries of Gatling and Parrott guns, and farther on were placed exhibits of safes from several noted firms. The next sections were occupied with the beautiful and costly displays of furnishing goods, costumes, etc., from the principal merchants of New York and Philadelphia. Then came an exhibit of vases, pedestals, and fountains, in terra cotta; then the sections set apart for threads, cordage, and cables; and south of these, beyond the principal avenue, the massive display of the Centennial Safe Deposit Company and the beautiful department of American clocks.

On the line of the main aisle, between the eastern entrance and the greater transept, were arranged the fine collections of cut and ground glass, the best being from the works of Wheeling and Pittsburgh. In the adjacent sections stood the glittering show-cases of the Meriden Britannia Company with their beautiful specimens of silver, plated wares, and bronzes. But more magnificent still was the jewelers' pavilion—Moorish in its style—standing at the southeast angle of the principal nave and transept. In this were displayed the almost priceless treasures of the leading American jewelers—Starr and Marcus, Caldwell of Philadelphia, and the Gorham Manufacturing Company of Providence. Among the articles exhibited by the latter was the celebrated CENTURY VASE, representing by its beautiful allegories and emblems in raised silver the progress of America from barbarism to renown. Here also were the matchless show-cases of Tiffany, starlit with diamonds, and blazing with all manner of precious stones. It was here, moreover, that the observer found the best view overhead; for at this point, by the bisection of the principal nave and transept, abundant room was afforded above for the display of art. Each of the four sides of the vaulted space was occupied with an immense allegorical painting. That on the east represented America, with Washington and Franklin for its central figures. The piece emblematical of Europe stood opposite, with Charlemagne and Shakespeare as its typical heroes. Asia was represented at the south curve of the transept by a group of figures and emblems, with Confucius and Mohammed in the midst; while in the north division was set the painting of Africa, Rameses II. and Sesostris occupying the center.

In the section south and east of the jewelers' pavilion were placed the exhibits of ores, paints, and chemicals. The display of printing-inks was made near by; and further to the east stood the perfume-fountains with their jets of cologne and halos of fragrant mist. Still eastward were set the cases containing the exhibit of philosophical and surgical instruments; and in the same vicinity, to the south, were the sections allotted to furniture, much of which was of the richest woods and most elaborate finish known to that branch of art. And before the observer had finished his examination of these superb apartments—for here the courts were fitted up after the manner of a suite of rooms—his car was saluted with strains of music, and turning about, he found himself face to face with the finest display of piano-fortes ever made in the world. All of the great makers had here done their best, under the stimulus of the sharpest competition—Steinway, Chickering, Decker, Steck, Knabe, Weber,— each with his claims of peculiar excellence, and each anxious for the supreme award.—So ended a ramble through the seven acres of space apportioned on the ground-floor of the Main Building to the exhibits of the United States.

But the Saxon's Island Empire, mother of English liberty, was also there with her arts and industries. Over the northwest angle of the main aisle and transept hung the Red banner of Lancaster, bearing the words "GREAT BRITAIN AND IRELAND." There were the courts apportioned to the British commission. In the first of these was placed the celebrated exhibit of the Elkingtons, silver smiths of Birmingham. Their collection embraced several pieces worthy to rank among the highest products of human skill and patience. The work was mostly in the new style of art called *Repoussé*—the process of developing figures in relief upon metallic surfaces by hammering. Here stood THE HELICON VASE with its infinite stories from the legends of Greece. Here hung THE MILTON SHIELD, bearing upon its ample disc the sublime visions of *Paradise Lost*.[38] Here

---

[38] It was a matter of oft-repeated inquiry among the visitors at the Centennial, why these superb specimens of workmanship exhibited by the Elkingtons, as well as the Tiffany *Bryant Vase* and the Gorham *Century Vase*, were not transferred to Memorial Hall along with other works of art in no respect superior.

a great number of less valuable works in silver and bronze gave extent and variety to one of the richest collections in the whole Exhibition.

Nearer to the northern projection of the Main Building were placed the British porcelains and potteries, embracing some of the finest specimens of ceramic art. Farther northward was the display of ornamental iron-work, and to the west an extensive exhibit of tiles. Next came the department of British furniture, rivaling that of the United States in the elaborate and sumptuous character of its specimens. Near by, the pavilion of the Royal School of Art and Needlework attracted a constant throng of visitors. For the queen herself and the members of her family were the makers of those splendid embroideries. Farther to the west was the magnificent display of the British carpet-dealers. Then came the exhibit of fire-arms, cutlery, philosophical instruments, stained glass, jewelry—chiefly Scottish—and then the superb collection of cotton and woolen goods, Irish poplins, cloths, silks, and laces, with which the section was filled along the main avenue.

The British Colonies had emulated the zeal of the mother-country. The Canadian exhibit was of the highest order. The educational system of Ontario was fully and meritoriously displayed by models, plans, and drawings illustrative of the methods and work of the public schools. The geological department was enriched with a full collection of ores, especially plumbago, coal, and granite. The Canadian Indians had sent a large contribution of peltry, bead-work, and apparel; and this display was contrasted with the richer and more extensive exhibit of furs made by the Company of Hudson Bay. In another section specimens of furniture from the shops of Quebec and Toronto gave token of tastefully furnished homes in the Dominion. Models of Canadian vessels showed commercial enterprise; cotton and woolen goods told of extensive factories; sewing-machines and pianos repeated the music of the Northern household.

Far Australia had also remembered the jubilee of Independence. The flocks on her hill-sides had contributed their magnificent fleeces to surprise the Western nations. The Argonauts of the South Pacific were home again with the richest of treasures! Here stood an obelisk of phantom gold, showing in cubic inches the quantity of *real* gold taken from the mines of New South Wales since 1851. Here were bars of New Zealand tin and blocks of coal; sections of beautiful timber and cocoons of silk; ores of antimony and copper; native wines and heaps of precious stones. Excellent photographs of Australian cities and scenery added much to the interest of the exhibit.

British India had also contributed specimens of her arts and industries. Photographs of her dusky people—oldest of the Aryan races—whose ancestors and *our* ancestors, in the far hill-country of Bactria, abode together, watching the same flocks, gazing at the same stars, and dreaming the same dream of destiny in the ages agone,—and photographs of Hindu homes as well, made the display of special interest. India carpets, gems from Bombay, and Delhi embroidery added brilliancy to the exhibit. Here, too, were jeweled weapons, native pottery, and precious stones; shawls and laces; silks and woolens; cereals and cotton from the banks of the Indus.

The colony of New Zealand was chiefly represented by paintings and drawings. But an important display of copper ores, lead, and coal was also made. The section of the Cape of Good Hope was occupied with a collection of native wines and brandies; gems and weapons; costumes and ores; and specimens illustrating the natural history of the country. Gold-dust, skins of animals, idols, ornaments, and weapons composed the display from the Gold Coast. Jamaica sent her rums and sugars, native woods and hemp. Tasmania had also come with an exhibit of zoological and mineral specimens. The Bahamas, Bermudas, Trinidad, and Guiana were represented by their various products, ranging from shells and corals to sugars, tobacco, and manufactures.

La Belle France—for the third time a republic! After a hundred years the land of LaFayette had come to do homage at the shrine which his blood had helped to consecrate. The space allotted to the French Commission was located between the main aisle and the north wall of the building, east of the central transept. The section of chief importance was that containing the exhibit of porcelains, rivaling in beauty and excellence the choicest work of the East. In glassware, too, the French display was of the highest order. The superb mirrors and chandeliers, exhibited by Brocard of Paris, were a delight to thousands who thronged around them. The section set apart for the display of bronzes and antiques was also crowded with admiring multitudes. Here stood an elegant mantel-piece of black marble, fifteen feet in height, exquisitely embellished with statues and reliefs; and here were grouped artistic cabinets, quaint figures, and articles in gilt.

Another department of great beauty was that in which were exhibited the treasures of French fashion—laces, gloves, silks, velvets, satins, and costumes. In this dazzling court Lyons and Paris were rivals. Near by was a second department of apparel, where courtly wax-figures, dressed to the excess of magnificence, did obeisance to other figures in splendid shawls and laces. Further on, stood the pavilion of the book publishers of France; and opposite to this was the court of engravings. The walls of the booksellers' pavilion were hung with the most elegant tapestries; and many of the publications displayed within were in the highest style of art. North of these sections, was the department of French vehicles—a unique collection, ranging from the quaint Cynofere, or dog-car, to carriages of state.

In the matter of personal ornaments and articles of household economy, the French exhibit was of great excellence. The display of the Paris jewelers was exceptional in its beauty and tastefulness. Of mantel ornaments there was an almost infinite variety, ranging from little ivory sprites and phantoms in ebony to elaborate clocks and bronzes. Of musical instruments—violins, flute's, cornets, music-boxes, and mimic birds—the exhibit was elegant after its kind. But the French pianos and organs were hardly comparable with the magnificent instruments displayed by the United States. In the department of cutlery a fine collection was presented, but the display was inferior to the corresponding exhibit made by Great Britain. The comparison turned the other way, however, in the section of plate glass; for in that department the French specimens were peerless.[39]

---

[39] The manufacture of American plate glass is yet in its incipiency, and is beset with special difficulties. Chief among the embarrassments which have attended the enterprise is the want of adequate protection, and the inveterate determination of foreign establishments to prevent the success of such manufacture in the United States.

West of the central transept and south of the principal aisle were the sections allotted to the German Empire. Across the avenue, directly opposite the American jewelers' pavilion, was placed the magnificent exhibit of the Royal Factory of Berlin. Here stood an imposing crescent-shaped case, with black columns at either end, bearing upon their summits the golden eagles of empire—the empire of Cæsar and Charlemagne restored in Hohenzollern. In this case were displayed the German porcelains, next to the French in excellence and beauty. Here were plates, busts, and statuettes, elaborate in design and intensely national in every part. Here were the three superb emblematical pieces called THE GERMANIA, THE AURORA, and THE OTHO VASES—queenly rivals of the splendid works of the Elkingtons, Tiffany, and Gorham. Further to the west was the section of plate glass; then the exhibit of the German jewelers; and then the court of armory, where were displayed the uniforms, accouterments, and weapons of the German soldiery, from the Crusading times to the present. Next came a section filled with toys from Nürnberg, and next the displays of Elberfeld silks and Saxon hosiery. On the southern aisle the objects of chief interest were the ivories exhibited by Meyer of Hamburg, the woven wire goods of Dresden, the gold and silver leaf exhibit of Bavaria, and the perfumes of Cologne. Nearer to the southern wall was the display of the German chemists. Then came the Leipsic lamps and lanterns, and then the Linden pavilion of velvets.

The southwest section of the German department was occupied with what musical instruments soever are played upon in Fatherland. But here again, as in the department of France, the inadequacy of the pianos and organs to compete with the instruments of the United States was plainly apparent. Along the southern wall was placed an interesting collection of articles illustrating the appliances and methods of a German army hospital. Near by was the exhibit of the Schwartzwold clock-makers—a

---

Nevertheless, it is known to the author that but for the serious misfortune of breaking the finest plate in packing, the Honorable W. C. De Pauw, president of the Star Glass Works of New Albany, Indiana, would have contributed to the Exposition specimens of his work fairly rivaling the best of the French exhibit. The largest of the De Pauw collection was a magnificent plate having a *superficial area* of 21,095 *square inches*.

quaint and beautiful collection. Models of the Hamburg steamships were found in the southeastern sections, and, finally, the elegant pavilion of the German booksellers—best of the kind from Europe.

A description of the departments of the leading Western nations, and of the exhibits made thereby, is in some measure a description of the rest. True, the beholder as he wandered from court to court was ever impressed with the multifarious aspects of human life and the ever-varying phases of civilization. Still, so far as the displays made by the different branches of the Aryan race were concerned, there was unity in variety—a generic similarity with specific modifications. As to the Oriental nations, there was a wider departure from the common type, but a noticeable similarity of features among their own displays. The thoughtful observer rarely failed to find in the various courts an exhibit typical of a known civilization, but he also found more than that. Thus, for instance, the Austrian sections presented the expected treasures of Bohemian cut-glass; of amber work and meerschaums; of pipes *ad infinitum*; of Viennese portemonnaies, diaries, and albums and the *un*expected treasures of the silk-weavers of the Danube. Also in the Italian court-were found the anticipated reproductions of ancient art; trophies commemorative of the Italian Radicals from Columbus to Garibaldi; the religious halo over every thing; and the *un*anticipated display of Venetian pottery. The Belgian section presented the finest of Brussels linens, laces, and tapestries; and, as if in contrast with these, an elaborate display of fire-arms and an illuminated advertisement of the mineral waters of Spa. Holland made an exhibit of what things soever the Netherlander prizes—from dikes to pipe-stems, from magnificent bridges to humble roofs of thatch. Nor had the conquerors of the North Sea forgotten the refinements of letters; for the Dutch booksellers' pavilion was among the finest at the Exposition.

Here stood the cuckoo clocks of Switzerland. Geneva, city of political philosophy and quaint watches, was present with all her arts. The embroidered lace curtains of St. Gall hung tastefully over photographs of the Alpine glens, and the Swiss pavilion of education stood near by. Sweden contributed a court of exceptional elegance, well filled with the products of her arts and industries. The chief attractions of the display were the specimens of Bessemer steel and cutlery, Swedish arms and armor, woolens and silks, safety-matches and pottery. Norway presented her glassware from Christiana. Ancient weapons were placed in contrast with a modern Norwegian school-house, and old coins and medals with modern jewels and silverware.

Among the sections of chief interest were the courts of Denmark, Egypt, and Spain. These were set contiguous, fronting the main aisle, and representing in their style and contents three diverse types of civilization. The articles most attractive in the Danish court were terra cotta ornaments, silverware from Copenhagen, Esquimau apparel, and a rich collection of furs. Across the entrance-way to the Egyptian court was this inscription: "EGYPT—SOUDAN—THE OLDEST PEOPLE OF THE WORLD SENDS ITS MORNING GREETING TO THE YOUNGEST NATION." Entering, the visitor was confronted with a bust of Rameses the Great and a model of the Pyramid of Gizeh. Then came a gorgeous display of the caparisons and gold-studded harness of the steeds of the modern Pharaohs; then cabinets of ebony, costly and quaint; and then an exhibit of Arabic books and manuscripts. The court of Spain was richly hung with Spanish trophies and curtains of velvet. Within were the portraits of those daring adventurers, Cortez, De Leon, De Soto, and Pizarro. The articles displayed were typical of the country and people. Scarfs and shawls, silks and woolens, porcelain tiles and glassware, chemicals and fire arms, were the chief products exhibited.

Opposite the departments allotted to Sweden stood the court of Japan. The contents surpassed description. The display of bronzes attracted universal attention and universal praise. The porcelains were, beyond comparison, the finest of the whole Exposition—finest in quality and in the immense variety of the exhibit. Richness of coloring—vivid hues of scarlet, green, and gold—prevailed everywhere. Lacquered ware of every variety, superb cabinets, and silken screens embroidered with figures infinite, curious faces, and Japanese costumes, made up a display which astonished the Western mind with the profusion of Eastern art.

China did not half so well—yet well. About the whole display were the anticipated characteristics of overdone conservatism. Here was the expected array of drawings without perspective and designs, consisting wholly of color. Here was a pagoda painted in fantastic hues, and here that China ware a rich profusion of plates and vases for which the Celestial empire has had immemorial fame. Here, too, were the beautiful silks, and cloths with gold embroidery, and elaborate bedsteads carved with dragons' heads, and woven forms unnamable in tapestry and screen. The polite and impassive man of the almond eyes and cue—manager of the exhibit—walked among the trophies of his civilization and did reverence before a wooden image of Fo.

The Russian court was placed between the sections of Spain and Austria. An iron statue of the inspired barbarian, Peter the Great, stood like a grim sentinel to guard the treasures of his empire. Much fine silverware, of excellent design and workmanship, was displayed as the exhibit of Moscow. A magnificent piece in *Repoussé*, called THE ADORATION OF THE MAGI, elicited universal praise. St. Petersburg had sent a similar collection, and also a unique group of bronzes illustrative of the life and manners of the Russian peasants. Another section contained a superb chandelier, together with statuettes, caskets, cabinets, and mantels. The exhibit of Russian furs was unsurpassed; and the display of embroidered cloths, velvets, and silks was well calculated to excite the jealousy of more favored lands.

The section of Portugal was found in the rear of the court of Egypt. Glassware, porcelain, and pottery constituted a large part of the exhibit. The life, costumes, and manners of the Portuguese peasantry were here represented by groups of statuary in plaster. The Azores made a beautiful display of phantom ships and flower-baskets woven of the fiber of the fig-tree. Along the south wall of the section was placed a fine collection of geological and topographical maps and charts illustrating the physical aspect of Portugal. The exhibit of raw silk, cotton goods, blankets, and embroidery, was exceptionally good.

Of the African kingdoms—after Egypt—the best and only displays were made by the Orange Free State and Tunis. The court of the latter was located in the rear of the sections of Denmark and Turkey, and was almost exclusively occupied with the personal exhibit made by the Dey. The collection consisted of articles illustrative of the manners and customs of the Bedouins, and of antiquities from the ruins of Carthage.

The court of the Orange Free State occupied the southwestern angle of the building, and was wholly devoted to the governmental exhibit made by the authorities of that country. An unexpected array of minerals, native woods, ivory, grains, mohair, and wool, composed the chief part of the collection. But the cases containing the wealth of the feathery races of South-eastern Africa, from the infinitesimal humming-birds of Madagascar to the straggling descendants of the dinornis, were of still greater interest and beauty.

No department in the Main Building was more admired and praised than the court of Brazil. Dom Pedro and his queen had no cause of shame in the presence of their national exhibit. The Brazilian pavilion was located between the courts of the Netherlands and Belgium, and was characterized throughout by elegant magnificence of structure and contents. At the entrance was a brilliant display of flowers and designs delicately woven from the plumage of Brazilian birds. Topographical maps and photographs illustrated the physical aspect of the country; while the splendid display of tropical woods, together with the finest of coffees, yams, ginger, and rice, revealed the true riches of the empire.

The minor South American States were also fairly represented. The pavilion of Peru was tastefully ornamented; the contents, of value and interest. Gold, silver, cinnabar, copper, iron, and lead, were the principal minerals exhibited; coffee, pepper, cinnamon, cocoa, caoutchouc, and cinchona, the chief vegetable products. The court of Chili was of similar sort, and contained some fine specimens of silk and worsted-work; but the most interesting part was the case filled with the stuffed skins of Chilian wild animals. The exhibit of the Argentine Confederation was chiefly of ores—gold, silver, copper, and lead. The display also embraced fine specimens of building stone, quartz, and plumbago. The manufactures were, for the most part, of leather; and handicraft was mainly illustrated in a collection of native weapons.—Far Hawaii, also, had a pavilion of considerable interest, containing a collection of birds, shells, and sea-weed; fans, ferns, and feather-work.

Mexico, with her pseudo-Latin civilization and anarchic republicanism, had pitched her court next to that of the United States. The pavilion was Aztec in its style, with hints of a more modern date.

The exhibit was principally historic, consisting of antiquities and remains. The display of manufactures embraced some fine silks and elegant leather goods. Here were effigies of Mexican cavaliers, formidable as Quixote in armor. Here were native wines and medicinal plants, and here a fine collection of ores—silver, galena, and iron. But the exhibit in its entirety was neither striking nor extensive.

In the Carriage Annex the observer found much to instruct and amuse. For here were the ridiculous vehicles which the fathers made their journeys in—old Virginia or Concord coaches, heavy enough for a fortification. But here, in contrast, was the full triumph of modern art in the combination of the ornate and the useful. All things elegant and luxurious of silver-palace car or private carriage studded with gold, and all things prosy of spokes and hubs and harness, were here displayed in profusion. Here again Brazil, competing with Pullman and Woodruff, presented a splendid coach from the Rio Janeiro Railway. Here Canadian sleighs and sledges were contrasted with the diminutive coaches of Italy and the substantial vehicles of Old England.—And so the rambler, passing under the western arches of the Main Building, found himself in the open air, facing the Bartholdi Fountain.

Interior View of Machinery Hall.

The way across the beautiful esplanade led to Machinery Hall. Entering at the southeastern portal of that great edifice, the observer came at once into the department of the German Empire. Immediately before him stood the famous Krupp guns, gigantic twelve hundred pounders, black and terrible as the Miltonic artillery. Several rifled cannon of smaller caliber were set in contrast; and just across the aisle was a pyramid of iron-ore, showing the material out of which the great guns were cast. On the opposite side of the battery was exhibited a brick-making machine from Berlin. Near the southeastern angle of the building, the Gas Motor Factory of Deutz displayed a peculiar engine in which the piston is propelled by the explosion of gas. The best steam-engines exhibited in the German section were from the works of Leipsic.

The department of France embraced the northeastern division of the ground-floor. Near the entrance thereto was placed an elegant pavilion in which were illustrated the processes of working in brass and copper. The confectioners' section, where bon-hons were made and sold, came next, and then the department of Parisian soaps and cosmetics. In this part also stood the silk-looms of Lyons, and further to the north a set of machines illustrating the processes of lithography. An apparatus for the manufacture of beet-sugar was also exhibited, and an ice-making machine from Paris. The rest of the French contrivances had respect, for the most part, to fashionable wants and the avocations of polite society.

Further westward was placed the section of Belgium. Chaudron of Brussels led the exhibit with an effective and tremendous machine for boring wells.[40] Car-wheels and axles from Louvain, a trip-hammer and steam shears from Marcinelle, and models of machinery for the manufacture of stearine, were the next attractive features of the display. A splendid exhibit of wool-carding apparatus was presented as the contribution of Verviers; and the city of Ghent added a superb horizontal engine, built for the mint at Brussels.

The Northern nations had contributed little in the way of machinery: Denmark nothing at all. Sweden made a small but

---

[40] It is clear that, in respect to machines for upland excavation, the Americans have much to learn. That whole line of contrivance, beginning with the plow and ending with the dredging-machine, is subject to great and radical improvements.

respectable display in the way of trip-hammers, stationary engines, one small locomotive, a fire-engine, and several sewing-machines. The contribution of Norway consisted of some odd-looking machinery for working in wood and metal. The Russian display was almost wholly of artillery—partly good, partly indifferent in its quality. In the same vicinity was the fine exhibit made by Brazil, consisting of models of dry docks and men-of-war; military and naval enginery; arms, accouterments, and munitions; stationary, locomotive, and fire-engines; pumps, pin-making apparatus, and machinery employed in the Imperial mint.

The best of the exhibits made by foreign nations was that of Great Britain. Two of the Rochester traction-engines, standing near the eastern entrance to the hall, were much wondered at and praised. So, also, the fine carding-machine just opposite. Manchester made a fine display of steam hammers, circular saws, and enginery of coinage and stamping dies. The armor-plate exhibited here was the best ever produced, ranging from nine inches to twenty-two inches in thickness, seemingly impenetrable. The Applebys of London exhibited two of their tremendous cranes—giants after their kind. English sewing machines—mostly of the hand-power pattern—were plentifully displayed. In the sections near by, the spinning and winding of cotton thread was illustrated, and further on, the delicate looms for weaving silken badges were in operation. Gadd of Manchester exhibited an engine capable of printing calicoes in eight colors at one impression. An effective system of railway switching and signaling was shown by Brierly and Reynolds of London. In an adjoining square stood a fine model of an Inman steamship, and east of this a Walter printing-press in operation. Farther on, Tait and Watson of London displayed a collection of machines, including a sugar-mill, a valveless engine, and centrifugal drying-pans.—Across the aisle was the exhibit of Canada, New Brunswick, and Nova Scotia,—embracing turbine wheels, a set of railway signals, quartz-mills from Halifax, Toronto marbles, fire-engines, sewing-machines, and Indian canoes.

Of the American department—three-fourths of the whole in extent—the greatest trophy was the Corliss vertical engine, standing in the middle of the central aisle. The platform was fifty-six feet in diameter; the stroke of the piston, ten feet; the weight of the fly-wheel, a hundred and twelve thousand pounds. It required twenty tubular boilers of large capacity to furnish the proper amount of steam. The periphery of the fly-wheel was geared with cogs into the underground line of shafting, and the power applied was equivalent to that of fourteen hundred horses; but the movements of the great engine were smooth and noiseless.

From the central station, the observer, glancing down the south transept, had a full view of the Hydraulic Annex. Here pumps of every grade and fashion were pouring their torrents into a vast tank having a capacity of sixty-three thousand cubic feet of water. An interesting display of steel ware was made in a section near by, and further on, an exhibit of metal piano-frames by the Steinways. Here the process of making nails and tacks was illustrated, and there a machine was cutting corks. On this hand was an extensive collection of files and screws, and on that a pyramid of grindstones. Farther on, to the west, was an exhibit of rolled iron, and next, a large display of axles and machinists' tools. A huge brick-making machine, capable of moulding four thousand bricks in an hour, was fairly matched with a mammoth planing machine, weighing a hundred and sixty-two thousand pounds, and having a traverse of forty-four feet. In an adjacent section, paper envelopes were made by an automatic apparatus at the rate of a hundred and twenty per minute. Worcester, Massachusetts, contributed a collection of edged tools, dies, and presses; and Paterson, New Jersey, a machine for spinning silk. On the central aisle model steamers, men-of-war, yachts, and life-boats were exhibited. Next came the sections occupied with Hoe and Bullock printing-presses; then the book-binding, stereotyping, and electrotyping display, and then the splendid roller-drum book-press of Cottrell and Babcock, New York. A type-writer stood near by, and farther on was a section where all the steam- and sailing-vessels owned in the ports of Massachusetts were exhibited by models.

In the department of confections the American display rivaled that of France. Close to the bon-bon section were placed some fine wheat-cleaning and centrifugal sugar-drying apparatuses. Then came an old

Virginia tobacco factory, where all the processes of making were exhibited. And the colored people, as they wrought, made the hall resound with the weird plantation melodies of the Southland. Farther east the manufacture of India-rubber shoes of all sorts and sizes was illustrated by the actual processes of the art. Then came the glass-blowers' exhibit, and then an excellent display of wall paper by the Howells of Philadelphia. A collection of washing- and wringing-machines caught the attention for a moment, and then the observer found himself before the huge sugar-refining apparatus exhibited by the Colwell Iron Works of New York. The Wharton automatic switch was exhibited near by, and then came a splendid display of common and platform scales. Mining machinery was shown by the Dickinson Company of Scranton, and American loco motives—unsurpassed by any in the world—by the Baldwin Works and the Pennsylvania Railway. In the adjacent section the Westing house air-brake and the Henderson hydraulic-brake were exhibited in sharp competition. The Backus water-motor here attracted much attention, as did also an odd hydraulic-ram near the western entrance. The department of American power-looms—rivaling those of the best European factories—was constantly thronged with visitors, and the section where Waltham watches were made was a similar scene of eager interest. The Pyramid Pin Company of New Haven exhibited a quaint little machine for sticking pins in papers. A powerful hydraulic cotton-press was shown by the Taylor Iron Works of Charleston, and a magnificent collection of wire ropes and cables by the Roeblings of Trenton.

The display of railway bars—iron and steel—was, for the most part, made by the works of Pittsburgh. Among the western sections of the hall some fine ditching and draining engenery was exhibited; and near by was the display of American knitting-machines. Of sewing-machines the exhibit was unrivaled. The competition reminded the observer of that among the piano-fortes in the Main Building. Every form of patent, from the original Howe to the most recent in novation, was duly praised by its group of advocates and admirers. The American Steamship Company exhibited their vessels by models, and eastward from their section stood a handsome pavilion containing an unlimited assortment of saws. The department of fire-engines and extinguishers was adjacent; and near by, the famous Weimar blowing-engine and an apparatus for charging blast-furnaces were displayed.

Many relics of old machinery were exhibited in various parts of the hall. Chief of these antiquated contrivances was a section of THE FIRST STEAM-ENGINE ever used in the United States,—an odd piece of mechanism of the Cornish pattern, which was brought to America in 1753 and set in operation in a copper-mine near Newark, New Jersey. The first saw-maker's anvil, imported in 1819, was exhibited near by. In another section were several pieces of excellent workmanship from the mechanical department of Cornell University. An automatic shingle-machine, having a working capacity of twenty-five thousand shingles per day, was an attractive object in an adjoining division; and in the same space the work of dovetailing, moulding, carving, and paneling by machinery was illustrated. Then came the work of barrel-making, shown by the actual processes; then an exhibit of scroll-saws in operation; then blast-furnaces by models, steam drills, gas apparatus of every variety, and a machine for crushing anthracite coal.—Taken all in all, the exhibit of American machinery was the finest display of the kind ever made by man.

On his way from the western entrance of Machinery Hall to the Government Building of the United States, the observer would hardly fail to pause and admire the Roman Catholic Total Abstinence Fountain, one of the most beautiful of the outdoor works of Fairmount Park. Thence a brief walk northward on Belmont Avenue brought him to the edifice erected by Congress for the exhibition of the functions of the American Government in times of peace, and its resources in war. The building itself has already been described. Without, to the east, stood a model monitor, having the same dimensions and appearance as the original. In the same vicinity a huge Rodman twenty-inch gun and others hardly less formidable were exhibited. On the south, also, many pieces of heavy artillery were displayed, together with shot, shells, and projectiles of various kinds. Here, too, were the boats *Faith* and *Advance*, used by De Haven and Kane in their Arctic voyages. Near by, two postal cars, for the fast-mail service of the United States, were exhibited by the Post-office Department. On the north, the War

Department made a display of pontoons, bridge trains, and army wagons. Within, the south division of the principal transept was occupied with the Centennial Post-office. Here the mails were regularly received and distributed with systematic precision. The subordinate sections of this department were named respectively the divisions of Topography, of Books and Blanks, of Mail Equipment, and of Stamps. In the last section a machine of unimaginable ingenuity was displayed, having an automatic capacity to cut, fold, gum, stamp, count, and pack, the Government envelopes.

Another large display in the Government Building was made under the auspices of the Agricultural Bureau. The subordinate divisions of this exhibit were of Statistics, Chemistry, Botany, Microscopy, Entomology, and Horticulture. In the first named of these sections were large outline maps of the United States, showing the areas of forest and farming-lands, the various products and capacities of soils, the distribution of animals, etc. In the department of chemistry was a fine and well-arranged exhibit of the earths, together with illustrations of the processes of growth, fermentation, distillation, and the like, as well as the methods of manufacturing vegetable products. In the botanical division the various woods of the United States were exhaustively exhibited. The collection was very extensive and valuable, embracing sections of nearly every species of wood growing between Central America and Canada, and from Passamaquoddy to the Golden Gate. The microscopic section was occupied with a series of charts and drawings illustrative of vegetable diseases. The entomological division was chiefly devoted to an exhibit of insect eating birds and of what creatures soever prey upon the farmer's fruits and grains. In the horticultural section a display was made of those plants which have an economic and commercial value, such as corn tobacco, cotton, and flax.

The exhibit made by the Department of the Interior was composed chiefly of the well-known treasures of the Patent Office and the National Museum at Washington. In addition to these, special displays were made by the Land and Indian offices, and by the Bureaus of Education and Pensions. Here, also, was exhibited a complete set of the census reports from 1790 to 1870, inclusive. But surpassing all in interest and value was the magnificent exhibit made by the Smithsonian Institution. This extraordinary display embraced, first of all, a classified collection of the animals of America. These animals were grouped according to the relation which they bear to man, as *useful* or *injurious*; and the exhibit included all those contrivances and implements which man employs in capturing them when wild, or subjecting and controlling them when domesticated. The collection illustrative of the fishery resources of the United States was equally complete and full of interest. In the department of American ethnology an extensive exhibit was made of aboriginal implements and contrivances peculiar to the primitive modes of life. The last branch of the Smithsonian contribution was that illustrating the mineral resources of the United States—a collection of great extent and value.

Interior View of the United States Government Building.

The first section under the auspices of the Treasury Department was devoted to the exhibition of the money, money-making, and medals of the national mint. The special display, made by the Lighthouse Board, of lanterns, reflectors, sea-signals, and electrical and calcium lights, fairly rivaled the great exhibit of similar apparatus made in the government building of France. The whole collection was of the highest order, and gave token that no branch of humanitarian science is making more rapid strides than that which appertains to the perfection of light-houses and the safety of mariners.

The Navy Department made an exhibit of torpedoes, and of the methods of using them in naval warfare. The collection embraced all of the patterns of that terrible engine, from the original as invented by Fulton, to the more modern forms produced by Ericsson and Lay. Another section was devoted to marine arms and armor, shot, shells, munitions, uniforms, and what weaponry soever is peculiar to men-of-war. The Naval Observatory exhibited—besides its own publications—a fine collection of photographs and chronometers. Here, too, were found most of the precious relics of the Arctic explorations, from the voyage of De Haven to that of Hall.

The exhibit made by the War Department was still larger and more complete. In this division was arranged the splendid display of the Signal Service under direction of General Albert J. Meyer, chief signal officer of the army. Here were exhibited all of the delicate instruments and tentative apparatus peculiar to the half-formed science of meteorology; and here the methods of observing and recording the multiform and many times capricious phenomena of earth, air, and sky, were fully illustrated. The Engineering Corps also contributed an interesting exhibit, chiefly composed of maps and drawings illustrative of the coast, lake, and river improvements of the United States during the past century. The section of the Ordnance Service was devoted to the display of fire-arm manufacture as the same is carried on at the Government Armory at Springfield, Massachusetts. The making of cartridges was also fully illustrated by the actual processes. Next came the exhibits made by the Post Hospital and the Laboratory—full of interest after their kind—and, last of all, the model light-house standing at the northeast angle of the building, without, and not far off the tremendous fog-horn called the *Siren*.

In the extensive exhibits of Agricultural Hall—varied and full of interest, as they were—there was, of course, a less display of human skill and a greater revelation of the beneficence of nature. For here the products exhibited were, for the most part, the offspring of the ground—the fruits of air, water, and sunshine. In this vast hall, the agency of man extended but little further than the modification and utilization of the gratuitous riches of the world. The display, therefore, was in a large measure limited to the collection and exhibition of things uncommon and prodigious.— A brief summary of the objects of principal interest in the various departments of the hall may here suffice.

The products of the United States occupied more space than did those of all other nations combined. And the general superiority of American exhibits over those of foreign lands was noticeable from the first. In the northeastern division of the hall were placed the sections of agricultural implements, plows being a specialty. The exhibit made by Speer and Sons of Pittsburgh, as well as that by Oliver Ames and Sons of North Easton, Massachusetts, was specially varied and excellent. In a section to the north were shown rakes and threshers of the most approved patents, and in the same collection a specimen of Foust's hay-lifting machine, which called forth many commendations. Near by stood the superb plows manufactured by the Oliver Chilled-Plow Company of South Bend, Indiana.[41] Farther on was another collection, by the Higganum Plow Company of Connecticut; and then came a section of gang-plows, exhibited by Collins and Company of New York.

In the department of reapers and mowers all the great makers were fully represented. The Sweepstakes, Harvester, McCormick, Champion, and Buckeye machines were specially conspicuous in the exhibit. The Union Corn Planter, from the shops of Peoria, Illinois, attracted much attention, and the superb Westinghouse steam thresher was greatly praised. An excellent reaper, called the Planet, was shown by the Wayne Agricultural Works of Richmond, Indiana. Slosaser's self-loading excavator—a powerful ditch-digging machine—stood close by; and near the eastern entrance was exhibited one of the well-known Adams Power Cornshellers.

---

[41] One plow exhibited by this firm was perhaps *the finest ever made*. The metallic parts were plated with nickel, and the rosewood frame was splendidly embossed with agricultural emblems.

Grain-drills next attracted attention, especially the display made by the Farmers' Friend Company of Dayton, Ohio. In the south end of the central transept several excellent cider-mills were exhibited in operation—that of Boomer and Boschert leading the collection. Farm scales were shown by the Howe Manufacturing Company, and farm saw-mills by Harbert and Raymond of Philadelphia. In this vicinity two models of stables—one of wood, and the other of iron—were exhibited, and also some fine horse-powers from Racine, Wisconsin.

Interior View of Agricultural Hall.

The observer next found himself in other scenes, amid the American wine-growers' exhibit; near the northern entrance. The California display was first in excellence and extent. After the Vintage of the Pacific Slope came the fine exhibits of Ohio, Missouri, and New York. South of the wine collection, at the bisection of the nave and transept, stood a large bronze fountain, throwing high its cooling waters; and at the four angles round about was set the display of canned fruits and meats, hops, malts, and spices. Here, too, was a splendid exhibit of starches, chief of which was the fine perfumed starch manufactured by Erkenbrecher of Cincinnati. Here, moreover, the appetite of whatsoever creatures live by bread was provoked by the bountiful display of that article. Close by, in the middle of the avenue, stood a huge windmill, purposely old-fashioned, thirty feet in height, dated 1776. Next came the zoological exhibit, composed of stuffed animals and birds, but more especially of a magnificent museum of plaster casts prepared by Professor Henry A. Ward of Rochester University. Along the western wall of the building all varieties of edible fishes, out of the fresh and salt waters of the United States, were exhibited alive in a series of aquaria.

The northwestern courts of the building were occupied with the tobacconists' pavilions. The display was very extensive, embracing every variety and caprice of manufacture. North of the tobacco section the Delta Moss Company of New Orleans exhibited a tree bearing a rich array of Southern moss; and the prepared product was shown in bales near by. A huge evaporator for drying fruits, and a massive road-roller driven by steam, next caught the attention; and then came the sections set apart for the general display of the woods, grains, vegetables, and fruits of the various States—perhaps the largest and most imposing collection of such articles ever brought together. In the court of New Hampshire were exhibited, along with other wonders, two enormous swine, stuffed, stupid, and prodigious as nature and taxidermy could make them. Farther on was the fish and fishery exhibit of Massachusetts, and farther still, the silk-worm display of California. South of the central transept the rich soils of Iowa were exhibited in large glass cylinders; and beyond was placed a fine collection of the minerals of Nevada.—Such were the objects of chief interest in the departments allotted to the United States.

The exhibit of Great Britain occupied the southeast division of the hall. First of all, the display of condiments was equal to the expectancy of the most accomplished epicure. Equally commendable were the exhibits of preserved meats, patent coffees and teas, preparations of milk, sugar, and the like, presented by the Colonial Produce Company of London. An adjoining section contained a full assortment of the famous English ales; and farther south was placed the department of British agricultural machinery, embracing some fine road-wagons, portable engines, and the smaller implements peculiar to field, orchard, and garden. Last of all came a display of mill stones, tiles, and ornaments in terra cotta.

The Canadian section, in the southwest quarter of the hall, was well filled with interesting products. And the exhibit was specially well arranged. The front line of cases was occupied with an extensive display of root vegetables, pulse, and cereals. In the next line, secondary products, such as wool, feathers, and pelts, were shown; and in the third tier of cases, prepared animal and vegetable materials—cured fish, flour, salt, pickles, and cheese—were displayed. Of agricultural implements the list was varied and extensive. Plows, rivaling the best of the American collection, were exhibited by Spardle of Stratford, Ontario, and by Ross of Chatham. Fine threshing machines, adjustable platform reapers, and turnip-drills of superior pattern, were the other objects of chief interest in the collection.—British Columbia, also, made a creditable display of her products, consisting chiefly of wheat and oats, woods, barks, and woolen goods of Indian manufacture.

France displayed her vintage. The exhibit was complete, embracing the whole list of vinous liquors from claret to brandy. In the same section were shown the unrivaled chocolates manufactured by Menier and Company of Paris. Vilmorin and Andrieux of the same city exhibited the products of their famous flower-gardens; and Strasbourg displayed her preserved fruits, sardines, and condiments. The process of manufacturing mineral waters was illustrated by Gazaubon of Paris, and near by was shown the method of bottling wine. Millstones, crucibles, cements, and artificial stone, were displayed in another department; and last of all, the fine cocoons and raw silks for which Southern France is so justly celebrated.

Along the south wall of the building was arranged the exhibit of the German Empire. Here, again, the display of wines was pre-eminent. The vintage of the Rhine elicited most praise. Nor did Gambrinus the king look down displeased from the florid labels of the Bavarian and Prussian beer-mugs. The exhibit of smoking and chewing-tobacco was next in extent and importance; after that, the display of confections. Then came a palm-tree with the mowing scythes of Wurtemberg for its branches; then specimens of curled hair out of the shops of Frankfort, and then some beautiful tufts of wool from the sheepcotes of Silesia.

The products of Austria and Hungary were displayed together. The cereals of the different parts of the empire were well exhibited. Vienna sent a fine collection of canned fruits, Pesth her boxes of nuts, and Prague her offering of wine and raisins. Flax, and wool, and hemp, were the staples of the Hungarian section, and leather of the exhibit of Bohemia.

On the south side of the central transept lay the court of Russia. And the display was unexpectedly complete and well arranged. The strictly agricultural element predominated throughout the whole exhibit, only a small space being devoted to wines and liquors. Wheat, oats, rye, and barley—all of the finest quality—constituted the major part of the display, and gave token of abundant wealth in the almost sunless fields of the Muscovite. The fiber-producing plants, of many and superior kinds, were shown; and excellent candied fruits and confections—the contribution of Poland—completed one of the most interesting divisions of the hall.

Among the best of the exhibits made by the Southern nations, was that of Spain, located on the south side of the central transept, adjoining the Russian court. Here, again, the true agricultural idea was maintained, and the wine and liquor exhibit given a secondary rank. The display of Spanish cereals, fruits, pulse, and nuts, was set in glass-encased panels, around the sides of the court, presenting a fair summary of the field and garden products of the kingdom. The exhibit of wools was among the finest of the Exposition, and the collection of wines admirable after its kind. Specimens of the gum and resin-bearing trees of the Philippine Islands were exhibited in an adjoining section; and near by, Havana displayed her cigars and chocolates. The space allotted to Portugal was well filled with her products, the exhibit being similar to that of Spain, and equally meritorious.

The Italian court occupied the southeast division of the hall. The collection embraced specimens of all those products for which the peninsula has been immemorially famous. Here were grains, and fruits, and nuts; olive-oil and raisins; oranges, figs, and lemons; citrons, pomegranates, and liquorice; and wine—such as the Latin wits and poets quaffed when Britain belonged to the Druids.

The court of the Netherlands joined that of Austria on the south. The Dutch display was arranged with much skill and tastefulness; and neither Gambrinus nor the grape was the be-all and the end-all of the exhibit. But the collection was as intensely national as those of Germany. The products were mostly shown under the auspices of the Gülderland and Zealand agricultural societies. The various sections presented a full array of grains, plants, and pulse, as well as the more valuable woods, especially those used in the manufacture of dyes. Fine specimens of the famous Holland cheese and flour were shown, and in the sections to the west an assortment of chocolates and cod-liver oil. The Dutch fishing interests were also well illustrated with tackles, seines, and boats. The beet-sugar makers of Arnhem made a fine display of their product, as did also the manufacturers of those peculiar pungent beers, gins, and heavy liquors, which are so popular in Holland.

In the court of Norway the section of greatest interest was that containing the exhibit of her fisheries. The collection of fishing vessels and apparatus was extensive and complete. Cured specimens of nearly all the fishes known in the Norwegian marts were included in the display. The space devoted to agricultural implements contained some rude but characteristic machines and tools from the fields and shops of the North. But the display of leather was excellent, and that of the waterfowl of Norway especially interesting.—Similar in sort were the exhibits made by Sweden and Denmark.

In the Japanese court the principal product displayed was tea a large and varied collection. Here, again, the fishing interest was well represented, nets and tackle being a specialty: Then came illustrations of the silk culture, by the actual processes, from the worm to the web. The woods of Japan were displayed to good advantage as were also the grains and vegetables of the empire.—No exhibit of their agricultural resources was made by the other nations of the East.

Among the South American States, Brazil here—as elsewhere was preëminent. Before the, Brazilian court stood a much admired rustic pavilion so flecked on post and rafter with tufts of fleecy cotton as to look like the greatcoat of St. Nicholas. Within was the coffee exhibit—a full and complete display of the leading industry of the empire. Leaf-tobacco was also shown, and near by was an unsurpassed collection of the tropical woods for which Brazil is famous. In a section farther on were exhibited fine Brazilian sugars, rivaling those of Cuba and the United States. Last of all came the display of the silk interest of Brazil, beginning with the mild-mannered worm peculiar to that country, and ending with the finished fabric.—Venezuela and the Argentine Republic also made small but interesting exhibits of their resources, ranging from feathers, waxes, and native gums to leather-work, silk, and liquors. Here, too, Liberia made a display of her resources and industries.

Entering the Mauresque doorways of the Horticultural Building, the rambler stopped to admire the Foley Fountain in the center of the hall. Around him was the luxuriance of the tropics. Fragrance bathed the air, and silence sat like a plumed but songless bird on all the motionless leaves of this green world of wonders. Here was the great central conservatory, filled with the choicest plants and richest flowers culled out of every clime where sunshine and air are woven into leaf and petal. Here were the date-tree and the palm, fern, and cactus, lemon shrub and banana a wilderness of blossoms and fruits, cool and silent as the bowers visited in dreams.

Along the sides of the main conservatory were the green-houses for the propagation of plants. The floors were sunk ten feet below the level of the main hall, and the aisle in each was a hundred feet in length. Passing up and down these avenues, the observer found on either side an indescribable array of whatever the hand of nature has done of quaint or beautiful in moss, or fern, or flower. No extended account will here be attempted of the variety and beauty of this, the kingdom of the plants.— The collections of Horticultural Hall were the floral offering of the United States—a wreath for the altar of Independence. But the leaves of the garland were gathered from all climes.

No structure of Fairmount Park was more characteristic of the epoch than the Woman's Pavilion. The building and its contents illustrated one of the grandest tendencies of American civilization the complete emancipation of woman. In ancient times her chains were forged; the Middle Age re-riveted them upon her; the Modern Era—even the Reformation—has mocked her with the *semblance* and the *show* of liberty. America sets her free and lifts her to the seat of honor.

Interior View of Horticultural Hall.

The collections of the Pavilion were rich and varied. The southeast division was set apart for the display of woman's inventions. The contrivances were mostly of such sort as appertain to domestic economy and the improvement of home. Now and then, however, some capricious apparatus of fashion, invented in the realm of whim, attracted the gaze of the curious. Photographs of such benevolent institutions as are under the conduct of women formed an interesting exhibit, as did also the worsted and silk embroideries which were displayed in an adjoining court. The art collection embraced some creditable—even excellent—specimens of drawing, a fair display of paintings, and several commendable pieces of statuary. In the center of the hall was an elegant printing office, where *The New Century for Women* was published and distributed during the Exposition.

The southwestern quarter was occupied by foreign exhibitors. Here, too, the display of woman's work was varied and of a high order of merit. The royal ladies of the Old World had contributed much to the excellence and interest of the exhibit. Queen Victoria's School of Art and Needlework made some splendid offerings of embroidery. Many contributions of similar sort were presented by the women of France, Sweden, and Canada. Egypt had its section of artistic designs in gold and silver thread-work; even the queen of Tunis had heard of Independence and sent some superb gold-embroidered velvets as a token of her good will. The Japanese exhibit was composed for the most part of silken screens, writing desks, and cabinets, delicately ornamented after the style of the country. The Brazilian women, also, had honored the pavilion with some beautiful specimens of gold lace, shell work, and silk and worsted embroideries.

But it was among the art treasures of Memorial Hall that the stranger in Fairmount Park tarried longest: and then came again and again. For the variety was wellnigh infinite–the pageant ever new. Here were the bright ideals which flit for a moment across the vision of genius, and in that moment are made immortal. Here was a scene where the human imagination had transfused itself into the radiant imagery of the canvas and the imperishable forms of marble. Here, for a season, the scales fell from the sordid eyes of Utility, and the gaze was lifted up in the serener air of the True and the Beautiful.

In the arrangement of the exhibits in the Art Gallery, Italy was given the preference. The main hall, before the southern entrance, was set apart for her treasures. Here the best of the Italian sculptors were represented by their works. Caroni of Florence exhibited his *Africaine* and several other fine pieces of statuary. *The Boy Franklin* from the studio of Zocchi and *Washington and his Hatchet* from that of Romanetti attested how much American legends are loved in Italy; and a colossal bust by Gaurnerio of Milan showed the heroic estimate placed upon the Father of his Country in that land. The humorous in art was well represented in *The Forced Prayer* by the same noted artist. The Milanese sculptor, Baroaglio, was represented by several fine pieces, chief of which was a colossal statue called *Flying Time*. Hardly less attractive were the *Berenice* by Peduzzi, and *Sunshine* and *Storm* by Popatti. The Florentine Torelli presented *Eva St. Clair* as a specimen of his work; and Ropi of Milan contributed a bust of Garibaldi. *The Night of October* 11*th* was the name of a piece by D'Amore, illustrating the discovery of Guanahani; while a number of child-statues were shown as the work of the Milanese sculptor Pereda. A Miltonic *Lucifer* from the studio of Corti was a work of the highest order of merit, as was also the beautiful *Madonna* by Romanelli. A *Psyche* by Pagani attracted much attention; and a *Bacchus* by Braga was greatly praised.

Of Italian paintings—mostly copies from the famous productions of the old masters—the collection was large and attractive. One of the finest of the exhibit was *Galileo before the Inquisition*, after Raphael. The original pictures, mostly of the *Renaissance*, were of various degrees of merit, the *Columbus in Chains* by Fumigalli deserving special praise.—Nor must mention be omitted of the famous Castellani Museum of Antiquities, which was exhibited in the northeastern quarter of the hall—a display unsurpassed in interest by any other of the whole Exposition. The exhibit embraced one of the rarest, most valuable, and best classified collections of ancient and mediaeval gems, classic busts, and personal ornaments, now in existence. The museum was under the care of Professor Castellani himself, and the section was the especial haunt of scholars and antiquaries.

The American exhibit in Memorial Hall was divided between the main edifice and the annex. The collection was very extensive, embracing several thousand works in painting and statuary. The chief display of paintings was made in the great north corridor of the main hall. Here were exhibited a vast number of pieces, ranging from second-class and mediocrity to the highest productions of genius. The eastern end of the corridor was wholly occupied with Rothermel's immense painting of *The Battle of Gettysburg*. Page's *Farragut in Mobile Bay* was also exhibited as a historic sketch; and as an allegorical work, Thorpe's *Westward the Star of Empire takes its Way* was shown. Here, also, were exhibited six of Bierstadt's famous landscapes—splendid scenes from the Pacific coast. Then came a numberless array of portraits, landscapes, sketches, and ideal works, by well-known American artists and new aspirants for fame, among whose productions, though furnishing abundant room for comment and criticism, it would be invidious, within this narrow limit, to discriminate.

Of American statuary, also, a large exhibit was made—chiefly in the central hall. Under the dome was set a fine group in terra cotta, being the allegory of *America* from the Albert Memorial in Hyde Park, London. Not far off stood Connelly's *Thetis with the Infant Achilles*, much and justly admired. Story's *Medea* gave proof of that artist's genius; and Margaret Foley's *Cleopatra* was a work of great beauty. Several busts of Americans by Americans, attested the skill of the artists, especially that of Charles Sumner by Preston Powers. In the northwest corridor was exhibited *The Dying Cleopatra*—a work of remarkable beauty and power—by Edmonia Lewis, the colored sculptress.

Rotunda of Memorial Hall.

Too much praise could hardly be bestowed upon the British collection of paintings. It was generally conceded that the exhibit, both in the merit of the works themselves and in the admirable grouping which had been effected by the managers, was the best of the Exposition. If any doubt existed as to whether the first artists had contributed their choicest works to the American collection, no such doubt existed in respect to the genius of England. For here was *The Battle of Naseby* by

Sir John Gilbert; a *Summer Moon* by Frederick Leighton; *The Railway Station* by Powell; Armitage's *Julian the Apostate*; Sir Edwin Landseer's *Lions and Marriage of Griselda*; Maclise's *Banquet Scene in Macbeth*; Sir Thomas Lawrence's *Three Partners of the House of Baring*; William Powell Frith's *Marriage of the Prince of Wales*; West's *Death of Wolfe*; and a vast number of landscapes, sketches, portraits, drawings, watercolors, pencilings and crayon-work—making a collection so complete and meritorious as to awaken the pride of every Briton.

The art department of France was hardly representative of the genius of that country. Still, the collection embraced many pieces deserving of high praise. Among the best was *Rizpah protecting the Bodies of her Sons*, by George Becker; *The Conspiracy of the Medici*, by Louis Adan; and *The Death of Cæsar*, by Clement. Hillemacher's *Napoleon I. with Goethe and Wieland*, and Viger's *Josephine in* 1814, were notable pieces of portraiture. *Leda and the Swan*, by Jules Saintin, and *The First Step in Crime*, by Pierre Antigua, received many commendations, and Duran's exquisite portrait of Mademoiselle Croixette of the Theatre Français was universally praised.

In the German collection the most striking picture was Steffeck's *Crown Prince in the Front of Battle*. Louis Braun and Count Harras each contributed a *Surrender of Sedan*—striking sketches of that historic event. *The Arrest of Luther*, likewise by Harras, was a picture of great merit, as was also *Elizabeth signing the Death Warrant of Mary Stuart*, by Julius Schrader. In the way of humorous pictures, *After the Church Festival* was exhibited by Ferdinand Meyer, and the *Village Gossips* by Meyer of Bremen. Nor should mention be omitted of *The Flight of Frederick V. from Prague*, by Faber du Tour—one of the best historic pieces in Memorial Hall. Another work of the same sort, and almost equally meritorious, was Brücke's *Discovery of America*. Last of all—exhibited in a separate corridor—was Wagner's great painting, *A Scene in the Circus Maximus at Rome*. In the way of portraits, that of Pauline Lucca by Begas, and of George Bancroft by Gustave Richter, were worthy of special praise.

In the eastern gallery was placed the collection of Austria. Here was John Makart's magnificent picture, entitled *Venice Paying Homage to*

Catharine Cornaro—a historic study of great interest. As specimens of figure-painting Ernest Lafitte contributed a *Girl of Upper Austria*, and Aloysius Schönn a *Siesta of an Oriental Woman*. Of similar sort were the two fine pictures *A Page* and *A Girl with Fruit*, by Canon of Vienna—works in imitation of Rembrandt. Friedlauder was represented in the collection by *Tasting the Wine*, and Müller by an *English Garden at Palermo*.—Several fine pieces of statuary were shown as a part of the Austrian exhibit. The principal of these were the busts of Francis Joseph, Maximilian I., and Charles V. To this collection also belonged *The Freedman*, by Pezzicar—a bronze statue emblematical of the emancipation of the slaves by Lincoln.

In the Spanish department *The Landing of Columbus* was the subject of two paintings—the first by Gisbert, and the second by Puebla. Here also was shown a *Christ on the Cross* by Murillo. *Columbus before the monks of La Rabida* was the title of a large and striking work by Gano. But the painting most esteemed in the Spanish exhibit was a superb production called *The Burial of St. Lorenzo*, by Alejo Vera of Rome.— The Portuguese painters and sculptors were not represented in the collections of the hall.

The Northern nations—Sweden, Norway, Denmark—made a creditable showing of their art. The Swedish collection was arranged along the eastern wall of the western gallery, and was composed of several fine and some commonplace productions. One of the best was *The Burning of the Royal Palace at Stockholm*—a painting by Hockert. Then came *The Winter Day*, *The First Snow*, and *The Poor People's Burying Ground*, by Baron Hermelin, the Swedish art commissioner at the Exposition. A fine work called *Dark Moments* was exhibited by Baron Cederström, and *Sigurd Ring* by Severin Nilsson. Several other legends of the Vikings were represented in the works of Winge, exhibited near by; while a *Market Day in Düsseldorf* illustrated the genius of August Jernberg.–The Norwegian collection was made up of two fine pieces by Professor Gude; one excellent picture entitled *A Scene in Romsdalsfiord*, by Norman; *The Hardengerfiord*, from the studio of Thurman; and several productions of less conspicuous merit.—The Danish group embraced *The Discovery of Greenland in A. D. 1000*, by

Rasmussen; *Two Greenland Pilots*, by the same artist; and *A Midsummer Night under Iceland's Rough Weather*, by Wilhelm Melby.

The Belgian pictures constituted a notable collection. Here, first of all, was *Autumn on the Meuse*, by Asselberg—a work of great excellence; as was, also, *Rome from the Tiber*, by Bossuet. De Keyser's *Dante and the Young Girls of Florence* attracted much admiration. Then came *The Sentinel at the Gate of the Harem*, by St. Cyr; *Sunday at the Convent*, by Meerts; Xavier Mellery's *Woman of the Roman Campagna*; Mols's *Dome of the Invalides*; Smits's *War*; Stallaert's *Cave of Diomede*; and *After the Rain*, by Van Luppen. The *Desdemona* of Van Kiersbilck, and *The Deception* by Jean Portaels, were works deserving the highest praise.

Next in interest was the art exhibit of the Netherlands. Nor did the collection in its entirety suffer by comparison with the best at the Exposition. Here again the observer was constantly reminded of the nationality—both of the artist and his work. Every thing was distinctly marked with the characteristics of Lowland life, method, and manners. First in the display were four large pieces by Altmann of Amsterdam—all excellent paintings—entitled respectively *The Banquet of the Civic Guards, The Five Masters of the Drapers, The Masters of the Harlem Guild*, and *The Young Bull*—a copy from Paul Potter. Then came Koster's *View on the Yo*, Rust's *Amsterdam in the Sixteenth Century*, and *A Landscape on the Mediterranean Coast* by Hilverdink. The other principal pieces of the collection were *Four Weeks after St. John's Day* by Huybers, Bosboom's *Church of Trier*, and Mesdag's *Evening on the Beach*. Besides these, many minor paintings in the exhibit testified of the genius of the Lowland artists.

In the eastern galleries of the annex were placed a few meritorious pictures by the painters of Brazil and Mexico. But the collections were comparatively unimportant. Among the Brazilian productions the best were *The Defense of Cabrito* and *The Battle of Humaita*—both scenes from the recent war with Paraguay. In the Mexican gallery the most interesting pieces were *The Valley of Mexico* by Valesquez, and portraits of Bartholomew de las Casas and Donna Isabella of Portugal.—Such is a brief survey of the art treasures of Memorial Hall.

During the months of early summer, every day brought its throng to Fairmount Park. The enthusiasm of the people rose with the occasion. The fame of the great Exposition spread through all the land. Success had crowned the enterprise. As the Anniversary of Independence drew near preparations were made for an elaborate celebration at Philadelphia. The day came. Countless multitudes thronged the streets.[42] The city was alive with flags and banners. Battery answered battery with thunderous congratulation. The scene was set in Independence Square, in the rear of the old Hall, on the very spot where liberty was proclaimed a century ago. Platforms were erected and awnings spread above them, where four thousand invited guests could be seated to witness the ceremonies. The people crowded into the open space to the south until the whole square was a sea of upturned faces. Senator Ferry of Michigan, acting Vice-President of the United States, was the presiding officer. General Hawley and other members of the Centennial Commission acted as his assistants. Dom Pedro II. and Prince Oscar of Sweden sat near by, and distinguished citizens of many nations were present. At ten o'clock the exercises were formally opened. Centennial hymns were sung, and the national airs were played by the finest bands of the country. Richard Henry Lee, grandson of him who offered the famous Resolution of Independence, then read the Declaration from the original manuscript. Other music followed; and then came the reading of *The National Ode* by Bayard Taylor. Last of all came *The Centennial Oration* by William M. Evarts of New York. The throng receded, and the ceremonies were at an end. But the pageant was revived at night with a display of fireworks and a brilliant illumination of the city.

The daily attendance at the Exhibition grounds during the summer varied from five thousand to two hundred and seventy-five thousand. And the interest in the Centennial was intensified near its close. The whole number of visitors attending the Exposition, as shown by the registry of the gates, was nine million seven hundred and eighty-six thousand one hundred and fifty-one. The daily average attendance was

---

[42] It was estimated that on the night of the 3d of July there were fully two hundred and fifty thousand strangers in Philadelphia.

sixty-one thousand nine hundred and thirty-eight. The grounds were open for one hundred and fifty-eight days, and the total receipts for admission were three million seven hundred and sixty-one thousand five hundred and ninety-eight dollars.

On the 10th of November—in accordance with the purpose of the Centennial Commissioners—the International Exhibition of 1876 was formally closed. At two o'clock in the afternoon the President of the United States attended by General Hawley, Director-General Goshorn—upon whom for his successful management of the Exposition too great praise can hardly be bestowed—other members of the Commission, and distinguished foreigners—ascended the platform, and the ceremonies began. Theodore Thomas's magnificent orchestra again furnished music worthy of the occasion. A hundred thousand people were present to witness the closing exercises. Brief addresses were delivered by the Honorable Daniel J. Morrell of Pennsylvania and the Honorable John Welch, president of the Board of Finance. The history of the Exposition and of its management was then recounted in appropriate orations by Major Goshorn and General Hawley. The hymn *America* was sung by the audience, led by the orchestra and then President Grant arose and said:—

"I DECLARE THE INTERNATIONAL EXHIBITION CLOSED."

The valves of the great Corliss engine were shut, and the work was done. In its general character and results the Exposition had outranked all of its predecessors, and had left an impress upon the minds of the American people likely to endure for a generation and then become a patriotic tradition with posterity.[43]

---

[43] Since the close of the Exhibition steps have been taken to secure as far as practicable the *permanency* of the Centennial display. Machinery Hall has been purchased by the Common Council of Philadelphia, and is to stand intact. The Main Building also, has been sold by auction, and the purchasers have decided that it shall remain as a permanent Exposition hall. The Woman's Executive Committee have voted that their Pavilion shall also stand in its present state. The authorities of Great Britain, Germany, and France have given their respective Government Buildings to the city of Philadelphia as permanent ornaments of the grounds and as tokens of

Sioux Indians in Battle With Emigrants.

During the last year of President Grant's administration the country was disturbed by a WAR WITH THE SIOUX INDIANS. These fierce savages had, in 1867, made a treaty with the United States agreeing to relinquish all the territory south of the Niobrara, west of the one hundred and fourth meridian, and north of the forty-sixth parallel of latitude. By this treaty the Sioux were confined to a large reservation in southwestern Dakota, and upon this reservation they agreed to retire by the 1st of January, 1876. Meanwhile, however, gold was discovered among the Black Hills—a region the greater part of which belonged, by the terms of the treaty, to the Sioux reservation. But no treaty could keep the hungry horde of gold-diggers and adventurers from overrunning the interdicted district. This gave the Sioux a good excuse for gratifying their native disposition by breaking over the limits of the reservation and roaming at large through Wyoming and Montana, burning houses, stealing horses, and murdering whoever opposed them.

---

international good will; and it seems not unlikely that the principal features of the delightful park, where so many thousand people have spent the holiday hours of the Centennial summer, will be preserved as they were during the Exposition.

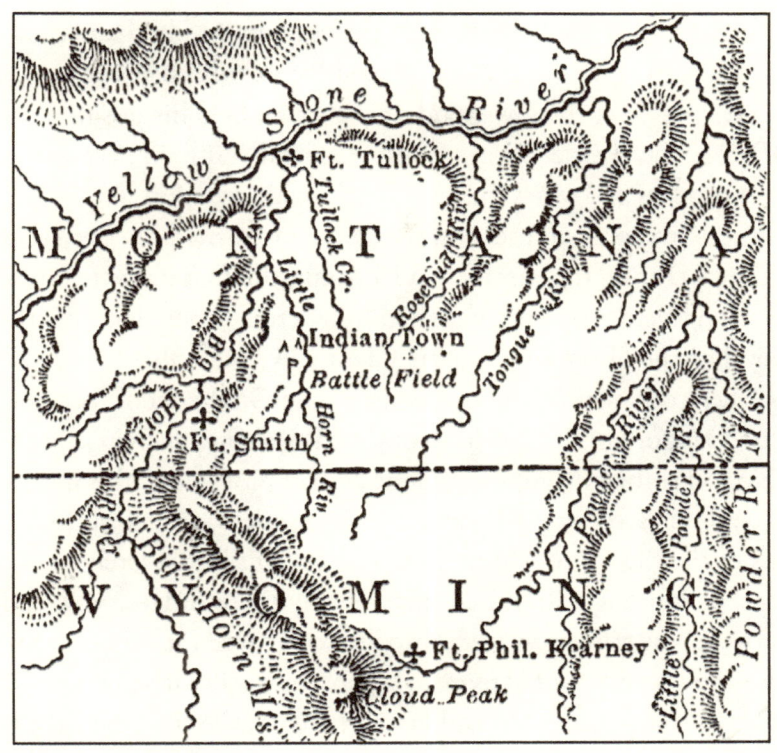

Scene of the Sioux War, 1876.

The Government now undertook to drive the Sioux upon their reservation. A large force of regulars, under Generals Terry and Crook, was sent into the mountainous country of the Upper Yellowstone, and the savages to the number of several thousand, led by their noted chieftain Sitting Bull, were crowded back against the Big Horn Mountains and River. Generals Custer and Reno, who were sent forward with the Seventh Cavalry to discover the whereabouts of the Indians, found them encamped in a large village extending for nearly three miles along the left bank of the Little Horn. On the 25th of June, General Custer, without waiting for reinforcements, charged headlong with his division into the Indian town, and was immediately surrounded by thousands of yelling warriors. Of the details of the struggle that ensued very little is known. For General Custer and every man of his command fell in the fight. The conflict equaled, if it did not surpass, in desperation and disaster any other Indian battle ever fought in America.

The whole loss of the Seventh Cavalry was two hundred and sixty-one killed, and fifty-two wounded. General Reno, who had been engaged with the savages at the lower end of the town, held his position on the bluffs of the Little Horn until General Gibbon arrived with reinforcements and saved the remnant from destruction.

Other divisions of the army were soon hurried to the scene of hostilities. During the summer and autumn the Indians were beaten in several engagements, and negotiations were opened looking to the removal of the Sioux to the Indian Territory. But still a few desperate bands held out against the authority of the Government; besides, the civilized Nations of the Territory objected to having the fierce savages of the North for their neighbors. On the 24th of November, the Sioux were decisively defeated by the Fourth Cavalry, under Colonel McKenzie, at a pass in the Big Horn Mountains. The Indians lost severely, and their village, containing a hundred and seventy-three lodges, was entirely destroyed. The army now went into winter-quarters at various points in the hostile country; but active operations were still carried on by forays and expeditions during December and January. On the 5th of the latter month, the savages were again overtaken and completely routed by the division of Colonel Miles.

Soon after this defeat, the remaining bands, under Sitting Bull and Crazy Horse, being able to offer no further serious resistance, escaped across the border and became subject to the authorities of Canada. Here they remained until the following autumn, when the Government opened negotiations with them for their return to their reservation in Dakota. A commission, headed by General Terry, met Sitting Bull and his warriors at Fort Walsh, on the Canadian frontier. Here a conference was held on the 8th of October. Full pardon for past offenses was offered to the Sioux on condition of their peaceable return and future good behavior. But the irreconcilable Sitting Bull and his savage chiefs rejected the proposal with scorn; the conference was broken off, and the Sioux were left at large in the British dominions north of Milk River.[44]

---

[44] The result of the Fort Walsh conference was by no means distasteful to the Government. By formally refusing to return to their reservation, the Indians virtually

The excitement occasioned by the outbreak of the war with the Sioux, and even the interest felt in the Centennial celebration, was soon overshadowed by the agitation of the public mind, attendant upon the twenty-third Presidential election. Before the close of June the national conventions were held and standard-bearers selected by the two leading parties. General Rutherford B. Hayes of Ohio and William A. Wheeler of New York, were chosen as candidates by the Republicans; Samuel J. Tilden of New York and Thomas A. Hendricks of Indiana, by the Democrats. A third—THE INDEPENDENT GREENBACK—party also appeared, and presented as candidates Peter Cooper of New York and Samuel F. Cary of Ohio. The canvass began early and with great spirit. The battle-cry of the Democratic party was *Reform*—reform in the public service and in all the methods of administration. For it was alleged that many of the departments of the Government and the officers presiding therein had become corrupt in practice and in fact. The Republicans answered back with the cry of *Reform,*—averring a willingness and an anxiety to correct public abuses of whatsoever sort, and to bring to condign punishment all who dared to prostitute the high places of honor to base uses. To this it was added that the nationality of the United States, as against the doctrine of State sovereignty, must be upheld, and that the rights of the colored people of the South must be protected with additional safeguards. The Independent party echoed the cry of *Reform*—monetary reform first, and all other reforms afterwards. For it was alleged by the leaders of this party that the measure of redeeming the national legal-tenders and other obligations of the United States in gold—which measure was advocated by both the other parties—was a project unjust to the debtor-class, iniquitous in itself, and impossible of accomplishment. And it was further argued by the Independents that the money-idea itself ought to be revolutionized, and that a national paper currency ought to be provided by the Government, and be based, not on specie, but on a bond bearing a low rate of interest, and interconvertible, at the option of the holder, with the currency itself.

---

renounced all relations with the United States, and the authorities were thus, by an unexpected stroke of good fortune, freed from the whole complication. Canada can hardly be congratulated on such an accession to her population!

But the advocates of this theory had only a slight political organization, and did not succeed in securing a single elect oral vote. The real contest lay—as it had done for twenty years—between the Republicans and the Democrats. The canvass drew to a close. The election was held; the general result was ascertained, *and both parties claimed the victory!* The election was so evenly balanced between the two candidates, there had been so much irregularity in the voting and subsequent electoral proceedings in the States of Florida, Louisiana, South Carolina, and Oregon, and the powers of Congress over the votes of such States were so vaguely defined, under existing legislation, that no certain declaration of the result could be made. The public mind was confounded with perplexity and excitement; and more than once were heard the ominous threatenings of civil war.

When Congress convened in December, the whole question 0f the disputed presidency came at once before that body for adjustment. The situation was seriously complicated by the political complexion of the Senate and the House of Representatives. In the former body the Republicans had a majority sufficient to control its action; while in the House the Democratic majority was still more decisive and equally willful. The debates began and seemed likely to be interminable. The question at issue was as to whether the electoral votes of the several States should, at the proper time, be opened and counted by the presiding officer of the Senate, in accordance with the immemorial and constitutional usage in such cases, or whether, in view of the existence of duplicate and spurious returns from some of the States, and of alleged gross irregularities and frauds in others, some additional court ought to be constituted to open and count the ballots. Meanwhile the necessity of doing *something* became more and more imperative. The great merchants and manufacturers of the country and the boards of trade in the principal cities grew clamorous for a speedy and peaceable adjustment of the difficulty. The spirit of compromise gained ground; and after much debating in Congress it was agreed that all the disputed election returns should be referred to A JOINT HIGH COMMISSION, consisting of five members to be chosen from the United States Senate, five from the House of Representatives, and five from the Supreme

Court. The judgment of this tribunal should be final in all matters referred thereto for decision. The Commission was accordingly constituted. The counting was begun as usual in the presence of the Senate and the House of Representatives. When the disputed and duplicate returns were reached they were referred, State by State, to the Joint High Commission; and on the 2d of March, *only two days before the time for the inauguration*, a final decision was rendered. The Republican candidates were declared elected. One hundred and eighty-five electoral votes were cast for Hayes and Wheeler, and one hundred and eighty-four fox Tilden and Hendricks. The greatest political crisis in the history of the country passed harmlessly by without violence or bloodshed.

CHAPTER LXIX.

Hayes's Administration, 1877-1881.

RUTHERFORD B. HAYES, nineteenth President of the United States, was born in Delaware, Ohio, on the 4th day of October, 1822. His ancestors were soldiers of the Revolution. His primary education was received in the public schools. Afterwards, his studies were extended to Greek and Latin at the Norwalk Academy and in 1837 he became a student at Webb's preparatory school, at Middletown, Connecticut. In the following year, he entered the Freshman class at Kenyon College, and in 1842 was graduated from that institution with the highest honors of his class. Three years after his graduation, he completed his legal studies at Harvard University, and soon afterward began the practice of his profession, first at Marietta, then at Fremont, and finally as city solicitor, in Cincinnati. Here he won distinguished reputation as a lawyer. During the Civil War he performed much honorable service in the Union cause, rose to the rank of major general, and in 1864, while still in the field, was elected to Congress. Three years later he was chosen governor of his native State, and was reelected in 1869, and again in 1875. At the Cincinnati convention of 1876, he had the good fortune to be nominated for the presidency over several of the most eminent men of the nation.

President Hayes.

In his inaugural address, delivered on the 5th of March,[45] President Hayes indicated the policy of his administration. The patriotic and conciliatory utterances of the address did much to quiet the bitter spirit of partisanship which for many months had disturbed the country. The distracted South was assured of right purposes on the part of the new chief-magistrate; a radical reform in the civil service was avowed as a part of his policy; and a speedy return to specie payments was recommended as the final cure for the deranged finances of the nation. The immediate effect of these assurances—so evidently made in all good faith and honesty—was to rally around the incipient administration the better part of all the parties and to introduce a new "Era of Good Feeling" as peaceable and beneficent in its character as the former turbulence had been exciting and dangerous.

On the 8th of March, the President named the members of his cabinet. Here, again, he marked out a new departure in the policy of the government. For the cabinet, though exceptionably able and statesmanlike, was noticeably non-partisan in its character. As secretary of state William M. Evarts, of New York, was chosen; John Sherman, of Ohio, was named as secretary of the treasury; George W. McCrary, of Iowa, secretary of war; Richard W. Thompson, of Indiana, secretary of the navy; Carl Schurz, of Missouri, secretary of the interior; Charles E. Devens, of Massachusetts, attorney-general; and David M. Key, of Tennessee, postmaster-general. These nominations were duly ratified by the Senate; and the new administration and the new century of the republic were ushered in together.

In the summer of 1877 occurred the great labor disturbance known as THE RAILROAD STRIKE. For several years the mining districts of the country had been vexed with disputes and outbreaks having their origin in the question of wages. The manufacturing towns and cities had witnessed similar troubles, and the great corporations having control of the lines of travel and commerce were frequently brought to a stand-still

---

[45] The 4th of March fell on Sunday. The same thing has happened in the following years: 1753, 1781, 1821 (Monroe's inauguration, second term), 1849 (Taylor's inauguration), 1877 (Hayes's inauguration); and the same will hereafter occur as follows: 1917, 1945, 1973, 2001, 2029, 2057, 2088, 2125, 2153.

by the determined opposition of their employés. The workingmen and the capitalists of the country had for some time maintained towards each other a kind of armed neutrality alike hurtful to the interests of both. In the spring of this year, the managers of the great railways leading from the seaboard to the West declared a reduction of ten per cent in the wages of their workmen. This measure, which was to take effect at the middle of July, was violently resisted by the employés of the companies, and the most active steps were taken to prevent its success. The workmen of the various roads entered into combinations, and the officers stood firm. On the 16th of July, the employés of the Baltimore and Ohio Railroad left their posts and gathered such strength in Baltimore and at Martinsburg, West Virginia, as to prevent the running of trains and set the authorities at defiance. The militia was called out by Governor Matthews and sent to Martinsburg, but was soon dispersed by the strikers who, for the time, remained masters of the line. The President then ordered General French to the scene with a body of regulars, and the blockade of the road was raised. On the 20th of the month, a terrible tumult occurred in Baltimore; but the troops succeeded in scattering the rioters of whom nine were killed and many wounded.

Meanwhile the strike spread everywhere. In less than a week the trains had been stopped on all the important roads between the Hudson and the Mississippi. Except in the cotton-growing States the insurrection was universal. Travel ceased, freights perished en route, business was paralyzed. In Pittsburgh the strikers, rioters, and dangerous classes gathering in a mob to the number of twenty thousand, obtained complete control of the city and for two days held a reign of terror unparalleled in the history of the country. The lawless violence and madness of the scene recalled the fiery days of the French Revolution. The Union Dépôt and all the machine shops and other railroad buildings of the city were burned. A hundred and twenty-five locomotives, and two thousand five hundred cars laden with valuable cargoes, were destroyed amid the wildest havoc and uproar. The insurrection was finally suppressed by the regular troops and the Pennsylvania militia, but not until nearly a hundred lives had been lost and property destroyed to the value of more than three millions of dollars.

On the 25th of the month, a similar but less terrible riot occurred at Chicago. In this tumult fifteen of the insurgents were killed by the military of the city. On the next day, St. Louis was for some hours in peril of the mob. San Francisco was at the same time the scene of a dangerous outbreak which was here directed against the Chinese immigrants and the managers of the lumber yards. Cincinnati, Columbus, Louisville, Indianapolis, and Fort Wayne were for a while in danger, but escaped without serious loss of life or property. By the close of the month, the alarming insurrection was at an end. Business and travel flowed back into their usual channels; but the sudden outbreak had given a great shock to the public mind, and revealed a hidden peril to American institutions.

In the mean time, a war had broken out with the Nez Percé Indians of Idaho. This tribe of natives had been known to the Government since 1806, when the first treaty was made with them by the explorers, Lewis and Clarke. Afterwards, missionary stations were established among them, and the nation remained on friendly terms until after the war with Mexico. In 1854 the authorities of the United States, purchased a part of the Nez Percé territory, large reservations being made in North-western Idaho and North-eastern Oregon; but some of the chiefs refused to ratify the purchase and remained at large. This was the beginning of difficulties.

The war began with the usual depredations by the Indians. General Howard, commanding the Department of the Columbia, marched against them with a small force of regulars; but the Nez Percés, led by their noted chieftain Joseph, fled first in this direction, and then in that, avoiding battle. During the greater part of the summer the pursuit continued; still the Indians could not be overtaken. In the fall they were chased through the mountains into Northern Montana, where they were confronted by other troops commanded by Colonel Miles.

The Nez Percés, thus hemmed in, were next driven across the Missouri River, near the mouth of the Musselshell, and were finally surrounded in their camp, north of the Bear Paw Mountains. Here, on the 4th of October, they were attacked by the forces of Colonel Miles. A hard battle was fought, and the Indians were completely routed. Only a few, led by the chief White Bird, escaped. All the rest were either killed or made prisoners. Three hundred and seventy-five of the captive Nez Percés were brought back to the American post on the Missouri. The tr00ps of General Howard had made forced marches through a mountainous country for a distance of *sixteen hundred miles!*–The campaign was crowned with complete success.

During the year 1877, the public mind was greatly agitated concerning THE REMONETIZATION OF SILVER. By the first coinage regulations of the United States, the standard unit of value was the American Silver Dollar, containing three hundred and seventy-one and one-fourth grains of pure silver. From the date of the adoption of this standard, in 1792, until 1873, the quantity of pure metal in this standard unit had never been changed, though the amount of alloy contained in the dollar was several times altered. Meanwhile, in 1849, a gold dollar was added to the coinage, and from that time forth the standard unit of value existed in both metals. In the years 1873-'74, at a time when, owing to the premium on gold and silver, both metals were out of circulation, a series of acts were adopted by Congress bearing upon the standard unit of value, whereby the legal tender quality of silver was first abridged and then abolished. These enactments were completed by the report of the Coinage Committee in 1874, by which the silver dollar was finally omitted from the list of coins to be struck at the national mints. The general effect of these acts was to leave the gold dollar of twenty-three and twenty-two–hundredths grains the single standard unit of value in the United States.

In January of 1875, THE RESUMPTION ACT was passed by Congress, whereby it was declared that on the 1st of January, 1879, the Government of the United States should begin to redeem its outstanding legal-tender notes *in coin*. As the time for resumption drew near, and the premium on gold fell off, the question was raised as to the meaning of "coin" in the act for resuming specie payments; and now, for the first time the attention of the people at large was aroused to the fact that by the acts of 1873-'74 the privilege of paying debts in silver had been taken away, and that after the beginning of 1879 all obligations must be discharged according to the measure of the gold dollar only. A great agitation followed. The cry *for the remonetizetion of silver* was heard everywhere. The question reached the Government, and early in

1878 a measure was passed by Congress for the restoration of the legal tender quality of the old silver dollar, and providing for the compulsory coinage of that unit at the mints at a rate of not less than two millions of dollars a month. The President returned the bill with his objections, but the veto was crushed under a tremendous majority; for nearly three-fourths of the members of Congress, without respect to party affiliations, gave their support to the measure; and the old double standard of values was restored.

In the summer of 1878, several of the Gulf States were scourged with a YELLOW FEVER EPIDEMIC, unparalleled in the history of the country. The disease made its appearance in New Orleans in the latter part of May, and from thence was quickly scattered among the other towns along the Mississippi. Unfortunately, the attention of the people in the Gulf country had been but little given to sanitary precautions, and the Southern cities were nearly all in a condition to invite the presence of the scourge. The terror soon spread from town to town, and the people began to fly from the pestilence. The cities of Memphis and Grenada became a scene of desolation. At Vicksburgh the ravages of the plague were almost equally terrible; and even in the parish-towns remote from the river, and as far north at Nashville and Louisville, the horrors of the scourge were felt. All summer long the disease held on unabated. The helpless populations along the Lower Mississippi languished and died by thousands. A regular system of contributions was established in the Northern States, and men and treasure were poured out without stint to relieve the suffering South. The efforts of the Howard Association at New Orleans, Memphis, and elsewhere, were almost unequaled in heroism and sacrifice. After more than twenty thousand people had fallen victims to the plague, the grateful frosts of October came at last and ended the pestilence.

By the XVIIIth Article of the Treaty of Washington,[46] it was agreed that the right of the inhabitants of the United States in certain sea-fisheries which had hitherto belonged exclusively to the subjects of Great Britain, should be acknowledged and maintained. It was conceded,

---

[46] See page 669.

moreover, that the privilege of taking fish of every kind—except shellfish—on the sea-coasts and shores, and in the bays, harbors, and creeks of the provinces of Quebec, Nova Scotia, New Brunswick, Prince Edward's Island, and the islands thereunto adjacent, without restriction as to distance from the shore, should be guaranteed to American fishermen, without prejudice or partiality. On the other hand, the government of the United States agreed to relinquish the duties which had hitherto been charged on certain kinds of fish imported by British subjects into American harbors. Several other concessions of minor importance were mutually made by the contracting parties; and in order to balance any discrepancy that might appear in the aggregate of such concessions, and to make the settlement of a vexed question full, fair, and final, it was further agreed that any total advantage to the United States arising from the treaty, might be compensated by a sum in gross to be paid by the American government to Great Britain. And in order to determine what such sum should be, a Commission was provided for, the same to consist of one commissioner to be appointed by the Queen, one by the President, and a third (provided the Queen and the President should not agree on a third) by the Austrian ambassador at the Court of St. James![47] Accordingly, in the summer of 1877, the Commission was constituted, and the sittings began at Halifax. But little attention was given to the proceedings of the body until November, when the country was startled by the announcement that by the casting vote of Mr. Delfosse, Belgian minister to the United States, who had been named as third commissioner by the Austrian ambassador at London, *an award of five millions of dollars had been made against the American government!* The decision was received with general surprise, both in the United States and in Europe; and for a while it seemed probable that the

---

[47] A strange and inexplicable provision. As a matter of fact, it came to pass that the man who by the terms of the treaty held the power of appointing, and who did appoint, the umpire in the Halifax Commission, was Count Von Beust, a Bourbon of the Bourbons in politics, a Saxon renegade, an upholder of the House of Hapsburg by choice, and a hater of all republican institutions. It thus happened that a question which had proved too much for the Joint High Commission itself, was remanded for settlement to a political adventurer temporarily resident *in London*! To understand the proceeding requires the wisdom of a—statesman!

arbitration might be renounced as iniquitous. It was decided, however, that the award, whether just or unjust, would better stand; and accordingly, in November, 1878, the amount was paid—not without great popular dissatisfaction—to the British government.

The year 1878 witnessed the establishment of a RESIDENT CHINESE EMBASSY at Washington. For twenty years the great and liberal treaty negotiated by Anson Burlingame had been in force between the United States and China. Under the protection of this compact, the commercial relations of the two countries had been vastly extended, and a knowledge of the institutions, manners, and customs prevalent in the Celestial Empire so widely diffused as to break down in some measure the race-prejudice existing against the Mongolians. The enlightened policy of the reigning emperor had also contributed to establish more friendly intercourse with the United States, and to promote such measures as should make that intercourse lasting. The idea of sending resident ambassadors to the American government had been entertained for several years. The emperor had been assured that the people of China—more particularly her ministers—would be received with all the courtesy shown to the most favored nation. The officers chosen by the imperial government as its representatives in the United States were Chen Lan Pin, minister plenipotentiary, Yung Wing, assistant envoy, and Yung Tsang Siang, secretary of legation. On the 28th of September the embassy was received by the President. The ceremonies of the occasion were among the most novel and interesting ever witnessed in Washington. The speech of Chen Lan Pin was equal in dignity and appropriateness to the best efforts of a European diplomatist. Addressing the President the Chinese minister said:

"MR. PRESIDENT: His Majesty, the Emperor of China, in appointing us to reside at Washington as ministers, instructed us to present your Excellency his salutations, and to express his assurances of friendship for you and the people of the United States. His Majesty hopes that your administration may be one of signal success, and that it may bring lasting peace and prosperity to the whole country. On a former occasion the Chinese government had the honor to send an embassy to Washington on a special mission, and the results were most beneficent. His Majesty cherishes the hope that this embassy will not only be the means of establishing on a firm basis the amicable relations of the two countries, but may also be the starting-point of a new diplomatic era which will eventually unite the East and West under an enlightened and progressive civilization."

The history of modern times contains many pleasing evidences of the growing estimate placed by civilized states upon the value of human life. In the legislation of Congress several important acts bear witness to the general interest felt in the United States on the subject of better protection for those who are exposed by land and sea. The question of affording adequate succor to shipwrecked sailors has especially engrossed the attention of the government, and many measures have been proposed with a view of giving greater security to "them that go down to the sea in ships." During the last session of the Forty-fifth Congress a bill was brought forward by S. S. Cox, of New York, for the reorganization of THE LIFE-SAVING SERVICE OF THE UNITED STATES, under the patronage and control of the government. This service had existed as a private enterprise since 1871. The plan proposed and adopted June 18, 1878, embraced the establishment of regular stations and light-houses on all the exposed parts of the Atlantic coast and along the great lakes. Each station was to be manned by a band of surfmen experienced in the dangers peculiar to the shore in times of storms, and drilled in the best methods of rescue and resuscitation. Boats of the most approved pattern—capable of surviving any storm that ever lashed the sea—were provided and equipped. A hundred appliances and inventions suggested by the wants of the service—life-cars with hawsers, and mortars for firing shot-lines into vessels foundering at a distance from the shore—were supplied and their use skillfully taught to the brave men who were employed at the stations. The success of the enterprise has been so great as to reflect the highest credit on its promoters. The number of lives saved through the direct agency of the service reaches to thousands annually, and the amount of human suffering and distress alleviated by this beneficent movement is beyond computation. So carefully are the exposed coasts of the United States now guarded that it is almost impossible for a foundering ship to be driven within sight of the shore without at once beholding through the darkness of the otherwise hope less night the sudden glare of the red-light signal flaming up from the beach, telling the story of friends near by and rescue soon to come.

On the 1st of January, 1879, THE RESUMPTION OF SPECIE PAYMENTS was formally accomplished by the treasury of the United States. For more than seventeen years, owing to the disorders arising from the Civil War, gold and silver coin had been at a premium over the legal-tender notes of the Government. During this whole period the monetary affairs of the Nation had been in a state of distraction. As a matter of fact, the monetary unit had been so fluctuating as to render legitimate business almost impossible. The actual purchasing power of a dollar could hardly be predicted from one week to another. Resulting from this, a spirit of rampant speculation had taken possession of most of the market values of the country. The lawful transactions of the street, carried forward in obedience to the plain principles of political economy, suffered shipwreck, while *parvenu* statesmen gave lectures on the nature of debt and the evils of overproduction! After the passage of the Resumption Act, in 1875, owing to the steady and rapid appreciation of the value of the monetary unit, the debtor classes of the country entered a period of great hardship; for their indebtedness constantly augmented in a ratio beyond the probability, if not the possibility, of payment. It was an epoch of financial ruin and bankruptcy, which was only checked, but not ended, by the abrogation of the Bankrupt Act, in 1878. With the near approach of Resumption, however, a certain degree of confidence supervened; and the actual accomplishment of the fact was hailed by many as the omen of better times.

The presidential election of 1880 was accompanied with the usual excitement attendant upon great political struggles in the United States. The congressional elections of 1878 had generally gone against the Republican party, insomuch that in both houses of the Forty-sixth Congress the Democrats had a clear majority. It was therefore not unreasonable to expect that in the impending contest for the presidency the Democratic party would prove successful. The leaders of this party were hopeful of success and entered the campaign with renewed zeal and energy. The Republican national convention was held in Chicago on the 2d and 3d of June. A platform of principles was adopted largely retrospective. The history of the party during the twenty years of its supremacy in the government was recited as the best reason why its lease of power should be continued by the people. The platform reaffirmed and emphasized the doctrine of nationality as opposed to the theory of states' rights; declared in favor of popular education; advocated a system of discriminating duties in favor of American industries; called on Congress to limit Chinese immigration; avoided the question of finance; complimented the administration of President Hayes; and arraigned the Democratic party as unpatriotic in its principles and fraudulent in its practices. Upon this platform—after the greater part of two days had been consumed in balloting—General James A. Garfield, of Ohio, was nominated for President, and Chester A. Arthur, of New York, for Vice-President.

The Democratic national convention assembled in Cincinnati, on the 22d of June. The platform of principles declared adherence to the doctrines and traditions of the party opposed the tendency to centralization in the government; adhered to gold and silver money and paper convertible into coin; advocated a tariff for revenue only; proclaimed a free ballot; denounced the administration as the creature of a conspiracy; opposed the presence of troops at the polls; complimented Samuel J. Tilden for his patriotism; declared for free ships and an amendment to the Burlingame treaty as against Chinese immigration; and appealed to the acts of the Forty-sixth Congress as proof and illustration of Democratic economy and wisdom. After adopting this platform the convention nominated for the presidency General Winfield S. Hancock, of New York, and for the vice-presidency William H. English, of Indiana.

Meanwhile the National Greenback party had held a convention in Chicago, on the 9th of June, and nominated as standard-bearers General James B. Weaver, of Iowa, for President, and General Benjamin J. Chambers, of Texas, for Vice-President. The platform of principles declared in favor of the rights of the laborer, as against the exactions of capital; denounced monopolies and syndicates; proclaimed the sovereign power of the government over the coinage of metallic and the issuance of paper money; advocated the abolition of the National banking system and the substitution of legal-tender currency; declared for the payment of the bonded debt of the United States as against all refunding schemes; denounced land-grants; opposed Chinese immigration and an increase of the standing army; favored the equal taxation of all property and unrestricted suffrage; demanded reform in the methods of congressional proceedings; and appealed for support to the sense of justice in the American people.

The canvass had not progressed far until it became evident that the contest lay between the Republican and the Democratic party, and that the long-standing sectional division into North and South was likely once more to decide the contest in favor of the former. That part of the Democratic platform which declared for a tariff for revenue only, alarmed the manufacturing interests and consolidated them in support of the Republican candidates. The banking and bond-holding classes rallied with great unanimity to the same standard, and the old war spirit, aroused at the appearance of a "solid South" insured a solid North against the Democracy. The election resulted in the choice of Garfield and Arthur. Two hundred and fourteen electoral votes, embracing those of all the Northern States except New Jersey, Nevada, and four out of the five votes of California, were cast for the Republican candidates, and one hundred and fifty-five votes, including those of every Southern State, were given to Hancock and English. The candidates of the National party secured no electoral votes, though the popular vote given to Weaver and Chambers aggregated 307,000 as against 81,000 cast for Cooper and Cary in 1876.

The administration of President Hayes and the last session of the Forty-sixth Congress expired together on the 4th of March, 1881. The closing session had been chiefly occupied with the matter of refunding the national debt. About seven hundred and fifty millions of dollars of five and six per cent. bonds became due during the year; and to provide for the payment or refunding of this large sum was the most important matter claiming the attention of Congress. Late in the session a bill was passed by that body providing for the issuance by the government of new bonds of two classes, both bearing three per cent.; the first class payable in from five to twenty years, and the second class in from one to ten years. The latter bonds were to be issued in small denominations, adapted to the conditions of a popular loan. One provision of the bill required the national banks holding five and six per cent. bonds to surrender the same—the bonds having fallen due—and to receive instead the new three per cents. This clause of the law aroused the antagonism of the banks and by every possible means they sought to prevent the passage of the bill. On the last day of the session, the measure having been adopted by both houses of Congress, the act was laid before the President for his approval, which was withheld. A veto message was returned to Congress; the advocates of the bill being unable to command a two-thirds majority in its favor, the bill failed to become a law, and the session closed without any provision for the refunding of the 750,000,000 dollars of bonds falling due in 1881.

Soon after retiring from the presidency, General Grant with his family and a company of personal friends, set out to visit the countries of Europe and Asia, and to make a tour of the world. Though the expedition was intended to be private it could but attract the most conspicuous attention both at home and abroad. The departure from Philadelphia on the 17th of May, 1877, was the beginning of a pageant which, in its duration and magnificence, was never before extended to any citizen of any nation of the earth. Wherever the distinguished ex-President went he was welcomed with huzzas and dismissed with plaudits. First in England—at Liverpool, Manchester, London—and afterwards, in midsummer, in Belgium, Switzerland, Prussia, and France, everywhere the General's coming was announced by the thunder of cannon, the thronging of multitudes, and a chorus of cheers. A short stay in Italy was followed by a voyage to Alexandria, and a brief sojourn in Egypt. Thence the company proceeded to Palestine and afterwards to Greece. The following spring found the ex-President and his party again in Italy—at Rome, Florence, Venice, and Milan; and the summer carried them into Denmark, Sweden, and Norway. The next countries visited were Austria and Russia, while for the winter the distinguished tourists chose the south of France and Spain. Ireland was visited, and in January of 1879 the company embarked from Marseilles for the East. The following year was Spent in visiting the great countries of Asia—India first; then Burmah and Siam; then China; and then Japan. In the fall of 1879 the party returned to San Francisco, bearing with them the highest tokens of esteem which the great nations of the Old World could bestow upon the honored representative of the civilization of the New.

The census of 1880 was undertaken with more system and care than ever before in the history of the country. The work was entrusted to the general superintendency of Professor Francis A. Walker, under whose direction the admirable census of 1870 was conducted. During the decade the same astounding progress which had marked the previous history of the United States was more than ever illustrated. In every source of national power, in every element of national vigor, the development of the country had continued without abatement. The total population of the states and territories of the Union now amounted to 50,152,866—an increase since 1870 *of more than a million inhabitants a year!* New York was still the leading state, having a population of 5,083,173. Nevada was least populous, showing an enumeration of but 62,265. Of the 11,584,188 added to the population since the census of 1870, 2,246,551 had been contributed by immigration, of whom about 85,000 annually came from Germany alone.

The number of cities having a population of over 100,000 inhabitants had increased during the decade from fourteen to twenty.[48]

---

[48] The following table will show the population and rate of increase in the ten leading cities in the United States, according to the censuses of 1870 and 1880:

CITY.	STATE.	Population 1870	Population 1880	Per cent. of increase.
New York	New York	942,292	1,206,590	28
Philadelphia	Pennsylvania	674,022	846,984	25
Brooklyn	New York	396,099	586,689	48
St. Louis	Missouri	310,864	350,522	13
Chicago	Illinois	298,977	503,304	72
Baltimore	Maryland	267,354	333,190	24
Boston	Massachusetts	250,526	362,535	44
Cincinnati	Ohio	216,239	255,708	22
New Orleans	Louisiana	191,418	216,140	13
San Francisco	California	149,473	233,956	56

The center of population had moved westward about fifty miles, and now rested at the city of Cincinnati.

The statistics of trade and industry were likewise of a sort to gratify patriotism, if not to excite national pride. The current of the precious metals which for many years had flowed constantly from the United States to foreign countries turned strongly, in 1880, towards America. The importation of specie during the year just mentioned amounted to $93,034,310 while the exportation of the same during the year reached only $17,142,199. During the greater part of the period covered by the census abundant crops had followed in almost unbroken succession, and the overplus in the great staples peculiar to our soil and climate had gone to enrich the country, and to stimulate to an unusual degree those fundamental industries upon which national perpetuity and individual happiness are ultimately founded.[49]

During the administration of President Hayes several eminent Americans passed from the scene of their earthly activities. On the 1st of November, 1877, the distinguished Senator Oliver P. Morton, of Indiana, after battling for many years against the deadly encroachments of paralysis, died at his home in Indianapolis. His death, though not unforeseen, was much lamented. Still more universally felt was the loss of the great poet and journalist, William Cullen Bryant, who, on the 12th of June, 1878, at the advanced age of eighty-four, passed from among the living. For more than sixty years his name had been known and honored wherever the English language is spoken. His life had been an inspiration, and the brightest light of American literature was extinguished in his death. On the 19th of December, in the same year, the illustrious Bayard Taylor, who had recently been appointed American minister to the German Empire, died suddenly in the city of Berlin. His life had been exclusively devoted to literary work; and almost every department of letters, from the common tasks of journalism to the highest charms of poetry, had been adorned by his genius. His death, at the early age of fifty-four, left a gap not soon to be filled in the shining ranks of literature. On the 1st day of November, 1879, Senator

---

[49] At the date of sending this edition to the press, only the preliminary results of the census of 1880 have been given to the public.

Zachariah Chandler, of Michigan, one of the organizers of the Republican party, and a great leader of that party in the times of the civil war, died suddenly at Chicago; and on the 24th day of February, 1881, another senator, the distinguished Matt. H. Carpenter, of Wisconsin, after a lingering illness, expired at Washington. One by one the strong men who battled for the preservation of American nationality in the stormy days of the civil war are passing or have passed into the land of rest.

CHAPTER LXX.

ADMINISTRATIONS OF GARFIELD AND ARTHUR.

JAMES A. GARFIELD, twentieth President of the United States, was born at Orange, Cuyahoga county, Ohio, November 19th, 1831. By the death of his father he was left in infancy to the sole care of his mother and to the rude surroundings of a backwoods home. Blest with great native energy and an abundance of physical vigor, the boy gathered from country toil a sound constitution, and from country schools the rudiments of education. In boyhood his services were in frequent demand by the farmers of the neighborhood—for he developed unusual skill as a mechanic. Afterwards he served as a driver and pilot of a canal boat plying the Ohio and Pennsylvania canal. At the age of seventeen he attended the High School in Chester, where he applied himself with great diligence, extending his studies to algebra, Latin, and Greek. In the fall of 1851, he entered Hiram College, in Portage county, Ohio, where he remained as student and instructor until 1854. In that year he entered Williams College, from which, in August of 1856, he was graduated with honor. He then returned to Ohio, and was made first a professor and afterwards president of Hiram College. This position he held until the outbreak of the civil war when he left his post to enter the army. Meanwhile he had studied

James A. Garfield

law, imbibed a love for politics, and been elected to the Ohio State Senate.

As a soldier Garfield was first made lieutenant-colonel and afterwards colonel of the Forty-second regiment of Ohio volunteers. Advancing with his men to the front he was soon promoted to a brigadier generalship, and did good service in Kentucky and Tennessee. He was made chief of staff to General Rosecrans, and bore a distinguished part in the battle, of Chickamauga. Soon afterwards, while still in the field, he was, in 1862, elected by the people of his district to the lower house of Congress, where he continued to serve as a member for seventeen years. In 1879 he was elected to the United States Senate, and hard upon this followed his nomination and election to the presidency. American history has furnished but few instances of a more steady and brilliant rise from the poverty of an obscure boyhood to the most distinguished elective office in the gift of mankind.

On the 4th of March, 1881, President Garfield, according to the custom, delivered his inaugural address. A retrospect of the progress of American civilization during the last quarter of a century was given and the country congratulated on its high rank among the nations. The leading topics of politics were briefly reviewed, and the policy of the executive department of the government with respect to the great questions likely to engross the attention of the people, set forth with clearness and precision. The public school system of the United States should be guarded with jealous care; the old wounds of the South should be healed and the heartburnings of the civil war be buried in oblivion; the present banking system should be maintained; the practices of polygamy should be repressed; Chinese immigration should be curbed by treaty; the equal rights of the enfranchised blacks should be asserted and maintained.

On the day following the inauguration the President sent to the Senate for confirmation the names of the members of his cabinet. The nominations were, for secretary of state, James G. Blaine of Maine; for secretary of the treasury, William Windom, of Minnesota; for secretary of war, Robert T. Lincoln, of Illinois; for secretary of the navy, William H. Hunt, of Louisiana; for secretary of the interior, Samuel J. Kirkwood, of Iowa; for attorney-general, Wayne MacVeagh, of Pennsylvania; for postmaster-general Thomas L. James, of New York. These nominations were promptly confirmed, and the new administration entered upon its course with omens of an auspicious future.

One of the first issues which engaged the attention of the government after Garfield's accession to the Presidency, was the question of REFORM IN THE CIVIL SERVICE. This question had been inherited from the administration of Hayes, by whom several spasmodic efforts had been made to introduce better methods in the selection of men to fill the appointive offices of the United States. The real issue was whether the choice of the officials of the government should be made on the grounds of the character and fitness of the candidate, or on the principle of distributing political patronage to those who had best served the party—whether men should be promoted from the lower to the higher grades of official life, and retained according to the value and proficiency of the service rendered, or be elevated to position in proportion to their success in carrying elections and maintaining the party in power. The members of Congress to whom the help of efficient supporters in their own districts and states seemed essential, and by whom the patronage of the government had been dispensed since the days of Jackson, held stoutly to the old order, unwilling to relinquish their influence over the appointing power. President Hayes, after vainly attempting to establish the opposite policy, abandoned the field near the close of his administration. The national Republican platform of 1880, however, vaguely endorsed "civil service reform" as a principle of the party, and some expectation existed that President Garfield would follow the policy of his predecessor. With the incoming of the new administration the rush for office was unprecedented in the previous history of the country. The politicians and place-seekers, who claimed to have "carried the election," swarmed into Washington and thronged the executive mansion, clamoring for office, until, for the time, all plans and purposes of reform in the civil service were quite crushed out of sight and forgotten. As always hitherto, ambition for political power and hunger for the spoils of office triumphed over the better sense of the American people.

The prospects of the new administration were soon darkened with political difficulties. A division arose in the ranks of the Republican party, threatening the disruption and ruin of that organization. The two wings of the Republicans were nicknamed the "Half breeds" and the "Stalwarts:" the latter, headed by Senator Conkling, of New York, being the division which had so resolutely supported General Grant for the Presidency in the Chicago Convention; the former, led by Mr. Blaine, now Secretary of State, and indorsed by the President himself, had control of the government, and were numerically stronger than their opponents. The Stalwarts claimed the right of dispensing the appointive offices of the Government, after the manner which prevailed for several preceding administrations; that is, the distribution of the offices in the several States, under the name of patronage, by the Senators and Representatives of those States in Congress. The President, supported by his division of the party, and in general by the reform element in politics, insisted on naming the officers in the various States according to his own wishes and what he conceived to be the fitness of things.

The chief clash between the two influences in the party occurred in respect to the offices in New York. The collectorship of customs for the port of New York is the best appointive office in the gift of the Government. To fill this position the President appointed Judge William Robertson, and the appointment was bitterly antagonized by the New York Senators, Roscoe Conkling and Thomas C. Platt, who, failing to prevent the confirmation of Robertson, resigned their seats, returned to their State, and failed of a reëlection. The breach thus effected in the Republican ranks was such as to threaten the dismemberment of the party.

Such was the condition of affairs at the adjournment of the Senate in June. A few days afterward the President made arrangements to visit Williams College, where his two sons were to be placed at school, and to pass a short vacation with his sick wife at the sea-side. On the morning of July 2d, in company with Secretary Blaine and a few friends, he entered the Baltimore depot at Washington, preparatory to taking the train for Long Branch, N. J. A moment afterward he was approached by a miserable political miscreant named Charles Julius Guiteau, who, from behind, and unperceived, came within a few feet of the company, drew a pistol, and fired upon the chief-magistrate of the Republic. The aim of the assassin was too well taken, and the second shot struck the President centrally in the right side of the back, inflicting a dreadful wound. The bleeding chieftain was quickly borne away to the executive mansion, and the vile wretch who had committed the crime was hurried to prison.

For a week or two the hearts of the American people vibrated between hope and fear. The best surgical aid was procured, and bulletins were daily issued containing a brief outline of the President's condition. The conviction grew day by day that he would ultimately recover. Two surgical operations were performed with a view of improving his chances for life but a series of relapses occurred, and the President gradually weakened under his sufferings. As a last hope he was, on the 6th of September, carefully conveyed from Washington City to Elberon, where he was placed in a cottage only a few yards from the surf. Here, for a brief period, hope again revived, but the symptoms were aggravated at intervals, and the patient sank day by day.

At half past ten on the evening of September 19th, the anniversary of the battle of Chickamauga, in which President Garfield had won his chief military reputation, his vital powers suddenly gave way under the destructive influence of blood poisoning and exhaustion, and in a few moments death closed the scene. For eighty days he had borne the pain and anguish of his situation with a fortitude and heroism rarely witnessed among men. The dark shadow of the crime which had laid him low heightened rather than eclipsed the luster and glory of his great and exemplary life.

On the day following this deplorable event Vice-President Arthur took the oath of office in New York, and immediately repaired to Washington. For the fourth time in the history of the American Republic the duties of the presidency had been devolved by death upon the man constitutionally provided for such an emergency. The heart of the people, however, clung for a time to the dead rather than to the living President. The funeral of Garfield was observed first of all at Washington, whither the body was taken and placed in state in the rotunda of the Capitol. Here it was viewed by tens of thousands of people during the 22d and 23d of September. In his life-time the illustrious dead had chosen as the place of his burial the Lakeview Cemetery, at Cleveland, Ohio, and thither, on the 24th of the month, the remains were conveyed by way of Philadelphia and Pittsburgh. As in the case of the dead Lincoln, the funeral processions and ceremonies were a pageant, exhibiting every-where the loyal respect and love of the American people for him who had so lately been their pride. On the 26th of September his body was laid in its final resting-place. The day of the burial was observed throughout the country in great assemblies gathered from hamlet and town and city, all anxious to testify, by some appropriate word or token, their sorrow for the great national calamity, and their appreciation of the grand example of James A. Garfield's life.

Chester A. Arthur, called by this sad event to be the President of the United States, was born in Franklin County, Vermont, October 5, 1830. He is of Irish descent, and was educated at Union College, from which institution he was graduated in 1849. For a while he taught school in his native State, and then came to New York City to study law. Here he was soon admitted to the bar and rapidly rose to distinction. During the Civil War he was Quartermaster-General of the State of New York, a very important and trying office, which he filled with great credit to himself and the government. After 1865 he returned to the practice of law, and was appointed Collector of Customs for the port of New York in 1871. This position he held until July, 1878 when he was removed by President Hayes. Again he returned to his law practice, but was soon called by the voice of his

Chester A. Arthur.

party to be a standard-bearer in the presidential canvass of 1880. His election to the vice-presidency followed, and then, by the death of President Garfield, he rose to the post of chief honor among the American people.

The assumption of the duties of his high office by President Arthur was attended with but little ceremony or formality. On the 22d of September the oath of office was again administered to him in the Vice-President's room, in the Capitol, Chief-justice Waite officiating. After this, in the presence of the few who were gathered in the apartment, he delivered a brief and appropriate address, referring, in a touching manner, to the death of his predecessor. Those present—including General Grant, ex-President Hayes, Senator Sherman, and his brother the General of the army—then paid their respects, and the ceremony was at an end.

In accordance with the custom, the members of the Cabinet, as constituted so recently by President Garfield, immediately tendered their resignations. These were not at once accepted, the President instead inviting all of the members to retain their places as his constitutional advisers. For the time all did so except Mr. Windom, Secretary of the Treasury, who was succeeded by Judge Folger, of New York. Mr. MacVeagh, the Attorney General, also resigned a short time afterward, and the President appointed as his successor Hon. Benjamin H. Brewster, of Philadelphia. The next to retire from the Garfield Cabinet were Mr. Blaine, Secretary of State, and Mr. James, Postmaster General, who were succeeded in their respective offices by Hon. F. T. Frelinghuysen, of New Jersey, and Hon. Timothy A. Howe, of Wisconsin. Mr. Lincoln—so great was the charm of that illustrious name—remained, as if by common consent, at the head of the Department of War. Besides those changes in his constitutional advisers, not much disposition to revolutionize the policy of the Government was manifested by the new administration and the people generally, without respect to party lines, gave a tolerably cordial support to him who had been so suddenly called to the chief magistracy of the Union.

From its predecessor the administration of President Arthur inherited not a few complications and troubles. The chief of these was the series of important State trials relating to the alleged STAR ROUTE CONSPIRACY. Under the recent conduct of affairs in the Post-office Department of the Government there had been organized a class of fast mail routes, known as the Star Routes, the ostensible object being to carry the mails with rapidity and certainty into certain distant and almost inaccessible portions of the Western States and Territories. The law governing the letting of mail contracts was of such sort as to restrict the action of the Postmaster General and his subordinates to definite limits of expense; but one clause of the law gave to the Department the discretionary power to "expedite" such mail routes as seemed to be weaker and less efficient than the service required. This gave to certain officers of the Government the opportunity to let the contracts for many mail lines at a *minimum*, and then under their discretionary power to *expedite* the same lines into efficiency at exorbitant rates—the end and aim being to divide the spoils with the contractors.

This alleged Star Route conspiracy to defraud the Government was unearthed during the Garfield administration, and Attorney-General MacVeagh was directed by the President to prosecute the reputed conspirators. Indictments were found by the Grand Jury against ex-United States Senator Stephen W. Dorsey, of Arkansas; second assistant Postmaster-General Thomas J. Brady, of Indiana, and several others of less note. Mr. MacVeagh, however, seemed in the conduct of the Department of Justice to act with little spirit and no success; but on the coming into office of Attorney-General Brewster, matters were quickened into sharp activity, and those indicted for conspiracy were brought to trial. After several weeks of stormy prosecution and defence, the case went to the jury, who brought in a verdict absurdly convicting certain subordinates of participating in a conspiracy which could not have existed without the guilt of their superiors. This scandal, occupying the public mind in the summer of 1882, contributed much to the defeat of the Republican party in the State elections of the November following—a defeat so general as to remand by overwhelming majorities the control of the Congress of the United States to the Democrats.

It is fortunate that the pen of history is sometimes occupied with events of a nature and tendency wholly different from the public affairs of the State. Perhaps the most striking feature of the civilization of our times is exhibited in THE ADVANCEMENT OF SCIENCE, as illustrated in the thousand applications of discovery and invention to the wants of mankind. At no other age in the history of the world has the practical knowledge of nature's laws been so rapidly and widely diffused; and at no other epoch has the subjection of natural relations to the will of man been so wonderfully displayed. The old life of the human race is giving place to the new life, based on science, and energized by the knowledge that the conditions of man's environment are as benevolent as they are immutable.

Vain would it be to attempt to enumerate all the ways in which the beneficent work of science has been extended in our day; but perhaps a specification of a few of the most remarkable of the recent applications of scientific knowledge may prove of interest to the reader of our current history.

It has remained for the present to solve the problem of oral communication between persons at a distance. A knowledge of the laws of sound and electricity has enabled the scientists of our day to transmit, or at least reproduce, the human voice at a distance of hundreds or even thousands of miles. The history of the TELEPHONE will ever stand as a perpetual reminder to after ages of the inventive skill and scientific progress of the last quarter of the nineteenth century. This instrument, like many similar inventions, seems to have been the work of several ingenious minds directed at nearly the same time to the same problem. The solution, however, may be properly accredited to Mr. Elisha P. Gray, of Chicago, and Professor A. Graham Bell, of the Massachusetts Institute of Technology. It should be mentioned, however, that Professor A. C. Dolbear, of Tufts College, Massachusetts, and Mr. Thomas A. Edison, of Menlo Park, New Jersey, have also succeeded in solving the original difficulties in the way of telephonic communication, or at least in answering practically some of the minor questions in the way of success.

The Telephone may be defined as an instrument for the reproduction of sounds, particularly the sounds of the human voice, by the agency of electricity, at long distances from the origin of the vocal disturbance. It is now well known that sound consists of a wave agitation, communicated through some medium to the organ of hearing. Every particular sound has its own physical equivalent in the system of waves in which it is written. The only thing that is necessary in order to carry a sound in its integrity to any distance is to transmit its physical equivalent, and to redeliver that equivalent to some organ of hearing capable of receiving it. Upon this idea the Telephone is created. Every sound which falls by impact upon the sheet-iron disk of the instrument communicates thereto a sort of tremor; this tremor causes the disk to approach and recede from the magnetic pole placed just behind the diaphragm. A current of electricity is thus induced, pulsates along the wire to the other end, and is delivered to the metallic disk of the second instrument, many miles away, just as it was produced in the first. The ear of the hearer receives from the second instrument the exact physical equivalent of the sound or sounds which were delivered against the disk of the first instrument, and thus the utterance is received at a distance just as it was given forth.

The Telephone.

As already said, the invention of the Telephone stands chiefly to the credit of Professors Gray and Bell. It should be recorded that as early as 1837 the philosopher Page succeeded, by means of electro-magnetism, in transmitting *musical* tones to a distance. It was not, however, until 1877 that Professor Bell, of the Massachusetts Institute of Technology, at a public lecture given at Salem, astonished his audience, and the whole country as well, by receiving and transmitting vocal messages from Boston, twenty miles away. Incredulity had no more a place, as it respected the feasibility of talking to others at a distance. The experiments of Mr. Gray at Chicago, a few days later in the same month, were equally successful. Messages were distinctly transmitted between that city and Milwaukee, a distance of eighty-five miles nor could it be longer doubted that a new era in the means of communication had come. The Bell Telephone, with many modifications and improvements, has sprung into rapid use. Within reasonable limits of distance the new method of transmitting intelligence by direct vocal utterance is rapidly taking the place of all slower and less convenient means of inter-communication. The appearance of this simple instrument is one of the many harbingers of that auspicious time when the constant interchange of thought and sentiment between man and man, community and community, nation and nation, shall conduce to the peace of the world and the goodfellowship of all mankind.

From the Telephone to the PHONOGRAPH was but a step. Both instruments are based upon the same principle of science. The discovery that every sound has its physical equivalent in a wave or agitation which affects the particles of matter composing the material through which the sound is transmitted, led almost inevitably to the other discovery of *catching* and *retaining* that physical equivalent or wave in the surface of some body, and to the reproduction of the original sound therefrom. Such is the fundamental principle of the interesting, but thus far little useful, instrument known as the Phonograph. The same was invented by Thomas A. Edison in the year 1877. The Phonograph differs considerably in structure and purpose from the Vibrograph and the Phonautograph which preceded it. The latter two instruments were made simply to *write* sound vibrations; the former to reproduce *audibly* the sounds themselves.

The Phonograph consists of three principal parts: the sender, or funnel-shaped tube, with its open mouth-piece standing toward the operator; the diaphragm and stylus united therewith, which receive the sound spoken into the tube and, thirdly, the revolving cylinder, with its sheet-coating of tin-foil laid over the surface of the spiral groove, to receive the indentations of the point of the stylus. The mode of operation is very simple. The cylinder is revolved and the point of the stylus when there is no sound-agitation in the funnel or mouth-piece makes a smooth continuous depression in the tin-foil over the spiral groove. But when any sound is thrown into the mouth-piece the iron disk or diaphragm is agitated; this agitation is carried through the stylus and written in irregular marks, dots, and peculiar figures in the tin-foil groove. When the utterance which is to be reproduced has been completed the instrument is stopped, the stylus thrown back from the groove, and the cylinder revolved backward to the place of starting. The stylus is now returned to its place in the groove, and the cylinder is revolved at the same rate of rapidity as before. As the point of the stylus plays up and down in the indentations and through the figures of the tin-foil produced by its own previous agitation, a quiver exactly equivalent to that which was produced by the utterance in the mouth-piece is now communicated backward to the diaphragm, and by it is flung through the mouth-piece into the air. This agitation is, of course, the exact physical equivalent of the original sound, or more properly *is* the sound itself. Thus it is that the Phonograph is made to talk, to sing, to cry, to utter, in short, any sound sufficiently powerful to produce a perceptible tremor in the mouth-piece and diaphragm of the instrument.

Some experiments have already been made looking to the utilization of the Phonograph as a practical addition to the civilizing apparatus of our times. It has been proposed to stereotype the tin-foil record of what has been uttered in the mouth-piece, and thus to preserve in a permanent form the potency of vanished sounds. If this could be successfully and perfectly accomplished the invention of the Phonograph would, doubtless, take rank with the greatest of the age, and might possibly revolutionize the whole method of learning. It would seem, indeed, that nature has intended the *ear*, rather than the *eye*, as the organ of education. It seems to be against the everlasting fitness of things that the eyes of all mankind should be strained, weakened, permanently injured, in childhood with the unnatural tasks which are imposed upon that delicate organ. It would seem to be more in accordance with the nature and capacities of man and the general character of the external world to reserve the eye for the discernment and appreciation of beauty, and to impose upon the ear the tedious and hard tasks of education. The Phonograph makes it possible to read *by the ear*, instead of by the eye; and it is not beyond the range of probability that the book of the future, near or remote, will be written in phonographic plates and made to reveal its story to the waiting ear rather than through the medium of print to the enfeebled and tired eye of the reader.

Perhaps the most marked and valuable invention of the age—the one best calculated to affect favorably the welfare of the people, especially in great cities—is that of THE ELECTRIC LIGHT. The introduction of this superior system of illumination marks an epoch more interesting and important in the history of our country than is any political conflict or mere change of rulers. About the beginning of the last decade the project of introducing the electric light for general purposes of illumination began to be agitated. It was at once perceived that the advantages of such lighting were as conspicuous as they were obvious. The light is so powerful as to render practicable the performance of many mechanical operations as easily by night as by day. Again, the danger of fire from illuminating sources is obviated by the new system. The ease and expedition of all kinds of night employment are greatly enhanced. A given amount of illumination can be produced much more cheaply by electricity than by any means of gas-lighting or ordinary combustion.

Among the first to demonstrate the feasibility of Electric Lighting was the philosopher Gramme, of Paris. In the early part of 1875 he successfully lighted his laboratory by means of electricity. Soon afterward the foundry of Ducommun & Company, of Mulhouse, was similarly lighted. In the course of the following year the apparatus for lighting by means of carbon candles was introduced into many of the principal factories of France and other leading countries of Europe. It may prove of interest in this connection to sketch briefly the principal features of the Electric Light system, and to trace in a few paragraphs the development of that system in our own and other countries.

Lighting by electricity is accomplished in several ways. In general, however, the principle by which the result is accomplished is one, and depends upon *the resistance which the electrical current meets in its transmission through various substances.* There are no perfect conductors of electricity. In proportion as the non-conductive quality is present in a substance, especially in a metal, the resistance to the passage of electricity is pronounced, and the consequent disturbance among the molecular particles of the substance is great. Whenever such resistance is encountered in a circuit, the electricity is converted into heat; and when the resistance is great the heat is in turn converted into light; that is, the substance which offers the resistance glows with the transformed energy of the impeded current.

Upon this simple principle all the apparatus for the production of the Electric Light is constructed. Among the metallic substances the one best adapted by its low conductivity to such resistance and transformation of force is platinum. The high degree of heat necessary to fuse this metal adds to its usefulness and availability for the purpose indicated. When an electrical current is forced along a platinum wire too small to transmit the entire volume it becomes at once heated, first to a red and then to a white glow, and is thus made to send forth a radiance like that of the sun. Of the non-metallic elements which offer similar resistance the best is carbon. The infusibility of this substance renders it greatly superior to platinum for purposes of the Electric Light.

As much as seventy years ago it was discovered by Sir Humphry Davy that carbon points may be rendered incandescent by means of a powerful electrical current. That philosopher in 1809 made the discovery here referred to while experimenting with the great battery of the Royal Institution in London. He observed, rather by accident than by design or previous anticipation, that a powerful electrical current, passing between two pointed bits of wood charcoal, produces tremendous heat and a light like that of the sun. It appears, however, that the philosopher regarded the phenomenon rather in the nature of an interesting display of force than as a suggestion of the possibility of turning night into day.

For nearly three quarters of a century the discovery made by Sir Humphry lay dormant among the great mass of scientific facts revealed in the laboratory. In the course of time, however, the potency of the new fact began to be apprehended. The electric lamp in many forms was proposed and tried. The scientists Niardet, Wilde, Brush, Fuller, and many others of less note busied themselves with the work of invention. Especially did MM. Gramme and Siemens devote their scientific genius to the work of turning to good account the knowledge now fully possessed of the transformability of the electric current into light.

The experiments of these two distinguished inventors seemed to bring us to the dawn of a new era in artificial lighting. The Russian philosopher Jablochkoff carried the work still further by the practical introduction of the carbon candle. Other scientists—Carré, Foucault, Serrin, Rapieff, and Werdermann—had at an earlier or later day thrown much additional information into the common stock of knowledge relative to the illuminating possibilities of electricity. Finally this accumulated material of science fell into the hands of our own untutored but remarkably brilliant and radical inventor, Thomas A. Edison, who gave himself with the utmost zeal to the work of removing the remaining difficulties in the problem. He began his investigations in this line of invention in September of 1878, and in December of the following year gave to the public his first formal statement of results. After many experiments with platinum, he abandoned that material in favor of the carbon-arc *in vacuo*. The latter is, indeed, the essential feature of the Edison light. A small semicircle or horseshoe, of some substance reduced to the form of pure carbon, the two ends being attached to the poles of the generating machine, or "dynamo," as the engine is popularly called, is enclosed in a glass bulb from which the air has been carefully withdrawn, and is rendered incandescent by the passage of an electric current. The other important features of Edison's discovery relate to the divisibility of the current and its control and regulation in volume by the operator. These matters have been so fully mastered in the Edison invention as to render the apparatus as completely subject to the management of even an unskilled manipulator as are the other varieties of illuminating apparatus.

It were vain to speculate upon the future of electric lighting. Doubtless the old systems of illumination are destined soon to give place altogether to the splendors of the electric glow. The general effects of the change upon society will, no doubt, be as marked as they are salutary. Darkness, the enemy of good government and morality in great cities, will in a great measure be dispelled by the beneficent agent over which the genius of Davy, Gramme, Brush, Edison, and a host of other explorers in the new continents of science has so nearly triumphed. The case, comfort, happiness, and welfare of mankind will be vastly multiplied; and we shall ever be reminded in the glow of the "light of the future" of that splendid fact, that the progress of civilization depends in a large measure upon the knowledge of nature's laws and the diffusion of that knowledge among the people.

The Brooklyn Bridge.

The last decade has also been conspicuous for the number and character of THE PUBLIC WORKS which have been projected or brought to completion within the period. In these the immense physical capacity of our country and people has been amply illustrated. Among the most important of the enterprises here referred to may be mentioned the great suspension bridge over the strait known as the East River, between New York and Brooklyn. The completion and formal opening of this work, which occurred on the 24th of May, 1883, was an event of such interest as to evoke universal attention and elicit many descriptions.

The Brooklyn Bridge is the longest and largest structure of the kind in the world. The design was the work of the distinguished John A.

Roebling, the originator of wire suspension bridges, under whose supervision and that of his son, Washington A. Roebling the structure was completed.[50]

The East River structure is what is known as a suspension bridge, being supported by four enormous wires or cables stretching from pier to pier a distance of 1,595 feet. From the main towers to the anchor ages on either side is 930 feet. From the anchorages outward to the *termini* of the approaches is, on the New York side a distance of 1,562 feet, and on the Brooklyn side 972 feet, giving a total length of bridge and approaches of 5,989 feet. The total weight of the structure is 6,470 tons. The estimated capacity of support is 1,740 tons, though the ultimate resistance is calculated at 49,200 tons.

The Brooklyn Bridge was first projected by William C. Kingsley, president of the bridge trustees, and his predecessor in that office, Henry C. Murphy; the first plans and estimates were prepared in 1865. The company for the construction was organized two years afterward. The capital was fixed at $5,000,000. The enterprise was not pressed with due vigor until 1875, when the work was taken up by the State of New York. A Board of Managers was appointed to bring the bridge to completion at as early a date as possible. Congress also patronized the enterprise to the extent of authorizing the construction of the work, which act was passed in June of 1869. The formal opening of the bridge in May of 1883 drew the attention of the whole nation to the metropolis, and proved by

---

[50] The personal history of the Roeblings, father and son, in connection with the great bridge, is as pathetic as it is interesting. The elder engineer was injured while laying the foundation of one of the shore piers on the 22d of July, 1869, and died of lockjaw. W. A. Roebling then took up his father's unfinished task. He continued the work of supervision for about two years, when he was prostrated with a peculiar form of paralysis known as the "caisson disease," from which he never fully recovered. His mental faculties, however, remained unimpaired, and he was able to direct with his eye what his hands could no longer touch. While thus prostrated his wife discovered a genius almost equal to that of her husband and her father-in-law. The palsied engineer, thus re-enforced, continued for live years to furnish plans for the work which had been projected by his father. These plans were almost all drawn by his wife, who never flagged in the great work which had fallen to her prostrate husband. In 1876 he was partly restored to health, and lived to hear the applause which his genius and enterprise had merited.

the interest which the event excited that the American people are still able to appreciate a great enterprise in art and mechanics, and to show by such appreciation that, even in America, politics is not the best vocation of mankind.

On the whole, the administration of President Arthur proved to be uneventful. The government pursued the even tenor of its way, and the progress of the country was unchecked by serious calamity. In the domain of politics we may note the gradual obliteration of those sharply defined issues which for the last quarter of a century have divided the two great parties. As a consequence there has been a healthful abatement of partisan rancor. It is becoming every year more apparent that the questions at issue in the political arena are merely factitious, and that the clamor of partisanship is kept up for the most part by those who hope to gather the spoils of the political battle field. How much longer these ill-founded cries of alarm will serve the purpose of holding the people in line under the old party names is a question which none may solve with certainty. Meanwhile, the man who plows, or keeps the flock—the mechanic, the artisan, the merchant—will for the present, no doubt, continue to come forth at the call of the party leaders and vote as has been his wont on issues that are more imaginary than real, and whose only merit consists in the fact that a certain residue of patriotism is still the motive-force in the average American election.

To the general fact, that party questions are no longer vital and distinct, there is one general exception. It cannot be doubted that the American people are really and sincerely divided on the question of THE TARIFF. Whether the true policy of the United States is that of free trade or of a protective system is a fundamental issue, and the decision is not yet. Ever and anon, from the very foundation of the government to the present hour, this question has obtruded itself upon the attention of the people. It may be well, therefore, in this connection to state the various views which may be entertained on the subject.

First, we have the doctrine of FREE TRADE pure and simple. The theory is this: The indications of profitable industry are founded in nature. A rich soil means agriculture; a barren soil means something else. Beds of ore signify mining; veins of petroleum, oil wells; a headlong river, water-power; a hill of silicon, glass works a forest of pine, ship masts and coal-tar; bays, havens, and rivers, commerce. Free trade says that these things are the hints of the natural world as to how human industry shall be exerted. The way to wealth, prosperity, happiness, is to follow nature whithersoever she leads. To go against nature is to go against self-interest and common sense. "Let alone" is the motto of the system—hands off and no meddling with the plain conditions which are imposed on man by his environment. Let him who lives in the fecund valley till the soil and gather a hundred-fold. Let him who inhabits the rocky upland by river-side or bed of pent-up coal devote his energies to manufacturing. Let each procure from the other by exchange the necessities and conveniences of life which he could not himself produce but at a great disadvantage. Let the producer of raw material send it near or far to the manufacturer and receive in return the fabric which he must wear; the food wherewith he must sustain his life. Why should he do otherwise? It is intended that men should live together in amity. Neighbors should be at peace. Different communities should not quarrel. Nations should not fight. The harmonious order of civilization requires a world-wide exchange of products. Men are happier and richer when they give themselves freely to the laws of their environment, and toil in those fields of industry to which both their own dispositions and the benevolent finger of nature points the way.

All contrivances of law which controvert or oppose these fundamental conditions of legitimate industry are false in theory and pernicious in application. If civil society assume to direct the industries of her people against the plain indications of nature, she becomes a tyrant. All laws which tend to divert the industrial energies of a nation from these pursuits which are indicated by the natural surroundings are hurtful, selfish, self-destructive, and, in the long run, weakening and degrading to the people. A tariff duty so laid as to build up one industry at the expense of another is a piece of barbarous intermeddling alike with the principles of common sense and the inherent rights of man. If free trade makes one nation dependent on another, then it also makes that other nation dependent on the first. The one can no more afford to fight the other than the other can afford to fight it. Hence free trade. It is beneficent and just. Hence a tariff for revenue only. It is the true policy of government relative to the interests of the people. Such is the theory of the free trader.

The first remove from the doctrine of free trade proper is that of INCIDENTAL PROTECTION. The primary assumptions of this theory are nearly identical with those above presented. Nearly all of the propositions advanced by the free trader are accepted as correct by the incidental protectionist. The latter, however, holds some peculiar doctrines of his own. He claims that men—as the doctrine of free trade teaches—should labor according to the indications of nature, and that the attempt on the part of government to divert the industries of the people from one channel to another is contrary to right reason and sound policy. But he also holds that since a tariff is the common means adopted by most of the civilized States of the world to produce the revenue whereby the expenses of the State are met and sustained, the same should be so levied as to be incidentally favorable to those industries of the people which are placed at a natural disadvantage. He does not hold that any tariff should be levied with the *intention* of protecting and fostering a given industry, but that in every case the tax should be laid for public purposes only—that is, with the *intention of sustaining the State*, and be only incidentally directed to the protection of the weaker industry. These last assumptions furnish the ground of political divergence between free traders proper and incidental protectionists. The latter take into consideration both the fundamental conditions of the argument and the peculiar character of the industries of the people. They claim that given pursuits may thus be strengthened and encouraged by legislative provisions, and that natural and political laws may be made to co-operate in varying and increasing the productive resources of the State.

The third view as relative to this question is that of LIMITED PROTECTION. The fundamental difference between this theory and the preceding is this: The incidental protectionist denies, and the limited protectionist affirms, the wisdom of levying tariff duties with the *intention* and *purpose* of protecting home industries. The limited protectionist would have the legislation of the State take particular cognizance of the character of the industries of the people, and would have the laws enacted with constant reference to the encouragement of the weaker—generally the manufacturing—pursuits. The doctrine of incidental protection would stop short of this; would adopt the theory of "let alone," so far as the original purpose of legislation is concerned, but would at the same time so shape the tariff that a needed stimulus should be given to certain industries. The limited protectionist agrees with the free trader in certain assumptions. The former as well as the latter assents to the proposition that the original condition of industry is found in nature—in the environment of the laborer. But he also urges that the necessity for a varied industry so great, so important, to the welfare and independence of a people as to justify the deflection of human energies by law to certain pursuits which could not be profitably followed but for the fact of protection. This he makes a reason for tariff legislation. He would make the weaker industry live and thrive by the side of the stronger. He would modify the crude rules of nature by the higher rules of human reason. He would not only adapt man to his environment but would adapt the environment to him. He would keep in view the strength and dignity of the State, and would be willing to incur temporary disadvantages for the sake of permanent good. In the course of time, when, under the stimulus of a protective system, the industries of the State have become sufficiently varied and sufficiently harmonized with original conditions, he would allow the system of protective duties to expire and freedom of trade to supervene, but until that time he would insist that the weaker, but not less necessary, industries of a people should be encouraged and fostered by law. He would deny the justice or economy of that system which in a new country, boundless in natural resources but poor in capital, would constrain the people to bend themselves to the production of a few great staples, the manufacture of which by foreign nations would make them rich and leave the original producers in perpetual vassalage and poverty.

The fourth view is embodied in the theory of HIGH PROTECTION. In this the doctrine is boldly advanced that the assumptions of free trade are specious and false. The influence of man upon his environment is so great as to make it virtually whatever the law of right reason would suggest. The suggestion of right reason is this: Every nation should be independent. Its sovereignty and equality should be secured by every means short of injustice. In order that a State may be independent and able to mark out for itself a great destiny, its industries must afford employment for all the talents and faculties of man, and yield products adapted to all his wants. To devote the energies of a people to those industries only which are suggested by the situation and environment is to make man a slave to nature instead of nature's master: It may be sound reason for the people inhabiting a fertile valley to devote themselves principally to agricultural pursuits; but to do this to the exclusion of other industries is merely to narrow the energies of the race, make dependent the laborer, and finally exhaust those very powers of nature which for the present seem to suggest one pursuit and forbid all others. On the contrary it is the duty of society to build up many industries in every locality, whatever may be the environment. If nature furnishes no suggestion of blast furnaces and iron-works, then nature should be constrained by means of human law. The production of manufactured products should be so encouraged by tariff duties as to become profitable in *all* situations. Not only should every State, but every community be made comparatively independent. Every community should be able, by its own industries, to supply at least the larger part of its own wants. The spindle should be *made* to turn; the forge *made* to glow; the mill wheel *made* to turn; the engine *made* to pant; and the towering furnace to fling up into the darkness of midnight its volcanic glare—all this, whether nature has or has not prepared the antecedents of such activities. And this cannot be accomplished, or at least not well accomplished, in any other way than by the legal protection of those industries which do not flourish under the action of merely natural laws. It is, in brief, the theory of the high protectionist that every community of men, by means of its varied and independent activities—fostered and encouraged by the protective system—should become in the body politic what the ganglion is in the nerve system of man—an independent, local power, capable of originating its own action and directing its own energies.

There is still a fifth position occasionally assumed by publicists and sometimes by nations. This is the doctrine and practice of PROHIBITOBY TARIFFS. The idea here is that the mutual interdependence of nations is, on the whole, disadvantageous, and that each should be rendered *wholly* independent of the other. If in any State or nation certain industrial powers and conditions are wanting, then these powers and conditions should be produced by means of law. Internal trade is, according to this doctrine, the principal thing; and commercial intercourse with foreign States a matter of secondary or even dubious advantage. If the price of the given home product be not sufficient to stimulate its production in such quantities as to meet all the requirements of the market, then that price should be raised by means of legislation, and raised again and again, until the foreign trade shall cease and home manufacture be supplied in its place. True, there are not many who now carry the doctrine of protection to this extreme; but it is also true that in the endeavor to prepare protective schedules under the system of limited or high protection it not infrequently happens that the tariff is fixed at such a scale as to *act* as a prohibitory duty, and turn aside entirely the foreign commerce in the article on which the tariff is laid.

Such, then, is the question which from time to time has arisen in the political history of our country. The second statute ever enacted by Congress under the Constitution was passed for the purpose of "providing a revenue and *affording protection to American industry.*" Even the very necessity which gave rise to the Constitution itself was one relating to commerce and interwoven with the tariff. From the beginning the question would not down. During the fourth and fifth decades of the century the leading political agitations were produced by the revival of the tariff issue in our politics. Every one is acquainted with the "American system" which was so earnestly promoted by Henry Clay. Every one knows that in general the Whigs of the ante bellum epoch were in favor of the protective system, and that the Democrats opposed it. After the war the question slumbered for a season. In 1880 a paragraph in the national platform of the Democratic party was inserted—not, indeed, with the intention of evoking an old controversy from the shadows of oblivion—which by declaring in favor of "a tariff for revenue only," unexpectedly precipitated the whole issue, and contributed to, if it did not determine, the defeat of the Democratic ticket. Even in those States where Democracy was in the ascendant the growth of great manufacturing establishments had in the meantime brought in a vast army of artisans, who, in spite of all party affiliation, refused to support a platform which, according to their belief, was calculated to injure, if not destroy, the very business in which they were engaged. Both the Democrats and the Republicans during the last four years have made a strenuous effort to align their party followers on this question, but neither have been successful. Neither are the Democrats unanimous for free trade, nor are the Republicans unanimous for a system of protection. Perhaps unanimity has been more nearly attained in the Republican than in the Democratic ranks, though it is not to be denied that many of the most eminent and thoughtful Republican leaders, in the East, are in favor of free trade.

During the whole of Arthur's administration this question gathered head, and the white crests of conflicting tides were seen along the whole surface of the presidential contest of 1884. The ultimate settlement of the question will be determined by self-interest rather than by abstract argument. When the party in power, whatever that party may he, shall become convinced that the *interest* of the United States requires the abolition of all protective duties and the substitution therefor of a system of tariff for revenue only, then, and not till then, will the English theory of political economy take the place of that which has thus far prevailed on this side of the sea.

The quadrennial agitation of the American people relative to the presidency began at an early date of Arthur's administration. Hardly had the crime of Garfield's murder been perpetrated and the presidency transferred to Mr. Arthur until the issue of naming a successor was raised by the ever-busy swarm of American politicians. The year 1882 had hardly furnished a breathing-time for the subsidence of the party passions of two years before, until the great army of the interested went forth on an expedition to arouse the country for another contest. It cannot be doubted that the managers of both the leading political organizations have been for some years alarmed lest through the failure of living issues the old combinations which have divided the country for a quarter of a century should go to pieces and leave the field to the people. But thus far the skill of partisans has been sufficient to cajole the masses into the belief that the old questions are still vital, and thus to keep alive the fires of a well-nigh extinct party strife.

During the year 1883 many eminent men were named in connection with the presidential office. Among those most prominently and warmly advocated by the Republicans were James G. Blaine, of Maine; George F. Edmunds, of Vermont; President Arthur, of New York; Joseph R. Hawley, of Connecticut; John Sherman, of Ohio; John A. Logan and Robert T. Lincoln, of Illinois; and General William T. Sherman, of Missouri. Among the Democrats, the statesmen most frequently urged for the nomination in 1884 were General B. F. Butler, of Massachusetts; Samuel J. Tilden and Grover Cleveland, of New York; Samuel J. Randall, of Pennsylvania; Thomas F. Bayard, of Delaware; Allen G. Thurman, of Ohio John G. Carlisle, of Kentucky; Joseph E. M'Donald and Thomas A. Hendricks, of Indiana. Early in 1884 Chicago was selected as the place of both the national conventions. Meanwhile the Greenback-Labor party held its convention at Indianapolis in the month of April, and nominated Gen. B. F. Butler as a candidate for the presidency, and A. M. West, of Mississippi, for the vice-presidency, of the United States. The Republican convention met on the 3d of May, and after a spirited session of three days' duration brought its labors to an end by the nomination of James G. Blaine, of Maine, for president, and Gen. John A. Logan, of Illinois, for vice-president; the Democratic delegates assembled on the 9th of July, and on the 11th of the month concluded their session by the nomination of Gov. Grover Cleveland, of New York, for the first place, and Thomas A. Hendricks, of Indiana, for the second, on the national ticket. Both the Republican and Democratic nominations were received with general enthusiasm, but large and powerful factions in both parties refused to support the nominee; nor could it well be foreseen at the opening of the canvass of 1884 which party was likely to come out victorious in the battle of the ensuing autumn.

As the summer wore away and the issues which the political parties had attempted to create were discussed before the people, the uncertainty became still greater. When the election drew nigh every thing seemed to depend upon the electoral votes of New York and Indiana. A close study of the situation revealed the fact that the latter State was Democratic, and would so record her vote. This fact narrowed the contest to the great State of New York. The event proved favorable to the Democrats, though their majority in the popular vote of the State was only 1,142. This small preponderance, however, was sufficient to determine the result; it gave the vote of the Empire State to Cleveland and Hendricks, assuring to them 219 ballots in the Electoral College against 182 votes for Blaine and Logan.

The sequel of the presidential election of this year was less happy than generally happens under like circumstances. It could hardly be expected that the Republican managers and office-holders long occupying the places of power would abdicate without expressions of displeasure. Mr. Blaine himself soon after the election delivered a speech which, so far from being pacific in its tone, was, for the most part, a bitter invective against the South. The Republican newspapers, especially in the West, took up the hue and cry, and for a while filled their columns with such matter as might well have appeared in the first year after the Civil War. By degrees, however, this feeling subsided and near the close of Arthur's administration the office-holders as a class began to trim their sails with the evident hope that the breezes of Civil Service Reform, to which the President-elect was pledged, might waft them still farther on the high seas of power and emolument.

Before the retirement of President Arthur the command of the Army of the United States was transferred from General William T. Sherman to General Philip H. Sheridan. The former distinguished officer, one of the most talented and eminent soldiers of the century, having reached the age at which, according to an act of Congress, he might retire from active service, availed himself of the provision and laid down his command. The formal papers with which he concluded his official relations with the army were marked with the same fervor and patriotism which had characterized all of his utterances since the time when he gave his services to the country in the dark days of disunion. Nor could it be said that the new chieftain, to whom the command of the American army was now given, was less a patriot and soldier than his illustrious predecessor.

General Philip H. Sheridan.

The recurrence of the birthday of Washington, 1885, was noted for the dedication of the great monument which had been a-building for so many years at the capital. The erection of such a structure was suggested as early as 1799. It was not, however, until 1835 that an organization was effected with a view to undertaking the work. For many years after the incipiency of the enterprise the building lagged, and it was not until the work had been energized by Congress that it was brought to completion. The cost of the completed monument was about a million five hundred thousand dollars. The structure is the highest in the world. The shaft itself, without reckoning the foundation, is five hundred and fifty-five feet in height, being thirty feet higher than the Cathedral at Cologne, and seventy-five feet higher than the Pyramid of Cheops. The structure is composed of more than eighteen thousand blocks of stone. They are mostly of white marble and weigh several tens each. One hundred and eighty-one memorial stones, contributed by the different States of the Union and by friendly foreign nations, are set at various places in the structure. The dedication occurred on Saturday, the 21st of February. The ceremonies were of the most imposing character. A procession of more than six thousand persons proceeded from the base of the monument along Pennsylvania Avenue to the Capitol, while salutes were fired from the batteries of the Navy Yard. At the Capitol the procession was reviewed by the President of the United States. The concluding ceremonies were held in the House of Representatives, where a great throng had assembled to honor the memory of the Father of his Country. The principal oration, written by the Honorable Robert C. Winthrop, as well as the less formal addresses of the occasion, was well worthy of the event and calculated to add—if aught could add—to the fame of him who was "first in war, first in peace, and first in the hearts of his countrymen."

CHAPTER LXXI.

CLEVELAND'S ADMINISTRATION, 1885–

GROVER CLEVELAND, twenty-second President of the United States, was born at Caldwell, New Jersey, on the 18th of March, 1837. Three years afterward he was taken by his father and mother to Fayetteville, near Syracuse, New York. Here in his boyhood he received such limited education as the schools of the place afforded. For a while in his youth he was clerk in a village store. Afterward the family removed first to Clinton and then to Holland Patent. At the latter place his father died, and young Cleveland, left to his own resources, went to New York and became a teacher in a blind asylum, in which an elder brother held a like position. After a short time, however, the young man finding such a pursuit uncongenial to his tastes, went to Buffalo and engaged in the study of law. He was admitted to the bar in 1859, and four years afterward began his public-career as assistant district-attorney. In 1869 he was elected sheriff of Erie County, and in 1881 was chosen mayor of Buffalo.

Mr. Cleveland's next promotion by his fellow-citizens was to the governorship of New York, to which position he was elected in 1882 by the astonishing majority of

Grover Cleveland.

192,854 — the majority being, perhaps, unparalleled in the history of American elections. It was while he still held this office that, in July of 1884, he was called by the Democratic national convention to be the standard-bearer of his party in the presidential contest.

The first duty of the new chief executive was to frame his cabinet. Public interest was not a little excited with the probabilities of the President's choice. On the day following the inauguration the nominations were sent to the Senate and were as follows: for secretary of state, Thomas F. Bayard, of Delaware; for secretary of the treasury, Daniel Manning, of New York; for secretary of the interior, Lucius Q. C. Lamar, of Mississippi; for secretary of war, Wm. C. Endicott, of Massachusetts; for secretary of the navy, Wm. C. Whitney, of New York; for postmaster-general, Wm. F. Vilas, of Wisconsin; for attorney-general, Augustus H. Garland, of Arkansas. The peculiarity of the appointments was that two of them were from New York but the prejudice which might arise on this account was fully counter-balanced by the high character and undoubted abilities of the men whom the President had chosen as the responsible advisers of his administration.

Thomas F. Bayard.

The most serious question which confronted the new President, was the distribution of official patronage. The Democratic party had come into power on a platform distinctly enunciating the doctrine of reform in the civil service. From almost the beginning of the government, it had been the custom of the party in power to distribute to its own partisans all the appointive offices. This usage, well established since the days of

Thomas A. Henrdicks.

President Jackson, had been the origin and cause of the greater part of the abuses which had existed in the various departments of government. Extreme party men had claimed always that "to the victors belong the spoils" of office. Of late years, however, the best political opinion of the country has turned with disgust from the gross practice of rewarding men for mere party services; and in the evenly balanced presidential contests of 1880 and 1884 it became all important that both the dominant parties should conciliate, at least by professions of sympathy, the growing phalanx of civil service reformers. They it was who, in the late election, believing in the sincerity of Mr. Cleveland, had thrown their influences in his favor and thereby secured his elevation to the presidency. He went into office pledged to carry out the views of those by whose suffrages he had been raised to power. These views, moreover, were his own, and it thus happened that the new administration was launched with "Civil Service Reform" inscribed on its pennon. It was soon seen, however, that the President would have serious

George B. McClellan.

difficulty in carrying out his purpose. From the day of the inauguration, a great crowd of office-seekers thronged the capital, and the chief magistrate was besieged by hundreds and thousands of those whose principal claims to preferment were that they had served the party. During the first year of the new administration it was a grave question whether or not the President would be able to stand by the flag of reform, or whether he would be driven to re-adopt the cast-off policy of satisfying with official appointments the hungry horde that surged around the presidential mansion.

Ambrose E. Burnside.

Joseph Hooker.

The last years of the Republic have been noted for two circumstances, both of historical interest and both relating to the Civil War. The first of these is the revival of the memory of that conflict, in authoritative publications, by some of the leading participants. This work, so important to the right understanding of the great struggle for and against the Union, was begun by General William T. Sherman, who, in 1875, published his

Memoirs, narrating the story of that part of the war in which he had been a leader. This had been preceded by the history of the WAR BETWEEN THE STATES, by Alexander H. Stephens, late Vice-President of the Confederacy. In 1884 General Grant began the publication of a series of war articles in the *Century Magazine,* which attracted universal attention, and which led to the preparation and publication of his *Memoirs* in 1885-86. Similar contributions by other eminent commanders of the Union and Confederate armies followed in succession, until a large amount of able and impartial literature was left on record for the instruction of after times.

Winfield S. Hancock.

The second fact referred to is the death, within the compass of a single year, of a number of the great Union generals who had led their armies to victory in the War of the Rebellion. It was in the early summer of 1885 that the attention of the people was called away from public affairs by the announcement that the veteran General Ulysses S. Grant had been stricken with a fatal malady, and that his days would be but few among the living. The heart of the Nation was greatly saddoned by the intelligence; but not even the sympathy of a great people could prevail against or even postpone the approaching hour of fate. The hero of Vicksburg and Appomattox sank under the ravages of a malignant cancer, which had fixed itself in his throat, and, on July 23, died at a summer cottage on Mount McGregor, New York. His last days were hallowed by the sympathies of the Nation which he had so gloriously defended. The news of his death passed over the land like the shadow of a great cloud. Almost every city and hamlet showed, in some appropriate way, its emblems of grief. The funeral ceremonies equaled, if they did not surpass, any which had ever been witnessed. The procession in New York city was, perhaps, the most solemn and imposing pageant ever exhibited in honor of the dead. On August 8, the body of General Grant was laid to rest in Riverside Park, overlooking the Hudson. There, on a summit, from which may be seen the great river and the metropolis of the Nation, is the tomb of him whose courage and magnanimity in war will forever give him rank with the few master spirits who, by their heroic deeds, have honored the human race and changed the course of history.

George G. Meade.

Within less than three months from the funeral of Grant another distinguished Union general fell. On the 29th of October, General George B. McClellan, first commander of the Army of the Potomac, at one time general-in-chief, subsequently Democratic candidate for the presidency, and at a later period governor of New Jersey, died at his home at St. Cloud, in that State. The conspicuous part which he had borne during the first two years of the Civil War, his eminent abilities as a soldier and civilian, and his unblemished character as a man and citizen, combined to heighten the estimate of his life and services, and to evoke the sincerest expressions of national sorrow on the occasion of his death.

After another brief interval a third great military leader fell, in the person of General Winfield S. Hancock. This brave and generous commander was, at the time of his death, the senior major-general of the American army. Always a favorite with the people, he had, since the close of the war, occupied a conspicuous place before the public. In 1880 he was the Democratic candidate for the presidency, and though defeated by General Garfield, the defeat was without dis honor. His death, which occurred at his home on Governor's Island, on the 9th of February, 1886, was universally deplored, and the people omitted no mark of respect to the memory of him who, in the great struggle for the preservation of the Union, had been honored with the title of "Hero of Gettysburg." Thus have passed away the gallant generals of the Army of the Potomac. George B. McClellan, Ambrose E. Burnside, Joseph Hooker, George G. Meade, and Winfield S. Hancock have one by one joined

> "The innumerable caravan that moves
> To that mysterious realm where each shall take
> His chamber in the silent halls of death."

Before the close of the year 1886 still another, worthy to rank among the greatest of the Union commanders of the Civil War, ended his career on earth. Late in December, Major-General John A. Logan, United States Senator from Illinois, fell sick at his home, called Calumet Place, in Washington City. His disease was rheumatism, to which he had been subject at intervals since his exposure and hardships in the early Western campaigns of the war. After a few days' illness he became suddenly worse, sank into a comatose condition, and on the 26th of the month quietly breathed his last. His military and civil career had been distinguished in the highest degree. At the outbreak of hostilities, in 1861, few men did more than Logan to strengthen and unify the Union sentiment in the wavering Border States. His voice was a clarion, heard shrill and far above the confusion and uproar of the times. Resigning his seat in Congress he joined the first advance of the Union army, and fought in the battle of Bull Run. Without previous military training he rose rapidly to distinction, and became the volunteer general *par excellence* of the war. After the close of the conflict he returned to political life, and was chosen United States Senator from Illinois. In 1884 he was nominated for the vice-presidency on the Republican ticket with James G. Blaine. That ticket being defeated, he resumed his duties in the Senate, and remained at his post until his death. The ceremonies of his funeral and the general voice of the American press indicated in an unmistakable manner the enduring place which he had merited and won in the affections of the people.

In the meantime a great civilian had fallen at his post of duty. On Nov. 25, 1885, Vice-President Thomas A. Hendricks, after what was supposed to be a trifling illness of a single day, died suddenly at his home in Indianapolis. The fatal message came in the form of paralysis. Not a moment's warning was given of the approach of that pale courier who knocks impartially at the door of the peasant and the portal of the great. The life of Mr. Hendricks had been one of singular purity, and the amenities of his character had been for many years conspicuous in the stormy arena of American politics. The goodness and greatness of the man, combined with his distinction as governor, senator, and vice-president, served to draw from the people every evidence of public and private respect

John A. Logan.

for his memory. The body of the dead statesman was buried in Crown Hill Cemetery, near Indianapolis, the funeral pageant surpassing in grandeur and solemnity any other display of the kind ever witnessed in the Western States, except the funeral of Lincoln.

The death of the Vice-President was soon followed by that of Horatio Seymour, of New York. On the 12th of February, 1886, this distinguished citizen, who had been governor of the Empire State, and, in 1868, candidate of the Democratic party for the presidency against General Grant, died at his home in Utica. He had reached the age of seventy-six, and, though for many years living in retirement, had never ceased to hold a large share of the attention of his fellow-citizens. Still more distinguished in reputation and ability was Samuel J. Tilden, also of the Empire State, who died at his home, called Greystone, at Yonkers, near New York City, on the 4th of August, 1886. Mr. Tilden had lived to make a marked—perhaps ineffaceable—impression on the political thought of the epoch. He had acquired within the lines of his own party an influence and ascendency far greater than that of any other statesman of his times. His intellectual force could not be doubted, nor could it be claimed that he failed to apply his faculties assiduously to the greatest political questions of the age.

Mr. Tilden was born on the 14th of February, 1814, and was thus in the 73d year of his age at the time of his death. He had been a prominent figure in his native State for fully forty years, and had held many places of public trust and honor. In 1870-71 he was

Samuel J. Tilden.

among the foremost in unearthing the astounding frauds and robberies which had been perpetrated on the city of New York, and in the following year was sent to the General Assembly, where his services were invaluable. In 1874 he was elected Governor of New York by a majority of more than 50,000 votes. In the executive office he was one of the ablest and most thorough-going who ever occupied the gubernatorial chair of the State. In 1876 he was nominated for the presidency, and at the election of that year received a large majority of the popular vote, only failing of a majority in the electoral college because of the tactics of the leaders of the party in power. Neither he nor General Hayes was clearly elected, the Democrats having carried two or three States with the shot-gun, and the Republicans, by the aid of the Electoral Commission, having counted in the electoral votes of a State or two which they did not carry at all. After the contest Mr. Tilden retired to private life, but continued to guide the counsels of his party and to influence public opinion up to the date of his death. Perhaps one of his ablest—as it was his last—public paper was a general letter on the subject of "The Coast and Harbor Defenses of the United States," a publication which clearly led to the legislation of the Forty-ninth Congress on that important subject. Thus, within the space of less than eleven months, four of those eminent American statesmen who had been candidates of the Democratic party for the presidency of the United States, and the distinguished Vice-President recently chosen by that party to the second place of honor in the Government, had fallen from their places in the ranks of the living.

To this list of the American great whose earthly activities have recently ended in death must still be added the illustrious name of Henry Ward Beecher. To him, with little reservation, must be assigned the first place among our orators and philanthropists. Nor is it likely that his equal in most of the sublime qualities of energy and manhood will soon be seen again on the great stage of life. His personality was so large, so unique, and striking, as to constitute the man in some sense *sui generis*. His kind is rare in the world, and the circumstances which aided in his development have passed away. That fact in American history—the institution of slavery—which brought out and displayed the higher

Henry Ward Beecher.

moods of his anger and stormy eloquence cannot again arouse the indignation of genius. The knight and his dangerous foil sleep together in the dust.

Mr. Beecher had the happy fortune to retain his faculties unimpaired to the very close of his career. On the evening of the 5th of March, 1887, at his home in Brooklyn, surrounded by his family, with no premonition or portent, the message came by apoplexy. An artery broke in the magnificent, heavy brain, that had been for more than forty years one of the greatest batteries of thought and action in the world, and the aged orator, nearing the close of his seventy-fourth year, sank into that deep sleep from which no power on earth could wake him. He lived until the morning of the 8th, and quietly entered the shadows. The sentiments awakened by his death, the circumstances of his sepulture, and the common eulogium of mankind, proved beyond doubt the supreme place which he had occupied in the admiring esteem, not only of his own countrymen, but of all the great peoples of the world.

Another distinguished name to be added to the American necrology of the decade is that of Morrison Remich Waite, Chief Justice of the United States. His death occurred at his home, in Washington City, on the 23d day of March, 1888. The event suggests and justifies the addition of a few paragraphs relative to the history and *personnel* of that great tribunal over which Judge Waite presided during the last fourteen years of his life.

In the formation of the Constitution of the United States it was intended that the three general departments of the Government should be of correlative rank and influence. The sequel, however, as developed and illustrated in the actual working of our national system, has shown that the executive and legislative departments predominate, naturally, perhaps inevitably, over the judicial branch, and that, in the popular estimate, at least, the supreme court is of small importance as compared with the presidency and the two houses of Congress. This disesteem of the judiciary is not verified by a broader and more philosophical view of the subject. The importance, especially, of the conservative opinion of our great national court, in determining, at least negatively, the final validity of all legislation and of all subordinate judicial decisions, can hardly be overestimated. The same may be said of the supreme bench, considered as the only immovable breakwater against the unscrupulous and rampant spirit of party. It is fortunate, moreover, that the offices of our chief justice and of the associate justiceships are appointive, and are thus removed, in great measure, from the perfidy of the convention and the passion of a partisan election. It may be of interest to glance for a moment at some of the vicissitudes through which the supreme court has passed since its organization, in 1789.

Morrison Remich Waite.

The court was then instituted by the appointment of John Jay as chief justice,[51] who held the office until 1796, when he gave place to Oliver Ellsworth. The latter presided over the court until, in 1800, the infirmities of age compelled his resignation. Then came the long and

---

[51] For the organization of the first supreme bench see page 427.

honorable ascendency of Chief Justice John Marshall, who held the office from his appointment, in 1801, to his death, in 1835. This was the golden age of the supreme court. From 1835 to 1837 there was an interregnum in the chief justiceship, occasioned by the disagreement of President Jackson and the Senate of the United States; but, at the latter date, the president secured the confirmation of Judge Roger B. Taney as chief justice, who entered upon his long term of twenty-seven years. It was his celebrated decision in the case of the negro, Dred Scott, relative to the status of the slave race in America, that applied the torch to that immense heap of combustibles whose explosion was the Civil War.

At the death of Chief Justice Taney, in 1864, President Lincoln appointed as his successor Salmon P. Chase, recently secretary of the treasury, and author of most of the great financial measures and expedients by which the national credit had been buoyed up and preserved during the rebellion. His official term extended to his death, in 1873, and covered the period when the important issues arising from the Civil War were under adjudication. To Chief Justice Chase fell also, by virtue of his office, the duty of presiding at the impeachment trial of President Andrew Johnson. In 1874 the appointment of Morrison R. Waite as chief justice was made by President Grant; and the death of this able jurist devolved on President Cleveland and the Senate the duty of naming his successor.

Chief Justice Waite was born at Lyme, Connecticut, on the 29th of November, 1816. From the public school he was transferred to Yale College, and was graduated from that institution in 1837. He then became a student of law, and, after completing his course, removed to Ohio, where he entered upon the practice of his profession at Maumee City. After serving one term, 1849-50, in the Legislature of the State, he removed to Toledo, which became henceforth his home, until his duties as chief justice called him to Washington City. He had been frequently solicited to become a candidate for office, but had adhered to his profession until 1871-72, when he accepted from President Grant the appointment as member of the celebrated Board of Arbitration, to sit at Geneva, in the adjudication of the Alabama Claims. Here he was associated with Charles Francis Adams, Caleb Cushing and Wm. M.

Evarts; and, though he was less known to the public than they, he nevertheless bore himself with honor among his colleagues. Shortly after his return the death of Chief Justice Chase opened the way for Mr. Waite's appointment to the highest and most important judicial seat in America; and to this august position he brought a character, talents and attainments equal to the responsibilities of his office.

During his occupancy of the supreme bench Chief Justice Waite steadily rose in the esteem and confidence of the nation. He was not, perhaps, a man of the highest order of genius or of the very highest rank as a jurist. But, on the whole, the office of chief justice was rarely, if ever, more worthily borne than by its latest occupant. He was a man of equable and judicial temper, little disposed, if disposed at all, to look beyond the supreme bench to a possibly higher seat. His death was from pneumonia, and was so sudden as to be announced to the country, by the same dispatches which gave first information of his serious sickness. He died peacefully, at his home. His funeral was held first in the hall of the House of Representatives, and afterward from his old residence in Toledo, at which city his remains were finally committed to the tomb.

The death of Chief Justice Waite made way for the return to the supreme judicial office in the United States of some member of the political party which has long been out of power. Since the epoch of the Civil War the court has been filled almost exclusively with judges who, by political affiliation, have belonged to the Republican party. The first distinctly Democratic appointment which has been made in the last quarter of a century was the recent one of Judge Lucius Q. C. Lamar, who by the nomination of President Cleveland was transferred from the secretaryship of the interior to the supreme bench. It has thus happened, in the vicissitude of things, that the two political theories which were opposed to each other in the war for the Union, and are still opposed by party name, have become confluent in the high court of the nation. This circumstance has been to some a source of alarm and prejudice: but the hope may be well entertained that partisan dispositions are less potent and dangerous—if indeed they assert themselves at all—on the supreme bench of the United States. Thus far in its history the court has, as a rule, been as pure in its administration and methods as it has been great in reputation. The muddy waters of party conflict have only occasionally reached as high as the threshold of our honored tribunal; and the fear that it may be otherwise hereafter may hopefully be put aside as a groundless and spectral chimera of the hour. On May 1, 1888, the President appointed Melville W. Fuller, of Chicago, to the vacant chief justiceship.

The impression produced by the death of Chief Justice Waite had scarcely passed when the decease of another citizen, most noted for high character and great talents, again called the public attention to the rapid disappearance of the nation's most distinguished representatives. On the 18th of April, at the Hoffman House, New York city, Hon. Roscoe Conkling, ex-Senator of the United States, died after a brief and painful illness. A local inflammation resulting in the formation of a pus-sack under the mastoid bone of the skull led to the cutting of the skull in hope of saving Mr. Conkling's life; but he succumbed to the fatal malady and shock of the operation.

Roscoe Conkling was born in Albany, N. Y., on the 30th of October, 1829. After the completion of an academic course of study he went as a student of law to Utica in 1846. On reaching his majority he was admitted to the bar, and was soon afterward appointed to the office of County Attorney. From the beginning of his career his great talents and remarkable force of character were manifest. He made

Roscoe Conkling.

a profound impression first upon the local and then upon the general society of New York. In 1858 he was Mayor of Utica, and in the same year was sent to the national House of Representatives. He had already become an able politician, and was soon recognized as the leader of the Republican party in his native State. His rise was rapid, and his influence became marked in the affairs of the Government. He served for six years in the lower House, and in 1866 was elected to the Senate. In that body he aspired to leadership and gradually attained it, though not without many struggles and contests with the great men of the epoch. He was twice re-elected Senator—in 1872 and 1878; but in his third term, namely, in 1881, he found himself in such relations with the Garfield administration as induced him to resign his seat. This step was regarded by many as the mistake of his political life. At any rate, he failed of a re-election, the administration party getting control of the Legislature of New York and sending another in his place. After that date Mr. Conkling retired to private life and took up with the greatest success the practice of his profession in New York city.

Roscoe Conkling was a man of the highest courage and stanchest convictions. He never shone to greater advantage than when leading the forces of General Grant in the Chicago Convention of 1880. He was a born political general. His will and persistency and pride gave him a power which, if it had been tempered with greater urbanity, could hardly have failed to crown his life with the highest honors of the nation. His talents rose to the region of genius, and his presence was magnificent—an inspiration to his friends, a terror to his enemies. As a summary of the results of his career it may be said that at the time of his death none except his eminent rival, Mr. Blaine, might justly contest with him the proud rank of most distinguished private citizen of the United States.

Meanwhile, in the spring of 1886, had occurred one of the most serious labor agitations which had ever been witnessed in the United States. It were difficult to present an adequate statement of the causes, general and special, which produced these alarming troubles. Not until after the close of the Civil War did there appear the first symptoms of a renewal, in the New World, of the struggle which has been going on for so long a time in Europe between the laboring classes and the capitalists. It had been hoped that such a conflict would never be renewed in the countries west of the Atlantic. Such a hope, however, was doomed to disappointment. The first well-marked symptoms of the appearance of serious labor strikes and insurrections occurred as early as 1867. The origin of these difficulties was in the coal and iron producing regions of Pennsylvania and in some of the great manufactories of New England. For a while the disturbances produced but little alarm. It was not until the great railroad strike of 1877 that a general apprehension was excited with respect to the unfriendly relations of labor and capital. In the following year much uneasiness existed, but the better times, extending from 1879 to 1882, with the consequent favorable rate of wages, tended to remove, or at least to postpone, the renewal of trouble.

A series of bad crops ensued, and the average ability of the people to purchase was correspondingly diminished. The speculative mania, however, did not cease, and the large amounts of capital withdrawn from legitimate production and lost in visionary enterprises still further reduced the means of employing labor. Stagnation ensued in business; stocks declined in value; manufactories were closed, and the difficulty of obtaining employment was greatly enhanced.

While these causes, half-natural, half-artificial, were at work, others, wholly fictitious, but powerful in their evil results, began to operate in the creation of strife and animosity. Monopolies grew and flourished to an extent hitherto unknown in the United States. On the other hand, labor discovered the salutary but dangerous power of combination. A rage for organizing took possession of the minds of the laboring men of the country, and to the arrogant front of monopoly was opposed the insurrectionary front of the working classes.

More serious still than the causes here referred to was the introduction into the United States of a large mass of ignorant foreign labor. The worst elements of several European States contributed freely to the manufactories and workshops of America, and a class of ideas utterly un-American became dominant in many of the leading establishments of the country. Communistic theories of society and anarchic views of government began to clash with the more sober republican opinions and practices of the people. To all this must be added the evils and abuses which seem to be incident to the wage system of labor, and are, perhaps, inseparable therefrom. The result has been a growing jealousy of the two great parties to production, the laborer and the capitalist.

The opening of trade for the season of 1886 witnessed a series of strikes and labor imbroglios in all parts of the country. Such troubles were, however, confined for the most part to the cities and towns where labor was aggregated. The first serious trouble occurred on what is known as the Gould system of railways, reaching from the Mississippi to the south-west. A single workman, belonging to the Knights of Labor, and employed on a branch of the Texas Pacific Railway, at that time under a receivership, and therefore beyond the control of Jay Gould and his subordinates, was discharged from his place. This action was resented by the Knights, and the laborers on a great part of the Gould system were ordered to strike. The movement was, for a season, successful, and the transportation of freights from St. Louis to the south-west ceased. Gradually, however, other workmen were substituted for the striking Knights; the movement of freights was resumed, and the strike ended in comparative failure; but this end was not reached until a severe riot in East St. Louis had occasioned the sacrifice of several innocent lives.

Far more alarming was the outbreak in Chicago. In that city the socialistic and anarchic elements were sufficiently powerful to present a bold front to the authorities. Processions bearing red flags and banners, with communistic devices and mottoes, frequently paraded the streets, and were addressed by demagogues who avowed themselves the open enemies of society and the existing order. On the 4th of May a vast crowd of this reckless material collected in a place called the Hay market, and were about to begin the usual inflammatory proceedings, when a band of policemen, mostly officers, drew near, with the evident purpose of controlling or dispersing the meeting. A terrible scene ensued. Dynamite bombs were thrown from the crowd and exploded among the officers, several of whom were blown to pieces and others shockingly mangled. The mob was, in turn, attacked by the police, and many of the insurgents were shot down. Order was presently restored in the city; several of the leading anarchists were arrested and held for trial on the charge of inciting to murder, and measures were taken to prevent the recurrence of such tragedies as had been witnessed in the Haymarket Square. On the following day a similar, though less dangerous, outbreak occurred in Milwaukee; but in this city the insurrectionary movement was suppressed without serious loss of life. The attention of the American people—let us hope to some good end—was called, as never before, to the dangerous relations existing between the upper and nether sides of our municipal populations.

The summer of 1886 is memorable on account of that great natural phenomenon, known as the Charleston earthquake. On the night of the 31st of August, at ten minutes before ten o'clock, it was discovered at Washington City, and at several other points where weather and signal stations were established, that communications with Charleston, S. C., were suddenly cut off. The discovery was made by inquiries relative to the origin of a shock which had that moment been felt with varying degrees of violence throughout nearly the whole country east of the Mississippi and south of the great lakes. In a few minutes it was found that no telegraphic communication from any side could be had with Charleston, and it was at once perceived that that city had suffered from the convulsion. Measures were hastily devised for further investigation, and the result showed that the worst apprehensions were verified. Without a moment's warning the city had been rocked and rent to its very foundations. Hardly a building in the limits of Charleston or in the country surrounding had escaped serious injury, and perhaps one-half of all were in a state of semi-wreck or total ruin. No such scene of devastation and terror from a like cause had ever before been witnessed within the limits of the United States.

Many scientists of national reputation hurried to the scene and made a careful scrutiny of the phenomenon with a view of contributing something to the exact knowledge of mankind respecting the causes and character of earthquakes. One or two points were determined with tolerable accuracy. One was, that the point of origin, called the epicenter, of the great convulsion had been at a place about twenty miles from Charleston, and that the motion of the earth immediately over this, center had been nearly up and down—that is, vertical. A second point tolerably well established was that the isoseismic lines, or lines of equal disturbance, might be drawn around the epicenter in circles very nearly concentric, and that the circle of greatest disturbance was at some distance from the center. Still a third item of knowledge tolerably well established was that away from the epicenter—as illustrated in the ruins of Charleston—the agitation of the earth was not in the nature of a single shock or convulsion, as a dropping or sliding of the region to one side, but rather a series of very quick and violent oscillations, by which the central country of the disturbance was in the course of some five minutes settled somewhat to seaward.

The whole coast in the central region of the disturbance was modified with respect to the sea, and the ocean itself was thrown into turmoil for leagues from the shore. The people of the city were in a state of utmost consternation. The people fled from their falling houses to the public squares and parks and far into the country. Afraid to return into the ruins they threw up tents and light booths for protection and abode for weeks away from their homes. The convulsion was by far the greatest that this continent has experienced within the historical epoch. Nothing before in the limits of our knowledge has been at all comparable with it in extent and violence except the great earthquake of New Madrid, in 1811. The disaster to Charleston served to bring out some of the better qualities of our civilization. Assistance came from all quarters, and contributions poured in for the support and encouragement of the afflicted people. For several weeks a series of diminishing shocks continued to terrify the citizens and paralyze the efforts at restoration. But it was discovered in the course of time that these shocks were only the dying away of the great convulsion, and that they gave cause for hope of entire cessation rather than continued alarm. In a lapse of a few months the *débris* was cleared away, business was resumed, and the people were again safe in their homes.

On the 4th of March, 1887, the second session of the Forty-ninth Congress expired by statutory limitation. The work of the body had not been so fruitful of results as had been desired and anticipated by the friends of the government; but some important legislation had been effected. On the question of the tariff nothing of value was accomplished. True, a serious measure of revenue reform had been brought forward at an early date in the session, but owing to the opposition of that wing of the Democratic party headed by Hon. Samuel J. Randall, and committed to the doctrine of protection, as well as to the antagonism of the Republican majority in the Senate, the act failed of adoption. In fact, by the beginning of 1887 it had become apparent that the existing political parties could not be forced to align on the issue of free trade and tariff, and as a result no legislation looking to any actual reform in the current revenue system of the United States could be carried through Congress.

On the question of extending the Pension List, however, the case was different. A great majority of both parties could always be counted on to favor such measures as looked to the increase of benefits to the soldiers. At the first, only a limited number of pensions had been granted, and these only to actually disabled and injured veterans of the War for the Union. With the lapse of time, however, and the relaxation of party allegiance, it became more and more important to each of the parties to secure and hold the soldier vote, without which it was felt that neither could maintain ascendency in the government. Nor can it be denied that genuine patriotic sentiment and gratitude of the nation to its defenders coincided in this respect with political ambition and selfishness. The Arrears of Pensions Act, making up to those who were already recipients of pensions such amounts as would have accrued if the benefit had dated from the time of disability, instead of from the time of granting the pension, was passed in 1879, and at the same time the list of beneficiaries was greatly enlarged.

The measure presented in the Forty-ninth Congress was designed to extend the pension list so as to include all regularly enlisted and honorably discharged soldiers of the Civil War who had become in whole or in part dependent upon the aid of others for their maintenance and welfare. The measure was known as the Dependent Pensions Bill, and though a few had the courage to oppose the enactment of a law which appeared to fling away the bounty of the government to the deserving and the undeserving, the evil and the just alike, and to compel the worthy and honorable recipients of pensions who had actually suffered in the war to rank themselves in the same category with the thriftless, the unpatriotic, and the improvident, who, having been in the army, had afterward come to grief through their own lack of enterprise and frugality; yet a majority was easily obtained for the measure in both Houses, and the act was passed. President Cleveland, however, interposed his veto, and the proposed law fell to the ground. A strenuous effort was made in the House of Representatives to pass the bill over the veto; but the movement failed.

By far the most important and noted piece of legislation of the session was incorporated in the act known as the Inter-State Commerce Bill. For some fifteen years complaints against the methods and management of the railways of the United States had been heard on many sides, and in cases not a few the complaints had originated in actual abuses, some of which were willful, but most were merely incidental to the development of a system so vast and, on the whole, so beneficial to the public. In such a state of affairs the lasting benefit is always forgotten in the accidental hurt. That large class of people who, in despite of the teachings of history, still believe in the cure of all things by law, and that mankind are always about to perish for want of more legislation, became clamorous in their demand that Congress should take the railways by the throat and compel them to accept what may be called the system of uniformity as it respects all charges for service rendered. It was believed in Congress that to take up this call, and champion the alleged cause of the people, would be one of the most popular measures of the period. The Inter-State Commerce Bill was, accordingly, prepared, with a multitude of lengthy and involved clauses requiring a commission of great lawyers for their interpretation. It was enacted that all freight carriage across State lines within the Union should be at the same rate per hundred for all distances, and between all places, and under substantially the same conditions, and that passenger fares should be uniform for all persons. It must be borne in mind that, in the very nature of things, railways are unable to carry freight at as small a rate per hundred, or passengers at as small a charge per mile, between places approximate as between places at great distances. It must also be remembered that in some regions it is many times more expensive to build and operate a railroad than in others. To carry one of these great thoroughfares over the Rocky

Mountains is a very different thing from stretching a similar track across the level prairies of Illinois. It must still further be considered that, in the nature of the case, competition will do its legitimate and inevitable work at an earlier date and more thoroughly between great cities, even when remotely situated, than between unimportant points, however near together. The traffic and travel between two villages is not sufficient to create competition among the carriers. It is as absurd to suppose that railway tariffs can be the same between New York and Chicago as they are between two Missouri towns, as it is to suppose that butter can command the same price in an Iowa village that it does in the Quincy Market of Boston. What should be said of an attempt in Congress to make the price of wheat and pork uniform throughout the United States?

The Inter-State Commerce Bill was conceived against all the natural, manifest and undeniable principles of the commercial world. It was passed with the belief that all discriminations in the charges made by railways doing business in more than one State could be prevented by law. It was passed as if to amend or abrogate those natural laws of trade and traffic which in their kind are as absolute, and as beneficial, as the law of gravitation. It was passed with the ulterior design of securing to its promoters the support of that ignorant and embittered race of men whose prejudices are out of all proportion to their knowledge of human rights, or their recognition of the paramount interests of the whole people. It was passed under the pernicious anti-democratic, theory of governmental paternalism, which says that men are infants or imbeciles, unable to care for themselves unless they are fed and led and coddled by some motherly government of which they are the irresponsible offspring. It is safe to say that no other measure ever adopted by the American Congress has been so difficult of application, or has thrown the commercial affairs of the country into so great disorder. The one redeeming feature of the case has been, and is, that they who, by the passage of so preposterous a series of enactments, thought to crown themselves with laurel, came forth wearing a diadem of weeds and cactus.

During the whole of Cleveland's administration the public mind was swayed and excited by the movements of politics. The universality of partisan newspapers, the combination in their columns of all the news of the world with the invectives, misrepresentations, and countercharges of party leaders, kept political questions constantly uppermost, to the detriment of social progress and industrial interests. Scarcely had President Cleveland entered upon his office as chief magistrate when the question of the succession to the Presidency was agitated. The echoes of the election of 1884 had not died away before the rising murmur of that of 1888 was heard.

By the last year of the current administration it was seen that there would be no general break-up of the existing parties. It was also perceived that the issues between them must be *made*, rather than found in the existing state of affairs. The sentiment in the United States in favor of the Constitutional prohibition of the manufacture and sale of intoxicating liquors had become somewhat extended and intensified since the last quadrennial election. But the discerning eye might perceive that the real issue was between the Republican and Democratic parties, and that the questions involved were to be rather those of the past than of the future.

One issue, however, presented itself which had a living and practical relation to affairs, and that was the question of PROTECTION to AMERICAN INDUSTRY. Since the campaign of 1884, the agitation had been gradually extended. At the opening of the session, in 1887 the President, in his annual message to Congress, departed from all precedent, and devoted the whole document to the discussion of the single question of a *Reform of the Revenue System* of the United States. The existing rates of duty on imported articles of commerce had so greatly augmented the income of the Government that a large surplus had accumulated, and was still accumulating, in the treasury of the United States. This fact was made the basis of the President's argument in favor of a new system of revenue, or at least an ample reduction in the tariff rates under the old. It was immediately charged by the Republicans that the project in question meant the substitution of the system of free trade in the United States as against the system of protective duties. The question thus involved was made the bottom issue in the Presidential campaign of 1888.

As to the nominees of the various parties, it was from the first a foregone conclusion that Mr. Cleveland would be nominated for re-election by the Democrats. The result justified the expectation. The Democratic National Convention was held in St. Louis, on the 5th day of June, 1888, and Mr. Cleveland was re-nominated by acclamation. For the Vice-Presidential nomination there was a considerable contest; but, after some balloting, the choice fell on ex-Senator Allen G. Thurman, of Ohio. The Republican National Convention was held in Chicago, on the 19th day of June. Many candidates were ardently pressed upon the body, and the contest was long and spirited. It was believed, up to the time of the Convention, that Mr. Blaine, who was evidently the favorite of a great majority, would be again nominated for the Presidency. But the antagonisms which that statesman had awakened in his own party made it imprudent to bring him forward again as the nominee. His name was accordingly not presented to the Convention, The most prominent candidates were Senator John Sherman, of Ohio; Judge Walter Q. Gresham, of Chicago; Chauncey M. Depew, of New York; ex-Governor Russel A. Alger, of Michigan; ex-Senator Benjamin Harrison, of Indiana; and Senator William B. Allison, of Iowa. The voting was continued to the eighth ballot, when the choice fell upon Benjamin Harrison, of Indiana. In the evening Levi P. Morton, of New York, was nominated for the Vice-Presidency on the first ballot.

In the meantime the Prohibition party had held its National Convention at Indianapolis, and on the 30th of May had nominated for the Presidency General Clinton B. Fisk, of New Jersey, and for the Vice-Presidency John A. Brooks, of Missouri. The Democratic platform declared for a reform of the revenue system of the United States, and re-affirmed the principle of adjusting the tariff on imports with strict regard to the actual needs of governmental expenditure. The Republican platform declared also for a reform of the tariff schedule, but at the same time stoutly affirmed the maintenance of the protective system, as such, as a part of the permanent policy of the United States. Both parties deferred to the patriotic sentiment of the country in favor of the soldiers, their rights and interests, and both endeavored by the usual incidental circumstances of the hour to gain the advantage of the other before the American people. The Prohibitionists entered the campaign on the distinct proposition that the manufacture and sale of intoxicating liquors should be prohibited throughout the United States by Constitutional amendment. To this was added a clause in favor of extending the right of suffrage to women.

As the canvass progressed during the summer and autumn of 1888 it became evident that the result was in doubt. The contest was exceedingly close. As in 1880 and 1884, the critical States were New York, Connecticut, New Jersey, and Indiana. In all of the other Northern States the Republicans were almost certain to win, while the Democrats were equally certain of success in all the South. In the last weeks of the campaign General Harrison grew in favor, and his party gained perceptibly to the close. The result showed success for the Republican candidate. He received 233 electoral votes, against 168 votes for Mr. Cleveland. The latter, however, appeared to a better advantage on the popular count, having a considerable majority over General Harrison. General Fisk, the Prohibition candidate, received nearly three hundred thousand votes; but under the system of voting no electoral vote of any State was obtained for him in the so-called "College," by which the actual choice is made. As soon as the result was known the excitement attendant upon the campaign subsided and political questions gave place to other interests.

The last days of Cleveland's administration and of the Fiftieth Congress were signalized by the admission into the Union of FOUR NEW STATES, making the number forty-two. Since the incoming of Colorado, in 1876, no State had been added to the Republic. Meanwhile the tremendous tides of population had continued to flow to the west and north-west, rapidly filling up the great Territories. Of these the greatest was Dakota, with its area of 150,932 square miles. In 1887 the question of dividing the Territory by a line running east and west was agitated, and the measure finally prevailed. Steps were taken by the people of both sections for admission into the Union. Montana, with her 145,776 square miles of territory, had meanwhile acquired a sufficient population; and Washington Territory, with its area of 69,994 square miles, also knocked for admission. In the closing days of the Fiftieth Congress a bill was passed raising all these four Territories—South Dakota, North Dakota, Montana, and Washington—to the plane of Statehood. The Act contemplated the adoption of State Constitutions, and a proclamation of admission by the next President. It thus happened that the honor of bringing in this great addition to the States of the Union was divided between the outgoing and incoming administrations.

Another Act of Congress was also of national importance. Hitherto the government had been administered through seven departments, at the head of each of which was placed a Cabinet officer, the seven together constituting the advisers of the President. No provision for such an arrangement exists in the Constitution of the United States; but the statutes of the Nation provide for such a system as most in accordance with the republican form of government. Early in 1889 a measure was brought forward in Congress and adopted for the institution of a new department, to be called the Department of Agriculture. Practically the measure involved the elevation of what had previously been an Agricultural Bureau in the Department of the Interior to the rank of a Cabinet office. Among foreign nations France has been conspicuous for the patronage which the Government has given to the agricultural pursuits of that country. Hitherto in the United States, though agriculture has been the greatest of all the producing interests of the people, it has been neglected for more political and less useful departments of American life and enterprise. By this act of Congress the Cabinet offices were increased in number to eight instead of seven.

CHAPTER LXXII.

Harrison's Administration, 1889—

Benjamin Harrison, twenty-third President of the United States, was born at North Bend, Ohio, on the 20th of August, 1833. He is the son of John Scott Harrison, a prominent citizen of his native State grandson of President William Henry Harrison; great-grandson of Benjamin Harrison, signer of the Declaration of Independence. In countries where attention is paid to honorable lineage the circumstances of General Harrison's descent would be considered of much importance; but in America little attention is paid to one's ancestry, and more to himself.

Benjamin Harrison.

Harrison's early life was passed as that of other American boys, in attendance at school and at home duties on the farm. He was a student at the institution called Farmers' College for two years. Afterwards he attended Miami University, at Oxford, Ohio, and was graduated therefrom in June, 1852. He took in marriage the daughter of Dr. John W. Scott, President of the University. After a course of study he entered the profession of law, removing to Indianapolis and establishing himself in that city. With the outbreak of the War he became a soldier of the Union, and rose to the rank of Brevet Brigadier-General of Volunteers. Before the close of the War he was elected Reporter of Decisions of the Supreme Court of Indiana.

In the period following the Civil War General Harrison rose to distinction as a civilian. In 1876 he was the unsuccessful candidate of the Republican party for Governor of Indiana. In 1881 he was elected to the United States Senate, where he won the reputation of a leader and statesman. In 1884 his name was prominently mentioned in connection with the Presidential nomination of his party, but Mr. Blaine was successful. After the lapse of four years, however, it was found at Chicago that General Harrison, more than any other, combined in himself all the elements of a successful candidate; and the event justified the choice of the party in making him the standard-bearer in the ensuing campaign.

General Harrison was, in accordance with the usages of the Government, inaugurated President on the 4th of March, 1889. He had succeeded better than any of his predecessors in keeping his own counsels during the interim between his election and the inauguration. No one had discerned his purposes, and all waited with interest the expressions of his Inaugural Address. In that document he set forth the policy which he should favor as the chief executive, recommending the same general measures which the Republican party had advocated during the campaign.

James G. Blaine.

On the day following the in augural ceremonies President Harrison sent in the nominations for his Cabinet officers, as follows: for Secretary of State, James G. Blaine, of Maine; for Secretary of the Treasury, William Windom, of Minnesota; for Secretary of War, Redfield Proctor, of Vermont; for Secretary of the Navy, Benjamin F. Tracy, of New York; for Postmaster-General, John Wanamaker, of Pennsylvania; for Secretary of the Interior, John W. Noble, of Missouri; for Attorney-General, William H. H. Miller, of Indiana; and for Secretary of Agriculture—the new department—Jeremiah Rusk, of Wisconsin. These appointments were immediately confirmed by the Senate, and the members of the new administration assumed their respective official duties.

Within two months after Harrison's inauguration an event occurred which might well recall to the mind of the American people the striking incidents in the history of the Revolutionary Epoch. The event in question was the gr eat Centennial Celebration of the Inauguration of Washington, first President of the United States. The same was commemorated in many parts of the country but the supreme event was in New York city, and the ceremonies connected there with were associated, as far as practicable, with the scenes of the first inauguration. These circumstances may well call forth not only some descriptive account of the celebration itself, but also a brief review of those events and incidents on which the same was based.

The period extending from the year 1776 to the year 1789 was marked in the colonial history of the United States by several crises, different in kind, but each so well defined in character as to be worthy of commemoration by the people of another and distant age. These crises were:

1. The Declaration of Independence.
2. The Formation of the Constitution of the United States.
3. The Adoption of the Constitution.
4. The Institution of the New Government.

The dates of these successive events are well known, the first occurring in midsummer of 1776; the second, in the summer of 1787; the third, in the years 1787 and 1788; and the fourth, in 1789. It is to the events of the last-named year that the attention of the reader will now be more particularly called.

As we have said, each of these crises has a philosophical place and character in American history, and the reader may be interested to note the same as preliminary to an understanding of the Centennial exercises in New York city.

First, the Declaration of Independence was a *democratic* and *popular* revolution. It was the act by which the allegiance of the old Thirteen Colonies to the mother country was broken. It was essentially destructive in its character. The first stages of all revolutions have this distinctive aspect. They destroy. It remains for a subsequent movement to rebuild. The revolution, in the first place, abolishes and destroys an existing order. It implies that the people have borne as long as possible some system which presses upon them as if it were of chains and fetters. It is to break the chains, to throw off the fetters that the revolution begins its career. Sometimes it is carried forward under a government which is able to survive the shock; more frequently it attacks the government itself, and, if successful, overthrows it. Such was the case with the destructive Revolution of 1776. It was leveled against the existing order, and was most happily successful.

Second, it was not long after the achievement of independence until the Revolutionary patriots, at least the more thoughtful and conservative of them, came to see that mere independence was not enough; that mere destruction of popular abuses could not suffice for the future of America. Acting from these sentiments the Fathers began to consult about re-building, or building anew, a structure in which civil liberty in America might find an abiding-place. These discussions began almost as soon as independence was clearly gained. Within a year after the treaty of peace Washington and his friends began to discuss the feasibility of a better system of government. Conferences were held first at Mount Vernon, then at Annapolis, and finally a great convention of delegates was assembled at Philadelphia. This occurred, as we have said, in the summer of 1787. The result of the labors of this convention is well known. That strange compromise called the Constitution of the United States was produced and signed by the delegates, with Washington as their president. This, then, was the epoch of the Formation of the Constitution.

Third, immediately after this event a period of political agitation, the first real and general agitation known in the history of the United States, occurred. The new Constitution laid before the States was the bottom fact from which the stormy discussions of the next two years sprang.

Should that Constitution be adopted? Or should it be rejected and the old confederative system of government be continued? On these questions there was a division of parties. The controversy waxed violent. All the old Thirteen States were shaken from center to boundary line.

In a former part of the present work[52] the story of the Adoption of the Constitution by the several States has been narrated; nor is it necessary here to repeat the well-known account of how State after State carried a majority of its delegates for the new system of government. This epoch of agitation, of controversy, and the final adoption is the third of the three crises to which we have made reference as belonging to our Revolutionary history.

Fourth, and last of all, after the Constitution was adopted by nine or ten of the States, came the striking event of the Institution of the New Government. The paper model of that Government existed in the Constitution itself. How Washington was unanimously chosen as first chief magistrate of the new republic is known to all the world. A Congress was constituted by the election of a House of Representatives and a Senate, in accordance with the provision of the new instrument. All things were made ready, as an architect might prepare the materials for a structure. Then came the actual building of the temple. The scene was in old New York; the New York of one hundred years ago.

It is worth while, before proceeding with the account of the Washingtonian inauguration, and of the commemorative events of 1889, to notice briefly the manner and spirit in which the preceding centennials were observed by the people of the United States. We have already seen with what enthusiasm the Centennial Anniversary of the great democratic Revolution of 1776 was marked by the masses. The people of the United States are warm in their affections toward the destructive revolution which was accomplished by the Declaration of Independence and the war which followed. There can be no doubt that, so far as the masses are concerned, they have taken more interest, not only in our own independence and the means by which it was accomplished, but in the destructive aspect of all other revolutionary

---

[52] See Chapter XLV.

movements. With what zeal and success the Centennial Anniversary of Independence was observed in the city of Philadelphia has already been narrated in a previous chapter of the present work.[53] The second Centennial—that is, the Centennial of the Formation of the Constitution, did not awaken in the United States any considerable degree of enthusiasm. From this it is to be plainly inferred that the people as a whole rejoice more in the fact of independence, in the destruction of old forms, and in the events by which independence was achieved, than they do in the structural part of the history of the country—that is, in the history of those new institutions which have been planted in place of the old.

There was in the city of Philadelphia, where the Constitution was adopted, an effort in 1887 to commemorate the anniversary, and some local interest was excited in the event; but there was no wide-spread zeal, no throbbing of the popular heart over the coming of the hundredth year of our national charter. The same may be said with respect to observing the intermediate period of the adoption of the Constitution. No celebrations of more than local importance were had in any of the States in commemoration of this important event. At the first it was even doubted whether the era of the institution of a government itself, dating from the 30th of April, 1789, could awaken sufficient public enthusiasm to warrant a national celebration. Events such as the formation of our Constitution, its adoption by the people of the States, and the institution of the new form instead of the old are not sufficiently spectacular and heroic to set the masses aglow, to produce the requisite heat of a great national commemoration. Nevertheless in the case of the institution of the Government it was believed by the people of New York city that the event could not by any means be allowed to pass without an effort to impress upon the minds of the present generation the great events of a century gone by.

Sufficiently striking in all respects was the contrast between the actual inauguration of Washington and the ceremonies attendant upon the beginning of the Government of the United States in 1789, on the

---

[53] See page 679.

one hand, and the commemorative exercises after the lapse of a century. It may be appropriate in this connection to review briefly the circumstances of Washington's inauguration in order that the reader may have the contrast well in mind.

According to the Constitution of the United States the new Government which had been provided for was to have been instituted on the 4th of March—the day which has ever since been retained as the quadrennial beginning of the successive administrations.

But the first setting up of the Government was attended with many difficulties. The seat of the new Republic, so far as its governmental machinery was concerned, was to be, at least for the time, in New York city. To reach that colonial metropolis, especially in the early spring, was a difficult and tedious process; the members of Congress had to come from what were then distant regions to reach the place appointed. So the work lagged. On the 25th of March, 1789, a quorum had not yet appeared in either House of Congress. Nor should the reader forget that the old Congress of the Confederation had not yet expired. It met from day to day in the old Federal Hall in Wall Street.

The coming of a greater Congress was at hand. Near the close of the month Fisher Ames wrote to a friend in Boston, as follows:

"We have 26 representatives, and as 30 are necessary to make a quorum we are still in a state of inaction. ... I am inclined to believe that the languor of the old Confederation is transfused into the members of the new Congress. This city has not caught the spirit, or rather the want of spirit, I am vexing myself to express to you. Their ball will cost £20,000 York money. They are pre paring fireworks and a splendid barge for the President, which last will cost £200 to £300. We lose £1,000 a day revenue. We lose credit, spirit, every thing. The public will forget the Government before it is born. The resurrection of the infant will come before its birth. Happily the federal interest is strong in Congress. The old Congress still continues to meet, and it seems to be doubtful whether the old Government is dead or the new one alive. God deliver us speedily from this puzzling state, or prepare my will, if it subsists much longer, for I am in a fever to think of it."

On the 1st of April, however, the House of Representatives had a quorum. Shortly afterwards the Senate also was sufficiently full to proceed to business. On the 6th of April both Houses were organized in the same Hall where the old Confederative Congress of the Colonies had been sitting. It will be remembered that this so-called Federal Hall was the old historic City Hall of New York, which had been used as the seat of legislative affairs since the close of the seventeenth century.

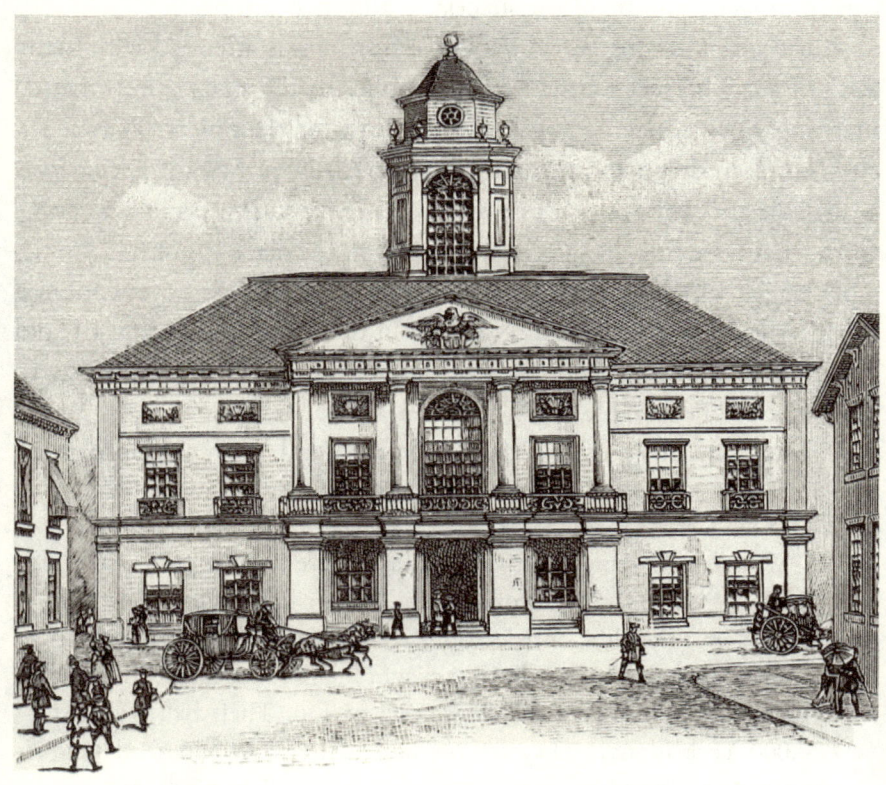

Old Federal Hall, Wall Street, at the Head of Broad, 1789.

The Constitution had devolved upon Congress the duty of opening and counting the ballots for President of the United States. This was first of all attended to. It was found that George Washington, of Virginia, had a unanimous vote from all the States. The next highest on the list was John Adams, of Massachusetts, who, as the Constitution then stood, was to serve as Vice-President. But neither the President-elect nor the Vice-President-elect had as yet arrived in New York. Events in those days went forward like a stately minuet. There was neither hurrying nor excitement; or if the latter existed it was suppressed under the formal regularities of the times.

Charles Thompson was dispatched by Congress to Mount Vernon to notify General Washington of his election to the Presidency. The messenger rode on horseback. For fifteen years he had been secretary of Congress. Nor is it uninteresting to notice that his wife, Hannah Harrison, was a sister of Benjamin Harrison, the signer of the Declaration of Independence, great-grandfather of him who was destined, in the course of events, to be the Centennial President of the United States. Washington was thus notified, and preparations were begun for his departure to the seat of government.

Sylvanus Bourne was a like messenger to Vice-President Adams. The latter left home sooner than did Washington, and presently, on the 20th of April, arrived at New York. But the General's coming was delayed until late in April. Even then his progress was slow; the people retarded his course. In the proper place we have already noticed the manner in which he was received *en route*—how, especially at Trenton, passing under triumphal arches, thirteen young girls strewed the way before him with flowers. Washington's course from Trenton was across New Jersey by the old stage-route to Elizabethtown, where he was met by a deputation from Congress to escort him to the city.

The passage of the harbor was sufficiently beautified with civic ceremonies; the boats were decorated with flags, and gay barges glided through the shining water. The President himself crossed over in a barge. It is said that every vessel in the great harbor was in full dress of streamers and flags, while at several points groups of singers saluted the President with music as he passed. Governor George Clinton, of New York, had been commissioned to receive Washington at the ferry. The stairs were carpeted leading up from the water to the shore; there Clinton received the Father of his Country. As soon as Washington's figure rose to view the assembled people broke out in shouts long continued and the excitement swirled through the city when it was known that the new President had really arrived. This was on the 23d of April, 1789.

New York at the time of which we speak was limited to the lower end of Manhattan Island. It was no more than a speck in comparison with the Centennial Metropolis of the nation. Its northern limits were marked by the building of the New York *Times*. Immediately north of this lay a lake, called the Collect Pond, about sixty feet in depth, covering that part of the city now occupied by the Tombs. It is said that the capitalists, even the adventurers, of that day, were without faith as to the future extension of the city northward. The population was approximately forty thousand. Water was distributed to the citizens in hydrants and drawn from what was known as the Old Tea Water Pump standing at the head of Pearl Street. No system of public street cleaning had been adopted. The streets were lighted with oil lamps. Much of the work was done by slaves, and slave auctions were at that time still a common occurrence.

General Washington was conducted to the residence which had been prepared for him in Franklin Square, and a programme was made out by Congress for the inauguration, which was set for the 30th of April. The stately and yet successful formalities of the occasion are fully set forth in the following memorandum from the first records of Congress:

> April 29th, 1789. The committees of both houses of Congress, appointed to take order for conducting the ceremonial of the formal reception, &c., of the President of the United States, on Thursday next, have agreed to the following order thereon, viz.:
>
> That General Webb, Colonel Smith, Lieutenant Colonel Fish, Lieutenant Colonel Franks, Major L'Enfant, Major Bleecker, and Mr. John R. Livingston, be requested to serve as assistants on the occasion.
>
> That a chair be placed in the Senate Chamber for the President of the United States. That a chair be placed in the Senate Chamber for the Vice-President, to the right of the President's chair; and that the Senators take their seats on that side of the chamber on which the Vice-President's chair shall be placed. That a chair be placed in the Senate Chamber for the Speaker of the House of Representatives, to the left of the President's chair—and that the Representatives take their seats on that side of the chamber on which the Speaker's chair shall be placed.
>
> That seats be provided in the Senate Chamber sufficient to accommodate the late president of Congress, the governor of the

Western territory, the five persons being the heads of three great departments, the Minister Plenipotentiary of France, the Encargado de negocios of Spain, the chaplains of Congress, the persons in the suite of the President, and also to accommodate the following Public Officers of the State, viz.: The Governor, the Lieutenant-Governor, the Chancellor, the Chief Justice, and other judges of the Supreme Court, and the Mayor of the city. That one of the assistants wait on these gentlemen, and inform them that seats are provided for their accommodation, and also to signify to them that no precedence of seats is intended, and that no salutation is expected from them on their entrance into, or their departure from, the Senate Chamber.

That the members of both houses assemble in their respective Chambers precisely at twelve o'clock, and that the representatives preceded by the Speaker, and attended by their clerk, and other officers, proceed to the Senate Chamber, there to be received by the Vice-President and the senators rising.

That the Committees attend the President from his residence to the Senate Chamber, and that he be there received by the Vice-President, the senators and representatives rising, and be by the Vice-President conducted to his chair.

That after the President shall be seated in his chair, and the Vice-President, senators and representatives shall be again seated, the Vice-President shall announce to the President, that the members of both houses will attend him to be present at his taking the Oath of Office required by the Constitution. To the end that the Oath of Office may be administered to the President in the most public manner, and that the greatest number of the people of the United States, and without distinction, may be witnesses to the solemnity, that therefore the Oath be administered in the outer gallery adjoining to the Senate Chamber.

That when the President shall proceed to the gallery to take the Oath, he be attended by the Vice-President, and be followed by the Chancellor of the State, and pass through the middle door; that the Senators pass through the door on the right; and the Representatives, preceded by the Speaker, pass through the door on the left; and such of the persons who shall have been admitted into the Senate Chamber, and may be desirous to go into the gallery, are then also to pass through the door on the right. When the President shall have taken the Oath, and returned into the Senate Chamber, attended by the Vice-President, and shall be seated in his chair, that the Senators and the Representatives also return into the Senate Chamber, and that the Vice-President and they resume their respective seats.

Both Houses having resolved to accompany the President, after he shall have taken the Oath, to St. Paul's Chapel, to hear divine service, to be performed by the chaplain of Congress, that the following order of procession be observed, viz.: The door-keeper and messenger of the House of Representatives. The clerk of the House. The Representatives. The Speaker. The President, with the Vice-President at his left hand. The Senators. The Secretary of the Senate. The door-keeper, and messenger of the Senate.

That a pew be reserved for the President, Vice-President, Speaker of the House of Representatives, and the Committees; and that pews be also reserved sufficient for the reception of the Senators and Representatives.

That after divine service shall be performed, the President be received at the door of the Church, by the Committees, and by them attended in carriages to his residence.

That it be intrusted to the assistants to take proper precautions for the keeping the avenues to the Hall open, and that for that purpose, they wait on his Excellency, the Governor of this State, and in the name of the Committees request his aid, by an order of recommendation to the Civil Officers, or militia of the city, to attend and serve on the occasion, as he shall judge most proper.

New York, as New York then was, had made great preparations to receive the Chief Magistrate. On the morning of the 30th, a national salute was fired; the bells burst out merrily from all the steeples of the city. The newspapers of the day described the scene as especially impressive. The people were called to attend church at nine o'clock in the morning. The beginning of the inaugural procession was set for noon-day; and promptly at that hour the President's carriage, followed by a train of attendants, proceeded from the house in Cherry Street, which had been appointed as his residence, through what was then Queen, Great Dock, and Broad Streets to the Old Federal Hall, where the ceremonies of the inauguration were to take place. The order of march is worthy of commemoration; for this, as well as many other circumstances, tends to set in strongest contrast the first inauguration with that of its Centennial recurrence.

Col. MORGAN LEWIS,
Attended by two officers.

Capt. STAKES,
With the Troop of Horse.

Artillery.
Maj. VAN HORNE.

Grenadiers, under Capt. HARSIN.
German Grenadiers, very gayly attired, under Capt. SCRIBA.
Major BIEKER.

The Infantry of the Brigade.
Major CHRYSLIE.

Sheriff.

Committee of the Senate.

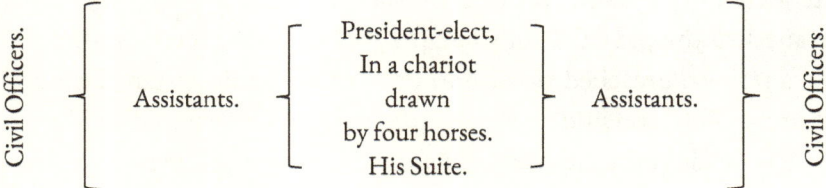

Civil Officers. { Assistants. { President-elect, In a chariot drawn by four horses. His Suite. } Assistants. } Civil Officers.

Committee of the Representatives.

Hon. Mr. JAY, Secretary of Foreign Affairs.

Gen. KNOX, Secretary of War.

Chancellor LIVINGSTON.

Several gentlemen of distinction.

Arrangements had been made for the reception of Washington in the Senate Hall. Thither he was conducted, and, when seated, was addressed by Vice-President Adams. After these preliminaries, the President-elect, with the Chief Officers of the new Republic, the Senate and House of Representatives, repaired by the left and right to the balcony in front of the Hall, looking down in Wall Street, where the assembled throng awaited the administration of the oath of office. To this duty Chancellor Robert R. Livingston, Chief-justice of New York, had been appointed. Perhaps no scene of public induction into office was ever more solemn or impressive. The chief figure was that of the Father of his Country, conspicuous by his height, and still more conspicuous by the grandeur and impressiveness of his demeanor. The oath of office was administered on the Bible, opened before Washington, whereon he laid his hand, and to which he pressed his lips at the conclusion of the oath. This done, Chancellor Livingston raised his voice, and with a gesture cried: "Long live George Washington, President of the United States." Immediately afterward the throng burst out in wild cheering; shouts echoed through the city, and the bells rang out their peal of gladness at the auspicious event. Returning to the Senate Chamber Washington delivered an inaugural address, not elaborate and formal, as such papers have become in the course of our history, but brief, and affecting to those who heard it.[54]

As soon as the exercises at the Federal Hall were over Washington, attended by the chief officers of the government, and the Senate, repaired to the old St. Paul's Chapel, where divine services were held, and a sermon preached by Bishop Provost of the Protestant Epis copal Church. This concluded the formal exercises of the day. With the coming of night the city was brilliantly illuminated. The people poured into the streets; shouts rang out on the evening air, and a universal joy seemed to prevail, which was but the conspicuous example of the common rejoicing in all the States.

---

[54] It is worthy of note that Washington, at the time of the inauguration, though only 57 years of age was already an old man. He had gone into the Revolution a young man, but was now aged, gray, enfeebled by the strenuous services and great anxieties to which he had been subjected through a period of fourteen years. He was still erect, majestic, firm in his step, with a certain serene dignity of countenance which has hardly had a parallel among all the great men who have risen on this side of the sea. But it was noticed by those in the Senate Chamber, on the day of his inauguration, that his voice was not a little enfeebled. He spoke in a low tone and could be heard only by those who were sitting near. Perhaps the premonitory shadows of the serious and long-continued illness, which fell upon him within two months after his inauguration, were already gathering on the day of his accession to the Presidency.

Baron Steuben, Gov. Arthur St. Clair, Chancellor Robert R. Livingston, Secretary Samuel A. Otis, George Washington, Roger Sherman, John Adams, Gov. George Clinton, Gen. Henry Knox.

Washington taking the oath as President,
April 30, 1789, on the Site of the Present Treasury Building, Wall Street, New York City.

Old St. Paul's Church, Broadway, New York.

It is fitting to note once more that Washington furnishes the only purely and absolutely non-partisan figure in the history of the United States of America. Already in the Colonial times local divisions had given rise to local partisan controversy, and at the time of Washington's inauguration—even before that inauguration—a great dispute, relative first of all to the Constitution itself, whether it should or should not be, and after that, relative to the *construction* of the great instrument, had broken out in all the States. Little jets of flame were already springing through the placid surface of public affairs, indicative of the great Federal and Democratic partisan disputes which have hardly yet ceased to agitate the American mind. But in this Washington had no part or lot. He stood proudly above it. His theory was to introduce into his administration the diverse elements of political belief, and to harmonize under his benign, fatherly influence the opposing forces which threatened to distract, if not to destroy, the very system to which he had now pledged his all.

Turning from the actual inauguration of the first President to the commemoration of that event one hundred years afterward, we notice first of all the incipiency of the enterprise. As early as March of 1883, a resolution was introduced into the Legislature of Tennessee requesting Congress to make a suitable appropriation for the observance of the Centenary of the American government. The measure is said to have originated with Colonel J. E. Peyton of New Jersey, who, though an Englishman by birth, had for a number of years been prominent as a mover and deviser of Centennial celebrations. It is perhaps true that to him the first movement in favor of the commemorative exercises of 1889 must be attributed.

Practically, however, the celebration originated with the New York Historical Society. In March of 1884 that body passed a resolution to undertake the enterprise. The project was then espoused by the Chamber of Commerce; and Congress and the State of New York were asked to indorse and support the measure. So far as the citizens of New York were concerned, their first public interest was excited by Colonel Peyton and Algernon S. Sullivan. A meeting was held at the Fifth Avenue Hotel, on the 1st of September, 1884, and formal steps began to be taken for the celebration. It was not, however, until 1887, and near the close of that year, that a committee of forty-nine citizens, with Mayor Abram S. Hewitt as chairman, was appointed for general supervision of the project. Many prominent citizens of New York, capitalists, military men, merchants, and others espoused the cause, and by the beginning of 1888 the enterprise was well under way.

At an early date it was determined that the commemorative celebration should conform as nearly as practicable to the actual inauguration of Washington. To this end it was decided to invite the President of the United States, whoever he should be, to visit New York, going approximately by the same route which had carried Washington thither one hundred years ago, to be received in like manner conducted across the harbor in a similar vessel, and to be presented in Wall Street, on the very spot where Washington was inaugurated, and where a Centennial oration commemorative of the progress and glory of the American people was to be delivered. About this central idea all the other features of the celebration were clustered. The event was totally different in character from the great expositions which had been connected with most Centennial celebrations. The Jubilees of France; the great World's Fairs of England; and our own Centennial Exposition at Philadelphia, in 1876, were of this kind. But in the case of the commemoration of the American government, now undertaken, the feature of exposition was wholly omitted. Every thing was made truly commemorative—designed to point backward to the events of a century ago, and to evoke, through the shadows of several generations, a vivid recollection of the condition of the American people and the American Republic, when the latter was instituted.

During the whole of 1888, and the first months of 1889, the preliminaries were prosecuted with zeal by the Citizens' Committee of New York. Meanwhile the presidential election had been held in which the temporary ascendency of the Democratic party was replaced by Republican success. Benjamin Harrison, of Indiana, was chosen President. Ex-President Cleveland retired at the close of his administration to New York city, and became a resident of that metropolis. Happily enough, the incoming Chief Magistrate was intimately associated in his family relations with the great events of the Revolution. His great-grandfather, also named Benjamin Harrison, had presided in the Colonial Congress when the Declaration of Independence was adopted, Mr. Hancock being absent from the chair on that ever memorable day. The son of that distinguished statesman had become ninth President of the United States, and now the great-grandson was chosen by the election of the American people to the same high office and dignity.

It was foreseen that the celebration would bring to New York city a vast concourse of people, and the event justified the expectations. It had been decided by the committee to devote two days to the commemorative exercises, namely, the 30th of April, and the 1st of May. For perhaps two weeks before these days the great trains on the many railways centering in the metropolis began to pour out an unusual cargo of human life. They grew longer, and darker with their burden, until, by the 29th of April, the city of New York was a mass of living beings gathered from all parts of the Republic, but principally from the old thirteen States. Next after these, the five great States composing what was a hundred years ago the territory north-west of the river Ohio were best represented. It is probable that at the time of the celebration New York proper held for her own population about 1,750,000 inhabitants, and a fair estimate would perhaps place the strangers then in the city at fully a half million.

For three days before the formal opening of the celebration, the Atlantic coast in the region of New York was visited with a great rain storm, which threatened to mar all that had been attempted, but on the 29th of the month the skies cleared, the air became fresh, and the sunshine bright. The morning of the Centennial day was ushered in as auspiciously as could be desired, and the metropolis was early astir for the great event.

Meanwhile arrangements had been made for President Harrison, Vice-President Morton, the members of the Cabinet, and other prominent men connected with the government, to go to the city from Washington. To this end a magnificent train was prepared by the managers of the Pennsylvania Railroad, and a little after midnight on the morning of the 29th the President and his companions left Washington. They were received at several points *en route* with much enthusiasm, and as the train drew near New York the stations and towns were crowded with people. At Elizabethtown the real imitation of the Washington inaugural began. Here a committee sent out from New York met the President and prepared to conduct him across the bay. A steamer called the *Despatch* had been prepared for this especial purpose. She was gaily decked with flags and streamers. The upper harbor of New York had been given up to the shipping, which was placed under the command of Admiral Porter. The scene presented from the observatory of the Field Building erected on the site of Washington's old head-quarters at the lower end of the island, was one of the finest ever witnessed. The broad harbor was covered with vessels, and gaily decorated ships of foreign nations vied with the American craft in flinging their streamers to the breeze.

We may here speak of the general appearance of the city. Every pains had been taken to put the metropolis into gala dress and to present to the eye the most inspiring spectacle. Never was a city more completely clad in gay apparel. Every street on both sides as far as the eye could reach was ornamented with flags and streamers, mottoes, and emblems of jubilee. In this respect Broadway and Fifth Avenue were the most elaborately and beautifully adorned. It is doubtful whether in the history of mankind a finer display has been made in the streets of any city. The decorations extended to every variety of public and private edifices. Scarcely a house on Manhattan Island but had its share in the display. Indeed, if one had been lifted in a balloon above old Castle Garden, sweeping northward with his glass he would have seen flags on flags from the Battery to Spuyten Duyvil. Along both sides of the North River and East River and in the islands of the bay the universal emblems were flung to the breeze. And the purest of sunshine glorified the scene with a blaze of morning light. The convoy of the *Despatch*, under command of Captain Ambrose Snow, of the New York Marine Society, was rowed by twelve venerable retired sea captains. The scene was sufficiently picturesque as they brought the President safely to land in the barge called the *Queen Kapiolani*.

The landing was effected a little after noon-day. The President was received by Mayor Grant, Governor Hill, and Stuyvesant Fish. The procession had been arranged from the foot of Wall Street to the great building of the Equitable Assurance Company in Broadway, where, under the auspices of the Lawyers' Club of New York, the first formal reception of the President occurred. As soon as General Harrison had taken his carriage the procession moved to the Equitable Building, where, on a raised platform, the President, the Vice-President, and Governor Hill were introduced to the invited guests, most of whom had taken part in the procession. In the next place the President lunched in an adjoining private room, the ornamentation of which, for this occasion, is said to have cost nearly $5,000. At this time the narrow streets in the lower part of the metropolis were packed with eager people. It was with difficulty that the troops, drawn up in a hollow square in front of the Equitable building, were able to keep back the crowds. Meanwhile many bands, especially those of Gilmore and Cappa, discoursed national airs, while in distant parts of the city the hum and roar of the rising excitement could be distinctly heard.

It must be borne in mind that the part assigned to President Harrison in these commemorative exercises was the part of Washington. He was to impersonate the Father of his Country. The next movement of the concourse was from the Equitable Building to the City Hall, where another reception was given. A splendid platform, covered with plush materials, railed in with brass, was erected on the spot where the bodies of Abraham Lincoln and General Grant had lain in state in death, and where the Marquis of Lafayette had stood on his visit to New York in 1824. About 5,000 persons at this place were received by the President. After the close of the exercises at City Hall the President was taken to the residence of Vice-President Morton on Fifth Avenue, whither his wife had already preceded him. In the evening he dined with Mr. Stuyvesant Fish in Gramercy Park, and at a later hour attended the great ball in the Metropolitan Opera House, which had been prepared in imitation and commemoration of the Washingtonian ball given on the occasion of the first inauguration, at which the Father of his Country led the first cotillon. Thus closed the ceremonies of the 29th of April, the day preceding the commemorative exercises proper.

On the following morning the inhabitants of New York, and hundreds of thousands of strangers, poured into the streets to witness the great military parade which was to be the feature of the day. Meanwhile in the lower part of the city the exercises which had been planned in imitation and commemoration of Washington's accession to the presidency were under way. Wall Street and Broad Street were packed with people. A great platform had been erected in front of the Treasury building, now occupying the site of old Federal Hall, and marked by the presence of Ward's colossal statue of Washington. It was here that the oratorical and literary exercises were to take place. These were to consist of a Centennial oration by Hon. Chauncey M. Depew, also of an address by President Harrison, of a poem by John Greenleaf Whittier, and of such religious services as were appropriate to the occasion. Several of the leading clergymen of the metropolis were present on the stand. Archbishop Corrigan, Dr. Richard S. Storrs, and Dr. Henry C. Potter, bishop of New York, were the most distinguished of the group.

Sub-Treasury, Wall and Nassau Streets, New York.

The exercises were opened by Mr. Elbridge T. Gerry, who in a few explanatory words introduced Dr. Storrs, who pronounced the invocation. The accessories were all in keeping with the occasion. President Harrison sat in a chair which had been much used by Washington. The table also was Washington's, and the Bible which was laid thereon was that on which the Father of his Country had taken the solemn oath to support and defend the Constitution of the United States. The Whittier poem was then read by Mr. C. W. Bowen, secretary of the Citizens' Committee, as follows:

THE VOW OF WASHINGTON.

By John Greenleaf Whittier.

The sword was sheathed; in April's sun
Lay green the fields by freedom won;
And severed sections, weary of debates,
Joined hands at last, and were United States.

O, city sitting by the sea!
How proud the day that dawned on thee;
When the New Era, long desired, began,
And in its need the hour had found the Man!

One thought the cannon's salvos spoke;
The resonant bell-tower's vibrant stroke;
The voiceful streets, the plaudit-echoing halls,
And prayer and hymn borne heavenward from St. Paul's.

How felt the land in every part
The strong throb of a nation's heart
As its great leader gave, with reverent awe,
His pledge to Union, Liberty, and Law.

That pledge the heavens above him heard;
That vow the sleep of centuries stirred;
In world-wide wonder listening peoples bent
Their gaze on freedom's great experiment.

Could it succeed? Of honor sold
And hopes deceived all history told;

Above the wrecks that strewed the mournful past
Was the long dream of ages true at last?

Thank God! The people's choice was just;
The one man equal to his trust;
Wise beyond lore and without weakness good,
Calm in the strength of flawless rectitude.

His rule of justice, order, peace,
Made possible the world's release;
Taught prince and serf that power is but a trust,
And rule alone which serves the ruled is just.

That freedom generous is, but strong
In hate of fraud and selfish wrong—
Pretense that turns her holy truths to lies,
And lawless license masking in her guise.

Land of his love! with one glad voice
Let thy great sisterhood rejoice;
A century's suns o'er thee have risen and set
And, God be praised! we are One Nation yet.

And still we trust the years to be
Shall prove his hope was destiny;
Leaving our flag with all its added stars
Unrent by faction and unstained by wars.

Lo! where with patient toil he nursed
And trained the new set plant at first,
The widening branches of a stately tree
Stretch from the sunrise to the sunset sea.

And in its broad and sheltering shade,
Sitting with none to make afraid,
Were we now silent through each mighty limb
The winds of heaven would sing the praise of him.

Our first and best! his ashes lie
Beneath his own Virginian sky.
Forgive, forget, O true and just and brave,
The storm that swept above thy sacred grave.

> Forever in the awful strife
> And dark hours of the nation's life,
> Through the fierce tumult pierced his warning word;
> Their father's voice his erring children heard.
>
> The change for which he prayed and sought
> In that sharp agony was wrought;
> No partial interest draws its alien line
> 'Twixt North and South, the cypress and the pine.
>
> One people now, all doubt beyond.
> His name shall be our union bond;
> We lift our hands to heaven, and here and now
> Take on our lips the old Centennial vow.
>
> For rule and trust must need be ours;
> Chooser and chosen both are powers;
> Equal in service as in rights, the claim
> Of duty rests on each and all the same.
>
> Then let the sovereign millions where
> Our banner floats in sun and air,
> From the warm palm-lands to Alaska's cold,
> Repeat with us THE PLEDGE a century old!

The oration of Mr. Depew was of a high order, eulogistic of the present—the voice of a patriot who believes in the past and trusts the future. The address by the President was also able and patriotic. The exercises were closed with a benediction by Archbishop Corrigan, of the archdiocese of New York.

In the meantime the great military parade—the greatest of all such displays in the United States, with the single exception of the review of the soldiers at Washington at the close of the war—was in preparation for the march. The principal streets in the lower part of the city had been assigned for the formation of the various divisions of the parade. At last the procession was ready to move. A number of magnificent carriages bearing the President, the Vice-President, the members of the Cabinet, and other distinguished representatives of the government, swept up to the head of the column and led the way to the great reviewing stand which had been prepared on the west side of Madison Square, looking down into Fifth

Avenue. Here the President and his companions took their places to review the column as it passed, and for six hours the chief magistrate stood up to recognize, in his official capacity, the passing squadrons of the greatest parade ever known in a time of peace west of the Atlantic.

It were difficult to describe the great procession. It was admirably managed—wholly military. The different divisions were arranged in files from eighteen to twenty-two men abreast. In many places the marching was in close rank, so that the knees of those in the rear rank fitted almost geometrically into those of the men in front. The passage was at the rate of more than 9,000 per hour. The best estimates place the number in line at over 52,000. Major General John M. Schofield was commander-in-chief. The course of march was from Wall Street into Broadway; up Broadway to Waverly Place; through Waverly Place into Fifth Avenue; along that magnificent thoroughfare to Fourteenth Street; thence around Union Square, through to Fifth Avenue and thence northward to Central Park.

Memorial Arch, Fifth Avenue and Waverley Place, New York.

Through all this distance and on both sides of the street was a solid wall of human beings, rising to the rear by every kind of contrivance which human ingenuity could invent, so as to gain a view of the procession. The mass on the sidewalks was from twenty to fifty persons deep. In every advantageous position scaffolding with ascending seats had been erected for the accommodation of the multitudes, and not a seat was left unoccupied. At the street crossings every variety of vehicle had been drawn up, and the privilege of standing on boxes or sitting in carts, wagons, or hacks was sold at high figures to the eager people who pressed into the crowd. Windows and every other available point of view, housetops, balconies, stoops, verandas, were crowded to their utmost capacity. In favorite localities fabulous prices were charged for the privilege of looking from a window upon the passing cavalcade. The latter was, as we have said, preceded by the Presidential company. General Schofield, senior Major-General of the American Army, as chief marshal, rode at the head of the column. After him, and leading the van of the procession proper, were over 2,000 regulars, infantry and cavalry, drawn from the Army; then came the cadets from West Point, whose marching and uniform and bearing were of such excellence as to excite a chorus of cheers from end to end of the long march. Next followed the artillery and batteries of the regular army. Many of the guns and much of the armor was resplendent for its brilliancy. After these came the marines and naval cadets, a vast column of apprentices, whose march, by its peculiar rolling movement, denoted that the column had been recently gathered from the decks of ships.

John M. Schofield.

Thus closed the first division of the procession—that is, those who were taken from the Army and Navy of the United States. Then followed the militiamen—the National Guard of the different States. At the head was a column of 370 men from Delaware; for Delaware had been first of the old thirteen States to adopt the Constitution, and was thus given a place of honor on the centennial anniversary. The Governor of each State represented in the parade rode at the head of the division from his own Commonwealth. Most of the governors were in civil attire. General Beaver, of Pennsylvania, General Fitzhugh Lee, of Virginia, and General John B. Gordon, of Georgia, were conspicuous at the head of their divisions. It was noticed that those who were present from the Southern States were received with unstinted applause. Governor Beaver rode at the head of the Pennsylvania troops, numbering fully 8,000 men. Then came Governor Green, with the soldiers of New Jersey 3,700 strong; then Georgia, with General Gordon and his staff. The Foot Guards from Connecticut, preceded by the Governor, numbered 600. Governor Ames, of Massachusetts, headed the column of 1,500 from the old Bay State—a noble division, containing the Ancient and Honorable Artillery of Boston, all uniformed after the most antique pattern. The men of Maryland were 500 strong. Then came New Hampshire; then Vermont, with a division of 700. Governor Richardson, of North Carolina, followed with a body of 500 men. This division was fortunate in bearing an old flag belonging to North Carolina in the pre-Revolutionary epoch. After this came the great division of New York. Twelve thousand men, arranged in four brigades of eighteen regiments, one battalion, and five batteries, were the contribution of the Empire State to the great display. At the head of the line rode Governor David B. Hill.

In this column the Seventh Regiment, made up of prominent men of New York city, and numbering over was, perhaps, the most conspicuous single body in the whole procession. The Twenty-second Regiment vied with its rival; and it might be difficult to decide whether the palm for marching and other evidences of elegant training should be awarded to the West Point Cadets, the Seventh Regiment of New York, the Twenty-second Regiment of the same State, the squadron from the Michigan Military Academy, or the Twenty-third Regiment, of Brooklyn.

Behind this magnificent display of the military came the veterans of the Civil War, the men of the Grand Army of the Republic, headed by their commander-in-chief, General William Warner. These were arranged column after column to an aggregate of 12,000 according to the locality from which they were gathered, the rear being closed with a magnificent body of old soldiers, numbering nearly 4,000 from Brooklyn and Kings County. It was already nightfall when this extreme left of the column passed the reviewing stand, and the parade for the day was at an end.

The evening of the 30th was occupied with one of the most elaborate and sumptuous banquets ever spread in the United States. For this purpose the Metropolitan Opera House, in Broadway, had been procured and decorated. It was claimed by those experienced in such matters that the floral ornamentation of the hall was far superior in costliness and beauty to any thing of like kind ever before displayed in the country. The boxes of the theater were adorned with the national colors, with the shields and coats-of-arms of the various States of the Union. Over the proscenium arch was a portrait of Washington, arranged in a cluster of evergreens and flowers. The auditorium was brilliantly illuminated, and the scene of splendor on every hand might well dazzle the eye and surprise the imagination of the beholder. The banqueters, embracing many of the chief men of the nation, were seated at a series of tables, the first and principal one being occupied by the President of the United States, the Governor of New York, the Vice-President, the Lieutenant-Governor, Chief-Justice Fuller, Judge Andrews, General Schofield, Admiral Porter, Senator Evarts, Senator Hiscock, Ex-President Hayes, Ex-President Cleveland, Bishop Potter, Speaker Cole, of the New York Assembly, Secretary Proctor, Hon. S. S. Cox, General William T. Sherman, Clarence W. Bowen, and Elbridge T. Gerry, the last two representing the Citizens' Committee. At this table Mayor Grant presided, and read the toasts of the evening.

The feast began at 9 o'clock in the evening. At the close a series of brief addresses were delivered by the Governor of New York, Ex-President Cleveland, Ex-President Hayes, General Sherman, Senator Evarts, President Eliot, of Harvard; James Russell Lowell, Senator Daniel, and others. The closing address was by the President of the United States. Nearly all the speeches were faultless in their subject matter, eloquent in delivery, and worthy to be regarded as classics of the occasion.

The programme prepared by the Citizens' Committee embraced a general holiday of three days' duration, during which business was suspended throughout the city. On the 29th and 30th of April and on the 1st day of May the restriction was faithfully regarded. One might traverse Broadway and find but few business establishments open to the public. This was true particularly of the two principal days of the festival.

It now remains to notice the great civic parade of the 1st of May, with which the commemorative exercises were concluded. The design was that this should represent the industries, the progress, and in general the civic life of the Metropolis of the Nation and of the country at large, as distinguished from the military display of the preceding day. It was found from the experience of the 30th that the line of march was too lengthy, and the second day's course was made somewhat shorter. It is not intended in this connection to enter into any elaborate account of the civic procession of the third day. It was second only in imp0rtance to the great military parade which had preceded it. The procession was composed, in large part, of those various civic orders and brotherhoods with which modern society so much abounds. In these the foreign nationalities which have obtained so large a footing in New York city were largely prevalent. The German societies were out in full force. Companies representing almost every nation of the Old World were in the line, carrying gay banners, keeping step to the music of magnificent bands, and proudly lifting their mottoes and emblems in the May-day morning.

The second general feature of this procession was the historical part. The primitive life of Manhattan Island the adventures of the early explorers and discoverers along the American coast, the striking incidents in the early annals of the old Thirteen States, were allegorized and mounted in visible form on chariots and drawn through the streets. All the old heroes of American History, from Columbus to Peter Stuyvesant, were seen again in mortal form, received obeisance, and heard the shouts of the multitudes From ten o'clock in the forenoon till half-past three in the afternoon the procession was under way, the principal line of march being down Fifth Avenue and through the principal squares of the city. With the coming of evening the pyrotechnic display of the preceding night was renewed in many parts of the metropolis, though it could hardly be said that the fireworks were equal in brilliancy, beauty, and impressiveness to the magnificent day pageants of the streets.

One of the striking features of the celebration was the ease and rapidity with which the vast multitudes were breathed into and breathed out of the city. In the principal hotels fully 150,000 strangers were registered as guests. More than twice this number were distributed in the smaller lodging-houses and private dwellings of New York and Brooklyn. Yet the careful observer abroad in the streets saw neither the coming nor the going. With the appearance of the days of the celebration the throngs were present; on the following days they were gone. The great railways centering in the metropolis had done their work noiselessly, speedily, effectively. It may well be recorded as one of the marvels of modern times that only two persons are said to have lost their lives in this tremendous assemblage, extending through several days, and that at least one of these died suddenly from heart disease, while the manner of the death of the other was unknown. Such is the triumph which the mastery of the human mind over the forces of the material world has easily achieved in our age, under the guidance of that beneficent science by which the world is at once enlightened and protected from danger.

The close of the year 1888 and the beginning of 1889 were marked by a peculiar episode in the history of the country. An unexpected and even dangerous complication arose between the United States and Germany relative to the Samoan Islands. This comparatively unimportant group of the South Pacific lies in a south-westerly direction, at a distance of about five thousand miles from San Francisco and nearly two thousand miles eastward from Australia. The long-standing policy of the government, established under the administration of Washington and ever since maintained, to have no entanglements with foreign nations, seemed in this instance to be strangely at variance with the facts.

During 1888 the civil affairs of the Samoan Islands were thrown into extreme confusion by what was really the progressive disposition of the people, but what appeared in the garb of an insurrection against the established authorities. The government of the islands is a monarchy. The country is ruled by native princes, and is independent of foreign powers. The capital, Apia, lies on a bay of the same name on the northern coast of the principal island. It was here that the insurrection gained greatest headway.

The revolutionary movement was headed by an audacious chieftain called Tamasese. The king of the island was Malietoa, and his chief supporter, Mataafa. At the time the German Empire was represented in Samoa by its Consul-General, Herr Knappe; and the United States was represented by Hon. Harold M. Sewall. A German armed force virtually deposed Malietoa and set up Tamasese on the throne. On the other hand, the representative of the United States, following the policy of his government, stood by the established authority, supporting the native sovereign and Mataafa. The American and German authorities in the island were thus brought into conflict, and serious difficulties occurred between the ships of the two nations in the harbor.

When the news of this state of affairs reached Germany, in April, 1889, several additional men-of-war were sent out to the island to up hold the German cause. Mataafa and the Germans were thus brought to war. Meanwhile the American government took up the cause of its consul and of King Malietoa as against the insurrection. A section of the American navy was dispatched to the distant island, and the ships of war of two of the greatest nations of Christendom were thus set face to face in a harbor of the South Pacific Ocean.

In this condition of affairs, on the 22d of March, 1889, one of the most violent hurricanes ever known in the islands blew up from the north, and the American and German war-vessels were driven upon the great reef which constitutes the only break-water outside of the harbor of Apia. Here they were wrecked. The American war-ships *Nipsic*, *Trenton*, and *Vandalia* were dashed into ruins. The German vessels *Adler*, *Olga*, and *Eber* were also lost. The English vessel *Calliope*, which was caught in the storm, was the only war-ship which escaped by steaming out to sea.

Serious loss of life accompanied the disaster: 4 American officers and 46 men, 9 German officers and 87 men sank to rise no more.

Meanwhile England had become interested in the dispute, and had taken a stand with the United States as against the decision of Germany. The matter became of so great importance that President Harrison, who had in the meantime acceded to office as chief magistrate, appointed, with the advice of the Senate, an Embassy Extraordinary, to go to Berlin and meet Prince Bismarck in a conference with a view to a peaceful solution of the difficulty. The embassadors appointed for this purpose were J. A. Kasson, of Iowa; William W. Phelps, of New Jersey; and G. H. Bates, of Delaware. The commissioners set out on the 13th of April, and on their arrival at the capital of the German Empire opened negotiations with the Chancellor Bismarck and his son. The attitude and demand of the American government was that the independence of Samoa, under its native sovereign, should be acknowledged and guaranteed by the great nations concerned in the controversy. The conference closed in May, 1889, with the restoration of King Malietoa and the recognition of his sovereignty over the island.

The closing week of May, 1889, was made forever memorable in the history of the United States by the destruction of Johnstown, Pennsylvania. The calamity was caused by the bursting of a reservoir and the pouring out of the deluge in the valley below. A large artificial lake had been constructed in the ravine of the South Fork River, a tributary of the Conemaugh. It was a fishing lake, the property of a company of wealthy sportsmen, and was about five miles in length, varying in depth from fifty to one hundred feet. An immense volume of water was thus accumulated in a gorge at the foot of the mountains, and was, as it were, suspended over the valley of Conemaugh. The country below the lake was thickly peopled. The city of Johnstown, with a population of more than ten thousand, lay at the junction of the South Fork with the Conemaugh. In the last days of May unusually heavy rains fell in all that region, swelling every stream to a torrent. The South Fork Lake became full to overflowing. The dam had been imperfectly constructed. On the afternoon of May 31 the dam of the reservoir burst wide open in the center and a solid wall of water from twenty to fifty feet in height rushed down the valley with terrific violence. The country was already inundated, and on top of the swollen streams was poured a veritable flood.

The destruction which ensued was among the greatest which the modern world has witnessed. In the path of the deluge every thing was swept away. The manufacturing city of Johnstown was totally wrecked, and was thrown in an indescribable heap of horror against the aqueduct of the Pennsylvania railway, which spanned the river below the town. Here the ruins caught fire, and the wild shrieks of hundreds of miserable victims were drowned in the holocaust. According to the best estimates more than 5,000 people perished in the flood or were burned to death in the ruins. The heart of the nation responded quickly to the sufferings of the survivors, and millions of dollars in money and supplies were poured out to relieve the despair of those who survived the calamity.

Thus has the History of the United States been traced from the beginning of our national career to the dawn of yesterday. The Republic has passed through stormy times, but has at last entered her second century in safety and peace. The clouds that were recently so black above her have sunk behind the horizon. The equality of all men before the law has been written with the iron pen of war in the Constitution of the Nation. The union of the States has been consecrated anew by the blood of patriots and the tears of the lowly. The temple of freedom, reared by the fathers, still stands in undiminished glory. THE PAST HAS TAUGHT ITS LESSON, THE PRESENT HAS ITS DUTY, AND THE FUTURE ITS HOPE.

CHAPTER LXXIII.

Conclusion.

WHAT, then, of the outlook for the American Republic? What shall another century bring forth? What is to be the destiny of this vigorous, aggressive, self-governing Anglo-American race? How will the picture, so well begun, be completed by the annalists of posterity? Is it the sad fate of humanity, after all its struggles, toils, and sighing, to turn forever round and round in the same beaten circle, climbing the long ascent from the degradation of savage life to the heights of national renown only to descend again into the fenlands of despair? Is Lord Byron's gloomy picture of the rise and fall of nations indeed a true portrayal of the order of the world?—

> Here is the moral of all human tales,—
> 'Tis but the same rehearsal of the past,
> First freedom and then glory—when that fails,
> Wealth, vice, corruption, barbarism at last;
> And History with all her volumes vast
> Hath but *one* page!

Or has the human race, breaking the bonds of its servitude and escaping at last from its long imprisonment, struck out across the fields of sublime possibility the promised pathway leading to the final triumph? There are still doubts and fears—perplexities, anxieties, and sometimes anguish—arising in the soul of the philanthropist as he turns his gaze to the future. But there are hopes also, grounds of confidence, auspicious omens, tokens of the substantial victory of truth, inspirations of faith welling up in the heart of the watcher as he scans the dappled horizon of the coming day.

As to present achievement the American people have far surpassed the expectations of the fathers. The visions and dreams of the Revolutionary patriots have been eclipsed by the luster of actual accomplishment. The territorial domains of the Republic enclose the grandest belt of forest, valley, and plain that the world has in it. Since the beginning of time no other people have possessed such a territory—so rich in resources, so varied in products, so magnificent in physical aspect. Soil and climate, the distribution of woods and lakes and rivers, the interposition of mountain ranges, and the fertility of valley and prairie, here contribute to give to man a many-sided and powerful development. Here he finds bays for his shipping, rivers for his steamers, fields for his plow, iron for his forge, gold for his cupidity, landscapes for his pencil, sunshine enough for song, and snow enough for courage. Nor has the Anglo-American failed to profit by the advantages of his surroundings. He has planted a free government on the largest and most liberal scale known in history. He has espoused the cause of liberty and right. He has fought like a hero for the freedom and equality of all men. He has projected a civilization which, though as yet but dimly traced in outline, is the vastest and grandest in the world. Better than all, he believes in the times to come. So long as man is anxious about the future the future is secure. Only when he falls into apathy, sleeps at his post, and cares no longer for the morrow, is the world in danger of relapse and barbarism.

To the thoughtful student of history several things seem necessary to the perpetuity and complete success of American institutions. The first of these is the prevalence of THE IDEA OF NATIONAL UNITY. Of this spake Washington in his Farewell Address, warning his countrymen in solemn words to preserve and defend that government which constituted them *one people*. Of this wrote Hamilton and Adams. For this pleaded Webster in his great orations. Upon this the far seeing statesmen of the present day, rising above the strifes of party and the turmoils of war, plant themselves as the one thing vital in American politics. The idea that *the United States are one Nation,* and not thirty-eight nations, is the grand cardinal doctrine of a sound political faith. State pride and sectional attachment are natural passions in the human breast, and are so near akin to patriotism as to be distinguished from it only in the court of a higher reason. But there is a nobler love of country—a patriotism that rises above all places and sections, that knows no County, no State, no North, no South, but only native land;

that claims no mountain slope; that clings to no river bank; that worships no range of hills; but lifts the aspiring eye to a continent redeemed from barbarism by common sacrifices and made sacred by the shedding of kindred blood. Such a patriotism is the cable and sheet-anchor of our hope.

A second requisite for the preservation of American institutions is THE UNIVERSAL SECULAR EDUCATION OF THE PEOPLE. Monarchies govern their subjects by authority and precedent; republics by right reason and free will. Whether one method or the other will be better, turns wholly upon the intelligence of the governed. If the subject have not the knowledge and discipline necessary to govern himself, it is better that a king, in whom some skill in the science of government is presupposed, should rule him. As between two stupendous evils, the rational tyranny of the intelligent few is preferable to the furious and irrational tyranny of the ignorant many. No force which has moved among men, impelling to bad action, inspiring to crime, over-turning order, tearing away the bulwarks of liberty and right, and converting civilization into a waste, has been so full of evil and so powerful to destroy as a blind, ignorant, and factious democracy. A republic without intelligence—even a high degree of intelligence—is a paradox and an impossibility. What means that principle of the Declaration of Independence which declares the consent of the governed to be the true foundation of all just authority? What kind of "consent" is referred to? Manifestly not the passive and unresisting acquiescence of the mind which, like the potter's clay, receives whatever is impressed upon it; but that active, thinking, resolute, conscious, personal consent which distinguishes the true freeman from the puppet. When the people of the United States rise to the heights of this noble and intelligent self-assertion, the occupation of the party leader—most despicable of all the tyrants–will be gone forever; and in order that the people may ascend to that high plane, the means by which intelligence is fostered, right reason exalted, and a calm and rational public opinion produced, must be universally secured. The public FREE SCHOOL is the fountain whose streams shall make glad all the lands of liberty. We must educate or perish.

A third thing necessary to the perpetuity of American liberties is TOLERATION—toleration in the broadest and most glorious sense. In the colonial times intolerance embittered the lives of our fathers. Until the present day the baleful shadow has been upon the land. The proscriptive vices of the Middle Age have flowed down with the blood of the race and tainted the life that now is, with a suspicion and distrust of freedom. Liberty in the minds of men has meant the privilege of agreeing with the majority. Men have desired free thought, but fear has stood at the door. It remains for the United States to build a highway, broad and free, into every field of liberal inquiry, and to make the poorest of men who walks therein, more secure in life and reputation than the soldier who sleeps behind the rampart. Proscription has no part nor lot in the American system. The stake, the gibbet, and the rack, thumb-screws, sword, and pillory, have no place on this side of the sea. Nature is diversified; so are human faculties, beliefs, and practices. Essential freedom is the right to *differ*; and that right must be sacredly respected. Nor must the privilege of dissent be conceded with coldness and disdain, but openly, cordially, and with good will. No loss of rank, abatement of character, or ostracism from society must darken the pathway of the humblest of the seekers after truth. The right of free thought, free inquiry, and free speech, is as clear as the noonday and bounteous as the air and ocean. Without a full and cheerful recognition of this right, America is only a name, her glory a dream, her institutions a mockery.

The fourth idea, essential to the welfare and stability of the Republic, is THE NOBILITY OF LABOR. It is the mission of the United States to ennoble toil and honor the toiler. In other lands to labor has been considered the lot of serfs and peasants; to gather the fruits and consume them in luxury and war, the business of the great. Since the medieval times European society has been organized on the basis of a *nobility* and a *people*. To be a nobleman was to be distinguished from the people; to be one of the people was to be forever debarred from nobility. Thus has been set on human industry the stigma of perpetual disgrace. Something of this has been transmitted to the new civilization in the West—a certain disposition to renew the old order of lord and laborer. Let the odious distinction perish: the true lord is the laborer and the true laborer the lord. It is the genius of American institutions, in the fullness of time, to wipe the last opprobrious stain from the brow of toil and to crown the toiler with the dignity, luster, and honor of a full and perfect manhood.

The scroll of the century is rolled together. The work is done. Peace to the memory of the fathers! Green be the graves where sleep the warriors, patriots, and sages! Calm be the resting-place of all the brave and true! Gentle be the summer rains on famous fields where armies met in battle! Forgotten be the animosities and heart-burnings of the strife! Sacred be the trusts committed to our care, and bright the visions of the coming ages!

APPENDIX A.

SIR JOHN MANDEVILLE'S ARGUMENT ON THE FIGURE OF THE EARTH.

[Since the paragraph in the text has been the subject of some doubts and criticism, the original of Sir John Mandeville's argument is here appended. The orthography and phraseology are not more quaint than the logic is invincible. In order that the argument may be more easily followed and clearly understood, a translation or paraphrase, is added. It must not be forgotten that the date of Sir John's book is 1356—a hundred and thirty-six years before the discovery of America by Columbus.—THE AUTHOR.]

In that Lond, ne in many othere bezonde that, no man may see the Sterre transmontane, that is clept the Sterre of the See, that is unmevable, and that is toward the Northe, that we clepen the Lode Sterre. But men seen another Sterre, the contrarie to him, that is toward the Southe, that is clept Antartyk. And right as the Schip men taken here Avys here, and governe hem be the Lode Sterre, right so don Schip men bezonde the parties, be the Sterre of the Southe, the whiche Sterre apperethe not to us. And this Sterre, that is toward the Northe, that wee clepen the Lode Sterre, ne apperethe not to hem. For whiche cause, men may wel perceyve, that the Lond and the See ben of rownde schapp and forme. For the partie of the Firmament schewethe in o Contree, that schewethe not in another Contree. And men may well preven be experience and sotyle compassement of Wytt, that zif a man fond passages be Schippes, that wolde go to serchen the World, men myghte go be Schippe alle aboute the World, and aboven and benethen. The whiche thing I prove thus, aftre that I have seyn. For I have ben toward the parties of Braban, and beholden the Astrolabre,[55] that the Sterre that is clept the Transmontayne, is 53 Degrees highe. And more forthere in Almayne and Bewme, it hathe 58 Degrees. And more forthe toward the parties septemtrioneles, it is 62 Degrees of heghte, and certeyn Mynutes. For I my self have mesured it by the Astrolabre. Now schulle ze knowe, that azen the Transmontayne, is the tether Sterre, that is clept Antartyke; as I have seyd before. And the 2 Sterres ne meeven nevere. And be hem turnethe alle the Firmament, righte as dothe a Wheel, that turnethe be his Axille Tree: so that tho Sterres beren the Firmament in 2 egalle parties; so that it hathe als mochel aboven, as it hathe benethen. Aftre this, I have gon toward the parties meridionales, that is toward the Southe: and I have founden, that in Lybye, men seen first the Sterre Antartyk. And so fer I have gon more forthe in tho Contrees, that I have founde that Sterre more highe; so that toward the highe Lybye, it is 18 Degrees of heghte, and certeyn Minutes (of the whiche, 60 Minutes maken a Degree). Aftre goynge be See and be Londe, toward this Contree, of that I have spoke, and to other Yles and Loudes bezonde that Contree, I have founden the Sterre Antartyk of 33 Degrees of heghte, and mo mynutes. And zif I hadde had Companye and Schippynge, for to go more bezonde, I trowe wel in certeyn, that wee scholde have seen alle the roundnesss of the Firmament alle aboute. * * * * * * Be the whichs I seye zou certeynly, that men may envirowne alle the Erthe of alle the World, as wel undre as aboven, and turnen azen to his Contree, that hadde Companye and Schippynge and Conduyt: and alle weyes, he scholde fynde Men, Londes, and Yles, als wel as in this Contree. For zee wyten welle, that thei that ben toward the Antartyk, thei ben streghte, feet azen feet of hem, that dwellen undre transmontane; als wel as wee and thei that dwellyn under us, ben feet azenst feet. For alle the parties of See and of Lond han here appositees, habitables or trepassables, and thei of this half and bezond half. * * * * * * And whan men gon bezonde tho iourneyes, toward Ynde and to the foreyn Yles, alle is envyronynge the roundnesse of the Erthe and of the See, undre oure Contrees on this half. And therfore hathe it befallen many tymes of 0 thing, that I have

---

[55] In Mandeville's time, Astronomers had attained but very little accuracy in taking observations.

herd cownted, whan I was zong; how a worthi man departed somtyme from oure Contrees, for to go serche the World. And so he passed Ynde, and the Yles bezonde Ynde, where ben mo than 5000 Yles: and so longe he wente be See and Lond, and so enviround the World be many seysons, that he fond an Yle, where he herde speke his owne Langage, callynge on Oxen in the Plowghe, suche Wordes as men speken to Bestes in his owhe Contree: whereof he hadde gret Mervayle: for he knewe not how it myghte be. But I seye, that he had gon so longe, be Londe and be See, that he had envyround alle the erthe, that he was comen azen envirounynge, that is to seye, goynge aboute, unto his owne Marches, zif he wolde have passed forthe, til he had founden his Contree and his owne knouleche. But he turned azen from thens, from whens he was come fro; and so he loste moche peynefulle labour, as him self seyde, a gret while aftre, that he was comen hom. For it befelle aftre, that he wente in to Norweye; and there Tempest of the See toke him; and he arryved in an Yle; and whan he was in that Yle, he knew wel, that it was the Yle, where he had herd speke his owne Langage before, and the callynge of the Oxen at the Plowghe: and that was possible thinge. But how it semethe to symple men unlerned, that men ne mowe not go undre the Erthe, and also that men scholde falle toward the Hevene, from undre! But that may not be, upon lesse, than wee mowe falle toward Hevene, fro the Erthe, where wee ben. For fro what partie of the Erthe, that men duelle, outher aboven or benethen, it semethe alweys to hem that duellen, that thei gon more righte than ony other folk. And righte as it semethe to us, that thei ben undre us, righte so it semethe hem, that wee ben undre hem. For zif a man myghte falle fro the Erthe unto the Firmament; be grettere resoun, the Erthe and the See, that ben so grete and so bevy, scholde fallen to the Firmament: but that may not be. * * * And alle be it that it be possible thing, that men may so envyronne alle the World, natheles of a 1000 persones, on no myghte not happen to returnen in to his Contree. For, for the gretnesse of the Erthe and of the See, men may go be a 1000 and a 1000 other weyes, that no man cowde redye him perfitely toward the parties that he cam fro, but zif it were be aventure and happ, or be the grace of God. For the Erthe is falle large and fulls gret, and bolt in roundnesse and aboute envyroun, be aboven and be benethen 20425 Myles, aftre the opynycun of the olde wise Astronomeres. And here Seyenges I repreve noughte. But aftre my lytylle wytt, it semethe me, savynge here reverence, that it is more. And for to have bettere understondynge, I seye thus, Be ther ymagyned a Figure that hathe a gret Compas; and aboute the poynt of the gret Compas, that is clept the Centre, be made another litille Compas: than aftre, be the gret Compas devised be Lines in manye parties; and that alle the Lynes meeten at the Centre; so that in as many parties, as the grete Compas schal be departed, in als manye schalle be departed the litille, that is aboute the Centre, alle be it that the spaces ben lesse. New thanne, be the gret compas represented for the firmament, and the litille compas represented for the Erthe. Now thanhs the Firmament is devysed, be Astronomeres, in 12 Signes; and every Signe is devysed in 30 Degrees, that is 360 Degrees, that the Firmament hathe aboven. Also, be the Erthe devysed in als many parties, as the Firmament; and lat every partye answere to a Degree of the Firmament: and wytethe it wel, that aftre the Auctoures of Astronomys, 700 Furlonges of Erthe answeren to a Degree of the Firmament; and the ben 87 Miles and 4 Furlonges. Now be that here multiplyed by 360 sithes; and than thei ben 31500 Myles, every of 8 Furlonges, aftre Myles of cure Contree. So moche hathe the Erthe in roundnesse, and of heghte enviroun, aftre myn opynyoun and myn undirstondynge.

CHART
SHOWING THE RATIO OF
CHURCH ACCOMMODATION
To the Population over 10 years of age,

With the proportion of such church accommodation furnished by each of the largest four denominations within each State, and by each of the largest eight denominations within the United States.

COMPILED FROM THE SOCIAL STATISTICS OF THE UNITED STATES
BY FRANCIS A. WALKER.

NOTE.—The interior square represents the proportion of the population which is provided for by the aggregate sittings in churches of all denominations. The blank interval between the inner and outer square represents the population for which no church accommodation is provided. Where the aggregate church accommodation equals or exceeds the population over 10 years of age the interval disappears.

- Methodist
- Baptist
- Presbyterian
- Roman Catholic
- Congregational
- Episcopal
- Lutheran
- Christian
- Dutch Reformed
- Universalist
- Mormon
- All other Denominations

THE UNITED STATES
DELAWARE
FLORIDA
GEORGIA
ALABAMA
ILLINOIS
ARKANSAS
INDIANA
CALIFORNIA
IOWA
CONNECTICUT

[PARAPHRASE.]

In that land and in others beyond no man may see the fixed star of the North which we call the Lode Star. But there men see another star called the Antarctic, opposite to the star of the North. And just as mariners in this hemisphere take their reckoning and govern their course by the North Star, so do the mariners of the South by the Antarctic. But the star of the North appears not to the people of the South. Wherefore men may easily perceive that *the land and the sea are of round shape and figure.* For that part of the firmament which is seen in one country is not seen in another. And men may prove both by experience and sound reasoning that if a man, having passage by ship, should go to search the world, *he might with his vessel sail around the world, both above and under it.* This proposition I prove as follows: I have myself in Prussia seen the North Star by the astrolabe fifty-three degrees above the horizon. Further on in Bohemia it rises to the height of fifty-eight degrees. And still farther northward it is sixty-two degrees and some minutes high. I myself have so measured it. Now the South Pole Star is, as I have said, opposite the North Pole Star. And about these poles the whole celestial sphere revolves like a wheel about the axle; and the firmament is thus divided into two equal parts. From the North I have turned southward, passed the equator, and found that in Lybia the Antarctic Star first appears above the horizon. Farther on in those lands that star rises higher, until in southern Lybia it reaches the height of eighteen degrees and certain minutes, sixty minutes making a degree. After going by sea and by land towards that country [Australia perhaps] of which I have spoken, I have found the Antarctic Star more than thirty three degrees above the horizon. *And if I had had company and shipping to go still further, I know of a certainty that I should have seen the whole circumference of the heavens.* * * * * * * *And I repeat that men may environ the whole world, as well under as above, and return to their own country, if they had company, and ships, and conduct.* And always, as well as in their own land shall they find inhabited continents and islands. For know you well that they who dwell in the southern hemisphere are feet against feet of them who dwell in the northern hemisphere, *just as we and they that dwell under us are feet to feet.* For every part of the sea and the land hath its antipode. * * * * * * Moreover when men go on a journey toward India and the foreign islands, they do, on the whole route, circle the circumference of the earth, even to those countries which are under us. And therefore hath that same thing, which I heard recited when I was young, happened many times. Howbeit, upon a time, a worthy man departed from our country to explore the world. And so he passed India and the islands beyond India—more than five thousand in number— and so long he went by sea and land, environing the world for many seasons, that he found an island where he heard them speaking his own language, hallooing at the oxen in the plow with the identical words spoken to beasts in his own country. Forsooth, he was astonished; for he knew not how the thing might happen. But I assure you that he had gone so far by land and sea that he had actually gone around the world and was come again through the long circuit to his own district. It only remained for him to go forth and find his particular neighborhood. Unfortunately he turned from the coast which he had reached, and thereby lost all his painful labor, as he himself afterwards acknowledged when he returned home. For it happened by and by that he went into Norway, being driven thither by a storm; and there he recognized an island as being the same in which he had heard men calling the oxen in his own tongue: and that was a possible thing. And yet it seemeth to simple unlearned rustics that men may not go around the world, and if they did *they would fall off*! But that absurd thing never could happen unless we ourselves from where we are should fall toward heaven! For upon what part soever of the earth men dwell, whether above or under, it always seemeth to them that they walk more perpendicularly than other folks! And just as it seemeth to us that our antipodes are under us head downwards, just so it seemeth to them that we are under them head downwards. If a man might fall from the earth towards heaven, by much more reason the earth itself, being so heavy, should fall to heaven—an impossible thing. * * * * * Perhaps of a thousand men who should go around the world, not one might succeed in returning to his own particular neighborhood. For the earth is indeed a body of great size, its circumference being—according to the old wise astronomers—twenty thousand four hundred and twenty-five miles. And I do not reject their estimates: but according to my judgment, saving their reverence, the circumference of the earth *is somewhat more than that*. And in order to have a clearer understanding of the matter, I use the following demonstration: Let there be imagined a great sphere, and about the point called the center another smaller sphere. Then from different parts of the great sphere let lines be drawn meeting at the center. It is clear that by this means the two spheres will be divided into an equal number of parts having the same relation to each other; but between the divisions on the smaller sphere the absolute space will be less. Now the great sphere represents the heavens and the smaller sphere the earth. But the firmament is divided by astronomers into twelve Signs, and each Sign into thirty degrees, making three hundred and sixty degrees in all. On the surface of the earth there will be, of course, divisions exactly corresponding to those of the celestial sphere, every line, degree and zone of the latter answering to a line, degree or zone of the former. And now know well that *according to the authors of astronomy*[56] seven hundred furlongs, or eighty-seven miles and four furlongs, answer to a degree of the firmament. Multiplying eighty-seven and a half miles by three hundred and sixty—the number of degrees in the firmament—we have thirty-one thousand five hundred English miles. And this according to my belief and demonstration is the true measurement of the circumference of the earth.

---

[56] An everlasting shame be to the "olde wise Astronomeres"! If they had given Sir John the correct measurement of a degree of latitude, he would not have missed the circumference of the world *by as much as ten miles!* His argument is absolutely correct. This, too, in A. D. 1856.

APPENDIX B.

A PLAN OF PERPETUAL UNION, FOR HIS MAJESTY'S COLONIES IN NORTH AMERICA; PROPOSED BY BENJ. FRANKLIN, AND ADOPTED BY THE COLONIAL CONVENTION AT ALBANY, JULY 10TH, 1754.

[This document will be found of special interest as containing the germ of the Articles of Confederation and the Constitution of the United States. It should be remembered that this "Plan of Union," though adopted by the Congress at Albany–Only the delegates from Connecticut dissenting—was rejected both by the colonial assemblies and the British Board of Trade,—by the former as being too despotic a constitution and by the latter as a piece of high-handed presumption.— THE AUTHOR.]

THAT the general government of His Majesty's Colonies in North America be administered by a President-General, to be appointed and supported by the crown; and a Grand Council, to be chosen by the representatives of the people of the several colonies met in their respective Assemblies;

Who shall meet for the first time at the city of Philadelphia, in Pennsylvania, being called by the President-General as soon as conveniently may be after his appointment;

That there shall be a new election of the members of the Grand Council every three years; and on the death or resignation of any member, his place should be supplied by a new choice at the next sitting of the Assembly of the colony he represented;

That after the first three years, when the proportion of money arising out of each colony to the general treasury can be known, the number of members to be chosen for each colony shall from time to time, in all ensuing elections, be regulated by that proportion, yet so as that the number to be chosen by any one province be not more than seven, nor less than two;

That the Grand Council shall meet once in every year, and oftener if occasion require, at such time and place as they shall adjourn to at the last preceding meeting, or as they shall be called to meet at by the President-General on any emergency; he having first obtained in writing the consent of seven of the members to such call, and sent due and timely notice to the whole;

That the Grand Council have power to choose their speaker; and shall neither be dissolved, prorogued, nor continued sitting longer than six weeks at one time, without their own consent or the special command of the crown;

That the members of the Grand Council shall be allowed for their service ten shillings per diem, during their session and journey to and from the place of meeting; twenty miles to be reckoned a day's journey;

That the assent of the President-General be requisite to all acts of the Grand Council, and that it be his office and duty to cause them to be carried into execution;

That the President-General, with the advice of the Grand Council, hold or direct all Indian treaties, in which the general interest of the colonies may be concerned; and make peace or declare war with Indian nations;

That they make such laws as they judge necessary for regulating all Indian trade;

That they make all purchases, from Indians for the crown, of lands not now within the bounds of particular colonies, or that shall not be within their bounds, when some of them are reduced to more convenient dimensions;

That they make new settlements on such purchases, by granting lands in the king's name, reserving a quit-rent to the crown for the use of the general treasury;

That they make laws for regulating and governing such new settlements, till the crown shall think fit to form them into particular governments;

That they raise and pay soldiers and build forts for the defence of any of the colonies, and equip vessels of force to guard the coasts and protect the trade on the ocean, lakes, or great rivers; but they shall not impress men in any colony, without the consent of the legislature;

That for these purposes they have power to make laws, and lay and levy such general duties, imposts, or taxes, as to them shall appear most equal and just (considering the ability and other circumstances of the inhabitants in the several colonies,) and such as may be collected with the least inconvenience to the people; rather discouraging luxury, than loading industry with unnecessary burthens;

That they may appoint a General Treasurer and Particular Treasurer in each government, when necessary; and from time to time may order the sums in the treasuries of each government into the general treasury or draw on them for special payments, as they find most convenient;

Yet no money to issue but by joint orders of the President-General and Grand Council except where sums have been appropriated to particular purposes, and the President-General is previously empowered by an act to draw such sums;

That the general accounts shall be yearly settled and reported to the several Assemblies;

That a quorum of the Grand Council, empowered to act with the President-General, do consist of twenty-five members; among whom there shall be one or more from a majority of the colonies;

That the laws made by them for the purposes aforesaid shall not be repugnant, but, as near as may be, agreeable to the laws of England, and shall be transmitted to the King in Council for approbation, as soon as may be after their passing; and if not disapproved within three years after presentation, to remain in force;

That, in case of the death of the President-General, the Speaker of the Grand Council for the time being shall succeed, and be vested with the same powers and authorities to continue till the King's pleasure be know;

That all military commission officers, whether for land or sea service, to act under this general constitution, shall be nominated by the President-General; but the approbation of the Grand Council is to be obtained, before they receive their commissions; and all civil officers are to be nominated by the Grand Council, and to receive the President General's approbation before they officiate;

But, in case of vacancy by death or removal of any officer civil or military under this constitution, the Governor of the province in which such vacancy happens, may appoint, till the pleasure of the President-General and Grand Council can be known;

That the particular military as well as civil establishments in each colony remain in their present state, the general constitution notwithstanding; and that on sudden emergencies any colony may defend itself; and lay the accounts of expense thence arising before the President-General and General Council, who may allow and order payment of the same, as far as they judge such accounts just and reasonable.

APPENDIX C.

THE DECLARATION OF INDEPENDENCE, ADOPTED BY CONGRESS, JULY 4, 1776.

A Declaration by the Representatives of the United States of America, in Congress Assembled.

WHEN, in the course of human events, it becomes necessary for one people to dissolve we political bands which have connected them with another, and to assume among the powers of the earth the separate and equal station to which the laws of nature and of nature's God entitle them, a decent respect to the opinions of mankind requires that they should declare the causes which impel them to the separation.

We hold these truths to be self-evident, that all men are created equal; that they are endowed by their Creator with certain inalienable rights; that among these are life, liberty, and the pursuit of happiness; that, to secure these rights, governments are instituted among men, deriving their just powers from the consent of the governed; that, whenever any form of government becomes destructive of these ends, it is the right of the people to alter or abolish it, and to institute a new government, laying its foundation on such principles, and organizing its powers in such form, as to them shall seem most likely to effect their safety and happiness. Prudence, indeed, will dictate that governments long established should not be changed for light and transient causes; and, accordingly, all experience hath shown that mankind are more disposed to suffer, while evils are sufferable, than to right themselves by abolishing the forms to which they are accustomed. But when a long train of abuses and usurpations, pursuing invariably the same object, evinces a design to reduce them under absolute despotism, it is their right, it is their duty, to throw off such a government, and to provide new guards for their future security. Such has been the patient sufferance of these Colonies; and such is now the necessity which constrains them to alter their former systems of government. The history of the present King of Great Britain is a history of repeated injuries and usurpations, all having in direct object the establishment of an absolute tyranny over these States. To prove this, let facts be submitted to a candid world:–

He has refused his assent to laws the most wholesome and necessary for the public good.

He has forbidden his governors to pass laws of immediate and pressing importance, unless suspended in their operations, till his assent should be obtained; and, when so suspended, he has utterly neglected to attend to them.

He has refused to pass other laws for the accommodation of large districts of people, unless those people would relinquish the right of representation in the legislature; a right inestimable to them, and formidable to tyrants only.

He has called together legislative bodies at places unusual, uncomfortable, and distant from the repository of their public records, for the sole purpose of fatiguing them into compliance with his measures.

He has dissolved representative houses repeatedly for opposing, with manly firmness, his invasions on the rights of the people.

He has refused, for a long time after such dissolutions, to cause others to be elected; whereby the legislative powers, incapable of annihilation, have returned to the people at large, for their exercise; the State remaining, in the mean time, exposed to all the dangers of invasions from without, and convulsions within.

He has endeavored to prevent the population of these States; for that purpose, obstructing the laws for the naturalization of foreigners; refusing to pass others to encourage their migration hither, and raising the conditions of new appropriations of lands.

He has obstructed the administration of justice by refusing his assent to laws for establishing judiciary powers.

He has made judges dependent on his will alone, for the tenure of their offices, and the amount and payment of their salaries.

He has erected a multitude of new offices, and sent hither swarms of officers, to harass our people, and eat out their substance.

He has kept among us, in times of peace, standing armies, without the consent of our legislatures.

He has affected to render the military independent of, and superior to, the civil power.

He has combined with others to subject us to a jurisdiction foreign to our constitution, and unacknowledged by our laws; giving his assent to their acts of pretended legislation:–

For quartering large bodies of armed troops among us;

For protecting them, by mock trial, from punishment for any murders which they should commit on the inhabitants of these States;

For cutting off our trade with all parts of the world;

For imposing taxes on us without our consent;

For depriving us, in many cases, of the benefits of trial by jury;

For transporting us beyond seas to be tried for pretended offences;

For abolishing the free system of English laws in a neighboring province, establishing therein an arbitrary government, and enlarging its boundaries, so as to render it at once an example and fit instrument for introducing the same absolute rule into these Colonies;

For taking away our charters, abolishing our most valuable laws, and altering, fundamentally, the powers of our governments;

For suspending our own legislatures, and declaring themselves invested with power to legislate for us in all cases whatsoever.

He has abdicated government here, by declaring us out of his protection, and waging war against us.

He has plundered our seas, ravaged our coasts, burned our towns, and destroyed the lives of our people.

He is at this time transporting large armies of foreign mercenaries to complete the works of death, desolation, and tyranny, already begun with circumstances of cruelty and perfidy scarcely paralleled in the most barbarous ages, and totally unworthy the head of a civilized nation.

He has constrained our fellow-citizens, taken captive on the high seas, to bear arms against their country, to become the executioners of their friends and brethren, or to fall themselves by their hands.

He has excited domestic insurrections amongst us, and has endeavored to bring on the inhabitants of our frontiers, the merciless Indian savages, whose known rule of war fare is an undistinguished destruction of all ages, sexes, and conditions.

In every stage of these oppressions, we have petitioned for redress in the most humble terms; our repeated petitions have been answered by repeated injury. A prince whose character is thus marked by every act which may define a tyrant, is unfit to be the ruler of a free people.

Nor have we been wanting in attentions to our British brethren. We have warned them, from time to time, of attempts by their legislature to extend an unwarrantable jurisdiction over us. We have reminded them of the circumstances of our emigration and settlement here. We have appealed to their native justice and magnanimity, and we have conjured them, by the ties of our common kindred, to disavow these usurpations, which would inevitably interrupt our connections and correspondence. They, too, have been deaf to the voice of justice and of consanguinity. We must, therefore, acquiesce in the necessity, which denounces our separation, and hold them, as we hold the rest of mankind, enemies in war; in peace, friends.

We, therefore, the representatives of the UNITED STATES OF AMERICA, in general congress assembled, appealing to the Supreme Judge of the world for the rectitude of our intentions, do, in the name and by the authority of the good people of these Colonies, solemnly publish and declare, that these United Colonies are, and of right ought to be, *Free* and *Independent States;* that they are absolved from all allegiance to the British crown, and that all political connection between them and the State of Great Britain is, and ought to be, totally dissolved; and that, as *Free* and *Independent States,* they have full power to levy war, conclude peace, contract alliances, establish commerce, and do all other acts and things which *Independent States* may of right do. And for the support of this Declaration, with a firm reliance on the protection of DIVINE PROVIDENCE, we mutually pledge to each other our lives, our fortunes, and our sacred honor.

JOHN HANCOCK.

NEW HAMPSHIRE.—Josiah Bartlett, William Whipple, Matthew Thornton.

MASSCHUSETTS BAY—Samuel Adams, John Adams, Robert Treat Paine, Elbridge Gerry.

RHODE ISLAND, ETC.—Stephen Hopkins, William Ellery.

CONNECTICUT.—Roger Sherman, Samuel Huntington, William Williams, Oliver Wolcott.

NEW YORK.—William Floyd, Philip Livingston, Francis Lewis, Lewis Morris.

NEW JERSEY.—Richard Stockton, John Witherspoon, Francis Hopkinson, John Hart, Abraham Clark.

PENNSYLVANIA.—Robert Morris, Benjamin Rush, Benjamin Franklin, John Morton, George Clymer, James Smith, George Taylor, James Wilson, George Ross.

DELAWARE.—Cash Rodney, George Read, Thomas M'Kean.

MARYLAND.—Samuel Chase, William Paca, Thomas Stone, Charles Carroll of Carrollton.

VIRGINIA.—George Wythe, Richard Henry Lee, Thomas Jefferson, Benjamin Harrison, Thomas Nelson, Jr., Francis Lightfoot Lee, Carter Braxton.

NORTH CAROLINA.—William Hooper, Joseph Hewes, John Penn.

SOUTH CAROLINA.—Edward Rutledge, Thomas Hayward, Jr., Thomas Lynch, Jr., Arthur Middleton.

GEORGIA.—Button Gwinnett, Lyman Hall, George Walton.

APPENDIX D.

ARTICLES OF CONFEDERATION.

[The Articles of Confederation were drawn up by a committee of gentlemen, who were appointed by Congress for this purpose, June 12, 1776, and finally adopted, November 15, 1777. The committee were Messrs. Bartlett, Samuel Adams, Hopkins, Sherman, R. R. Livingston, Dickinson, M'Kean, Stone, Nelson, Howes, E. Rutledge, and Gwinnet.]

ARTICLES OF CONFEDERATION AND PERPETUAL UNION

Between the States of New Hampshire, Massachusetts Bay, Rhode Island and Providence Plantations, Connecticut, New York, New Jersey, Pennsylvania, Delaware, Maryland, Virginia, North Carolina, South Carolina, and Georgia.

Article I.

The style of this confederacy shall be, "THE UNITED STATES OF AMERICA."

Article II.

Each State retains its sovereignty, freedom, and independence, and every power, jurisdiction, and right, which is not by this confederation expressly delegated to the United States in Congress assembled.

Article III.

The said States hereby severally enter into a firm league of friendship with each other, for their common defence, the security of their liberties, and their mutual and general welfare, binding themselves to assist each other against all force offered to, or attacks made upon them, or any of them, on account of religion, sovereignty, trade, or any other pretence whatever.

Article IV.

SECTION I.—The better to secure and perpetuate mutual friendship and intercourse among the people of the different States in this union, the free inhabitants of each of these States—paupers, vagabonds, and fugitives from justice excepted—shall be entitled to all privileges and immunities of free citizens in the several States; and the people of each State shall have free ingress and egress to and from any other State, and shall enjoy therein all the privileges of trade and commerce, subject to the same duties, impositions, and restrictions, as the inhabitants thereof respectively; provided, that such restrictions shall not extend so far as to prevent the removal of property imported into any State, to any other State, of which the owner is an inhabitant; provided also, that no imposition, duties, or restriction, shall be laid by any State on the property of the United States, or either of them.

SEC. 2.—If any person, guilty of, or charged with treason, felony, or other high misdemeanor, in any State, shall flee from justice, and be found in any of the United States, he shall, upon the demand of the Governor or executive power of the State from which he fled, be delivered up and removed to the State having jurisdiction of his offence.

SEC. 3. Full faith and credit shall be given, in each of these States, to the records, acts, and judicial proceedings of the courts and magistrates of every other State.

Article V.

SECTION 1.—For the more convenient management of the general interests of the United States, delegates shall be annually appointed in such manner as the legislature of each State shall direct, to meet in Congress on the first Monday in November in every year, with a power reserved to each State to recall its delegates, or any of them, at any time within the year, and to send others in their stead, for the remainder of the year.

SEC. 2.—No State shall be represented in Congress by less than two, nor more than seven members; and no person shall be capable of being a delegate for more than three years, in any term of six years; nor shall any person, being a delegate, be capable of holding any office under the United States, for which he, or any other for his benefit, receives any salary, fees, or emolument, of any kind.

SEC. 3.—Each State shall maintain its own delegates in a meeting of the States, and while they act as members of the committee of these States.

SEC. 4.—In determining questions in the United States in Congress assembled, each State shall have one vote.

SEC. 5.—Freedom of speech and debate in Congress shall not be impeached or questioned in any court or place out of Congress, and the members of Congress shall be protected in their persons from arrests and imprisonments during the time of their going to and from, and attendance on Congress, except for treason, felony, or breach of the peace.

Article VI.

SECTION 1.—No State, without the consent of the United States in Congress assembled, shall send any embassy to, or receive any embassy from, or enter into any conference, agreement, alliance, or treaty with any king, prince, or State, nor shall any person holding any office of profit or trust under the United States, or any of them, accept of any present, emolument, office, or title, of any kind whatever, from any king, prince, or foreign state; nor shall the United States in Congress assembled, or any of them, grant any title of nobility.

SEC. 2.—No two or more States shall enter into any treaty, confederation, or alliance whatever, between them, without the consent of the United States in Congress assembled, specifying accurately the purposes for which the same is to be entered into, and how long it shall continue.

SEC. 3.—No State shall lay any imposts or duties which may interfere with any stipulations in treaties entered into by the United States in Congress assembled, with any king, prince, or State, in pursuance of any treaties already proposed by Congress to the courts of France and Spain.

SEC. 4.—No vessels of war shall be kept up in time of peace by any State, except such number only as shall be deemed necessary by the United States in Congress assembled, for the defence of such State, or its trade; nor shall any body of forces be kept up by any State, in time of peace, except such number only as, in the judgment of the United States in Congress assembled, shall be deemed requisite to garrison the forts necessary for the defence of such State; but every State shall always keep up a well-regulated and disciplined militia, sufficiently armed and accoutred, and shall provide and constantly have ready for use, in public stores, a due number of field-pieces and tents, and a proper quantity of arms, ammunition, and camp equipage.

SEC. 5.—No State shall engage in any war without the consent of the United States in Congress assembled, unless such State be actually invaded by enemies, or shall have received certain advice of a resolution being formed by some nation of Indians to invade such State, and the danger is so imminent as not to admit of delay till the United States in Congress assembled can be consulted nor shall any State grant commissions to any ships or vessels of war, nor letters of marque or reprisal, except it be after a declaration of war by the United States in Congress assembled, and then only against the kingdom or State, and the subjects thereof, against which war has been so declared, and under such regulations as shall be established by the United States in Congress assembled, unless such State be infested by pirates, in which case vessels of war may be fitted out for that occasion, and kept so long as the danger shall continue, or until the United States in Congress assembled shall determine otherwise.

Article VII.

When land forces are raised by any State for the common defence, all officers of or under the rank of colonel, shall be appointed by the legislature of each State respectively by whom such forces shall be raised, or in such manner as such State shall direct, and all vacancies shall be filled up by the State which first made the appointment.

Article VIII.

All charges of war, and all other expenses that shall be incurred for the common defence or general welfare, and allowed by the United States in Congress assembled, shall be defrayed out of a common treasury, which shall be supplied by the several States, in proportion to the value of all land within each State, granted to or surveyed for any person, as such land and the buildings and improvements thereon shall be estimated, according to such mode as the United States in Congress assembled shall, from time to time, direct and appoint. The taxes for paying that proportion shall be laid and levied by the authority and direction of the legislatures of the several States within the time agreed upon by the United States in Congress assembled.

Article IX.

SECTION 1.–The United States in Congress assembled shall have the sole and exclusive right and power of determining on peace and war, except in the cases mentioned in the sixth article, of sending and receiving ambassadors; entering into treaties and alliances, provided that no treaty of commerce shall be made, whereby the legislative power of the respective States shall be restrained from imposing such imposts and duties on foreigners, as their own people are subjected to, or from prohibiting the exportation or importation of any species of goods or commodities whatsoever; of establishing rules for deciding in all cases what captures on land or water shall be legal, and in what manner prizes taken by land or naval forces in the service of the United States shall be divided or appropriated; of granting letters of marque and reprisal in times of peace; appointing courts for the trial of piracies and felonies committed on the high seas; and establishing courts for receiving and determining finally appeals in all cases of capture; provided that no member of Congress shall be appointed a judge of any of the said courts.

SEC. 2.—The United States in Congress assembled shall also be the last resort on appeal in all disputes and differences now subsisting, or that hereafter may arise between two or, more States concerning boundary, jurisdiction, or any other cause whatever; which authority shall always be exercised in the manner following: Whenever the legislative or executive authority or lawful agent of any State in controversy with another, shall present a petition to Congress, stating the matter in question, and praying for a hearing, notice thereof shall be given by order of Congress to the legislative or executive authority of the other State in controversy, and a day assigned for the appearance of the parties by their lawful agents, who shall then be directed to appoint, by joint consent, commissioners or judges to constitute a court for hearing and determining the matter in question; but if they can not agree, Congress shall name three persons out of each of the United States, and from the list of such persons each party shall alternately strike out one, the petitioners beginning, until the number shall be reduced to thirteen; and from that number not less than seven, nor more than nine names, as Congress shall direct, shall, in the presence of Congress, be drawn out by lot; and the persons whose names shall be so drawn, or any five of them, shall be commissioners or judges to hear and finally determine the controversy, so always as a major part of the judges, who shall hear the cause, shall agree in the determination: and it either party shall neglect to attend at the day appointed, without showing reasons which Congress shall judge sufficient, or being present, shall refuse to strike, the

Congress shall proceed to nominate three persons out of each State, and the secretary of Congress shall strike in behalf of such party absent or refusing; and the judgment and sentence of the court, to be appointed in the manner before prescribed, shall be final and conclusive; and if any of the parties shall refuse to submit to the authority of such court, or to appear or defend their claim or cause, the court shall nevertheless proceed to pronounce sentence, or judgment, which shall in like manner be final and decisive; the judgment or sentence and other proceedings being in either case transmitted to Congress, and lodged among the acts of Congress, for the security of the parties concerned: provided that every commissioner, before he sits in judgment, shall take an oath, to be administered by one of the judges of the supreme or superior court of the State where the cause shall be tried, "well and truly to hear and determine the matter in question, according to the best of his judgment, without favor, affection, or hope of reward." Provided, also, that no State shall be deprived of territory for the benefit of the United States.

SEC. 3.—All controversies concerning the private right of soil claimed under different grants of two or more States, whose jurisdiction, as they may respect such lands, and the States which passed such grants are adjusted, the said grants or either of them being at the same time claimed to have originated antecedent to such settlement of jurisdiction, shall, on the petition of either party to the Congress of the United States, be finally determined, as near as may be, in the same manner as is before prescribed for deciding disputes respecting territorial jurisdiction between different States.

SEC. 4.–The United States in Congress assembled shall also have the sole and exclusive right and power of regulating the alloy and value of coin struck by their own authority, or by that of the respective States; fixing the standard of weights and measures throughout the United States; regulating the trade, and managing all affairs with the Indians, not members of any of the States; provided that the legislative right of any State, within its own limits, be not infringed or violated; establishing and regulating post offices from one State to another throughout all the United States, and exacting such postage on the papers passing through the same, as may be requisite to defray the expenses of the said office;

appointing all officers of the land forces in the service of the United States, excepting regimental officers; appointing all the officers of the naval forces, and commissioning all officers whatever in the service of the United States; making rules for the government and regulation of the said land and naval forces, and directing their operations.

SEC. 5.—The United States in Congress assembled shall have authority to appoint a committee to sit in the recess of Congress, to be denominated, *"A Committee of the States,"* and to consist of one delegate from each State; and to appoint such other committees and civil officers as may be necessary for managing the general affairs of the United States under their direction; to appoint one of their number to preside; provided that no person be allowed to serve in the office of president more than one year in any term of three years; to ascertain the necessary sums of money to be raised for the service of the United States, and to appropriate and apply the same for defraying the public expenses; to borrow money or emit bills on the credit of the United States, transmitting every half-year to the respective States an account of the sums of money so borrowed or emitted; to build and equip a navy; to agree upon the number of land forces, and to make requisitions from each State for its quota, in proportion to the number of white inhabitants in such State, which requisition shall be binding; and thereupon the legislature of each State shall appoint the regimental officers, raise the men, clothe, arm, and equip them, in a soldier-like manner, at the expense of the United States; and the officers and men so clothed, armed, and equipped, shall march to the place appointed, and within the time agreed on by the United States in Congress assembled; but if the United States in Congress assembled shall, on consideration of circumstances, judge proper that any State should not raise men, or should raise a smaller number than its quota, and that any other State should raise a greater number of men than the quota thereof, such extra number shall be raised, officered, clothed, armed, and equipped, in the same manner as the quota of such State, unless the legislature of such State shall judge that such extra number can not be safely spared out of the same, in which case they shall raise, officer, clothe, arm, and equip, as many of such extra number as they judge can be safely spared, and the officers and men so clothed, armed, and equipped, shall march to the place appointed, and within the time agreed on by the United States in Congress assembled.

Sec. 6.—The United States in Congress assembled shall never engage in a war, nor grant letters of marque and reprisal in time of peace, nor enter into any treaties or alliances, nor coin money, nor regulate the value thereof, nor ascertain the sums and expenses necessary for the defence and welfare of the United States, or any of them, nor emit bills, nor borrow money on the credit of the United States, nor appropriate money, nor agree upon the number of vessels of war to be built or purchased, or the number of land or sea forces to be raised, nor appoint a commander-in-chief of the army or navy, unless nine States assent to the same: nor shall a question on any other point, except for adjourning from day to day, be determined, unless by the votes of a majority of the United States in Congress assembled.

Sec. 7.—The Congress of the United States shall have power to adjourn to any time within the year, and to any place within the United States, so that no period of adjournment be for a longer duration than the space of six months, and shall publish the journal of their proceedings monthly, except such parts thereof relating to treaties, alliances, or military operations, as in their judgment require secrecy; and the yeas and nays of the delegates of each State, on any question, shall be entered on the journal, when it is desired by any delegate; and the delegates of a State, or any of them, at his or their request, shall be furnished with a transcript of the said journal, except such parts as are above excepted, to lay before the legislatures of the several States.

Article X.

The Committee of the States, or any nine of them, shall be authorized to execute in the recess of Congress, such of the powers of Congress as the United States, in Congress assembled, by the consent of nine States, shall, from time to time, think expedient to vest them with; provided that no power be delegated to the said committee, for the exercise of which, by the Articles of Confederation, the voice of nine States, in the Congress of the United States assembled, is requisite.

Article XI.

Canada, acceding to this Confederation, and joining in the measures 0f the United States shall be admitted into and entitled to all the advantages of this Union: But no other colony shall be admitted into the same, unless such admission be agreed to by nine States.

Article XII.

All bills of credit emitted, moneys borrowed, and debts contracted by or under the authority of Congress, before the assembling of the United States, in pursuance of the present Confederation, shall be deemed and considered as a charge against the United States, for payment and satisfaction whereof the said United States and the public faith are hereby solemnly pledged.

Article XIII.

Every State shall abide by the determination of the United States in Congress assembled, in all questions which by this Confederation are submitted to them. And the articles of this Confederation shall be inviolably observed by every State, and the union shall be perpetual; nor shall any alteration at any time hereafter be made in any of them; unless such alteration be agreed to in a Congress of the United States, and be afterwards confirmed by the legislature of every State.

And whereas it hath pleased the great Governor of the world to incline the hearts of the legislatures we respectively represent in Congress to approve of, and to authorize us to ratify the said Articles of Confederation and Perpetual Union, Know ye, that we, the undersigned delegates, by virtue of the power and authority to us given for that purpose, do by these presents, in the name and in behalf of our respective constituents, fully and entirely ratify and confirm each and every of the said Articles of Confederation and Perpetual Union, and all and singular the matters and things therein contained. And we do further solemnly plight and engage the faith of our respective constituents, that they shall abide by the determinations of the United States in Congress assembled, in all questions which by the said Confederation are submitted to them; and that the articles thereof shall be inviolably observed by the States we respectively represent, and that the union shall be perpetual. In witness whereof we have hereunto set our hands in Congress.

Done at Philadelphia, in the State of Pennsylvania, the 9th day of July, in the year of our Lord 1778, and in the third year of the Independence of America.

NEW HAMPSHIRE.—Josiah Bartlett, John Wentworth, Jr.

MASSACHUSETTS BAY.—John Hancock, Samuel Adams, Elbridge Gerry, Francis Dana, James Lovel, Samuel Holton.

RHODE ISLAND, ETC.—William Ellery, Henry Marchant, John Collins.

CONNECTICUT.—R0ger Sherman, Samuel Huntington, Oliver Wolcott, Titus Hosmer, Andrew Adams.

NEW YORK.—James Duane, Francis Lewis, William Duer, Gouverneur Morris.

NEW JERSEY.—John Witherspoon, Nath. Scudder.

PENNSYLVANIA.—Robert Morris, Daniel Roberdeau, Jona Bayard Smith, William Clingan, Joseph Reed.

DELAWARE.—Thomas M'Kean, John Dickinson, Nicholas Van Dyke.

MARYLAND.—John Hanson, Daniel Carroll.

VIRGINIA. —Richard Henry Lee, John Banister, Thomas Adams, John Harvie, Francis Lightfoot Lee.

NORTH CAROLINA.—John Penn, Cons. Harnett, John Williams.

SOUTH CAROLINA.—Henry Laurens, Wm. Henry Drayton, John Matthews, Richard Hutson, Thomas Heyward, Jr.

GEORGIA.—J0hn Walton, Edward Tel fair, Edward Langworthy.

APPENDIX E.

CONSTITUTION OF THE UNITED STATES.

WE, the People of the United States, in order to form a more perfect union, establish justice, insure domestic tranquillity, provide for the common defence, promote the general welfare, and secure the blessings of liberty to ourselves and our posterity, do ordain and establish this Constitution for the United States of North America.

Article I.

SECTION 1.—All legislative powers herein granted shall be vested in a Congress of the United States, which shall consist of a Senate and House of Representatives.

SEC. 2.—The House of Representatives shall be composed of members chosen every second year by the people of the several States, and the electors in each State shall have the qualifications requisite for electors of the most numerous branch of the State legislature.

No person shall be a representative who shall not have attained to the age of twenty-five years, and been seven years a citizen of the United States, and who shall not, when elected, be an inhabitant of that State in which he shall be chosen. Representatives and direct taxes shall be apportioned among the several States which may be included within this Union, according to their respective numbers, which shall be determined by adding to the whole number of free persons, including those bound to service for a term of years, and excluding Indians not taxed, three-fifths of all other persons. The actual enumeration shall be made within three years after the first meeting of the Congress of the United States, and within every subsequent term of ten years, in such manner as they shall by law direct. The number of representatives shall not exceed one for every thirty thousand; but each State shall have at least one representative; and until such enumeration shall be made, the State of New Hampshire shall be entitled to choose three, Massachusetts, eight, Rhode Island and Providence Plantations, one, Connecticut, five, New York, six, New Jersey, four, Pennsylvania, eight, Delaware, one, Maryland, six, Virginia, ten, North Carolina, five, South Carolina, five, and Georgia, three.

When vacancies happen in the representation from any State, the executive authority thereof shall issue writs of election to fill such vacancies.

The House of Representatives shall choose their speaker and other officers; and shall have the sole power of impeachment.

SEC. 3.—The Senate of the United States shall be composed of two senators from each State, chosen by the legislature thereof, for six years; and each senator shall have one vote. Immediately after they shall be assembled in consequence of the first election, they shall be divided, as equally as may be, into three classes. The seats of the senators of the first class shall be vacated at the expiration of the second year, of the second class, at the expiration of the fourth year, and of the third class at the expiration of the sixth year, so that one-third may be chosen every second year; and if vacancies happen, by resignation or otherwise, during the recess of the legislature of any State, the executive thereof may make temporary appointments until the next meeting of the legislature, which shall then fill such vacancies.

No person shall be a senator who shall not have attained to the age of thirty years, and been nine years a citizen of the United States, and who shall not, when elected, be an inhabitant of that State for which he shall be chosen.

The Vice-President of the United States shall be president of the Senate, but shall have no vote, unless they be equally divided. The Senate shall choose their other officers, and also a president *pro tempore*, in the absence of the Vice-President, or when he shall exercise the office as President of the United States.

The Senate shall have the sole power to try all impeachments. When sitting for that purpose, they shall be on oath or affirmation. When the

President of the United States is tried, the chief-justice shall preside; and no person shall be convicted without the concurrence of two-thirds of the members present.

Judgment, in cases of impeachment, shall not extend further than to removal from office, and disqualification to hold and enjoy any office of honor, trust, or profit under the United States; but the party convicted shall, nevertheless, be liable and subject to indictment, trial, judgment, and punishment, according to law.

SEC. 4.—The times, places, and manner of holding elections for senators and representatives, shall be prescribed in each State by the legislature thereof; but the Congress may, at any time, by law, make or alter such regulations, except as to the places of choosing senators.

The Congress shall assemble at least once in every year; and such meeting shall be on the first Monday in December, unless they shall by law appoint a different day.

SEC. 5.—Each house shall be the judge of the elections, returns, and qualifications of its own members; and a majority of each shall constitute a quorum to do business; but a smaller number may adjourn from day to day, and may be authorized to compel the attendance of absent members, in such manner and under such penalties as each house may provide.

Each house may determine the rules of its proceedings, punish its members for disorderly behavior, and, with the concurrence of two-thirds, expel a member.

Each house shall keep a journal of its proceedings, and from time to time publish the same, excepting such parts as may in their judgment require secrecy; and the yeas and nays of the members of either house, on any question, shall, at the desire of one fifth of those present, be entered on the journal.

Neither house, during the session of Congress, shall, without the consent of the other, adjourn for more than three days, nor to any other place than that in which the two houses shall be sitting.

SEC. 6.—The senators and representatives shall receive a compensation for their services, to be ascertained by law, and paid out of the treasury of the United States. They shall, in all cases except treason, felony, and breach of the peace, be privileged from arrest during their attendance on the session of their respective houses, and in going to and returning from the same; and, for any speech or debate in either house, they shall not be questioned in any other place.

No senator or representative shall, during the time for which he was elected, be appointed to any civil office under the authority of the United States which shall have been created, or the emoluments whereof shall have been increased, during such time; and no person holding any office under the United States shall be a member of either house during his continuance in office.

SEC. 7.—All bills for raising revenue shall originate in the House of Representatives; but the Senate may propose or concur with amendments, as on other bills. Every bill which shall have passed the House of Representatives and the Senate, shall, before it become a law, be presented to the President of the United States; if he approve he shall sign it but if not he shall return it, with his objections, to that house in which it shall have originated, who shall enter the objections at large on their journal, and proceed to reconsider it. If, after such reconsideration, two-thirds of that house shall agree to pass the bill, it shall be sent, together with the objections, to the other house, by which it shall likewise be reconsidered, and, if approved by two-thirds of that house, it shall become a law. But, in all such cases, the votes of both houses shall be determined by yeas and nays; and the names of the persons voting for and against the bill shall be entered on the journal of each house respectively. If any bill shall not be returned by the President within ten days (Sundays excepted) after it shall have been presented to him, the same shall be a law in like manner as if he had signed it, unless the Congress by their adjournment prevent its return, in which case it shall not be a law.

Every order, resolution, or vote, to which the concurrence of the Senate and House of Representatives may be necessary (except on a question of adjournment), shall be presented to the President of the United States; and, before the same shall take effect, shall be approved by him, or, being disapproved by him, shall be repassed by two thirds of the Senate and House of Representatives, according to the rules and limitations prescribed in the case of a bill.

Sec. 8.—The Congress shall have power:–

To lay and collect taxes, duties, imposts, and excises, to pay the debts, and provide for the common defence and general welfare, of the United States; but all duties, imposts, and excises shall be uniform throughout the United States;

To borrow money on the credit of the United States;

To regulate commerce with foreign nations, and among the several States, and with the Indian tribes;

To establish an uniform rule of naturalization, and uniform laws on the subject of bankruptcies throughout the United States;

To coin money, regulate the value thereof, and of foreign coin, and fix the standard of weights and measures;

To provide for the punishment of counterfeiting the securities and current coin of the United States;

To establish post-offices and post-roads;

To promote the progress of science and useful arts, by securing for limited times, to authors and inventors, the exclusive right to their respective writings and discoveries;

To constitute tribunals inferior to the Supreme Court;

To define and punish piracies and felonies committed on the high seas, and offences against the law of nations;

To declare war, grant letters of marque and reprisal, and make rules concerning captures on land and water;

To raise and support armies; but no appropriation of money to that use shall be for a longer term than two years;

To provide and maintain a navy;

To make rules for the government and regulation of the land and naval forces;

To provide for calling forth the militia to execute the laws of the Union, suppress insurrections, and repel invasions;

To provide for organizing, arming, and disciplining the militia, and for governing such part of them as may be employed in the service of the United States, reserving to the States respectively, the appointment of the officers, and the authority of training the militia according to the discipline prescribed by Congress;

To exercise exclusive legislation, in all cases whatsoever, over such district (not exceeding ten miles square) as may, by cession of particular States, and the acceptance of Congress, become the seat of government of the United States, and to exercise like authority over all places purchased by the consent of the legislature of the State in which the same shall be, for the erection of forts, magazines, arsenals, dockyards, and other needful buildings:—And

To make all laws which shall be necessary and proper for carrying into execution the foregoing powers, and all other powers vested by this Constitution in the government of the United States, or in any department or officer thereof.

SEC. 9.—The migration or importation of such persons, as any of the States now existing shall think proper to admit, shall not be prohibited by the Congress prior to the year one thousand eight hundred and eight; but a tax, or duty, may be imposed on such importation, not exceeding ten dollars for each person.

The privilege of the writ of *habeas corpus* shall not be suspended, unless when in cases of rebellion or invasion the public safety may require it.

No bill of attainder or *ex post facto* law shall be passed.

No capitation or other direct tax shall be laid, unless in proportion to the census or enumeration, hereinbefore directed to be taken.

No tax or duty shall be laid on articles exported from any State. No preference shall be given by any regulation of commerce or revenue to the ports of one State over those of another; nor shall vessels bound to or from one State be obliged to enter, clear or pay duties, in another.

No money shall be drawn from the treasury but in consequence of appropriations made by law; and a regular statement and account of the receipts and expenditures of all public money shall be published from time to time.

No title of nobility shall be granted by the United States; and no person holding any office of profit or trust under them shall, without the consent of the Congress, accept of any present, emolument, office, or title of any kind whatever, from any king, prince, or foreign state.

SEC. 10.—No State shall enter into any treaty, alliance, or confederation; grant letters of marque and reprisal; coin money; emit bills of credit; make any thing but gold and silver coin a tender in payment of debts; pass any bill of attainder, *ex post facto* law, or law impairing the obligation of contracts; or grant any title of nobility.

No State shall, without the consent of the Congress, lay any imposts or duties on imports or exports, except what may be absolutely necessary for executing its inspection laws; and the net produce of all duties and imposts laid by any State on imports or exports, shall be for the use of the treasury of the United States; and all such laws shall be subject to the revision and control of the Congress. No State shall, without the consent of Congress, lay any duty of tonnage, keep troops or ships of war in time of peace, enter into any agreement or compact with another State or with a foreign power, or engage in war, unless actually invaded, or in such imminent danger as will not admit of delay.

Article II.

SECTION 1—The executive power shall be vested in a President of the United States of America. He shall hold his office during the term of four years, and together with the Vice-President, chosen for the same term, be elected as follows:—

Each State shall appoint, in such manner as the legislature thereof may direct, a number of electors equal to the whole number of senators and representatives to which the State may be entitled in the Congress; but no senator or representative, or person holding an office of trust or profit under the United States, shall be appointed an elector.

The electors shall meet in their respective States, and vote by ballot for two per sons, of whom one, at least, shall not be an inhabitant of the same State with themselves. And they shall make a list of all the persons voted for, and of the number of votes for each; which list they shall sign and certify, and transmit sealed to the seat of the government of the United States, directed to the president of the Senate. The president of the Senate shall, in the presence of the Senate and House of Representatives, open all the certificates; and the votes shall then be counted. The person having the greatest number of votes shall be the President, if such number be a majority of the whole number of electors appointed; and if there be more than one who have such majority, and have an equal number of votes, then the House of Representatives shall immediately choose, by ballot, one of them for President; and if no person have a majority, then, from the five highest on the list, the said house shall, in like manner, choose the President. But, in choosing the President, the votes shall be taken by States; the representation from each State having one vote; a quorum for this purpose shall consist of a member or members from two-thirds of the States; and a majority of all the States shall be necessary to a choice. In every case, after the choice of the President, the person having the greatest number of votes of the electors shall be Vice-President. But, if there should remain two or more who have equal votes, the Senate shall choose from them, by ballot, the Vice-President.

The Congress may determine the time of choosing the electors, and the day on which they shall give their votes; which day shall be the same throughout the United States.

No person except a natural born citizen, or a citizen of the United States at the time of the adoption of this Constitution, shall be eligible to the office of President: neither shall any person be eligible to that office who shall not have attained to the age of thirty-five years, and been fourteen years a resident within the United States.

In case of the removal of the President from office, or of his death, resignation, or inability to discharge the powers or duties of the said office, the same shall devolve on the Vice-President; and the Congress may, by law, provide for the case of removal, death, resignation, or inability, both of the President and Vice-President, declaring what officer shall then act as President; and such officer shall act accordingly, until the disability be removed, or a President shall be elected.

The President shall, at stated times, receive for his services a compensation, which shall neither be increased nor diminished during the period for which he shall have been elected; and he shall not receive within that period any other emolument from the United States or any of them.

Before he enter on the execution of his office, he shall take the following oath or affirmation:—

"I do solemnly swear (or affirm) that I will faithfully execute the office of President of the United States, and will, to the best of my ability, preserve, protect, and defend the Constitution of the United States."

SEC. 2.—The President shall be commander-in-chief of the army and navy of the United States, and of the militia of the several States, when called into the actual service of the United States; he may require the opinion, in writing, of the principal officer in each of the executive departments, upon any subject relating to the duties of their respective offices, and he shall have power to grant reprieves and pardons for offences against the United States, except in cases of impeachment.

He shall have power, by and with the advice and consent of the Senate, to make treaties, provided two-thirds of the senators present concur; and he shall nominate, and by and with the advice and consent of the Senate, shall appoint, ambassadors, other public ministers, and consuls, judges of the Supreme Court, and all other officers of the United States, whose appointments are not herein otherwise provided for, and which shall be established by law: but the Congress may, by law, vest the appointment of such inferior officers as they think proper, in the President alone, in the courts of law, or in the heads of departments.

The President shall have power to fill up all vacancies that may happen during the recess of the Senate, by granting commissions, which shall expire at the end of their next session.

SEC. 3.—He shall, from time to time, give to the Congress information of the state of the Union, and recommend to their consideration such measures as he shall judge necessary and expedient; he may, on extraordinary occasions, convene both houses, or either of them, and, in case of disagreement between them with respect to the time of adjournment, he may adjourn them to such time as he shall think proper; he shall receive ambassadors and other public ministers; he shall take care that the laws be faithfully executed; and shall commission all the officers of the United States.

SEC. 4.—The President, Vice-President, and all civil officers of the United States, shall be removed from office on impeachment for and conviction of treason, bribery, or other high crimes and misdemeanors.

Article III.

SECTION 1.—The judicial power of the United States shall be vested in a Supreme Court, and in such inferior courts as the Congress may from time to time ordain and establish. The judges, both of the supreme and inferior courts, shall hold their offices during good behavior; and shall, at stated times, receive for their services a compensation, which shall not be diminished during their continuance in office.

SEC. 2.—The judicial power shall extend to all cases, in law and equity, arising under this Constitution, the laws of the United States, and treaties made, or which shall be made, under their authority; to all cases affecting ambassadors, other public ministers and consuls; to all cases of admiralty and maritime jurisdiction; to controversies to which the United States shall be a party; to controversies between two or more States, between a State and citizens of another State, between citizens of different States, between citizens of the same State claiming lands under grants of different States, and between a State, or the citizens thereof, and foreign States, citizens, or subjects.

In all cases affecting ambassadors, other public ministers and consuls, and those in which a State shall be a party, the Supreme Court shall have original jurisdiction. In all the other cases before mentioned, the Supreme Court shall have appellate jurisdiction both as to law and fact, with such exceptions, and under such regulations as the Congress shall make.

The trial of all crimes, except in cases of impeachment, shall be by jury; and such trial shall be held in the State where the said crimes shall have been committed: but, when not committed within any State, the trial shall be at such place or places as the Congress may by law have directed.

SEC. 3.—Treason against the United States shall consist only in levying war against them, or in adhering to their enemies, giving them aid and comfort. No person shall be convicted of treason unless on the testimony of two witnesses to the same overt act, or on confession in open court.

The Congress shall have power to declare the punishment of treason, but no attainder of treason shall work corruption of blood or forfeiture, except during the life of the person attainted.

Article IV.

SECTION 1.—Full faith and credit shall be given in each State to the public acts, records, and judicial proceedings of every other State. And the Congress may by general laws prescribe the manner in which such acts, records, and proceedings shall be proved, and the effect thereof.

SEC. 2.—The citizens of each State shall be entitled to all privileges and immunities of citizens in the several States.

A person charged in any State with treason, felony, or other crime, who shall flee from justice, and be found in another State, shall, on demand of the executive authority of the State from which he fled, be delivered up, to be removed to the State having jurisdiction of the crime.

No person held to service or labor in one State under the laws thereof, escaping into another, shall, in consequence of any law or regulation therein, be discharged from such service or labor, but shall be delivered up on claim of the party to whom such service or labor may be due.

SEC. 3.—New States may be admitted by the Congress into this Union; but no new State shall be formed or erected within the jurisdiction of any other State; nor any State be formed by the junction of two or more States, or parts of States, without the consent of the legislature of the States concerned, as well as of the Congress.

The Congress shall have power to dispose of and make all needful rules and regulations respecting the territory or other property belonging to the United States; and nothing in this Constitution shall be so construed as to prejudice any claims of the United States, or of any particular State.

SEC. 4.—The United States shall guarantee to every State in this Union a republican form of government, and shall protect each of them against invasion; and on application of the legislature, or of the executive (when the legislature can not be convened), against domestic violence.

Article V.

The Congress, whenever two-thirds of both houses shall deem it necessary, shall propose amendments to this Constitution, or, on the application of the legislatures of two-thirds of the several States, shall call a convention for proposing amendments, which, in either case, shall be valid, to all intents and purposes, as part of this Constitution, when ratified by the legislatures of three-fourths of the several States. or by conventions in three-fourths thereof, as the one or the other mode of ratification may be proposed by the Congress; Provided, that no amendment, which may be made prior to the year one thousand eight hundred and eight, shall in any manner affect the first and fourth clauses in the ninth section of the first article; and that no State, without its consent, shall be deprived of its equal suffrage in the Senate.

Article VI.

All debts contracted, and engagements entered in to, before the adoption of this Constitution, shall be as valid against the United States under this Constitution, as under the Confederation.

This Constitution, and the laws of the United States which shall be made in pursuance thereof; and all treaties made, or which shall be made, under the authority of the United States, shall be the supreme law of the land; and the judges in every State shall be bound thereby, any thing in the constitution or laws of any State to the contrary notwithstanding.

The senators and representatives before mentioned, and the members of the several State legislatures, and all executive and judicial officers, both of the United States and of the several States, shall be bound by oath or affirmation to support this Constitution; but no religious test shall ever be required as a qualification to any office or public trust under the United States.

Article VII.

The ratification of the conventions of nine States shall be sufficient for the establishment of this Constitution between the States so ratifying the same.

Done in Convention by the unanimous consent of the States present, the seventeenth day of September, in the year of our Lord one thousand seven hundred and eighty-seven, and of the Independence of the United States of America the twelfth. In witness whereof we have hereunto subscribed our names.

GEORGE WASHINGTON, *President, and Deputy from Virginia.*

NEW HAMPSHIRE.—John Langdon, Nicholas Gilman.
MASSACHUSETTS.—Nathaniel Gorham, Rufus King.
CONNECTICUT.—William Samuel Johnson, Roger Sherman.
NEW YORK.—Alexander Hamilton.
NEW JERSEY.—William Livingston, David Bearly, William Patterson, Jonathan Dayton.
PENNSYLVANIA.—Benjamin Franklin, Thomas Mifflin, Robert Morris, George Clymer, Thomas Fitzsimons, Jared Ingersoll, James Wilson, Gouverneur Morris.
DELAWARE.—George Read, Gunning Bedford, Jr., John Dickinson, Richard Bassett, Jacob Broom.
MARYLAND.—James McHenry, Daniel of St. Thomas Jenifer, Daniel Carroll.
VIRGINIA.—John Blair, James Madison, Jr.
NORTH CAROLINA.—William Blount, Richard Dobbs Spaight, Hugh Williamson.
SOUTH CAROLINA.—John Rutledge, Charles Cotesworth Pinckney, Charles Pinckney, Pierce Butler.
GEORGIA.—William Few, Abraham Baldwin.

Attest:

WILLIAM JACKSON, *Secretary.*

Amendments to the Constitution.

Article I.

Congress shall make no law respecting an establishment of religion, or prohibiting the free exercise thereof; or abridging the freedom of speech or of the press; or the right of the people peaceably to assemble, and to petition the government for a redress of grievances.

Article II.

A well-regulated militia being necessary to the security of a free State, the right of the people to keep and bear arms shall not be infringed.

Article III.

No soldier shall, in time of peace, be quartered in any house without the consent of the owner; nor in time of war, but in a manner to be prescribed by law.

Article IV.

The right of the people to be secure in their persons, houses, papers, and effects, against unreasonable searches and seizures, shall not be violated; and no warrants shall issue but upon probable cause, supported by oath or affirmation, and particularly describing the place to be searched and the person or things to be seized.

Article V.

No person shall be held to answer for a capital or otherwise infamous crime, unless on a presentment or indictment of a grand jury, except in cases arising in the land or naval forces, or in the militia when in actual service in time of war or public danger; nor shall any person be subject, for the same offence, to be twice put in jeopardy of life or limb; nor shall be compelled, in any criminal case, to be a witness against himself; nor be deprived of life, liberty, or property, without due process of law; nor shall private property be taken for public use without just compensation.

Article VI.

In all criminal prosecutions, the accused shall enjoy the right to a speedy and public trial, by an impartial jury of the State and district wherein the crime shall have been committed, which district shall have been previously ascertained by law; and to he informed of the nature and cause of the accusation; to be confronted with the witnesses against him; to have compulsory process for obtaining witnesses in his favor and to have the assistance of counsel for his defence.

Article VII.

In suits at common law, where the value in controversy shall exceed twenty dollars, the right of trial by jury shall be preserved and no fact tried by a jury shall be otherwise re-examined in any court of the United States than according to the rules of the common law.

Article VIII.

Excessive bail shall not be required, nor excessive fines imposed, nor cruel and unusual punishments inflicted.

Article IX.

The enumeration in the Constitution of certain rights, shall not be construed to deny or disparage others retained by the people.

Article X.

The powers not delegated to the United States by the Constitution, nor prohibited by it to the States, are reserved to the States respectively, or to the people.

Article XI.

The judicial power of the United States shall not be construed to extend to any suit in law or equity, commenced or prosecuted against one of the United States by citizens of another State, or by citizens or subjects of any foreign State.

Article XII.

The electors shall meet in their respective States, and vote by ballot for President and Vice-President, one of whom, at least, shall not be an inhabitant of the same State with themselves; they shall name in their ballots the person voted for as President, and in distinct ballots the person voted for as Vice-President; and they shall make distinct lists of all persons voted for as President, and of all persons voted for as Vice-President, and of the number of votes for each, which lists they shall sign and certify, and transmit sealed to the seat of the government of the United States, directed to the president of the Senate; the president of the Senate shall, in the presence of the Senate and House of Representatives, open all the certificates, and the votes shall then be counted; the person having the greatest number of votes for President shall be the President, if such number he a majority of the whole number of electors appointed; and if no person have such, majority, then from the persons having the highest numbers, not exceeding threw on the list of those voted for as President, the House of Representatives shall choose immediately, by ballot, the President. But, in choosing the President, the votes shall be taken by States, the representation from each State having one vote; a quorum for this purpose shall consist of a member or members from two-thirds of the States, and a majority of all the States shall be necessary to a choice. And if the House of Representatives shall not choose a President, whenever the right of choice shall devolve upon them, before the fourth day of March next following, then the Vice-President shall act as President, as in the case of the death or other constitutional disability of the President.

The person having the greatest number of votes as Vice-President, shall be the Vice-President, if such number be a majority of the whole number of electors appointed; and if no person have a majority, then from the two highest numbers on the list, the Senate shall choose the Vice-President; a quorum for the purpose shall consist of two thirds of the whole number of senators, and a majority of the whole number shall be necessary to a choice.

But no person constitutionally ineligible to the Office of President, shall be eligible to that of Vice-President of the United States.

Article XIII.

SECTION 1.—Neither slavery nor involuntary servitude, except as a punishment for crime, whereof the party shall have been duly convicted, shall exist within the United States, or any place subject to their jurisdiction.

SEC. 2.—Congress shall have power to enforce this Article by appropriate legislation.

Article XIV.

SECTION 1.—All persons born or naturalized in the United States, and subject to the jurisdiction thereof, are citizens of the United States and of the State wherein they reside. No State shall make or enforce any law which shall abridge the privileges or immunities of citizens of the United States; nor shall any State deprive any person of life, liberty, or property, without due process of law, nor deny to any person within its jurisdiction the equal protection of the laws.

SEC. 2.—Representatives shall be apportioned among the several States, according to their respective numbers, counting the whole number of persons in each State, excluding Indians not taxed. But when the right to vote at any election for choice of electors for President and Vice-President of the United States, representatives in Congress, the executive and judicial officers of a State, or the members of the legislature thereof, is denied to any of the male inhabitants of such State being twenty-one years of age, and citizens of the United States, or in any way abridged, except for participation in rebellion or other crime, the basis of representation therein shall be reduced in the proportion which the number of such male citizens shall bear to the whole number of male citizens twenty-one years of age in such State.

SEC. 3.—No person shall be a senator, or representative in Congress, or elector of President and Vice-President, or hold any office, civil or military, under the United States, or under any State, who, having previously taken an oath as a member of Congress, or as an officer of the United States, or as a member of any State legislature, or as an executive or judicial officer of any State, to support the Constitution of the United States, shall have engaged in insurrection or rebellion against the same, or given aid or comfort to the enemies thereof; but Congress may, by a vote of two-thirds of each house, remove such disability.

SEC. 4.—The validity of the public debt of the United States authorized by law, including debts incurred for payment of pensions, and bounties for services in suppressing insurrection or rebellion, shall not be questioned. But neither the United States, nor any State, shall assume or pay any debt or obligation incurred in aid of insurrection or rebellion against the United States, or any claim for the loss or emancipation of any slave; but all such debts, obligations, and claims shall be held illegal and void.

SEC. 5.—The Congress shall have power to enforce by appropriate legislation the provisions of this Article.

Article XV.

SECTION 1.—The right of citizens of the United States to vote shall not be denied or abridged by the United States, or by any State, on account of race, color, or previous condition of servitude.

SEC. 2.—The Congress shall have power to enforce this Article by appropriate legislation.

APPENDIX F.

WASHINGTON'S FAREWELL ADDRESS.

FRIENDS AND FELLOW-CITIZENS:—

THE period for a new election of a citizen to administer the executive government of the United States being not far distant, and the time actually arrived when your thoughts must be employed in designating the person who is to be clothed with that important trust, it appears to me proper, especially as it may conduce to a more distinct expression of the public voice, that I should now apprise you of the resolution I have formed, to decline being considered among the number of those out of whom a choice is to be made.

I beg you, at the same time, to do me the justice to be assured that this resolution has not been taken without a strict regard to all the considerations appertaining to the relation which binds a dutiful citizen to his country; and that, in withdrawing the tender of service, which silence in my situation might imply, I am influenced by no diminution of zeal for your future interest; no deficiency of grateful respect for your past kindness; but am supported by a full conviction that the step is compatible with both.

The acceptance of, and continuance hitherto in, the office to which your suffrages have twice called me, have been a uniform sacrifice of inclination to the opinion of duty, and to a deference for what appeared to be your desire. I constantly hoped that it would have been much earlier in my power, consistently with motives which I was not at liberty to disregard, to return to that retirement from which I had been reluctantly drawn. The strength of my inclination to do this, previous to the last election, had even led to the preparation of an address to declare it to you; but mature reflection on the then perplexed and critical posture of our affairs with foreign nations, and the unanimous advice of persons entitled to my confidence, impelled me to abandon the idea.

I rejoice that the state of your concerns, external as well as internal, no longer renders the pursuit of inclination incompatible with the sentiment of duty or propriety; and am persuaded, whatever partiality may be retained for my services, that, in the present circumstances of our country, you will not disapprove of my determination to retire.

The impressions with which I first undertook the arduous trust were explained on the proper occasion. In the discharge of this trust, I will only say that I have, with good intentions, contributed towards the organization and administration of the government the best exertions of which a very fallible judgment was capable. Not unconscious in the outset of the inferiority of any qualifications, experience, in my own—eyes perhaps still more in the eyes of others—has strengthened the motives to diffidence of myself; and every nay the increasing weight of years admonishes me, more and more, that the shade of retirement is as necessary to me as it will be welcome. Satisfied that if any circumstances have given peculiar value to my services they were temporary, I have the consolation to believe that, while choice and prudence invite me to quit the political scene, patriotism does not forbid it.

In looking forward to the moment which is intended to terminate the career of my public life, my feelings do not permit me to suspend the deep acknowledgment of that debt of gratitude which I owe to my beloved country for the many honors it has conferred upon me; still more for the steadfast confidence with which it has supported me; and for the opportunities I have thence enjoyed of manifesting my inviolable attachment, by services faithful and persevering, though in usefulness unequal to my zeal. If benefits have resulted to our country from these services, let it always be remembered to your praise, and as an instructive example in our annals, that, under circumstances in which the passions, agitated in every direction, were liable to mislead; amidst appearances sometimes dubious, vicissitudes of fortune often discouraging; in situations in which, not unfrequently, want of success has countenanced the spirit of criticism the constancy of your support was the essential prop of the efforts, and a guarantee of the plans, by which they were effected. Profoundly penetrated with this idea, I shall carry it with me to my grave, as a strong incitement to unceasing wishes, that Heaven may continue to you the choicest tokens of its beneficence; that your union and brotherly affection may be perpetual; that the free Constitution, which is the work of your hands, may be sacredly maintained; that its administration, in every department, may be stamped with wisdom and virtue; that, in fine, the happiness of the people of these States, under the auspices of liberty, may be made complete, by so careful a preservation and so prudent a use of this blessing as will acquire to them the glory of recommending it to the applause, the affection, and adoption of every nation which is yet a stranger to it.

Here, perhaps, I ought to stop; but a solicitude for your welfare, which can not end but with my life, and the apprehension of danger natural to that solicitude, urge me, on an occasion like the present, to offer to your solemn contemplation, and to recommend to your frequent review, some sentiments which are the result of much reflection, of no inconsiderable observation, and which appear to me all-important to the permanency of your felicity as a people. These will be offered to you with the more freedom, as you can only see in them the disinterested warnings of a parting friend, who can possibly have no personal motive to bias his counsels; nor can I forget, as an encouragement to it, your indulgent reception of my sentiments on a former and not dissimilar occasion.

Interwoven as is the love of liberty with every ligament of your hearts, no recommendation of mine is necessary to fortify or confirm the attachment.

The Unity of Government, which constitutes you one people, is also now dear to you. It is justly so; for it is a main pillar in the edifice of your real independence—the support of your tranquillity at home, your peace abroad, of your safety, of your prosperity, of that very liberty which you so highly prize. But as it is easy to foresee that, from different causes and from different quarters, much pains will be taken, many artifices employed, to weaken in your minds the conviction of this truth; as this is the point in your political fortress against which the batteries of internal and external enemies will be most constantly and actively (though often covertly and insidiously) directed—it is of infinite moment that you should properly estimate the immense value of your National Union to your collective and individual happiness; that you should cherish a cordial, habitual, and immovable attachment to it; accustoming yourselves to think and speak of it as the palladium Of your political safety and prosperity; watching for its preservation with jealous anxiety; discountenancing whatever may suggest even a suspicion that it can, in any event, be abandoned; and indignantly frowning upon the first dawning of every attempt to alienate any portion of our country from the rest, or to enfeeble the sacred ties which now link together the various parts.

For this you have every inducement of sympathy and interest. Citizens by birth or choice, of a common country, that country has a right to concentrate your affections. The name of *American*, which belongs to you in your national capacity, must always exalt the just pride of patriotism, more than any appellation derived from local discriminations. With slight shades of difference, you have the same religion, manners, habits, and political principles. You have, in a common cause, fought and triumphed together; the independence and liberty you possess are the work of joint counsels and joint efforts—of common dangers, sufferings, and successes.

But these considerations, however powerfully they address themselves to your sensibility, are greatly outweighed by those which apply more immediately to your interest: here every portion of our country finds the most commanding motives for carefully guarding and preserving the union of the whole.

The North, in an unrestrained intercourse with the South, protected by the equal laws of a common government, finds, in the productions of the latter, great additional resources of maritime and commercial enterprise, and precious materials of manufacturing industry. The South, in the same intercourse, benefiting by the agency of the North, sees its agriculture grow, and its commerce expand. Turning partly into its own channels the seamen of the North, it finds its particular navigation invigorated; and while it contributes, in different ways, to nourish and increase the general mass of the national navigation, it looks forward to the protection of a maritime strength to which itself is unequally adapted. The East, in a like intercourse with the West, already finds, and in the progressive improvement of interior communications, by land and water, will more and more find a valuable vent for the commodities which it brings from abroad, or manufactures at home. The West derives from the East supplies requisite to its growth and comfort—and what is perhaps of still greater consequence, it must of necessity owe the secure enjoyment of indispensable outlets for its own productions to the weight, influence, and the future maritime strength of the Atlantic side of the Union, directed by an indissoluble community of interest as one nation. Any other tenure by which the West can hold this essential advantage, whether derived from its own separate strength, or from an apostate and unnatural connection with any foreign power, must be intrinsically precarious.

While, then, every part of our country thus feels an immediate and particular interest in Union, all the parts combined can not fail to find in the united mass of means and efforts, greater strength, greater resource, proportionably greater security from external danger, a less frequent interruption of their peace by foreign nations; and what is of inestimable value, they must derive from Union an exemption from those broils and wars between themselves, which so frequently afflict neighboring countries, not tied together by the same government; which their own rivalships alone would be sufficient to produce, but which opposite foreign alliances, attachments, and intrigues would stimulate and embitter. Hence, likewise, they will avoid the necessity of those overgrown military establishments, which under any form of government are inauspicious to liberty, and which are to be regarded as particularly hostile to Republican Liberty. In this sense it is, that your Union ought to be considered as the main prop of your liberty, and that the love of the one ought to endear to you the preservation of the other.

These considerations speak a persuasive language to every reflecting and virtuous mind, and exhibit the continuance of the Union as a primary object of patriotic desire. Is there a doubt whether a common government can embrace so large a sphere? Let experience solve it. To listen to mere speculation in such a case were criminal. We are authorized to hope that a proper organization of the whole, with the auxiliary agency of governments for the respective subdivisions, will afford a happy issue to the experiment. It is well worth a fair and full experiment. With such powerful and obvious motives to Union affecting all parts of our country, while experience shall not have demonstrated its impracticability, there will always be reason to distrust the patriotism of those who in any quarter may endeavor to weaken its bands.

In contemplating the causes which may disturb our Union, it occurs as matter of serious concern, that any ground should have been furnished for characterizing parties by geographical discriminations—*Northern* and *Southern*, *Atlantic* and *Western*; whence designing men may endeavor to excite a belief that there is a real difference of local interests and views. One of the expedients of party to acquire influence, within particular districts, is to misrepresent the opinions and aims of other districts. You can not shield yourselves too much against the jealousies and heart-burnings which spring from these misrepresentations; they tend to render alien to each other those who ought to be bound together by fraternal affection. The inhabitants of our Western country have lately had a useful lesson on this head: they have seen, in the negotiation by the executive, and in the unanimous ratification by the Senate, of the treaty with Spain, and in the universal satisfaction at the event throughout the United States, a decisive proof how unfounded were the suspicions propagated among them of a policy in the general government, and in the Atlantic States, unfriendly to their interests in regard to the Mississippi: they have been witnesses to the formation of two treaties, that with Great Britain and that with Spain, which secure to them every thing they could desire, in respect to our foreign relations, towards confirming their prosperity. Will it not be their wisdom to rely for the preservation of these advantages on the UNION by which they were procured? Will they not henceforth be deaf to those advisers, if such there are, who would sever them from their brethren, and connect them with aliens?

To the efficacy and permanency of your Union, a government for the whole is indispensable. No alliances, however strict, between the parts can be an adequate substitute; they must inevitably experience the infractions and interruptions which all alliances in all times have experienced. Sensible of this momentous truth, you have improved upon your first essay, by the adoption of a Constitution of government better calculated than your former for an intimate Union, and for the efficacious management of your Common concerns. This government, the offspring of your own choice, uninfluenced and unawed, adopted upon full investigation and mature deliberation, completely free in its principles, in the distribution of its powers, uniting security with energy, and containing within itself a provision for its own amendment, has a just claim to your confidence and your support. Respect for its authority, compliance with its laws, acquiescence in its measures, are duties enjoined by the fundamental maxims of true liberty. The basis of our political systems is the right of the people to make, and to alter their constitutions of government. But the constitution which at any time exists, until changed by an explicit and authentic act of the whole people, is sacredly obligatory upon all. The very idea of the power and the right of the people to establish government, presupposes the duty of every individual to obey the established government.

All obstructions to the execution of the laws, all combinations and associations, under whatever plausible character, with the real design to direct, control, counteract or awe the regular deliberation and action of the constituted authorities, are destructive of this fundamental principle, and of fatal tendency. They serve to organize faction, to give it an artificial and extraordinary force—to put in the place of the delegated will of the nation, the will of a party, often a small but artful and enterprising minority of the community and, according to the alternate triumphs of different parties, to make the public administration the mirror of the ill-concerted and incongruous projects of faction, rather than the organ of consistent and wholesome plans digested by common councils and modified by mutual interests.

However combinations or associations of the above description may now and then answer popular ends, they are likely, in the course of time and things, to become potent engines, by which cunning, ambitious, and unprincipled men will be enabled to subvert the power of the people, and to usurp for themselves the reins of government; destroying afterward the very engines which have lifted them to unjust dominion.

Towards the preservation of your government, and the permanency of your present happy state, it is requisite, not only that you steadily discountenance irregular opposition to its acknowledged authority, but also that you resist with care the spirit of innovation upon its principles, however specious the pretexts. One method of assault may be to effect in the forms of the Constitution alterations which will impair the energy of the system, and thus to undermine what can not be directly overthrown. In all the changes to which you may be invited, remember that time and habit are at least as necessary to fix the true character of governments, as of other human institutions; that experience is the surest standard by which to test the real tendency of the existing constitution of a country—that facility in changes upon the credit of mere hypothesis and opinion, exposes to perpetual change from the endless variety of hypothesis and opinion; and remember, especially, that for the efficient management of your common interests, in a country so extensive as ours, a government of as much vigor as is consistent with the perfect security of liberty, is indispensable. Liberty itself will find in such a government, with powers properly distributed and adjusted, its surest guardian. It is, indeed, little else than a name, where the government is too feeble to withstand the enterprises of faction, to confine each member of the society within the limits prescribed by the laws, and to maintain all in the secure and tranquil enjoyment of the rights of person and property.

I have already intimated to you the danger of parties in the state, with particular reference to the founding of them on geographical discriminations. Let me now take a more comprehensive view, and warn you in the most solemn manner against the baneful effects of the spirit of party, generally.

This spirit, unfortunately, is inseparable from our nature, having its root in the strongest passions of the human mind. It exists under different shapes in all governments, more or less stifled, controlled, or repressed but in those of the popular form, it is seen in its greatest rankness, and it is truly their worst enemy. The alternate domination of one faction over another, sharpened by the spirit of revenge, natural to party dissension, which in different ages and countries has perpetrated the most horrid enormities, is itself a frightful despotism. But this leads at length to a more formal and permanent despotism. The disorders and miseries which result, gradually incline the minds of men to seek security and repose in the absolute power of an individual; and sooner or later the chief of some prevailing faction, more able or more fortunate than his competitors, turns this disposition to the purposes of his own elevation, on the ruins of public liberty.

Without looking forward to an extremity of this kind (which, nevertheless, ought not to be entirely out of sight), the common and continual mischiefs of the spirit of party are sufficient to make it the interest and the duty of a wise people to discourage and restrain it.

It serves always to distract the public councils, and enfeeble the public administration. It agitates the community with ill-founded jealousies and false alarms; kindles the animosity of one part against another, foments occasionally riot and insurrection. It opens the door to foreign influence and corruption, which find a facilitated access to the government itself through the channels of party passions. Thus the policy and the will of one country are subjected to the policy and will of another.

There is an opinion that parties in free countries are useful checks upon the administration of government, and serve to keep alive the spirit of liberty. This within certain limits is probably true; and in governments of a monarchical cast, patriotism may look with indulgence, if not with favor, upon the spirit of party. But in those of the popular character, in governments purely elective, it is a spirit not to be encouraged. From their natural tendency it is certain there will always be enough of that spirit for every salutary purpose. And there being constant danger of excess, the effort ought to be, by force of public opinion, to mitigate and assuage it. A fire not to be quenched, it demands a uniform vigilance to prevent its bursting into a flame, lest, instead of warming, it should consume.

It is important, likewise, that the habits, of thinking, in a free country, should inspire caution in those intrusted with its administration, to confine themselves within their respective constitutional spheres, avoiding in the exercise of the powers of one department to encroach upon another. The spirit of encroachment tends to consolidate the powers of all the departments in one, and thus to create, whatever the form of government, a real despotism. A just estimate of that love of power, and proneness to abuse it, which predominates in the human heart, is sufficient to satisfy us of the truth of this position. The necessity of reciprocal checks in the exercise of political power, by dividing and distributing it into different depositories, and constituting each the guardian of the public weal against invasions by the others, has been evinced by experiments ancient and modern; some of them in our country and under our own eyes. To preserve them must be as necessary as to institute them. If, in the opinion of the people, the distribution or modification of the constitutional powers be in any particular wrong, let it be corrected by an amendment in the war which the Constitution designates. But let there be no change by usurpation; for though this, in one instance, may be the instrument of good, it is the customary weapon by which free governments are destroyed. The precedent must always greatly overbalance in permanent evil any partial or transient benefit which the use can at any time yield.

Of all the dispositions and habits which lead to political prosperity, religion and morality are indispensable supports. In vain would that man claim the tribute of patriotism, who should labor to subvert these great pillars of human happiness, these firmest props of the duties of men and citizens. The mere politician, equally with the pious man, ought to respect and to cherish them. A volume could not trace all their connections with private and public felicity. Let it simply be asked, where is the security for property, for reputation, for life, if the sense of religious obligation desert the oaths which are the instruments of investigation in courts of justice? And let us with caution indulge the supposition, that morality can be maintained without religion. Whatever may be conceded to the influence of refined education on minds of peculiar structure, reason and experience both forbid us to expect that national morality can prevail in exclusion of religious principle.

It is substantially true, that virtue or morality is a necessary spring of popular government. The rule indeed extends with more or less force to every species of free government. Who that is a sincere friend to it, can look with indifference upon attempts to shake the foundation of the fabric?

Promote then, as an object of primary importance, institutions for the general diffusion of knowledge. In proportion as the structure of a government gives force to public opinion, it is essential that public opinion should be enlightened.

As a very important source of strength and security, cherish public credit. One method of preserving it is to use it as sparingly as possible, avoiding occasions of expense by cultivating peace; but remembering also that timely disbursements to prepare for danger, frequently prevent much greater disbursements to repel it; avoiding likewise the accumulation of debt, not only by shunning occasions of expense, but by vigorous exertions in time of peace to discharge the debts which unavoidable wars may have occasioned, not ungenerously throwing upon posterity the burden which we ourselves ought to bear. The execution of these maxims belongs to your Representatives, but it is necessary that public opinion should co-operate. To facilitate to them the performance of their duty, it is essential that you should practically bear in mind, that toward the payment of debts there must be revenue; that to have revenue there must be taxes; that no taxes can be devised which are not more or less inconvenient and unpleasant; that the intrinsic embarrassment inseparable from the selection of the proper objects (which is always a choice of difficulties) ought to be a decisive motive for a candid construction of the conduct of the government in making it, and for a spirit of acquiescence in the measures for obtaining revenue which the public exigencies may at any time dictate.

Observe good faith and justice towards all nations, cultivate peace and harmony with all; religion and morality enjoin this conduct, and can it be that good policy does not equally enjoin it? It will be worthy of a free, enlightened, and, at no distant period, a great nation, to give to mankind the magnanimous and too novel example of a people always guided by an exalted justice and benevolence. Who can doubt but that in the course of time and things, the fruits of such a plan would richly repay any temporary advantage which might be lost by a steady adherence to it? Can it be that Providence has not connected the permanent felicity of a nation with its virtue? The experiment, at least, is recommended by every sentiment which ennobles human nature. Alas! is it rendered impossible by its vices?

In the execution of such a plan, nothing is more essential than that permanent, inveterate antipathies against particular nations, and passionate attachments for others, should be excluded; and that in place of them just and amicable feelings towards all should be cultivated. The nation which indulges toward another an habitual hatred or an habitual fondness, is in some degree a slave. It is a slave to its animosity or its affection, either of which is sufficient to lead it astray from its duty and its interests. Antipathy in one nation against another, disposes each more readily to offer insult and injury, to lay hold of slight causes of umbrage, and to be haughty and intractable, when accidental or trifling occasions of dispute occur. Hence frequent collisions, obstinate, envenomed, and bloody contests. The nation, prompted by ill-will and resentment, sometimes impels to war the government, contrary to the best calculations of policy. The government sometimes participates in the national propensity, and adopts through passion what reason would reject; at other times, it makes the animosity of the nation subservient to projects of hostility instigated by pride, ambition, and other sinister and pernicious motives. The peace often, sometimes perhaps the liberty, of nations has been the victim.

So, likewise, a passionate attachment of one nation for another produces a variety of evils. Sympathy for the favorite nation, facilitating the illusion of an imaginary common interest in cases where no real common interest exists, and infusing into one the enmities of the other, betrays the former into a participation in the quarrels and wars of the latter, without adequate inducement or justification. It leads also to concessions to the favorite nation of privileges denied to others, which is apt doubly to injure the nation making the concessions, by unnecessarily parting with what ought to have been retained; and by exciting jealousy, ill-will, and a disposition to retaliate, in the parties from whom equal privileges are withheld. And it gives to ambitious, corrupted, or deluded citizens (who devote themselves to the favorite nation) facility to betray or sacrifice the interests of their own country, without odium, sometimes even with popularity; gilding with the appearance of a virtuous sense of obligation a commendable deference for public opinion, or a laudable zeal for public good, the base or foolish compliances of ambition, corruption, or infatuation.

As avenues to foreign influence in innumerable ways, such attachments are particularly alarming to the truly enlightened and independent patriot. How many opportunities do they afford to tamper with domestic factions; to practice the arts of sedition, to mislead public opinion, to influence or awe the public councils! Such an attachment of a small and weak, towards a great and powerful nation, dooms the former to be the satellite of the latter. Against the insidious wiles of foreign influence (I conjure you to believe me, fellow-citizens,) the jealousy of a free people ought to be constantly awake; since history and experience prove that foreign influence is one of the most baneful foes of Republican Government. But that jealousy be useful must be impartial; else it becomes the instrument of the very influence to be avoided, instead of a defence against it. Excessive partiality for one foreign nation, and excessive dislike of another, cause those whom they actuate to see danger only on one side, and serve to veil and even second the arts of influence on the other. Real patriots, who may resist the intrigues of the favorite, are liable to become suspected and odious; while its tools and dupes usurp the applause and confidence of the people, to surrender their interest.

The great rule of conduct for us, in regard to foreign nations, is, in extending our commercial relations, to have with them as little *political* connection as possible. So far as we have already formed engagements, let them be fulfilled with perfect good faith. Here let us stop.

Europe has a set of primary interests, which to us have none, or a very remote relation. Hence she must be engaged in frequent controversies, the causes of which are essentially foreign to our concerns. Hence, therefore, it must be unwise in us to implicate ourselves, by artificial ties, in the ordinary vicissitudes of her politics, or the ordinary combinations and collisions of her friendships or enmities.

Our detached and distant situation invites and enables us to pursue a different course. If we remain one people, under an efficient government, the period is not far off when we may defy material injury from external annoyance; when we take such an attitude as will cause the neutrality we may at any time resolve upon to be scrupulously respected; when belligerent nations, under the impossibility of making acquisitions upon us, will not lightly hazard the giving us provocation; when we may choose peace or war, as our interest, guided by justice, shall counsel.

Why forego the advantages of so peculiar a situation? Why quit your own to stand upon foreign ground? Why, by interweaving our destiny with that of any part of Europe, entangle our peace and prosperity in the toils of European ambition, rivalship, interest, humor, or caprice?

It is our true policy to steer clear of permanent alliances with any portion of the foreign world—so far, I mean, as we are now at liberty to do it; for let me not be understood as capable of patronizing infidelity to existing engagements. I hold the maxim no less applicable to public than to private affairs, that honesty is always the best policy. I repeat it, therefore, let those engagements be observed in their genuine sense. But, in my opinion, it is unnecessary, and would be unwise to extend them.

Taking care always to keep ourselves, by suitable establishments, on a respectable defensive posture, we may safely trust to temporary alliances for extraordinary emergencies.

Harmony, and liberal intercourse with all nations, are recommended by policy, humanity, and interest.

But even our commercial policy should hold an equal and impartial hand; neither seeking nor granting exclusive favors or preferences;—consulting the natural course of things; diffusing and diversifying by gentle means the streams of commerce, but forcing nothing; establishing, with powers so disposed, in order to give trade a stable course, to define the rights of our merchants, and to enable the government to support them, conventional rules of intercourse, the best that present circumstances and mutual opinion will permit, but temporary, and liable to be from time to time abandoned or varied, as experience and circumstances shall dictate; constantly keeping in view, that it is folly in one nation to look for disinterested favors from another; that it must pay with a portion of its independence for whatever it may accept under that character; that by such acceptance, it may place itself in the condition of having given equivalents for nominal favors, and yet of being reproached with ingratitude for not giving more. There can be no greater error than to expect, or calculate upon, real favors from nation to nation. It is an illusion which experience must cure, which a just pride ought to discard.

In offering to you, my countrymen, these counsels of an old and affectionate friend, I dare not hope they will make the strong and lasting impression I could wish—that they will control the usual current of the passions, or prevent our nation from running the course which has hitherto marked the destiny of nations. But if I may even flatter myself that they may be productive of some partial benefit, some occasional good; that they may now and then recur to moderate the fury of party spirit, to warn against the mischiefs of foreign intrigue, to guard against the impostures of pretended patriotism; this hope will be a full recompense for the solicitude for your welfare by which they have been dictated.

How far in the discharge of my official duties I have been guided by the principles which have been delineated, the public records and other evidences of my conduct must witness to you and to the world. To myself, the assurance of my own conscience is, that I have at least believed myself to be guided by them.

In relation to the still subsisting war in Europe, my proclamation of the 22d of April, 1793, is the index to my plan. Sanctioned by your approving voice, and by that of your Representatives in both Houses of Congress, the spirit of that measure has continually governed me, uninfluenced by any attempts to deter or divert me from it.

After deliberate examination, with the aid of the best lights I could obtain, I was well satisfied that our country, under all the circumstances of the case, had a right to take, and was bound in duty and interest to take, a neutral position. Having taken it, I determined, as far as should depend upon me, to maintain it with moderation, perseverance, and firmness.

The considerations which respect the right to hold this conduct, it is not necessary on this occasion to detail. I will only observe, that, according to my understanding of the matter, that right, so far from being denied by any of the belligerent Powers, has been virtually admitted by all.

The duty of holding a neutral conduct may be inferred, without any thing more from the obligation which justice and humanity imposes on every nation, in cases in which it is free to act, to maintain inviolate the relations of peace and amity towards other nations.

The inducements of interest for observing that conduct will best be referred to your own reflections and experience. With me, a predominant motive has been to endeavor to gain time to our country to settle and mature its yet recent institutions, and to progress, without interruption, to that degree of strength and consistency which is necessary to give it, humanly speaking, the command of its own fortunes.

Though, in reviewing the incidents of my administration, I am unconscious of intentional error, I am nevertheless too sensible of my defects, not to think it probable that I may have committed many errors. Whatever they may be, I fervently beseech the Almighty to avert or mitigate the evils to which they may tend. I shall also carry with me the hope that my country will never cease to view them with indulgence; and that after forty-five years of my life dedicated to its service, with an upright zeal, the faults of incompetent abilities will be consigned to oblivion, as myself must soon be to the mansions of rest.

Relying on its kindness in this as in other things, and actuated by that fervent love towards it, which is so natural to a man who views in it the native soil of himself and his progenitors for several generations; I anticipate with pleasing expectation that retreat, in which I promise myself to realize, without alloy, the sweet enjoyment of partaking, in the midst of my fellow-citizens, the benign influence of good laws under a free government—the ever favorite object of my heart, and the happy reward, as I trust, of our mutual cares, labors, and dangers.

G. WASHINGTON.

UNITED STATES, 17*th September*, 1796.

APPENDIX G.

THE EMANCIPATION PROCLAMATION.
BY THE PRESIDENT OF THE UNITED STATES OF AMERICA.

[If the Emancipation Proclamation is to be regarded as *the cause* of the freedom of the African race in the United States, then indeed must it be considered as among the most important documents known in history: perhaps the most important of all. The truer view of the case, however, seems to be this: The inexorable Logic of Events Was rapidly bringing about the emancipation of the slaves. The National government fell under a stringent necessity to strike a blow at the labor system of the Southern States. With every struggle of the war the sentiment of abolition at the North rose higher and higher. The President himself and the chief supporters of his administration had for years made no concealment of their desire that all men everywhere should be free. The *occasion* was at hand. Mr. Lincoln seized and generalized the facts, embodied them in his own words, and became for all time the oracle and interpreter of *National Necessity.*—THE AUTHOR.]

WHEREAS, on the twenty-second day of September, in the year of our Lord one thousand eight hundred and sixty-two, a Proclamation was issued by the President of the United States, containing among other things the following, to wit:

"That on the first day of January, in the year of our Lord one thousand eight hundred and sixty-three, all persons held as slaves within any State, or designated part of a State, the people whereof shall then be in rebellion against the United States, shall be then, thenceforward and forever free, and the executive government of the United States, including the military and naval authority thereof, will recognize and maintain the freedom of such persons, and will do no act or acts to repress such persons, or any of them, in any efforts they may make for their actual freedom."

"That the executive will, on the first day of January aforesaid, by proclamation, designate the States and parts of States, if any, in which the people thereof respectively shall then be in rebellion against the United States, and the fact that any State, or the people thereof, shall on that day be in good faith represented in the Congress of the United States by members chosen thereto at elections wherein a majority of the qualified voters of such State shall have participated, shall, in the absence of strong countervailing testimony, be deemed conclusive evidence that such State and the people thereof are not then in rebellion against the United States."

Now, therefore, I, ABRAHAM LINCOLN, President of the United States, by virtue of the power in me vested as Commander-in-Chief of the Army and Navy of the United States in time of actual armed rebellion against the authority and government of the United States, and as a fit and necessary war measure for suppressing said rebellion, do, on this first day of January, in the year of our Lord one thousand eight hundred and sixty-three, and in accordance with my purpose so to do, publicly proclaim for the full period of one hundred days from the day the first above mentioned, order and designate, as the States and parts of States wherein the people thereof respectively are this day in rebellion against the United States, the following, to wit:

ARKANSAS, TEXAS, LOUISIANA, (except the parishes of St. Bernard, Plaquemines, Jefferson, St. John, St. Charles, St. James, Ascension, Assumption, Terre Bonne, Lafourche, St. Mary, St. Martin, and Orleans, including the city of New Orleans), MISSISSIPPI, ALABAMA, FLORIDA, GEORGIA, SOUTH CAROLINA, NORTH CAROLINA, and VIRGINIA (except the forty-eight counties designated as West Virginia, and also the counties of Berkley, Accomac, Northampton, Elizabeth City, York, Princess Ann, and Norfolk, including the cities of Norfolk and Portsmouth), and which excepted parts are, for the present, left precisely as if this Proclamation were not issued.

And by virtue of the power and for the purpose aforesaid, I do order and declare that all persons held as slaves within said designated States and parts of States are, and henceforward shall be free; and that the executive government of the United States, including the military and naval authorities thereof, will recognize and maintain the freedom of said persons.

And I hereby enjoin upon the people so declared to be free, to abstain from all violence, unless in necessary self-defence, and I recommend to them that in all cases, when allowed, they labor faithfully for reasonable wages.

And I further declare and make known that such persons of suitable condition will be received into the armed service of the United States to garrison forts, positions, stations, and other places, and to man vessels of all sorts in said service.

And upon this act, sincerely believed to be an act of justice, warranted by the Constitution, upon military necessity, I invoke the considerate judgment of mankind and the gracious favor of Almighty God.

In testimony whereof, I have hereunto set my name, and caused the seal of the United States to be affixed.

[L. S.]   *Done at the City of Washington, this first day of January, in the year of our Lord one thousand eight hundred and sixty-three, and of the Independence of the United States the eighty-seventh.*

ABRAHAM LINCOLN.

By the President:
WILLIAM H. SEWARD,
Secretary of State.

PRONUNCIATION OF PROPER NAMES.

[E., English; E, French; S., Spanish; P., Portugese; It., Italian; G., German; N., Norse; Sw. Swedish; Pol., Polish; L., Latin; I., Indian]

Abenaki [I.], ăb-ĕ-**nah**-kĭ.
Abercrombie [E.], **ăb-ĕr**-krŭm-bĭ.
Adet [F.], ah-**dā**.
Adolphus [L.], ă-**dŏl**-fŭs.
Aix-la-Chapelle [F.], āks-lah-shah-**pĕl**.
Algonquin [I.], ăl-gŏn-**kĕn**.
Almonte [S.], ăl-**mon**-tĕ.
Alvarado [S.], ăl-v ă-**rah**-dō.
Ambrister [E.], ăm-**brĭs**-tĕr.
Amerigo Vespucci [It.], ah-mĕr-ē-gō vĕs-**poot**-chĕ.
Amidas [E.], **ăm**-ĭd-ăs.
Ampudia [S.], ăm-**poo**-dĭ-ā
André [F.], **ăn**-drā.
Antietam [E.], ăn-**tĕ**-tăm.
Antonio de Espego [S.], ahn-**tō**-nĭ-ō dā ĕs-pā-hō.
Arbuthnot [E.], **ahr**-bŭth-nŏt.
Arista [S.], ah-**rĭs**-tă.
Armada [S.], ahr-**mah**-dă.
Ashe [E.], **ăsh**.
Au Glaize [F.], ō-**glāz**.
Ayavalia [S.], ĭ-ah-**vahl**-yă.
Ayotla [S.], ĭ-**ŏt**-lă.
Aztecs [I.], **ăz**-tĕks.
Bahia [S.], bah-**ē**-ă.
Balfour [E.], băl-**foor**.
Barron [E.], **bahr**-rŏn.
Baum [E.], **bawm**.

Baumarchais [F.], bō-mahr-**shā**.
Bayard [E.], **bĭ**-ahrd.
Beaujeu [F.], bō-**zhŭ**.
Beauregard [F.], **bō**-rā-gahrd.
Beau-Sejour [F.], bō-sā-**zhoor**.
Bellomont [E.], **bĕl**-ō-mŏnt.
Bernard [E.], bĕr-**nahrd**.
Bienville [F.], bĕ-ong-**vĕl**.
Blennerhasset [E.], blĕn-nĕr-**hăs**-sĕt.
Blyth [E.], **blĭth**.
Boscawen [E.], bŏs-**kaw**-ĕn.
Buddhist [Sanscrit], **bood**-dĭst.
Bulkeley [E.], **bŭlk**-lĭ.
Burgoyne [E.], bŭr-**goin**.
Cabot [E.], **kăb**-ŏt.
Cadwallader [E.], kăd-**wahl**-lă-dĕr.
Canonchet [I.], kā-**nŏn**-shĕt.
Canonicus [I.], kā-**nŏn**-ĭ-kŭs.
Canseau [F.], kăn-**sō**.
Carleton [E.], **kahrl**-tŭn.
Cartier [F.], kahr-tĭ-**ā**.
Casimer [Sw.], **kăs**-ĭ-mĕr.
Castin [F.], kăs-**tăn**.
Chabot [F.], shă-**bō**.
Cham [Tartar], **kăm**.
Champe [E.], **kămp**.
Champlain [F.], shăm-**plăn**.
Chapultepec [S.], kah-pool-tā-**pĕk**.
Chaudiere [F.], shō-dĕ-**ār**.
Chauncey [E.], **chawn**-sĕ.
Cherbourg [F.], **shĕr**-boorg.
Cherokee [I.], **chĕr**-ō-kĕ.
Chickamauga [E.], chĭk-ă-**maw**-gă.
Chickasaws [I.], **chĭk**-ă-sawz.
Chicora [S.], chĕ-**kō**-ră.

Chignecto [I.], shĕ-**nĕk**-tō.
Chihuahua [S.], shĕ-**wah**-wah.
Choctaws [I.], **chŏk**-tawz.
Christison [Sw.], **krĭs**-tĭ-sŭn.
Christophe [S.], krĭs-**tō**-fĕ.
Chrysler [E.], **krĭs**-lĕr.
Churubusco [S.], koo-roo-**boos**-kō.
Clarendon [E.], **klăr**-ĕn-dŭn.
Cochrane [E.], **kŏk**-răn.
Coligni [F.], kō-**lēn**-yē.
Columbus [L.], kō-**lŭm**-bŭs.
Comanches [I.], kō-**măn**-chĕz.
Condé [F.], kŏn-**dā**.
Contreras [S.], kōn-**trā**-răs.
Copernicus [L.], kō-**pĕr**-nĭ-kŭs.
Copley [E.], **kōp**-lĕ.
Corees [I.] **kō**-rēz.
Cornwallis [E.], kawrn-**wahl**-lĭs.
Credit Mobilier [F.], crā-dĭ-mō-bĭl-ĭ-**ār**.
Croghan [E.] **krōg**-hăn.
Dacres [E.], **dăk**-ĕrz.
Dahlgren [E.], **dăl**-grĕn.
Darrah [E.], **dahr**-rah.
D'Anville [F.], dŏng-**vēl**.
D'Aubrey [F.], dō-**brā**.
Daye [E.], **dā**.
De Barras [F.], dŭ-bahr-**rah**.
Decatur [E.], dĕ-**kā**-tŭr.
De Fleury [F.], dŭ **flŭr**-ĭ.
De Grasse [F.], dŭ **grăs**.
De Kalb [F.], dŭ-**kahlb**.
Delaplace [F.], dŭ-lă-**plăs**.
De Monts [F.], dŭ **mong**.
D'Estaing [F.], d-**stăng**.
De Ternay [F.], dŭ-tĕr-**nā**.

De Vaca [S.], dā **vah**-kă.
De Vergor [F.], dŭ-vār-**gōr**.
De Villiers [F.], dŭ-věl-**yār**.
De Vries [F.], dŭ **vrēz**.
Dieskau [F.], dĕ-ĕs-kō.
Dominic de Gourges [F.], dō-măn-ēk dŭ **goorg**.
Dongan [E.], **dŭn**-găn.
Doniphan [E.], **dōn**-ĭ-făn.
Dupont [E.], dŭ-**pōnt**.
Du Quesne [F.], dē-**kān**.
Dyar [E.], **dĭ**-ăr.
Eldorado [S.], ĕl-dō-**rah**-dō.
Elkswatawa [I.], ĕlks-**wah**-tah-wah.
Emucfau [I.], ĕ-**mook**-faw.
Endicott [E.], **ĕn**-dĭ-kŏt.
Ericsson [E.], **ĕr**-ĭks-sŭn.
Erskine [E.], **ĕr**-skĭn.
Esopus [E.], ĕ-**sō**-pŭs.
Esquimaux [I.], **es**-kĭ-mōz.
Farragut [E.], **fahr**-ră-gŭ.
Ferdinand de Soto [S.], **fĕr**-dĭ-nahnd dā **sō**-tō.
Ferdinand Gorges [E.], **fĕr**-dĭ-nănd **gŏr**-jĕz.
Ferdinand Magellan [P.], **fĕr**-dĭ-nĕnd ma-**jel**-lăn.
Ferguson [E.], **fŭr**-gŭ-sŭn.
Fernandez de Cordova [S.], fĕr-**nahn**-dĕth dā **kōr**-dō-vă.
Fernando Cortez [S.], fĕr-**nahn**-dō **kōr**-tĕth.
Fouchet [F.], foo-**shā**.
Fraser [E.], **frā**-zĕr.
Freneau [E.], frĕ-**nō**.
Frobisher [E.], **frōb**-ĭsh-ĕr.
Frontenac [E.], frŏn-tĕ-**năk**.
Gabarus [E.], gă-**băr**-ŭs.
Galileo [It.], gah-lĭ-**lā**-ō.
Gambier [F.], gahm-bĭ-**ā**.
Ganowanian [I.], gahn-ō-**wahn**-ĭ-ăn.

Gaspar Cortereal [P.], **gahs**-pahr kōr-tā-rā-**ahl**
Gaspé [F.], găs-**pā**.
Gawen [E.], **gaw**-ĕn.
Genet [F.], zhĕ-**nā**.
Gillis [G.], **gĭl**-lĭs.
Gladwyn [E.], **glăd**-wĭn.
Gloucester [E.], **glŏs**-tĕr.
Godyn [E.], gō-**dĭn**.
Goffe [E.], **gawf**.
Gorgeana [E.], gŏr-jĕ-**ăn**-ă.
Gosnold [E.], **gŏs**-nōld.
Goulburn [E.], **gool**-bŭrn.
Grierson [E.], **grĕr**-sŭn.
Grijalva [S.], grĕ-**hahl**-vă.
Guerriere [F.], gĕr-rĭ-**ār**.
Gustavus [L.], gŭs-**tā**-vŭs.
Hakluyt [E.], **hăk**-loot.
Havre de Grace [F.], hahver-dŭ-**grăs**.
Hayne [E.], **hān**.
Heister [G.], **hĭs**-tĕr.
Herjulfson [N.], **hār**-yoolf-sōn.
Herkimer [E.], **hŭr**-kĭ-mĕr.
Hertel [F.], hĕr-**tĕl**.
Hochelaga [I.], hōk-ĕ-**lah**-gă.
Hosset [G.], **hōs**-sĕt.
Houston [E.], **hows**-tŭn.
Hovenden [E.], **hō**-vĕn-dĕn.
Hugenost [F.], **hū**-gĕ-nŏts.
Iroquois [I.], ĭr-ō-**kwah**.
Isabella [S.], ĭz-ă-**bĕl**-lă.
Isle-aux-Noix [F.], ĕl-ō-**nooah**.
Iuka [E.], ĭ-**yoo**-kă.
Jameson [E.], **jăm**-ĕ-sŭn.
Joris [G.], **yō**-rĭs.
Juan Ponce de Leon [S.], **hwahn pōn**-thā dā lā-**ōn**.

Juarez [S.], **hwah**-rĕth.
Jumonville [F.], zhē-mŏng-**vēl**.
Kamtchatkans [I.], kăm-**tchăt**-kănz.
Kearney [E.], **kahr**-nĕ.
Kearsarge [E.], **kahr**-sahr-gĕ, or **kĕr**-sahrj.
Kieft [E.], **kēft**.
Klamaths [I.], **klăm**-ăths.
Knowlton [E.], **nōl**-tŭn.
Knyphausen [G.], **nēp**-how-sĕn.
Kosciusko [Pol.], kŏs-sĭ-**ŭs**-kō.
Kossuth [G.], kōs-**shoot**.
Koszta [Hungarian], **kōt**-tă.
La Colle [F.], lă-**kŏl**.
La Fayette [F.], lă-fā-**ĕt**.
La Fitte [F.], lă-**fĭt**.
La Roche [F.], lă-**rōsh**.
La Roque [F.], lă-**rōk**.
La Salle [F.], lă-**săl**.
Lathrop [E.], **lā**-thrŭp.
Laudonière [F.], lō-dōn-nĭ-**ār**.
Laurie [E.], **law**-rĭ.
La Vega [S.], lah-**vā**-gă.
Le Bœuf [F.], lŭ-**bŭf**.
Leddra [E.], **lĕd**-ră.
Ledyard [E.], **lĕd**-yahrd.
Leisler [G.], **lĭs**-lĕr.
Leitch [E.], **lēch**.
Leverett [E.], **lĕv**-ĕr-ĕt.
Leyden [G.], **lī**-dĕn.
Lief Erickson [N.] **lēf ĕr**-ĭk-sŭn.
Lionel [S.], **lī**-ō-nĕl.
Lopez [S.], **lō**-pĕth.
Loudoun [E.], loo-**doon**.
Lucas Vasquez de Ayllon [S.], **loo**-kahs **vahs**-kĕth dā īl-**yōn**.
Lützen [G.], **lētz**-ĕn.

Luzerne [Swiss], loo-**zĕrn**.
Macdonough [E.], măk-**dŏn**-ŏ.
Macdougall [E.], măk-**doo**-găl.
Macomb [E.], mā-**kōm**.
Magaw [E.], mă-**gaw**.
Mandeville [E.], **măn**-dĕ-vĭl.
Manteo [I.], **mahn**-tĕ-ō.
Manuel [P.], **mahn**-oo-ăl.
Markham [E.], **mahrk**-ăm.
Marlborough [E.], **mahrl**-brŭ.
Massasoit [I.], măs-**săs**-ō-ĭt.
Mather [E.], **măthe**-ĕr.
Matoaka [I.], măt-ō-**ăk**-ă.
Matthews [E.], **măth**-ūz.
Maurepas [F.], mō-rĕ-**pah**.
Maximilian [G.], măx-ĭ-**mĭl**-yăn.
McCullough [E.], măk-**kul**-lō.
McIntosh [E.], **măk**-ĭn-tŏsh.
Meacham [E.]**,** **mē**-chăm.
Meigs [E.], **mĕgz**.
Meta Incognita [L.], **mē**-tă ĭn-**cŏg**-nĭ-tă.
Miantonomoh [I.], mĭ-ăn-tō-**nō**-mō.
Micanopy [I.], mĭ-**kăn**-ō-pĭ.
Minuit [G.], **mĭn**-oo-ĭt.
Mohegan [I.] mō-**hē**-găn.
Monckton [E.], **mŭnk**-tŭn.
Monk [E.], **mŭnk**.
Montcalm [F.], mŏnt-**kahm**.
Monteano [S.], mōn-tā-**ahn**-ō.
Montezuma [I.], mŏn-tĕ-**zoo**-mă.
Montmorenci [F.], mŏnt-mō-**rĕn**-sĭ.
Mosley [E.], **mŏs**-lĕ.
Moultrie [E.], **mōl**-trĭ.
Nairne [E.], **nārn**.
Nassau [F.], năs-**sō**.

Naumkeag [I.], nawm-kĕ-ăg.
Nipmucks [I.], nĭp-mŭks.
Nueces [S.], nwā-sĕs.
Okclawaha [I.], ŏk-lă-wāh-hah.
Odeneal [E.], ō-dĕn-ĕl.
Oglethorpe [E.], ō-gĕl-thŏrp.
O'Hara [E.], ō-hahr-ră.
Ojeda [S.], ō-hā-dă.
Okeechobee [I.], ō-kē-chō-bē.
Oldham [E.], ōld-ām.
Olustee [E.], ō-lŭs-tĕ.
Opecancanough [I.], ō-pĕ-kăn-kăn-ŏ.
Orapax [I.], ŏr-ă-păkx.
Osceola [I.], ŏs-sē-ō-lā.
Oswald [E.], ŏs-wawld.
Ouatanon [I.], waht-ă-nŏn.
Oxenstiern [Sw.] ōks-ēn-stērn.
Pamphilo de Narvaez [S.], pahm-fē-lō dā nahr-vah-ĕth
Pascua Florida [L.], pahs-koo-ă flōr-ĭ-dă.
Pauw [G.], paw.
Pedro Menendez [S.], pā-drō mā-lĕn-dĕth.
Pemaquid [I.], pĕm-ă-kwĭd.
Pepperell [E.], pĕp-pĕr-ĕl.
Pequod [I.], pē-kwōd.
Perote [S.], pă-rō-tĕ.
Pigot [E.], pĭg-ŏt.
Pitcairn [E.], pĭt-kărn.
Pizarro [S.], pē-thahr-rō.
Pocahontas [I.], pōk-ă-hŏn-tăs.
Poictiers [F.], pwah-tē-ă.
Point au Trembles [F.], pwăn tō trahmbl.
Pontchartrain [F.], pōn-shahr-trăn.
Powhatan [I.], pow-hăt-an.
Presque Isle [F.], prĕsk ēl.
Prevost [E.], prĕv-ōst.

Prideaux [F.], prē-**dō**.
Pulaski [Pol.], poo-**lahs**-kĭ.
Quantrell [E.], **kwahn**-trĕl.
Queretaro [S.], kā-rā-**tah**-rō.
Rahl [G.], **rahl**.
Releigh [E.], **raw**-lĭ.
Ratcliffe [E.], **răt**-klĭf.
Rawdon [E.], **raw**-dūn.
Raymbault [F.], rām-**bō**.
Revere [E.], rĕ-**vĕr**.
Riall [E.], **rī**-ăl.
Ribault [F.], rē-**bō**.
Roberval [F.], rōb-ĕr-**vahl**.
Rochambeau [F.], rō-shăm-**bō**.
Rochelle [F.], rō-**shēl**.
Roderigo Triana [S.], rōd-**rē**-gō trē-**ah**-nă.
Rosecrans [G.], **rōs**-ĕ-krahns.
Ryswick [G.], **rēs**-wĭk.
Saltillo [S.], sahl-**tēl**-yō.
Samosset [I.], **săm**-ō-sĕt.
Santa Maria [S.], **sahn**-tă mah-**rē**-ă.
Sassacus [I.], **săs**-săk-ŭs.
Sayle [E.], **sāl**.
Schuyler [E.], **skī**-lĕr.
Selish [I.], **sē**-lĭsh.
Seminoles [I.], **sĕm**-ĭ-nōlz.
Sheaffe [G.], **shăf**-fĕ.
Shoshonees [I.], shō-**shō**-nēz.
Sicklemore [E.], **sĭk**-ĕl-mōr.
Sloughter [E.], **slō**-tĕr.
Squanto [I.], **skwahn**-tō.
St. Croix [F.], sānt-**kroi**.
Steuben [G.], **stū**-bĕn.
Stirling [E.], **stŭr**-lĭng.
St. Leger [F.], săn lā-**zhā**.

Stoughton [E.], **stō**-tŭn.
St. Pierre [F.], săn pē-**ār**.
Stuyvesant [G.], **stĭ**-věs-ănt.
Subercase [F.], sē-bēr-**kahs**.
Talladega [I.], tahl-lă-**dē**-gă.
Tamaulipas [S.], tahm-aw-lē-păs.
Tanacharisson [L.], tăn-ă-**kăr**-ĭs-sŭn.
Tecumtha [I.], tĕ-**kŭm**-thă.
Theresa [G.], tēr-**ĕs**-ă.
Thorfinn Karlsefne [N.], **tōr**-fĭn **kahrl**-sĕf-nĕ.
Thorstein Erickson [N.], **tōr**-stĭn **ĕr**-ĭk-sŭn.
Tituba [I.], tĭ-**too**-bă.
Tohopeka [I.], tō-hō-**pē**-kă.
Tomo-Chichi [I.], **tō**-mō-**chē**-chĭ.
Van Rensselaer [E.], văn **rĕns**-sĕ-lahr.
Van Twiller [G.], văn **twēl**-lĕr.
Vasco de Gama [P.], **vahs**-kō dā **gah**-mă.
Vasco Nunez de Balboa [S.], **vahs**-kō **noon** yĕth dā bahl-**bō**-ă.
Vaudreuil [F.], vō-drū-**ēl**.
Vaughan [E.], **vawn**.
Vergennes [F.], vĕr-**zhĕn**.
Verhulst [G.], **vār**-hoolst.
Verrazzani [It.], vĕr-răt-**tsah**-nĕ.
Wainman [E.], **wān**-măn.
Walloons [G.], wahl-**loonz**.
Wampanoags [I.], wahm-păn-**ō**-agz.
Warwick [E.], **wahr**-rĭck.
Waymouth [E.], **wā**-muth.
Welde [E.], **wel**-dĕ.
Weitzel [G.], **wīt**-zĕl.
Whalley [E.], **hwahl**-lĭ.
Whinyates [E.], **hwin**-yāts.
Whitefield [E.], **hwĭt**-fēld.
Wingina [I.], wĭn-**gē**-nă.
Worcester [E.], **woos**-tĕr.

Wouter [G.], **woos**-tĕr.
Xeres [S.], **hā**-rĕth.
Yamacraws [I.], **yahm**-ă-kraws.
Yeamans [E.], **yē**-mănz.
Yeardley [E.], **yŭrd**-lĭ.
Youghiogheny [I.], yōh-hō-gā-**nĭ**.
Yusef [Moorish], **yoo**-sĕf.
Zenger [G.], **zĕn**-gĕr.

www.ingramcontent.com/pod-product-compliance
Lightning Source LLC
Chambersburg PA
CBHW020414010526
44118CB00010B/252